The Waite Group's
GW-BASIC®
Primer Plus

The Waite Group's
GW-BASIC®
Primer Plus

D. R. Mackenroth

SAMS

A Division of Macmillan Computer Publishing
11711 North College, Carmel, Indiana 46032 USA

© 1991 by The Waite Group, Inc.

FIRST EDITION
FIRST PRINTING—1991

All rights reserved. No part of this book shall be reproduced, stored in a retrieval system, or transmitted by any means, electronic, mechanical, photocopying, recording, or otherwise, without written permission from the publisher. No patent liability is assumed with respect to the use of the information contained herein. Although every precaution has been taken in the preparation of this book, the publisher and author assume no responsibility for errors or omissions. Neither is any liability assumed for damages resulting from the use of the information contained herein. For information, address SAMS, 11711 N. College Ave., Carmel, IN 46032.

International Standard Book Number: 0-672-22739-8
Library of Congress Catalog Card Number: 90-63394

From The Waite Group, Inc.
Development Editors: Mitchell Waite and Scott Calamar
Editorial Director: Scott Calamar
Managing Editor: Karen Marcus
Content & Technical Editor: Harry Henderson

From SAMS
Acquisitions Editor: Dan Derrick
Manuscript Editor: Susan Christophersen
Illustrator: Don Clemons
Production Assistance: Jeff Baker, Jill D. Bomaster,
    Martin Coleman, Sandy Grieshop, Bob LaRoche,
    Sarah Leatherman, Howard Peirce, Cindy L. Phipps,
    Joe Ramon, Tad Ringo, Dennis Sheehan, Johnna
    VanHoose, Lisa A. Wilson
Indexer: Jill D. Bomaster
Technical Reviewer: Rob Casserotti

Printed in the United States of America

To the memory of Barney Mackenroth, for giving me curiosity about machines and respect for the tools used to explore them.

Overview

1	Introduction to GW-BASIC	*1*
2	Control Flow	*71*
3	Arrays	*113*
4	Data and Numeric Functions	*153*
5	String Functions	*209*
6	Taking Control with GW-BASIC	*233*
7	Input and Output to Files and Devices	*273*
8	The BASIC Screen, Graphics, and Sound	*349*
9	Advanced GW-BASIC	*429*
10	The Fabulous Fractal	*495*
A	BASIC Quick Reference Guide	*523*
B	Numbering Systems	*561*
C	ASCII—Numeric Conversions and Keyboard Scan Codes	*585*
D	Tips to Save Memory	*597*
E	Speed Hints	*601*
F	Exponential (Scientific) Notation	*603*
G	Information for Graphics	*609*
H	Answers to Review Questions	*615*
	Index	*625*

Contents

1 Introduction to GW-BASIC   3

    What Is BASIC?   3
    Many BASIC Dialects   4
    BASIC Applications   4
        Business Applications   4
        Entertainment Applications   5
        Educational Applications   6
        Scientific Applications   7
    What You'll Learn in this Chapter   8
    Getting Started   9
        What You'll Need: Your Minimum Configuration   9
        The System Disk   10
        Booting with the System Disk   10
        Want to Learn More About DOS?   12
    Making a BASIC Work Disk   12
        On a Hard Disk   13
        On a Floppy Disk   14
    Starting the Computer from the Working Disk   19
    How to Start BASIC   20
    The BASIC Screen   20
        Soft Keys   21
        Turning Soft Keys On and Off   21
        Clearing the Screen   22
    Getting Back to DOS   23
    Using BASIC in Direct Mode   23
    What BASIC Understands   24
        Your First Program   25
    Line Numbers   26

LIST	28
RUN Line Number	29
STOP and END	30
Inserting BEEPs	32
Automatic Line Numbers	32
Editing Your Program	35
EDIT Line Number	35
Renumbering a Program	36
Math Functions	37
Figuring in BASIC	39
Exponentiation	40
PRINT with Commas	41
Double Commas	44
PRINT with Semicolons	45
BASIC Variables	46
Leaving Off LET	50
Variable Names	50
String Variables	51
Concatenation of Strings	53
Input	53
TAB	56
Reserved Words	58
Printing the Date and Time	58
Putting It All Together: The Loan Program	59
Documenting Your Program with Remarks	63
Saving and Loading Program Files	65
Saving Programs with SAVE	65
Retrieving a Program with LOAD	66
Review Questions	67

2   Control Flow   73

What You'll Learn in this Chapter	73
The Decision-Making Statements	74
FOR...NEXT, the Programmed Loop	74
IF...THEN, Conditional Branches	76
ELSE—An Alternative to THEN	78
Breaking Lines without Starting Anew	79
Easy Looping with WHILE...WEND	79
Simple Function Statements	81

Using INT to Convert Numbers to Integers	82
Finding Prime Numbers	83
ABS, The Absolute Value Function	85
How to Generate Random Numbers	85
Going Places—and Getting Back	89
GOTO: the Unconditional Branch	89
Tracing Your Program's Execution	93
Enhancing the Loan Program	94
ON...GOTO, Indexed Branching	99
Expense Account Program	99
The All-Important Subroutine	103
ON...GOSUB, Indexed Subroutine Branching	105
Error-Checking Subroutine	106
Review Questions	111

3 Arrays   115

What You'll Learn in this Chapter	115
Arrays and Subscripted Variables	116
Dimension with DIM	119
Using DIM to Provide Space	121
When Can You Omit a DIM Statement?	122
Using OPTION BASE	122
How ERASE Gets Your Memory Back	123
Using an Expense Account Program	125
Your Expense Account Program: Where to Begin?	126
Designing the Program	128
The Overall Flowchart	128
Initialization and Menu Display	129
Inputting an Expense	134
The General Input Subroutine	136
Displaying the Expenses	139
Ending the Program	143
Running the Expense Account Program	143
Review Questions	150

4 Data and Numeric Functions   155

What You'll Learn in this Chapter	155
DATA and READ Statements	155

The Data Pointer	157
Restoring the Data Pointer	160
Initializing Arrays with DATA and READ	161
What Happens When You Run Out of DATA	162
A Metric Conversion Program	162
Variable Types: Integers, Single and Double Precision, Strings	168
What is Precision, Anyway?	169
Integer Variables	169
Single-Precision Variables	170
Integer versus Single-Precision Variables	174
Double-Precision Variables	175
Type Declaration Characters	176
How to Define Variable Types Automatically	178
Type Conversion	181
Automatic Type Conversion	182
Numeric Functions and How to Use Them	183
Finding Square Root with SQR	183
Trigonometric Functions	184
LOG and EXP	191
Finding the Altitude	192
Double-Precision Results	193
The SGN Function	193
Rounding and Truncating: INT, FIX, and CINT	194
Integer Division	196
MOD Operator	197
Finding Prime Numbers with MOD	198
The Logical Operators	199
Review Questions	206

5 String Functions   211

What You'll Learn in this Chapter	211
Single-Character ASCII-String Conversions	212
The ASC Function	212
Using ASC to Detect Oddball Characters	213
The CHR$ Function	214
Shuffling Substrings!	215
The LEFT$ Function	215
The RIGHT$ Function	216
The MID$ Function	217
Complete Conversions of Strings and Numbers	217

Contents

	The VAL Function	218
	Why Do You Use VAL?	218
	The STR$ Function	219
	Finding String Length with LEN	220
	Reading More Keystrokes with INPUT$	223
	Using LINE INPUT to Enter Anything	225
	Searching for Strings with INSTR	227
	Finding the Real Word	229
	Adding Up Strings	229
	Review Questions	230

6 Taking Control with GW-BASIC 235

	What You'll Learn in this Chapter	235
	Prettying Up Your Printed Output	235
	Using the PRINT USING Statement	236
	Printing Borders with STRING$	240
	The Payroll Program	241
	Advanced Display Functions	244
	SPACE$—All Spaced Out	244
	Centering Titles	245
	Submarine Hunt	245
	Scaling a Random Number	248
	Printing Spaces with SPC	249
	Keys at Your Command	250
	Listing Function Keys with KEY LIST	250
	Writing Your Own Key Labels with KEY	251
	Using a Key within a Program	252
	Trapping Exotic Key Combinations	254
	Other Vital BASIC Features	257
	Time to the Nearest Nanosecond with TIMER	257
	Minding Memory with FRE	262
	Using DELETE	262
	Finding the Cursor with POS	264
	Adding to BASIC's Vocabulary with DEF FN	265
	Exchanging Contents Using SWAP	267
	The Bubble Sort	268
	Review Questions	270

7 Input and Output to Files and Devices 275

	What You'll Learn in this Chapter	276
	Getting Hardcopy Output from Your Printer	276

xiii

Using the LLIST Command	277
If Your Printer Won't Print...	277
LPRINT and LPRINT USING	279
A Word About Files	280
More About LOAD and SAVE	281
Your Program as an ASCII File	284
Logging Your BASIC "Session"	285
Protected Files	287
Building and Using Sequential Data Files	288
Sequential versus Random-Access Data Files	289
Putting Data into a Sequential File	291
Bringing Data In from a Sequential File	294
Further Commands for Sequential Files	297
A Sequential Telephone Number File	302
Random Access Files	318
What Is a Random Access File?	318
Putting Data into a Random Access File	319
Getting Data from Random Access File	324
Additional Things You Should Know About Files	328
More About OPEN	328
Finding Where You Are with LOC	331
The Length of File (LOF) Function	331
Protecting Data Files with LOCK	332
Other Devices	333
Still More About OPEN	333
Trap Those Devices!	334
Using a Light Pen	335
Getting Happiness from a Joystick	337
Using STICK with a Joystick	337
Increasing BASIC Communications Skills	338
Other I/O Aids	341
Returning a Device Error	341
File Management	341
Counting Files	342
Changing Names	342
Killing Files Softly	342
Setting the Environment	344
Review Questions	345

8 The BASIC Screen, Graphics, and Sound — 351

What You'll Learn in this Chapter	351
Using the Text Screen	352
About the Standard Text Screen	352
Video Plotting with TAB	352
Plotting the SIN on the Screen	355
Switching Line Length with WIDTH	356
If Your Display Isn't IBM...	357
Going Where You Want—And Finding Where You've Been	358
BASIC Graphics	361
BASIC's Other Screens	361
Changing the SCREEN Mode	361
Plotting Points	363
Coordinates—Your Way	369
What If You Use a Different Screen?	373
Drawing Lines and Boxes	373
Drawing Circles and Arcs	377
Colorful Graphics	392
Changing Colors	392
Everything You Wanted to Know About SCREEN	392
The COLOR Statement	396
Applying Other Palettes of Color (EGA Only)	401
The PALETTE Statement	401
PALETTE USING	402
What About Color on SCREEN 2?	403
Filling Large Areas with Color	404
Fancy Things with Windows	409
What a VIEW!	409
Setting Text Boundaries with VIEW PRINT	411
Other Graphics Statements	411
Looking for People Who Like to DRAW	412
Using PUT and GET	415
Copying Pages with PCOPY	419
Using the POINT Function	419
Translating Coordinates with PMAP	420
Making Music and Sound	421
The SOUND Machine	421
The Music Writer	421
How to PLAY Music	424
Using ON PLAY for Background Music	426
Review Questions	427

9 Advanced GW-BASIC — 431

What You'll Learn in this Chapter	431
Using Conversions for Economy	432
Number-String Conversions with MKl$, MKS$, and MKD$	432
String-Number Conversions with CVI, CVS, and CVD	432
Multiple BASIC Programs	434
Using Chain to Link Programs	434
Using COMMON	437
Nondestructive Merging with CHAIN MERGE	438
Hexadecimal and Octal Conversions	448
Manipulating Memory Directly	450
A Little About Memory	450
Saving and Loading Chunks of Memory	452
Using PEEK and POKE	458
Using Mixed-Language Routines	465
Another Way to Call Assembly Language Programs	465
Locating Variables with VARPTR	467
How BASIC Variables Are stored	467
Using VARPTR with Files and Devices	475
Finding a Variable with VARPTR$	475
How SHELL Summons DOS Commands and Other BASIC Programs	476
Accessing I/O Ports	478
Dealing with Errors—Creatively	481
ON ERROR GOTO and RESUME—Confronting Your Errors	482
ERR and ERL—What Was the Error, and Where Did It Happen	484
ERROR—Stirring Up Trouble	486
Having GW-BASIC Your Way	490
The BASIC Command Line	490
The CLEAR Statement	492
Review Questions	493

10 The Fabulous Fractal — 497

What You'll Learn in this Chapter	497
Initial Planning	498
Minimum Requirement	499
Two Considerations: Speed and Size	499
Choosing the Fractal	500

Pseudocode or Flowchart?	500
Pseudocode Is the Real Thing	500
Flowcharting	502
Adding to the General Program	503
Dynamic Design	504
The Final Flowchart	506
Biting the Bullet—Writing the Program	507
The Main Program Loops	507
Saving the Fractal to Disk	508
Flash and Dazzle	509
Initialization and Dynamic Design	511
A View from the Bottom Up	512
Gaining Speed	512
CGA Changes	513
Other Fractal Formulas	514
Presenting—The Fabulous Fractal Programs	514
Fractals for EGA/VGA	514
Fractals for CGA	515
Triangular Fractals	517
Viewing the Fractal Again	518
Suggested Reading List	519

A   BASIC Quick Reference Guide   **523**

B   Numbering Systems   **561**

C   ASCII—Numeric Conversions and Keyboard Scan Codes   **585**

D   Tips to Save Memory   **597**

E   Speed Hints   **601**

F   Exponential (Scientific) Notation   **603**

G	**Information for Graphics**	**609**
H	**Answers to Review Questions**	**615**
	Chapter 1	615
	Chapter 2	616
	Chapter 3	617
	Chapter 4	618
	Chapter 5	619
	Chapter 6	619
	Chapter 7	621
	Chapter 8	622
	Chapter 9	623
	Index	**625**

Preface

BASIC is an easy-to-use computer programming language that uses simple commands written in English. You can sit down at a personal computer and write your first program in a matter of moments. But BASIC isn't a toy—in fact, applications such as word processors, spreadsheets, graphics, games, and databases are written in BASIC, and they're used by millions of people.

This book is for anyone who has a version of BASIC, such as GW-BASIC or BASICA, that is often included with the purchase of a personal computer. Most versions of BASIC are similar, and you can use this book with almost any version. Here are some of the ways this book can help you:

Teach yourself to program. If you're new to programming, this is the book for you. You don't have to know anything about computers; just start on the first page and you'll teach yourself. The book takes you slowly, step by step, from simple exercises to writing complete, detailed, fully-formed programs in BASIC. Along the way you'll learn how to use each new command, and there are plenty of examples to help you understand. At the end of each chapter, you'll find review questions to test your understanding, and a programming exercise to test your skills.

Use this book as a complete, up-to-date reference. There are descriptions and examples for virtually every GW-BASIC statement—including comprehensive chapters on getting the most from graphics and files. You'll find a complete quick reference guide for a fast overview, coupled with a detailed index that directs you right to the page where a concept is explained.

Find prewritten programs you can use. You'll find dozens of prewritten programs to use or modify. There are business applications such as expense accounts, telephone directories, and customer lists; games such as a submarine hunt and a reflex tester; and colorful graphics illustrating the principles of computer animation. Chapter 10 is entirely devoted to producing stunning full-screen pictures known as fractals—using all the colors of the rainbow, if you have a color monitor.

This book was written to supply everything you need to know to program in BASIC. To get the most from it, don't just read the pages; try the examples, modify them, change them to suit your own personal style. Because programming is—and should be—very personal.

Acknowledgments

My special thanks to Harry Henderson for guidance and for careful and eminently constructive editing that helped me at every stage. Thanks, too, to Robert Arnson for virtually all of Chapter 10, including the program code and description of the colorful fractal programs; and to Ethan Winer of Crescent Software for the save routines used in those programs. And finally, my appreciation and admiration to Scott Calamar of The Waite Group for pulling together all the pieces of the writing, editing, and production that went into this book.

Trademarks

All terms mentioned in this book that are known to be trademarks or service marks are listed below. In addition, terms suspected of being trademarks or service marks have been appropriately capitalized. Howard W. Sams & Company cannot attest to the accuracy of this information. Use of a term in this book should not be regarded as affecting the validity of any trademark or service mark.

MS-DOS and GW-BASIC are registered trademarks of Microsoft Corporation.

IBM-PC is a registered trademark of International Business Machines Corporation.

About the Author

 **D. R. Mackenroth**. A full-time free-lance writer and BASIC programmer, D.R. Mackenroth is a former electronic technician who has held technical positions with Shell Oil, McDonnell-Douglas, and Western Electric. He first learned BASIC while employed at Hewlett-Packard, and is the author of that company's self-study course in using BASIC to control instrumentation. When not hunched over a computer screen, he enjoys tennis, long-distance cycling, and the study of foreign languages. He lives in Silicon Valley, California, co-authored the *Encyclopedia of Electronic Circuits*, and the *Encyclopedia of Solid State Circuits and Applications*, both published by Prentice-Hall.

Chapter **1**

Introduction to GW-BASIC

Chapter *1*

Introduction to GW-BASIC

What Is BASIC?

BASIC is a programming language for computers. It is especially easy to learn and has quickly become the most popular language among computer users in the world today. The reason for the popularity of BASIC has to do with its origins. The language was developed at Dartmouth College so that students with no background in programming could learn to use a computer. You don't need to become a computer scientist to learn how to use a computer. The BASIC language is designed for students and professionals alike. It has all the power of a full-fledged computer language but is inherently simple to learn and to use.

BASIC has been called the "all-purpose" computer language. This is because it can be applied in hundreds of areas ranging from the sciences to the arts to industrial control. Today, literally millions of PC-compatible systems come with BASIC ready to run.

BASIC is not the only language for computers being used today. Many other languages exist and each has its own particular merits and shortcomings. FORTRAN, for example, is a scientific language, used to perform advanced calculations and aid laboratory work. COBOL is best used in business data processing applications. And then there are C, Pascal, SNOBOL, FOCAL, RPG, APL, PILOT, PL/M and LISP. Don't let these exotic names confuse you. It is not necessary to know them to learn BASIC. Furthermore, none of these other languages can offer the simplicity and gentleness that makes BASIC so easy to learn.

Chapter 1

Many BASIC Dialects

Just as there are variations of a language when spoken in different areas of a country, there are several variations in the structure and content of the BASIC language. We call these differences "dialect" variations. Most of the differences are minor, and due mainly to the fact that there is no fixed "standard" for the elements of the BASIC language.

Since its creation at Dartmouth College, BASIC has undergone several modifications but still maintains its overall structure. What this means to you, the user of BASIC, is that each manufacturer will add features to its BASIC that are not necessarily found in another version of the language. For example, manufacturer A might include commands that make it easier to use graphics with BASIC, whereas manufacturer B might include complex mathematical functions. Or manufacturer A might allow variable names to be up to 31 characters in length whereas manufacturer B might allow only two-character variable names. Also, if you decide to adapt BASIC programs originally written for the IBM-PC to another system—perhaps an Apple Macintosh—you will find that some keywords might be different in the "other" BASIC.

But for the most part, the differences between the various BASICs are such that they can be easily identified and worked around. Microsoft's GW-BASIC is the closest thing to a "standard" version of BASIC that exists. It's simple and easy to use, and doesn't chew up a lot of computer memory. GW-BASIC is often included in the package right along with a personal computer's disc operating system, or DOS.

BASIC Applications

The list of things we can program in BASIC is almost endless, but for clarity, we can lump applications into four broad categories. These categories are business, entertainment, education, and science. In this section we will examine some of the types of programs we can create in each of these areas. Later in the book we will explore some of these in more detail.

Business Applications

Although BASIC was never specifically intended to be a business data processing language, it has nonetheless become a popular language for creating business solutions with the computer. Some business program applications include the following:

General Ledger

Order Processing

Inventory Control

Customer Billing

Mailing Label Preparation

A General Ledger (or G/L for short) is a program or group of programs that automates all the accounting needs of a company. A G/L replaces the error-prone manual method of bookkeeping. Business transactions are entered just as they would be entered into a book. They are "posted" to certain accounts, and then summarized into meaningful financial statements or reports. Financial transactions can be entered from data on check stubs, invoices, or deposit slips; or they can be noncash entries such as depreciation. A G/L in BASIC helps a company keep track of where its money is being spent and how to make the best use of its financial resources. It also helps to prepare income tax forms at the end of the year. These G/Ls are often sold by independent software vendors in a form that can be adapted to a particular type of business.

Order processing programs allow the user to enter customer orders into the computer and to make up shipping and billing invoices for certain products or services. A BASIC Order Entry program can check inventory stock almost instantly and shipments can be made on a "same day" basis.

Inventory Control programs keep track of the number of items a company has in stock, and allow specific information about the movement of stock items to be displayed. The programs help a business maintain tight control over the volume of merchandise stored in the company warehouses. This in turn helps to increase the inventory turnover rate and save the company money.

Customer Billing programs are used to generate invoices and billing forms for a product or service. They maintain a list of customers and produce bills for these accounts on a periodic basis.

Mailing Label Preparation programs are used to produce mailing addresses for sending bills, invoices, and other data to customers or clients. A mailing label program usually involves some sorting of addresses according to ZIP code, and so on. Enormous amounts of time are saved by having BASIC print the mailing labels instead of having employees do it manually.

Entertainment Applications

Even if you purchased your computer for a "serious" purpose such as a business or scientific application, the chances are that sooner or later you will find yourself using it for entertainment. BASIC's fast information processing ability and the dazzling graphics displays it is capable of (in color, if you have a color monitor) make it a natural medium for many different kinds of games. It can be very rewarding, and sometimes fun, to write your own game programs. Although they may lack some of the sophistication of a commercial game, you will have the satisfaction of having created them from scratch, and you can "customize" them any way you want to. Because BASIC is the primary language supplied with most personal computers, and because it is easy to learn and to use, it is a natural tool for writing game programs. Many commercial game programs are written in BASIC (although those that require very high speed graphics displays are often written in a much more complicated language called "assembler").

Many traditional games have been written in BASIC, including chess, checkers, backgammon, Othello, tic-tac-toe, hangman, and Nim. There is also a variety of card games such as blackjack and bridge. In some versions of these games you play against the computer, and in others you play against another human while the computer keeps track of the moves and the score.

Several new kinds of games have also appeared, based on BASIC's particular abilities. Some of these games make use of the computer's arithmetic speed to "model" or imitate complex physical situations. With BASIC you can, for example, simulate an airplane, which you "fly" using the keyboard and the monitor screen. Or you can command a submarine, or a spaceship, or try to land a "lunar lander" on the moon without crashing.

Some games are designed to test your manual dexterity. You might have to drive a car along a winding road, escape from dangerous creatures in a maze, or shoot down approaching hordes of alien spaceships. Many of these games that are available for personal computers are versions of the games popular in video arcades across the country.

Other games involve you in a variety of different fantasy situations. In the famous "adventure" games, you find yourself in a mazelike castle or a haunted house, from which you must find your way out while avoiding various dangers, such as trap doors and evil dwarfs. Other games let you create fantasy characters who grow in skill and power as they overcome dangers. And, in war simulation games, you command an army or a fleet, and reenact famous historical battles.

There is an incredible variety of games to choose from, and new ones are appearing all the time. You can buy them, or, using BASIC, you can write your own version of your favorite game, or perhaps create an entirely new game!

Educational Applications

Educational applications are becoming increasingly important in the personal computer field, as more and more educators learn to appreciate the advantages of computers in the classroom. Computers can produce animated color graphics which are almost guaranteed to capture a student's attention; they can provide a student with individual instruction at exactly the level he or she needs; they can create their own questions as they go along and provide instant feedback if a student doesn't understand something; and, above all, they are very patient and do not become annoyed or upset, no matter how many mistakes the student makes.

Introduction to GW-BASIC

For very young children there is a variety of educational programs which are so much like games that often a child can be learning without even realizing it. Such programs may use color graphics and a simplified keyboard to teach the difference between left and right, or the recognition of patterns. For slightly older children the alphabet and simple arithmetic can be taught with graphics displays featuring the child's favorite cartoon characters, or with educational versions of popular computer games.

Computer programs have been devised for almost every grade school and high school subject: math, spelling, grammar, geography, typing, foreign languages—the list can go on and on. There is also a variety of programs to help teachers prepare exams (sometimes tailoring them for each individual student) and grade the results. In more advanced courses, computers can be used for creating pictures of DNA molecules, for analyzing the stresses on a bridge, and for a myriad of other applications.

As with games, educational programs can either be purchased or written by the user. Many teachers create their own BASIC language educational programs for use in special learning situations. In this way, they can produce a program which is tailored to the specific needs of a group of children in a particular learning situation.

BASIC is also the perfect language for teaching programming, because it is so easy to write—in just a few lines—a program which can actually perform useful tasks. Even a one-line program can do something interesting, as you will see in the next few pages. Many other computer languages, such as Pascal, require every program to start with a group of complicated statements to define what variables are to be used and to perform other functions. This makes them harder to learn. In BASIC you can write your first program almost instantly!

Scientific Applications

Computers programmed in the BASIC language have been used in scientific and laboratory environments for quite some time. Traditionally, BASIC programs are used in scientific and lab applications to perform complicated mathematical functions in a specific logical sequence to produce solutions to equations that would take years to solve by hand. BASIC programs can model the natural laws of hundreds of physical processes, and the model can be changed and studied by simply changing the program.

In what are called "real time" applications, computers programmed in BASIC can monitor, sense, and control external events such as the regulating of temperatures, the weighing of materials, or the movement of mechanical devices. Such applications usually involve some sort of "hardware interface," a device that converts signals from the "real world" to a form that the computer can deal with. You don't really need to understand the interface device to use it.

As an example, a BASIC program can be designed to measure and keep track of the rotational velocity of a wind anemometer (a spinning device that measures

Chapter 1

wind speed) if a hardware interface is attached to it that produces pulses of electricity each time the anemometer turns. The computer program can count these pulses at predetermined intervals throughout the day, scale them to represent wind speed in miles per hour or feet per second, and store the values inside the memory of the computer for later analysis. The computer program can even draw charts and graphs from the data. What is more, the program can be made to work in such a way that each time the measurement is made it takes only a few seconds of computer time and leaves the computer free to do other things.

On the other hand, a BASIC program can be made to control external events rather than to simply monitor them. Lamps can be turned on and off at predefined intervals throughout the day. Valves can be opened and closed based on some internal or external event. Motors can be turned in particular directions for specific periods of time. In fact, just about anything you can imagine that contains some kind of switch or electric power source can be controlled by the computer. Again, a hardware interface device is needed, but in some cases the device may be extremely simple, such as a single relay or a single lamp.

You can see that the computer is a universal kind of "programmed regulator." You can use it to regulate the flow of water to your house plants, or to regulate the flow of chemicals to an industrial process cycle.

We have seen BASIC applications span an enormous range of possibilities, and BASICally the sky's the limit. In the next sections we will begin to explore how to program in BASIC.

What You'll Learn in this Chapter

In this chapter you'll learn the rudiments of BASIC, including:

- Making a working disk and getting BASIC running on your computer
- Getting back and forth between DOS and BASIC
- Calculating at the keyboard and simple math functions
- Writing and running a program
- Listing and renumbering a program
- Saving a program to disk
- Controlling how your output looks
- Adding beeps
- Handling variables
- Calculating loan interest with a "real-world" program

Getting Started

Okay, it's time to begin learning BASIC! First, follow these simple instructions:

1. Turn on your computer. (The computer's manual should tell you how.)
2. Sit down in front of it.

In front of you is the computer keyboard. It looks like a standard typewriter keyboard, with a few additions. Near the keyboard is the screen of the computer. It's usually called the monitor, and it's where all the information appears. It takes the place of typewriter paper.

What You'll Need: Your Minimum Configuration

To run BASIC, your computer must be at least what's called a *minimum configuration*. In this case, it means you'll need an IBM or IBM-compatible computer, one that's an XT, AT, or PS2 model. The computer will need at least one floppy disk drive—a hard drive is optional.

You'll also need the BASIC program itself. It's called "GW-BASIC" or "BASICA," and it probably came along with the computer you bought. If you have a so-called compatible or clone computer, GW-BASIC is probably on a separate disk that came with DOS. If your computer is actually from IBM, BASICA is already provided in the computer, and you can skip right down to "How to Start Basic" below. Incidentally, BASICA works only on IBM machines, although some other manufacturers, such as Compaq, provide their own versions.

Look at the monitor display. You should see an "A" or "C" with a "greater than" symbol (or maybe some other symbols), as follows:

```
A:\>
```

Or:

```
C:\>
```

This is a *prompt* for the operating system. It tells you that the computer's operating system is running and the computer is ready for you to type commands. In PC-compatible computers, the operating system is almost always a form of DOS, such as MS-DOS (Microsoft Disk Operating System) or PC-DOS (IBM's version).

When you turn on the computer, if you don't see the operating system prompt—the "A" or "C" or even "B"—you'll probably see an error message like the following:

```
Non-system disk or disk error. Strike any key when ready
```

Chapter 1

Don't worry—this won't hurt your computer. It just means you'll have to use a system disk to "boot up." That's computerese for turning on the operating system.

If you already have a system prompt—the A> or B> or C>—skip directly down to "Making a BASIC Work Disk" below.

The System Disk

If your computer has a system disk available when you turn it on, the operating system starts automatically. A system disk contains the operating system software. If your computer has a hard disk, it is probably the system disk. With a hard disk you don't have to worry about finding and inserting the system disk. (If you have a hard disk but DOS doesn't start automatically from it, see your DOS manual for instructions on how to install DOS on the hard disk.)

If your computer doesn't have a hard disk, you'll have to insert a disk containing the DOS operating system into the computer's disk drive, then turn the computer on. No matter what kind of computer you have, you must start the operating system before you can start BASIC (see fig. 1-1).

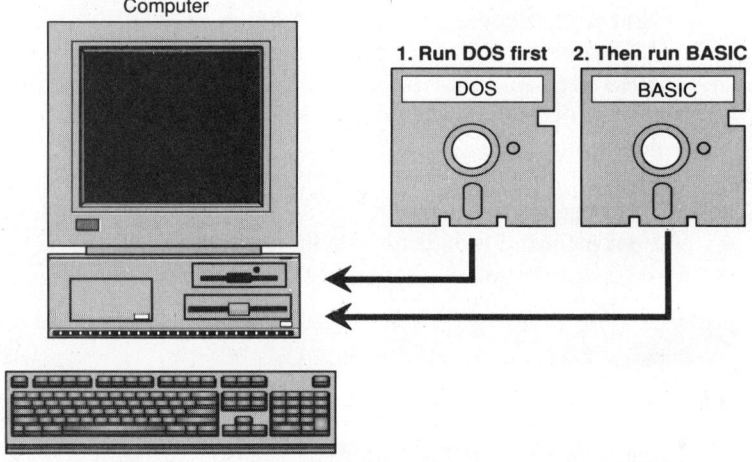

Fig. 1-1:   Start off by running DOS, then run BASIC.

Booting with the System Disk

Where do you find a system disk? Look for a floppy disk for your computer, the one that has a label with the word "DOS" on it in big letters. It might say something like "MS-DOS 3.3 System Disk."

Introduction to GW-BASIC

Be careful! The system disk is precious. Handle it gently by the edges, and keep it away from dirt, heat, magnetism, coffee and kids. Now follow these instructions for inserting the disk:

1. Turn the little lever of the computer's floppy disk drive sideways. If there's another disk in there, remove it.
2. Insert the system disk into the computer's disk drive. Make sure the label on the disk is up and facing away from you (see fig. 1-2).

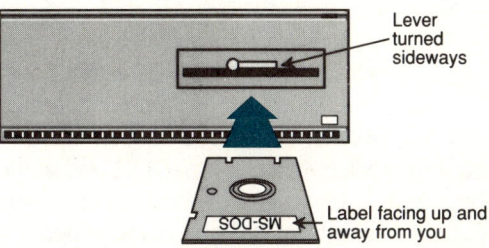

Fig. 1-2:   Inserting a disk.

If Your Computer Has 3 1/2-Inch Disks

If your computer takes the smaller 3 1/2-inch disks, by all means use them! You insert these disks with the label up and the metal portion of the disk away from you. To remove a disk from the computer, press the small button (see fig. 1-3).

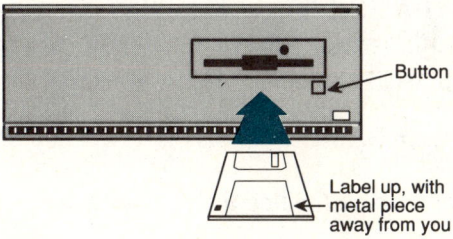

Fig. 1-3:   3 1/2-inch disk.

Turn the computer's power off, then on. (Or you can simply press these three keys at the same time: Ctrl, Alt, Del. These three keys, when pressed at the same time,

Chapter 1

"reboot" the computer. They're located in different parts of the keyboard so that you won't accidentally press them while you're working.)

Now you should have a prompt on your screen that looks like the following:

```
A:\>
```

The prompt might be A> rather than A:\>. It all depends on how DOS is configured, and it doesn't really matter now.

Want to Learn More About DOS?

In this book we can show you only enough about DOS to help you start and use BASIC. As you work with your computer, you might want to learn more about the many features of DOS itself. A good introduction, similar in style to this book, is The Waite Group's *Understanding MS-DOS*, available from your bookstore or from Howard W. Sams & Company. Another recommended book is The Waite Group's *Using PC DOS*, which provides an encyclopedic reference and extensive tutorial exercises.

Making a BASIC Work Disk

Both BASIC and the DOS operating system are shipped to you on floppy disks. Now think about this: What if you lost those disks, or they got wet, or the dog mistook one of them for a bone? What if you came home and found your children boomeranging them back and forth across the room? Those disks are delicate. And, although small, they're still very valuable. Without an operating system, your computer is just a big metal-and-plastic paperweight!

That's why you should make a *work disk*. This is a disk containing the operating system and BASIC. It's what you will use for everyday operation of your computer. You'll keep the original, master disks somewhere safe, and use the work disk instead. If anything happens to the work disk, you can easily use the master disks to make another one.

Making a BASIC work disk is a two-step process:

1. Format the disk (adding the operating system if necessary).
2. Copy BASIC to the work disk.

How you actually do these steps depends on whether your computer has a hard disk, or on how many floppy disk drives it has.

Introduction to GW-BASIC

On a Hard Disk

If your computer has a hard disk, you can use it to keep the working version of BASIC. (The hard disk probably has the operating system on it already.) You can copy BASIC to the hard disk using the following steps:

1. Find the floppy disk containing BASIC. It may be labeled "GW-BASIC" or "MS-DOS Supplemental Programs" or something else.
2. Insert the disk in disk drive A on your computer. Drive A is usually the top or left-hand floppy disk drive. If you're not sure, refer to your computer's manual.
3. Type the following exactly as shown (don't forget the colon):

```
A:
```

Then press the Return or Enter key on the computer keyboard. You should see a prompt on the screen that looks something like the following:

```
A:\>
```

4. Type:

```
DIR
```

Then press Return (or Enter) again.

You should see a list (a "directory") of the files on the floppy disk. Find the file GWBASIC.EXE or other BASIC.EXE file.

```
GWBASIC     EXE       (This is the GW-BASIC program)
```

Do you see it? If the file names disappear off the top of the screen too quickly for you to read them, you can modify the DIR command to show only one screenful (or "page") at a time:

```
DIR /P
```

To see the next screenful, press any key.

If you don't see something that looks like BASIC, try another disk until you've seen the file names on all the disks that came with your computer.

5. Once you've located the BASIC file, copy it to the hard disk. Type exactly as shown (use the file name for your version of BASIC):

Chapter 1

```
COPY GWBASIC.EXE C:
```

When the computer has copied BASIC to your hard disk, it displays the message:

```
1 File(s) copied
```

And that's it! BASIC is now on your hard disk and ready to run. Skip a few pages down to the section, "How to Start BASIC."

On a Floppy Disk

If your computer doesn't have a hard disk, you'll need to make a working disk containing the operating system and BASIC. The procedure is easy, but it's slightly different depending on whether your computer has two floppy disk drives or only one. In either case, follow the procedure exactly, so that you don't accidentally wipe out the BASIC master disk.

If Your Computer Has Two Disk Drives

1. If your computer has two floppy disk drives, begin by removing any disks that are in the drives.
2. Type the following:

```
FORMAT A: /S
```

Then press the Enter key. The computer displays a message telling you to insert a blank floppy disk.

```
Insert new disk for drive A:
and strike ENTER when ready
```

3. Insert a blank, unformatted disk in your computer's drive A. This is usually the top or left-hand drive. If you're not sure, refer to the computer's manual.

   Remember, formatting a disk will destroy any data you now have on that disk. So, before formatting, make sure that the disk is new, or that you don't have any valuable programs or data on it.

4. Press Enter (or Return). You'll see messages on the screen showing that the disk is being formatted. They'll change continually, but depending on your version of DOS, they'll probably look something like this:

```
Head: 0      Cylinder: 16
```

Introduction to GW-BASIC

After a few minutes (be patient!) you'll see a message showing that formatting is finished:

```
Format complete
System transferred
Format another (Y/N)?
```

5. Type N for "No" because you need to format only one disk.
6. Find the floppy disk containing BASIC. It might be labeled "GW-BASIC" or "MS-DOS Supplemental Programs" or something else.
7. Insert the disk in disk drive B on your computer. Drive B is usually the lower or the right-hand floppy disk drive.
8. With the new, formatted disk in drive A, and the disk containing BASIC in drive B, type the following, exactly as shown (don't forget the colon):

```
B:
```

Then press the Return or Enter key on the computer keyboard. You should see a prompt on the screen that looks something like the following:

```
B:\>
```

9. Type:

```
DIR
```

Then press Return (or Enter) again.

You should see a list (a *directory*) of the files on the floppy disk. Find the file GWBASIC.EXE or other BASIC.EXE file.

```
GWBASIC     EXE         (This is the GW-BASIC program)
```

Do you see it? If the file names disappear off the top of the screen too quickly for you to read them, you can modify the DIR command to show only one screenful (or "page") at a time:

```
DIR /P
```

To see the next screenful, press any key.

If you don't see something that looks like BASIC, try another disk until you've seen the file names on all the disks that came with your computer.

15

Chapter 1

10. Once you've located the BASIC file, copy it to the working disk. Type exactly as shown here (use the file name for your version of BASIC):

```
COPY GWBASIC.EXE A:
```

When the computer has finished copying, the display shows the following:

```
1 File(s) copied
```

And that's it! BASIC and the operating system are now on the working disk in drive A. To use this disk, skip the next few pages and start the computer using this working disk as explained in the section, "Starting the Computer from the Working Disk."

If Your Computer Has Only One Disk Drive

Even if your computer has only a single floppy disk drive, you can copy BASIC from its disk to another floppy disk. The procedure is just as if you were using two floppy drives—except that you have to insert first the disk for drive A, then the disk for drive B, then the disk for drive A again, and so on. You'll have to keep track of which disk should be in the drive at any given time (see fig. 1-4).

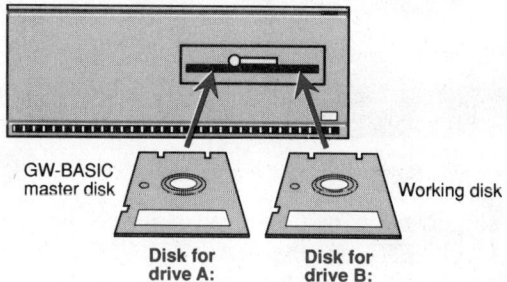

Fig. 1-4: Using two disks with one drive.

Use the following steps to copy BASIC from its master disk to the working disk using only one drive:

1. Begin by removing any disk that is in the computer's disk drive.
2. Type the following:

```
A:
```

Introduction to GW-BASIC

Don't forget the colon. Press Enter to make sure the prompt is for drive A. You should see the prompt for A; chances are it looks like the following:

```
A:\>
```

3. Now you're going to format a new disk. This destroys any information on the disk, so be careful, and follow the procedure exactly as shown here. Type the following:

```
FORMAT B: /S
```

Then press the Enter key. The computer displays a message telling you to insert a blank floppy disk.

```
Insert new disk for drive B:
and strike ENTER when ready
```

4. Insert a blank, unformatted disk in your computer's disk drive. Remember, formatting the disk will destroy any data you now have on that disk. So, before formatting, make sure that the disk is new or that you don't have any valuable programs or data on it.

5. Press Enter (or Return). You'll see messages on the screen showing that the disk is being formatted. The messages will change continually, but depending on your version of DOS, they'll probably look something like the following:

```
Head: 0        Cylinder: 16
```

After a few minutes (be patient!) you'll see a message that shows formatting is finished:

```
Format complete
System transferred
Format another (Y/N)?
```

6. Type N for "No" because you need to format only one disk.

7. Find the floppy disk containing BASIC. It was probably shipped with your computer, and it may be labeled "GW-BASIC" or "MS-DOS Supplemental Programs" or something else.

8. Remove the formatted disk from the drive, and insert the floppy disk containing BASIC.

9. With the disk containing BASIC in the drive, make sure that you still have the A:\> prompt on the screen, like this:

Chapter 1

```
A:\>
```

Then type the following:

```
DIR
```

Then press Return (or Enter) again. The computer might now ask you to insert a disk for the A: drive:

```
Insert disk for drive A: and strike
any key when ready
```

10. Because you've already inserted the disk, just press Enter. You should see a list (a *directory*) of the files on the floppy disk. Find the file GWBASIC.EXE, or other BASIC.EXE file.

```
GWBASIC     EXE      (This is the GW-BASIC program)
```

Do you see it? If the file names disappear off the top of the screen too quickly for you to read them, you can modify the DIR command to show only one screenful (or "page") at a time:

```
DIR /P
```

To see the next screenful, press any key.

If you don't see something that looks like BASIC, try another disk until you've seen the file names on all the disks that came with your computer.

11. Once you've located the BASIC file, copy it to the working disk. Type exactly as shown here (use the file name for your version of BASIC and don't forget the colons and spaces):

```
COPY A:\GWBASIC.EXE B:
```

Now the computer prompts you to change disks:

```
Insert disk for drive B: and strike
any key when ready
```

12. Okay, now you're going to have to keep track of the two disks. Remember:

- The master disk is the one for drive A:
- The new, formatted work disk is the one for drive B:

Introduction to GW-BASIC

Follow the instructions on the screen. When they ask for the disk for drive B, insert the new, formatted disk, then press Enter. When the instructions ask for the disk for drive B, insert the BASIC master disk. You'll probably have to switch the disks a couple of times.

13. When the computer has finished copying, the display shows:

```
1 File(s) copied
```

BASIC and the operating system are now on the working disk, and you're ready to go on to the next section, "Starting the Computer from the Working Disk."

Starting the Computer from the Working Disk

The working disk contains both the DOS operating system and BASIC. To start the computer using the working disk, use the following steps:

1. Insert the working disk into the computer's floppy disk drive and turn the computer off, then on (or leave the computer on, then press the Ctrl, Alt, and Del keys all at the same time).

   After a few moments, the computer screen may show something like the following message:

   ```
   Current date is Wed 3/21/1990
   Enter new date (mm-dd-yy):
   ```

   (If you don't see this, and instead see the DOS prompt A:\> or something like it, don't despair. It just means this part has been taken care of for you. You can go on to the next section, "How to Start BASIC.")

2. The computer has an internal clock that always keeps track of the current date and time. Later you'll see how you can print the date and time, and use them to mark your programs and output. If the date you see is OK, just press Enter to accept this date. If you want to change the computer's internal date, type the date using two digits for the month and follow this with a hyphen, then type two digits for the date followed by another hyphen, and finally four digits for the year—just use the same format that's displayed, only with a new date.

   Now the computer lets you change the internal clock time, or use the current time. The display shows:

   ```
   Current time is 7:40:47:07
   Enter new time:
   ```

Chapter 1

3. Press Enter to use the current time, or type the time with hours first, followed by minutes and seconds. Separate them with colons.

How to Start BASIC

To run GW-BASIC, or any version of BASIC, make sure that the GW-BASIC program or other BASIC program has been copied to your hard disk, or make sure that the working disk is inserted in the disk drive. Then type the name of BASIC's .EXE file. For instance, if the file name is GWBASIC.EXE, you type:

GWBASIC   *(Or whatever the file name of BASIC is)*

Now press Enter.

After a few moments, you'll see that BASIC is now loaded in your computer. It has "taken over" the computer, so that from now on, the computer understands only BASIC commands.

The BASIC Screen

Let's look at the BASIC screen on your computer. It probably looks something like the one shown in figure 1-5.

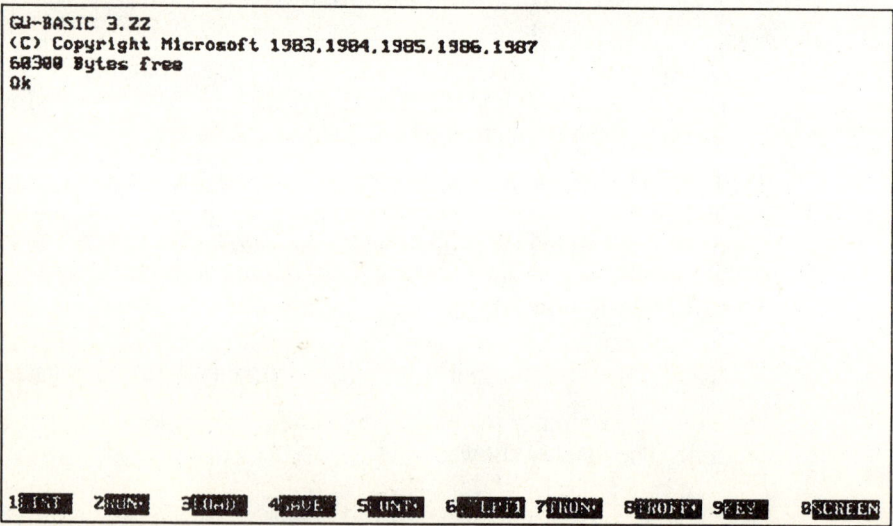

Fig. 1-5: GW-BASIC screen.

20

Introduction to GW-BASIC

When you first "turn on" BASIC, you see some information at the top of the screen. This information is there to help you use your computer wisely.

At the very top, you can see the version number of BASIC that you're using. When a manufacturer improves a program, or changes it in some way, a new version number is often assigned. If you have several versions, you should always try to use the latest version at all times.

Next you see some copyright information. This shows the company that "owns" the program.

Next you see a line something like "60300 Bytes free." This shows how much of your computer's internal memory is free for use by BASIC. (This is different from the amount of memory you have available on disks.)

Finally, you can see the message, "Ok." This prompt shows that it's "Ok" for you to enter BASIC commands now. The blank area after the "Ok" is where you'll type commands and program instructions.

Soft Keys

At the bottom of the screen, you can see a row of numbers and names. These actually correspond to keys on your computer. Look at the very top row of your keyboard. Do you see the keys labeled "F1," "F2," "F3," and so on? (On some older computers, these keys may be on the left-hand side of the keyboard instead of across the top.) These keys are called *function* keys (see fig. 1-6). These keys are also called user-definable, or *soft* keys. They perform different functions depending on the software you're using, but in BASIC, you can actually define them to be anything you want. When BASIC first "wakes up," they're set to perform the functions you see written.

You can think of these keys as aids to help your typing. For instance, if you press the F1 key, you see the word LIST appear on the screen. If you press F5, you see the word CONT. These words are BASIC commands, and it's just as if you'd typed them on the screen yourself—except that it took you only one keystroke!

Turning Soft Keys On and Off

Now that you've seen the soft keys, let's make them disappear. You can use a couple of commands called KEY OFF and KEY ON to control the display of the soft keys. To try it, type the following:

```
KEY OFF
```

Now press Enter. See what happened? The display of keys at the bottom of the screen was turned off. But don't worry—to get the display back again, just type:

```
KEY ON
```

Chapter 1

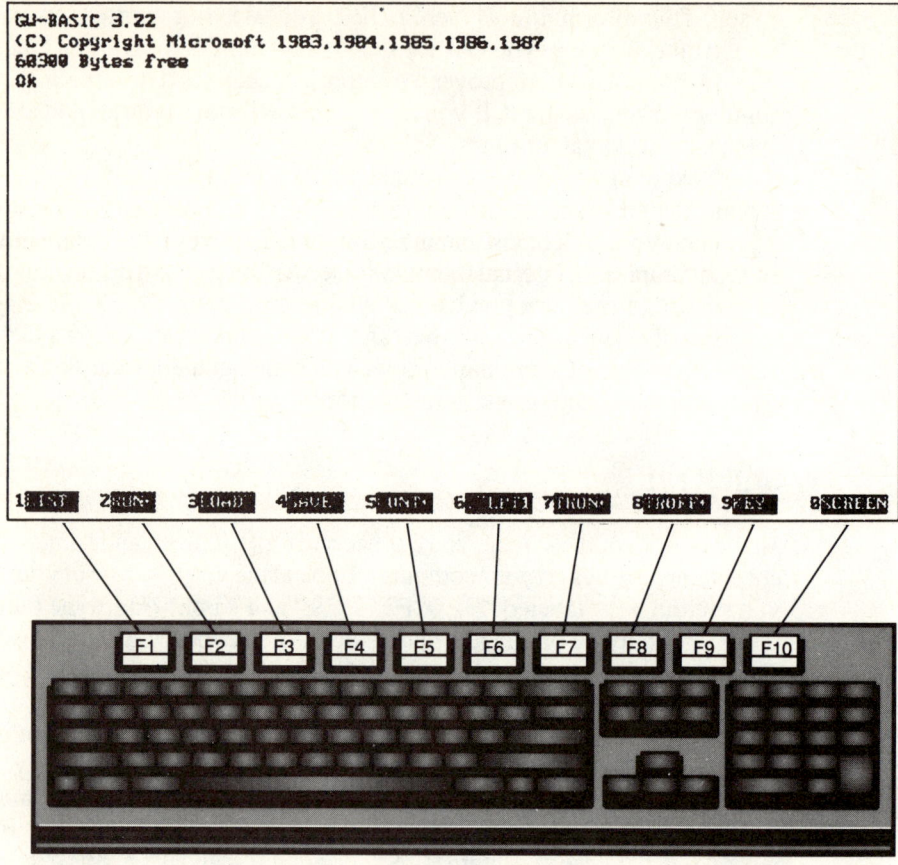

Fig. 1-6: Screen labels correspond to function keys on the keyboard.

As usual, press the Enter key after you type any command. Later, after you've memorized what each function key does, you may want to turn the key display off to use that extra line for your valuable program listings.

Clearing the Screen

Wouldn't it be nice if you could get rid of everything on the screen at once? You can—thanks to BASIC's CLS (clear screen) command. Just type CLS, and you get a "clean slate" to work with. Try it:

```
CLS
```

Introduction to GW-BASIC

CLS only clears the screen. It doesn't kill any programs, or erase any program information or memory contents. And, as you can see, it doesn't affect the user-definable function keys, either.

Getting Back to DOS

All this BASIC stuff is pretty interesting. But remember that BASIC now has control of your computer. Your machine no longer recognizes DOS commands such as DIR or COPY; instead, it understands only BASIC commands. Can you think of a way to turn off BASIC and turn the DOS operating system back on? Answer quickly, now.

If you said "Turn the computer off, then on," you're right. Any time the computer's power is turned off, it "wakes up" back in DOS. But this isn't very elegant, is it? It takes time, and frankly, it puts wear and tear on the computer's power supply.

Happily, there's a better way: the SYSTEM command. When you're in BASIC and you type SYSTEM, the computer jumps back to DOS. Try it:

```
SYSTEM
A:\>
```

Now you no longer see the BASIC screen. Instead, you're back at the DOS prompt. (It might be anything from A:\> to D:\>, depending on where the system was located when you first turned on the computer.)

There's something you should know about SYSTEM: it kills any programs you have in BASIC. If you had just typed a 50-line program, and then typed SYSTEM, all that work would be lost. So be aware of this, and save your work on disk first, as described later in this book.

Using BASIC in Direct Mode

Even if the word "programming" is new to you, BASIC can go to work for you right away. That's because there are actually two ways that you can use this language: *direct mode* and *program mode*.

First, type GWBASIC (or whatever you need to type for your version) so that your computer is up and running BASIC.

Now, let's try telling the computer something it understands how to do. Type the following:

```
PRINT "ISN'T THIS NEAT"
```

Chapter 1

Now press the Enter key on the keyboard. See what happens? The computer prints everything that was in quotation marks:

```
ISN'T THIS NEAT
Ok
```

The first word you typed, PRINT, happens to be a command that is part of the BASIC language. When the computer sees this word as the first item in the line, followed by something in quotation marks, it no longer balks. In fact, it now knows just what you want to do, and it "prints" the phrase on the monitor screen.

Because PRINT is part of the BASIC language, it's called a "keyword." Whenever BASIC sees a keyword as the first word in a line, it recognizes it as a command and tries to execute it.

Let's try something else with PRINT. Type the following:

```
PRINT 2+2
```

Then hit Enter. You see that BASIC actually computes the answer for you:

```
 4
Ok
```

Here, the computer knew that you wanted to print the answer. BASIC is so smart and easy to use that it can do your mathematics problems for you, even if you don't program a keystroke! In fact, so many people use BASIC this way that sometimes this direct mode is called "calculator" mode, because it makes BASIC act just like a calculator.

Incidentally, BASIC doesn't care whether you type capital letters or lowercase ones. When BASIC understands a word, it understands it no matter how you type the word. Try this:

```
print 2+2
 4
```

Later on you'll learn about all the other math functions available in BASIC. For now, though, it's time to learn the second way to use BASIC—programming.

What BASIC Understands

Let's get the feel for the way a computer works. We can simply type something and see what happens. Remember, BASIC has control of the computer now. Suppose that you type:

Introduction to GW-BASIC

> HI COMPUTER

When you finish typing, press the carriage return key. This key might be labeled Return, CR, or Enter.

What happens now is that BASIC will give you an error message in response to what you typed. It might look like figure 1-7.

Fig. 1-7:   Error messages tell what you've done wrong.

Ok is also printed. It means everything is fine with BASIC and it is ready to continue.

The computer typed "Syntax error" because it didn't understand what we wanted it to do. The point is that computers that understand plain English have not yet been designed. So, to make the computer do something, we use a computer "language," like BASIC, to enter our instructions to the computer. The word "Ok" just means that everything is all right, and the computer is ready for more work.

Understand that a "Syntax error" message doesn't mean you have done any harm to the computer. The computer simply ignores you until you type something it understands, something in the vocabulary of the BASIC language.

Your First Program

There's another way to use BASIC, remember? It's called *program mode*.

Usually we start a session in BASIC by typing the word *new*, as shown in figure 1-8.

Fig. 1-8:   NEW gets BASIC ready for a new program.

Now any previous instructions that were in the computer memory have been "cleared" or "scratched," and the computer is ready to accept NEW instructions. The memory is the place where all the work in the computer occurs. It is where the BASIC program is kept. The memory is erased by typing NEW, so do not type NEW unless you wish to erase your program.

25

Chapter 1

Now type this:

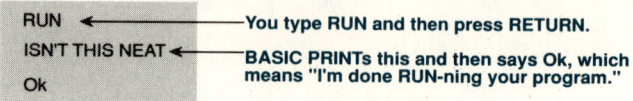

When you are done, hit the Return key.

Now type the word *run* and then press Return again. Figure 1-9 shows what happens.

RUN ← ——————— You type RUN and then press RETURN.
ISN'T THIS NEAT ← ———— BASIC PRINTs this and then says Ok, which
Ok   means "I'm done RUN-ning your program."

Fig. 1-9: RUN executes your program.

Congratulations are now in order. You have just entered a "computer program" in BASIC and caused BASIC to RUN or "execute" your program. The program is kind of small and doesn't do anything great; nonetheless, it is a program.

What we have done here is told BASIC to PRINT what was inside the quotation marks. Our program was the statement, `10 PRINT "ISN'T THIS NEAT."` We caused the program to execute once by typing RUN. The computer responded by typing ISN'T THIS NEAT and then Ok to tell us it was done. The word *Ok* is printed after every normal execution of a BASIC program. (Programs with errors in them cause "Syntax error" to be printed.)

Line Numbers

Line numbers are used so that BASIC can determine the order in which it is supposed to execute *statements*. When you tell BASIC to RUN a program, it starts by following or executing the statement or instruction with the smallest *line number*. The instruction you gave in line 10 is called a PRINT statement. When you typed RUN and pressed Return, BASIC responded by printing the information between the quotation marks. The information between the quotation marks is called a *string*.

Figure 1-10 shows what the pieces of the print statement we used previously are called.

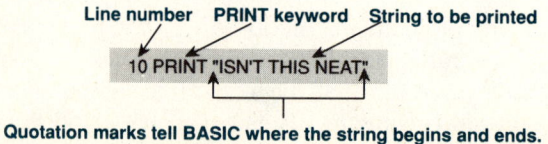

Fig. 1-10: Pieces of a PRINT statement.

Introduction to GW-BASIC

A statement that isn't executed as soon as you enter it is called an *indirect statement*. In a BASIC program, an indirect statement always begins with a line number, like this:

```
10 PRINT "ISN'T THIS NEAT"
```

A line number may be any positive number between 0 and 65529.

In BASIC, these are examples of *direct statements*:

```
NEW
```

or

```
RUN
```

Direct statements like these are not part of the program and therefore do not require line numbers. Most of the statements we will learn about are indirect statements, the kind with line numbers. Direct statements are more in the area of programming "aids," so we will save the bulk of them for later. Sometimes direct statements are called BASIC "commands" because they immediately command the computer to do something for us, whereas with indirect statements we must wait for the computer to RUN them.

A program is made up of several indirect statements, each with its own unique line number. The statement with the lowest line number gets executed first. When BASIC is finished doing, or executing, the first statement, it goes on to the next statement in numerical order.

For an example of how line numbers work, enter the program shown in figure 1-11 (remember to type NEW since this is a new program) and then RUN it.

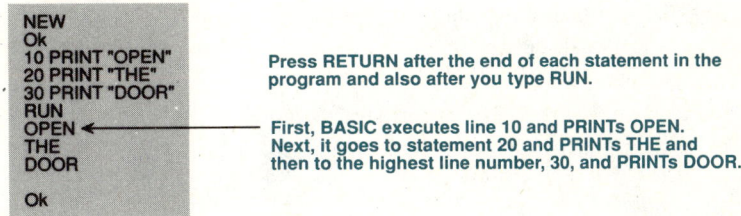

Press RETURN after the end of each statement in the program and also after you type RUN.

First, BASIC executes line 10 and PRINTs OPEN. Next, it goes to statement 20 and PRINTs THE and then to the highest line number, 30, and PRINTs DOOR.

Fig. 1-11:   Entering and running a multi-line program.

Now let us examine line numbers more closely. First of all, to enter a program, you don't have to enter it in line number order. That is, you can enter line numbers in any order you want, say 30 first, then 20, then 10, and the computer will put them in the proper "line number order" for you. This means we can easily insert more statements in a program already stored in the computer's memory.

27

Chapter 1

Note how we numbered the statements by 10's. This clever idea makes it easy for us to add more statements between existing line numbers. For example, nine more statements can be added between lines 10 and 20. To prove this to yourself, type the following new program shown in figure 1-12. Notice how the line numbers are not entered in order.

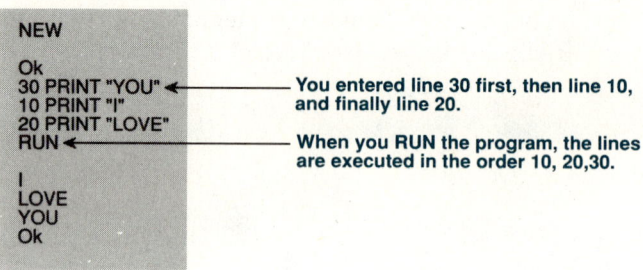

Fig. 1-12: You don't have to enter line numbers in order.

As you can see, BASIC ran the program in the order dictated by the line numbers, not the order we entered them.

LIST

To see how BASIC has rearranged the program statements we can use the direct statement:

```
LIST
```

LIST does just what it says—it causes the BASIC program in the memory of the computer to be displayed on the screen as a list of statements. Try it:

```
LIST
10 PRINT "I"
20 PRINT "LOVE"
30 PRINT "YOU"
```

Note that LIST listed each statement in the program in line number order. You can LIST a program any time the computer is not running a program. Don't forget to hit return after typing LIST.

To see how easy it is to add statements, type the following (don't type NEW this time because we are adding to our current program, not starting a new one):

```
15 PRINT "DON'T"
```

28

Introduction to GW-BASIC

Now list the program to see what happens to line 15 (see fig. 1-13).

```
LIST
10 PRINT "I"
15 PRINT "DON'T"   ← See how BASIC inserts line 15 between
20 PRINT "LOVE"       lines 10 and 20. Easy, huh?
30 PRINT "YOU"

RUN
I
DON'T
LOVE
YOU

Ok
```

Fig. 1-13: BASIC inserts lines in the correct order.

See how easy it is? Removing statements from your program is just as simple. To remove a statement, type the line number of that statement and then press Return. This removes that line from the program. For example, to remove line 30 (PRINT "YOU") from our program, type the following line number. (The CR stands for Carriage Return—it's there to remind you to press the Return or Enter key. Don't type CR!)

```
30 (CR)
```

Now if we list the program with LIST, look what has happened:

```
LIST

10 PRINT "I"
15 PRINT "DON'T"
20 PRINT "LOVE"

Ok
```

RUN Line Number

Sometimes we would like to RUN the program so that it starts somewhere other than at the beginning line number. This comes up when you are *debugging* or testing a program. (A *bug* means that something is wrong with the way the program works. Debugging is removing bugs. No DDT is required!)

In order to make a program RUN at a specific line number, type the following:

```
RUN line number
```

Chapter 1

The *line number* is the number of the line where we want the program to start. For example, in our last program we could make it start at line 15 by typing:

```
RUN 15
DON'T
LOVE
Ok
```

As you can see, the program started with line 15, then executed line 20. You can RUN at any line that actually exists in the program. But if you type "RUN 50" and line 50 does not exist, you will receive the following message:

```
RUN 50
Undefined line number
Ok
```

Because there is no line 50 in our current program in memory, BASIC told us so and stopped.

STOP and END

So far we've seen how to start a program, but what about stopping the program? In all our previous examples, the program stopped after it executed the last statement in the last line number. Some BASICs require that you end all programs with the statement called END, and it's a good habit to always include END. (In Microsoft GW-BASIC, the END statement is not mandatory, but is still useful.)

END causes BASIC to stop and return to the command level. (Remember, the command level is when BASIC has printed Ok, and is ready for you to command it.) The END statement should usually be at the end of your program, but it can be used elsewhere in the program.

No matter where the END statement is located, as soon as END is executed, BASIC stops dead in its tracks. To see how END works, first LIST the current program in memory (or reenter it if it is not still in memory):

```
LIST
10 PRINT "I"
15 PRINT "DON'T"
20 PRINT "LOVE"
Ok
```

Now add the statement shown in figure 1-14 (remember, you simply type the new line number followed by the new statement).

30

Introduction to GW-BASIC

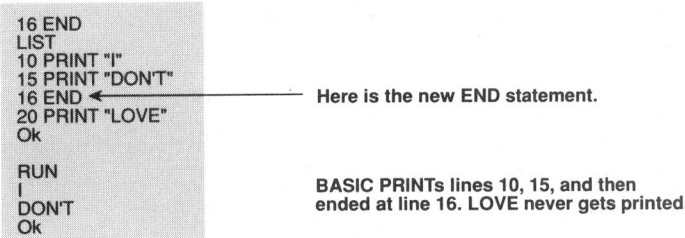

Fig. 1-14: END tells BASIC it's reached the end of a program.

Notice what happened here. BASIC executed line 10 and PRINTed "I," executed line 15 and PRINTed "DON'T," and then found line 16, which said "END," so BASIC ended the program. This is evident by the "Ok" that was printed.

In general, if you come upon a program that has been running and the last thing printed on the screen was Ok, then BASIC is probably done and in the command mode. In fact, some versions of BASIC return to the command mode and print the words READY or DONE, or just show some kind of character such as the "greater than" sign (>) or the open bracket ([). The point is that END may appear anywhere in the program, and it will cause the program to end when it is executed. Normally END is at the end of the program.

There is another useful statement for terminating program execution. Let's replace line 16; to replace a line, simply type a new line with the same number.

Enter this in place of the END statement and then RUN the program:

```
16 STOP
RUN
I
DON'T
Break in 16
Ok
```

What happened here is that BASIC found the STOP statement, which, like the END statement, stopped the program. However, STOP also made BASIC print "where" it stopped. "Break in 16" means "I stopped running your program at line 16," or, in other words, BASIC took a "break."

Use STOP whenever you wish the program to end prematurely. For example, during debugging you might wish to stop somewhere in the middle of the program so that you can isolate the part that is not working right. STOP will help you here. For now, keep STOP in mind as another form of END.

31

Chapter 1

Inserting BEEPs

To modify an old axiom, "Faint heart and the BASIC PRINT statement never convinced a beloved." Simply printing "I love you" may not be enough to get the attention you desire. Why not add something that can be heard as well as seen? You can use the BEEP statement.

Like most BASIC statements, BEEP does just what it says—it makes the computer "beep." Try this small program:

```
NEW
Ok
10 PRINT "I LOVE YOU"
20 BEEP
30 END
RUN
I LOVE YOU (BEEP!)
```

Did you hear the beep? To make it longer, just add more beeps. Type the following:

```
21 BEEP
22 BEEP
23 BEEP
24 BEEP
25 BEEP
RUN

I LOVE YOU (BEEEEEEP!)
```

Use the beep to add spice to your programs, or to signal that a long program is finished. Many programmers include the BEEP to signal errors or subtle changes of execution within a program.

Automatic Line Numbers

Just now you may be thinking, "If computers are supposed to save me work, why do I have to type line numbers every time?" Luckily for you, BASIC has a command to handle that very task. It's the AUTO command. When you type AUTO, the computer automatically types the line numbers for you.

Introduction to GW-BASIC

To see how it works, start a new program and type AUTO:

```
NEW
AUTO
10
```

When you type the AUTO command, the computer knows you want auto-numbering. The first line number, 10, is typed automatically for you, and the cursor is indented one space, ready for you to type a statement.

Now type the rest of the first line and press Enter:

```
10 PRINT "YOU CAN TALK OF GIN AND BEER"
20
```

When you typed the rest of the line and pressed Enter, the next line number (20) was typed automatically, and the cursor was poised for you to type the statement. You didn't have to indent it yourself.

Finish typing the program using auto-numbering:

```
10 PRINT "YOU CAN TALK OF GIN AND BEER"
20 PRINT "WHEN YOU'RE QUARTERED SAFE OUT HERE"
30 END
40
```

BASIC is expecting you to keep typing statements. But you're done, and you need to tell it so. To turn off auto-numbering and get back to normal operation, press the Ctrl (Control) key and the C key; or press the Ctrl key and the Break key. (You can use Pause if it's located on the same key as Break.) You have to press them at the same time.

```
10 PRINT "YOU CAN TALK OF GIN AND BEER"
20 PRINT "WHEN YOU'RE QUARTERED SAFE OUT HERE"
30 END
40
Ok
```

When you type Ctrl-C or Ctrl-Break, that line is not saved. So, in this example, line 40 is lost. LIST the program to make sure:

```
LIST
10 PRINT "YOU CAN TALK OF GIN AND BEER"
20 PRINT "WHEN YOU'RE QUARTERED SAFE OUT HERE"
30 END
Ok
```

Chapter 1

When using AUTO, make sure you're on a new line before you turn off auto-numbering with Ctrl-C or Ctrl-Break.

Incidentally, you don't have to use line numbers in increments of 10, nor start with line number 10. You can specify a starting line number and an increment, as follows:

```
AUTO 100, 20
```
This begins auto-numbering with line number 100, in increments of 20

If you use a period instead of the line number, it means, "begin with the current line." For example:

```
AUTO.,5
```
This begins auto-numbering with the current line and gives increments of 5

If AUTO comes to a line number that's already being used, you see an asterisk right after the number. Try this:

```
AUTO 30,10
30*
```

The AUTO 30,10 command means "begin auto-numbering with line 30, in increments of 10 lines." The asterisk you see means that something is already in that line. Now, remember what happens if you type a line with a number that's already been used? That's right, the old line is erased and your new line replaces it. Typing a line erases whatever was there before and replaces it with your new statement. To change line 30, all you have to do is type the new statement, as follows:

```
30 PRINT
```

A PRINT statement with nothing after it will simply print a blank line. Now LIST the program:

```
LIST
10 PRINT "YOU CAN TALK OF GIN AND BEER"
20 PRINT "WHEN YOU'RE QUARTERED SAFE OUT HERE"
30 PRINT
Ok
```

If your AUTO command shows you a line with an asterisk and you want to skip the line without changing it, just press Enter.

Editing Your Program

By now you've had a chance to type a few programs. And, if you're like most people, you didn't always get them right the first time. Or perhaps you wanted to modify them later. BASIC has a couple of features that make it easier for you to edit and renumber programs.

EDIT Line Number

Imagine for a moment that you're the software censor for the town of Fallentotter. You know that the PRINT statements in the previous example program are going to cause an uproar in your community, unless you can change them.

Your first tool is the EDIT command. EDIT jumps you directly to the specified line, ready for changing it. To edit line 10, type:

```
EDIT 10
10 PRINT "YOU CAN TALK OF GIN AND BEER"
```

Well, this line simply will not do! Use the right arrow key to move the cursor to the word "gin." Then change it by overtyping, and press Enter, as shown here:

```
10 PRINT "YOU CAN TALK OF MILK AND WATER"
```

That's better! Now make this little poem more specific to your local market:

```
EDIT 20
20 PRINT "WHEN YOU'RE QUARTERED SAFE OUT HERE"
```

Change the line to something more suitable, such as:

```
20 PRINT "WHEN YOU LIVE IN FALLENTOTTER"
```

To delete a line, you can simply type the line number, then press Enter. To delete line 30, just type the following:

```
30          (followed by the Enter key)
```

The modified program should now be safe to run in Fallentotter:

```
RUN
YOU CAN TALK OF MILK AND WATER
WHEN YOU LIVE IN FALLENTOTTER
Ok
```

Now LIST the program to see your changes:

```
LIST
10 PRINT "YOU CAN TALK OF MILK AND WATER"
20 PRINT "WHEN YOU LIVE IN FALLENTOTTER"
Ok
```

Renumbering a Program

Another way you might want to modify a program is to renumber the lines. Suppose that you wanted to add, oh, 30 new instructions between lines 10 and 20. How would you do it? Only nine "empty" lines exist between 10 and 20. Or, suppose that you wanted your program to begin at line 100 instead of line 10. You can deal with all these problems using the RENUM (renumber) command.

Try this RENUM command on the program now in the computer:

```
RENUM 100,10
Ok
```

This `RENUM 100,10` command means "renumber the program so that its first line number is 100; begin the renumbering with line 10." LIST the program to see the results:

```
LIST
100 PRINT "YOU CAN TALK OF MILK AND WATER"
110 PRINT "WHEN YOU LIVE IN FALLENTOTTER"
Ok
```

Try another RENUM command:

```
RENUM 1000,100,200
Ok

LIST
1000 PRINT "YOU CAN TALK OF MILK AND WATER"
1200 PRINT "WHEN YOU LIVE IN FALLENTOTTER"
Ok
```

Here, the `RENUM 1000, 100, 200` command renumbered the program so that the first new line was line 1000. The first old line to be renumbered was line 100, and the increment between new lines was 200.

If you don't specify any intervals or line numbers for RENUM, all conditions are preset to 10. (We say the default condition is 10.) So, simply typing RENUM

Introduction to GW-BASIC

renumbers your program so that the first new line number will be 10, and line numbers increase in increments of 10. Try it now:

```
RENUM
LIST
10 PRINT "YOU CAN TALK OF MILK AND WATER"
20 PRINT "WHEN YOU LIVE IN FALLENTOTTER"
Ok
```

You can use RENUM to clean up your programs, making them easier to read. RENUM also lets you insert loads of new lines wherever you want.

Math Functions

You remember that PRINT "message" causes the string of characters enclosed by the quotation marks to be printed on the screen. BASIC can also handle numbers with considerable ease. Enter the program shown in figure 1-15 and RUN it.

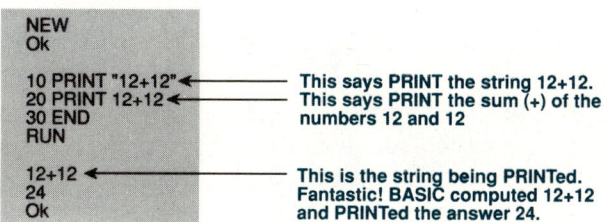

Fig. 1-15:   Using BASIC's math functions.

Note that in this program we have done something new. The statement, PRINT 12+12, has NO quotation marks around it. When the statement was executed, it calculated 12+12 and printed "24." Or, as is said in computer talk, the computer "evaluated the expression" and PRINTed the results.

BASIC can perform the kind of arithmetic found on a standard pocket calculator. Here are some rules about BASIC arithmetic:

• To ADD on the computer use +

• To SUBTRACT on the computer use –

37

Chapter 1

- To MULTIPLY on the computer use *
- To DIVIDE on the computer use /

In programming, we call these four symbols (+, –, *, /) the BASIC *arithmetic operators*. The operators operate on numbers. Try typing the following program:

```
NEW
Ok

10 PRINT 12+12
20 PRINT 12-12
30 PRINT 12*12
40 PRINT 12/12
50 END
RUN
 24
 0
 144
 1

Ok
```

There are several things to notice about this program. First, BASIC printed the results of four expressions, one after the other. Note that the numbers are printed with a space in front of each. This can be seen by the fact that the answers are shifted one space to the right of the RUN command and the word Ok. This space contains the "sign" of the number, but because the numbers are all positive, the + sign is not printed. The only time the sign of the number actually gets printed is when the number is negative. For example, add this statement and RUN the program:

```
45 PRINT 12-13
RUN

 24
 0
 144
 1
-1

Ok
```

38

Here the answer to PRINT 12–13 is –1, and the – sign got printed. The rule is that if the number is positive (greater than one) then a space is made for an "invisible" plus sign (+). On the other hand, if the number is negative (less than one), then a minus sign (–) is printed in front of the number.

Figuring in BASIC

Try the line shown in figure 1-16 in *direct mode*.

```
PRINT 3+3*4          Direct mode has no line number.
 15
Ok
```

Fig. 1-16: Which happens first: addition or multiplication?

Now try this slightly different version of the same expression:

```
PRINT (3+3)*4
 24
Ok
```

Whoa! What happened? There are a few things to note here. In the first statement, BASIC multiplied before it added, even though the + sign came before the * sign. In the second statement, we used left and right parentheses to make the addition happen before we multiply. We say multiplication (and division) have precedence over addition and subtraction.

But you don't need to worry about precedence if you use parentheses. Suppose that you wanted to evaluate the following expression:

3+3/2–1

First, try it without parentheses:

```
PRINT 3+3/2-1
 3.5
Ok
```

Chapter 1

Wrong answer! What happened is that BASIC did the division first, followed by addition and subtraction. So, it did things this way:

Step 1:   3 + 3/2 – 1

Step 2:   3 + 1.5 – 1

Step 3:   3.5

Add parentheses to make certain that the expression is evaluated the way you want, as follows:

```
PRINT (3+3)/(2-1)
  6
Ok
```

This time, thanks to the parentheses, you got the right answer.

```
PRINT 4*4/2/2
  4
Ok
```

Here the operators are * and /. These operators have "equal" precedence, and in this case, BASIC evaluates the expression from left to right. In our example, BASIC multiplies 4 by 4, divides by 2 to get 8 and divides by 2 again to get 4. That's it!

Exponentiation

How do you raise a number to a power, such as 2^5 or 3^3? There is a special arithmetic operator in BASIC for raising a number to a power. Try these two examples in the direct mode:

```
PRINT 2*2*2*2*2
 32
Ok

PRINT 2^5
 32
Ok
```

The two statements do the same thing. The symbol is called the circumflex character. As you can see in the second example, it means, "Multiply a number by

Introduction to GW-BASIC

itself as many times as specified by the number after the symbol." Now try the following:

```
PRINT 3^3
 27
Ok
```

Obviously, this is the same as 3*3*3, or 27. We call the operation caused by the operator "exponentiation," or raising a number to a power. In this last example, we say "3 raised to the third power." Here is 4 raised to the second power:

```
PRINT 4^2
 16
Ok
```

We will see more of the exponentiation operator later.

PRINT with Commas

Let us take our knowledge with PRINT and calculations a little further. Type the program shown in figure 1-17 and RUN it.

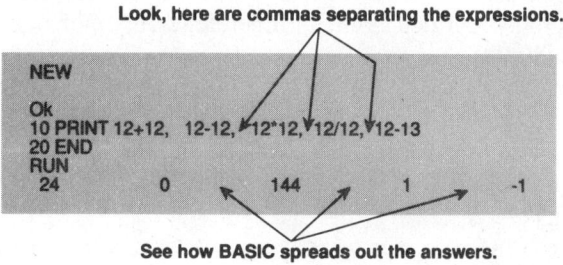

Fig. 1-17: Use commas to separate items in a PRINT statement.

Note how BASIC spreads out the answers.
This time we entered five expressions all in a single PRINT statement, using commas to separate them. You can see from the RUN of the program that the commas caused the results to be spread across the screen, with lots of space being inserted between the answers.

41

Chapter 1

Commas make our answers look pretty by spreading them across the page neatly and precisely. BASIC takes care of the spacing for us. Now type the following program and RUN it:

```
NEW
Ok
10 PRINT
20 PRINT "TIMES SEVEN TABLE"
30 PRINT 7*1, 7*2, 7*3, 7*4, 7*5, 7*6, 7*7, 7*8, 7*9
40 END
RUN
TIMES SEVEN TABLE
 7      14      21      28      35
 42     49      56      63

Ok
```

There are several new things to notice about this program and the results that were printed. As you can see, using commas to separate items of expressions in a single PRINT statement gives you five *columns*, *places*, or *print zones* across the line.

Also, when we exceed the number of columns in a line, the computer simply overflows the additional information onto the columns on the next line.

A *line* is defined as any number, letter, symbol, or single space. In BASIC, you can specify 80-character lines and 40-character lines.

In GW-BASIC, on an 80-column terminal, a line contains 72 character positions, so that is the value we will use in this book.

Now a little detail about the five columns. Each column is exactly 14 character positions wide. BASIC calls the first character position 0 and the last 71. The last two positions (70 & 71) are not used.

To get a feeling for the spacing that commas cause, figure 1-18 shows the output of our previous program printed with a row of numbers underneath it so that you can see the columns and where the commas cause the answers to be PRINTed. Read the numbers we printed up and down, as follows:

2 means 20, 5 means 56, and so on.

Introduction to GW-BASIC

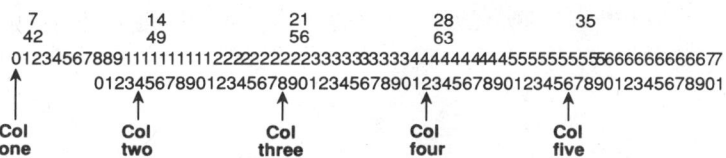

Fig. 1-18: How commas affect spacing.

As you can see by the numbers below the output, the columns start in positions 0, 14, 28, 42, and 56. When you look at how the actual numbers get printed, you can see that the number always has a leading blank space in front of it. The blank is the space for the assumed plus sign.

Note how numbers start in the left-hand edge of the column and expand to the right as the number of digits increases. In computer talk, we say the numbers are *left-justified*.

Now we know a little about making our numeric answers look pretty. But guess what—commas work with letters (strings of characters) as well as numbers.

```
NEW

Ok
10 PRINT "JOHN", "HARRY", "JOE", "FRANK", "BILL"
RUN
JOHN          HARRY         JOE           FRANK         BILL

Ok
```

See how the computer spread out the strings? Like numbers, the strings begin in successive columns. The first word starts at print position 0, the next at 14, and so on.

Does this ability to columnize suggest anything to you? How about using strings with commas to label the columns, and then using expressions in a PRINT statement with commas so that the values come out under the desired string labels. Try the following program:

```
NEW

Ok
10 PRINT
20 PRINT "RATE=$11 PER HOUR"
30 PRINT " $/HR", " $ PER DAY", " $ PER WEEK",
   " $ PER MONTH", " $ PER YEAR"
40 PRINT 11, 11*8, 11*40, 11*40*4, 11*40*52
```

Chapter 1

```
RUN

RATE=$11 PER HOUR
$/HR      $ PER DAY     $ PER WEEK     $ PER MONTH     $ PER YEAR
11        88            440            1760            22880

Ok
```

Notice that we added a space between the quotation mark and the dollar sign ($), so the columns line up. Now this is pretty neat, but it's not very useful yet. This does give us an idea of how we can "columnize" the results of our programs. Notice statement 10 (10 PRINT). This makes the computer move down one line and puts space between the word RUN and the beginning of the program output. If you wish to have more spacing, simply add more PRINT statements, as follows:

```
11 PRINT
12 PRINT
   .
   .
   .
      etc
```

Line 20 (20 PRINT "RATE=$11 PER HOUR") causes the computer to print the message about the amount of the hourly rate used in the rest of the program. Line 30 prints the titles or labels for the columns. Line 40 evaluates the five expressions based on the $11 hourly rate, and prints the results under the proper columns. That's it!

Double Commas

You can use all the commas you want in a PRINT statement, and each will simply cause the computer to move a column to the right before displaying. Try the following:

```
10 PRINT,,"I FOUND IT!"
RUN
                              I FOUND IT!
Ok
```

Or, how about this:

```
10 PRINT, "GOOD",,"BYE"
RUN
              GOOD                        BYE
Ok
```

Introduction to GW-BASIC

PRINT with Semicolons

Commas are used to put our output in precise, predefined columns. The semicolon has a different but similar use. Type and RUN this new program as shown in figure 1-19:

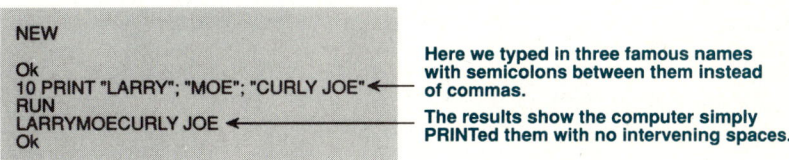

```
NEW
Ok
10 PRINT "LARRY"; "MOE"; "CURLY JOE"      ← Here we typed in three famous names
RUN                                          with semicolons between them instead
LARRYMOECURLY JOE      ←                     of commas.
Ok                                           The results show the computer simply
                                             PRINTed them with no intervening spaces.
```

Fig. 1-19:   Use semicolons if you want things PRINTed close together.

As you can see, in our program the semicolon was used instead of the commas. Rather than printing the results in columns, the computer PRINTed the three names as one string of characters. Try changing the program by putting two blank spaces before each name, as follows:

```
10 PRINT "  LARRY"; "  MOE"; "  CURLY JOE"
RUN
  LARRY  MOE  CURLY JOE
Ok
```

In this example, we changed line 10 so that each name contains two blank spaces before it. Because the semicolon forces the output to be squeezed together, the blank spaces are counted as characters and separate the individual names, so we can read them more easily now.

We can mix strings with numbers. Try typing and RUNning this program:

```
NEW
Ok
10 PRINT "10+10="; 10+10
RUN
10+10= 20
Ok
```

Can you figure out how this works? Here is a diagram of the statement, shown in figure 1-20.

45

Chapter 1

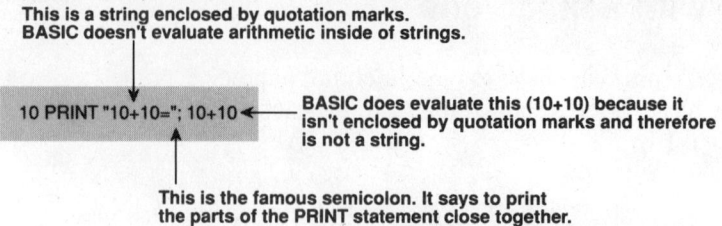

Fig. 1-20:   Mixing strings and numeric expressions in a PRINT statement.

That is enough about semicolons for now. Throughout the book we will see how they come to the rescue to make our programming life "more better."

BASIC Variables

Imagine for a moment that way down inside the computer there are stacks of tiny boxes. Each box has two compartments. The left side holds the *variable*. The right side of the box holds a number called the *value of the variable* (see fig. 1-21).

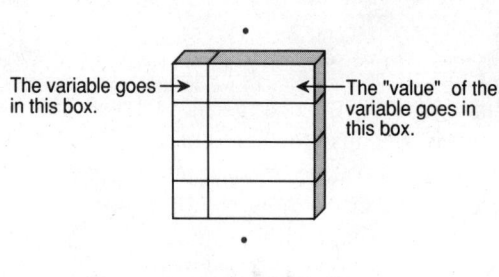

Fig. 1-21:   Variables and their values in memory.

Take a look at the little boxes that follow in figure 1-22. Some of the boxes have the variable labels filled in, and with values "assigned" to the variables. We have LET variable B have the value 12. That means the value 12 is placed in the box called B, or in simple terms, B=12. Variable X is assigned the value of -4.5, or X=-4.5. Similarly, the variable Q is assigned the value of 102 in the last box.

46

Introduction to GW-BASIC

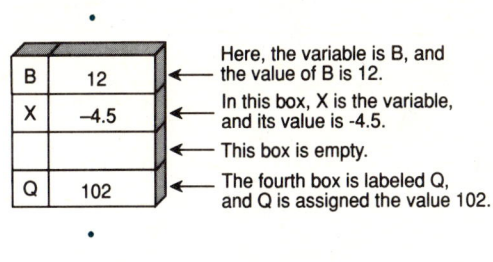

Fig. 1-22: Each variable has one value assigned to it.

Now we will learn a way to get BASIC to fill in the little boxes, that is, to assign values to variables. Try this program:

```
NEW
Ok
10 LET A=64
20 PRINT A

RUN
 64
Ok
```

When we ran the program, a little box was set up by the LET statement (line 10) and the statement assigned, or *Let*, the variable A have the value 64. Now the box looks like that shown in figure 1-23.

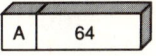

Fig. 1-23: The variable A is assigned the value of 64.

Change statement 10 to the following:

```
10 LET A=128
RUN
 128
Ok
```

47

Chapter 1

Now see that, by changing the value assigned to the variable A to 128, we also changed the value in the little box; and when we went PRINT A, the new value of 128 got printed. The box looks like that shown in figure 1-24.

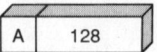

Fig. 1-24: Now the variable A is assigned the value 128.

You can have one value in the box at a time. The new value replaces the old value.

Let us try a little program that shows off how LET is used. Enter and RUN this program:

```
NEW

Ok
10 LET A=5
20 LET B=10
30 LET C=15
40 LET D=(A+B+C)/3
50 PRINT "THE AVERAGE IS"; D
RUN
THE AVERAGE IS 10
Ok
```

Here we used three LET statements to assign values to the three variables A, B, and C. Statement 40 added them together and divided the sum by 3 to obtain the average, and then the LET statement assigned the result to the variable D. Statement 50 printed the message, THE AVERAGE IS, and printed the value assigned to D. Before line 40 is executed, the boxes look like those shown in figure 1-25.

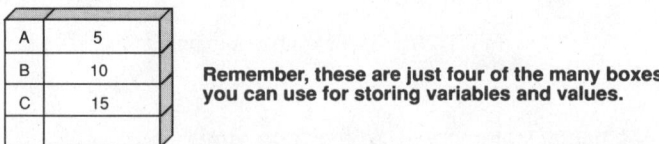

Fig. 1-25: Before line 40, D does not exist.

After we calculate the average and a value for the variable D, the boxes look like the ones shown in figure 1-26.

Introduction to GW-BASIC

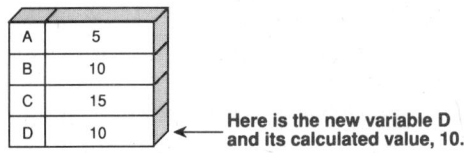

Fig. 1-26: After line 40 is executed, the result is placed in the variable D.

As you can see, D has its own little box now and the value (10) we calculated and assigned to D is in the box. Here is more practice using LET:

```
10 LET X=2
20 LET Y=10
30 LET Z=X^Y
40 PRINT "X", "Y", "X^Y"
50 PRINT X, Y, Z
RUN
X         Y         X^Y
 2        10        1024
Ok
```

Here we used the LET statement to create and assign values to the variables X and Y. Statement 30 (LET Z=X^Y) multiplies X by itself Y times. In this example, because X equals 2 and Y equals 10, the value of X^Y is:

2*2*2*2*2*2*2*2*2*2 or 1024

Can you see why LET Z=X^Y makes things easier for us?

Here is another fact to know about variables. Sometimes in our programs we wish to assign the same special value to several variables. We can do so as follows:

```
10 LET P=3.14159
20 LET C=P
30 LET D=P
40 LET E=P
50 PRINT C, D, E
RUN
 3.14159        3.14159        3.14159
Ok
```

Here we are assigning the same value to three variables, and the value we are assigning is itself a variable. In this example, the value is 3.14159 (which is pi).

Chapter 1

Leaving Off LET

The keyword LET is sometimes helpful in understanding how a program works, but you don't really need it. In fact, these two statements give exactly the same results:

```
10 LET A=75
10 A=75
```

Most BASIC programmers omit LET, and we'll leave it off later in this book. But this so-called "implied LET" can cause confusion if you're not careful. See if you can predict the results of this program:

```
10 A=1
20 B=2
30 B=A
40 PRINT B
50 END
```

There's a simple rule to remember here, and it holds true throughout BASIC:

The variable on the left of the equal sign always receives the value of whatever is on the right.

So, in line 30, the variable B receives the value of variable A, not the other way around. Here's the output, if you enter and RUN the program:

```
RUN
 1
```

Did you get it right?

Variable Names

Thus far, we have used single letters to stand for numeric variables. But GW-BASIC allows any length variable up to 40 characters. The first character must always be a letter and the second can be a letter or a number. The rest of the characters in the name can be letters or numbers. Figure 1-27 shows some legal numeric variables.

Introduction to GW-BASIC

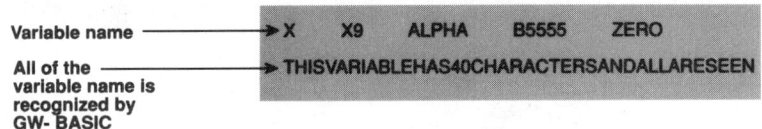

Fig. 1-27: Variable names can be short or long.

What happens if you try to use lowercase letters? You can type variables as capital letters or lowercase letters—it doesn't matter. BASIC changes them all to uppercase letters for you.

To be sure about what is allowed in your version of BASIC, consult your BASIC manual. If you want your programs to work on all versions of BASIC, stick with single characters, or, at most, a letter and a number for variable names. Longer names will help you tell what the variable does, and you can use long variable names in most versions of BASIC in use today.

Compare the two programs. Which is easier to understand?

Version #1: Single-letter variables:

```
10 A=25
20 B=78
30 C=55
40 D=(A+B+C)/3
50 PRINT "THE CLASS AVERAGE IS"; D
```

Version #2: Multiple-letter variables:

```
10 MYAGE = 25
20 YOURAGE = 78
30 HERAGE = 55
40 AVERAGE = (MYAGE + YOURAGE + HERAGE)/3
```

String Variables

As you might have already suspected, there is more to variables than just putting numbers in boxes. Instead of a number, a variable box can contain a string of letters or characters. This type of variable is called a *string variable*. In order for BASIC to know that we are dealing with a string variable and not a numeric variable, the label or variable name ends with a dollar sign ($); for example, X$ or A1$. The string that is being assigned to the string variable is enclosed by quotations, just as in the PRINT

Chapter 1

statement. Remember our program that printed the names of three famous comedians? Here is how we could do it with string variables:

```
10 LET A$="LARRY"
20 LET B$="MOE"
30 LET C$="CURLY JOE"
40 PRINT A$; B$; C$
RUN
LARRYMOECURLY JOE
Ok
```

Just as in the case of numeric variables, string variables can be imagined as being held in little boxes (see fig. 1-28).

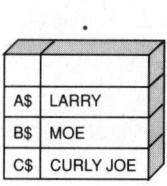

Fig. 1-28:   String variables and their contents.

The only thing wrong with our program is that there is no separation between the three names. Can you think of a remedy? Figure 1-29 shows two answers.

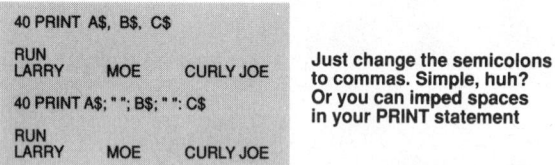

Fig. 1-29:   Separate items with commas, or by embedding strings of spaces between your variables.

In this trick, we printed A$ followed by two spaces, followed by B$, followed by two spaces, then the word AND, then two more spaces, and finally C$. Whew! In computer talk, you are embedding your string variables within strings of spaces—a creative approach to displaying results.

Introduction to GW-BASIC

Concatenation of Strings

Believe it or not, strings can be joined together as one happy unit with the plus symbol (+). No, this doesn't mean addition; it is just another way of saying that you are joining two things together. (Probably the inventors of BASIC could think of no better symbol than +.) In computer talk, we call joining two strings *concatenation* (pronounced con-ca-ten-a-shon). Here's an example:

```
10 A$="EVERYBODY"
20 B$="NEEDS"
30 C$="SOMEBODY"
40 D$=A$+B$+C$
50 PRINT D$
RUN
EVERYBODYNEEDSSOMEBODY
Ok
```

What happened is that we defined three separate strings to three separate string variables, and then in line 40 we *concatenated* them with A$+B$+C$, called this D$, and PRINTed it out. Neat, huh?

Input

There is another way of putting labels in little boxes and assigning them values. The INPUT statement allows us a way to get values and variables into BASIC after the program is started by RUN. Try the example shown in figure 1-30.

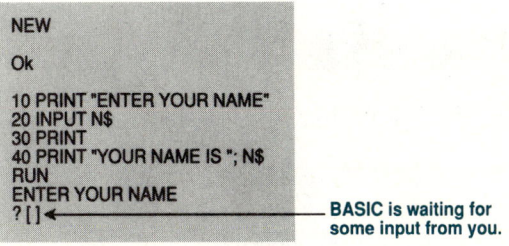

Fig. 1-30: INPUT causes the program to wait for your input.

Notice the question mark. This was caused by the INPUT statement, which says, "INPUT something." In this case, that something is a string of characters,

53

Chapter 1

because the variable after the INPUT is a string variable. (Some BASICs require a semicolon after the INPUT, as follows: `INPUT ;N$`.)

BASIC is waiting for you to INPUT so that it can put something in the little box inside the computer marked `N$`. You must respond by typing a name (or any string) and then pressing the Return key:

```
ENTER YOUR NAME
? GYRO GEARLOOSE

YOUR NAME IS GYRO GEARLOOSE
Ok
```

Here BASIC made `N$` equal `GYRO GEARLOOSE`, and we didn't even need quotation marks like most strings do (see fig. 1-31).

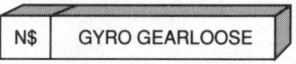

Fig. 1-31: The string variable N$ holds the string "GYRO GEARLOOSE."

The only times we need quotations around our string INPUTs is when there is a comma in the string, or if we want to have spaces at the end of a string. Try this:

```
RUN
ENTER YOUR NAME
? "EINSTEIN, ALBERT"

YOUR NAME IS EINSTEIN, ALBERT
Ok
```

You need to use quotation marks when entering a string that contains commas.

Note that in our program we used a PRINT statement to tell us what the INPUT statement wanted, in this case a string name. The question mark by itself doesn't tell us much. We can eliminate the PRINT statement in the program by putting it inside the INPUT statement, as shown in figure 1-32.

Introduction to GW-BASIC

```
10 INPUT "ENTER YOUR NAME"; N$
20 PRINT
30 PRINT "YOUR NAME IS "; N$          Note the space and the semicolon.

RUN
ENTER YOUR NAME? HARCOMB MUD

YOUR NAME IS HARCOMB MUD
Ok
```

Fig. 1-32:   Putting a prompt string in the INPUT statement.

We call this an INPUT statement with a "prompt" string. It makes our programming simpler and eliminates an extra PRINT statement. You can also INPUT numbers into little boxes with INPUT, like this enhancement of our previous program:

```
10 INPUT "ENTER YOUR NAME"; MYNAME$
20 INPUT "ENTER YOUR AGE IN YEARS"; Y
30 LET D=Y*365.25
40 PRINT "YOU'RE"; D; "DAYS OLD, " MYNAME$
RUN
ENTER YOUR NAME? MITCH
ENTER YOUR AGE IN YEARS? 32
YOU'RE 11688 DAYS OLD, MITCH
Ok
```

Here we used INPUT in line 20 to ask the user to enter his age in years. This number is then assigned to the variable Y. Next, in line 30 we multiply Y times the number of days in a year (365.25), and assign this value to D. In line 40 we PRINT the value of D, a short string, and the name of the person (MYNAME$). Figure 1-33 shows how the boxes look.

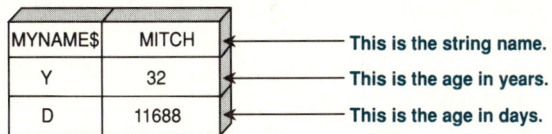

Fig. 1-33:   Variables and their contents after running the program.

Sometimes when BASIC is requesting input for an INPUT statement, you might not wish to answer the question. To abort the INPUT and return BASIC to the

Chapter 1

command mode (direct mode) type Control-C. This will terminate the INPUT, and BASIC will print Break and then Ok, as shown in figure 1-34.

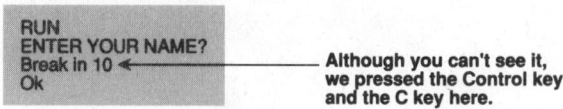

Fig. 1-34:   Control-C terminates input.

A simple way to remember the rule for input is that you can enter numbers into a string variable but you can't enter letters into a numeric variable. This is because a string variable will accept any character. An example would be a phone number or street address; you would not want to add these numbers together, so you would use a string variable. Just remember that BASIC can't perform arithmetic on numbers that are in strings.

TAB

TAB is a keyword that is always used with PRINT. Its purpose is to cause the cursor to move horizontally a specific number of positions before printing the information in the PRINT statement. The form of TAB is as follows:

```
PRINT TAB (var) var, var, . . .
```

You are already familiar with the PRINT statement. When TAB appears in a PRINT statement, the variables `var, var . . .` after TAB are printed on the screen, starting at the horizontal column position specified by the value of variable (`var`) in the TAB parentheses. It is assumed that the variable (`var`) is greater than zero and less than the width of your screen. In some BASICs, if the value of `var` exceeds the screen width, the information is printed on the next line until the number of column positions specified by `var` has been reached. In essence, TAB is like the Tab on a typewriter; it moves the print head to the right by so many spaces. In the case of the computer, we have a special control of the movement of the cursor (which is analogous to the print head on the typewriter) through the variable `var`. It is also assumed that var is an *integer* variable because there is no such thing as a fractional cursor position. An actual number can be used instead of a variable.

As an example, consider that you wish to print a heading for a program so that it is centered on the terminal or screen page. There are two ways to do this. One way is to simply place the correct number of blanks inside the quotation marks around the string you wish to display. The blanks precede the message and cause the message to be printed to the right of the first column position, as shown in figure 1-35.

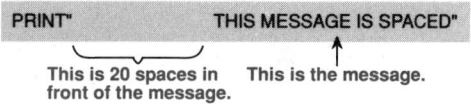

Fig. 1-35: Inserting blank spaces puts the message where you want it.

When the PRINT statement is executed in BASIC, the message appears as shown in figure 1-36.

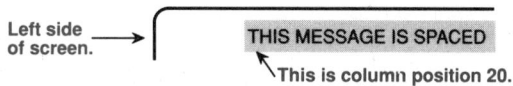

Fig. 1-36: Message displayed on the monitor screen.

We can accomplish the same thing and shorten our statement by using TAB and making the value of the variable var 20, as follows:

```
PRINT TAB(20) "THIS MESSAGE IS SPACED"
```

This statement makes the message begin at column position 20. If we wanted to move the message frequently, or test its spacing at various positions, we could do this:

```
10 INPUT I
20 PRINT TAB(I) "THIS MESSAGE IS SPACED"
RUN
? 10
          THIS MESSAGE IS SPACED
RUN
?5
     THIS MESSAGE IS SPACED

RUN?1
 THIS MESSAGE IS SPACED
```

Chapter 1

The program allows us to INPUT a TAB value and see how the string, THIS MESSAGE IS SPACED, gets printed. Note that when we entered a TAB value of 1, the string began in the first column position. TAB(1) put the message in Column 1, which is the same as no TAB at all.

The use of TAB is not restricted to string messages. We can force a TAB on any item in a PRINT statement. For example, consider a case in which you wish to print several numbers in column positions that are different than the ones set by the comma:

```
100 A=10
101 B=20
102 C=30
110 PRINT TAB(5) A;" ";B;" ";C
RUN
      10    20    30
```

Note that the entire group of three numbers (A, B, and C) was shifted five spaces to the right by TAB(5). The semicolon and the string " " were used to place two spaces between each number. TAB affects the group of characters A, B, and C, but the spacing relationship between the values of A, B, and C remain fixed.

Reserved Words

As we mentioned earlier, GW-BASIC allows variables to be given names longer than one or two characters. For example, we can call a variable XVALUE. This longer name option is really nice except for a subtle danger. The danger is that you cannot name a variable with a name that is already used in GW-BASIC for some statement command or function.

For example, if you call a variable RUN5, the computer will think you mean to *run*, or execute, line 5. Or, if you have a statement, FORMAT=10, when BASIC executes this, it may think that this is a FOR...NEXT loop because it sees the letters FOR; thus, you may get an error of some kind.

In order to avoid these problems, BASIC has *reserved words*. These are all the words that BASIC reserves for its own purposes. You should not use any of these words in your variable names. In GW-BASIC, they're all the words found in Appendix A, the quick reference guide.

Printing the Date and Time

What time is it now? And what's the date? Before you look at your fancy digital watch, type the following:

Introduction to GW-BASIC

```
PRINT DATE$
03-25-1990
Ok
```

And this:

```
PRINT TIME$
13:19:38
Ok
```

That's right, BASIC can keep you on time and up to date. You can use the handy DATE$ and TIME$ statements to add date or time "stamps" to your programs. Here's an example:

```
10 INPUT "HOW MANY YEN TO THE DOLLAR TODAY";YEN
20 PRINT
30 PRINT "TODAY,";DATE$;", YOU'LL GET";YEN;"YEN PER DOLLAR"
40 END
RUN
HOW MANY YEN TO THE DOLLAR TODAY? 145
TODAY,03-25-1990, YOU'LL GET 145 YEN PER DOLLAR
Ok
```

The $ sign at the end of DATE$ and TIME$ means that these statements are string variables, not numbers, so you can use them as you would any string variable.

Putting It All Together: The Loan Program

With just three simple keywords of the BASIC language (INPUT, LET, and PRINT), and five arithmetic operators (+, −, *, /, ^), we now have the ability to perform complicated and useful programs by simply combining them in some logical order, according to a predetermined plan we devise.

Let us step back for a moment and take a look at what we've learned. Computers operate using three main functions:

1. They *input* information.

2. They *process* the information.

3. They *output* the results of the process.

All three of these functions have their own variations, which provide you with a huge variety of program techniques.

Chapter 1

Although there are literally hundreds of things you could think up to program in BASIC, the ones that BASIC is most suited for involve operations that would be difficult to do with a calculator and almost impossible to do by hand.

As an example of a practical program for which you could use the computer, consider the everyday problem of borrowing money. Almost everyone at one time or another has had to take out a loan from a bank, credit union, or other lending institution. Have you ever wondered how the bank figures your monthly payment? Or, did you ever wish you could check to see whether the figure was right, or whether you could determine the payment on your own without having to call the bank? The program we are about to introduce pulls together everything we have learned so far to calculate the total monthly payment of a loan. The program illustrates the three laws of computing, and the way that a complex formula can be simplified into a LET statement.

The way banks figure out your monthly payment for a loan is to use special tables of figures that chart out the various payment schedules for certain loan amounts, spread over a specified number of years or months, and carrying a certain interest rate. There is also a special formula that can be used to compute the loan payment for any combination of loan amount, term or length, and interest.

The special formula is called an *amortization loan* formula. Amortization refers to the fact that the monthly payment is based on interest computed each month on the unpaid balance. A *simple loan* formula, on the other hand, would just take a percentage of the total borrowed amount, add it to the amount borrowed, and divide the total by the number of months of the loan, called the *term*.

When written down on paper, the amortization formula looks like the one shown in figure 1-37.

$$p = iA\left(\frac{(2+i)^n}{(1+i)^n - 1}\right)$$

Fig. 1-37: Loan amortization formula.

In this formula, you take 1 plus the monthly interest rate, i, and raise it to the number of payments, n. Once you've calculated this quantity, you divide it by the same quantity minus 1. You multiply the result by the interest rate, i, and by the total amount of the loan, A.

Here are a couple of things to remember about this formula: For one thing, the interest rate, i, is expressed in a percentage, but it isn't the yearly interest rate. Instead, it's a monthly interest rate. So, you'll have to take the yearly interest rate, divide it by 12, then divide the result by 100 to come up with a value for a monthly interest rate that you can use in the calculation, as follows:

i=Yearly interest rate/12/100

Here's another point: The number of monthly payments, n, is found by multiplying the number of years of the loan by 12, as follows:

n=Years * 12

How can we write a program to calculate the loan payment? We begin by using the INPUT statement to ask for the needed quantities:

```
10 INPUT "Amount";A
20 INPUT "Interest rate";RATE
30 INPUT "Years";YEARS
```

Notice that we ask for the interest rate as a yearly rate, called RATE. (We'll need to convert this to the monthly rate used in the formula.) Also, we asked for the number of YEARS of the loan, which we'll also have to convert to something we can use—the total number of monthly payments.

After the needed quantities are INPUT, we then convert the interest RATE to the quantity I needed in the formula:

```
40 LET I=RATE/12/100
```

And we convert the years of the loan to the number of payment periods:

```
50 LET N=YEARS*12
```

Now that we have all the information, we can calculate the monthly payment. Here goes:

```
60 LET P=I*A*(((1+I)^N)/(((1+I)^N)-1))
```

This is really the same as the formula you saw earlier. If you have trouble visualizing how line 60 corresponds to the formula, try looking at it from the innermost set of parentheses and working outward. We calculate 1 + I and raise it to the N power using exponentiation. We divide that by the same quantity (1 + I raised to the N power) minus 1. Finally, we multiply that result by the amount, A, and the monthly interest rate, I. This gives us the monthly payment.

Chapter 1

We're not quite finished yet. We still have to generate the output. Output is the only part of your program that most people ever see, and you want answers to be clear and easy to read. So, make sure to label the output:

```
70 PRINT "The monthly payment for a loan of $";A
80 PRINT "at a rate of ";RATE;"%"
90 PRINT "for";YEARS;"years is $";P
```

That's it! The program is ready to go to work for you. Let's suppose that you wanted a car loan of $8200. The dealer will handle the financing, and will give you a four-year loan at an annual interest rate of 15%. LIST the entire program, and RUN it to find the payment for your automobile loan.

```
LIST
10 INPUT "Amount";A
20 INPUT "Interest rate";RATE
30 INPUT "Years";YEARS
40 LET I=RATE/12/100
50 LET N=YEARS*12
60 LET P=I*A*(((1+I)^N)/(((1+I)^N)-1))
70 PRINT "The monthly payment for a loan of $";A
80 PRINT "at a rate of ";RATE;"%"
90 PRINT "for";YEARS;"years is $";P
100 END
Ok
RUN

Amount? 8200
Interest rate? 15
Years? 4
The monthly payment for a loan of $ 8200
at a rate of  15 %
for 4 years is $ 228.2113
```

Well, that's not so bad. Since you can easily handle a payment of $228.21 per month, what about purchasing a house, too? The little cottage you have your eye on is just $400,000. If you make a down payment of $80,000, you can finance the remaining $320,000 with a 30-year loan at a 10.5% annual interest rate. Here's how to figure your monthly payment:

```
RUN
Amount? 320000
Interest rate? 10.5
```

Introduction to GW-BASIC

```
Years? 30
The monthly payment for a loan of $ 320000
at a rate of  10.5 %
for 30 years is $ 2927.168
Ok
```

Documenting Your Program with Remarks

Suppose that you wrote a program in 1990, and then in 1993 you came back to it and attempted to modify its design. Because few of us have photographic memories, what we have to do is "relearn" how the program works. Although BASIC is a simple language, one cannot just look at a program listing and immediately tell how it works. Furthermore, the program lacks information to point out what it actually accomplishes when it is run. Unless you are really sharp, deciding what statements perform what functions can be very difficult.

In order to alleviate this problem, BASIC provides a special statement, called REM, which stands for REMark. REM allows us to add program *documentation* information, which appears in the program listing but has no effect on the way the program works. REMs are called nonexecutable statements, because when the computer encounters a REM in the program flow, it simply ignores it and goes to the next line.

The form of the REM statement is as follows:

```
line REM a message goes here about the program . . .
```

For example, in our Loan program, we can use a REM statement right away in line 1 to tell us the name of the program, as follows:

```
REM LOAN AMORTIZATION PROGRAM
```

Now when we come back to the program at a later date and read the listing, the first REM statement will tell us the name and purpose of the program. The REM statement is therefore used throughout the program to explain to you, or to an outsider, what the statements in the program actually do to complete the total job.

Keep in mind that the REM statements do not get executed by the computer. When one is encountered, the computer knows that it is to ignore the statement and execute the next statement after the REM. But when we list the program with the LIST command, the information in the REM statement will be displayed for us.

There's another way to put remarks into GW-BASIC programs. You use the apostrophe (') character. This works just like REM—everything on the line after the apostrophe is ignored by the computer when it runs the program.

Chapter 1

You can (and should) use remarks to put detailed information in your programs. This is called *documenting the program*, and it's as important as the actual program instructions that you write.

Look at how you might document the loan amortization program:

```
1 REM LOAN AMORTIZATION PROGRAM
2 REM Last modified 3/15/90
3 REM This program calculates the monthly payment
4 '    for a loan. The user is asked for the loan
5 '    amount, A, the interest rate, I, and the
6 '    number of years, Y, of the loan. The payment,
7 '    P, is calculated and printed.
```

Notice how the apostrophes are used like REM statements. The apostrophe is particularly useful for adding a remark to a line containing an instruction. For instance, you might want to add information to remind you what's happening in lines 40 and 50:

```
40 LET I=RATE/12/100        'Convert yearly interest rate to monthly
50 LET N=YEARS*12           'Convert years to number of payments
```

Remember, the computer ignores everything on a line after the apostrophe. So you can add an apostrophe to a program line, then type remarks to tell you what the line does. (You can't do this with REM, because REM needs to be on its own separate line.)

Now LIST the program to show how much easier it is to read and understand:

```
LIST
1 REM LOAN AMORTIZATION PROGRAM
2 REM Last modified 3/15/90
3 REM This program calculates the monthly payment
4 '    for a loan. The user is asked for the loan
5 '    amount, A, the interest rate, I, and the
6 '    number of years, Y, of the loan. The payment,
7 '    P, is calculated and printed.
10 INPUT "Amount";A
20 INPUT "Interest rate";RATE
30 INPUT "Years";YEARS
40 LET I=RATE/12/100 ' Convert yearly interest rate to monthly
50 LET N=YEARS*12 ' Convert years to number of payments
60 LET P=I*A*(((1+I)^N)/(((1+I)^N)-1))
70 PRINT "The monthly payment for a loan of $";A
```

```
80 PRINT "at a rate of ";RATE;"%"
90 PRINT "for";YEARS;"years is $";P
100 END
```

One thing you will certainly discover as your programming experience grows is that "the other guy" never seems to document his program well enough for you to understand. In fact, the secret of good programming is super documentation, but most programmers are weak in this area. A program without adequate REM statements is like a machine with no operator's manual. If you get stuck or if you want to change something, you must reinvent what the original maker had in mind when it was designed.

So, to be an especially accomplished programmer, strive to document your programs with REM. The only negative things about REMs is they consume extra memory without adding any computing power to the program—and, if they're too long, they can be tedious to read. In the case of excessively long programs, the additional memory consumption by the REMs can be a problem. So, you should at least place REMs in the critical parts of the body of the program.

Saving and Loading Program Files

By now you're probably getting a little tired of typing a new program each time you start BASIC. And, maybe after you've gone to all the work to create the loan program, you'd like to save it.

Luckily for you, BASIC has a pair of statements, SAVE and LOAD, that let you store your programs on disk, then retrieve them later.

Saving Programs with SAVE

SAVE stores a copy of your program on disk for you, so you don't have to reenter it every time you turn on the computer. All you have to do is give the program a name. Here's how you use the SAVE statement:

```
SAVE "NAME
```

This means, "take all program lines currently in memory and save them in the file called NAME." You can substitute any name for NAME; in fact, the name can be up to eight letters, followed by a dot and three more letters. So, the following are all OK:

```
SAVE "LOANFILE
SAVE "LOANFILE.1
SAVE "LOAN.FIL
```

Chapter 1

You need quotation marks in front of the name, but not after it. For speed, you can use the function key F4 at the top of the keyboard—this types SAVE" for you—and then type a name.

Retrieving a Program with LOAD

Once you've saved a program with SAVE, you can bring it back into the computer again with the LOAD statement. The general form of LOAD is as follows:

```
LOAD "NAME
```

This means, "look for the program file called NAME and load it in the computer." As with SAVE, you can use the function key (this time it's F3) as a typing aid to speed things up.

When you LOAD a program, it erases any program lines that you had in your computer. Even if you have 100 lines of program code and you LOAD a program of only 10 lines, your 100-line program is all gone, replaced by the 10-line program.

Try a LOAD and a SAVE now. First, enter the following simple program:

```
NEW
Ok
10 PRINT "I went away and now I'm back"
```

Now save the file as DEMOFILE. Use the function key F4 as a typing aid, if you like:

```
SAVE "DEMOFILE
Ok
```

Your program is now saved under the name DEMOFILE. You can retrieve it with the LOAD statement. First, for purposes of this demonstration, erase the program lines now in the computer:

```
NEW
Ok
LIST
Ok
```

LIST shows what's in the computer now—which is nothing. (Note that you didn't really have to erase those lines, because the new program would kick them out of there for you. But this proves beyond the shadow of a doubt that there's nothing in memory, nothing up our sleeve.)

Now LOAD the program DEMOFILE:

```
LOAD "DEMOFILE
Ok
LIST
10 PRINT "I went away and now I'm back"
Ok
```

There's your program, back again! To RUN it, just enter RUN:

```
RUN
I went away and now I'm back
Ok
```

You'll learn more about how to save your programs later in this book.

Now we have a good idea of the three simplest BASIC keywords—INPUT, LET, and PRINT—as well as some special-purpose characters for formatting our output (semicolons and commas). We also know a little about numbers and variables. As you saw with the loan amortization program, you can write a number of useful programs with just these few statements. In the next chapter, however, we will take a bigger step into BASIC and learn how programs can be increased greatly in power and flexibility by some new BASIC keywords called program control statements.

Review Questions

1. Which of the following statements are legal in GW-BASIC?

    a. 100 PRINT "HELLO THERE"

    b. –10 A=A+1

    c. 334 PRINT A$ + B

    d. LIST 50-200

2. Consider this short program:

```
10 WORD1$=" BASIC"
20 WORD2$=" IS"
30 WORD3$=" FOR"
40 WORD4$=" EVERYONE"
```

Add a line 50 with a PRINT statement that generates the following sentence on the screen:

EVERYONE IS FOR BASIC

Chapter 1

3. Write a PRINT statement that will produce the correct answer for this equation: 5[28–7(8+2)]/2.

4. Which of the following are legal variable names?

   a. L

   b. LIST

   c. LISTING

   d. ALISTCANBEDONEFROMWITHINAPROGRAM

5. After a single RUN of the following program, what is the value of C?

```
10 A=10
20 B=20
30 END
40 C=30
```

6. What statement should you normally use to halt program execution?

7. This is a BASIC version of the old shell game. The variables A, B, and C are the "shells," and the value 1 is the "pea." Two shells always are empty (that is, they contain zero). At the end of the program, which variable has the value of 1?

```
10 C=1
20 A=0
30 B=0
40 B=A
50 B=C
60 C=A
70 A=B
80 B=C
90 PRINT A,B,C
```

8. What statement would you write to renumber a program so that what is now line 100 becomes line 500, what is now the next line becomes line 600, and so on?

9. Name two ways to show line 80 of a program for editing on the screen.

10. Exercise: In aerobic exercise, the object is to try to get your heart rate up to a so-called "target range" and keep it there for several minutes. The target range is given by the formula:

    60% to 90% of (220 – Age)

    Write a program that will:

    a. Ask the user for his or her name

b. Ask the user for his or her age.

c. Calculate and display that person's target heart rate.

A single RUN of the program might look like this:

```
RUN
AEROBIC TARGET HEART RATE
What is your name?
Adonis

How old are you, Adonis?
45

Adonis, your target heart rate
is from 105 beats per minute
to 167.5 beats per minute
```

Chapter 2

Control Flow

Chapter *2*

Control Flow

Have you ever made a decision? Silly question—you probably make hundreds of them each day. Some are based solely on fact; others may be more emotional. Like you and me, BASIC can also make decisions—and unlike us, BASIC bases its decisions only on the facts at hand. These facts may be something like, "Which of two numbers is the greater?" or "Is the name I've been given the same name that I stored a while ago?" As long as BASIC has sufficient, accurate information, it can evaluate the information and make a completely unbiased decision.

What You'll Learn in this Chapter

In this chapter, you'll learn about BASIC's decision-making powers and a few other helpful BASIC statements and commands, including:

- FOR...NEXT loops
- IF...THEN conditional branches
- Easy looping with WHILE...WEND
- Some simple functions
- The GOTO statement
- ON...GOTO branches
- Tracing program execution
- Subroutines and how to use them

Most of BASIC's decisions are of the "yes or no" variety: If a statement is true, BASIC takes one path and executes a sequence of instructions; and if the same

Chapter 2

statement is false, BASIC takes a different path and a different sequence. Although that doesn't sound like much compared to our own sophisticated decision-making powers, BASIC can make thousands of these decisions per second. Certain statements also let BASIC make a choice among several different paths.

In this section we will discuss the BASIC statements that provide the program with a way to "change course" based upon the evaluation of some information. This concept is what really makes BASIC a powerful tool.

The Decision-Making Statements

There are several BASIC statements that come under the category of decision-making statements. Each has a specific use and function. In many cases these statements can be combined to offer even greater decision-making power to BASIC.

FOR...NEXT, the Programmed Loop

In most programming applications, you'll need to do the same steps over and over again. This process is known as *iteration*. It is also referred to quite often as *looping* because it usually involves setting up the program so that it will loop back and repeat itself. Depending on how a program is written, it can easily get stuck in the loop and keep on repeating itself forever. For this reason, there is usually some means of getting out of the loop, whether by keeping track of just how many times the loop is supposed to repeat itself, or by looping until a condition changes.

One way of determining how many times a loop will be executed is with the FOR and NEXT statements. The FOR statement sets up the beginning of the loop and determines how many times it will be repeated. The NEXT statement marks the end of the loop, and causes the program to go back and repeat itself if necessary.

To use a simple example: Let's suppose that we want our program to INPUT four numbers from the keyboard, add them together, and PRINT the total on the screen. Now, the four numbers could easily be entered using just one INPUT statement, but, for the sake of the example, let us say that the numbers are to be entered separately. The program looks like this:

```
10 T = 0
20 FOR I = 1 to 4      'Begins a FOR...NEXT loop from 1 to 4.
30     INPUT N
40     T = T + N
50 NEXT I              'NEXT I represents the end of the loop.
60 PRINT T             'PRINTS the total of the four numbers you input
70 END
```

Control Flow

Now we'll take a closer look at this program, line by line. At line 10, we begin by setting the variable T equal to zero. This is the variable that we will use to accumulate the total of the four numbers to be INPUT. At line 20 we see the FOR statement, which controls how many times the following statements will be performed. The FOR statement specifies that the *index* number I will be initially set to the value of 1, and the loop will continue until I has reached a value of 4. Statement 30 lets us INPUT a number into the variable called N. At line 40, another implied LET statement is used to replace the current value of T (the running total), with the sum of T and the value of the variable N.

Now, at line 50, the NEXT statement defines the end of the loop and causes the value of I to be increased by 1. At this point, if I is greater than 4, the next statement in the program will be performed. That would be the PRINT statement at 60, which causes the total of the four numbers stored in variable T to be PRINTed on the screen. If, however, I is less than or equal to 4 after the NEXT I statement has increased I by one, the program will return to the first statement following the FOR statement where the loop begins. Another number will be read from the keyboard into variable N. It will then be added to the current value of the total stored in variable T, and so on. Figure 2-1 shows the FOR...NEXT loop.

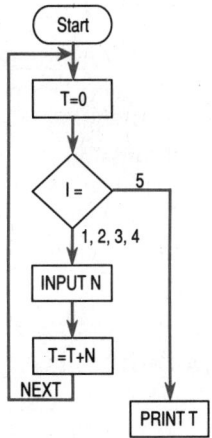

Fig. 2-1:   The FOR...NEXT loop continues until I is greater than 4.

Notice that in the program we've indented the statements within the loop. That's to make the program easier for you (and others) to read, because you can tell at a glance just where the loop is and what's in it. You can add these indents as you type programs by spacing over manually, or simply pressing the Tab key after you type the line number.

Chapter 2

Let's look at another, more powerful version of the FOR statement. FOR can allow the increment that is added to the "index" I to be some value other than one. This advanced FOR statement looks like the following:

```
FOR I = 1 to 50 STEP 3
```

Notice the addition of the word STEP to the statement. This statement would begin by initializing the index I to 1. Then when the NEXT I statement was encountered later in the program, the value of 3 would be added to I instead of 1. Then, as before, the value of I would be checked to see whether it had exceeded the termination value of the loop, 50.

Let's suppose that we want to write a program that will add up all the odd numbers between 0 and 100, and print the answer. The program could be done like this:

```
10 T = 0
20 FOR I = 1 TO 100 STEP 2    'I goes 1, 3, 5 ...
30    T = T + I
40 NEXT I
50 PRINT T
```

It's quite a simple program, really. First, at line 10, we set up a variable called T and initialize it to zero. The next line is the beginning of the FOR...NEXT loop, which starts at 1 and goes to 100 by 2s. Each time through the loop the value of I is added to the total being accumulated in T. Finally, when the value of I exceeds 100, the answer is printed.

Will I ever be equal to 1? Think about it. The loop progresses like this: 1, 3, 5,...95, 97, 99. When 2 is added to the value 99, the result is 101, which is greater than 100 and therefore causes the termination of the loop.

IF...THEN, Conditional Branches

Another way for BASIC to make decisions is with the IF...THEN combination. There are many forms of the IF...THEN statement, ranging from very simple data evaluation to complex combinations of conditions. To get a quick idea of what this statement is like, use a simple analogy:

IF today is Wednesday, THEN do the laundry.

Here we have set up a conditional decision. If the premise is true (that it is Wednesday), then the result of the decision causes the action of doing the laundry. Of course, the opposite situation (that it is NOT Wednesday) would cause no action to be taken. It is only when the premise is true that the part following the word THEN is carried out.

Control Flow

In BASIC, things work the same way. Here's a sample of a BASIC statement using IF...THEN:

```
IF A = 5 THEN PRINT "END OF JOB"
```

Here, the current value of the variable A is tested to see whether it is equal to 5. If it is, the program will output the message END OF JOB. Again, if A is not equal to 5, the message will not be printed.

Notice that the condition being tested in this statement is the value of the variable A. This is done by using one of the arithmetic operators (=) to indicate that it is equality that is being tested. The variety of different expressions that can be included as part of the premise is quite great. For example, the following are some other forms of the IF...THEN statement.

```
IF A + 3 = B THEN C = 0
IF 2*B-5 = C+2 THEN PRINT "MATCH"
```

Other relational operators that may be used in the IF...THEN statement are as follows:

```
<  less than
>  greater than
=< less than or equal to
>= greater than or equal to
<> not equal to
```

The following are some examples of these relational IF...THEN statements:

```
IF A < 3 THEN END
IF 2*B+4 > 20 THEN A = 1
IF B+C+6 <> 0 THEN PRINT "NOT EQUAL"
```

There are variations on the THEN side of the IF...THEN statement as well. We have already seen that we can cause something to be printed if the premise of the IF statement is true. We can also cause other things to happen; take a look at the following examples:

```
IF...THEN A = 125
IF...THEN B = A + C
IF...THEN INPUT N
```

You can see that there are many things that the program can do based upon the premise of the IF statement being true. Once again, if the premise is NOT true, the object of the statement (that part which follows the word THEN) will not be performed. Instead, the program will just proceed to the next statement in sequence.

To make this statement even more powerful, we can add variations that use what are known as "logical operators" to form compound IF...THEN statements. Some examples include:

```
IF A = 3 AND B < 4 THEN C = 10
IF B > 2 OR C < 2 THEN PRINT "INVALID"
```

In the first example, the object of the IF statement will be executed only if both conditions are true. That is, "A must be equal to 3," AND "B must be less than 4." If either of these premises is not true, then the THEN C=10 will not be performed.

In the second example, if either the first premise OR the second one is true—that is, if either "B is greater than 2," or "C is less than 2—then the message INVALID will be printed.

We can see that by using this type of IF...THEN statement, many conditions may be tested at once, and at the same time very complex logical decisions can be made.

ELSE—An Alternative to THEN

ELSE is an optional addition to an IF...THEN statement. It means, "IF the expression following the IF is not true, THEN do the statements following the ELSE."

You've already learned about IF...THEN conditional clauses. Remember, IF the premise (the expression following IF) is true, THEN the statements following the THEN will be executed. Otherwise nothing happens, and control goes to the next program line.

Now suppose we want to use IF...THEN to print an appropriate greeting: "Good morning" if the time is before noon, and "Good Afternoon" otherwise. Assume that T is the hour (in 24-hour time). We could write:

```
10 IF T < 12 THEN PRINT "Good morning!"
20 IF T >= 12 THEN PRINT "Good afternoon!"
```

But the expression T >= 12 in line 20 is really unnecessary—after all, it does nothing more than express the opposite of the comparison T < 12 in line 10. And it makes the program harder to read.

We can get rid of it if we use ELSE with IF...THEN. By using ELSE, we can let the program do one thing if the premise is true, and something ELSE if it is false:

```
10 IF T < 12 THEN PRINT "Good morning!"
20 ELSE PRINT "Good afternoon!"
```

Isn't that easier to read? Figure 2-2 shows how IF...THEN...ELSE works.

Control Flow

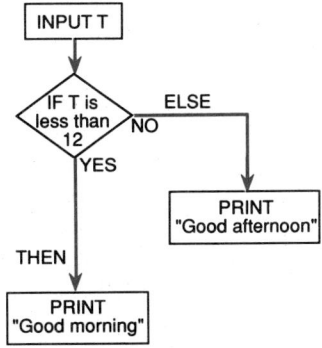

Fig. 2-2: IF...THEN...ELSE.

An IF...THEN...ELSE statement can also be used as the result of another IF...THEN...ELSE statement. Here's an example that prints an appropriate greeting depending on your age:

```
10 INPUT "ENTER YOUR AGE IN YEARS"; AGE
20 IF AGE < 18
        THEN PRINT "HI, KID!"
     ELSE IF AGE < 65
        THEN PRINT "HI!"
     ELSE PRINT "HELLO, SIR"
```

Notice the way the lines are indented to match the corresponding THENs and ELSEs. This makes the listing easier to read.

Breaking Lines without Starting Anew

BASIC automatically wraps lines around to the next line for you, so a single program line can occupy two or three lines on the screen. (But if you press Enter, it starts a new program line!) If you want to break lines without beginning a new line, press the Control and Enter keys at the same time. This Ctrl-Enter (or Ctrl-Return) can help make your listings easier to read.

Easy Looping with WHILE...WEND

Earlier you learned how to repeat an operation a certain number of times by using a FOR...NEXT loop. Another kind of loop is WHILE...WEND. The WHILE...WEND construction means, "WHILE something is true, execute the statements between the WHILE and the WEND." (WEND indicates the END of the WHILE...WEND loop.)

Chapter 2

As an example, let's write some routines to find the factorial of a number. The factorial of a number is simply the number multiplied by all the numbers smaller than itself. (For example, the factorial of 5 equals 5 * 4 * 3 * 2 * 1, or 120.)

Here's a factorial program that uses a FOR...NEXT loop:

```
10 INPUT"Number"; N
20 F = 1
30 FOR J = N TO 1 STEP -1
40    F = F*J
50 NEXT J
60 PRINT"Factorial is"; F
```

This gets the job done, but it's not very elegant. The FOR and NEXT statements clearly set off what's going to be done in the loop. But notice how we've had to introduce a new variable, J, just to count how many times to do the loop. The more variables in a program, the harder it is to understand, so this is a step in the wrong direction.

Using WHILE...WEND both does away with the need for a counting variable and makes for a clearer program. Here's how the program looks using WHILE...WEND:

```
10 INPUT"Number"; N
20 F = 1
30 WHILE N > 0
40    F = F*N
50    N = N-1
60 WEND
70 PRINT"Factorial is"; F
```

The N > 0 following the WHILE in line 30 is the third essential element of the WHILE...WEND loop, besides the WHILE and the WEND. When BASIC gets to the WHILE statement in the program, it remembers the expression N > 0. It then executes all statements down to the WEND.

When execution reaches the WEND statement, it evaluates the expression following the WHILE, which in this case is N > 0, to see whether it is true. If the statement is true, execution goes back up to the WHILE and cranks through all the statements in the loop again. If the expression is not true, it goes to the next statement following WEND. Figure 2-3 illustrates the WHILE...WEND loop.

Control Flow

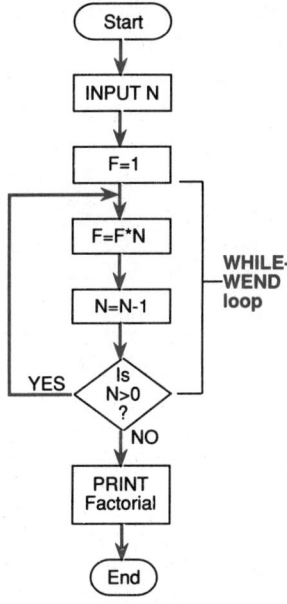

Fig. 2-3:   WHILE...WEND loop.

So, as long as N > 0 in this example, the WHILE...WEND loop will keep multiplying the product F by the number N, and then reducing N by one. When N = 0, the process stops, and execution "falls through" the loop to line 70, printing the factorial.

The WHILE...WEND loop makes for a more readable program, because we can see immediately that the statements between WHILE and WEND will be executed repeatedly as long as N > 0. (Indenting the lines between the WHILE and the WHEN makes it even easier to follow.)

Simple Function Statements

Many programming applications require the use of some common mathematical and other operations. Instead of making you laboriously write code for these operations, BASIC has provided many built-in functions for you to use. There are functions like square root, sine of a number, and so on. Some functions are for use with numeric data; others are for use with string data. We'll learn more about most functions in a later chapter, but at this point, we will take a look at a couple of the simplest numeric functions. They are easy to understand and can be used right away.

Using INT to Convert Numbers to Integers

The INT function is used to derive the closest whole number to a numeric value. Really, all it does (assuming that the number is greater than zero) is to truncate (cut off) all the digits that are to the right of the decimal point. For example,

```
INT(25.035) = 25
INT(.95) = 0
INT(100.9999) = 100
INT(-12.2) = -12
```

This provides a way of getting rid of unwanted decimal positions. The common form used for the INT statement is as follows:

```
A = INT(X)
```

in which X is either a numeric constant, a numeric variable, or a numeric expression, such as,

```
A = INT(12*B-2)
B = INT(.5*N)
```

One common usage of the INT statement is to allow for the rounding of numeric variables to the nearest whole number. This is done very easily in BASIC as follows:

```
X = INT(X + .5)
```

For example, if

$X = 3.49999$, then
$X + .5 = 3.99999$, so
INT $(X + .5) = 3$

However, if

```
X = 3.50001, then
X + .5 = 4.00001, so
INT(X + .5) = 4
```

Using this technique, we can always guarantee that an answer we are going to print will be printed as a whole number.

A more accurate explanation of what INT(X) does is that it "returns the largest integer that is less than (or equal to) X." For positive values of X, this is the same as chopping off the digits to the right of the decimal point; but for negative values of X it means chopping off the digits and then subtracting one.

For example,

```
PRINT INT (-4.222)
-5
PRINT INT (-13.75)
-14
```

Finding Prime Numbers

A prime number is a number that can only be divided by itself and one. Mathematicians consider prime numbers to be the fundamental building blocks for our number system, and they are important in such fields as cryptography—the use of codes for concealing information.

Here's a program that uses the WHILE...WEND and IF...THEN...ELSE statements along with the INT function to find out whether a number you enter is a prime number, and if not, what its divisors are.

```
10  PRINT "Prime Number Finder. Type 0 to terminate."
20  N=1
30  WHILE N<>0
40      INPUT "Number";N
50      I=2
60      WHILE N/I-INT(N/I) <>0
70          I=I+1
80      WEND
90      IF N=0 THEN PRINT "Finished"
            ELSE IF I=N AND N<>2 THEN PRINT N"is a prime"
            ELSE PRINT N"is divisible by"I"and is not a prime"
100 WEND
110 END
```

In this program, we've nested one WHILE...WEND loop inside another. The outer WHILE...WEND loop, from line 30 to line 100, does just one thing—it waits until you type a zero. If you type a zero, execution falls out of this loop and the program is terminated.

The inner WHILE...WEND loop, from line 60 to line 80, is what really does the work in this program. Beginning with an I of 2, each time through the loop the program checks to see whether N is exactly divisible by I. Here's how: the WHILE statement in line 60 divides N by I. Then it takes the integer part of N/I, using the INT function. (If you recall the INT function, you know it chops off any digits to the right of the decimal place.) Then the program subtracts the integer portion of N/I from N/I. If the difference is zero, guess what: it means N is exactly divisible by I, and execution falls out of the inner loop. This means that N is not a prime number UNLESS it's the same as I.

Let's look carefully at an example. Suppose that we INPUT an N of 10, so that N is 10 and I is 2. When we substitute these values in N/I we get 10/2, which is exactly 5; there are no digits to the right of the decimal point. Now the integer part of 5 is also exactly 5. So, N/I minus INT (N/I) is zero, and execution falls out of the inner loop.

Because execution has fallen out of the inner loop, we know that division has taken place. Now we need to test the results using the long IF...THEN statement in line 90. It looks complicated, but it's not.

First, if you typed an N of zero, it means you want to end the program, and the message "Finished" is printed.

Second, if division took place only when I reached the value N (that is IF I=N), then the number was a prime, so we print the number and the message, "is a prime." Because the number 2 is divisible by 2, it can't be a prime, so we have to eliminate it from consideration; that's what the AND N<>2 portion of this line does.

Third, if division took place before I reached the value of N, then the number couldn't be a prime, so we print the message, "is not a prime."

Let's try the program on some numbers and find out whether they are primes.

```
RUN
Prime Number Finder. Type 0 to terminate.
Number? 10
  10 is divisible by 2 and is not a prime

Number? 13
  13 is a prime

Number? 2
  2 is divisible by 2 and is not a prime

Number? 0
Finished
Ok
```

This program shows how you can use the INT function to see whether a number is exactly divisible by another number. The nested WHILE...WEND loops and the IF...THEN statement with multiple ELSEs let you make several decisions in just a few program lines.

ABS, The Absolute Value Function

The ABS function is used to get the *absolute value* of a number. This is defined as the actual numeric value of the number, ignoring the sign. The most common form of this statement looks like this:

```
A = ABS(X)
```

Here, the variable A is replaced with the *absolute value* of the variable X. For example,

```
ABS(5) = 5
ABS(13.25) = 13.25
ABS(-25) = 25
ABS(0) = 0
ABS(5-12) = 7
```

Notice that the absolute value of a number can never be negative. It is always a positive number equal to the actual numeric value of the contents within the parentheses. This can be a numeric constant, a numeric variable, or an expression of numeric terms, such as:

```
A = ABS(12*X-6)
```

or

```
B = ABS(I+J+(K/3))
```

This function is useful for finding the actual difference between two numbers without being concerned as to whether they are positive or negative. For example, you can check the distance to a target in a video game.

How to Generate Random Numbers

In games and other applications, you often want to be able to generate random numbers—that is, numbers that aren't at all predictable. You may use these numbers for cutting a deck of cards, spinning the wheel of fortune, or even throwing the dice.

RND, the Randomize Function

This function allows you to generate a random number. There is no way to know just what the result of the RND function will be. It will, however, always be returned as

Chapter 2

a number between 0 and 1. It might be .573 or .00941, or .0003 or any other number between 0 and 1.

This random number can then be used to generate other numbers in other ranges simply by using multiplication. For example, if we wanted to program a deck of cards being cut, we would want the result of the RND function to be a number from 1 to 52. This can be done by multiplying the number returned by the RND function by the numeric constant 52 and then adding a numeric 1 to that.

The general form of the RND function is as follows:

```
100 A = RND(X)
```

In this statement, the X serves as a "dummy" variable if it is a positive number (greater than 0); that is, no matter what value of X you use, the RND function will do the same thing—return a random number between 0 and 1. If X is 0, RND will return the same random number it did before.

Try typing and running the following program:

```
10 WHILE A <1
20     A=RND(1)
30     PRINT A
30 WEND

RUN
0.1213501
0.651861
0.8688611
0.7297625
```

Because the value of A is always between 0 and 1, A never becomes 1. If you let this program run, it will go on forever printing numbers similar to these. However, the sequence will always be the same.

Using RANDOMIZE

This function allows you to *reseed* the random number generator used in the RND function. What does *reseed* mean? Well, normally, every time you RUN your program, the RND function will start over generating the exact same sequence of random numbers. This isn't so good if, for example, you are using RND in a game to deal you a hand of cards; you don't want to get the same hand every time you RUN the program!

Control Flow

RANDOMIZE allows you to start over with a different sequence of random numbers each time you execute it: this is called *reseeding* the random number generator. RANDOMIZE has the following form:

```
RANDOMIZE S
```

in which S is a number between 32767 and −32768. For every different value of S that you use in the RANDOMIZE statement, the RND statement will create a different sequence of random numbers.

Randomizing with the TIMER

There's still a problem with RANDOMIZE and RND: in order to get truly random sequences, you have to reseed with a different number each time. Suppose that you have a betting game in which the player reseeds with his or her own choice of random numbers; some players might, just might, want to use the same "seed" so they could win every time.

One way to ensure random numbers is to reseed using the TIMER. GW-BASIC's TIMER function produces the number of seconds since midnight or the last system reset, like this:

```
PRINT TIMER
 25355.62
Ok
```

Later we'll learn to use the TIMER for other purposes. But for now, know that you can reseed a random number generator using the timer and the RANDOMIZE function, like this:

```
RANDOMIZE TIMER
```

This gives what is closer to a really "random" sequence of random numbers.

Combining Functions

In order to write even more sophisticated programs, it is possible to combine functions within one statement. For example, we can write a statement like the following:

```
A = INT(2*ABS(X-1))
```

Chapter 2

or

```
B = ABS(INT(X)-INT(Y))
```

Let's say that what we really want is to get a random number between 1 and 52 to simulate a deck of cards being cut. We can use a combination of the RND and INT functions, like this:

```
10 RANDOMIZE TIMER
20 C = INT(52*RND(1)) +1
```

The RND function is done first because of the way that the parentheses are arranged, so that a random number between 0 and 1 is generated. Then the multiplication follows, yielding a decimal number between 0 and 52. Next, the digits to the right of the decimal point are stripped off using the INT function, resulting in an integer with a value ranging from 0 through 51. Finally, we add 1 to the result so that we will end up with a number from 1 to 52.

We can use the same technique to simulate a throw of the dice as follows:

```
10 RANDOMIZE TIMER
20 T = INT(6*RND(1)) + 1
```

or we could "flip a coin," like this:

```
10 RANDOMIZE TIMER
20 F = INT(2*RND(1)) + 1
```

Notice that we are always randomizing using the TIMER so that we will get a new random sequence.

Random Number Guessing Game

Another entertaining application of the RND function is in a little program that plays a number guessing game with you. The RND function is used to generate a number from 1 to 1,000. Then you have to guess what the number is and enter your guess through the keyboard. The program will then let you know whether your guess was high or low, and give you another chance if you didn't guess it right. It also keeps track of how many chances it took for you to guess the number, and prints the total out at the end.

```
10 REM-RANDOM NUMBER GUESSING GAME
20 RANDOMIZE TIMER
30 N=INT(1000*RND(1))+1
```

Control Flow

```
40 T=0
50 PRINT "Start guessing"
60 WHILE G <> N
70      INPUT G
80      T=T+1
90      REM-Check for a high guess
100     IF G>N THEN PRINT "Your guess is high"
110     REM-Check for a low guess
120     IF G<N THEN PRINT "Your guess is low"
130 WEND
140 PRINT "You got it!"
150 PRINT "You guessed the number in";T;"tries."

RUN
Start guessing
?500
Your guess is high
?250
Your guess is low
?375
Your guess is high
?300
You got it!
You guessed the number in 4 tries.
Ok
```

The program uses a WHILE...WEND loop to keep track of whether you guess the number. When you do hit the number, execution falls out of the loop, and you see the total number of guesses (T) it took you to find the number.

Going Places—and Getting Back

Now that we've seen how to make decisions, we're going to examine what BASIC can do after the decision is made.

GOTO: the Unconditional Branch

First we're going to tell you about something, then we're going to tell you not to use it. It's the plain GOTO statement.

Chapter 2

GOTO is used to force the program to go to some other statement and perform the program lines there. By itself, the GOTO statement will simply cause the program to "branch" to another statement. For example,

```
GOTO 1200
```

This statement would cause the program to branch to the statement bearing the number 1200 and to execute it, then continue on with the next statement after 1200. This is known as an "unconditional branch" because it occurs every time, no matter what. Here's an example:

```
10 X=1
20 GOTO 50
30 PRINT "HELLO"
40 PRINT "GOODBYE"
50 PRINT "X IS"; X
```

In this example, execution begins with line 10. Then in line 20, the GOTO statement makes execution jump directly to line 50. Lines 30 and 40 are never executed (so you never see HELLO and GOODBYE), but line 50 is executed and you see the following output:

```
X IS 1
Ok
```

The Endless Loop

Maybe you've already figured out what can happen with an unconditional GOTO. Look at this code:

```
10 X = 1
20 GOTO 10
30 PRINT X
```

Now if you hit RUN, what's going to happen? The program begins at line 10 and sets X=1. Then it executes line 20—which sends it back to 10! The PRINT statement at line 30 will never be executed. When you tell your computer to RUN this program, it will appear to "fall asleep." The program runs forever, as shown in figure 2-4, and the "Ok" prompt will never be seen again in the program.

Control Flow

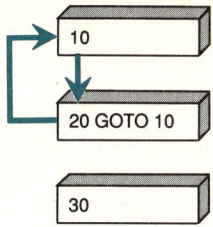

Fig. 2-4:   Endless loop.

This is known as an *endless loop*, and it's one of the main reasons you shouldn't use unconditional GOTOs in your programs. As you'll find out shortly, BASIC has ways for your programs to branch without using unconditional GOTO statements.

Getting Out of an Endless Loop—and Other Problems

All right, what happens if you are unlucky enough to fall into an endless loop, or another situation in which the program seems to "lock up"? BASIC has a way out—it will respond to the entry on the keyboard of a "control-break sequence." This is done by holding down the key labeled "Ctrl" and pressing the "Break" key at the same time. Control-Break will cause the BASIC program to be interrupted and the "Ok" prompt to be returned to the screen. Also, the line the program was executing when the Control-Break was entered is displayed on the screen:

```
Break in 20
Ok
```

At this point, you can examine the program to find the problem and then continue the execution of the program by typing the following:

```
CONT
```

Cont means "continue." Note that if the program is altered in any way (i.e., typing a new line) then CONT cannot be used to restart. Instead, RUN must be used.

In general, the Control-Break sequence may be used at any time that you want to interrupt a program. If a program does a lot of PRINTing, and you wish to stop the program before all of the printing has been completed, the Control-Break sequence may be used to abort the printing in progress and return control to BASIC.

Chapter 2

Using GOTO the Better Way

The truth is that GOTO is something of an outcast among modern programmers. That's because of the so-called "spaghetti code" that results from hopping around a program with GOTO. That's not to say you should never use it. Just be sure to use it carefully, and make it happen only as the result of some condition.

One type of conditional GOTO is when it's used as the object of an IF...THEN statement. For example,

```
IF A = 5 THEN GOTO 100
```

This is known as a "conditional branch" because it occurs only if the premise of the IF...THEN statement is true. If the current value of the variable A is equal to 5, the GOTO branch to statement 100 will occur; otherwise, the next statement after the IF...THEN statement will be executed.

Here's a program to illustrate the use of both the IF...THEN statement and the GOTO statement. This program will INPUT two numbers, and a single character string variable that will direct the program to either add (A) the two numbers together and print the result, or subtract (S) the second number from the first number and print the result.

```
10 REM -First input the two numbers and the command
20 INPUT "Input X, Y, then A (add) or S (subtract)"; X, Y, A$
30 REM -See which operation is to be done
40 IF A$ = "A" THEN GOTO 90
50 IF A$ = "S" THEN GOTO 120
60 REM -If neither, end the program
70 GOTO 170
80 REM -Add the numbers
90 Z = X + Y
100 GOTO 150
110 REM -Subtract the second number from the first
120 Z = Y-X
130 GOTO 150
140 REM -Print the answer and do it again
150 PRINT "THE ANSWER IS"; Z
160 GOTO 20
170 END
```

From this example, we can see how the IF...THEN and GOTO statements can be used in conjunction to provide extensive program control. And we can also see the result of using too many GOTOs.

What's Wrong with GOTO?

Remember the factorial you calculated earlier? Here's how you could do it using an IF statement and a GOTO:

```
10 INPUT"Number"; N
20 F = 1
30 F = F*N
40 N = N-1
50 IF N > 0 THEN GOTO 30
60 PRINT"Factorial is"; F
```

Try it! The program works all right, but using the IF statement and the GOTO means that in order to figure out what statements will be repeated N times in the loop, we have to read down to the IF statement, and then search back up to the line number it references.

This isn't hard in a short loop, but for long loops in larger programs it can be very confusing. Many programmers today try to avoid the use of GOTO statements for this reason.

Perhaps you've been on the kind of treasure hunt where you find a note that says, "Look for the next clue in a hollow tree," and when you find the hollow tree there's a note saying, "Go to the fourth fence post from the road." Trying to trace the execution of a program that uses too many GOTOs is a little like a treasure hunt: you're never quite sure what you're doing or where you're going next.

Tracing Your Program's Execution

One tool that can help you keep track of program branches is tracing. With all these jumps and branches, loops and end loops, it can be hard to tell how a program runs simply by looking at the code listing. And if you're like most of us, you've already made one or more typing errors that have caused a running program to "blow up" on you.

To help with understanding how a program works, and to aid you in troubleshooting your code, GW-BASIC gives you the TRON and TROFF switches. TRON, which means *trace on*, is one of the user-definable keys you see at the bottom of the screen when you first turn on GW-BASIC. This handy "switch" slows down execution so that you can see which line numbers are actually executed. You can trace program flow.

Let's try it using that factorial program:

```
10 INPUT "Number"; N
20 F=1
30 F=F*N
```

```
40 N=N-1
50 IF N > 0 THEN GOTO 30
60 PRINT "Factorial is";F
```

That's the program. Here's how it looks if you RUN it with trace on:

```
TRON
Ok

RUN
[10]Number? 3
[20][30][40][50][30][40][50][30][40][50][60]Factorial is 6
Ok
```

You can see how TRON works. The line number for each statement executed appears in the display, surrounded by square brackets. The program still works exactly as advertised, except that the line numbers are printed so that you can trace execution. You can see that execution starts with line 10. After you enter a number in response to the INPUT statement in line 10, lines 20, 30, 40, and 50 are executed in order. Then, if the number you entered is greater than 0, execution jumps back to line 30, where the number is multiplied by itself. Execution bounces between lines 30 and 50 until the number N reaches 0 and execution can finally go on to line 60, where the message "Factorial is" is printed.

The TRON command can be a big help in finding out why your programs don't run exactly the way you want. To turn off tracing and return to normal execution, use the TROFF (trace off) command:

```
TROFF
Ok
```

Enhancing the Loan Program

Think back on the loan program we used in Chapter 1 to illustrate the three laws of computing. Let's use what we've learned in this chapter to add some modifications, and supply some additional information. As we recall, the program required as INPUT the following:

The amount of the loan, A

The annual interest rate, RATE

The term of the loan in years, YEARS

With this information and the LET statement, we were able to compute the monthly payment, P.

Now, let's enhance the program so that for each payment, it will compute the amount that is paid as interest, and also the amount that is applied to the principal of the loan. In addition, we'll program it to accumulate the total amount of interest paid, and to compute the principal balance of the loan. Finally, we will have all this information printed in columns, one for each monthly payment.

This sounds like a good application for the program control statements. We'll use a FOR...NEXT loop to print the monthly information, and we'll use IF...THEN to make sure we print the final payment, after we've "fallen out" of the loop.

You see, depending upon the loan amount and the interest rate, the last payment might not always be equal to the other monthly payments. (You might have noticed this on your own personal loans.) Therefore, when we get down to computing the last payment, we will want to make sure that the amount of the payment that is applied to the principal is exactly equal to the outstanding balance.

Let's tackle the program. We'll break it up into logical segments for the purpose of illustration. First, the beginning of the program is very similar to the original version:

```
10 REM LOAN AMORTIZATION PROGRAM
20 ' This program calculates and prints the
30 ' loan schedule.
40 '
50 ' Input section
60 INPUT "Enter the amount of the loan";A
70 INPUT "Enter the interest rate";RATE
80 INPUT "Input the number of years of the loan";YEARS
90 ' Change annual interest rate to monthly rate
100 I=RATE/12/100
110 ' Convert years to number of monthly payments
120 N=YEARS*12
130 ' Compute and print the monthly payment
140 P=I*A*(((1+I)^N)/(((1+I)^N)-1))
150 PRINT "The monthly payment for a loan of $";A
160 PRINT "at a rate of ";RATE;"%"
170 PRINT "for";YEARS;"years is $";P
```

Next, the program has to get ready to print the amortization schedule. We will need to establish a variable for the current loan balance (B) after a payment has been

Chapter 2

made. We will also need a variable to accumulate the total interest paid (TI). And to dress up the output, we will also print some column headings.

```
180 ' Initialize the amortization schedule
190 B=A
200 TI=0
210 PRINT "NUM","INTEREST","PRINCIPAL","PRIN BAL","TOT INT"
```

Now comes the payment loop. We'll use the variable J as the "index" to the loop, and the number of monthly payments N as the "terminator" of the loop. For each payment, we will compute the amount that is paid as interest MI, and the amount which is applied to the principal. Also, we will subtract the amount applied to the principal from the loan balance B, and accumulate the total interest paid, TI.

```
220     ' Do the loop for the number of payments
230 FOR J=1 TO N
240         ' Compute the interest
250         MI=B*I
260         ' Compute the principal
270         PRINCIPAL=P-MI
280         ' Force out the last payment
290         IF J=N THEN PRINCIPAL=B
300         ' Update the loan balance
310         B=B-PRINCIPAL
320         ' Update the total interest
330         TI=TI+MI
```

Now, using the automatic column function of the PRINT statement, we will print all the information for the monthly payment and then end the loop.

```
340         ' Print the monthly payment detail
350         PRINT J,MI,PRINCIPAL,B,TI
360 NEXT J
```

At this point, let's add some statements that will provide the option of either going back to the beginning of the program to process another loan, or ending the program. See if you can figure out how this works.

```
370 ' See if the program is done
380 INPUT "DO YOU WANT TO SEE ANOTHER LOAN (YES/NO)?";A$
390 IF A$="YES" THEN GOTO 60
400 END
```

Notice that we are using a *string variable* here. Remember that this is denoted by the $ following the variable name. This means that we'll input a string of characters at statement 380, and if that string happens to be the word YES, then the program will go back to statement 60 where the entire process starts again. If the input string is not the word YES, then the program will proceed to the next statement, which is the END statement at line 400. This causes the program to terminate.

Now you have a very useful little program. You can use it to find out what your monthly payment would be on a particular loan, and also to see just how much monthly interest you will pay.

Look at the example of a printout for a sample loan amortization below. At the top of the table, the numbers that are underscored are those you enter when the program asks for information.

In this example, we are amortizing a loan of $8,200.00 at an annual interest rate of 15% over a term of four years. The program computes the monthly payment to be $228.2113 and prints that first. Then the program proceeds to print the amortization schedule according to the format that we decided upon earlier. Notice that the column headings are printed first, followed by one line for each monthly payment.

Look at the interest and the principal. At first the amount paid as interest is relatively large, and it decreases as the loan balance decreases. Likewise, the amount applied to the principal is relatively small at first, and then gets larger as the amount paid as interest decreases.

There are a few other things we should notice. One is that if we sum the amount paid as interest with the amount applied to the principal for each month, we do not always get the monthly payment, $228.2113, as the answer. This is because the numbers printed here have not been rounded off after BASIC performed the mathematics. For example, when the program converts the annual interest rate of 15% to a monthly interest rate, it comes out to a decimal fraction of .0125 (that is, 15/12/100). Now, when the program computes the amount paid as interest on the payment, the math actually comes out like this:

MONTHLY RATE X LOAN BALANCE = INTEREST AMOUNT

.0125 x 7974.006 = 99.67507

According to the table, the interest amount on payment 3 is 99.33757 (to seven significant digits). This apparent discrepancy is due to the accumulated error inherent in the least significant digit of the arithmetic processes of BASIC.

```
RUN
Enter the amount of the loan? 8200
Enter the interest rate? 15
Input the number of years of the loan? 4
The monthly payment for a loan of $ 8200
at a rate of  15 %
for 4 years is $ 228.2113
```

Chapter 2

NUM	INTEREST	PRINCIPAL	PRIN BAL	TOT INT
1	102.5	125.7112	8074.289	102.5
2	100.9286	127.2826	7947.006	203.4286
3	99.33757	128.8737	7818.132	302.7662
4	97.72664	130.4846	7687.648	400.4928
5	96.09559	132.1157	7555.532	496.5885
6	94.44414	133.7671	7421.765	591.0326
7	92.77206	135.4392	7286.325	683.8046
8	91.07906	137.1322	7149.193	774.8837
9	89.36491	138.8463	7010.347	864.2486
10	87.62933	140.5819	6869.765	951.8779
11	85.87206	142.3392	6727.426	1037.75
12	84.09282	144.1184	6583.307	1121.843
13	82.29134	145.9199	6437.387	1204.134
14	80.46733	147.7439	6289.643	1284.602
15	78.62053	149.5907	6140.052	1363.222
16	76.75065	151.4606	5988.591	1439.973
17	74.85738	153.3539	5835.237	1514.83
18	72.94046	155.2708	5679.966	1587.77
19	70.99958	157.2117	5522.754	1658.77
20	69.03443	159.1768	5363.577	1727.805
21	67.04472	161.1665	5202.411	1794.849
22	65.03014	163.1811	5039.23	1859.879
23	62.99037	165.2209	4874.009	1922.87
24	60.92511	167.2861	4706.723	1983.795
25	58.83404	169.3772	4537.345	2042.629
26	56.71682	171.4944	4365.851	2099.346
27	54.57313	173.6381	4192.213	2153.919
28	52.40266	175.8086	4016.404	2206.321
29	50.20505	178.0062	3838.398	2256.526
30	47.97998	180.2313	3658.167	2304.506
31	45.72708	182.4842	3475.682	2350.234
32	43.44603	184.7652	3290.917	2393.68
33	41.13646	187.0748	3103.842	2434.816
34	38.79803	189.4132	2914.429	2473.614
35	36.43037	191.7809	2722.649	2510.045
36	34.03311	194.1781	2528.47	2544.078
37	31.60588	196.6054	2331.865	2575.684
38	29.14831	199.0629	2132.802	2604.832
39	26.66002	201.5512	1931.251	2631.492
40	24.14063	204.0706	1727.18	2655.632
41	21.58975	206.6215	1520.559	2677.222
42	19.00698	209.2043	1311.354	2696.229
43	16.39193	211.8193	1099.535	2712.621

```
 44          13.74419         214.4671         885.0679         2726.365
 45          11.06335         217.1479         667.92           2737.429
 46           8.349           219.8623         448.0578         2745.778
 47           5.600722        222.6105         225.4472         2751.379
 48           2.81809         225.4472         0                2754.197
Do you want to see another loan (Yes/No)?? N
Ok
```

ON...GOTO, Indexed Branching

One place where GOTO can come in very handy is a special form of the GOTO statement that allows multiple options. Using ON...GOTO, the programmer can specify several possible destinations of the branch, and make the selection of the one to be taken based upon the value of a particular variable. The form of this type of GOTO statement is as follows:

```
10 ON I GOTO 100, 200, 300, 400, 500 etc.
```

Here the variable I is used as the "index" for the ON...GOTO statement. If the value of I is 1, then the GOTO will cause a branch to line 100. If I is equal to 2, then the branch will be to line 200, and so on.

Notice that the value of the index to the ON...GOTO statement must be an integer, a whole number. It must also be greater than zero, and not greater than the total number of lines listed after the GOTO. If the index is zero, or greater than the total number of lines in the list, the next statement after the ON...GOTO statement will be executed. If the index is negative, an error will result.

Expense Account Program

The ON...GOTO statement lends itself very well to making organized program branches based on a number entered to the program via the keyboard. For instance, the following program is an expense account that keeps four expenses: food, lodging, transportation, and miscellaneous.

The program has three major sections, which we will discuss separately. First, the program will provide us with a *menu* from which we can select the conversion we want. Then, the program will take our menu choice and branch to the proper statements to add to the correct subtotal. Finally, we'll want to print the results of each subtotal and of the overall grand total for our expenses.

The first part is the menu. You see a menu that tells what category each expense is, as follows:

```
10 REM-Expense Account Program
20 REM-Print the menu
30 CLS: PRINT "Enter the category of expense"
40 PRINT: PRINT "1 - Food"
50 PRINT "2 - Transportation"
60 PRINT "3 - Lodging"
70 PRINT "4 - Miscellaneous"
80 PRINT "5 to exit"
90 INPUT CATEGORY
100 ON CATEGORY GOTO 1000, 2000, 3000, 4000, 5000
110 GOTO 5000
```

Notice that we clear the screen before printing the menu, then we execute two PRINT statements in line 40. The first PRINT statement "prints" a blank line, to separate the menu from the headline telling you to "Enter the category of expense." When you INPUT the CATEGORY according to the menu number, the program uses that number as the index for the ON...GOTO statement. For instance, if you INPUT a 3 for CATEGORY, the program branches to line 3000, which is where the subtotals for LODGING are kept.

The sections containing the subtotals are all similar:

```
1000 REM-Keep subtotal for food
1010 INPUT "Enter the food expense";F
1020 FOOD=FOOD + F
1030 GOTO 30

2000 REM-Keep subtotal for transportation
2010 INPUT "Enter the transportation expense";T
2020 TRANSPORT=TRANSPORT + T
2030 GOTO 30

3000 REM-Keep the subtotal for lodging
3010 INPUT "Enter the lodging expense";L
3020 LODGING=LODGING + L
3030 GOTO 30

4000 REM-Keep the subtotal for miscellaneous expenses
4010 INPUT "Enter the miscellaneous expense"; M
4020 MISC=MISC + M
4030 GOTO 30
```

Each section asks you to "Enter the _____ expense" and places it in a variable (for instance, F for food, or T for transportation). Then the value you INPUT is added to a running subtotal: FOOD, TRANSPORT, LODGING, or MISC. You use meaningful variable names to make following the program easier.

When you've finished entering expenses, you answer the menu prompt with a 5, which causes a branch to line 5000. This section is the end of the program; all the subtotals are printed, then added together and printed so that you can see the whopping grand total:

```
5000 REM-Print the totals and end
5010 CLS: PRINT "Food:" FOOD
5020 PRINT "Transport:" TRANSPORT
5030 PRINT "Lodging:" LODGING
5040 PRINT "Miscellaneous:" MISC
5050 PRINT: PRINT "Total expenses:" FOOD+TRANSPORT+LODGING+MISC
5060 END
```

Here's a sample output for a day's expenses:

```
RUN
Enter the category of expense

1 - Food
2 - Transportation
3 - Lodging
4 - Miscellaneous
5 to exit
? 1
Enter the food expense? 2.73

Enter the category of expense
? 1
Enter the food expense? 14.82

Enter the category of expense
? 2
Enter the transportation expense? .75

Enter the category of expense
? 2
Enter the transportation expense? 6

Enter the category of expense
? 3
Enter the lodging expense? 99

Enter the category of expense
? 4
Enter the miscellaneous expense? 2.11
```

```
Enter the category of expense
? 5

Food: 17.55
Transport: 6.75
Lodging: 99
Miscellaneous: 2.11

Total expenses: 125.41
Ok
```

Here's a listing of the complete program. Notice that you can exit from the menu and print the totals in one of two ways: either by typing 5 in answer to the menu prompt, or by typing anything except 1, 2, 3, 4, or 5. If you type 6, for example, there's no provision made for that number in the ON CATEGORY GOTO sequence in line 100, so execution continues on (we say it "falls through") to line 110, which sends it off to the end of the program anyway.

When writing programs, you should always provide an exit—and you should always make a provision for those users who want to "experiment" with values other than those on your menu!

```
10 REM-Expense Account Program
20 REM-Print the menu
30 CLS: PRINT "Enter the category of expense"
40 PRINT: PRINT "1 - Food"
50 PRINT "2 - Transportation"
60 PRINT "3 - Lodging"
70 PRINT "4 - Miscellaneous"
80 PRINT "5 to exit"
90 INPUT CATEGORY
100 ON CATEGORY GOTO 1000, 2000, 3000, 4000, 5000
110 GOTO 5000
1000 REM-Keep subtotal for food
1010 INPUT "Enter the food expense";F
1020 FOOD=FOOD + F
1030 GOTO 30
2000 REM-Keep subtotal for transportation
2010 INPUT "Enter the transportation expense";T
2020 TRANSPORT=TRANSPORT + T
2030 GOTO 30
3000 REM-Keep the subtotal for lodging
3010 INPUT "Enter the lodging expense";L
```

```
3020 LODGING=LODGING + L
3030 GOTO 30
4000 REM-Keep the subtotal for miscellaneous expenses
4010 INPUT "Enter the miscellaneous expense"; M
4020 MISC=MISC + M
4030 GOTO 30
5000 REM-Print the totals and end
5010 CLS: PRINT "Food:" FOOD
5020 PRINT "Transport:" TRANSPORT
5030 PRINT "Lodging:" LODGING
5040 PRINT "Miscellaneous:" MISC
5050 PRINT: PRINT "Total expenses:" FOOD+TRANSPORT+LODGING+MISC
5060 END
```

The important things to learn from this example are the *menu* concept, and the use of the ON...GOTO statement to selectively branch to different parts of the same program. Finally, you have seen that a well-organized program is easy to read, and would be easy to modify.

The All-Important Subroutine

As your programs grow in size and complexity, you will find it desirable to chop them up into smaller parts. Sometimes it is just too difficult to write one big program that takes care of everything. Other times, there is one series of operations that must be performed several times throughout the entire program. It would be tedious to write this series into the program every place that it is needed, and the resulting program would be unnecessarily large. These are two very good reasons for the development of the *subroutine*.

As its name implies, a subroutine is a "subpart" of a program. It is a routine that is performed at some specified time, and does the same thing each time. The subroutine need be "written" only once, somewhere within the program, and then "called" by the program—via a special BASIC statement, the GOSUB—when its execution is necessary. As shown in figure 2-5, when the subroutine has completed its operation, it "returns" to the main program at the point right after the line where the main program called the subroutine. Subroutines are a much better way to handle branching than are GOTOs.

Chapter 2

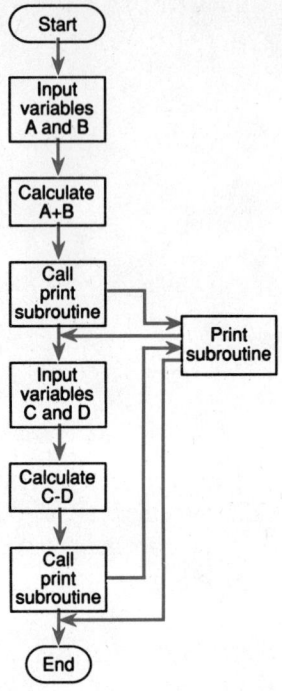

Fig. 2-5: Flowchart showing subroutine operation.

Subroutines are composed of BASIC statements just like any other part of a program. The statements all have line numbers and must follow all of the rules that apply to any program statement.

The form of the GOSUB statement is as follows:

```
100 GOSUB 2000
```

Directly following the word GOSUB must be a valid line number, which represents the first line of the part of the program that is to be considered the subroutine. When the GOSUB statement is executed, the program branches to the line number specified in the statement. All the subroutine statements are then executed until another special BASIC statement known as RETURN is encountered. At that time, the program branches back to the line directly following the GOSUB statement that caused the original branch.

Control Flow

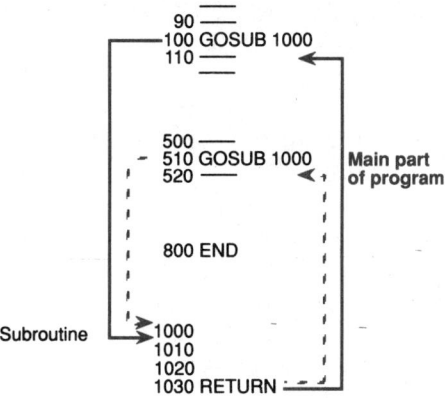

Fig. 2-6: A subroutine is called by GOSUB and ends with a RETURN to the line after the GOSUB.

In the example shown in figure 2-6, the statements through line 90 are normal BASIC statements. At line 100 we see the first GOSUB statement, which references line 1000. This is where the subroutine begins, and at line 100 we want to branch to the subroutine and perform whatever statements are there.

At the end of the subroutine, in line 1030, we see the RETURN statement, which causes the program to branch back to line 110, the line directly following the subroutine call. Here execution resumes normally.

Line 510 has another call to the same subroutine. The GOSUB 1000 statement causes another branch to line 1000. Again, the subroutine is executed until the RETURN statement at line 1030 is executed, then execution goes back to the next line after the calling GOSUB, which is line 520 this time. From here, the program keeps running until the END statement at line 800 is encountered.

In this particular example, we can see that if the statements that make up the subroutine are found only once within the program, and that if we can access these statements from several places in the main program, then the overall program has been made smaller through the use of the subroutine concept. Without the subroutine, we would have had to incorporate the same statements at two places in the main program, once at line 100 and again at line 510. In a sense, the GOSUB statement is like an unconditional branch—except that it has a return address telling it where to come back to when the RETURN statement is executed.

ON...GOSUB, Indexed Subroutine Branching

The ON...GOSUB statement works just like the ON...GOTO statement does, except that it refers to subroutines. That is, there is a variable that is used as the index for

Chapter 2

the ON...GOSUB statement, and there is a list of possible line numbers to which the subroutine branch is made depending upon the value of the index. The common form of the statement looks like this:

```
100 ON K GOSUB 1000,2000,3000,4000,...
```

Again, the value of the index variable K at the time that the ON...GOSUB statement is executed must be interpreted as an integer whole number greater than zero, and less than the number of line numbers in the list that follows the GOSUB part of the statement. In the example above, if the value of K is equal to one, the statement will cause a subroutine branch to line 1000. If the value is two, the branch will be made to line 2000, and so on.

If the value of K is zero or greater than the number of line numbers in the list, the program will ignore the ON...GOSUB statement completely, and resume execution at the next line in the program. If the value of K is negative, an error will result.

After the subroutine has finished execution, the RETURN statement at its end will cause the program to come back to the next statement after the ON...GOSUB that caused the branch in the first place. Here again, as with the ON...GOTO statement, the major advantage is that several different subroutines may be called depending upon the value of a variable in the program. This variable can be entered via an INPUT statement, or it can be computed in the program itself from some other data. In any case, its value at the time that the ON...GOSUB statement is executed will cause a controlled branch to a subroutine.

In the following pages, we will examine the use of the subroutine concept to validate input data to make sure that it is within certain limits.

Error-Checking Subroutine

An old programmer's proverb says, "garbage in, garbage out." This simply means that if you enter invalid information into a computer program, you can't depend on the results. In some situations, the program might be fooled by the invalid information, and go right ahead and process it anyway. This usually yields an invalid answer, or output—and it may happen without you knowing it. In other cases, the INPUTting of invalid information can cause a program error to occur, which might result in the total malfunction of the program. This is especially true if the INPUT information is to be used in a program-control statement such as a FOR...NEXT loop, in which the use of an invalid loop parameter could cause the loop to go on forever.

We can design a subroutine that will check for errors in INPUT data. The subroutine provides the most basic error-checking capability and can be used in programs like the loan program and the expense account program. What we want the subroutine to do is as follows:

1. Check for a positive, nonzero number.

2. Check that the number does not exceed some predetermined maximum value.
3. Display an error message if either of these conditions is not correct and ask the user to enter the data again.

The subroutine looks like this:

```
6000 REM-Numeric error-checking subroutine
6010 WHILE X < 0 OR X > MAX
6020    INPUT "INVALID ENTRY! TRY AGAIN"; X
6030 WEND
6040 RETURN
```

Within the subroutine, we use a WHILE...WEND loop that, with any luck, will never be executed. That is, in line 6010 a check is made to see whether the value of variable X is less than zero (that is, if it's a negative number). This line also checks to see whether X is greater than a variable called MAX (for *maximum*).

Now, if X is either greater than zero or less than MAX, it's within the limits we want and the WHILE...WEND loop is never executed. Execution simply "falls through" and returns to the calling program.

If, on the other hand, X is less than zero (that is, it's a negative number) or X is greater than MAX, execution goes into the WHILE...WEND loop and you see a prompt to TRY AGAIN! The INPUT statement waits until you type another number for X. If that number is also less than zero or greater than MAX, you stay in the loop. In fact, you'll stay there, inputting numbers, until you finally get it right.

We have some more work to do before we can use this subroutine, however. We have to make sure that the variable called X is set up in the main program to be equal to the current value of the INPUT data to be checked. Also, you'll have to specify how large you want MAX to be.

Let's tack this subroutine onto the expense account program we wrote. First, we know that our penny-pinching manager won't OK any single expense greater than $200, so we'll make MAX that value:

```
25 MAX=200
```

Next, we have to set X equal to the amount we INPUT in each of the sections (for food, lodging, transportation, and miscellaneous) before the subroutine call. Then, after we return from the subroutine, X might hold a new value, so we have to set the amount equal to X. Here's how we'd handle this for the food section:

```
1000 REM-Keep total for food
1010 INPUT "Enter the food expense";F
1015 X=F
1016 GOSUB 6000
```

Chapter 2

```
1017 F=X
1020 FOOD=FOOD + F
1030 GOTO 30
```

You can see that we added lines 1015, 1016, and 1017. Now, after you INPUT the food expense, F, line 1015 sets X equal to whatever your food expense was. Line 1016 branches execution to the subroutine.

What can happen in the subroutine? Well, one thing that can happen is that X is between 0 and MAX, and there's no change. But remember, if X is less than zero or greater than MAX, you'll be locked in the WHILE...WEND loop until you change its value by INPUTting a new value for X. This means that upon returning from the subroutine, X could well have a new value.

That's the reason for line 1017. Here we change the value of F by setting it equal to X; that is, we change F so that it's the new value you INPUT in the subroutine.

We'll have to change the other sections in a similar manner:

```
2000 REM-Keep total for transportation
2010 INPUT "Enter the transportation expense";T
2015 X=T
2016 GOSUB 6000
2017 T=X
2020 TRANSPORT=TRANSPORT + T
2030 GOTO 30

3000 REM-Keep the total for lodging
3010 INPUT "Enter the lodging expense";L
3015 X=L
3016 GOSUB 6000
3017 L=X
3020 LODGING=LODGING + L
3030 GOTO 30

4000 REM-Keep the total for miscellaneous expenses
4010 INPUT "Enter the miscellaneous expense"; M
4015 X=M
4016 GOSUB 6000
4017 M=X
4020 MISC=MISC + M
4030 GOTO 30
```

Here's how it works: Suppose that you have a fast-food lunch for $3.75, but get bollixed up and leave off the decimal point when you type it in. The program simply won't let you exceed your maximum expense:

```
RUN
Enter the category of expense

1 - Food
2 - Transportation
3 - Lodging
4 - Miscellaneous
5 to exit
? 1
Enter the food expense? 375
INVALID ENTRY! TRY AGAIN?
```

You'll have to keep trying until you finally INPUT a number from 0 to 200.

```
INVALID ENTRY! TRY AGAIN? 3.75
Enter the category of expense

1 - Food
2 - Transportation
3 - Lodging
4 - Miscellaneous
5 to exit
? 5
Food: 3.75
Transport: 0
Lodging: 0
Miscellaneous: 0

Total expenses: 3.75
Ok
```

Here's a listing for the complete expense account program, with the added error-checking subroutine:

```
10 REM-Expense Account Program
20 REM-Print the menu
25 MAX=200
30 CLS: PRINT "Enter the category of expense"
40 PRINT: PRINT "1 - Food"
50 PRINT "2 - Transportation"
60 PRINT "3 - Lodging"
70 PRINT "4 - Miscellaneous"
80 PRINT "5 to exit"
```

Chapter 2

```
90 INPUT CATEGORY
100 ON CATEGORY GOTO 1000, 2000, 3000, 4000, 5000
110 GOTO 5000
1000 REM-Keep total for food
1010 INPUT "Enter the food expense";F
1015 X=F
1016 GOSUB 6000
1017 F=X
1020 FOOD=FOOD + F
1030 GOTO 30
2000 REM-Keep total for transportation
2010 INPUT "Enter the transportation expense";T
2020 TRANSPORT=TRANSPORT + T
2030 GOTO 30
3000 REM-Keep the total for lodging
3010 INPUT "Enter the lodging expense";L
3020 LODGING=LODGING + L
3030 GOTO 30
4000 REM-Keep the total for miscellaneous expenses
4010 INPUT "Enter the miscellaneous expense"; M
4020 MISC=MISC + M
4030 GOTO 30
5000 CLS: PRINT "Food:" FOOD
5010 PRINT "Transport:" TRANSPORT
5020 PRINT "Lodging:" LODGING
5030 PRINT "Miscellaneous:" MISC
5040 PRINT: PRINT "Total expenses:" FOOD+TRANSPORT+LODGING+MISC
5050 END
6000 REM-Numeric error-checking subroutine
6010 WHILE X < 0 OR X > MAX
6020    INPUT "INVALID ENTRY! TRY AGAIN"; X
6030 WEND
6040 RETURN
```

We've learned a large number of powerful new BASIC statements and a couple of useful program methods. The next thing we will learn about will allow your programming to jump to a higher level of sophistication through the use of the "array" concept. So let's get moving.

Control Flow

Review Questions

1. What's the effect of the following program?

```
10 FOR LOOPCOUNTER = 100 to 50 STEP -1
20      PRINT LOOPCOUNTER
30 NEXT
```

2. Write a short program that uses a FOR...NEXT loop to calculate and print the sum of all even integers from 0 to 100.

3. What's wrong with this expression?

```
50 IF 10=XX THEN PRINT "TRUE"
```

4. What's the output on the screen of this program?

```
10 X=ABS(INT(-7.9))
20 Y=INT(ABS(-7.9))
30 IF X=Y THEN PRINT "EQUAL" ELSE PRINT "UNEQUAL"
```

5. Write a line 110 that ends the program if ANSWER$ is "Y" or "y."

```
100 INPUT "TERMINATE (Y/N)"; ANSWER$
110
```

6. Write a section of program code that asks you to INPUT a number and calls the subroutine beginning at line 50 if you input a 1, the subroutine at line 770 if you input a 2, or the subroutine at line 100 if you input a 3.

7. This program prints an amount you enter. Add a subroutine that adds 7% sales tax to the amount before it's printed.

```
10 INPUT AMOUNT
20 PRINT AMOUNT
30 END
```

8. How do you trace a program's execution?

9. When will this program halt execution?

```
10 INPUT N
20 X=N+5
30 GOSUB 100
40 T=X*7
50 GOTO 20
60 END
100 PRINT X
110 RETURN
```

111

Chapter 2

10. Exercise: Write a program for Big Ben's Bodacious Burger Barn that uses the ON...GOSUB structure to let the user choose one of four menu items. After the choice is made, the cost of that item is added to a total. When no more choices are needed, the program prints a bill. Here's what the menu could look like:

```
BIG BEN'S BODACIOUS BURGERS

Item                    Price           Press

Baby                    0.59            1
Ben's Bitable           1.49            2
Big Big Burger          2.15            3
Brobdingnagian          3.99            4

To exit and see the total       5

What's your choice?
```

When you respond to, "What's your choice?" with a menu number, the price is added to your bill. When you press 5 to exit, the total bill is displayed, like this:

```
Your total comes to $4.30. Thank you for eating at Ben's.
Have a nice forever.
```

Chapter 3

Arrays

Chapter **3**

Arrays

So far in our study of BASIC we have learned how to deal with information one piece at a time. We can manipulate numbers by giving each a variable name, or work with groups of letters by giving each string a string-variable name. But BASIC also lets you take a single variable name and use it to represent information that is made up of several parts. In this section we will explore the concept of *arrays and subscripted variables*, a method whereby information may be divided into several sub-elements or parts, so that each part can be organized and referenced by your program with ease. The array concept means we can represent information inside the computer in a more organized manner than is possible with single-value variables.

What You'll Learn in this Chapter

This chapter is devoted primarily to arrays and how to handle them. You'll learn about

- Subscripted variables and how to work with them
- Why you need to reserve space for arrays—and how to do it
- How to save memory when using arrays

Last but definitely not least, you'll learn how to create an expense account program using arrays. You'll follow along every step of the design process, from simple and more complex flowcharts to writing the actual program code. And when it's all done, you can use the expense account to keep track of your own expenses—whether for yourself or for the tax authorities.

Chapter 3

Arrays and Subscripted Variables

Arrays are items of data arranged and stored under a single variable name. Like a regular variable, an array has a simple name, but whereas a variable represents only a single value, an array represents several values. The parts that make up an array are called its *elements*. Each element can be a number or a string, depending on the type of array you have defined. An array element is identified by an array name followed by an integer number. In GW-BASIC you must use a DIM statement for arrays of more than 10 elements. (More about DIM in a moment.) The number is enclosed in parentheses and follows the array name. The number serves to identify a unique element in the array. We call a variable with a referencing number following it a *subscripted variable*. The general form of a subscripted variable looks like this:

```
ARRAYNAME (integer constant)
```

The `ARRAYNAME` part of a subscripted variable is any legal BASIC variable name as described in Chapter 1. The *subscript* is the integer constant following the `ARRAYNAME` and surrounded by parentheses. The subscript tells us which item of the variable we are referencing.

An array is really just a group of variables. But it's a very special group. The subscripts let you handle the entire group of variables all together.

Consider a situation in which you want to store and print the temperatures for the days of a week, then calculate their average. That's seven days, seven temperatures, seven values—plus the average. Here's what you want to save:

```
Mon  9
Tue  12
Wed  18
Thu  16
Fri  21
Sat  13
Sun  15
```

(It's not really that cold—these temperatures are in degrees Celsius, not Fahrenheit.)

To get the temperatures into BASIC, you could start writing a laborious program that would ask you to INPUT the temperatures, like this:

```
10 INPUT "Temperature 1"; T1
20 INPUT "Temperature 2"; T2
30 INPUT "Temperature 3"; T3
   .
   .
```

Arrays

You'd probably get tired of this exercise very quickly. Now let's see how you could handle that same situation with an array, which we'll call "T." Remember, an array is just a group of variables, so one way to fill the array would be the same way you started—slow and steady. You change the subscript (the number between parentheses) each time, but you still input the temperatures in the same way:

```
10 INPUT "Temperature 1"; T(1)
20 INPUT "Temperature 2"; T(2)
30 INPUT "Temperature 3"; T(3)
   .
   .
```

But thanks to the magic of the array, there's a better way. You just use a FOR...NEXT loop, like this:

```
10 FOR I=1 TO 7
20     INPUT "Temperature"; T(I)
30 NEXT
```

The first time through the FOR...NEXT loop, I is 1, so your INPUT of 9 will go into the variable T(1). The next time through the loop, when I is 2, the value you INPUT (12) is stored in variable T(2). You slash the number of program lines needed—and the resulting array shown in figure 3-1 is substantially more useful than 7 individual variables would be.

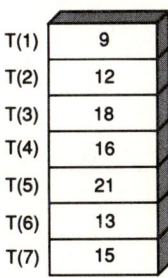

Fig. 3-1: The array of temperatures is made up of numeric variables.

Printing the temperatures is also easier. You just set up another FOR...NEXT loop, and presto—instant temperatures on the screen:

```
40 FOR I=1 TO 7
50     PRINT T(I)
60 NEXT
```

Chapter 3

This section of the program gives the following output:

```
9
12
18
16
21
13
15
```

Again, by using the loop counter I as an "index" into the array, you can print the entire group of variables using very little program code. The first time through the loop, the value of T(1) is printed, the second time T(2) is printed, and so on until all seven variables are on the screen.

Like other variables, arrays don't have to be only numeric. They can be strings as well. Here's a small section of code that asks you to input the days of the week in order:

```
40 FOR I=1 TO 7
50     PRINT "Input day"; I
60     INPUT D$(I)
70 NEXT
```

If you RUN this program, inputting a different day each time you're asked, you might wind up with an array like D$ in figure 3-2 that contains the days of the week.

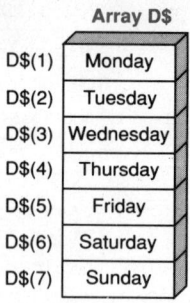

Fig. 3-2: Arrays can be strings, too.

Now here comes the real power of arrays and their subscripted variables. If you look at the T array and the D$ array, you can see that they look very much alike. D$(1) is Mon, and T(1) is the temperature for that day; D$(2) is Tue and T(2)

118

is that temperature, etc. Because the two arrays correspond, we can print them together, using only one loop counter. Here's how to print both arrays at once, and also to calculate the average:

```
80   FOR J=1 TO 7
90      PRINT D$(I); T(I)
100     X=X + T(I)
110  NEXT
120  PRINT "Average is";X/7
```

Each time through the FOR...NEXT loop, one subscripted D$ and one subscripted T are printed side by side. The latest T(J) is added to X to keep a total that's used to calculate the average temperature. When you RUN this program, you get:

```
Mon   9
Tue   12
Wed   18
Thu   16
Fri   21
Sat   13
Sun   15
Average is 14.85714
```

The temperatures are printed side by side with the appropriate days of the week.

We can make the subscript of the array an expression, as long as the results of the expression evaluate to an integer. (An array subscript must be an integer because there is no such thing as a fractional element—L(1.5) just doesn't exist.) An example of an expression for a subscript would be when we want to reference the elements in some special order, such as just the last 5 elements of a 10-element array, like this:

```
300  FOR I=1 to 5
310  L(I+5)=5
320  NEXT I
```

Obviously, array and subscripted variables make our programming job much easier and more flexible. But arrays are not limited to a series of linear parts. We can further divide an array with the aid of a concept called *dimension*.

Dimension with DIM

Arrays and subscripts are not limited to a single element. We can, for example, consider how a business, Lilliputian Industries, is organized. To find any employee,

Chapter 3

you have to specify not only a number, but also a section; therefore we have two items to specify. How is this done? The answer is to consider that the array used for employees has two *dimensions*. The first dimension is the number. The second dimension is the section. BASIC accomplishes this concept by allowing you to specify a second independent subscript between the parentheses. These two subscripts must be separated by a comma, like this:

```
L(I,J)
```

Here the subscript I indicates the number in L, Lilliputian Industries, and the subscript J indicates the section in L. For each section J there is a number of employees, I, which depends on the size of the array. We can call a dual-subscripted array a *two dimensional* array, because it has the equivalent of dimensions, like a room that has dimensions described by height and width.

Now when we specify Lilliputian Industries, we talk about a particular section and a particular employee in that section. For example, to specify section 2 and the third employee in that section, we write

```
L(3,2)=5
```

To help visualize the array, we can imagine that the elements are arranged in the computer like this (assuming there are three sections and five employees per section):

```
L(1,1)  L(2,1)  L(3,1)  L(4,1)  L(5,1)
L(1,2)  L(2,2)  L(3,2)  L(4,2)  L(5,2)
L(1,3)  L(2,3)  L(3,3)  L(4,3)  L(5,3)
```

For each of the five employees there is one particular section (from 1 to 3) which the employee is associated with. Thus we now have a total of 5 x 3 or 15 employees. In BASIC, we say that array L is an I by J array.

What is nice about BASIC arrays is that we can keep adding information, or dimensions, to the array by increasing the number of subscripts. For example, to specify a particular section, employee, and division, we could add a third subscript, like this:

```
L(I,J,K)
```

Here the subscript K stands for the division of the company and the subscripts I and J are as previously described. We now have a three-dimensional array, or an I by J by K array.

Visualizing three dimensions is certainly not as easy as two, but for convenience you can imagine that the third dimension is like the length of a space, and the other two stand for height and width, as shown in figure 3-3.

Arrays

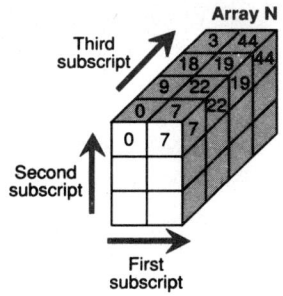

Fig. 3-3: A 3-Dimensional array.

Even though the array has 3 dimensions, you can still specify any element. So, in the array N shown in figure 3-3, the variable N(2,3,4) is 44.

Using DIM to Provide Space

In order for BASIC to set aside the proper amount of memory space for holding the element values of the array, we need to specify this before the array is used. BASIC provides a special keyword called DIM for this purpose. DIM appears at the beginning of a program that uses an array, and describes to the computer how many dimensions are in the array and how many elements are in each dimension. The general form of DIM is as follows:

```
DIM arrayname(I,J,K, . . . ), arrayname(I,J,K, . . . .
```

in which arrayname is the name of the array (this name follows the convention for all variable names) and I, J, and K stand for the *maximum elements* of the array dimensions. For example, the two-dimensional array Lilliputian Industries with three sections and five employees per section would be dimensioned as:

```
DIM L(5,3)
```

The 5 indicates that the first dimension has a maximum of five elements in it, and the 3 indicates that the second dimension has a maximum of three elements. Thus the computer sets aside 15 memory locations (or more if the values take up more than one byte each) for the array L.

For a three-dimensional array, we would write the following:

```
DIM L(5,3,10)
```

Chapter 3

in which the 10 indicates that there are 10 divisions, each containing 3 sections and 5 employees per section. Obviously the array needs 3 x 5 x 10 elements, or 150 total elements, to fully describe all combinations.

As the general form of the DIM statement shows, we can have several arrays dimensioned on the same DIM statement by simply separating each with a comma. This saves us from having to write separate DIM statements for each array we wish to dimension.

Is there any limit to the number of dimensions an array can have? The answer is "Yes"; in GW-BASIC, it's 255. GW-BASIC allows up to 255 dimensions.

When Can You Omit a DIM Statement?

We've said that the DIM statement reserves memory for an array to use later in the program. In GW-BASIC, you can create small arrays, with subscripts up to 10, without a DIM statement. So, the following program is OK:

```
10 FOR I = 1 TO 5
20    A(I) = I*I
30 NEXT I
```

However, if you change the value of I so that the program tries to create an array of, say, 20 subscripted variables, you'll have to add a DIM statement to reserve memory for the array, as shown here:

```
5 DIM A(20)
10 FOR I = 1 TO 20
20    A(I) = I*I
30 NEXT I
```

If you have any doubt that any subscript of your array will be larger than 10, be sure to use the DIM statement.

Using OPTION BASE

Suppose that you have a DIM statement like this in GW-BASIC:

```
10 DIM Z(100)
```

What this actually does is to reserve space for 101 subscripted variables—not 100! Why? Because right along with the space reserved for variables Z(1), Z(2), Z(3)...Z(99) and Z(100), there's also a place reserved for variable Z(0). Chances are you won't use variable Z(0), but its space has been reserved for you anyway.

Most of the time you can simply forget about the "extra" subscripted variable. But if you want to eliminate it altogether (whether to save that precious extra bit of memory space, or to keep your programs from getting all bollixed up), you can use the OPTION BASE statement, like this:

```
5   OPTION BASE 1
10  DIM Z(100)
```

Now the array Z begins with Z(1), Z(2), Z(3), etc., and continues to Z(100). There's no Z(0) element. OPTION BASE 1 means, "the first element of every array in this program is now 1, not 0."

GW-BASIC and most other versions of BASIC start with OPTION BASE set to 0. In GW-BASIC, you can set OPTION BASE 0 or OPTION BASE 1; you don't have any other choices.

How ERASE Gets Your Memory Back

Remember, the DIM statement reserves computer memory for use by arrays. And if you're finished with the array (or even if you don't ever use it!), that memory is still reserved. Neither you nor the program can use it for anything else.

Naturally, this can be a problem, especially if you have many large arrays. Luckily, GW-BASIC includes the ERASE statement that lets you release that reserved memory for other, more productive uses. Here's how you use ERASE to release the memory reserved for arrays:

```
ERASE array A, array B, array C, etc.
```

Now let's try an example. Although computers seem very fast to us, some tasks take longer than others. Arithmetic functions such as multiplication and division are relatively slow. To find the cube of a number using multiplication, for instance, the computer has to laboriously multiply the number by itself, then multiply that product by the number again. Now this doesn't sound too hard, especially for a powerful computer like yours, but if this type of calculation has to be performed over and over again in a program, it can chew up a lot of time.

Faced with the need to calculate similar numbers over and over again in a particular section of computer code, many programmers will create a *look-up table*. This table is an array of values that have already been calculated in some other part of the program. Now, when the program needs a value, it simply reads the value from the look-up table, rather than having to go off somewhere and use its relatively slow calculation routines.

For instance, if you knew your program was going to be needing the cubes of the numbers from 1 to 500, you could create a look-up table like that shown in Figure 3-4.

Chapter 3

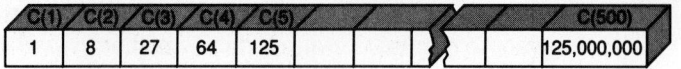

Fig. 3-4: The look-up table in an array.

When the program calls for the cube of 4, it simply "looks up" the variable A(4), and gets the value 64 very, very quickly.

Now try the following program to create a look-up table of cubes:

```
10 DIM C(500)
20 FOR I = 1 TO 500: C(I) = I*I*I: NEXT I
30 PRINT "The cube of 42 is" C(42)
40 PRINT "The cube of 500 is" C(500)
```

Before we proceed, take a good look at line 20. There are actually three BASIC statements on this single line. GW-BASIC lets you use the colon (:) symbol to separate statements and put them on the same line. Here the entire FOR...NEXT loop is included. Even when they're separated by colons, the computer expects the statements to occur in the same order you read them, from left to right, so line 20 is actually this:

```
FOR I = 1 TO 500
LET C(I) = I*I*I
NEXT I
```

Incidentally, it's not usually a good idea to put several statements on a single line because it makes a program listing harder to read. It does save memory, however, and it's useful in certain constructions (such as IF...THEN...ELSE) when you want to pack as much as you can into the statement.

Now RUN the program. After you've run it, you can use FRE to see how much free space is left on the computer, like this:

```
RUN
The cube of 42 is 74088
The cube of 500 is 1.25E+08
Ok

PRINT FRE (0)
 58068
```

The FRE(0) statement displays the number of bytes that are currently available ("free") for use. This illustration means that the computer used here now has

124

58,068 bytes of free memory. (The number may be different on your own computer.) Let's see what happens when we ERASE the look-up table and memory reserved for array C:

```
ERASE C
Ok
PRINT FRE(0)
 60081
Ok
```

See how ERASE released that extra memory for you? We now have 60,081 bytes available for use in our program. That's an extra 2,013 bytes!

ERASE also lets you redimension arrays while your program is running. Normally, once you've set an array size with a DIM statement, you can't change the size of the array. But ERASE lets you redimension "on the fly." Here's how you could create a look-up table of 500 cubes, then reduce it later to a 100-cube array:

```
10 DIM C(500)
20 FOR I = 1 TO 500: C(I) = I*I*I: NEXT I
.
.
.
1200 ERASE C
1210 DIM C(100)
1220 FOR I = 1 TO 100: C(I) = I*I*I: NEXT I
```

As your arrays expand and gobble up more and more memory, you'll want to make liberal use of ERASE to keep programs running at tip-top efficiency.

Using an Expense Account Program

You now have enough knowledge at your fingertips to write some pretty good BASIC programs. You can create simple games, do "computer-aided education," keep track of calories or expenses—all with just the few statements you've learned thus far in this book.

One useful program is an expense account, a program that prompts you for the amount of an expense, then adds the amount to a total. At the press of a key, you should then be able to display the total for expenses. Let's expand the expense account program of the previous chapter, using programming techniques and design that can be applied to virtually any programming problem.

Chapter 3

Your Expense Account Program: Where to Begin?

To write a program that's longer than a few lines, you don't just sit down and start entering program statements. As the size and complexity of your programs grow, you'll need to go about the task of writing them in a logical and ordered way. To begin cranking out program code without a plan is to invite disaster—even if you get a program that seems to work, it will probably be so unstructured that you'll never be able to sort it out, or to debug it when the inevitable problems occur. (And occur they will! Bugs are a fact of life in programming.)

So where do you begin your ordered, logical procedure? You start with the output from the program. Although it seems like the last place to start, determining what the output will be and what it will look like is the first step in creating a program.

Software companies that produce the popular game and business packages—and even languages such as GW-BASIC—often begin a project by creating what's called an *engineering specification*. This is a document, used by all members of the programming team, that clearly defines what the program will do and what the output will look like. Although it is not "locked in stone," the engineering specification starts everyone pointing in the same direction, and the larger the project, the more important it is that the engineering specification be clearly defined at the outset and closely followed.

Output Screen

Let's start with a kind of engineering specification for our expense account program. We want the output to look something like this:

```
                    EXPENSE REPORT

                    FOOD

   Date             Description             Amount
   xxx              xxx                     $xxx

          Expenses for food:                $xxx

                    TRANSPORTATION

   Date             Description             Amount
   xxx              xxx                     $xxx

          Expenses for transportation:      $xxx
```

```
                    LODGING

Date              Description           Amount

xxx               xxx                   $ xxx

            Expenses for Lodging:       $ xxx

                 MISCELLANEOUS

Date              Description           Amount

xxx               xxx                   $xxx

            Grand total:                $xxxxx
```

You can see that what we'll have to come up with is a screen that prints a main headline, followed by lists of expenses for individual categories. We'll show food, transportation, lodging, and miscellaneous, but of course there could be many more, depending on your own personal style. For each category of expense, we print the date of the expense, a description, and the amount. After displaying all the individual expenses, the program prints a subtotal for each category of expense, followed by a grand total.

Input Screen

Now that we know how we want the output to look, we can ponder what information we'll need to produce it. We'll want the user to be able to pick from a menu of categories, then type the date, description, and amount for that category. Some of us might have already arranged our receipts by date, or might use this program at the end of every day. So if the date is the same as the previous entry, we'll just hit Return to use the same date. The input for any category, then, will proceed like this:

```
Input your choice? 4

MISCELLANEOUS
Last date was xxx
Hit RETURN to use this date
or input new date?

Description? xxx
Amount? xxx
```

Chapter 3

The Menu Screen

Finally—or first, depending on your point of view—we'll want a menu that lets the user pick a category for entering an expense, displaying or printing the expense account, or exiting. Let's say that the menu is going to look like this:

```
EXPENSE-ACCOUNTER

What type of expense?
1 - Food
2 - Transportation
3 - Lodging
4 - Miscellaneous

8 to print the total
9 to exit
Input your choice?
```

This is what the program displays when it is run. By typing a number in answer to the prompt, the user selects what will happen next—entry of an expense, calculating and displaying the total, printing a list of expenses, or quitting for the day.

Designing the Program

Now we'll design the program, determining how we want it to be executed. One aid in program design is a flowchart, and if you've seen programming textbooks, you know they're chock full of flowcharts. For a detailed and complex program, you might want several levels of flowcharts.

The Overall Flowchart

An overall flowchart for our program, one that shows the major flow, is shown in figure 3-5.
    You can see that the program will begin by displaying a menu. There are six choices displayed in the menu. The first four choices are to input an expense for food, transportation, lodging, or miscellaneous, respectively. There's also a choice to print the totals. After any of these choices is executed, we want to go back and display the menu again.
    If the user wants to exit, we don't go back to the menu, but instead branch directly to the end of the program. Any program you write should have a beginning, a middle, and a way to end the program.

Arrays

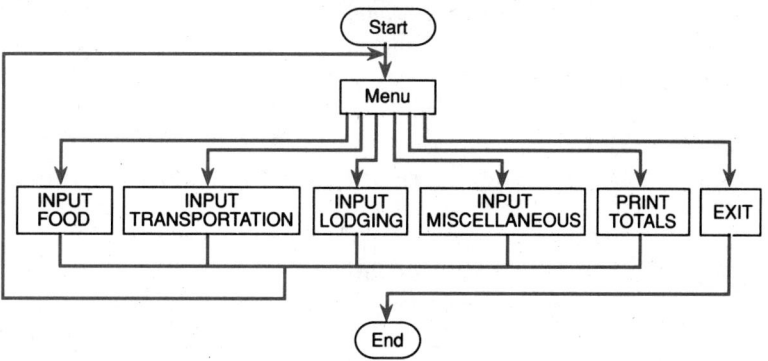

Fig. 3-5: Overall flowchart for the expense account program.

Initialization and Menu Display

Now let's flesh out the overall flowchart with flowcharts to cover more specific areas, and add the appropriate code after each flowchart. The first is initialization and menu display. Initialization means setting up the screen and everything in the program to make it the way you want it before you do any actual work (see fig. 3-6).

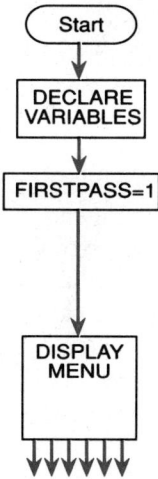

Fig. 3-6: Initialization and menu display.

Chapter 3

The first thing we'll do is declare all variables. In this section of the program, we'll determine which variables will be integers, which will be strings, and so on. This is a good area of the program to document your variables, too, so that other programmers who come across your code 100 years from now will be able to follow it more easily.

During initialization, one thing we'll do that's pretty important is set a variable (which we're calling `FIRSTPASS`) to 1. Remember, we said that we want the user to be able to hit Return if the date is the same, rather than having to input it again. But what if this is the first time the program has been run today? The user will not have entered any date at all, so the variable we're using for the date will be zero. To prevent this from happening, we'll set `FIRSTPASS` to 1 if this is the first time the program is run, then we'll use `FIRSTPASS` later to make a decision about how to handle the date.

The Variable List

Before you start writing code, you should make up a list of all the variables you think you'll be using, and what they are. Otherwise, you run the danger of writing an instruction in line 100 that specifies the variable AMT, then write another instruction in line 5000 that refers to AMOUNT. To you, with your human-oriented, "fuzzy logic" kind of thinking, they're the same thing, but to BASIC they're completely different.

Here's a list of the variables we'll use in the expense account program:

`M`	Maximum number of types of expenses. Set to 4 originally.
`TYPE`	Numeric variable specifying type of expense.
`DAY$`	String array containing the dates for all expenses.
`DESCRIP$`	String array containing descriptions of the expenses.
`AMT`	Array of numeric variables containing the amounts of expenses.
`FIRSTPASS`	Numeric variable that's a flag for whether it's the first run of the program or not.
`D$`	String variable containing the current date.
`I`	Numeric variable containing the number of the highest element of any array (that is, the total number of expense entries).
`SUBTOTAL`	Numeric variable to hold the subtotal when printing the amounts in each category.
`GRANDTOTAL`	Numeric variable to hold the grand total of all expenses.
`S`	Array size.
`N`	Menu number.
`J`	Loop counter.
`A$`	String variable to hold "Y" or "y".

Writing the Initialization and Menu Routine

Now it's time to put fingers on keys and start entering code. The first thing we'll do is input the initialization and menu routine—the main part of the program, as you'll see. Begin with a suitable title and the name of the file in which you'll store the program:

```
10 REM-EXPENSE-ACCOUNTER
20 REM-Save as "EXPACC"
30 REM-This program is an expense account.
40 REM-You can input expenses by category, and display the total.
50 REM
```

Now we move into the initialization section. We'll start by clearing the screen for action, and setting the key display at the bottom of the screen to off. Then we assign values to a couple of variables that need to be specified at the outset.

```
60 REM-Initialization section
70 CLS: KEY OFF
80 S=200
90 M=4
100 OPTION BASE 1
110 DIM TYPE(S), DAY$(S), DESCRIP$(S), AMT(S)
120 FIRSTPASS=1
130 REM
```

We set the variable S equal to 200; we'll use this number to dimension our arrays, so it means this is the maximum number of elements in any array. It also means that the maximum number of different expenses you can enter into this program will be 200. You can change this number if you like; because we've placed it in a variable, you can change the dimensions of all arrays by simply changing this one variable.

This is an important point. By using variables instead of constants as much as possible, you make it much easier to modify a program later.

The maximum number of categories available for our expense account is another place we're using a variable instead of a constant. Here the variable is M, and we'll set it to 4 to begin with. If you want to add menu choices later, using a variable like M will make it a lot easier than if you simply write the original program assuming that there are only 4 choices.

Now we'll dimension the arrays we'll need. We don't care about the first element (element 0) of any array, so we'll use the OPTION BASE 1 statement to begin every array at element #1. The arrays are

`TYPE`	Numeric variable specifying type of expense.
`DAY$`	String array containing the dates for all expenses.
`DESCRIP$`	String array containing descriptions of the expenses.
`AMT`	Array of numeric variables containing the amounts of expenses.

Notice that all these are dimensioned to 200 because of the value of `S`. If you change `S`, you also change the potential size of these arrays.

Now that our arrays are all ready to go, there's one other little housekeeping task to take care of. Remember the `FIRSTPASS` flag? We'll set it to 1, because the only time this section of code gets executed is the first time the program is run. As you'll see, we'll only use this flag once, but it plays an important role in our program nevertheless.

The Main Menu

Now we come to the menu loop. Once execution has entered this loop, there are only two ways out. (Sounds kind of ominous, doesn't it? But it's good programming practice both to provide exits from loops, and also to control those exits.)

We'll want to make several decisions in this loop, which is shown in figure 3-7. First, the user is going to INPUT a menu number, `N`. If that `N` is from 1 to 4, execution will branch to the appropriate subroutine for food, transportation, lodging, or miscellaneous expenses. Simple enough—sounds like a candidate for ON...GOTO or ON...GOSUB.

To actually print the subtotals for each category, and the grand total, we'll use menu selection 8. If the user inputs an `N` of 8, we'll print the totals and come back to the menu again. We could incorporate this into the diamond above it (and put it in the same ON...GOTO statement) but we want to leave some room to add other menu selections between 4 and 8.

Our available menu selections for now are 1 to `M` (`M` is 4, remember), 8, and 9. What if the user enters something that's outside this range? We'll want to print a gentle admonition and return to the menu for another try. Only if N=9 is the user allowed to exit; as you'll see, by controlling the exit this way, we can provide for some "housekeeping" that should be done, like clearing the screen.

Here's the actual code we'll use for the menu loop. It's made up of our old friend, the WHILE...WEND construction, surrounding several other statements.

```
140 REM-Wait for a menu selection
150 WHILE  N<S
160     REM
170     PRINT
180     REM-Show the menu
190     PRINT "EXPENSE-ACCOUNTER": PRINT
200     PRINT  "What type of expense?
```

```
210     PRINT "1 - Food"
220     PRINT "2 - Transportation"
230     PRINT "3 - Lodging"
240     PRINT "4 - Miscellaneous"
250     PRINT: PRINT "8 to print the total"
260     PRINT "9 to exit"
270     REM
280     REM-Branch to correct subroutine
290     INPUT "Input your choice";N
300     ON N GOSUB 1000, 2000, 3000, 4000
310     IF N=8 THEN GOSUB 5000
320     IF N=9 THEN GOTO 9000
330     CLS
340     IF M<N AND N<8 OR N>9 OR N<1 THEN PRINT:
        PRINT "Make a legitimate choice!":
        PRINT
350 WEND
```

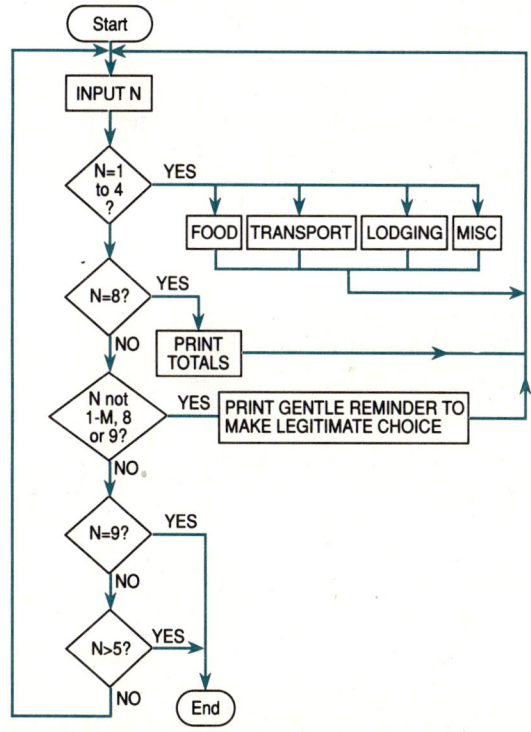

Fig. 3-7: The menu loop.

133

Chapter 3

The very first thing we do each time through the loop is print a heading and a menu that shows the user what choices are available. Then comes the famous INPUT statement, which suspends execution and waits for the user to type a value for N. This variable is used as a menu number, and we'll also store it in the TYPE array so that we know what type an expense is.

Once the user has input a value for N, everything else in the loop depends on that value. If N is 1, execution branches to the subroutine beginning at line 1000, which is the subroutine to input an expense for food. If N is 2, execution branches to the transportation subroutine beginning at line 2000, and so on for menu items 1 through 4.

If N is 8, execution branches to the subroutine beginning at line 5000; this is where the printing of the actual expense account is handled. With an N of 9, execution branches to 9000, which is the end of the program. Notice that this is a GOTO branch, not a subroutine—there's no return from it. Once you choose 9, it's all over.

What happens if the user, whether by design or through bad luck or bad typing, inputs an N that is none of the above? One way to handle this case is simply to ignore it; execution can't fall out of the loop (unless N becomes equal to or greater than the maximum number of array elements, S), so pretty soon your hapless user would probably get the idea and stumble onto a legal menu selection.

But it's better to provide messages in such cases. So, we include the IF...THEN statement. This statement is crammed with decisions, so let's look at it step by step. It prints the message "Make a legitimate choice!" if any of these conditions occur:

- N is between M (the maximum number for expense categories, currently set to 4) and 8
- N is greater than 9, or
- N is less than 1

If any of these conditions is true, the user's hand is slapped ever so gently.

If by some chance you fill up all the arrays so that N becomes equal to or greater than S, execution "falls out" of the WHILE...WEND loop. But look what's waiting for it: a message to tell you what's happened, followed by an END statement:

```
360 PRINT "Expense table full"
370 END
```

Inputting an Expense

Now let's discuss how we will handle things when execution branches to one of the subroutines to enter an expense, the ones beginning at lines 1000, 2000, 3000, and 4000. These are all the same, with the exception of the title, so we'll just look at one.

134

Figure 3-8 shows the flowchart for inputting an expense. When execution is transferred from the calling part of the program, we'll first want to print a title, something that will remind the user what kind of an expense to input here. Then we want to keep track of what kind of expense this is, so we'll set the TYPE equal to the value of N. Thus, all expenses for food will be type 1, those for transportation type 2, and so on.

If this is the first pass through one of the input subroutines, we need to have the user always input the date; but if it's the second pass or later, we want the user to be able to use the previous date if desired. So we look at FIRSTPASS. If FIRSTPASS is set to 1, it means "this is the very first time I'm being run," so we always have the user input the day into variable DAY$. Then we're done with FIRSTPASS, so we set it to zero and it is never used again.

We'll need to provide a way to keep the current day so that it can be used on later passes. We'll do that with a variable called D$, in which we'll always have a copy of the very latest day.

If this isn't the first pass through one of the input subroutines, we'll show the last day used, D$. The user has a choice of using it or not; if the choice is to use it, we'll assign DAY$ the value of D$. If the choice is to not use it, we'll have the user input a string to be assigned to DAY$.

After inputting the date, the user enters the description of the expense, followed by the amount, then returns to the calling program. With the exception of the title, which changes, this same operation will be duplicated in all the input subroutines.

Now let's look at the actual code for this operation. We'll examine the code for the "food" expense subroutine that begins in line 1000. Remember, we said that except for the title, all the rest of the program steps are virtually the same from one input subroutine to the next, so we just print the needed title, then blithely branch off to yet another subroutine:

```
1000 REM-Subroutine for food expense
1010 REM
1020 CLS
1030 PRINT "FOOD"
1040 GOSUB 6000 'Call general input subroutine
1050 RETURN
```

That's pretty simple. We clear the menu off the screen, print a title, then call a subroutine. When we come back from the subroutine, we return right away to the WHILE...WEND menu loop.

Not so fast! We'll also want to look over the general input subroutine, because that's where the real work is done. It's where all your expenses are placed into their arrays.

Chapter 3

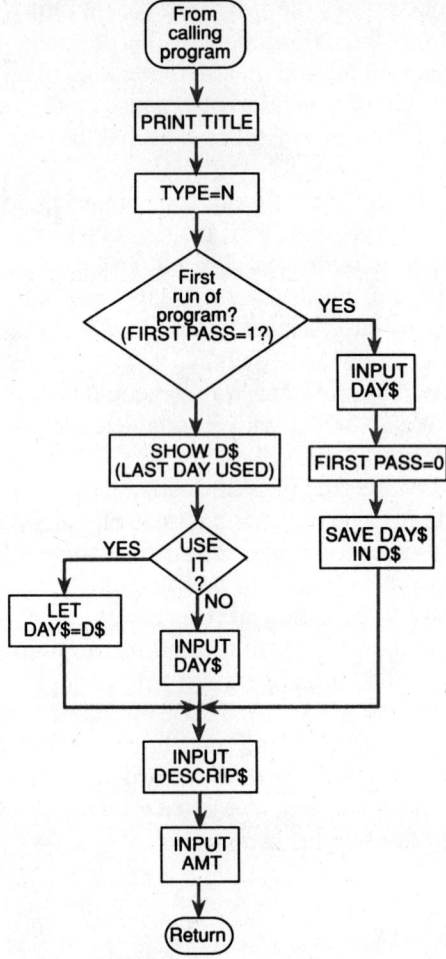

Fig. 3-8: Flowchart for inputting an expense.

The General Input Subroutine

After printing the headline for the category—food, transportation, lodging, or miscellaneous—the program calls the general input subroutine in line 6000. Here are the program statements that are executed:

Arrays

```
6000 REM-General input subroutine
6010 I=I+1
6020 TYPE(I)=N
6030 REM-Line to handle date input for first run of program
6040 IF FIRSTPASS=1 THEN INPUT "Input date";DAY$(I):
        FIRSTPASS=0:
        D$=DAY$(I):
        GOTO 6110
6050 REM-Ordinary case; not first run of program
6060 PRINT "Last date was ";D$
6070 PRINT "Hit RETURN to use this date"
6080 INPUT "or input new date"; DAY$(I)
6090 IF DAY$(I)="" THEN DAY$(I)=D$
6100 D$=DAY$(I)
6110 INPUT "Description"; DESCRIP$(I)
6120 INPUT "Amount"; AMT(I)
6130 RETURN
```

The first thing that happens in the subroutine is that we increment I. This variable is a counter that keeps track of how many entries are in our arrays. Each time this subroutine is called (that is, every time an expense is entered), this counter is increased by 1, which means that the number of the subscripts on our array variables is also increased.

Next, we set TYPE(I)=N. So, if this is the first entry of an expense and you pressed the 1 key to input an expense for food, you'll get the following:

```
TYPE(1)=1
```

Now we input a string for DAY$(I), and here is where we must make another decision. The big long IF...THEN statement handles the case if this is the first time through the input subroutine—that is, if the FIRSTPASS flag is set to 1. It says that if FIRSTPASS is set to 1, then all these things will be done:

- You are prompted to "Input date," and the program waits for you to INPUT a string, DAY$(I).
- The FIRSTPASS flag is set to 0.
- D$, which holds the latest date, is set to DAY$(I) (the string that you just typed).
- Execution branches to line 6110 for input of the description

If this isn't the first pass, FIRSTPASS is set to zero, so line 6040 isn't executed. Instead, execution picks up with line 6050. You see the current date D$ printed, then you have a choice: enter a new date, or press Return.

137

Chapter 3

The INPUT statement waits for a value for `DAY$(I)` to be INPUT from the keyboard. If `DAY$(I)` is a null string (that is, you simply press Return), then the date held in `D$` is used for `DAY$(I)`. If you actually enter a string in line 6080, it's used for the date, and `D$` is updated to this new string.

Let's say that this is the first time through this subroutine and you input the date 7/15/90. What happens is the same as if you had entered the following:

```
DAY$(1)= "7/15/90"
```

Next, the string for `DESCRIP$(I)` and the amount for numeric variable `AMT(I)` are input. If this is the first time through the loop and you're inputting an expense for a pizza that cost $9.50, it's as if the following statements had been entered:

```
DESCRIP$(1) = "PIZZA"
AMT(1) = 9.50
```

When you receive the prompt "Description," you enter a string that's stored in string variable `DESCRIP$(1)`. When you enter the "Amount," it's saved in numeric variable `AMT(1)`. After the amount has been stored, execution returns to the calling subroutine, and then returns to the WHILE...WEND menu loop.

Now suppose that the second time this subroutine is called, you're recording an expense for lodging, and you input the following information:

- When prompted for "Input date?" you press Return
- When prompted for "Description?" you input PRIVACY PLACE
- When prompted for "Amount" you type 45.00

The array variables are affected like this:

```
TYPE(2)=3
DATE$(2)="7/15/90"  (the previous date)
DESCRIP$(2)="PARK PLACE"
AMT(2)=45.00
```

So, the arrays of expense information are beginning to fill up. After your first two inputs, they look like the diagram in figure 3-9.

Arrays

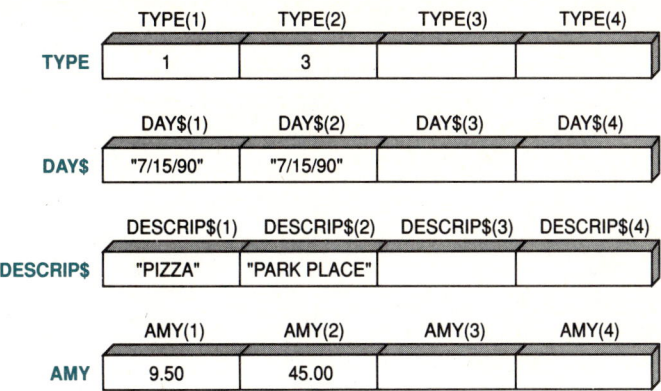

Fig. 3-9:   Filling the arrays.

You can continue filling the arrays as long as you like, until you reach the 200-element limit set by S. Now let's see how we can read what's in the arrays.

Displaying the Expenses

Getting data out of the arrays is a fairly simple proposition. In fact, you don't actually get data out—you simply read what's in there. Displaying or printing the value of arrays is just like displaying or printing any variable, and it doesn't affect the contents.

To read the data, we'll set up a series of loops, shown in figure 3-10. First we'll want to read and print only those array elements that are for food items, then transportation, then lodging, and finally miscellaneous.

For instance, when we're calculating and printing the expenses for food, we want to examine the TYPE to see whether it's a 1. If it isn't a 1, then we look at the next TYPE variable in the array; but if it is a 1, that means this TYPE (and the elements of the other arrays with the same subscript) make up a food expense. We'll print the date, description, and amount, and we'll also keep a subtotal of the amounts for this type.

Notice that we don't care about sorting the actual elements of the array. All we want to do is look at each TYPE in turn, and, if the type is what we want, to print all the information that was saved at the same time as that particular element.

When we've tried all the elements to see if they're one type, we add the subtotal for this type to a grand total. Then we reset the SUBTOTAL variable to zero so we can use it again.

Chapter 3

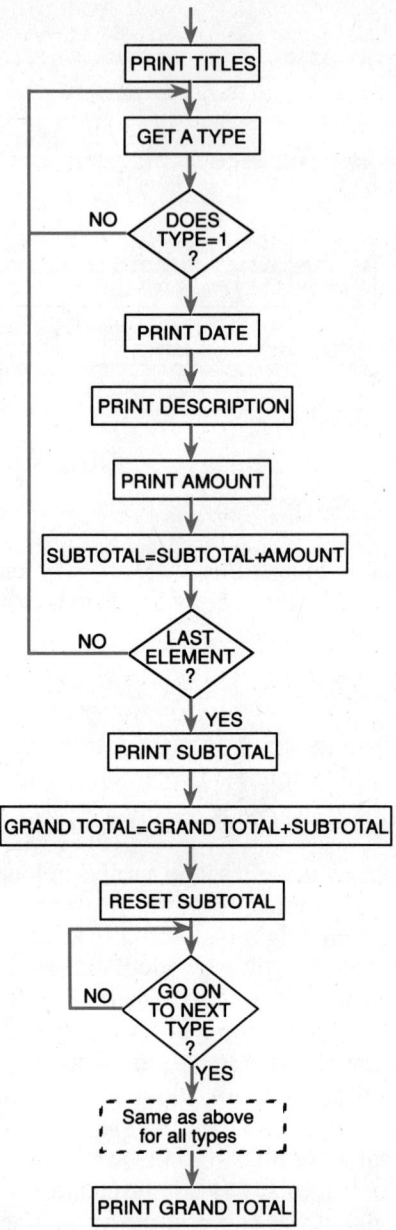

Fig. 3-10:   Loops print data from the arrays.

Arrays

Some of these totals can fly by pretty fast, so we'll put a small loop in that waits for you to look over the subtotal before going on to print the next type. Finally, when we're done with all the TYPEs, we'll print a grand total of all our expenses so that we can tell just how bad things are.

Here's the code for printing the general heading and one TYPE of output, that for food expenses:

```
5000 REM-Subroutine to print totals
5010 REM
5020 CLS
5030 PRINT: PRINT TAB(20) "EXPENSE REPORT"
5040 PRINT: PRINT TAB(20) "FOOD"
5050 PRINT: PRINT "Date" TAB(20) "Description" TAB(40) "Amount"
5060 PRINT
5070 FOR J=1 TO I
5080     IF TYPE(J)=1 THEN GOSUB 7000
5090 NEXT
5100 PRINT: PRINT TAB(10) "Expenses for food:" TAB(40)
     "$"SUBTOTAL
5110 SUBTOTAL=0 'Reset subtotal
5120 GOSUB 8000 'Call subroutine to wait for answer
5130 REM
5140 REM-Print transportation subtotals
5150 PRINT: PRINT TAB(20) "TRANSPORTATION"
5160 PRINT: PRINT "Date" TAB(20) "Description" TAB(40) "Amount"
5170 PRINT
5180 FOR J=1 TO I
5190     IF TYPE(J)=2 THEN GOSUB 7000
5200 NEXT
```

We first clear the screen and print a general heading that tells what's coming up. We know that the maximum element in the TYPE array (or any array) has the subscript I, so we use the FOR J=1 TO I loop to count up from 1 to I, checking each element of the TYPE array for 1's.

When we find a TYPE that's a 1, we branch to the subroutine to print subtotals in line 7000. Here's what happens there:

```
7000 REM-Subroutine to print subtotals
7010 PRINT DAY$(J) TAB(20) DESCRIP$(J) TAB(40) "$"AMT(J)
7020 SUBTOTAL=SUBTOTAL + AMT(J)
7030 GRANDTOTAL=GRANDTOTAL + SUBTOTAL
7040 RETURN
```

Chapter 3

Because we know that `TYPE(J)=1`, we know we want to print all the array elements with that same I subscript. For instance, suppose that `ARRAY(15)` turns out to be equal to 1. We branch to line 7000 and print `DAY$(15)`, `DESCRIP$(15)`, and `AMT(15)` across the screen. Then execution returns to the calling FOR...NEXT loop until another `TYPE(J)=1` occurs.

The subroutine beginning in line 7000 is also where we update both the `SUBTOTAL` and the `GRANDTOTAL`. The `SUBTOTAL` gets reset to zero after each category of expense has been printed, but we keep adding to the `GRANDTOTAL`, so we can print it at the end.

After we print a `SUBTOTAL`, we need a way to "freeze" the screen so you can examine it. For this purpose, we call a WHILE...WEND loop that's in subroutine 8000:

```
8000 REM-Subroutine to wait for a "Y" or "y" answer
8010 PRINT
8020 WHILE A$ <> "Y" AND A$ <> "y"
8030     INPUT "Show next (Y/N)";A$
8040 WEND
8050 A$=""
8060 RETURN
```

This is nothing more than another WHILE...WEND loop that waits until you enter a "Y" or a "y" (for "Yes"). Execution stays in the loop—and the subtotals stay on the screen—until you INPUT a single "Y" or a "y" for the variable `A$`. Then execution drops out of the loop and continues with the next portion of the program after the subroutine call. Notice that you need to reset `A$` to something other than "Y" or "y" before returning, or else the next time this subroutine is called, execution will fall through the WHILE...WEND loop.

All the `TYPE`s of expenses are printed in the same manner. When all is done, we print the `GRANDTOTAL` and return to the main menu loop:

```
5450 REM-Print grand total
5460 PRINT: PRINT TAB(10) "Grand total:"TAB(40)"$"GRANDTOTAL
5470 PRINT
5480 WHILE A$ <> "Y" AND A$ <> "y"
5490     INPUT "Return to menu (Y/N)";A$
5500 WEND
5510 RETURN
```

Arrays

Like the subtotals, we want to be able to view the grand total before returning, so we include a WHILE...WEND loop with the same action but a slightly different message from that in subroutine 8000.

Ending the Program

When you answer the menu prompt with a 9, execution branches to line 9000. This illustrates how you should clean up the screen for the next program when you exit. Because you turned the function key display off, you'll turn it back on; and you'll also clear the screen to its formerly pristine state:

```
9000 REM-Routine to clean up screen and exit
9010 CLS
9020 PRINT "Program terminated"
9030 KEY ON
9040 END
```

Running the Expense Account Program

Now try running the expense account program to see whether the output is anything like we want. Fire it up and take a look at the menu:

```
RUN
EXPENSE-ACCOUNTER

What type of expense?
1 - Food
2 - Transportation
3 - Lodging
4 - Miscellaneous

8 to print the total
9 to exit
Input your choice?
```

Looks good so far. Put in some expenses incurred at the sumptuous lunch you had today:

Chapter 3

```
Input your choice? 1

FOOD
Input date? 7/15/90
Description? CORN CHIPS
Amount? 1.35

EXPENSE-ACCOUNTER

What type of expense?
1 - Food
2 - Transportation
3 - Lodging
4 - Miscellaneous

8 to print the total
9 to exit
Input your choice?
```

Perfect. Now try out the part of the program that lets you press Return to enter the date:

```
Input your choice? 1

FOOD
Last date was 7/15/90
Press RETURN to use this date
or input new date?    (You press RETURN here...)
Description? PIZZA
Amount? 9.80
```

Input some other expenses from a few fun-filled days:

```
Input your choice? 2

TRANSPORTATION
Last date was 7/15/90
Press RETURN to use this date
or input new date? 7/16/90
Description? TAXI
Amount? 12.50
```

```
Input your choice? 3

LODGING
Last date was 7/16/90
Press RETURN to use this date
or input new date?
Description? PARK PLACE
Amount? 45.00

Input your choice? 4

MISCELLANEOUS
Last date was 7/16/90
Press RETURN to use this date
or input new date?
Description? VIDEO
Amount? 5.25

Input your choice? 4

MISCELLANEOUS
Last date was 7/16/90
Press RETURN to use this date
or input new date?
Description? HAIR RESTORER
Amount? 3.45
```

Now let's print the results and see how much our good times have cost.

```
Input your choice? 8

                EXPENSE REPORT

                FOOD

Date            Description         Amount

7/15/90         CORN CHIPS          $ 1.35
7/15/90         PIZZA               $ 9.8

        Expenses for food:          $ 11.15
```

Chapter 3

```
Show next (Y/N)? Y

                TRANSPORTATION

Date            Description         Amount

7/16/90         TAXI                $ 12.5

        Expenses for transportation:   $ 12.5

Show next (Y/N)? Y

                LODGING

Date            Description         Amount

7/16/90         PARK PLACE          $ 45

        Expenses for lodging:       $ 45

Show next (Y/N)? Y

                MISCELLANEOUS

Date            Description         Amount

7/16/90         VIDEO               $ 5.25
7/16/90         HAIR RESTORER       $ 3.45

        Miscellaneous expenses:     $ 8.7

        Grand total:                $ 83.95

Return to menu (Y/N)? Y
```

   Notice that, like the loan program in the previous chapter, not all the numbers appear as only two digits. Later on in this book you'll learn how to round off numbers, and how to employ a statement called PRINT USING that can display numbers just the way you want to see them.
   You'll find a complete listing of the expense account here.

```
10 REM-EXPENSE-ACCOUNTER
20 REM-Save as "EXPACC"
30 REM-This program is an expense account.
40 REM-You can input expenses by category, and display the total
50 REM
60 REM-Initialization section
70 CLS: KEY OFF
80 S=200
90 M=4
100 OPTION BASE 1
110 DIM TYPE(S), DAY$(S), DESCRIP$(S), AMT(S)
120 FIRSTPASS=1
130 REM
140 REM-Wait for a menu selection
150 WHILE  N<S
160      REM
170      PRINT
180      REM-Show the menu
190      PRINT "EXPENSE-ACCOUNTER": PRINT
200      PRINT  "What type of expense?
210      PRINT "1 - Food"
220      PRINT "2 - Transportation"
230      PRINT "3 - Lodging"
240      PRINT "4 - Miscellaneous"
250      PRINT: PRINT "8 to print the total"
260      PRINT "9 to exit"
270      REM
280      REM-Branch to correct subroutine
290      INPUT "Input your choice";N
300      ON N GOSUB 1000, 2000, 3000, 4000
310      IF N=8 THEN GOSUB 5000
320      IF N=9 THEN GOTO 9000
330      CLS
340      IF M<N AND N<8 OR N>9 OR N<1 THEN PRINT:
         PRINT "Make a legitimate choice!":
         PRINT
350 WEND
360 PRINT "Expense table full"
370 END
380 REM
1000 REM-Subroutine for food expense
1010 REM
1020 CLS
```

```
1030 PRINT "FOOD"
1040 GOSUB 6000 'Call general input subroutine
1050 RETURN
2000 REM-Subroutine for transportation expense
2010 REM
2020 CLS
2030 PRINT "TRANSPORTATION"
2040 GOSUB 6000 'Call general input subroutine
2050 RETURN
3000 REM-Subroutine for lodging expense
3010 REM
3020 CLS
3030 PRINT "LODGING"
3040 GOSUB 6000 'Call general input subroutine
3050 RETURN
4000 REM-Subroutine for miscellaneous expense
4010 REM
4020 CLS
4030 PRINT "MISCELLANEOUS"
4040 GOSUB 6000 'Call general input subroutine
4050 RETURN
4060 REM
5000 REM-Subroutine to print totals
5010 REM
5020 CLS
5030 PRINT: PRINT TAB(20) "EXPENSE REPORT"
5040 PRINT: PRINT TAB(20) "FOOD"
5050 PRINT: PRINT "Date" TAB(20) "Description" TAB(40) "Amount"
5060 PRINT
5070 FOR J=1 TO I
5080     IF TYPE(J)=1 THEN GOSUB 7000
5090 NEXT
5100 PRINT: PRINT TAB(10) "Expenses for food:" TAB(40)
     "$"SUBTOTAL
5110 SUBTOTAL=0 'Reset subtotal
5120 GOSUB 8000 'Call subroutine to wait for answer
5130 REM
5140 REM-Print transportation subtotals
5150 PRINT: PRINT TAB(20) "TRANSPORTATION"
5160 PRINT: PRINT "Date" TAB(20) "Description" TAB(40) "Amount"
5170 PRINT
5180 FOR J=1 TO I
5190     IF TYPE(J)=2 THEN GOSUB 7000
```

```
5200 NEXT
5210 PRINT: PRINT TAB(10) "Expenses for transportation:" TAB(40)
     "$"SUBTOTAL
5220 SUBTOTAL=0 'Reset subtotal
5230 GOSUB 8000 'Call subroutine to wait for answer
5240 REM
5250 REM-Print lodging subtotals
5260 PRINT: PRINT TAB(20) "LODGING"
5270 PRINT: PRINT "Date" TAB(20) "Description" TAB(40) "Amount"
5280 PRINT
5290 FOR J=1 TO I
5300     IF TYPE(J)=3 THEN GOSUB 7000
5310 NEXT
5320 PRINT: PRINT TAB(10) "Expenses for lodging:" TAB(40)
     "$"SUBTOTAL
5330 SUBTOTAL=0 'Reset subtotal
5340 GOSUB 8000 'Call subroutine to wait for answer
5350 REM
5360 REM-Print subtotals for miscellaneous
5370 PRINT: PRINT TAB(20) "MISCELLANEOUS"
5380 PRINT: PRINT "Date" TAB(20) "Description" TAB(40) "Amount"
5390 PRINT
5400 FOR J=1 TO I
5410     IF TYPE(J)=4 THEN GOSUB 7000
5420 NEXT
5430 PRINT: PRINT TAB(10) "Miscellaneous expenses:" TAB(40)
     "$"SUBTOTAL
5440 REM
5450 REM-Print grand total
5460 PRINT: PRINT TAB(10) "Grand total:" TAB(40) "$"GRANDTOTAL
5470 PRINT
5480 WHILE A$ <> "Y" AND A$ <> "y"
5490     INPUT "Return to menu (Y/N)";A$
5500 WEND
5510 RETURN
5520 REM
6000 REM-General input subroutine
6010 I=I+1
6020 TYPE(I)=N
6030 REM-Line to handle date input for first run of program
6040 IF FIRSTPASS=1 THEN INPUT "Input date";DAY$(I):
         FIRSTPASS=0:
```

Chapter 3

```
            D$=DAYS(I):
            GOTO 6110
6050 REM-Ordinary case; not first run of program
6060 PRINT "Last date was ";D$
6070 PRINT "Hit RETURN to use this date"
6080 INPUT "or input new date"; DAY$(I)
6090 IF DAY$(I)="" THEN DAY$(I)=D$
6100 D$=DAY$(I)
6110 INPUT "Description"; DESCRIP$(I)
6120 INPUT "Amount"; AMT(I)
6130 RETURN
6140 REM
7000 REM-Subroutine to print subtotals
7010 PRINT DAY$(J) TAB(20) DESCRIP$(J) TAB(40) "$"AMT(J)
7020 SUBTOTAL=SUBTOTAL + AMT(J)
7030 GRANDTOTAL=GRANDTOTAL + SUBTOTAL
7040 RETURN
7050 REM
8000 REM-Subroutine to wait for a "Y" or "y" answer
8010 PRINT
8020 WHILE A$ <> "Y" AND A$ <> "y"
8030     INPUT "Show next (Y/N)";A$
8040 WEND
8050 A$=""
8060 RETURN
8070 REM
9000 REM-Routine to clean up screen and exit
9010 CLS
9020 PRINT "Program terminated"
9030 KEY ON
9040 END
```

Review Questions

1. Explain how to reserve memory for a numeric array, N, that will contain at least 100 elements.

2. Use one statement to dimension three arrays to hold the following data:
    - The names of the months of the year
    - The square roots of the numbers from 1 to 99
    - The weekly amount paid to each of 10 workers for a year

Arrays

3. What are the two primary uses for ERASE?
4. What's wrong with the following program?

```
10 CLS
20 OPTION BASE 1
30 FOR X= 1 TO 20
40     A(X)=X*X*2
50 NEXT
60 FOR Y = 1 TO 20
70 PRINT A(Y)
80 END
```

5. Write a program that prompts for the month and the average temperature for that month, then prints the months, temperatures, and the average temperature for the year.
6. What's the effect of OPTION BASE 0 and OPTION BASE 1 on all arrays in a program?
7. Does the section of code that follows cause an error?

```
10 INPUT L
20 INPUT M
30 DIM N$(L,M)
```

8. In the EXPENSE-ACCOUNTER program, how could you eliminate the FIRSTPASS flag?
9. If the maximum number of dimensions for an array is 255, will this statement cause an error?

```
100 DIM ARRAY (300, 50)
```

10. Exercise: Write a program that uses arrays to store the names of 12 cities and their average rainfall, then prints a bar graph like the one shown in the example below:

```
City           Average Annual Rainfall (X = 1 inch)
New York       XXXXXXXX
Phoenix        XX
Portland       XXXXXXXXXXXXXXXX
```

Chapter 4

Data and Numeric Functions

Chapter **4**

Data and Numeric Functions

BASIC is the first language learned by many programmers, and sometimes it is looked down upon as a "beginner's language." But nothing could be further from the truth. In fact, even in its simpler forms such as GW-BASIC and BASICA, the BASIC language has plenty of powerful functions for getting the job done, including some not found in more "advanced" languages. You'll find you can write and use highly complex and sophisticated programs by taking advantage of BASIC's special features.

What You'll Learn in this Chapter

This chapter explains more about some of the features that will help you write better programs. You'll learn about

- The dynamic duo of DATA and READ, which allow information to be defined by the program
- Types of variables and their precision
- The numeric functions that deliver answers to mathematical problems

DATA and READ Statements

Thus far, to get information into a program, you've been using the INPUT statement to assign that information to variables. (BASIC can't use information unless it's been assigned to a variable first.) For each INPUT statement, the program halts and asks you to input the needed data, then assigns the data to a variable. A name, for instance, is kept in a string variable such as `MYNAME$`, while a number is assigned to a numeric variable like `X` or `MYNUMBER`.

This isn't always the most efficient way to handle information, though, especially if the data is the same each time the program is run. For instance, you might have a program that needs a fixed tax rate, a list of prices, dates, names, instructions, and so on. It would certainly be tedious to INPUT that same data over and over again. After all, aren't computers supposed to save us work?

Luckily we have DATA and READ to make it easier to get large amounts of fixed data into a program. DATA and READ assign values to variables from within a program. They work hand-in-hand: the READ statement "reads" whatever is in the DATA statement.

The format of the DATA statement is as follows:

```
DATA (information separated by commas)
```

The READ statement looks like this:

```
READ (list of variables separated by commas)
```

Look at the two statements together:

```
10 DATA 6.02
20 READ A
```

Line 10 places the number 6.02 in the computer's memory. The READ statement in line 20 then assigns that number to the variable `A`. It's just as if the computer had executed a LET statement:

```
10 A=6.02
```

So, what's the big deal? Well, you can "match up" and combine variables in READ statements and numbers in DATA statements, like this:

```
10 DATA 15, 30, 6.02
20 READ A, B, C
```

What happens here is that the READ statement "matches up" its first variable, `A`, with the first number in the DATA statement, which is `15`, and the number 15 is

Data and Numeric Functions

assigned to A. The second number, 30, is assigned to the second variable, B; and the remaining number, 6.02, is assigned to C. This is the same as three LET statements:

```
10 A=15
20 B=30
30 C=6.02
```

The data used by DATA and READ doesn't have to be numbers. You can use string data (that is, words), too. Take a look at this pair of statements:

```
10 DATA "January", "February", "March", "April", "May"
20 READ A$, B$, C$, D$, E$
```

In this example, the names of the five months in the DATA statement are assigned, in order, to the string variables in the READ statement.

When using READ with different kinds of data, be sure that the variable type matches the data. If you try to READ string data into a numeric variable, your program will stop, you'll get an error, and you'll be embarrassed beyond words.

The Data Pointer

The DATA and READ statements don't have to match up exactly. Here's another way you could read the names of the months above:

```
10 DATA "January", "February", "March", "April", "May"
20 READ A$, B$, C$
 .
 .
 .
130 READ D$, E$
```

You see, BASIC uses a "data pointer" to keep track of the data that has been processed by READ statements. In this example, the READ statement in line 20 assigns the first three months (January, February, March) to the variables A$, B$, and C$. The data pointer moves past each piece of data as it's processed, so after line 20, the pointer is set to the beginning of the fourth piece of data (see fig. 4-1).

Chapter 4

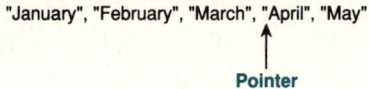

Fig. 4-1:   Data pointer.

When line 130 is executed, the computer reads the final two pieces of data, and the pointer is moved to the end of the data string (see fig. 4-2).

"January", "February", "March", "April", "May"
↑
Pointer

Fig. 4-2:   Pointer at the end of the data stream.

As you just have seen, you can use many READ statements to get data from a single DATA statement. You can also have many DATA statements and a single READ statement; in this case, the data are read in order:

```
10 READ A, B
20 DATA 43, 45, 47, 49, 51
30 READ C, D
40 READ E
```

This example illustrates something else about these two statements: It doesn't matter whether the READ is placed before or after the DATA in your program. What actually happens is that when you run the program, all the data from all DATA statements is first placed in a big long row in memory. Then, as the program executes, the READ statements gobble up the data one piece at a time.

Quickly try this little program:

```
10 DATA 1,2,3
20 READ A,B,C
30 PRINT A;B;C
40 DATA 4,5,6,7,8,9
50 READ A,B,C
60 PRINT A;B;C
70 READ A,B,C
80 PRINT A;B;C
90 END
```

When you run the program, the output should look like this:

```
1 2 3
4 5 6
7 8 9
```

What happened? First, the computer looked at all the DATA statements, and linked them to store a data stream in memory. The pointer was set at the beginning of the stream (see fig. 4-3).

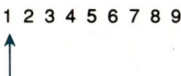

Fig. 4-3:   Pointer at beginning of data stream.

Later, during execution, the READ statement in line 20 read the first three numbers and placed them in variables A, B, and C. The pointer moved to the fourth piece of data (see fig. 4-4).

Fig. 4-4:   Pointer after reading the first three pieces of data.

Line 50 read the next three quantities, and also assigned them to variables A, B, and C. As the data was read, the pointer moved to the seventh piece of data (see fig. 4-5).

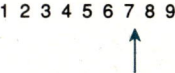

Fig. 4-5:   Pointer after reading six pieces of data.

Finally, line 70 read the last three quantities into variables A, B and C (see fig. 4-6).

Chapter 4

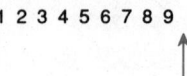

Fig. 4-6: Pointer after reading all data.

Restoring the Data Pointer

You've probably figured out that it's usually best to match up READ and DATA statements; trying to keep track of that elusive data pointer can be mind-boggling in a long program. BASIC, though, has a way for you to reset the data pointer: it's the RESTORE statement. The statement looks like this:

```
RESTORE (line number)
```

RESTORE resets the data pointer to the beginning of the data after the specified line number (or to the first DATA statement in the program, if you omit the line number). This means that after the RESTORE, the next READ statement gets data from the first DATA statement after the specified line number. To see how this works, try adding a line to the program you just ran, as follows:

```
61 RESTORE 40
```

Then run the program again. Now the output looks like this:

```
1 2 3
4 5 6
4 5 6
```

Here's what the modified mini-program looks like:

```
10 DATA 1,2,3
20 READ A,B,C
30 PRINT A;B;C
40 DATA 4,5,6,7,8,9
50 READ A,B,C
60 PRINT A;B;C
61 RESTORE 40
70 READ A;B;C
80 PRINT A,B,C
90 END
```

Before the program actually begins executing, the data from lines 10 and 40 is placed in a data stream in memory. At runtime, line 20 reads the first three numbers, and line 50 reads the second three. Line 61 restores the data pointer to the beginning of the data specified in line 40, so the next READ statement begins with that data again.

Initializing Arrays with DATA and READ

An array, you will remember, is a group of variables with the same variable name but different subscripts, such as M(1), M(2), M(3); or A$(1,3), A$(2,3), and so on. The DATA and READ statements make it easier for you to initialize arrays. (*Initialize* means to set to the initial value. For an array, it means loading up the array with the data you want to be in it.)

There are two ways to use DATA and READ to initialize an array. Here's one of them:

```
10 OPTION BASE 1
20 DIM M$(12)
30 DATA "Jan", "Feb", "Mar", "Apr", "May", "Jun"
40 DATA "Jul", "Aug", "Sep", "Oct", "Nov", "Dec"
50 READ M$(1), M$(2), M$(3), M$(4), M$(5), M$(6)
60 READ M$(7), M$(8), M$(9), M$(10), M$(11), M$(12)
```

Here we have split the data (the names of the months) into two DATA statements, and we're also using a matching pair of READ statements to put the data into array M. The READ statement in line 50 initializes the first six variables of the array using the DATA statement in line 30. This "uses up" all the data in line 30. Then the READ statement in line 60 initializes the variables M(7) through M(12), using the data from line 40.

Now, the method above works just fine. But there's an easier way to initialize an array, one that takes advantage of the fact that the array is an ordered group of variables. You can use a FOR...NEXT loop, like this:

```
10 OPTION BASE 1
20 DIM M$(12)
30 DATA "Jan", "Feb", "Mar", "Apr", "May", "Jun"
40 DATA "Jul", "Aug", "Sep", "Oct", "Nov", "Dec"
50 FOR I= 1 TO 12
60     READ M$(I)
70 NEXT I
```

Now isn't that easier? The single READ statement in the FOR...NEXT loop takes care of all the data. The first time through the loop, when I is set to 1, the READ

Chapter 4

statement gets Jan, the first piece of data in line 30, and uses it to initialize variable M(1). On the second time through the loop, when I is set to 2, variable M(2) is initialized to Feb, and so on. The READ statement in the loop is executed 12 times.

Here we've split the data into two DATA statements, but you could just as easily have a single DATA statement, or three, or four. The READ statement gets the first piece of data in a DATA statement, then the second, then the third, and keeps getting data until the loop is exited (or until all the data is used up).

You can see the advantages of using loops with DATA and READ statements to initialize array variables. When you have just a small array, you can load up the array by specifying each variable individually, as in the first example above. But think about getting data into an array of 100 variables or more! You would definitely want to use a single DATA statement in a loop, as in the second example.

What Happens When You Run Out of DATA

What's wrong with this little program?

```
10 DATA 4, 21, 99
20 FOR I=1 TO 10
30     READ N
40     PRINT N
50 NEXT
```

The problem is that there are three pieces of data in the DATA statement, but the FOR...NEXT loop will try to execute 10 READs. The result is as follows:

```
4
21
99
Out of DATA in 30
```

The good news is that BASIC will go ahead and READ as far as it can—until it runs out of data—and it can process the data normally. But when it tries to READ some DATA that isn't there, the program will "bomb", and you'll get an error message. So, make sure there's enough data to be read!

A Metric Conversion Program

Think for a minute about what you'd need for a program to convert units such as inches, pounds, and quarts into their metric equivalents, such as centimeters, kilograms, and liters. You'd want the user to choose the type of conversion. Then, based on that choice, you'd want a prompt message, a calculation, and an output message, like this:

Data and Numeric Functions

```
Inches to centimeters
Enter inches
```
(Do calculation)
```
1 inch is equal to 2.54 centimeters

Pounds to kilograms
Enter pounds
```
(Do calculation)
```
5 pounds is equal to 2.268 kilograms
```

See how alike the different conversions are? For any conversion, the prompt message, calculation, and output messages are different, but they always occur at the same time in the program. This looks like a good place to use arrays to hold the different-but-similar information we'll need. We'll store all the prompt messages in arrays of string variables, and we'll keep the conversion factors in a numeric array.

Begin by setting aside memory for the different arrays you'll need

```
10 REM -Initialize the arrays
20 N=3
30 DIM M$(N), Q$(N), A$(N), B$(N), F(N)
40 REM
```

In line 20, we use the variable N to specify the number of types of conversion the program can handle. In this little program we'll perform only three kinds of conversions (inches to centimeters, pounds to kilograms, and quarts to liters), but, as you'll see, the program is set up so that you can easily add other conversions to it.

Line 30 dimensions all the arrays you'll need. Each array is set up to the length defined by the variable N. Because we've used N to specify the number of conversions (rather than using a specific number to dimension all the arrays) we have to change only the value of N to add other conversions. If we had used a fixed number, then we'd have to change all those individual numbers in line 30.

The arrays are as follows:

M$ String array containing the menu.

Q$ String array containing the input question.

A$ String array containing the first part of the answer.

B$ String array containing the last part of the answer.

F   Numeric array containing the conversion factors.

Chapter 4

The next part of the program has the DATA statements that contain the data to be placed in the arrays:

```
50 REM -Data for arrays
60 DATA "1-Inches to centimeters", "Enter inches", "inches",
       "centimeters", 2.54
70 DATA "2-Pounds to kilograms","Enter pounds","pounds",
       "kilograms",.4536
80 DATA "3-Quarts to liters","Enter quarts","quarts",
       "liters",.9463
90 REM
```

You can see that there are three DATA statements (although there could be many more in a larger program with more conversions). Each DATA statement contains all the messages and data for one type of conversion, with everything separated by commas. First, there is the heading that shows the number you press to select this type of conversion. This is followed by the instruction to enter the quantity. The next two pieces of data are labels for the output. Finally, the numeric conversion factor is also here in the data stream.

All right, there's the data. Now let's add the statements needed to READ this data into the appropriate arrays:

```
100 REM -Read the arrays
110 FOR I=1 TO N:
    READ M$(I), Q$(I), A$(I), B$(I), F(I):
    NEXT I
120 REM
```

Notice how line 110 actually contains three statements, that together make up a complete FOR...NEXT loop:

```
FOR I=1 TO N:
    READ M$(I), Q$(I), A$(I), B$(I), F(I):
NEXT I
```

In this example, each time through the loop, the READ statement gobbles up the data from one DATA statement and places it in the correct array variables. The first time through the loop, READ fills the arrays with string and numeric information for inches-to-centimeters conversion; the second time, it loads the pounds-to-kilograms conversion; and so on.

Everything up to now has been done "behind the scenes." Now that the arrays are all initialized, let's look at the rest of the program, the part you actually see when you run it:

Data and Numeric Functions

```
130 REM -Display the menu
140 PRINT: PRINT "Metric Conversion Program":PRINT
150 FOR I=1 TO N: PRINT M$(I): NEXT I
160 PRINT "9-To end the program":PRINT
170 REM
```

Line 140 displays a general heading for the program, then line 150 displays the messages showing which numbers to press to choose the type of conversion. Line 160 gives you an option to end the program. Here's how the menu will look on the screen:

```
Metric Conversion Program

1-Inches to centimeters
2-Pounds to kilograms
3-Quarts to liters
9-To end the program
```

With all this information on the screen, we're ready to make a selection:

```
180 REM -Enter the selection
190 INPUT "Enter the number for your selection";S
200 IF S<1 OR S>N THEN GOTO 9999
210 REM
```

The INPUT statement in line 190 prompts you to enter a selection number, S. Then line 200 tests to see whether the value for S is outside the range of defined selections; if it is, the program branches to the end.

Here's the message that's displayed while the program waits for you to type S:

```
Enter the number for your selection?
```

Now it's time for the actual conversion:

```
220 REM -Do the conversion
230 PRINT: PRINT Q$(S): INPUT X
240 PRINT X; A$(S); " is equal to";X*F(S); B$(S)
250 GOTO 130
9999 END
```

Line 230 prints Q$(S), which is a string containing the message prompting you for "inches" or "pounds" or "quarts." The INPUT statement in the same line

Chapter 4

waits for you to enter X, which is the number of inches, pounds, or quarts. So, if you chose 2, "Pounds to kilograms", you'd see a message like this:

```
Enter the number for your selection? 2

Enter pounds
?
```

When you enter a value for X, line 240 prints the number you entered, followed by its classifier (inches, pounds, or quarts). This is followed on the same line by the words is equal to, and the calculated result, which is obtained by multiplying X by the conversion factor in array F. This line also prints the classifier (centimeters, kilograms, or liters) for the new quantity:

```
Enter pounds
? 2
  2 pounds is equal to .9072 kilograms
```

The complete program is listed below. It's easily expanded, too—you just change the number of functions (the value of N specified in line 20), then add a DATA statement for each new conversion. The new DATA statement contains all the needed data for that conversion.

```
1 REM METRIC CONVERSION PROGRAM
2 REM -This program uses the DATA and READ
3 REM -statements to initialize arrays for
4 REM -metric conversion.
5 REM
10 REM -Initialize the arrays
20 N=3
30 DIM M$(N), Q$(N), A$(N), B$(N), F(N)
40 REM
50 REM -Data for arrays
60 DATA "1-Inches to centimeters", "Enter inches", "inches",
        "centimeters", 2.54
70 DATA "2-Pounds to kilograms","Enter pounds","pounds",
        "kilograms",.4536
80 DATA "3-Quarts to liters","Enter quarts","quarts",
        "liters",.9463
90 REM
100 REM -Read the arrays
```

Data and Numeric Functions

```
110 FOR I=1 TO N:
        READ M$(I), Q$(I), A$(I), B$(I), F(I):
        NEXT I
120 REM
130 REM -Display the menu
140 PRINT: PRINT "Metric Conversion Program":PRINT
150 FOR I=1 TO N: PRINT M$(I): NEXT I
160 PRINT "9-To end the program":PRINT
170 REM
180 REM -Enter the selection
190 INPUT "Enter the number for your selection";S
200 IF S<1 OR S>N THEN GOTO 9999
210 REM
220 REM -Do the conversion
230 PRINT: PRINT Q$(S): INPUT X
240 PRINT X; A$(S); " is equal to";X*F(S); B$(S)
250 GOTO 130
9999 END
```

Now try a few examples. Begin by converting 2 pounds to kilograms:

```
Metric Conversion Program

1-Inches to centimeters
2-Pounds to kilograms
3-Quarts to liters
9-To end the program

Enter the number for your selection? 2

Enter pounds
? 2
   2 pounds is equal to .9072 kilograms

Metric Conversion Program

1-Inches to centimeters
2-Pounds to kilograms
3-Quarts to liters
9-To end the program
```

Chapter 4

Now try the program to see how many liters in four quarts:

```
Enter the number for your selection? 3

Enter quarts
? 4
 4 quarts is equal to 3.7852 liters

Metric Conversion Program

1-Inches to centimeters
2-Pounds to kilograms
3-Quarts to liters
9-To end the program
```

Now end the program:

```
Enter the number for your selection? 9
Ok
```

Actually, the program ends if you enter any number other than menu numbers 1 to N; for instance, try entering a number of 97:

```
RUN
Enter the number for your selection? 97
Ok
```

For now, we've pretty much just concentrated on the DATA and READ statements, and ignored the question of what happens if you input wrong data.

This metric conversion program shows how DATA and READ statements make it easy for you to turn a simple program into a much more extensive one.

Variable Types: Integers, Single and Double Precision, Strings

Earlier in this book, you learned the difference between string variables (like A$) and numeric variables (like A). You learned that the names of string variables are followed by a dollar sign, and that the value of a string variable is always a string of alphanumeric characters (such as "CAT" or "12 O'CLOCK"). You learned that a numeric variable is not followed by a dollar sign, and that its value is a numeric quantity like 2 or 10 or 6.123. In the program examples we have used so far, you have not needed to know more than these two kinds of variables, numeric and string. However, BASIC offers different types of numeric variables, including strings.

What is Precision, Anyway?

When we talk about *precision* of a value, we are referring to our level of confidence in its accuracy. For instance, suppose that your thermometer is reading somewhere between 41 and 42 degrees. If you look very closely, you might be able to say it's 41.5 degrees. But you'd never try to state that it was 41.4789567894 degrees! The precision of the thermometer is only the first two or three digits—all the other digits are meaningless.

It's the same way in BASIC. We can write a statement like the following easily enough:

```
A=12345.678901234567890
```

However, ordinary BASIC variables (called *single-precision*) are stored as seven digits, and are accurate out to only six digits. So, the value of A is stored like this:

A=12345.67

And its precision is only out to six digits, like this:

```
A=12345.6
```

When you look at a BASIC value, remember that although it's a little more precise than your thermometer, it has its limits, too.

The numbers in BASIC can be integers, single-precision, or double-precision. Here's a summary of how those numbers are stored:

Type	Stored As
Integer	Whole number only
Single-precision	7 digits
Double-precision	17 digits

Let's look at integer, single-precision, and double-precision variables, and explain the difference between these kinds of variables.

Integer Variables

Briefly, an *integer* is a number with no digits to the right of the decimal point. That is, it is a whole number, with no fractional part. Thus, 10 and 2 and −9 and 4096 are integers, while 4.7 and 2/3 and 0.002 are not. And so, not surprisingly, an integer variable is one whose value is an integer. In GW-BASIC, the value of an integer variable must not be larger than 32767 nor smaller than −32768.

Chapter 4

Single-Precision Variables

What are single-precision variables? In GW-BASIC, a single-precision variable is one whose value consists of digits (with the decimal point anywhere) and whose range (size) is between about 1E+38 and 1E−38. (These two numbers are written in exponential notation. If writing numbers this way is new to you, turn to Appendix F, *Exponential Notation*.)

It's easy to see how many digits your version of BASIC is working with. Just enter this line, in command mode:

```
PRINT 1/3
```

BASIC responds with a string of 3s and one lonely 4:

```
.3333334
```

Since 1 divided by 3 actually produces an infinite string of 3s following the decimal point, we can see at once just how many digits BASIC is working with by counting the number of 3s in this example. In this case, we can conclude that BASIC's single-precision routines are using 6 digits. The seventh digit (4) is not accurate, so don't count on using it.

Let's write a simple program to demonstrate the definition of single-precision variables:

```
10 J=1.23456789
20 PRINT J,
30 J = J * 10
40 GOTO 20
```

We start with a number J which is 9 digits long. We print it, multiply it by 10, print the result, multiply the result by 10, and so on. If you enter this program and RUN it, BASIC should print something like that seen here (press Ctrl-Break to stop it after the overflow):

```
1.234568
12.34568
123.4568
1234.568
12345.68
123456.8
1234568
1.234568E+07
1.234568E+08
1.234568E+09
1.234568E+10
```

```
     1.234568E+11
     1.234568E+12
     1.234568E+13
     1.234568E+14
     1.234568E+15
     1.234568E+16
     1.234568E+17
     1.234568E+18
     1.234568E+19
     1.234568E+20
     1.234568E+21
     1.234568E+22
     1.234568E+23
     1.234568E+24
     1.234568E+25
     1.234568E+26
     1.234568E+27
     1.234568E+28
     1.234568E+29
     1.234568E+30
     1.234568E+31
     1.234568E+32
     1.234568E+33
     1.234568E+34
     1.234568E+35
     1.234568E+36
     1.234568E+37
     1.234568E+38
Overflow
     1.701412E+38
Overflow
     1.701412E+38
Break in 30
```

The first thing to notice is the first number BASIC printed: 1.234568, rather than the 1.23456789 that we entered. Our variable J has been rounded off so it is only 7 digits long, instead of the 9 we entered. What happened to the other 2 digits? Well, unless someone tells it otherwise, GW-BASIC always assumes that the variables and the numbers you use in your programs are single precision. And since a single-precision number can only have seven digits, two are chopped off. Actually, there's no use even entering more than seven digits—anything more than that will be lost.

The second thing to notice about this output is, once the numbers reach a certain size, they are printed in exponential notation. Actually, BASIC stores single-precision variables in exponential form no matter what size their values are. It prints

Chapter 4

out the smaller numbers in the "normal" way (as 4123 instead of 4.123E+3, for example) merely as a convenience to you.

In exponential notation, part of the variable is used for storing the mantissa (the seven digits written before the E) and part is used to store the exponent (the two-digit number following the E). If the mantissa gets too big, the computer can't store the number at all and has to print an error message. That's what's happening in the printout: When the program tries to multiply 1.234568E+38 by 10, the error message results and you have to stop the programming with Ctrl-Break. Why? Because a single-precision value cannot be any larger than about 1.7x10E+38. (Remember that when a number's exponent is 38, then the number is 38 digits long! Because such large numbers are not often encountered, the fact that the computer can't deal with them is not such a serious limitation.) Here's what 1.234568E+38 looks like written out:

123,456,800,000,000,000,000,000,000,000,000,000

Here's another program. This one generates numbers that get smaller and smaller, since we divide by 10 each time we print the number (instead of multiplying, as in the example above). We add a line to STOP the program (line 30) when BASIC starts to think that J is zero. This is because BASIC, instead of causing an error message when the exponent goes from −38 to −39, simply decides that a number that small is the same as zero and would continue to print zeros from then until doomsday if we didn't stop the program.

```
10 J=6.02
20 PRINT J,
30 IF J=0 THEN STOP
40 J=J/10
50 GOTO 20
```

This shows the output from the program:

```
RUN
  6.02
  .602
  .0602
  .00602
  .000602
  .0000602
  6.02E-06
  6.02E-07
  6.02E-08
  6.02E-09
  6.02E-10
  6.02E-11
```

```
6.02E-12
6.02E-13
6.02E-14
6.02E-15
6.02E-16
6.02E-17
6.02E-18
6.02E-19
6.02E-20
6.02E-21
6.02E-22
6.02E-23
6.02E-24
6.02E-25
6.02E-26
6.02E-27
6.02E-28
6.02E-29
6.02E-30
6.02E-31
6.02E-32
6.02E-33
6.02E-34
6.02E-35
6.019999E-36
6.019999E-37
6.019999E-38
6.02E-39
0
Break in 30
Ok
```

Here's what 6.02E−39 looks like written out:

```
0.000,000,000,000,000,000,000,000,000,000,000,000,00602
```

Let's summarize the differences between an integer variable and a single-precision variable. An integer variable must lie in the range between +32767 and −32768 and must be a whole number, with no fractional part (that is, no digits to the right of the decimal point). A single-precision variable, on the other hand, can have any value between about 1−7E+38 and 3−0E−39, but can have only seven digits, of which only the first six are accurate.

Chapter 4

Integer versus Single-Precision Variables

As you have probably guessed, integer and single-precision variables are useful for different kinds of things. Integers are good for counting small numbers of discrete items such as how many oranges in a sack or how many months in a year—things that have no fractional part. Single-precision numbers are good for measuring continuous quantities that are not necessarily whole numbers, like the percentage of "Yes" voters, or how long a table is.

Why not always use single precision? After all, any number that can be expressed as an integer can also be expressed as single precision. (The reverse is not, of course, true.) The reason is that integers have two advantages—they're small, and they're fast.

Integers are small in the sense that they take up less room in your computer's memory than single-precision variables do. An integer value is stored in two bytes, while a single-precision value requires four bytes. So if you have a large program and not much memory left, it pays to use integer variables whenever possible. (For a further description of how computers store variables, read Appendix D, *Tips to Save Memory*.)

The second reason to prefer integers over single-precision variables is speed. Say you have a program with a FOR...NEXT loop in it, like this:

```
10 FOR J = 1 TO 10,000
       .
       .
(other program lines here)
       .
       .
100 NEXT J
```

If you don't tell it otherwise, BASIC assumes that all variables are single precision, including the J in the FOR...NEXT loop. But, when BASIC is actually executing a FOR...NEXT loop, it needs J to be an integer to use it for counting. So every time the FOR statement is executed (10,000 times in the example) BASIC changes J from a single-precision variable to an integer variable, increments the loop, and then changes it back so that it is available to other statements inside the loop as a single-precision variable. Naturally, all this changing back and forth takes time. So, if you want your FOR...NEXT loops to run as fast as possible, use integer variables for the loop counter and, if possible, in calculations performed inside the loop.

BASIC also performs arithmetic faster on integers than it does on single-precision variables. Actually, your BASIC has a complete set of routines for doing arithmetic with integers (add, subtract, multiply and divide) and another set of routines for doing arithmetic on single-precision variables. (There is a third set, too, for double precision, which we will discuss later.) Because integer variables are only two bytes long, rather than four, the routines to do arithmetic on them are much faster than the corresponding routines for single precision. So, if you have a lot of arithmetic to do, it pays to speed it up by using integers, provided of course that the numbers you are operating on lie between 32767 and −32768.

But how do we get a variable to be an integer, if BASIC assumes that all numeric variables are single precision? We'll find that out later.

Double-Precision Variables

What do you do if you need to write a program which deals with numbers that have more significant digits than the six or seven digits provided by single-precision variables? For example, suppose that you're in real estate and you've just earned a five percent commission on a house you sold for $12,345,678.90. (The house is in Beverly Hills.) You need to know to the penny just what your commission is. Write the following program:

```
10 P = .05
20 SP = 12345678.90
30 C = P * SP
40 PRINT C
```

Here, P is the percentage of your commission, SP is the selling price, and C is the commission you are trying to find. When you RUN the program you will get something like $617284. (This may be slightly different with a different version of BASIC.) Well, this is a lot of money, but it is the wrong answer. In fact, the program doesn't even print the last digits (for pennies).

How can we get a completely accurate answer? BASIC has another variable type we haven't used yet, called *double precision*. As the name implies, double precision gives us more digits in our answer than does single precision (actually more than twice as many).

To see the difference between single and double precision, write the following little program:

```
10 A = 1
20 B = 3
30 PRINT A/B
```

If you run this program, you'll get an answer like .3333334. As you can see, this answer is correct to six digits. (This is similar to the earlier example in the description of single precision.)

Now let's change this program to double precision. One way to make a double precision variable is to put a number sign (#) after it. (This is a *type declaration character*. You'll learn more about this character shortly.)

```
10 A# = 1
20 B# = 3
30 PRINT A#/B#
```

RUN that, and what do you get?

```
.3333333333333333
```

Sixteen digits! That's a lot of precision. We could handle the national debt, to the nearest penny, with that many digits.

Now we're ready to figure the commission in our real estate problem. We'll modify the program this way:

```
10 P# = .05
20 SP# = 12345678.90
30 C# = P# * SP#
40 PRINT C#
RUN
617283.9541982476
```

We can easily round off this number to $617,283.95. Now our answer is correct to the nearest penny—in fact, we had a lot more precision than we needed for this particular problem.

Double precision is most often used in financial programs involving large amounts of money, and in scientific and engineering problems. Even if you don't need sixteen digits of precision too often, it's nice to know they're there when you need them.

Naturally, there is a price to pay for using double precision. Just as single-precision variables are slower and take up more room in the computer's memory than do integer variables, so double precision variables are slower and take up more space than single precision variables. It requires eight bytes to store the value of a double-precision variable, twice that of a single-precision variable, which is itself twice as large as an integer. So, if you want to save memory space and computing time, don't use double precision unless it's absolutely necessary.

Type Declaration Characters

Type declaration characters are special symbols which are written immediately after a variable name to specify which of four types the variable is. These four types, and the character that specifies each one, are as follows:

- *Integer*, indicated by a percent sign (%).
  Examples: A%, Z3%, COUNTER%

- *Single Precision*, indicated by an exclamation point (!).
  Examples: B!, Q4!, AMOUNT!

- *Double Precision*, indicated by a number sign (#).
  Examples: D#, P9#, BEVERLY#

- *String*, indicated by a dollar sign ($).
  Examples: F$, S7$, NAMES$

Earlier, we talked about the advantages of using integer variables in some cases, and single-precision or double-precision variables in others. But how do we force a variable to be one of these types? One way is with type declaration characters. This long name simply means that we add one of the special characters listed above to the variable name to force the variable to be a particular type. You already learned to use the type declaration character for strings: it's a dollar sign. So you know that while `A1` is a numeric variable, `A1$` is a string variable.

Numeric variables also have type declaration characters. (Let's abbreviate them to T.D.C.s from now on.) The T.D.C. for integers is a percent sign (%), the T.D.C. for single-precision variables is an exclamation point (!), and the T.D.C. for double-precision variables is the number, or pound, sign (#). If you want to specify the type that a numeric variable is going to be, all you have to do is add the appropriate T.D.C. to the name every time you write it. Thus, `A%` and `B2%` are integer variables, and `A!` and `B2!` are single-precision variables. The T.D.C. actually becomes part of the name and can be used to distinguish two variables which would otherwise have the same name. Thus, `H2%` and `H2!` are completely different variables and can both be used in the same program. BASIC will keep them separate.

As an example of how to use T.D.C.s, and also as a demonstration of the advantages of using integers in certain situations, let's look at the following loop:

```
10 FOR J = 1 TO 10000
20 NEXT J
```

Because BASIC assumes that every variable is single precision unless told specifically otherwise, it will treat the loop variable `J` as single precision. But because it needs `J` to be an integer to use it as a loop variable, it will convert `J` to an integer each time it needs to increment it in the loop. This takes time and makes the program run slower. To see just how much slower, do this: run the program, and time it. If you have a stopwatch you can time it very accurately, but the second hand on your watch will do. Write down how long it took. (On our 386 computer it took 1.5 seconds, while on a portable computer it took 11 seconds.)

Now, change the program like this:

```
10 FOR J% = 1 TO 10000
20 NEXT J%
```

We've changed J to an integer variable by adding the percent sign. Now try running the program and timing it. It should be substantially faster than the example in which J is a single-precision variable. (On our 386 computer it took only 1.2 seconds, whereas on the portable it took only 7 seconds this time.)

Since variables are single precision unless otherwise specified, we don't often have to use the exclamation point (!) T.D.C. to force a variable to be single precision. Sometimes it is useful, though, as we'll see in the section coming up that discusses DEFINT, DEFSNG, etc.

Table 4-1 presents a summary of the four variable types.

Table 4-1: Variables types.

Variable Type	Type Declaration Character	Example of Variable	Example of Values	Range of Values	Bytes of Memory Used by Variable
STRING	$	A$ B2$ ZZ$	"CAT" "CHICKEN" "12 P.M." "4.234"	Strings from 0 to 255 chars	1 byte per character, plus 6 bytes for name.
INTEGER	%	A% B2% ZZ%	12 30000 –207	From –32768 to 32767	2 bytes for value, plus 3 bytes for name.
SINGLE PRECISION	!	A! B2! ZZ!	12.45 999999.9 3.2E + 19 –17.4	Mantissa: 7 digits exponent: –38 to +38	4 bytes for value, plus 3 bytes for name.
DOUBLE PRECISION	#	A# B2# ZZ#	12.45 7.7777777777777 1.24932434342E-9	Mantissa: 16 digits Exponent: –38 to +38	8 bytes for value, plus 3 bytes for name

How to Define Variable Types Automatically

The type declaration characters discussed in the last section accomplish their purpose of specifying which type a variable will be, but they also add an extra character to the variable name. So, if you are typing a long program, you may find it inconvenient and time-consuming to be constantly inserting dollar signs, percent signs, and so on into your listing. In many programs, for example, almost all the variables are defined as integers, which means a lot of percent signs to type.

Fortunately, BASIC comes to our rescue with a clever labor-saving device: type declaration definitions whose first three characters are "DEF." These definitions (DEFINT, DEFSNG, DEFDBL, or DEFSTR) let you define, in one statement, a whole group of variables as a particular type (integer, single precision, etc.). Once they're defined in this way, you no longer have to use the type declaration characters (!, %, #, and $) after each instance of the variable name.

Here are the type declaration definitions and how they work:

- DEFINT L means, "Define all variables beginning with the letter L to be integer variables."

- DEFSNG L means, "Define all variables beginning with the letter L to be single-precision variables."

- DEFDBL L means, "Define all variables beginning with the letter L to be double-precision variables."

- DEFSTR L means, "Define all variables beginning with the letter L to be string variables."

For instance, DEFINT N means that all variables whose names start with the letter N are now defined as integer variables. So, every time you write such a variable name in your program, like N, or N2, or NZ, BASIC will assume it is an integer. Similarly, DEFDBL Z defines all variables beginning with the letter Z to be double-precision variables, and DEFSTR Q defines all variables beginning with the letter Q to be strings. DEFSNG S defines all variables beginning with the letter S to be single precision, but since BASIC assumes that a variable is single precision unless told otherwise, it isn't usually necessary to use a DEFSNG statement. (We say the *default* variable type is single precision.)

You can also use a list of letters or a range of letters in a DEF statement. For example, DEFDBL A,G,P defines all variables starting with the letters A or G or P to be double precision, while DEFINT I-N defines all variables whose names start with I, J, K, L, M, or N to be integers. (In the FORTRAN programming language, the variables I, J, K, L, M, and N all default to integer variables. Some BASIC programmers follow this tradition by starting their programs with DEFINT I-N.)

Another common statement near the beginning of programs that use mostly integer variables is DEFINT A-Z. This defines all variables in the program to be integer, no matter what letter they begin with. Using this statement ensures that all FOR...NEXT loops will use integer variables, and that all arithmetic will be done with integer variables. Because using integers cuts down on memory space and increases speed, this statement reaps many benefits for very little effort.

But what happens if you want to use, say, a string variable in a program after you have already used the DEFINT A-Z statement? Easy: just use a type declaration character after the string variable name. Type declaration characters always take precedence over DEF statements; that is, no matter how you have defined a variable with a DEF statement, as soon as you use ! or # or $ or % after the name, BASIC will override the DEF statement and assign the variable to whatever type the character indicates (! for single precision, % for integer, and so on).

In the following program, for example, the variable A will be an integer variable, B will be a single-precision variable, P will be double precision, and Q will be a string.

```
10 DEFINT A-L : DEFDBL M-Z
20 A = 1/3
30 B! = 1/3
40 P = 1/3
50 Q$ = "1/3"
60 PRINT A, B!, P, Q$
```

When you RUN this program you'll get the following:

```
0        .3333334        .3333333432674408        1/3
```

The variable A is zero because it is defined as an integer type in the DEFINT A-L statement, and 1/3 rounded to the nearest integer is zero. B! is single precision, because even though variables beginning with B are defined to be integers by the DEFINT A-L statement, the type declaration character ! in line 30 takes precedence over the DEFINT statement; and the single-precision representation of 1/3 has six digits.

P is double precision because it is defined that way in the DEFDBL M-Z statement. Thus, P has 16 digits, but only six of them are accurate because BASIC used the single-precision division routine to divide 1 by 3, and then assigned the result to a double-precision number. Q$ is a string, because even though all variables beginning with the letter Q are defined as double precision by the DEFDBL M-Z statement, the type declaration character $ takes precedence over the DEFDBL statement. Q$ is not an arithmetic expression at all, but simply the string "1/3."

Array variables can also be any of the four variable types described above. (See the earlier description of arrays and array variables.) Their type can be defined with the type declaration characters !, %, #, and $, or it can be defined with a DEF statement.

Type Conversion

To *declare* the type of variable, you append characters (!, #, %) to numbers and variables. Once a variable type has been declared, BASIC also has three functions that *convert* one type of number to another type. These functions and their general forms are as follows:

```
CINT(X)
CSNG(X)
CDBL(X)
```

CINT converts a number to an integer, CSNG converts to single precision, and CDBL converts a number to double precision. Here is an example:

```
10 X# = 12345.6789012345
20 PRINT X#, CSNG(X#), CINT(X#)

RUN
12345.6789012345       12345.68       12346
Ok
```

In the example, the original value of `X#` remains unchanged, but `CSNG(X#)` and `CINT(X#)` are actually single-precision and integer quantities, respectively.

If you're not careful, type conversion can give an appearance of accuracy that's not really there. Try this:

```
10 X = 1202.39
20 PRINT X
30 PRINT X#
40 PRINT CDBL(X)
50 PRINT X

RUN
 1202.39
 0
 1202.390014648438
 1202.39
Ok
```

In line 10, you declare the quantity 1202.39 to be a normal, single-precision number. Attempting to change the number to double precision by adding a pound sign (#) in line 30 doesn't work; you have to use the `CDBL` function, as in line 40.

But look at the output from line 40! Shouldn't `CDBL(X)` be 1202.390000000000? It should—but because you originally declared the number as single precision, the last eight digits in `CDBL(X)` *have no meaning*. Now, if you didn't know better, and the number 1202.390014648438 popped out of a program, you'd probably think you had a super-accurate result. The moral of this little tale is to be careful when interpreting type-converted numbers!

Automatic Type Conversion

On occasion, BASIC will automatically change the variable type for you. You don't have to worry about it, because this happens only when different variable types are evaluated together, or when you specify too many digits for one type. And if this happens, BASIC evaluates with the highest precision.

For instance, enter the following program, then LIST it. As you'll see, you don't even have to RUN it to get results.

This is how you enter it:

```
10 A=12345
20 B=123456
30 C=1234567
40 D=12345678
```

And this is how it looks when you LIST it:

```
LIST
10 A=12345
20 B=123456!
30 C=1234567!
40 D=12345678#
Ok
```

As your quantities approach the boundary between single and double precision, BASIC automatically appends the type declaration character that it assumes you want. For variables B and C, BASIC appends an exclamation point to show that they are single precision. When you type a quantity with eight digits, as in line 40, BASIC knows you want double precision, and the pound sign (#) is added to show you that the quantity is double precision.

In this program, the variables themselves (including D in line 40) remain single precision unless you specify otherwise.

Data and Numeric Functions

Numeric Functions and How to Use Them

BASIC has a fistful of numeric functions that you can use in your programs. You've already learned about ABS, INT and RND, but there are many others as well. As you will see when you begin to write more complex programs, these numeric functions are not just for solving math problems. They come in handy in all types of applications, including business uses, games, graphics, and more. For now, we'll just show you how each operates, with a few simple examples. Keep these functions in mind as you expand your programming horizons.

Finding Square Root with SQR

One of the most useful of BASIC's functions is SQR (square root), which finds the square root of any positive number. Generally, you use the function like this:

```
100 Y=SQR(X)
```

The square root of number X is the number that, if multiplied by itself, gives X. Square roots are used in all kinds of calculations, including those based on the Pythagorean Theorem.

The Pythagorean Theorem says that for a right triangle, the hypotenuse is equal to the square root of the sum of the squares of the other two sides. You can use this in all sorts of ways.

For instance, suppose that you're swimming laps in a pool. You want to get the maximum workout, so you swim lengthwise, from one corner to the opposite corner. If the pool is 20 meters long and 5 meters wide, how far can you swim in each lap?

Figure 4-7 shows the right triangle formed by the sides of the pool and the hypotenuse.

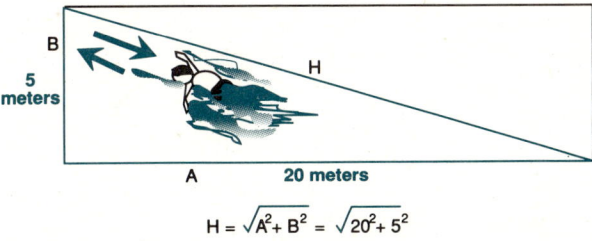

Fig. 4-7: The Pythagorean Theorem in the pool.

Chapter 4

To find the hypotenuse of this triangle, you add the sums of the squares of the other two sides, then determine the square root of that quantity. This is so simple, you don't even need to program it. Just enter the following:

```
A=20
Ok
B=5
Ok
PRINT SQR(A*A+B*B)
 20.61553
Ok
```

Pretty easy, huh? To square the two sides, A and B, you multiply them by themselves. Then you add those two quantities, and use SQR to take the square root of the result. The distance you can swim is the unknown hypotenuse of this right triangle, 20.61553 meters.

If you wish, you can use the circumflex (^) with the exponent 2 to indicate that the numbers should be squared.

```
PRINT SQR(A^2+B^2)
 20.61553
Ok
```

You can see that the result is the same. SQR is an important function, but it's not the only one in BASIC. Let's look at some others.

Trigonometric Functions

The trigonometric functions, which you might remember from high school or college, define the relationships between the sides of a right triangle and the angles themselves. BASIC provides four trigonometric functions for you to use: sine, cosine, tangent, and arctangent. Here's how to handle these functions:

```
100 X = SIN (angle in radians)
200 Y = COS (angle in radians)
300 Z = TAN (angle in radians)
400 A = ATN (tangent of angle A)
```

These functions are useful in a number of ways, and they're especially helpful when you get into BASIC's graphics commands. Let's take a closer look at the trigonometric functions now.

Calculating the Sine

To calculate the sine of an angle, you take the length of the side of the triangle that is opposite the angle, then divide that by the hypotenuse of the right triangle (see fig. 4-8).

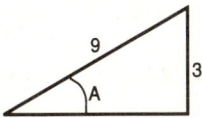

Fig. 4-8: Calculating the sine.

In the figure shown, the sine is calculated as follows:

SIN(A) = side opposite A/hypotenuse = 3/9 = 1/3 = .3333334

As with all functions, you can compute sines without writing a program. Just use the PRINT function from the keyboard, like this:

```
PRINT SIN(2)
 .9092975
Ok
```

This shows you that the sine of 2 radians is .9092975, which brings up an important point:
Trigonometric functions always assume that angles are in radians!
Before you can compute the sine, cosine, tangent, or arctangent of an angle in degrees, you'll have to change it to radians.

Converting Angles to Degrees

In trigonometry, you probably learned to measure angles in degrees. But in the real world, there are several ways to measure angles. One of the most often used is radians. The relationship between radians and degrees is expressed this way:

360 degrees = 2π radians

The value for pi, to six digits, is 3.14159. This means that you can easily convert radians to degrees using the formula that follows:

Chapter 4

$$\text{degrees} = 2\pi/360 = 2 * 3.14159/360 = 3.14159/180$$

A handy way to do this in your programs is to create a variable called PI, and a conversion called DEG2RAD, like this:

```
10 PI=3.14159
20 DEG2RAD=PI/180
```

Then insert `PI` into your program, and multiply the angle in degrees by `DEG2RAD` each time to convert it to radians. For instance, to find the sine of 90 degrees, you could use this instruction:

```
30 PRINT SIN(90*DEG2RAD)
RUN
 1
Ok
```

In working with angles, two formulas to remember are the following:

1. To convert radians to degrees, multiply radians by 180/PI.
2. To convert degrees to radians, multiply degrees by PI/180.

Now, if you remember your trigonometry textbooks at all, you remember pages and pages filled with fine-print tables of angles and their sines, cosines, tangents, etc. Thanks to BASIC, you can throw away all those tables because every function is at your fingertips. And if you're really hooked on tables, well, here's how to create a table of sines of all the angles from 1 to 90 degrees:

```
10 PI=3.14159
20 DEG2RAD=PI/180
30 FOR A=1 TO 90
40     PRINT "The sine of ";A;"degrees is";SIN(A*DEG2RAD)
50 NEXT
```

In this program, line 10 establishes the value of pi. Line 20 is the conversion factor, to convert angles in degrees (the way you will enter them) to radians (what the SIN function needs). The FOR...NEXT loop in lines 30-50 produces the sines of the angles from 1 to 90 degrees.

To see it work, press the RUN key, and presto: an instant sine table!

```
RUN
The sine of  1 degrees is .0174524
The sine of  2 degrees is 3.489947E-02
```

Data and Numeric Functions

```
The sine of    3 degrees is 5.233592E-02
.
.
.
The sine of   89 degrees is .9998476
The sine of   90 degrees is 1
Ok
```

Calculating the Cosine

The cosine of an angle is calculated by taking the value of the side adjacent to the angle, and dividing it by the hypotenuse, as shown in figure 4-9.

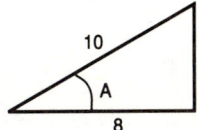

Fig. 4-9: Calculating the cosine.

Here, the cosine is calculated like this:

COS(A) = side adjacent/hypotenuse = 8/10 = .8

Suppose that you're standing at one end of a 250-yard-long bridge across a river, as shown in figure 4-10. You see a grain elevator upriver at an angle of 30 degrees from the bridge.

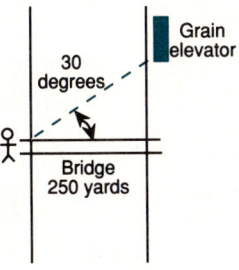

Fig. 4-10: Using the cosine to find distance to an object.

Chapter 4

Assuming that the river's banks form a 90-degree angle to the bridge, you can write a short program that uses the cosine function to find out how far it is to the grain elevator, like this:

```
10 PI=3.14159
20 DEG2RAD=PI/180
30 INPUT "Bridge distance"; BRIDGE
40 INPUT "Angle"; ANGLE
50 ANGLE=ANGLE*DEG2RAD
60 ELEVATOR=BRIDGE/COS(ANGLE)
70 PRINT "Distance to the elevator is";ELEVATOR;"yards"
```

The distance across the bridge is the side adjacent to the angle, and the hypotenuse is the distance you need to find. When you run the program, here's what you get:

```
Bridge distance? 250
Angle? 30
Distance to the elevator is 288.6751 yards
Ok
```

Voila! You've got the distance. You could easily modify this program to compute any similar distance—but you might want to change the prompts from "bridge" and "elevator" to something a little more generic.

Calculating the Tangent

You use the TAN function to calculate the tangent of an angle. The tangent is given by the side opposite the angle, divided by the side adjacent to the angle.

Using TAN to Figure Height

Here's how you can use the TAN function and a protractor (such as you can find in the school supply section of almost any store) to calculate the height of a building (see fig. 4-11).

You start by pacing off a known distance, D1, directly away from the building. From that spot, sight along the protractor to determine the angle, A, to the top of the building. You can see that the distance D1 is the side adjacent to angle A, while D2 is the side opposite the angle. Then use BASIC's TAN function to calculate D2 and determine the height of the building. The formula is as follows:

$\tan(A) = D2/D1$

Data and Numeric Functions

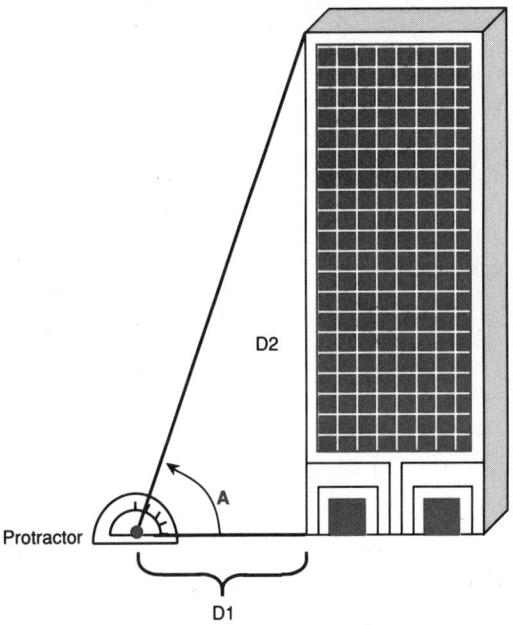

Fig. 4-11: Figuring height with TAN.

Or, to put it another way:

D2 = D1 * tan(A)

For instance, suppose that you paced off 100 feet from the building, set up the protractor, and read an angle of 75 degrees. Then you could use BASIC to find the distance D2, like this:

```
PI=3.14159
Ok
DEG2RAD=PI/180
Ok
D2 = 100 * (TAN(75*DEG2RAD))
Ok
PRINT D2
 373.2037
Ok
```

The height of the building is about 373 feet.

Chapter 4

Calculating the Arctangent

The arctangent is slightly different than the other trigonometric functions. If you know the tangent, the arctangent gives you the angle itself, like this:

angle A (in radians) = ATN (X)

As with all these functions, the angle is given in radians, so you have to convert it if you want to see or use the answer in degrees.

If you know the sides of a right triangle, you can use ATN and your knowledge of how TAN is computed to give you the angle. For instance, suppose that, as shown in figure 4-12, you're on a dirt bike in the desert, and you want to get to Greenville. Now, you can take the road to Brownsville, 80 miles away along a straight road, then turn 90 degrees left and travel 60 miles to Greenville. Or you can head cross-country, but there's no road and you'll have to follow your compass. What angle do you need to turn to get to Greenville?

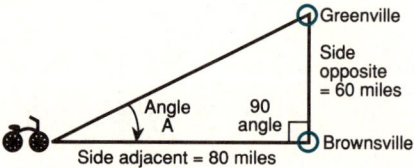

Fig. 4-12: Using ATN to find the angle.

Begin by finding the tangent of angle A.

TAN(A) = side opposite/side adjacent = 60/80

```
PRINT 60/80
 .75
Ok
```

Then use ATN to find the angle in radians.

```
PRINT ATN (.75)
 .6435011
Ok
```

Data and Numeric Functions

The angle is 0.643501 radians. Now convert that angle to degrees, so that you can use your compass.

```
PRINT .643501*180/3.14159
 36.86992
Ok
```

Turn 36.86992 degrees left, and head cross-country, straight for Greenville!

LOG and EXP

Now it's time to rack your brain once again and remember those halcyon days of high school math class—specifically, logarithms. Recall that a logarithm of a number is the power to which the "base" must be raised to obtain the number. For a natural logarithm, that base is known as "e", and it is defined as roughly 2.718. Although it might seem like a strange number on which to base natural logarithms, you can rest assured that it means a great deal to mavens of mathematics. Here's how logarithms work:

If $Y = e^x$, then $LOG(Y) = x$

GW-BASIC gives you two logarithmic functions: the natural logarithm (LOG), and the natural antilog (EXP). They are used like this:

```
100 X = LOG(Y)
200 Y = EXP(X)
```

Before BASIC, volumes of log tables were a hot-selling item in colleges and universities. But now, you have logarithms at your fingertips. For instance, to find the natural log of 10 type the following:

```
PRINT LOG(10)
 2.302585
Ok
```

EXP gives you back the number if you know the logarithm. (It actually generates the result of raising the base, e, to some power.) So EXP(X) is the reverse of LOG(X); in fact, it's actually the same as e^x. To get back to the original number, type

```
PRINT EXP(2.302585)
 9.999998
```

191

Chapter 4

See how LOG and EXP work? First you calculated the logarithm of 10 with LOG(10), and saw that it was 2.302585. Then you took the antilog of that number by entering EXP(2.302585), and you got your original number back. (9.999998 is pretty close to 10.)

Finding the Altitude

What good are logarithms, anyway? Before computers came along, they were useful because you could multiply two numbers by simply adding their logarithms, or divide them by subtracting the log of one number from that of another. Today, logarithms are still the basis for a number of mathematical formulas. Here's one that uses the barometric pressure to give an approximation of altitude:

$$\text{Altitude in feet} = 25{,}000 \left(\log \left(\frac{30}{\text{Pressure in millimeters of mercury}} \right) \right)$$

The tiny program that follows asks you to type the barometric pressure, then gives an approximation of the altitude:

```
10 REM HOW HIGH AM I?
20 PRINT "What's the barometric pressure in inches of mercury?"
30 INPUT BP
40 PRINT "You are approximately" (25000*(LOG(30/BP)))"feet high"
50 END
```

Try it to see what the approximate altitude is if your barometer reads 18.5 millimeters:

```
RUN
What's the barometric pressure in inches of mercury?
? 18.5
You are approximately 12085.67 feet high
Ok
```

Double-Precision Results

In GW-BASIC, if you need better precision with a mathematic or trigonometric function, you can use the /D switch when you first load it. From the DOS prompt, you just add /D after you type GWBASIC, like this:

```
GWBASIC/D
```

Now you get the added accuracy of double-precision results from any of these functions: SQR, SIN, COS, TAN, ATN, LOG, and EXP. Double-precision results take more memory and time to execute, though, so make sure you really need this kind of accuracy.

Later in this book you'll learn more about other switches you can use when you load GW-BASIC.

The SGN Function

The SGN function (it stands for *sign*) records the sign of a number. Although this doesn't help you much when you're using BASIC from the keyboard, it can be very useful in your programs.

The general form of the SGN function is like this:

```
100 X = SGN(A)
```

The value of X depends upon the sign of the variable A:

- If A is positive, X is set to +1.
- If A is negative, X is set to −1.
- If A is zero, X is set to 0.

To see how it works, try this from the keyboard:

```
X=3
Ok
X=X*SGN(X)
Ok
PRINT X
 3
Ok
```

Multiplying X times SGN(X) is a way of guaranteeing that the resulting number will always be positive or zero. Think about it: when X is a positive number, SGN(X) is +1. Multiplying X*SGN(X) is the same as multiplying X*1, which results in X.

When the original X is a negative number, SGN(X) is –1. Multiplying two negative numbers together (–X*–1) results in a positive X. Try it:

```
X=-3
Ok
X=X*SGN(X)
Ok
PRINT X
 3
Ok
```

When X is zero, SGN(X) = 0. So, multiplying 0*0 gives 0.

Some functions (such as LOG) cannot operate on a negative number. You might have to "trap" a negative variable before it gets to the function, or you might want to change how the program runs depending on whether a quantity is positive, negative, or zero. This small program shows how you can use SGN to make a programming decision:

```
10 INPUT "Type a positive number"; N
20 ON SGN(N)+2 GOSUB 1000, 2000, 3000
30 END
1000 PRINT "THAT'S A NEGATIVE NUMBER, CHUMP!": RETURN
2000 PRINT "NO, NO, THAT'S A ZERO!": RETURN
3000 PRINT "POSITIVE NUMBER. GOOD JOB!" : RETURN
```

In line 10, you are asked to enter a number, N. In line 20, if N is negative, then SGN(N) is –1, and +2 is added to that quantity to get 1. The number 1 "points" to the first subroutine call, GOSUB 1000, which is the message that gently chastises you for having entered a negative number.

If, in response to the INPUT statement in line 10, you enter a zero, then SGN(N) is 0, and 0+2=2; so the subroutine call in line 20 is to line 2000.

If you do as you're told and enter a positive number, SGN(N) in line 20 is +1. Since 1+2=3, line 20 branches to the third of the subroutine calls in the list—GOSUB 3000—which tells you that you're correct and supplies those positive strokes you so richly deserve.

Rounding and Truncating: INT, FIX, and CINT

Let's review integer variables for a moment. Remember, using some numbers as integers (that is, as whole numbers, with no fractional portion) can make your programs run faster, and can also save you memory space. You already learned how to use the INT function to round off a number to an integer. In fact, GW-BASIC has three functions for rounding off numbers, and together they let you either round or not round a number, as you choose. The functions are as follows:

- CINT(X) rounds X to the nearest whole number.
- FIX(X) truncates X without rounding; that is, it slices off the decimal point and everything to the right of it.
- INT(X) truncates X without rounding, but a negative number is set to the next lower integer value.

The easiest way to see the differences between these functions is to enter and run this little program:

```
10 INPUT "Type a number for X";X
20 PRINT "When X=";X
30 PRINT "INT(X)=";INT(X)
40 PRINT "FIX(X)=";FIX(X)
50 PRINT "CINT(X)=";CINT(X)

RUN
Enter a number for X? 3.1
When X= 3.1
INT(X)= 3
FIX(X)= 3
CINT(X)= 3
Ok

RUN
Enter a number for X? 3.9
When X= 3.9
INT(X)= 3
FIX(X)= 3
CINT(X)= 4
Ok

RUN
Enter a number for X? -3.1
When X=-3.1
INT(X)=-4
FIX(X)=-3
CINT(X)=-3
Ok
```

Chapter 4

```
RUN
Enter a number for X? -3.9
When X=-3.9
INT(X)=-4
FIX(X)=-3
CINT(X)=-4
Ok
```

You can see that these three functions all do the same thing: they turn a number into an integer. However, the integer that results depends on the original number and on the function.

INT turns 3.1 and 3.9 into the integer 3, without rounding. It turns –3.1 and –3.9 into the next lower number, –4 (again, without rounding.)

FIX simply lops off the decimal point and everything to the right. Therefore, no matter whether the number is 3.1, 3.9, –3.1 or –3.9, it is always converted to the integer 3.

CINT is a true "rounding" function. It rounds off to the nearest integer. So CINT rounds off 3.1 and –3.1 to 3 and –3, respectively. It rounds 3.9 and –3.9 to 4 and –4, respectively.

Integer Division

GW-BASIC uses the backslash (\) rather than the normal division symbol (/) to perform integer division. This means that the result of a division is just the integer portion of the answer. Here's an example:

```
PRINT 35/3
 11.66667
Ok
PRINT 35\3
 11
Ok
```

See the difference? When you used the slash for division, as in 35/3, the result was to the normal number of decimal places. But when you used the backslash (35\3), the result was truncated to a whole number.

In your programs, you'll normally want to use the slash for ordinary division (/). If you do choose to speed up execution by performing integer division with the backslash, it's a good idea to put a comment on that line.

```
100 Z=X\Y 'Integer division!
```

That's because integer division in the wrong place can give you the wrong results; and when you're debugging, it can be pretty hard to tell / from \ in a long code listing.

MOD Operator

The MOD operator is not some fashion holdover from the 1960s. It's actually a mathematics operator. It is similar to the slash (/) operator you use for division, except that instead of producing the full answer, MOD gives you only the remainder of the division. Here's how it works:

```
R = X MOD Y
```

You can read this example as "X divided by Y puts the remainder in R." MOD, which stands for *modulus*, gives you the remainder, rather than the quotient.

Here are a couple of examples you can try on your own computer:

```
PRINT 16/3
  5.333334
Ok
PRINT 16\3
  5
Ok
```

The first example was normal division, which produced the complete answer. In the second example, 16\3, you used the backslash (\) to produce an integer result, with the remainder thrown away. Now try modulus division:

```
PRINT 16 MOD 3
  1
Ok
```

When you used MOD rather than the division operator or the backslash, the computer printed just the number 1. That's because when you divide 16 by 3, you get 5, with a remainder of 1.

Here are some other examples of modulus division using MOD:

12 MOD 6 = 0
35 MOD 8 = 3
9 MOD 2 = 1

Finding Prime Numbers with MOD

If you worked through chapter 2 in this book, you discovered a way to find out whether a number was a prime or not. A prime number, remember, is one that can be divided only by 1 and by itself. (So 5 and 7 are prime numbers, but not 4 or 6.)

Here's another way to look for prime numbers. This program uses the MOD operator to test for a remainder; if there's no remainder, it means that the number can't be a prime.

```
10 INPUT "Type a positive integer";N
20 FOR I=2 TO N-1
30     IF N MOD I = 0 THEN GOTO 70
40 NEXT
50 PRINT N "is a prime number"
60 GOTO 90
70 PRINT N "is not a prime number"
80 PRINT "because it's divisible by"; I
90 END
```

Line 10 asks for you to enter a number, N. The FOR...NEXT loop begins with the integer 2 (since we know that every number can be divided by 1), and tries to divide the number N by every number from 2 to N-1. As long as division by an integer doesn't produce a remainder (that is, N MOD I is zero), the loop continues. However, when division results in a remainder (that is, N MOD I gives a number other than zero), the program branches out of the loop and signals that the number cannot be a prime number. On the other hand, if the number is a prime, the loop is executed completely, and execution "falls through" and prints the message in line 50 that tells you the number is a prime. The output looks like this:

```
RUN

Type a positive integer? 5
 5 is a prime number
Ok

RUN
Type a positive integer? 6
 6 is not a prime number
because it's divisible by 2
Ok
```

Data and Numeric Functions

```
RUN
Type a positive integer? 119
 119 is not a prime number
because it's divisible by 7
Ok

RUN
Type a positive integer? 137
 137 is a prime number
Ok
```

The Logical Operators

Now we come to something that gladdens the heart of real power programmers, and makes the rest of us quake in our sneakers. They're the "logical operators." They are sometimes called the "bitwise operators" or "Boolean logic operators" because they let you make logical decisions, and perform so-called "truth-table operations" on each bit of the bytes used as arguments.

The logical operators include the following:

AND

OR

XOR

EQV

IMP

NOT

A Bit about Bits and Bytes

When we talk about computers today, we invariably mean digital computers. The word "digital" means that all your variables are stored as *bits*, which can be either 1's or 0's. If a bit is a 1, we say that the bit is *on* or *true*; whereas if it's 0 we say that it's *off* or *false*.

To herd those millions of bits in computer memory into some semblance of order, they're organized as *bytes*, as illustrated in figure 4-13. In older computers, each byte was made up of 8 bits; today we're using what are called "16-bit machines" because every byte is an aggregate of 16 bits. The byte is the usual unit of measure;

Chapter 4

for instance, each character takes up one byte of memory. So to store a word like CAT, you need 3 bytes: one byte for C, one byte for A, and one byte for T.

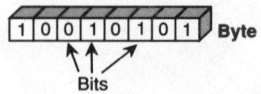

Fig. 4-13: A byte contains bits.

Usually you don't have to worry about what's happening to individual bits—or even bytes. But sometimes it's helpful if you can manipulate them.

If you aren't familiar with bytes, numbering systems, or binary numbers, take a look at Appendix B for more information before you go on.

Making Multiple Decisions

You may have already used logical operators in your decisions, but did you know they can be strung together? You just put all the decisions you need in one line, like this:

```
100 IF A < B AND C > D THEN GOSUB 1000
120 IF A$ = "AHHH" OR A$ = "OHHH" THEN GOSUB 4340
```

Although you don't usually need to know how these logical operators function internally, sometimes it's helpful to understand their exact operation. In lines 100 and 120 the AND and OR is comparing entire statements, but now you're going to use AND (and the other logical operators) in "truth table" declarations that look at quantities bit by bit.

Logical operators change their operands (that is, the numbers they work on) to 16-bit, signed, two's complement integers in the range from +32767 to –32768. If each operand is a 0 or a –1, the logical operators all return either a 0 or a –1.

Truth Tables

A *truth table* is a way of comparing two binary quantities—that is, quantities made up of 1's and 0's. You can compare individual bits or entire bytes. The basic rules for truth tables are pretty simple:

Data and Numeric Functions

If you AND one quantity with another, both have to be true for the result to be true. So,

1 AND 1 = 1

but

1 AND 0 = 0

If you OR one quantity with another, the result is true if either quantity is true. So,

1 OR 0 = 1

This should become more clear as you work through the examples of the logical operators.

And what if you don't care right now about logical operators and truth tables and bumping those bits around? Well, you can skip right over the next few pages with no sense of loss, then come back and learn the logical operators at a later date. Almost everything you want to do in BASIC can be done without the logical operators—it's just that under some circumstances they give you more control than "higher-level" statements.

The AND Operator

This is how the AND operator is used:

```
100 X = A AND B
```

This means, "do a logical AND of the bits in variable A and those in variable B, and put the result in the bits in X." You can see this on the keyboard:

```
PRINT 3 + 5
  8
Ok

PRINT 3 AND 5
  1
Ok
```

There's a big difference between the arithmetic + and the logical AND, isn't there? As shown in figure 4-14, the AND operator combines bits from the number

201

Chapter 4

3 and the number 5. According to truth-table rules, both bits must be 1 in order for the resulting bit to be a 1. If either bit is a 0, the resulting bit is a 0.

```
         Bits for 3   0011
AND      Bits for 5   0101      AND gives a "1" only when
Result:  Bits for 1   0001      both corresponding bits are "1".
```

Fig. 4-14: ANDing two numbers.

The OR Operator

The syntax of the OR operator is like this:

```
X = A OR B
```

This means "to perform a logical OR of the individual bits of variable A and those of B, and put the result in the bits of X." The OR operator yields a 1 if *either* of the ORed bits is a 1. For example:

```
PRINT 3 OR 5
   7
Ok
```

Figure 4-15 shows what happens when you OR 3 and 5.

```
         Bits for 3   0011
OR       Bits for 5   0101      OR operator gives a "1" if
Result:  Bits for 7   0111      either corresponding bit is a "1"
```

Fig. 4-15: ORing two numbers.

The XOR Operator

The XOR (*exclusive or*) operator combines the bits of two quantities. If both corresponding bits are the same, the result is a 0. If the corresponding bits are different, the result is a 1. Here's an example:

```
PRINT 3 XOR 5
   6
Ok
```

Data and Numeric Functions

Figure 4-16 illustrates an XOR of the numbers 3 and 5.

```
         Bits for 3    0011     Result of XOR is "0" both bits are
XOR      Bits for 5    0101     the same, "1" if bits are different.
Result:  Bits for 6    0110
```

Fig. 4-16: XORing two numbers.

The EQV Operator

You can think of EQV as the other side of the coin from XOR, because it produces a 1 only if *both* corresponding bits are the same (whether 1's or 0's). You use the EQV operator like this:

```
100 X = A EQV B
```

This means "combine the bits of A and B, and for each location where the corresponding bits are the same, put a 1 in X." To try it,

```
PRINT 5 EQV 3
 -7
Ok
```

Figure 4-17 shows the results of 5 EQV 3.

```
               Sign bit : "0" for positive number, "1" for negative.
                              ↓
         Bits for 3     0  000  0000  0000  0011
EQV      Bits for 5     0  000  0000  0000  0101
Result:  Bits for -7    1  111  1111  1111  0110
```

Fig. 4-17: EQVing two numbers.

The result of an EQV of two positive numbers is always a negative number. That's because the bit in the left-most position is used to carry the number's sign; this bit is 0 for positive numbers and 1 for negative numbers. If we use EQV to combine the two leftmost 0's, the result is a 1 in this position, making the result negative.

203

Chapter 4

The IMP Operator

The IMP operator is sensitive to which of the two quantities is evaluated first. It's used like this:

```
100 X = A IMP B
```

This means "for each bit position, if both corresponding bits are the same, put a 1 in that position in X; if the bits are different, look at the A bit, and put that bit in the corresponding position in X."

Here's how it works (see fig. 4-18)

```
              3 IMP 5
First number    0011
Second number   0101
Result          1011

              5 IMP 3
First number    0101
Second number   0011
Result          1101
```

Fig. 4-18:   IMP is sensitive to the order of the numbers.

Like EQV, the IMP of two positive numbers is always negative.

The NOT Operator

The NOT operator uses only a single number. It reverses the bits of the number, like this:

```
100 X = NOT A
```

This means "reverse every bit of A and put the result in the bits of X" (see fig. 4-19).

```
                     NOT 0
Bits of 0    0000  0000  0000  0000
NOT(0)
Result:-1    1111  1111  1111  1111
```

Fig. 4-19:   NOT of a number.

Data and Numeric Functions

Masking and Bit-Coding

In the computer world, "masking" has nothing to do with Halloween. A mask is something that you apply to a byte of data that lets you see only the bit or bits that you want.

One place you might want to use a mask is in communications over a serial or parallel port, when data comes in as a full byte, but you care about only a few bits. You can also use a mask in a technique known as *bit-coding*. For conditions that can be expressed as *true* or *false* (such as the status of a program or a file), bit-coding lets you keep track of the condition using one bit of data rather than an entire variable.

For instance, if you are interested in only the sixth bit of a given byte of data, you can use the AND function to mask the other bits, like this:

```
100 IF S AND 32 = 32 THEN PRINT "FILE IS UPDATED"
110 S = S AND 32
```

Here, you care about only the sixth bit of S (bits are numbered from right to left), so you mask the other bits by ANDing the quantity with 32. Look at the individual bits in figure 4-20 to see what's happening.

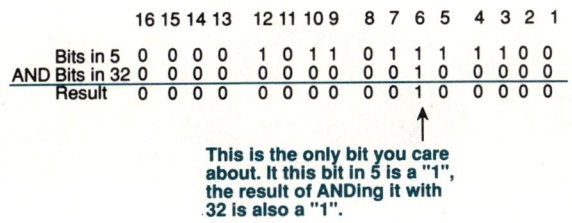

Fig. 4-20: Masking a quantity.

The result of the AND function yields the value of 32, which causes the message FILE IS UPDATED to be printed. If the sixth bit is a 0 then the result of the AND function yields all 0's, so the message isn't printed.

In bit-coding, you can use the OR operator to change a bit. For instance, if the indicator is a 0, indicating that the file has not been updated, and you want to change it to a 1 without disturbing any of the other bits in the variable, you can use OR, like this:

```
100 S = S OR 32
```

The resulting bits then look like those shown in figure 4-21.

Chapter 4

```
        Bits in 5      0000  1011  0100  1100
OR      Bits in 32     0000  0000  0010  0000
        Result         0000  1011  0110  1100
                                      ↑
                                      Only this bit is
                                      changed in the result.
```

Fig. 4-21: Changing a quantity with OR.

Review Questions

1. What will be the output of the following program?

   ```
   10 READ A, B, C, D
   20 PRINT A, D
   30 RESTORE
   40 DATA 10, 20, 30, 40
   50 PRINT B, C
   ```

2. Rewrite the program below to use a FOR...NEXT loop and DATA statements to READ the names of the months:

   ```
   10 OPTION BASE 1
   20 DIM M$(12)
   30 DATA "Jan", "Feb", "Mar", "Apr", "May", "Jun"
   40 DATA "Jul", "Aug", "Sep", "Oct", "Nov", "Dec"
   50 READ M$(1), M$(2), M$(3), M$(4), M$(5), M$(6)
   60 READ M$(7), M$(8), M$(9), M$(10), M$(11), M$(12)
   ```

3. As a golfer, you fear water hazards, and there's a big one between you and the 13th hole (see fig. 4-22). You know it's only 150 yards straight to the green, but you take the safe route and hit the ball off at an angle of 40 degrees, as far as point B. Then you can hit the ball from point B to the green. If the angle between the direct line and last shot you hit is 90 degrees, how far did your ball ultimately have to travel to get to the green?

4. Predict the result of this program line without trying it on your computer:

   ```
   100 PRINT 15\(5 MOD 3)
   ```

5. The following instruction masks all but what bit? (That is, which bit will be read by this instruction?)

   ```
   100 IF X AND 2 THEN PRINT "OK"
   ```

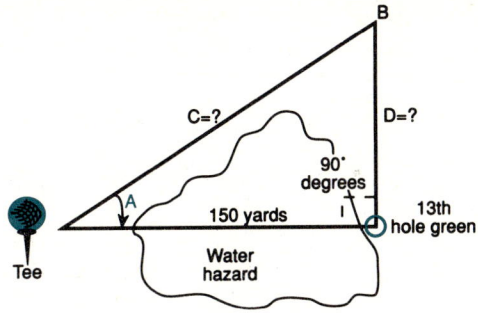

Fig 4-22: The water hazard.

6. In the following display, what is the significance of the 3 in the answer?

```
PRINT 104556/23
  4545.913
Ok
```

7. How many bytes of memory are used by single-precision variables?

8. What are the two advantages of using integer variables whenever possible?

9. Write an instruction that will declare as integer variables any variables beginning with A through M or X through Z.

10. Exercise: Write a program that keeps track of cash transactions. For each transaction, the program should print the item, the amount paid, the sales tax (computed with double-precision variables) and the total. At the end of the day, print the total sales and total sales tax, to two decimal places.

Chapter 5

String Functions

Chapter **5**

String Functions

In previous years, most people thought of computers as machines whose main purpose was to perform numerical calculations. It's true that computers got their start as "number crunchers"—devices that make numerical calculations as rapidly as possible. Early programming languages such as FORTRAN were oriented almost exclusively toward numbers; they had only a primitive capability to deal with anything else.

Over the years, however, people began to realize that computers could be used to process data other than numbers, such as pictures, sound, and words. BASIC has all these capabilities, but its ability to handle words (that is, strings) might be the most important.

String-handling capabilities are useful in business programs for data that is mostly text-oriented, such as mailing lists and inventory control. But strings have also made the use of computers possible for a variety of other kinds of programs: educational, entertainment, and even artistic. There are, for example, the "Adventure" games, in which, using short sentences like "Go North," you attempt to find your way out of various mazelike castles, haunted houses, and so forth. Then there is the famous "Eliza" program, which imitates a psychiatrist. A growing number of programs write short stories or poetry, and there are interactive computer stories in which you can take part in the story, talk to the other characters, and influence the plot.

What You'll Learn in this Chapter

In this section, you will learn how to handle strings and some BASIC functions that make manipulating strings faster and easier. With BASIC's string capabilities, you can manipulate words better than a politician! You'll learn about:

- Handling ASCII characters
- Converting strings to numbers and back

Chapter 5

- Finding string length
- Getting input of a single key or a whole line
- Combining strings

Like most BASIC languages, GW-BASIC has several functions that let you manipulate string variables and convert between string variables and numeric variables. This section shows you how to handle these string functions.

Single-Character ASCII-String Conversions

Strings and numeric variables, as you know, don't mix. If you try to INPUT a string to a numeric variable, for instance, you'll get a "Type mismatch" error message. But a special set of BASIC functions lets you convert strings to numeric quantities and back again.

Conversions are based on the ASCII table. (The name stands for *American Standard Code for Information Interchange*, which is a real mouthful; you can see why people just say *as-key*.) This table is the standard code used today on virtually all computers to represent characters of the alphabet, numerals, and several special characters. If you take a look at the ASCII table in Appendix C, you'll see that each character or number has a distinct decimal value associated with it.

These values are the key to converting between numeric and string quantities. They're used by the ASC and CHR$ functions to perform the conversions.

The ASC Function

The ASC function takes a string variable and produces the ASCII decimal value of the first character of that string. This is how it works:

```
100 X = ASC(A$)
```

This means, "look at the first character of string A$ and put its decimal value (based on the ASCII table) into X." Remember that this function gives you the value of only the first character in the string. The other characters are ignored.

Here's an example:

```
100 A$ = "SAN FRANCISCO"
200 X = ASC(A$)
300 PRINT X
```

When you RUN this little program, you get the following output:

```
RUN
 83
Ok
```

Do you see why the number 83 was printed for the value of X? If you look at the ASCII table in Appendix C, you can see that the ASCII decimal value for an uppercase *S* is 83. The ASC function sees only the first character of the string A$, so the program prints the ASCII decimal value for S, which is 83.

Using ASC to Detect Oddball Characters

The ASC function can be helpful when your program must handle characters that are not part of the normal alphabet. For instance, suppose that you want to abort program execution when the program sees an ESC (escape) character. Although ESC isn't a normal character, you look in the ASCII table and discover that its decimal value is 27. Therefore, your code might look like that shown in the following example. (The INPUT$ statement in line 100 is a special form of INPUT that handles *all* ASCII characters; you need it here if you want to run this demonstration. You'll find a further explanation of INPUT$ later in this chapter under "Reading More Keystrokes with INPUT$.")

```
90 PRINT "Input ESC to abort"
100 C$ = INPUT$(1)
110 IF ASC(C$) = 27 THEN GOSUB 500
120 END
500 FOR I = 1 TO 5
510     PRINT "Aborting program!"
520 NEXT
530 RETURN
```

Line 100 of this little program INPUTs one character into a variable called `C$`. Line 110 tests that to see whether it is equal to the Escape character. If the character isn't ESC, nothing happens and execution continues. But if the character is ESC (that is, an ASCII 27), the program executes the subroutine in lines 500-520 before ending. Here's what happens if you RUN it:

```
RUN
Input ESC to abort
```
(You hit the ESC key, then ENTER)
```
Aborting program!
Aborting program!
Aborting program!
Aborting program!
Aborting program!
Ok
```

ASC is especially useful in communications. For example, some communications software sends an STX (start text) character, which signals that text will follow. This character isn't printed, but because it has an ASCII value of 2, you can detect and process it.

The CHR$ Function

The CHR$ function is just the opposite of the ASC function. CHR$ takes an ASCII decimal value as the argument and converts it into a one-character string. The common form of the CHR$ function is shown here:

```
100 A$ = CHR$(X)
```

This means, "find the ASCII character for the number in X, and put that character into `A$`." This function is useful for dealing with characters that are not part of the "plain vanilla" normal character set—the alphabet, the numerals, and a few special characters.

For instance, the ASCII character set has a "bell" (a legacy from teletype days) that causes most computers and terminals to issue an audible alarm such as a bell, horn, buzzer, or beeper. It's often used to attract the operator's attention when displaying errors or other important messages. You can ring your computer's bell by sending a special ASCII character to it. This character is ASCII 7, so it can't be enclosed in quotes like a normal string variable. Instead, you generate it using the CHR$ function. Try it from the keyboard:

```
PRINT CHR$(7)
```
(Beep!)

String Functions

The CHR$ function converts the decimal value of 7 into the ASCII character for the bell and sends it to the computer. The computer recognizes this as the command to beep. Remember that the string created by the CHR$ function is only one character in length.

Shuffling Substrings!

BASIC has several functions that allow you to manipulate substrings—that is, portions of strings. LEFT$, MID$, and RIGHT$ are all used to break up string variables into substrings. Substrings can be useful for changing a name to "last name first, first name last" order, and for other kinds of text formatting.

The LEFT$ Function

LEFT$ copies a specified number of characters from the left end of a string variable into another string. The general form of the LEFT$ function is as follows:

```
100 B$ = LEFT$(A$,N)
```

This means, "beginning with the left end of A$, copy N characters and place them in B$." Within the parentheses of the LEFT$ function, A$ is the string variable upon which the function is performed. The numeric variable N defines just how many characters on the left end of A$ will be copied into the string B$. For example,

```
10 A$ = "Mountain View"
20 N = 8
30 B$ = LEFT$(A$,N)
40 PRINT B$
```

Before you RUN this, see whether you can figure out what will be printed by the PRINT statement at line 40. Then see whether you were right.

```
RUN
Mountain
Ok
```

Because the LEFT$ function copies only the leftmost 8 characters of the string A$ into the new string B$, only the word "Mountain" is printed. The characters in the string A$ are not altered.

In this function, the value of N cannot be negative, nor can it be larger than 255. If N is zero, the result is a "null string" (a string with no length and nothing in it).

The RIGHT$ Function

The RIGHT$ function allows the program to move characters from the right end of a string into another string—just the opposite of the LEFT$ function. The general form is as follows:

```
100 B$ = RIGHT$(A$,N)
```

This means, "beginning with the right end of A$, copy N characters and place them in B$." The same rules apply as for the LEFT$ function. For instance, here's how to copy just the right-hand word of "Mountain View":

```
100 A$ = "Mountain View"
200 N = 5
300 B$ = RIGHT$(A$,N)
400 PRINT B$

RUN
 View
Ok
```

This program copies the rightmost 5 characters from the argument string into B$, so B$ receives not only the word "View," but also the space that precedes it.

RIGHT$, like LEFT$, requires that the value of N not be negative nor larger than 255. If N is zero, a null string results.

Here's a program that combines RIGHT$ and LEFT$ to reverse the order of a name:

```
10 A$= "URIAH HEEP"
20 B$=RIGHT$(A$,4)
30 C$=LEFT$(A$,5)
40 PRINT B$", "C$
```

When you RUN this program, the result is

```
HEEP, URIAH
```

The MID$ Function

The MID$ function, as you have probably guessed, copies characters from the middle of one string and puts them into another string. The general form of the MID$ function is as follows:

```
100 B$ = MID$(A$,N,M)
```

This means, "look at string A$ and, beginning with the Nth character from the left, copy M characters into B$."

Notice that the MID$ function operates just a bit differently from the LEFT$ and RIGHT$ functions. Because MID$ copies from the middle of the string, it requires one additional argument. The variable N is used to define the starting position in A$ from which characters will be copied. (Starting position is relative to the left end of the string.) The variable M defines the number of characters to be moved. For example,

```
10 A$ = "Golden Gate Bridge"
20 N = 8: M =4
30 B$ = MID$(A$,N,M)
40 PRINT B$

RUN
Gate
Ok
```

Because of the values of the variables N and M, the MID$ function begins with the eighth character in the string A$ and copies four characters into the string B$. Therefore B$ contains only the word *Gate*.

The variable N must be positive and from 1 to 255. The variable M has to be in the range of 0 to 255.

Complete Conversions of Strings and Numbers

GW-BASIC gives you two functions, STR$ and VAL, to help convert complete strings to numeric values and vice versa. These are especially useful when you're programming for business applications and databases.

The VAL Function

The VAL function takes a string variable containing *characters* that represent a numeric value, and evaluates the characters to create an actual *number* (that is, a numeric variable). The general form of the VAL function is

```
100 X = VAL(A$)
```

This means, "see what characters are written into variable A$ and put their actual numeric value into X." Here's an example of how VAL works:

```
100 A$ = "152.40"
200 PRINT A$
300 X = VAL(A$)
400 PRINT X
```

The output of the little demonstration program looks like this:

```
RUN
152.40
 152.4
Ok
```

What's the difference between A$ and X? Just this: A$ is a string variable. It sees the numbers "152.40" as merely a series of individual characters, like "abc" or "4377 Melody Lane." After conversion by VAL, though, the number 152.40 in X is an actual number: You can crunch it to your heart's delight, using the mathematical operators for addition, subtraction, multiplication, etc.

Why Do You Use VAL?

What's the point of VAL, anyway? You put a number in, you get a number out. You put in 152.40, you get 152.4 out. So, why the fuss?

Imagine for a moment that you're a banker with a list of names and account balances, like this:

```
Creakle, James     $152.40
Traddles, Thomas    $73.50
```

Right now, this is all string data—you can't add interest to any of those balances, and you can't deduct monthly account charges. Before you can do any

218

mathematical operations on those balances, you have to convert them to numeric data. That's a job for VAL.

After conversion by VAL, the original string `A$` is not altered; it still contains the original characters. To convert negative values, place a minus sign in the first position of the string.

```
100 A$ = "-62"
```

VAL ignores any leading blanks, tabs, or line feeds. If the first actual character is anything other than a numeral, decimal point, or a minus sign, the string is evaluated as zero.

Another important use for VAL is in error-checking. Normally, if BASIC is expecting you to INPUT a number and you input a string, the program simply "crashes." So, to get a number into BASIC, you can ask for a string variable, then convert it to a number with VAL. This gets you past the "crash" that would normally happen if you input string data to a numeric variable, and lets you do your own error-handling and generate more meaningful error messages.

The STR$ Function

The STR$ function converts a numeric quantity into a string. (It's really the opposite of VAL.) The form of the STR$ function is as follows:

```
100 A$ = STR$(X)
```

This means, "look at numeric variable `X` and put its string characters in `A$`." Here's an example:

```
100 X = 79.4
200 A$ = STR$(X)
300 PRINT A$

RUN
 79.4
```

In line 100 of this example, `X` is set to the value 79.4. Since `X` is a numeric variable, you can perform arithmetic on this quantity. In line 200, the characters "79.4" are placed in string variable `A$`. One advantage of using string variables for numeric quantities is that you have much more flexibility in printing and displaying them than you do with numeric quantities.

219

Finding String Length with LEN

Because it can find out the current length of a string variable, LEN is one of the most useful of the string functions. The form of the LEN function is

```
100 N = LEN(A$)
```

This means, "count the number of characters and spaces in A$ and write that number in N." If the string A$ contains the characters "Grinby", then the LEN function returns a value of 6 in the variable N.

LEN is important because each time you alter a string variable, its length changes. Using a statement like INPUT A$ to read in a list of names, for instance, results in varying lengths for A$. Try this:

```
10 FOR I=1 TO 5
20    INPUT A$
30    PRINT "The name "A$" has"LEN(A$)"characters"
40 NEXT
50 END
```

Now run this program to see the length of three different names.

```
RUN
? Martin Chuzzlewit
The name Martin Chuzzlewit has 17 characters
? Sam Weller
The name Sam Weller has 10 characters
? Yourname
The name Yourname has 8 characters
```

Remember that LEN gives the current length of the string. If the string is changed within the program or by an INPUT statement, then the value returned by LEN changes, too.

When you are entering numbers or string data from the keyboard, usually you type the characters and then, because the program has no other way of telling when you're done, you press Return (or Enter) to tell the program to start processing the number or string. This works well in the usual case where several characters must be entered for each input. But what about the situation in which only a one-character input is necessary? If you know you're going to enter only one character and the program knows that, too, having to press Return after you enter it is just a nuisance.

String Functions

INKEY$ is a method of reading a single character in from the keyboard. INKEY$ is actually a variable; its general form looks like this:

```
C$ = INKEY$
```

This means, "input a single keystroke from the keyboard and assign it to C$." You don't have to end the input with Return.

INKEY$ is a good way to handle single-character responses, such as Y for Yes, or N for No. Take a look at this example of how you can do it:

```
LIST
10 PRINT "Do you want to continue? (Y/N)"
20 A$=INKEY$: IF A$="" GOTO 20
30 PRINT A$
40 IF A$= "Y" OR A$ = "y" GOTO 80
50 IF A$= "N" OR A$ = "n" GOTO 100 ELSE PRINT "Answer Y or N"
60 PRINT
70 GOTO 10
80 PRINT "You chose Y. Good choice! Program continues..."
90 GOTO 110
100 PRINT "You chose N. Program terminated"
110 END
```

This example illustrates how to handle Yes and No responses. In your earlier programs, the user was required to enter the word (or at least a letter), followed by Return. This program uses INKEY$ to process your one-character answer.

Line 10 asks whether you want to continue and prompts for a Yes or No input (that is, a Y or an N). Unlike INPUT, the INKEY$ doesn't let you add a prompt message with the statement, so you must PRINT the message first. Line 20 is a way of waiting for input—we'll explain more about that in a moment.

Lines 40 and 50 are where the decisions are made. If you press Y (or y) for Yes, the program branches immediately to line 80. But if you press N (or n) for No, execution branches to line 100. Notice that lines 40 and 50 also force you to choose between Yes and No—any other key just causes execution to "fall through" to line 70, which starts the loop all over again with line 10.

If you could be sure that the user would use only capital letters, or only lowercase letters, you wouldn't need to provide for both kinds of characters in lines 40 and 50. But as you know, the ASCII code for a lowercase letter is different from that for an uppercase letter. And because you can't be sure *what* the user will press, you have to be prepared for either uppercase or lowercase letters.

Now look at line 20:

```
20 A$ = INKEY$ : IF A$ = "" GOTO 20
```

As you can see, there are important differences between using INKEY$ and using INPUT. First, INKEY$ is not a complete BASIC statement as INPUT is; it is a BASIC function. Therefore, the first thing we do is to make the variable we want to examine, `A$` in this case, equal to (take on the value of) INKEY$. We do this in the first part of line 20, after we have printed the "Do you want to continue?" message in line 10.

So far so good. You probably expect that the next thing we'll do is to analyze `A$` to see whether it is Y, y, N, or n. But not so fast! What happens if, when the program gets to line 20, the user hasn't entered anything yet? Actually, this is a pretty good bet, because the time that elapses between line 10, when the program prints the prompt, and line 20, when it first checks for your input, is less than a millisecond. Unless you have very good reaction time, there won't be anything typed on the keyboard for INKEY$ to read. In this case there is no point for the program to try to analyze the input—there isn't any. We want to be able to wait until some key is pressed. That's what the second part of line 20 does: IF INKEY$ = "" THEN GOTO 20. The two quotation marks with nothing between them mean "no character." (This is sometimes called the "null string.") It is the same as saying that nothing was typed. So the statement says, "If nothing was typed, go execute line 20 again." Because the first part of line 20 simply reads the keyboard, the program will continue to execute this line until a character is typed on the keyboard—in other words, until INKEY$ becomes something other than the null string.

Once a character is typed, INKEY$ takes on the value of that character. The program finds that `A$` is no longer equal to " ", and goes on (finally!) to the next line number, 30. In this line, the first thing we do is print the character—because INKEY$ does not print (or *echo*) the character it has gotten from the keyboard, and the user would probably feel uncomfortable about typing something that doesn't appear on the screen.

Menu-selection routines such as this are typical situations in which the INKEY$ function is useful. Another use for INKEY$ is when you must read a large amount of text on the screen, and the program needs you to signal when you are done with each screenful so that it can print the next one.

You could write

```
1000 INPUT"PRESS RETURN TO CONTINUE"; X
```

but then the Return key is the only key that will work. Instead, let's use INKEY$:

```
1000 PRINT"PRESS ANY KEY TO CONTINUE: ";
1010 IF INKEY$ = "" THEN GOTO 1010
```

After printing the prompt in line 1000, the program will wait on line 1010 until some key, no matter what, is pressed so that the program can continue. Now, even someone who doesn't know where the Return key is can read the next screenful of instructions.

In the previous example, because we don't care what key was pressed, we don't need to store the character. Therefore we don't need to assign INKEY$ to another variable like `A$`—we can check directly to see whether it is equal to the null string and, if not, proceed with the rest of the program.

INKEY$ can also handle "extended" ASCII characters, such as BEL (ASCII 7) and SOH (ASCII 1) that are used in communications and other software. Use CHR$, with a zero before the character code, like this:

```
50 IF INKEY$ = CHR$(01) THEN PRINT "SOH"
```

To check for a special key such as ESC, you can use its ASCII code the same way.

```
50 IF INKEY$ = CHR$(27) THEN END
```

INKEY$ is also useful in game programs in which you might want to move something (a spaceship, for example) around the screen using the arrow (or cursor control) keys. The exact instructions for doing this kind of thing usually depend on the graphics capability of your computer.

Reading More Keystrokes with INPUT$

INPUT$ is like INKEY$ (see the preceding description) in that it reads the keyboard and does not need to be terminated by Return. However, whereas INKEY$ will read only one character, INPUT$ will read any number of characters (up to 255). Here's the general form:

```
A$ = INPUT$ (N)
```

This means, "INPUT N keystrokes from the keyboard (or other device) and put them in `A$`." It is not necessary to terminate this function with Return (or Enter). Exactly how many characters it will read is specified by the number N in the parentheses following the INPUT$. INPUT$ will wait until this many characters have been typed before it goes on to the next statement.

Here's an example of how we might use INPUT$. Suppose that we are writing a program in which we want to enter the day of the week. We then want to assign to a variable DW (Day of the Week) a number from 1 to 7, depending on the day.

Now, it's not really necessary to wait for the complete word (like "Wednesday") to be entered. The first two letters are sufficient to determine which day we

Chapter 5

have in mind. (One letter isn't enough because Saturday and Sunday both start with *S* and Tuesday and Thursday both start with *T*.)

We can write the following routine:

```
100 PRINT"PLEASE TYPE THE DAY OF THE WEEK"
110 DA$ = INPUT$(2)
120 IF DA$ = "SU" THEN DW = 1
130 IF DA$ = "MO" THEN DW = 2
140 IF DA$ = "TU" THEN DW = 3
150 IF DA$ = "WE" THEN DW = 4
160 IF DA$ = "TH" THEN DW = 5
170 IF DA$ = "FR" THEN DW = 6
180 IF DA$ = "SA" THEN DW = 7
190 PRINT"THANK YOU."
```

The program waits, in line 110, for us to type two letters. When we do, the program goes on to analyze the letters, without waiting for the rest of the word, and interrupts us (if we are still typing) with a "THANK YOU" message.

One difference to notice between INPUT$ and INKEY$ is that INPUT$ always waits for N characters to be typed, even if N is 1. It never returns the null string (as INKEY$ does), so we don't have to check for the null string and keep executing the statement again and again until we find a different character, as we do with INKEY$.

For example, if we want the program to pause until we press any key, we can write the following:

```
1000 PRINT"PRESS ANY KEY TO CONTINUE: ";
1010 INPUT $(1)
```

This is simpler than the corresponding example shown in the description of INKEY$.

The greatest usefulness of INPUT$ is in reading data from devices other than the keyboard, such as a telephone modem. This is because (like INKEY$) INPUT$ will accept any ASCII input without printing it, including control codes (except Ctrl-Break), backspaces, and so on. In communications over a telephone modem, these control codes may have different meanings than they do in normal BASIC. For example, receiving a Return character doesn't necessarily mean that the message is over. Using INPUT$ permits the program to analyze these characters and take appropriate action, rather than letting the regular INPUT statement do all the analyzing.

String Functions

Another application for INPUT$ is a text formatting program that doesn't necessarily want to interpret a single Return as a new line, or that wants to interpret two successive Returns as the end of a paragraph.

Remember that INPUT$ doesn't "echo" what's being typed, and this would be disconcerting to someone who is expecting to see letters and numbers on the screen as he or she presses keys on the keyboard.

Using LINE INPUT to Enter Anything

In many situations, INPUT is the only statement you need to enter information into your computer from the keyboard. But sometimes it can be a little awkward. LINE INPUT is often a better choice. The general form is as follows:

```
100 LINE INPUT A$
```

This means, "INPUT a LINE of characters (up to 255 characters), which can include commas, colons, and quotes. Assign this string to variable A$."

Why use LINE INPUT? So far in the examples in this book, the input to programs has been in the form of numbers or one-word character strings. But suppose you are writing a program that requires complete sentences for input, as "Eliza" does. "Eliza" is a game program that pretends to be a psychiatrist. It asks whether you have any problems, and you answer it in conversational English. For example, you might type, "My family doesn't understand me."

The trouble with using the INPUT statement in this situation is that if you include a comma in the sentence you are typing, INPUT will think they belong to a different variable. (The same is true of colons.)

Here's an example of what can happen:

```
10 PRINT"Tell me your problem."
20 INPUT A$
30 PRINT A$
RUN
Tell me your problem.
? Well, I don't get along with my boss.
? Redo from start
```

Notice how the computer can't handle any of the input sentence following "Well." You can avoid this problem if you always enclose your input in quotations, but that can get tedious after a while. Also, the question mark, which INPUT always prints before your input, looks out of place here.

225

Chapter 5

Substituting LINE INPUT A$ for INPUT A$ solves these problems.

```
10 PRINT"Tell me your problem."
20 LINE INPUT A$
30 PRINT A$
RUN
Tell me your problem.
Well, I don't get along with my boss.
Well, I don't get along with my boss.
```

Now the program "remembers" the entire input sentence. With LINE INPUT, you can input any characters you want, including leading blank spaces, commas, colons, and quotations, and they will all be assigned to the variable `A$`. Only pressing Return (or Enter or Ctrl-Break, etc.) can terminate the input line you are typing. LINE INPUT also does not automatically output the question mark as a prompt.

You can use a "prompt string" in LINE INPUT. Let's combine lines 10 and 20 from the above program. The result is the following:

```
10 LINE INPUT"Tell me your problem."; A$
```

This will work just the same as lines 10 and 20 did in the above program.

One of the most important uses for LINE INPUT is to make sure that, even if you make a mistake entering your input, you will receive an error message you can understand so that you will know how to correct your mistake.

```
2070 INPUT "ENTER YOUR SELECTION";S
```

For example, suppose that you have a program with an INPUT statement like that in line 2070, one that is expecting numeric input—say 1, 2, or 3. But your user types "Two" rather than "2". What will happen?

The INPUT statement is waiting for a numeric variable, either 1, 2, or 3. When it sees the "Two" it will immediately print:

```
?Redo from start
?
```

Now, what will your user make of this? He or she may figure out that "Redo from start" means to try again, but probably will not know exactly what the mistake was. Let's fix up the program to give a more self-explanatory error message.

First, change line 2070 to read:

```
2070 LINE INPUT"ENTER YOUR SELECTION "; S$
```

Then add these lines:

```
2075 IF S$ = "ONE" OR S$ = "TWO" OR S$ = "THREE"
     THEN PRINT"Please do not spell out the numbers. Use
          the digits 1, 2, or 3.": GOTO 2070
2077 S = VAL(S$)
```

Now if you spell out the numbers, the error message is readily understandable. Similarly, LINE INPUT can be used to *trap* other kinds of input errors (*trap* means to catch an error before it can cause trouble), such as inputting two variables when only one is expected).

You have probably noticed something else here: Because the input of a LINE INPUT statement is always assigned to a string variable (A$ in this example), if we want to turn it back into a number we have to change its type, using the VAL function as in line 2077.

You can turn this to your advantage with this more flexible approach:

```
2070 LINE INPUT"ENTER YOUR SELECTION"; S$
2075 S = VAL(S$)
2080 IF S = 0 OR S>3 THEN PRINT"PLEASE USE ONLY
     NUMBERS": GOTO 2070
```

Here we use VAL to convert the input to a numeric, then test to see whether that numeric is anything except the numbers 1-3. If words are typed as input, VAL returns a 0, so you don't have to test for all possible words.

Searching for Strings with INSTR

INSTR is a very useful and powerful function, usually used to look for the occurrence of a specific word or name in a sentence or data file. It has this general form:

```
X = INSTR(N,S$,W$)
```

This means, "look for the string `W$` (which might be a word) in the string `S$` (which might be a sentence), starting at character position `N` in string `S$`." It will return the character position in the string `S$` at which the match begins, or it will return 0 if no match is found. These numeric values will be assigned to the variable `X`.

The `N` is optional; if it is left out, the entire string `S$` will be searched. Either `S$` or `W$` can be replaced with string constants—that is, actual strings enclosed in quotations, like "MITCH."

Suppose that you're writing a "psychiatrist" program that first asks whether the user has any problems to discuss, then waits for a reply. Let's say that, if the user then

Chapter 5

types a sentence that contains the word "Mother," you want the program (playing the role of a psychiatrist) to respond with, "Tell me more about your family."

Here's how, using INSTR, you can accomplish this:

```
10 PRINT"Tell me your problem."
20 LINE INPUT S$
30 IF INSTR(S$,"MOTHER") THEN GOTO 100
50 PRINT"Please go on." : GOTO 20
100 PRINT"Tell me more about your family." : GOTO 20
```

Lines 10 and 20 ask for the user to enter a line of input. They're the same as in the example under LINE INPUT. Line 30, using INSTR, searches the input sentence S$ for the word "MOTHER." If it finds the word, control branches to line 100. If this word is not found, the program, not knowing what else to say, prints, "Please go on."

Although this program is perhaps not quite so clever as a real psychiatrist, it gives you an idea about how INSTR can be used. Incidentally, INSTR is sensitive to uppercase and lowercase. So here it responds to "MOTHER," but not to "mother" or even "Mother."

Notice that INSTR detects only the first occurrence of a word in a sentence (or a string in another string). If you want to see whether the word occurs more than once, you will have to search the sentence again, starting just past the point where the first match was found. That's where the variable N in the INSTR function comes in handy.

Here's a program that will count how many times the word "the" appears in a sentence that you enter:

```
10 LINE INPUT "TYPE SENTENCE: "; S$
20 W$ = "THE" : N = 1 : J = 0
30 P = INSTR(N,S$,W$)
40 IF P <> 0 THEN J = J + 1: N = P + 1 : GOTO 30
50 PRINT"THE WORD < THE > APPEARED" J "TIMES."
```

In this program, the variable J counts how many times "THE" has been found in the string S$; P is the position in S$ where a match is found; and N is the starting position of the search in S$.

N starts at 1 (the character position at the beginning of the sentence) and J starts at 0, since we haven't yet counted the THEs. Then, in line 30, we examine the input sentence S$ (which was typed in response to line 10), starting at position N (1 in this case) to see if the word "THE" occurs in the sentence. If a match is found,

String Functions

P will be the position of the match in S$, and P <> 0 will be true, so we increment J (J = J + 1), and set N equal to P + 1; that is, just past the starting position of the match. Then we go back to line 30 to search again. When no more matches are found, P = 0, and control goes to line 50 where the total number of matches is printed.

Finding the Real Word

You have to be careful with comparisons. To see why, try this:

```
RUN
TYPE SENTENCE: THEN SHE GOES "THEIR THEFT WAS THE LAST STRAW"
THE WORD <THE> APPEARED 4 TIMES.
```

You see what happened? BASIC looked only for the characters THE, regardless of whether they were part of another word or not. To help ensure that you find only THE, and not words like THEN, THEIR, or THEFT, you can add an extra space to the word as follows:

```
20 W$="THE ": N=1: J=0
```

Adding a space after THE and before the closing quotation marks should fix it. Why don't you give it a try? (Of course, this won't work if the word is followed by punctuation, such as a comma or period.)

Adding Up Strings

Did you know that BASIC lets you add strings together? It's simple; you just use the plus operator (+), like this:

```
10 A$ = "MADAM"
20 B$ = " I'M ADAM"
30 C$ = A$ + B$
40 PRINT C$
```

We added an extra space in after the first set of quotation marks in line 20 so that this will look better when we add the strings up. When you RUN this tiny little program, here's what you'll see:

```
MADAM I'M ADAM
```

229

Chapter 5

We haven't taken much time to show you this little trick. But it's important that you don't forget it. As your programs grow in power and complexity, you'll want to combine strings in this way. You can save memory and disk space by adding "boilerplate" text to material that changes.

Review Questions

1. What key would you press to make this program print "OUT OF LOOP"?

```
10 A$ = INKEY$: IF A$="" GOTO 10
20 IF A$ = CHR$(13) THEN PRINT "OUT OF LOOP"
```

2. You're writing a high-speed entry routine for a post office. What statement could you use to allow input of two-digit state codes such as CA and AZ? You want the routine to begin processing as soon as the second character is typed.

3. How many times will this little program say it found the word "and" if you type, "She commanded that we band together and read George Sand"?

```
10 LINE INPUT "TYPE SENTENCE: "; S$
20 W$="and":N=10:J=0
30 P=INSTR(N, S$, W$)
40 IF P <> 0 THEN J=J+1: N=P+1: GOTO 30
50 PRINT "The word <and> appeared" J "times."
```

4. The program below is an endless loop. What key must you press to break out of the loop and end the program? (No fair using Ctrl-C or Break!)

```
10 INPUT A$
20 IF ASC(A$) = 88 GOTO 40
30 GOTO 10
40 END
```

5. If the variable A$ = "LOOKOUT", write a program to use LEFT$ and RIGHT$ to print the word OUTLOOK.

6. What statement and argument could you use with CHR$ to produce the following output:

=

7. What statement would you use to find the ASCII value of the first character of the string "Queequeg"?

8. What statement do you think you'd use to send a "form feed" command to a printer? (Hint: It's similar to ringing a bell on the computer.)

9. What is the disadvantage of using INPUT$ for text input?

10. Exercise: Write a program that lets you type in alphabetic characters from the keyboard and that "echos" them on the screen. If you type a number or symbol, don't echo it, but display the message "Alphabetic characters only please." If you type Return, end the program.

Chapter 6

Taking Control with GW-BASIC

Chapter *6*

Taking Control with GW-BASIC

If you've dutifully worked through all the examples up to this point, you should have a good idea of the rudiments of using BASIC. You'll find that most versions of BASIC have nearly all the commands, statements, and functions that you've been putting to work.

What You'll Learn in this Chapter

In this chapter, you'll learn about some additional features of GW-BASIC that might or might not be present in other versions. Some of the more important topics covered in this chapter include

- Mastering the ins and outs of the keyboard
- The special BASIC statement that makes sorting a snap
- Prettying up your printed output
- Using the timer
- Writing your own functions

Prettying Up Your Printed Output

Whether you're writing programs for work or just for fun, the way your output looks is very important because that's the only part of your program that the "outside

Chapter 6

world" ever sees. You may know in your heart that a particular section of program code is elegant, but if the output on the screen or the printed page is sloppy or incomplete, that's how you'll be judged. Besides, clean, well-formatted prompts and output make your programs that much easier to use and to understand.

Earlier in this book you learned how to use commas and semicolons to control what your printed output looks like. But BASIC has other statements ready to help you make your output shipshape. PRINT USING is the one you'll use most often; it lets you format words and numbers just the way you want them. And STRING$ is a function that comes in handy when you want to print long rows of identical characters (to create a border of asterisks, say).

Using the PRINT USING Statement

To see how PRINT USING can help format your output, first remember how BASIC prints a number using PRINT:

```
PRINT 12.3456
 12.3456
Ok
```

Now try the PRINT USING statement on the same number:

```
PRINT USING "##.##"; 12.3456
12.35
Ok
```

See what happened? When you printed the number 12.3456 with the PRINT USING "##.##" statement, it was produced with two numbers before the decimal point, and two numbers after—just like in the "model." Each number sign (#) in the model means "print one digit." The PRINT USING "##.##" statement calls for two numbers, followed by a decimal point and then two more numbers, and that's what is printed.

How Does PRINT USING Affect the Number?

PRINT USING (or any PRINT statement) doesn't affect the actual value of the quantity being printed. So, although you see the number 12.3456 printed as 12.35, your computer is still using the full six-digit value for all calculations. PRINT USING controls how numbers and strings *appear*, but it doesn't affect their actual *value*.

PRINT USING helps you line up decimal points, insert numbers in long columns for readability, and control the number of digits that you see. You can also use this statement to make strings such as names and labels appear the way you want them to.

Here's the general form of the statement:

```
PRINT USING formatting string expression; list of
strings or numeric expressions to be printed[;]
```

The formatting string expression comes right after the words PRINT USING. It contains special characters that tell PRINT USING how to display or print the list of strings or numeric expressions that follow.

Printing Strings with PRINT USING

The string expression that follows the words PRINT USING contains special characters that specify how to print the data. You use certain characters to print strings, and other characters if you want to print numbers. Here are the characters you can include when you're printing strings with PRINT USING:

    !   Print only the first character in the string.
    \ \   Print the same number of characters as there are spaces. (Each backslash also counts as a space.)
    &   Print the string exactly as it is.

Now let's try a few of these PRINT USING formats to help understand them better. You don't even have to write a program to take advantage of PRINT USING. Try this from the keyboard:

```
PRINT USING "!"; "HELLO"
H
Ok
```

In this example, you specified an exclamation point (!) as the formatting expression, which told PRINT USING to print only the first letter of the word "HELLO." Try another one:

```
PRINT USING "\ \"; "HELLO"
HEL
Ok
PRINT USING "\    \";"HELLO"
HELLO
Ok
```

Chapter 6

In this example, you used backslashes. In the first PRINT USING statement, you typed a backslash, then a space, then another backslash; this resulted in the printing of three characters, "HEL." For the second PRINT USING statement, you typed a backslash, then three spaces, then another backslash. And presto, this printed the entire five-character word.

If you want to print an entire string, not just a portion of it, you can use the "and" sign (&), like this:

```
PRINT USING "&"; "HELLO"
HELLO
Ok
```

Printing Numbers with PRINT USING

The string expression that follows PRINT USING can contain a number of special characters that tell how you want the numbers to be printed. Here are the characters you use to format numbers:

#	Print one digit position here.
.	Print the decimal point here.
+	Print a plus or minus sign.
-	At the end of the formatting string expression, this means "print a minus sign at the end of the number."
**	Fill any leading spaces with asterisks.
$$	Print the number with a dollar sign.
,	To the left of the decimal point, this means "add commas to make long numbers easier to read."
^^^^	Print the number in exponential format.
_	Underscore means "print the next character as a literal character."

Now try a few of these formats from the keyboard to see how they work:

```
PRINT USING "##.##"; 12.3456789
12.35
Ok
```

This example illustrates how the pound sign works in PRINT USING. A pound sign represents each digit position that is printed, and if the entire number is not displayed, it's rounded off. (Remember, though, that the number maintains its full value inside the computer.)

```
PRINT USING "##.##"; 1234.5678
%1234.57
Ok
```

PRINT USING won't truncate numbers before the decimal point. The above example shows what happens if you try to force a number into a format that's too small for it. You specified a number with four places before the decimal point, but you put only two pound signs in front of the decimal point in the PRINT USING statement. So, you see all four leading digits, all right, but with a percent sign (%) to indicate that this number didn't fit your format.

```
10 A=1.2345
20 B=-76.543
30 C=45.6789
40 PRINT USING "+##.##   ";A, B, C
50 PRINT USING "##.##+   ";A, B, C

RUN
 +1.23   -76.54   +45.68
  1.23+   76.54-   45.68+
Ok
```

The example illustrates how you can choose to place the sign of a number in front of it or behind it. Notice, too, that rounding off occurs only when the next digit is 5 or greater, so A and B are truncated, but C is rounded off.

What about larger numbers? They're a lot easier to read with PRINT USING.

```
PRINT USING "#########,.##   "; 12345678, 888.888, 987654.321
12,345,678.00         888.89       987,654.32
Ok

PRINT USING "##.##^^^^   "; 123456789, 888.888, 987654.321
 1.23D+08    8.89E+02    9.88D+05
Ok
```

This example shows two ways to make large numbers more readable with PRINT USING. In the first example, a comma right before the decimal point in the format string causes all numbers to be printed with commas separating every third digit. The second example shows how you can use four circumflex characters (^^^^) to cause numbers to be printed in scientific notation.

Remember, all quantities maintain their full accuracy inside the computer, even though you don't see all the digits now. A quantity printed with an "E" for the exponent, such as 8.89E+02, is held internally as a single precision number. Quantities with a D to show the exponent, such as 9.88D+05 and 1.23D+08, are double precision.

Printing Borders with STRING$

If you've ever looked at professional computer printouts, you've probably seen that they're rarely just stark sheets of paper with numbers and letters on them. Good programmers include borders and *headers* containing significant information, and they clearly mark where one section ends and another begins.

One function that can help you print borders is STRING$. The general form of it is as follows:

```
A$ = STRING$(L,C)
```

This means, "make a string that is L characters long, consisting entirely of characters made up of ASCII character C, and put the string in A$." Another form of this function is as follows:

```
A$ = STRING$(L,X$)
```

This means, "make a string that is L characters long, consisting entirely of characters made up of the first character of X$, and put the resulting string into A$."

To see a demonstration of how to use the STRING$ function, run this little program.

```
10 A$=STRING$(51,42)
20 B$=STRING$(17,45)
40 PRINT A$:PRINT A$
50 PRINT B$ "RECORD COLLECTION" B$
60 PRINT A$: PRINT A$
```

Line 10 creates string A$ that consists of the asterisk (ASCII character 42) repeated 51 times. Line 20 creates string B$, which consists of the minus sign

(ASCII 45) repeated 17 times. Put these together with the headline "RECORD COLLECTION," and you come up with this:

Now isn't that easier than printing a row of asterisks or minus signs by laboriously typing out a LET statement? STRING$ makes your printed output look sharp, and it saves you typing time, too.

The Payroll Program

Many businesses use payroll programs that, for each employee, take the number of hours worked each month, multiply it by the hourly rate, and come up with the gross pay amount for that individual. Here is how one such program works:

```
RUN
How many hours did Wilkens Micawber work this month?
? 156.75
How many hours did Agnes Wickfield work this month?
? 179
How many hours did Dora Spenlow work this month?
? 211.3

NAME                    RATE            HOURS           PAY
Wilkens Micawber        12.5            156.75          1959.375
Agnes Wickfield         23.3333         179             4176.661
Dora Spenlow            7.4             211.3           1563.62
Ok
```

This program works—it gives the desired results—but the output isn't very professional-looking, is it? Let's see what we can do to make it more attractive and easier to read.

Chapter 6

We begin by setting up arrays for data.

```
10 REM PAYROLL PROGRAM
20 N=3
30 DIM N$(N), RATE(N), HOURS(N), PAY(N)
```

The current number of employees is set by the number N in line 20. It is an easy matter to change this number as employees are added or "excessed." Line 30 dimensions arrays containing these variables:

N$	Name of employee
RATE	Rate of pay of the employee
HOURS	How many hours the employee worked this month
PAY	The total pay of the employee

Next comes a FOR...NEXT loop to read the data into their arrays. Each time through the loop, the READ statement reads a name and a pay rate, then the user is prompted to enter the number of hours worked by that person. Notice that we put the DATA statements at the end of the program (after the END statement) to make it easy to add or subtract later.

```
40 FOR I= 1 TO N
50     READ N$(I), RATE(I)
60     PRINT "How many hours did "N$(I)" work this month?"
70     INPUT HOURS(I)
80     PAY(I)=HOURS(I)*RATE(I)
90 NEXT
100 PRINT
.
.
.
190 DATA "Wilkens Micawber", 12.50
200 DATA "Agnes Wickfield", 23.3333
210 DATA "Dora Spenlow", 7.40
```

Next we print a list of column headings, followed by the data itself.

```
110 PRINT "NAME"; TAB(20);" RATE"; TAB(40);"HOURS";
    TAB(60);"PAY"
120 FOR I=1 TO N
130     PRINT N$(I); TAB(20);
140     PRINT RATE(I); TAB(40);
```

242

```
150        PRINT HOURS(I); TAB(60)
160        PRINT PAY(I)
170 NEXT
180 END
```

You've seen how the output appears, and, looking at the statements in lines 130-160, you can see why. Let's change these lines so that the display or printed output is a little more palatable:

```
120 FOR I=1 TO N
130        PRINT N$(I); TAB(20)
140        PRINT USING "$$##.##"; RATE(I); :PRINT TAB(40);
150        PRINT USING "###.##"; HOURS(I); :PRINT TAB(60);
160        PRINT USING "**$######,.##"; PAY(I)
170 NEXT
```

Each time through the loop, line 130 prints the employee's name, N$(I), then tabs over to column 20. Line 140 prints the RATE, using the image $$##.##. This image puts a dollar sign before the quantity and displays it to two decimal places. You can't use TAB in PRINT USING, so you have to put a separate PRINT TAB(40) statement here to move to column 40.

Line 150 prints the number of HOURS with three places before and two after the decimal point. Again, the PRINT USING statement is followed by a PRINT TAB(60) statement on the same line to tab over to column 60.

Line 160 prints the PAY using the image **$######,.##, which fills the six-character field before the decimal point with leading asterisks, prints a dollar sign, and puts a comma after every three numbers to make them easier to read.

The output of the revised program looks like this:

```
RUN
How many hours did Wilkens Micawber work this month?
? 156.75
How many hours did Agnes Wickfield work this month?
? 179
How many hours did Dora Spenlow work this month?
? 211.3

NAME                 RATE           HOURS              PAY
Wilkens Micawber     $12.50         156.75        ****$1,959.38
Agnes Wickfield      $23.33         179.00        ****$4,176.66
Dora Spenlow          $7.40         211.30        ****$1,563.62
Ok
```

Chapter 6

That's much better, isn't it? Here's the complete listing for the entire program, after modification:

```
10 REM PAYROLL PROGRAM
20 N=3
30 DIM N$(N), RATE(N), HOURS(N), PAY(N)
40 FOR I= 1 TO N
50     READ N$(I), RATE(I)
60     PRINT "How many hours did "N$(I)" work this month?"
70     INPUT HOURS(I)
80     PAY(I)=HOURS(I)*RATE(I)
90 NEXT
100 PRINT
110 PRINT "NAME"; TAB(20);" RATE"; TAB(40);"HOURS"; TAB(60);"PAY"
120 FOR I=1 TO N
130     PRINT N$(I); TAB(20)
140     PRINT USING "$$##.##"; RATE(I); :PRINT TAB(40);
150     PRINT USING "###.##"; HOURS(I); :PRINT TAB(60);
160     PRINT USING "**$######,.##"; PAY(I)
170 NEXT
180 END
190 DATA "Wilkens Micawber", 12.50
200 DATA "Agnes Wickfield", 23.3333
210 DATA "Dora Spenlow", 7.40
```

Advanced Display Functions

When you start programming for others besides yourself, you have to worry about how things look on the screen or printout. You've already learned how to format numbers with PRINT USING. This chapter includes other BASIC functions to help make your printed output look sharp. SPACE$ and SPC add spaces where you need them, and POS can keep words from being broken at the edge of the screen or printout.

SPACE$—All Spaced Out

SPACE$(N) prints spaces in your output. The general form is

```
SPACE$(N)
```

This means, "Print N spaces on the screen (or printer)."

SPACE$(N) is a string function that produces N spaces. (N is always rounded to an integer.) You can use SPACE$ in a PRINT statement or anywhere else you would use a string variable. If you PRINT SPACE$(5), then 5 spaces will be printed on the screen. N itself can be a numerical variable or even an expression. That is, you can also use either of the following lines to print 5 spaces:

```
10 N = 5 : PRINT SPACE$(N);
10 PRINT SPACE$ (3 + 2);
```

Centering Titles

SPACE$ is useful for formatting output in a variety of situations. The example that follows shows how SPACE$ can be used to center a title in the middle of the screen. Assume that your screen is 80 characters wide. (If it isn't, change the 80 in line 20 to the appropriate value.)

```
10 T$ = "GW-BASIC PRIMER PLUS"
20 N = (80 - LEN(T$))/2
30 PRINT SPACE$(N); T$
```

In line 10 we let T$ represent the title. The title is LEN(T$) characters long, which leaves 80 minus LEN(T$) spaces left over on the line. To center the title, we want half these spaces to precede the title and half to follow it (although we don't need to worry about the ones that follow); so we divide 80 – LEN(T$) by 2. Then we print that many spaces (in line 30), followed by the title itself, and, presto, the title is centered.

Submarine Hunt

Here is a small but exciting game program that uses SPACE$ as the key to its display. It's your chance to test your mettle against the best submarine skippers in the world.

Here's the scenario: You're captain of the *Maguro*, a fast attack submarine equipped with all the latest electronic wizardry. You're playing a cat-and-mouse game with submarines from a rival nation; your job is to intercept them as they leave port and make them turn back.

The rival subs steam out underwater, using one of 10 sectors; you have to guess which one. It's a tough job, searching the miles of trackless ocean for the submerged ships, because you can't see them. However, you're aided by the Subfinder, a sophisticated electronic listening device and computer that tells how far away you are from the rival submarine.

Chapter 6

    As the rival submarine sallies forth, you pilot your ship to one of the 10 sectors using the Subfinder's number keys. Your ship appears on the Subfinder screen as a cross, and if you choose the wrong sector, the Subfinder tells how far away you are. Then you must quickly speed to another sector. When you intercept the rival sub, the Subfinder prints how well you're doing. You have to be quick, though; if you don't intercept it in time, the rival sub will escape and you are severely chastised.

    Let's fire up the Subfinder and try it out:

```
RUN
Press the number key for a sector
0    1    2    3    4    5    6    7    8    9
               +                              (You press 3)
                                              2 sector(s) off.
                                              Adjust and
                                              try again.


          +                                   (You press 2)
                                              1 sector(s)
                                              off.
                                              Adjust and
                                              try again.


     +                                        (You press 1)
     *                                        Interception!
You've intercepted 1 submarine(s)
out of 1 launched.
Press spacebar to continue.
```

    You began by pressing 3 because you guessed the rival sub might be in that sector. The Subfinder calculated you were 2 sectors away from the sub, so you tried sector 2. But your math was wrong, and you were still 1 sector off. Finally, when you tried sector 1, you had an intercept. (The rival sub finally appears as an asterisk.)

```
Press the number key for a sector
0    1    2    3    4    5    6    7    8    9
                         +
                                              1 sector(s)
                                              off.
                                              Adjust and
                                              try again.


                              +
                                              1 sector(s)
                                              off.
```

246

```
                                        Adjust and
                                        try again.

                  +
                                        2 sector(s)
                                        off.
                                        Adjust and
                                        try again.

                                        Too long!
                                        A sub got
                                        through!

You've intercepted 1 submarine(s)
out of 2 launched.
Press spacebar to continue.
```

As, usual, you can press Ctrl-Break to get out of the program. The program listing is below. If too many submarines are getting through, you can change the number 10,000 for J in line 60 to a larger number. If the game is too slow, change 10,000 to a smaller number.

```
10 REM -SUBMARINE HUNT
20 X=INT(RND*(9+1)) :S=S+1: CLS
30 PRINT "Press the number key for a sector"
40 PRINT "0     1     2     3     4     5     6     7     8     9"
50 REM -Start the timing loop
60 FOR J=1 TO 10000
70     A$=INKEY$
80     REM -If no key pressed, go to next
90     IF A$="" GOTO 200
100    REM -If key pressed, print a +
110    A=ASC(A$)-48 : PRINT SPACE$(A*5);"+"
120    REM -If number pressed is same as X
130    IF A=X THEN PRINT SPACE$(X*5); "*"
       TAB(50) "Interception!"
140    IF A=X THEN I=I+1: GOTO 250
150    REM -Number pressed is not x
160    PRINT TAB(50) ABS(A-X) "sector(s)"
170    PRINT TAB(50) "off."
180    PRINT TAB(50) "Adjust and"
190    PRINT TAB(50) "try again.":PRINT
200 NEXT J
```

```
210 REM -No key pressed in time
220 PRINT TAB(50) "Too long!"
230 PRINT TAB(50) "A sub got"
240 PRINT TAB(50) "through!"
250 REM -Print score and do again
260 PRINT "You've intercepted";I;"submarine(s)"
270 PRINT "out of";S;"launched."
280 PRINT "Press spacebar to continue."
290 IF INKEY$=" " THEN GOTO 20 ELSE GOTO 290
```

(Note: If you type this in, be sure to hit the spacebar between the quotation marks in line 290.)

Here's how the Subfinder works: The variable X represents the sector of ocean where the rival submarine is lurking. X is determined by using the random number function, RND, in line 20.

Scaling a Random Number

The random number function, RND, gives you a random number that's between 0 and 1. If you need a random number that's between, say, 0 and 9, you have to *scale* the function. Here's a general way to do it:

```
X=INT(RND*(N+1))
```

This means, "generate a random number that's in the range from 0 to N, and put the result in X."

RND actually gives "pseudo-random" numbers—it generates the same sequence of these so-called "random" numbers each time it's used. To get numbers that are more random, use the RANDOMIZE TIMER statement before RND, like this:

```
100 RANDOMIZE TIMER
110 X=INT(RND*(N+1)
```

Returning to the submarine hunt, the program prompts you to choose a sector and displays numbers for the 10 sectors (each separated by 5 spaces). Then the FOR...NEXT timing loop begins in line 60. The first thing the program does in the loop is to use the INKEY$ function to see whether a key has been pressed on the keyboard. If a key has not been pressed, then A$ equals " " as in line 90, so execution branches directly to the NEXT J statement in line 200. This counts as one pass through the loop, leaving 9,999 passes to go (assuming that the loop variable in line 60 is 10,000). The loop runs again and again; each time through, line 90 checks to see whether there's been an input, and if not, the loop keeps running without doing anything.

While this is all happening very quickly, you ponderously lift your fingers to the keyboard, in your slow human way, and press a number key to guess the sector where the rival submarine may be running. The INKEY$ statement in line 70 recognizes this input and assigns that number to A$.

In line 110, the statement A=ASC(A$) – 48 converts this value from a string character to a number. It uses the ASC function, then subtracts 48 (because in the ASCII code, the *character* zero is represented by ASCII 48, the *character* 1 by ASCII 49, and so on).

Also in line 110, the Subfinder prints a plus sign under the sector number you specified. How? By using the SPACE$ variable to print the number of spaces equal to A times 5, then printing the plus sign following the spaces. If you've guessed correctly and A=X, line 130 uses SPACE$ to print an asterisk, showing that you've intercepted the rival submarine. Also, if you've intercepted a submarine, the counter I (for "intercepted") is increased by one, and execution branches to line 250.

Lines 260-270 show the total number of submarines (S) and the number you've intercepted (I). Finally, line 290 waits for you to press the spacebar; when you do, execution jumps back to line 20 and another submarine is launched.

Incidentally, using a FOR...NEXT loop as the timing loop is a pretty good trick, but it's too dependent on the speed of your computer to make this program "portable" (capable of being used on all different computers). A better way to handle the timing loop is with BASIC's TIMER, which is discussed later in this chapter.

Printing Spaces with SPC

SPC(N) also prints spaces, but it can be used only in a PRINT (or LPRINT) statement. SPC(N) performs much the same function as SPACE$(N): It saves you the time required to type a row of spaces and also shortens your program. The difference is that SPACE$ can be used in such statements as X$ = SPACE$(5), whereas SPC(N) must be used in a PRINT (or LPRINT) statement. In this respect, SPC(N) is like the TAB(N) function; they are both used as formatting aids within the PRINT statement, but can't be assigned to variables.

The general form of SPC is as follows:

```
print statement SPC(N)
```

This means, "print N spaces in this PRINT, LPRINT, or PRINT# statement." Try this:

```
PRINT "WAR"; SPC(3); "AND"; SPC(3); "PEACE"
WAR    AND    PEACE
OK
```

Chapter 6

Keys at Your Command

If you've been using BASIC long, you've discovered the value of the so-called "soft" keys that are displayed at the bottom of BASIC's screen. As you know, each one of the tiny squares on your BASIC screen is tied to one of the function keys on the computer's keyboard. LIST is the display for key F1, RUN for key F2, and so on. You can turn the display on and off with the KEY ON and KEY OFF commands, but the functions of those keys remain unchanged.

Wouldn't it be nice if you could use those function keys for other purposes? (After all, they are *user-definable*. And you're a user!) Well, you can redefine them—or any other key on the keyboard—to type the message or perform the function that you desire. This section tells you how.

Listing Function Keys with KEY LIST

When you see the display of "soft key" functions at the bottom of the BASIC screen, you're actually viewing only a portion of the display for each key. Although you see only the first six characters, each key can in fact "type" up to 15 keystrokes. Use the KEY LIST statement to see the complete message for each key, like this:

```
KEY LIST
  F1    LIST
  F2    RUN<-
  F3    LOAD"
  F4    SAVE"
  F5    CONT<-
  F6    ,"LPT1:"<-
  F7    TRON<-
  F8    TROFF<-
  F9    KEY
  F10   SCREEN 0,0,0<-
Ok
```

Notice that you don't see all these characters on the BASIC key display at the bottom of the screen. You have to use KEY LIST to see them all.

See the little arrow that's printed next to some keys? That means you don't have to press Enter or Return after you press the key. Take RUN, for example. As soon as you press the F2 key on your keyboard, the word RUN is typed on the screen, Enter is also "pressed" automatically, and the computer begins RUNning your program.

Writing Your Own Key Labels with KEY

By now you've discovered that you use some of the user-definable function keys a lot, and others hardly at all. If you want to change the typed message from a key, you can use the KEY statement. The general form is

```
100 KEY N, "string expression"
```

This means, "assign the string expression to user-definable key N." (N, naturally, is a number from 1 to 10.) For instance, maybe you're toggling back and forth between BASIC and DOS a lot, and it's becoming wearisome to have to type S...Y...S...T...E...M each time. You can replace the CONT message for function key 5 with SYSTEM, like this:

```
KEY 5, "SYSTEM"
Ok
```

Now look at the display of keys at the bottom of the BASIC screen. As shown in figure 6-1, key 5 now types the SYSTEM command:

```
1LIST 2RUN← 3LOAD" 4SAVE" 5 SYSTEM 6"LPT1 7TRON← 8TROFF← 9KEY 0SCREEN
```

Fig. 6-1: SYSTEM has replaced CONT in key 5.

You can try it by hitting the F5 key. (You're going to go to the SYSTEM, so make sure you don't have any valuable program information to lose now.)

```
SYSTEM
```

Key F5 typed the command SYSTEM for you, saving you valuable time and keystrokes. To speed things up even more, you can make this key automatic by adding the Enter (that is, the CR or carriage return) at the end of the typed word. You just add the extra key with the plus sign and CHR$, like this:

```
KEY 5, "SYSTEM" + CHR$(13)
Ok
```

Now as soon as you press F5, BASIC returns to the DOS system. You don't have to hit Enter.

Chapter 6

Using a Key within a Program

Commercial software packages such as word processors, spreadsheets, and databases are actually just long programs that run forever, until you tell them to quit. If you've worked with any of these kinds of programs, you know that they make liberal use of the computer's function keys to perform some tasks. They may also have so-called "hotkey" routines, such as pressing the Alt key and the P key for "print," or pressing the down arrow key to jump down to the next paragraph.

Like all good programming languages, GW-BASIC lets you use function keys, cursor control keys, and Alt-key combinations in your programs. (You can even redefine the keyboard, so that, say, pressing the P key always means "print;" but this isn't really recommended. Your goal is to make your programs straightforward and easy to use, not obtuse and difficult.) Two statements, ON KEY and KEY ON, redefine keys in a running program.

Trapping Keys with ON KEY

The ON KEY statement "traps" the press of a key. That is, it registers as soon as a key is pressed, and branches execution. The general form is

```
100 ON KEY (N) GOSUB XXX
```

This means, "watch for a press of key N, and if it's pressed, execute the subroutine beginning with line XXX." After this statement (and if the key is turned on with the KEY ON statement), the program begins looking for a press of key N. As it executes a program, no matter how many lines, BASIC checks after each line to see whether key N has been pressed. When it is pressed, then execution immediately branches from that line, executes the subroutine, and returns to the next line after the subroutine. Figure 6-2 illustrates how key trapping is enabled and executed.

In key trapping, N can be from 1 to 20. Here's what these numbers mean in GW-BASIC. (There may be a few differences in other similar versions such as BASICA.)

N	Key
1-10	User-definable function keys F1 through F10
11	Cursor up (up-arrow key)
12	Cursor left (left-arrow key)
13	Cursor right (right-arrow key)
14	Cursor down (down arrow key)
15-20	Other user-defined keys

Numbers 15 through 20 let you redefine *any* key on the keyboard and use it in your program. More about this in a minute—for now, let's concentrate on the function keys (numbers 1-10) and the cursor keys (11-14). There's one more statement you need before your program will "trap" a function key: It's the KEY(N) statement.

Taking Control with GW-BASIC

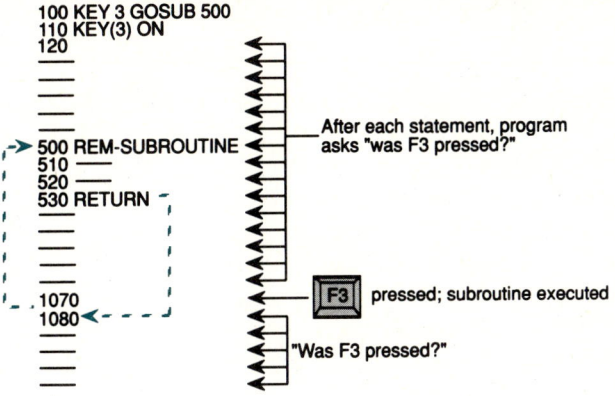

Fig. 6-2: Key trapping.

Controlling Key Trapping with KEY(N)

Once you've used ON KEY to define the key you're going to trap, you need to turn on the key with the KEY(N) statement. In fact, KEY(N) actually controls whether the key is trapped or not. The general form of this statement is as follows:

```
100 KEY(N) ON
500 KEY(N) OFF
700 KEY(N) STOP
```

The KEY(N) ON statement means, "turn on the trapping of this key." The KEY(N) OFF statement means, "turn off trapping of this key."
   The KEY(N) STOP statement means, "remember this key press but don't execute the subroutine in the ON KEY statement now; execute the subroutine as soon as the KEY(N) ON statement is executed again." KEY(N) STOP is a way of trapping key presses but deferring any action on them until later. This can be useful for times when the program shouldn't be interrupted.

A Simple Example of Key Trapping

Time is a fleeting commodity, which is all the more reason why we need to keep track of it. The following program is a simple example of key trapping that uses all the KEY statements you have just learned. It simulates the running of a much longer program, and shows how you can use the F5 key to print the time and date at any moment. Here's the code:

```
10 REM-TIME WHILE RUNNING
20 KEY 5, "Time's wasting"  'Typing aid and message
30 ON KEY (5) GOSUB 90      'Sets up the branch to subroutine
40 KEY (5) ON               'Turns on key F5
50 FOR I=1 TO 20000         'Loop simulates a running program
60 NEXT I
70 PRINT "DONE"
80 END
90 PRINT TIME$ TAB(15) DATE$
100 RETURN
```

Line 30 of this program contains the ON KEY statement. It will look for a press of function key F5, and when this key is pressed, the subroutine beginning with line 90 is executed. This subroutine immediately prints the current time and date on the screen.

Line 40 of the program is the KEY (5) ON statement that "turns on" key F5. Without this statement, the program won't detect the pressing of F5. Line 20 changes the normal display of F5's function to "Time's wasting"; if we didn't include this, the user would still see CONT as the display for this function key, and might forget which key to press to generate the time and date.

Here's the output from the program:

```
RUN
19:59:58    05-24-1990   (F5 pressed)
20:00:00    05-24-1990   (F5 pressed)
DONE
Ok
```

You can trap the cursor keys the same way. Trapping the four cursor keys is important in all types of programs, but especially in graphics and game software.

Trapping Exotic Key Combinations

If you've been following along, you now understand how to make those function keys and cursor keys usable in your programs. But what about the rest of the keyboard? Suppose that you want to sound a beep every time you hit the B key, or you want to prevent the user from halting a program with Ctrl-Break?

Remember that in the KEY(N) and ON KEY(N) statements, you could use an N of 1 through 10 for the function keys F1 through F10; and you could use an N of 11-14 for the cursor keys. The GW-BASIC language lets you use an N of 15 through 20 to trap any six keys or combinations of keys. But you need to supply some additional information, including the key's *scan code*. You also need the *keycode* if the key is preceded by Alt or Ctrl, or if it's a shifted key. Here's a general form showing how you set up the trap:

```
100 KEY(N), CHR$(K) + CHR$(S)
110 ON KEY(N) GOSUB XXX
120 KEY(N) ON
```

Line 100 means, "find the key referred to by scan code S (using the keycode K for a latched or extended key if necessary) and call it N." (A "latched" key is one that's pressed in conjunction with one of these other keys: Caps Lock, Alt, Ctrl, Left Shift, or Right Shift. *Extended* keys include the center set of cursor control keys on the IBM extended keyboard.) Line 110 means, "if key N is on and pressed, go execute subroutine XXX." And line 120 means, "trap key N if it's pressed."

The value for S is the *scan code*, a number that tells the computer hardware which key is being pressed. Although similar, scan codes differ from the ASCII codes for the keys. (Thus the ASCII code for a lowercase b is decimal 98, whereas the scan code for the b key is hexadecimal 30, or decimal 48.) There are at least two lists of scan codes you can use: a list of 84 keys for the old IBM PC/XT, and a newer list of 101 keys for the IBM enhanced keyboard. You'll find the newer list in Appendix C.

The value for K is the *keycode* that is needed to trap "latched" keys, such as those pressed in conjunction with Alt and Caps Lock. You need the decimal value because you're using CHR$. Here are the codes you'll use:

Latched Key	Keycode
Normal	0
Right shift	1
Left shift	2
CTRL n	4
ALT	8
NUM LOCK	32
CAPS LOCK	64
EXTENDED	128

Chapter 6

Here are a couple of examples of latched keys:

```
CHR$(0)  + CHR$(48)    "B" key
CHR$(4)  + CHR$(48)    "CTRL B" (keys pressed together)
CHR$(64) + CHR$(48)    "CAPS LOCK B"
```

Here's a short program that shows how you can make the b key beep every time it's pressed:

```
10 KEY 18, CHR$(0) + CHR$(48)
20 ON KEY (18) GOSUB 100
30 KEY (18) ON
40 WHILE INKEY$ <> " ": WEND
50 PRINT "DONE"
60 END
100 BEEP
110 PRINT "BEEPING"
120 RETURN
```

(Note: If you enter and run this program, type the spacebar key between the quotation marks in line 40. Also, if your keyboard's scan codes are different from those of the standard IBM 101-key keyboard, you will have to change the value of CHR$(48) in line 10. Make sure NUMLOCK, CAPS LOCK, etc., are off.)

Output from the program is shown below. Notice that the b key doesn't appear on the screen when you press it. You see only the message, "BEEPING."

```
RUN
BEEPING            (You press the "b" key)
BEEPING            (You press it again)
```

Here's how the program works: Line 10 specifies that you're assigning a lower-case b to something called key 18. (There's no real key 18 on the keyboard; this is just a number used by you and BASIC to refer to the b key, in this case.) Because it's to be lowercase, you follow KEY 18 with a keycode of 0—that is, CHR$(0). And because the scan code for the b key is hexadecimal 30 (decimal 48), you follow that with "+ CHR$(48)".

Once you've defined key 18, you use line 20 to tell BASIC what to do if a lowercase b is pressed: Go off and execute the "beep" subroutine beginning at line 100. Line 30 turns this key on, so that BASIC will trap the lowercase b if you press it. Line 40 is just an endless loop (it simulates a giant program that runs and runs and runs), which you can exit by pressing the spacebar key.

When you RUN this program, every time you press a lowercase b you'll hear a beep, and see the word "BEEPING." Try it with Caps Lock on and off, and try it while pressing the right and left shift keys at the same time you press the b.

Other Vital BASIC Features

This section shows you some additional BASIC statements and functions that increase your control and make your output more professional-looking.

Time to the Nearest Nanosecond with TIMER

The TIMER function in GW-BASIC gives you the number of seconds that have elapsed since the last system reset or since midnight. The general form of this function is the following:

```
100 T = TIMER
```

This means, "calculate the number of seconds since midnight and put that number in variable T." The number is a single-precision value; fractions of seconds are shown to the best possible accuracy.

So what good is knowing the number of seconds since midnight? The value of TIMER lies not in making a single measurement, but in making two. For instance, here's how you can use TIMER to see how long a loop takes:

```
10 T1 = TIMER
20 FOR I= 1 TO 10000: NEXT I
30 T2 = TIMER
40 PRINT T2-T1

RUN
 1.160156
```

Now do you see how to use TIMER like a lightning-fast stopwatch? In line 10, you "start" the stopwatch by setting T1=TIMER. Then you do some task; here, it's executing the loop in line 20. In line 30 you "stop" the stopwatch by setting T2=TIMER. Finally you subtract T1 from T2, and presto, you can print the number of seconds it took for the loop to run.

Another way to use the TIMER is to set the time for loops. Remember the Subfinder program? You could change the timing loop to a WHILE...WEND loop and use the TIMER to specify the exact number of seconds, like this:

```
55 T1 = TIMER
56 T2 = T1 + S
60 WHILE TIMER < T2
 .
 .
 .
200 WEND
```

Chapter 6

The number S is the number of seconds you want to allow the user to run the Subfinder.

Reflex Tester

Here's an example program that uses the TIMER function to test how good your reflexes are. When you RUN the program, as soon as you see the word "GO!", press the Enter key. You get five trials, and at the end, your reflex times are averaged. Here's what the output looks like:

```
RUN
This program tests your reflexes.
There are five tests.
Hit the [ENTER] key each time you see the word GO

GO!
GO!
GO!
GO!
GO!
Test 1 was .3320313 seconds
Test 2 was .4375 seconds
Test 3 was .390625 seconds
Test 4 was .390625 seconds
Test 5 was .328125 seconds
Your average reflex time was .3757813 seconds
```

Here is the code for the program, in case you want to type it and try it:

```
10 REM -REFLEX TESTER
20 PRINT "This program tests your reflexes."
30 PRINT "There are five tests."
40 PRINT "Hit the [ENTER] key each time you see the word GO"
50 PRINT
60 FOR I=1 TO 5
70      RANDOMIZE TIMER
80      OFFSET=INT(RND*(10000+1))
90      FOR J=1 TO 10000+OFFSET: NEXT J
95      CLS
100     T1=TIMER
110     PRINT "GO!"
120     WHILE INKEY$<>CHR$(13):WEND
```

```
130     T2=TIMER
140     RT(I)=T2-T1
150 CLS
160 NEXT
170 FOR I=1 TO 5
180     PRINT "Test";I;"was";RT(I);"seconds
190     TOTAL=TOTAL+RT(I)
200 NEXT
210 AVERAGE=TOTAL/5
220 PRINT "Your average reflex time was";AVERAGE;"seconds"
230 END
```

The heart of the program is a FOR...NEXT loop that executes five times. Each time through the loop, line 70 performs a RANDOMIZE TIMER function that sets a random "seed" for the RND function in the next line. (Without a random seed, RND simply repeats the same sequence of so-called "random" numbers over and over.) The RND function in line 80 provides a random offset between 0 and 10,000. This number is added to the number 10,000, which is the limit of the loop in line 90.

Line 90 contains a complete FOR...NEXT loop of its own. This is really a "random-delay" loop that gives a varying time between "GO!" signals, so that you can't anticipate when the next "GO!" is going to occur.

Lines 100-130 are the "stopwatch." Line 100 records the TIMER, then the display flashes "GO!" and line 120 waits until you press the Enter key, signified by CHR$(13) in this statement. When your sluggish finger finally manages to hit Enter, execution continues to line 130, where the new time is recorded in T2.

The array variable RT holds the reflex times for each iteration of the loop. Five times are recorded: RT(1), RT(2), RT(3), RT(4), and RT(5). The FOR...NEXT loop in lines 170-200 prints out these times and adds them together for the TOTAL time. Then the AVERAGE=TOTAL/5 statement in line 210 computes your average time, and you see how well—or how poorly—you did.

Trapping the TIMER

You can "trap" the timer, using the TIMER ON and ON TIMER statements, just as you trapped key presses with KEY ON and ON KEY. The general form of ON TIMER is

```
100 ON TIMER (S) GOSUB NNN
```

This means, "when the timer reaches S seconds after the TIMER ON statement, execute subroutine NNN; then reset the timer and start again."

Chapter 6

Here's a program that shows how to trap the timer. You choose an interval—it could be every hour or every 10 seconds. Then, as the program runs, at that interval it beeps, prints a message, and seems to suspend execution for a few seconds.

```
10 PRINT "Enter the interval at which you want things to happen"
20 INPUT "HOURS"; H
30 INPUT "MINUTES"; M
40 INPUT "SECONDS"; S
50 INTERVAL=H*3600 + M*60 + S
60 ON TIMER (INTERVAL) GOSUB 190
70 PRINT: PRINT "Press any key to start timer"
80 WHILE INKEY$ = ""
90      TIMER ON
100 WEND
110 '
120 REM-Simulate actual running program
130 WHILE INKEY$ = ""
140     PRINT: PRINT "This simulates a running program..."
150     PRINT "Press any key to exit."
160 WEND
170 END
180 '
190 REM-Timer indicator subroutine
200 REM-In this section put whatever you want to happen
210 REM-every INTERVAL seconds.
220 REM-For instance, a beep and a message...
230 '
240 BEEP
250 PRINT "Hi, sailor!"
260 '
270 REM-Loop waits for S seconds before returning
280 S=5
290 START=TIMER
300 WHILE TIMER < START + S
310 WEND
320 RETURN
```

You input an interval as hours, minutes, and seconds, and the program converts these all to seconds, adds them up, and assigns the value to the variable INTERVAL. Then a WHILE...WEND loop waits for you to start the timer by pressing any key.

Once the timer is running, the actual program begins. Here, the WHILE...WEND loop in lines 130-160 simulates a much larger program, like a word processor, spreadsheet, game, or anything else. As it runs, the timer silently ticks away in the background.

260

Every time INTERVAL is reached, the program branches to the subroutine that begins with line 190. There's a beep, a message (you may want to pick something other than "Hi sailor!"), and then a timed wait loop consisting of yet another WHILE...WEND structure.

The wait loop uses the TIMER differently than ON TIMER. Here we set one time for `START`, then count up to `S` seconds. The timer increases in 1-second increments, so the first hundred or so times through the WHILE...WEND loop, the value `START + S` is 5 seconds greater than that of TIMER. The next few hundred times through the loop, the TIMER has incremented, so `START + S` is only 4 seconds greater than TIMER. When the TIMER finally goes past `START + S`, that's when execution falls out of the WHILE...WEND loop and can return to the calling program. Here's a RUN of the program:

```
RUN

Enter the interval at which you want things to happen
HOURS? 0
MINUTES? 0
SECONDS? 10

Press any key to start timer

This simulates a running program...
Press any key to exit.

This simulates a running program...
Press any key to exit.

(Beep!)

Hi, sailor!

(Program waits 5 seconds before continuing)

This simulates a running program...
Press any key to exit.

This simulates a running program...
Press any key to exit.
```

You specified an interval of 10 seconds. So, every 10 seconds, execution branches to line 190, beeps and prints a message, then waits 5 seconds before returning. This continues as long as your main program is running.

Notice that if the wait loop starts just before midnight, you'll have problems. Suppose you started the wait loop at 23:59:57, that is, 3 seconds before midnight. Now, there are 86,400 seconds in a day, so that means START + S = 86,397 + 5 = 86,402. The TIMER can count up to only 86,400, so it will never be greater than START + S—and that means a big, fat endless loop!

Minding Memory with FRE

The command FRE(0) shows how much memory space remains unused by the program currently in memory. This is useful if you want to know how much memory your computer has before you start to write your program, and will also let you figure out how large your program is.

The general form of the FRE function is

```
100 X = FRE(0)
```

This means, "find out how many bytes of free memory remain in the computer, and put that number in X."

For instance, if you have a program named "BIGPROG," the following sequence of commands will tell you how long the program is

```
NEW
PRINT FRE(0)
 60225
LOAD"BIGPROG"
Ok
PRINT FRE(0)
 11105
```

Now you know that BIGPROG must be 49,120 bytes long, because with no program in memory there are 60,225 bytes of free space, and after you load BIGPROG there are only 11,105 bytes left. The difference, 60,225 less 11,105, is the size of the program.

Actually, a program will use some more bytes, for storing variables, when you RUN it. So, just because a program fits in memory when you first load it, that doesn't necessarily mean that it will fit when you start to run it. Also, if you reserve space for strings, this will be subtracted from the available memory.

Using DELETE

You can use DELETE to remove specific lines from your program. We have learned already that you can eliminate any line in a program by simply typing the line number and following it with a carriage return. DELETE allows us to eliminate several successive lines at one time. The most general form of DELETE is as follows:

```
DELETE beginning line number-ending line number
```

This form of DELETE will make the computer eliminate all lines from the specified beginning line number to the specified line number. You can also type

```
DELETE-line number
```

This will delete all lines of the current program, from the beginning line of the program to the specified line number. Be careful when using DELETE so that you do not accidentally delete your entire program.

You can use DELETE right in a program, and this is one way to keep your programs from growing larger than available memory. As a program executes, it can delete lines it no longer needs, as in this example:

```
10 PRINT "This little program stays lean and mean"
20 PRINT "Its first few lines soon leave the scene"
30 DELETE 10-20
40 END
```

When you RUN this program, then LIST it, here's what you'll see:

```
RUN
This little program stays lean and mean
Its first few lines soon leave the scene
Ok
LIST
30 DELETE 10-20
40 END
Ok
```

Lines 10 and 20 are present when you start the program, and they are executed normally. Then, their work done, they are rudely deleted and shipped off into number-crunching never-never land. The result is a smaller, more concise program.

DELETE, when used this way, is helpful if you have a program with a large array. A program can DELETE earlier program lines that you don't need to use again, then dimension and fill that memory-hogging array.

Chapter 6

Finding the Cursor with POS

Whatever you PRINT on the screen or INPUT from the user will be written starting at the screen location where the cursor is positioned. POS (position) detects the cursor position, and can be useful for making sure that input and output on the screen looks the way you want it to.

The general form is as follows:

```
X = POS(N)
```

This means, "find the current position of the cursor along the horizontal line and put that number in X." POS returns a number between 1 and whatever the width of your display screen is. This number tells you how many characters along the current line the cursor is positioned. (It gives no information on the vertical position of the cursor—that is, which line the cursor is on.) The N in parentheses after the POS is a "dummy" argument: It doesn't matter what number you put there.

Suppose, for example, that your program is PRINTing a list of numbers of different sizes from an array A: numbers like 403,629; 7.4; 0.000043; and so on. We want to PRINT as many of these numbers as we can on the same line, but when we get to the end of the line we don't want the number to be split, with half the number on one line and half on the next line. Because the PRINT statement doesn't care whether it splits a number this way, we'll use the POS function to make sure that every number is printed with all its digits on the same line.

Let's assume that none of the numbers will have more than 8 characters, including the decimal point, and that we will separate each pair of numbers with a space. Also, we'll suppose that we start off with 50 numbers in our array A, and that the screen is 80 characters wide. (Program lines 1 and 2 put the simulated data in array A.)

```
1   DIM A(50)
2   FOR I = 1 to 50: A(I) = I^4:
    NEXT I 'Simulates data in array A
10  FOR J = 1 TO 50
20  PRINT A(J);
30  PRINT " ";
40  IF POS(0) > 71 THEN PRINT
50  NEXT J
```

For each of the 50 numbers we are going to print, first we print the number and then a space in lines 20 and 30. By ending both these PRINT statements with semicolons, we keep our output on the same line. Because the 8 characters of the number, plus 1 for the space in between, makes 9, we want to make sure that we are no closer than 9 characters to the edge of the screen when we print each number. This will ensure that there's room to print the number without splitting it at the edge of the screen. (This is called *wraparound*.)

We do this in line 40, which asks whether POS(0) (the cursor position) is greater than 71 (because 80 minus 9 equals 71). If it is, we execute a PRINT statement, which has the effect of causing a linefeed—that is, moving the cursor down to the next line. If POS(0) is not greater than 71, we simply continue to print the next number on the same line. The loop continues on in this way until all 50 numbers have been printed.

Adding to BASIC's Vocabulary with DEF FN

Functions are an important part of BASIC. They're one of the things that make it easy to use—you don't have to compute the sine of an angle or the square root of a number because "canned" functions are present to handle these tasks for you.

What if you need a function and BASIC doesn't have it? You can write your own! The DEF FN statement lets you add functions to the BASIC language. The general form is

```
100 DEF FN N(A,B) = expression
```

This means, "define the function N, with the arguments A, B, as the *expression*." An example of a function is something like this:

```
DEF FN CUBE (A) = (A*A*A)
```

This BASIC statement means that we're defining the function CUBE to be the cube of A (that is, A times A times A, or A ^ 3). Instead of CUBE you can use any name, limited only by your own imagination and the restrictions on BASIC variable names.

In the FN CUBE function, A is the "argument." The DEF FN statement shows what will happen to that argument—that is, to whatever is in that "A" position when you actually use the function later.

Once you've defined a function like CUBE somewhere near the beginning of your program, you can use it any time you want, just the way you use SIN and SQR. To use the function, you write a statement like this:

```
C = FN CUBE (43)
```

This statement takes the number 43 and performs the operation you specified in the earlier DEF FN statement. So in this case, that means C will receive the value of 43*43*43. Or you can use another variable for the argument, like this:

```
Y = FN CUBE (X)
```

Chapter 6

Here the variable Y will receive the value X*X*X. Here's a RUN of a program that defines the CUBE function, then uses it in a couple of different ways:

```
10 DEF FN CUBE = A*A*A
20 PRINT FN CUBE (43)       'Using the CUBE function
30 M=5
40 N = FN CUBE (M)          'Using it again
50 PRINT N

RUN
 79507
 125
```

Figure 6-3 shows how to define and use a function. Notice that even though you define the function using A, when you use the function you can substitute any value in that position. The argument A in the definition is what's called a *formal parameter* that tells the function what kind of data to accept. The actual arguments you supply when you use the function (remember, you supplied 43 in line 20, and M in line 40) are the *actual parameters*.

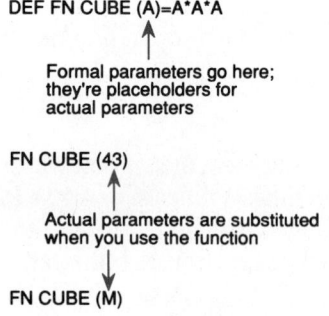

Fig. 6-3:   Defining and using a function.

The formal parameters are used only in the definition. They make it clear what kind of arguments are going to be used, and how the function will act on them, but they're not used at all outside the definition. In fact, if you use A somewhere else in your program as a regular variable, and then execute a DEF FN statement that uses A, the value you originally assigned to A won't be changed.

Exchanging Contents Using SWAP

How would you exchange the values of two variables—say, A and B? One way would be to create a temporary variable, T, to hold the value of A, copy B into A, then copy T into B. Sort of like this:

```
10 A = 10
20 B= 5
30 T = A
40 A = B
50 B = T
```

With BASIC, you don't have to go through these machinations, though. One of the most useful of GW-BASIC's statements is SWAP, which exchanges the values of two variables. The general form is as follows:

```
100 SWAP A, B
```

or

```
200 SWAP A$, B$
```

This means, "exchange the values of variables A and B (or A$ and B$)." Let's give it a try:

```
10 A$="Hello"
20 B$="Goodbye"
30 PRINT A$, B$
40 SWAP A$,B$
50 PRINT A$,B$
```

Knowing what you do about SWAP, can you predict the output of this program? See if you were correct:

```
RUN
Hello         Goodbye
Goodbye       Hello
Ok
```

Line 30 and line 50 both contain the same statement: PRINT A$, B$. But in between these two lines, the contents of variables A$ and B$ are exchanged by means of the SWAP statement in line 40. A$ originally contains "Hello," whereas "Goodbye" is in B$. After the SWAP, variable A$ contains "Goodbye" and B$ has "Hello."

Chapter 6

The Bubble Sort

If you've ever organized your records or recipes, or even if you've ever been to the library, you're familiar with sorting. You can sort items according to number, name, category, color, style, or a host of other indicators. Computers can sort, too, and they can do it much more quickly than humans. In fact, one of the most common computer tasks is sorting long lists of data or numbers.

You can find many ways to accomplish a computer sort, but one of the easiest to understand is the *bubble* sort. Picture a list of names, for example. In an alphabetical bubble sort, each name is compared to the one above it; if the lower name is actually closer to the front of the alphabet, the two names exchange places. Thus the name "Aardvark, Anthony A." isn't boosted to the top of the list all at once—instead, it "bubbles" gradually to the top, as it continues to replace the name above it.

Here is a routine that performs a simple bubble sort. We've used only three names to make it easy to follow, but the same principles apply if you're sorting a dictionary of 50,000 words.

```
10 REM BUBBLE SORT
20 OPTION BASE 1
30 N=3   'Number of names to sort
40 DIM A$(N)
50 GOSUB 1000 'Read in names
60 GOSUB 2000 'Sort names
70 GOSUB 3000 'Print names
80 END
1000 'Subroutine to read in names
1010 FOR I=1 TO N
1020    READ A$(I)
1030 NEXT
1040 RETURN
2000 '-Subroutine to sort names
2010 FOR I=1 TO N-1
2020    FOR J=I+1 TO N
2030        IF A$(I) > A$(J) THEN SWAP A$(I), A$(J)
2040    NEXT J
2050 NEXT I
2060 RETURN
3000 '-Subroutine to print names
3010 FOR I=1 TO N
3020    PRINT A$(I)
3030 NEXT I
3040 RETURN
4000 DATA "Gradgrind", "Sparsit", "Bounderby"
```

When you RUN this little program, you get

```
RUN
Bounderby
Gradgrind
Sparsit
Ok
```

Here's how it works: The number of names to sort is set to 3 in line 30. (You could just as easily set this to 3,000; or you could have N set by the actual number of names entered by a user.) Then the array A$ is dimensioned in line 40. The main part of the program is simple enough—it branches first to a subroutine to read in the names, next to a subroutine to sort them, and finally to a third subroutine that prints the names.

Names are read into array A$ by a simple FOR...NEXT loop in lines 1010-1030 that READs the data from line 4000. (As usual, we put the DATA statements at the end of the program to make it easy to modify or add data.) Then the program calls the sorting subroutine that begins with line 2000, and the real work begins.

The sorting routine consists of two FOR...NEXT loops, one "nested" inside the other. Let's see how they operate using the three names in A$. The first time through both loops, the names are in A$ just the way they were read in:

```
A$
(1) Gradgrind
(2) Sparsit
(3) Bounderby
```

The loop counters are set like this:

```
I    1
J    2
```

So, line 2030 asks the question, "Is A$(1) greater than A$(2)?" In the ASCII table, Gradgrind (capital G) is not greater than Sparsit (capital S), so the two names are not SWAPped. The next time through the J loop, the counters are set like this:

```
I    1
J    3
```

Now the comparison is, "Is A$(1) greater than A$(3)? Gradgrind is greater than Bounderby, so this time the names are SWAPped, resulting in

```
A$(1)       Bounderby
A$(2)       Sparsit
A$(3)       Gradgrind
```

That's it! The names are now sorted correctly. If there were more names, or if they were in a different order, the sort might take a little longer. But the principles are the same for all bubble sorts.

Review Questions

1. Write a PRINT USING statement that will result in the data being formatted as shown:

```
10 DATA 21.40, 79.995, 316, 5690.3, 3.8099
20 READ A, B, C, D, E
30 (Your PRINT USING statement here...)

RUN
*****$21.40*****$80.00****$316.00***$5,690.30******$3.81
```

2. What will the output of the following program be?

```
10 FOR I=10 TO 200 STEP 10
20    PRINT SPACE$(SQR(I)); "*"
30 NEXT I
```

3. Which key would you press to execute the BEEP subroutine?

```
200 ON KEY (12) GOSUB 1000
210 KEY (12) ON
---
1000 BEEP: RETURN
```

4. With the following section of code, which key on the keyboard will cause the message "Branch to hotkey" to be printed?

```
10 KEY 16, CHR$(8) + CHR$(35)
20 ON KEY (16) GOSUB 100
30 KEY (16) ON
40 WHILE INKEY$ <> " ": WEND
50 PRINT "DONE"
60 END
100 PRINT "Branch to hotkey"
110 RETURN
```

5. What statement would you use to change the function key F10 so that it types the command RENUM, then executes that command without requiring you to press Enter?

6. You type PRINT TIMER and see the display 25200. What time is it?

7. What command could you use to remove the FOR...NEXT loop from this program?

```
10 REM-TIMING LOOP
20 FOR I= 1 TO 1000000
30   PRINT "I'M COUNTING UP"; I
40 NEXT I
50 PRINT "THE TIMING LOOP IS FINISHED"
60 PRINT "CONTINUING WITH THE PROGRAM"
70 PRINT "STOPPING THE PROGRAM"
80 END
```

8. To convert degrees Fahrenheit to Celsius, we use the formula $C=5/9(F-32)$. Write a function that takes temperature in degrees Fahrenheit and converts it to degrees Celsius. Call the function "FTOC." Use the function to find the Celsius equivalent of 40 degrees Fahrenheit.

9. What statement do you use to print strings of identical characters?

10. Exercise: Write a program that will produce a series of random integers from 1 to 10, then use SWAP to sort them in ascending order.

Chapter 7

Input and Output to Files and Devices

Chapter **7**

Input and Output to Files and Devices

Up to this point, your routines and programs have received their input from either the keyboard, from DATA, or from implied LET statements inside the program itself. You've seen data output on the screen, but there's been no way to store data for future use, or to get data that's been stored. For many kinds of programs—and especially databases, spreadsheets, and word processors—having data in a program is not enough. They have to be able to go out and store that data, and retrieve it later when necessary, because it's being updated continually. And there are other reasons besides data storage to go beyond the bounds of the BASIC program.

In this chapter, you're going to learn to use peripheral devices—or, simply, *peripherals*. Peripherals are anything that's not part of the computer's central processing unit (CPU) or main memory.

The most common peripheral—one that's in all computers except those designed for use as terminals—is a disk drive. There are peripherals to which you send data, such as a printer or a plotter, and there are others that provide BASIC with data, such as a light pen, mouse, joystick, or trackball. You can even exchange data with other computers using a modem (MODulator-DEModulator, used for communications) and the computer's serial port. You might attach a separate floppy or hard disk drive, too. Figure 7-1 shows some of the peripherals you can control using BASIC.

Chapter 7

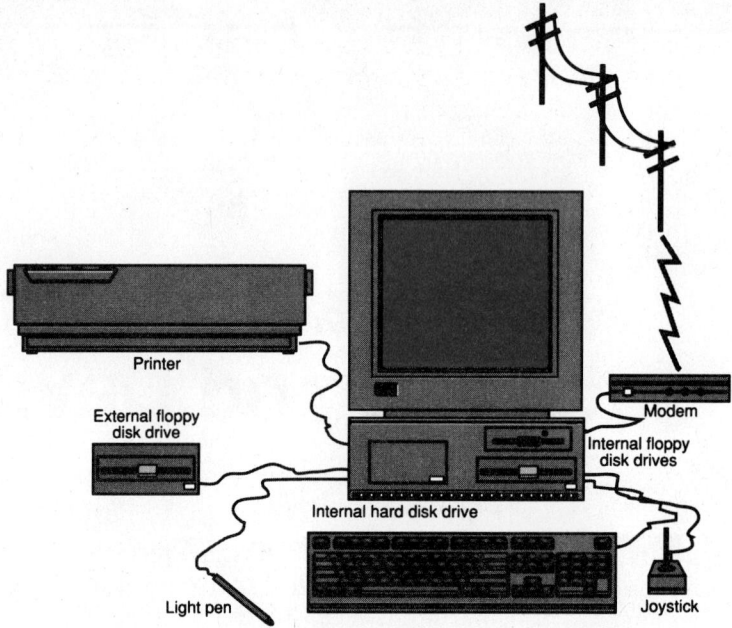

Fig. 7-1: Peripherals enhance the power of BASIC.

What You'll Learn in this Chapter

In this chapter you'll learn:

- How to output to the printer instead of the screen
- How to save your data in files, and how to retrieve it
- How to get other devices, such as a light pen or joystick, to "talk"

Getting Hardcopy Output from Your Printer

If you have a printer connected to your computer, you might think BASIC is trying to bollix you up. After all, the PRINT command doesn't have anything to do with the printer, does it? Instead, PRINT just "prints" on the monitor screen.

So what are you to do when you want a hard copy of your program listing to send to your mother? Or if you need to print expense data as proof for the tax man?

Input and Output to Files and Devices

If you have a printer connected to your computer, you can use it in much the same way you use your video screen—to print the output of your programs, and to list them. The printer has the advantage of creating a permanent record, but it is much slower than the video screen.

The statements you use to output information to the printer are very similar to those used with the video screen. These statements are LLIST, which is similar to LIST, LPRINT, which is similar to PRINT, and LPRINT USING, which is similar to PRINT USING.

Using the LLIST Command

The LLIST command will cause your program to be listed on the printer. If you try to execute this statement when you don't have a printer, or when the printer isn't ready to receive data (perhaps because it's not turned on), you may get an error message, or your computer might "hang up"—that is, go into an endless loop until you reset it. All variations in the ways to use LIST apply also to LLIST. For example, the following statements are all valid:

```
LLIST 10           List on the printer only line 10
LLIST 50-100       List on the printer lines 50 to 100
LLIST 1000-        List on the printer all the lines following 1000
LLIST -500         List on the printer all the lines up to 500
```

With certain combinations of computers and printers, a problem can arise when a program line to be listed is longer than the number of characters the printer can print. Sometimes the printer will come to the end of the line and keep typing the same place, without going on to the next line. Also, sometimes the printer will go back to the beginning of the same line and type over it, again and again. These and similar problems can be caused by "misunderstandings" between the computer and the printer. (For instance, the computer might assume that the printer will always execute a line feed every time it sends a carriage return, whereas the printer assumes that if the computer wants a carriage return, it will send one.) Sometimes the problems can be solved by resetting switches in the printer. You can look in your printer manual for an explanation of the various switch settings. Before you change any settings, however, you should make a note of the existing switch positions so that you can restore them later if necessary.

If Your Printer Won't Print...

Before you read this, try to LLIST a short program on your printer. If the printer produces the listing, then you can skip this little section. If you have problems, read on.

Chapter 7

Using a Laser Printer?

Laser printers take in all the data for one page at a time, then wait for a special "form feed" character to tell them to print the page. GW-BASIC doesn't automatically send a form feed signal to the printer when it's done sending information. So, if your listing or output is less than a page, the printer won't print it. In this case, use your printer's ON LINE and FORM FEED keys to generate the page, like this:

1. Press the printer's ON LINE button to take the printer off line.
2. Press the printer's FORM FEED button to print the page.
3. Press ON LINE again to put the printer back on line.

You can also put a statement in your program that sends a form feed to the printer; this statement is CHR$(12).

Printing to a Serial Port

When your computer "wakes up" in the DOS operating system (before you type GWBASIC or another command to load BASIC), it sets up the driver for the print device PRN. (PRN is usually the first parallel printer on your computer.) The commands and statements in GW-BASIC that print to the printer (such as LLIST) actually "print" to this reserved name in DOS.

There's usually no problem if your printer is connected to the first parallel port, LPT1. If, however, your printer is connected to a different parallel port, or to a serial port such as COM1 or COM2, you'll need a statement to redirect output. If you're trying without success to print to a computer connected to a serial port or to a parallel port other than LPT1, you might need to insert a redirection statement in your computer's AUTOEXEC.BAT file. You can try redirection in DOS from the keyboard like this:

1. From GW-BASIC, type SYSTEM to get the DOS prompt.
2. Type a MODE command to set up the printer. For example,

```
C> MODE COM1: 9600, N, 8, 1, P
```

This is only an example. It means

- 9600 bits per second data rate
- No parity
- 8 data bits

- 1 stop bit
- "P" makes the serial port the system printer port

    Look at your printer manual and the switches on the printer to help you set up the correct MODE command. (Be sure to record the current switch settings before you change them, though!)

3. Then type a MODE command to redirect LPT1 to that COM port. For example,

```
C> MODE LPT1: = COM1:
```

If this works, then you can insert these commands in the AUTOEXEC.BAT file. For more details, see your MS-DOS manuals or another reference, such as *The Waite Group's MS-DOS Bible*.

LPRINT and LPRINT USING

LPRINT is used in exactly the same way that PRINT is, and you can do all the things with LPRINT that you have already learned with PRINT. LPRINT will send your output to the printer in just the same way PRINT sends it to the screen.

For example, the following statements are all valid.

```
LPRINT 2 + 2
LPRINT A$, B, C$, D
LPRINT TAB(10); B$
LPRINT "ENTER YOUR NAME";
```

Similarly, you can replace PRINT USING with LPRINT USING statements to see formatted output from a printer instead of on the screen.

One of the main differences between LPRINT and PRINT is that the number of characters you can put on a single line is sometimes longer on a printer than it is on the video screen. You will have to keep this in mind if you want your output to the line printer to be formatted in a particular way. Another difference is that on many printers a line will not be printed until it is full (that is, if you have an 80-column printer, nothing will be printed until 80 characters have been sent), or until a line feed has been sent to the printer. This means that if you execute a statement such as the following:

```
LPRINT"HELLO, THERE.";
```

it will not be printed right away. To make the printer generate it, you will have to send enough text to fill up the line on the printer, or else execute another LPRINT statement (without a semicolon) to cause a carriage return.

Chapter 7

A Word About Files

When people talk about computer memory, they're usually speaking of the memory that's in the computer itself. As you have probably discovered by now, the contents of this memory are "volatile." They're lost when you turn the computer off. That's why you have to load BASIC and type a program each time you turn the computer back on. And that's why there are storage devices such as floppy disks and hard disks.

Disks are how you save valuable information. When you store information on a disk—and that includes the hard disk, if you have one inside your computer—the information stays there, pure and inviolate, even if you turn off the power. In the case of a floppy drive, you can even remove the disk and put it in a safe-deposit box! (See figure 7-2.)

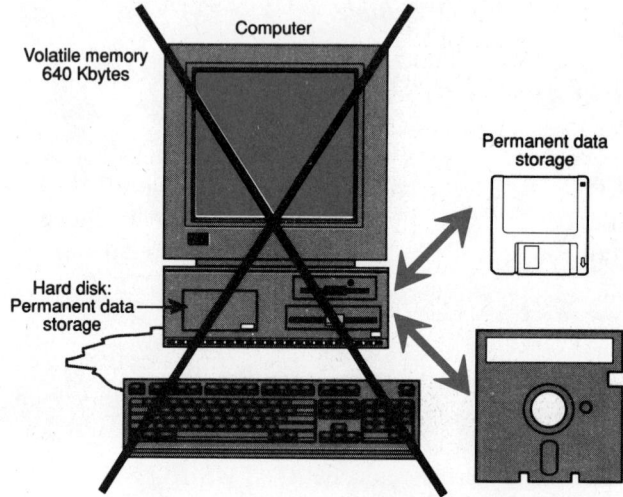

Fig. 7-2: Use disks for permanence.

Information is stored on a disk by means of *files*. A file contains one separate program, or a set of data (such as a list of names and addresses) used by a program. In fact, you can think of a computer disk as a *file cabinet* containing individual files. (See figure 7-3.)

There's an important distinction to make between two kinds of files.

1. *Program files* contain programs you write.
2. *Data files* contain data (such as names and addresses) that are used by a program.

Keep this distinction in mind as you learn how to save and retrieve files.

Input and Output to Files and Devices

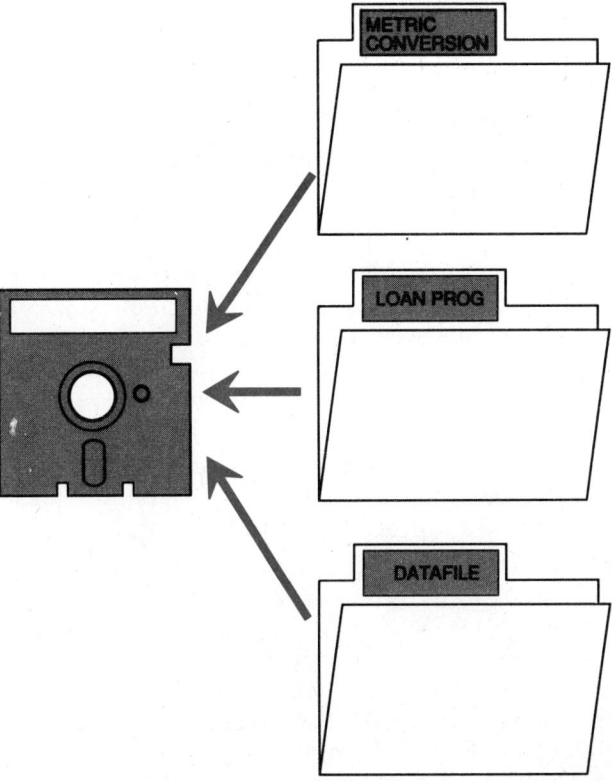

Fig. 7-3: Programs and data are stored as files.

More About LOAD and SAVE

In an earlier chapter, you learned how to SAVE and LOAD program files on disk. Now we'll learn a little more about these important statements. Remember, the SAVE statement saves your files on disk. Its general form is as follows:

```
10 SAVE "MYFILE
20 SAVE "MYFILE, A"
30 SAVE "MYFILE, P
```

This means, "take all program lines currently in memory and save them in the file called MYFILE.BAS." If MYFILE.BAS doesn't exist, BASIC creates it; if this file already exists, its contents are replaced by a copy of whatever program is now in your computer.

Chapter 7

The name is limited by the usual DOS naming conventions—that is, up to eight letters, followed by a period and a three-letter extension. GW-BASIC adds the period and the BAS extension for you if you don't specify an extension. This is to help you keep track of your BASIC program files. Therefore, typing the following

```
SAVE "MYFILE
```

produces a filename of MYFILE.BAS.

You need the quotation marks in front of the filename. As you know, for speed you can use the function key F4 at the top of the keyboard—this types SAVE" for you. (Also for speed, GW-BASIC lets you get by with putting in just the first set of quotation marks, and omitting the "closing" quotation marks, as shown in line 10. Most languages other than BASIC demand the closing marks, though; you've been warned.)

If you don't specify a directory, GW-BASIC saves your file in the current directory—that is, probably the one from which you loaded the BASIC program in the first place. As with any DOS file, however, you can specify a complete path, as follows:

```
SAVE "A:\PROGRAMS\PROG1
```

The statement above saves your program code as the file PROG1.BAS, in the directory called PROGRAMS, on the disk in drive A (which is almost always your computer's floppy disk drive).

(The "A" or "P" after the filename in a SAVE statement saves your file as an ASCII file or a protected file. You'll learn more about these in a moment.)

Once you've saved a program with SAVE, you can bring it back into the computer again with the LOAD statement. The general form of LOAD is

```
LOAD "MYFILE
LOAD "MYFILE", R
```

This means, "look for the program file called MYFILE.BAS and load it in the computer." If you add the closing quotation marks, the comma, and the "R", it means, "RUN the program as soon as it's loaded." As with SAVE, you can use the function key (this time it's key F3) as a typing aid to speed things up.

When you LOAD a program, it erases any program lines in your computer. Even if you have 100 lines of program code and you LOAD a program of only 10 lines, your 100-line program is all gone, replaced by the 10-line program.

Input and Output to Files and Devices

Try a LOAD and a SAVE now. First, type this simple program.

```
NEW
Ok
10 PRINT "LOAD EXAMPLE"
20 PRINT "I can start by myself, thank you"
```

Now save the file as MYFILE. Use the function key F4 as a typing aid, if you like.

```
SAVE "MYFILE
Ok
```

Your program is now saved on disk as MYFILE.BAS. You can retrieve it with the LOAD statement. First, erase the program lines now in the computer.

```
NEW
Ok
LIST
Ok
```

LIST shows what's in the computer now—which is nothing. Now LOAD the program MYFILE.

```
LOAD "MYFILE
Ok
LIST
10 PRINT "LOAD EXAMPLE"
20 PRINT "I can start by myself, thank you"
Ok
```

There's your program, back again! To RUN it automatically, add a closing quotation mark, a comma, and the letter "R" as follows:

```
LOAD "MYFILE", R
LOAD EXAMPLE
I can start by myself, thank you
Ok
```

The program runs automatically as soon as you load it.

Both LOAD and SAVE are programmable. Using the R with LOAD, you can link several programs together and automatically run them one after another.

283

Your Program as an ASCII File

The SAVE statement normally saves your code in a compressed form known as *binary* format. This form takes up less space on a memory device like a hard disk or a floppy disk. Binary format, however, makes the file more difficult to read by word processors or the TYPE command of MS-DOS.

You can also save a program as an ASCII file. This form of program storage takes a little more disk space than binary format. But it's a "plain vanilla" format that you can read with a word processor, with the TYPE command in MS-DOS, or even with other versions of BASIC. Saving a BASIC program in ASCII format gives it transportability—the ability to be read or used by applications other than the version of BASIC you have now.

Saving an ASCII Program File

If you type SAVE followed by the filename, then add closing quotation marks, a comma, and an "A" to the filename, it means, "save the program lines now in memory as an ASCII file." For instance, to save the current program this way, type the following:

```
SAVE "MYFILE.ASC", A
Ok
```

We've added the .ASC extension to the filename so that you can see the difference between MYFILE.BAS and MYFILE.ASC in your DOS directory listing. But you don't need the extension; to save the file as an ASCII file called MYFILE.BAS, just type SAVE "MYFILE", A.

Did you notice the important difference between how you typed the SAVE statement and filename for ASCII storage? That's right, you need the second (that is, the closing) quotation marks after the name. (Remember, you needed only the first quotation marks for ordinary binary storage.)

Loading an ASCII Program File

Whether a program has been saved as an ASCII file or an ordinary binary file, you retrieve it the same way—with the LOAD statement. LOAD doesn't care whether a program has been saved in binary or ASCII format. For instance, to get an ASCII program named MYFILE.ASC from a disk, you'd type

```
LOAD "MYFILE.ASC
```

Naturally, if you didn't specify a period and extension when you saved the program, it's saved with the extension .BAS. And whether it's a binary or ASCII file, you don't need to type the .BAS extension when you load the program, either.

Writing Programs in Your Word Processor

If you've been following us carefully, you've probably figured something out by now: Because GW-BASIC doesn't care whether a program file is saved in binary or ASCII format, you can use any ASCII file as a program file.

This means you don't have to load BASIC in order to write programs for it. You simply use your word processor, or any application that can save a so-called "plain text," or ASCII, file.

Follow the same rules that you do when you're writing a program in BASIC—that is, on each line, begin with a line number in the far-left column, leave a space, then type a valid BASIC keyword. You can use tabs to indent listings; they'll be converted to spaces. When you save the file from within the word processor, choose "ASCII" or "text" or a similar option. You can then load GW-BASIC, and LOAD and RUN the program just as if it's any other program file.

What's a Legal BASIC Program File?

BASIC will try to LOAD any file as a program, no matter what its size or name. You could LOAD a file called LETTERS.DOC or PROGRAM.TXT if you wanted. There's just one little "gotcha"—every line in the file has to look like a legal BASIC line. That means, every line has to begin with a line number and a space. Until you try to RUN the "program," BASIC doesn't care whether the statements in the lines are legal, or whether they're in order. But they do have to begin with a line number and a space, or BASIC gives you an error like this:

```
Direct statement in file
```

Logging Your BASIC "Session"

While we're on the subject of files, let's explore how you can record your keystrokes. Sometimes (particularly in long programs where you make many changes) it's advantageous to have a listing of everything you've done—what statements worked and what statements caused errors. By reviewing this list later, you know what you've done and how far you've gotten with a program.

Chapter 7

You save your steps in a file. GW-BASIC can record every step you take from the time you type "GWBASIC" to load it until you type "SYSTEM" to end the session. When you first load BASIC from DOS, you use the "greater than" symbol (>) to direct output to a file, as follows:

```
A> GWBASIC > SESSION.LOG
```

This means, "beginning at the DOS A prompt, load GWBASIC and record every action in the file SESSION.LOG on this disk." (You can use any name, and you can specify any legal path and file name.) Your actions appear on the screen, and they're also written into the file you specify. This is an ASCII file that you can examine with your word processor, or display using the TYPE command of DOS.

To see how this works, use SYSTEM to exit to DOS, then log all your keystrokes as you type and run a simple program:

```
SYSTEM
A>GWBASIC > MYFILE.LOG
Ok
```

Now you're back in BASIC, ready to program; but everything you do, every step you take, is being saved in the file MYFILE.LOG. Try this:

```
10 FOR I = 1 TO 5
20     PRINT "HELLO"
RUN
FOR without NEXT in 10
Ok
```

Whoops! You made a mistake. Better add that NEXT statement and try again.

```
30 NEXT
RUN
HELLO
HELLO
HELLO
HELLO
HELLO
Ok
```

Now if you exit to DOS and TYPE the file, you'll see an exact replica of your last BASIC session—complete with your error and its solution.

Input and Output to Files and Devices

```
SYSTEM
A> TYPE MYFILE.LOG
10 FOR I = 1 TO 5
20   PRINT "HELLO"
RUN
FOR without NEXT in 10
Ok
30 NEXT
RUN
HELLO
HELLO
HELLO
HELLO
HELLO
Ok
SYSTEM
```

Logging your display this way can be very helpful in debugging.

Protected Files

If you're developing a program for sale or for use by others, you probably don't want ordinary users to be able to modify it—or even to list the code. In this case, you can add the closing quotation marks, comma, and the letter "P" to the SAVE statement, like this:

```
SAVE "MYFILE", P
```

This means, "save the current program on disk as MYFILE.BAS, in protected mode." Protected mode is an encoded binary file format. You can load and run a protected file, but you can't list or modify it.

Try saving this simple one-line program in protected mode:

```
10 PRINT "I'm impregnable"
SAVE "IMMUNE", P
Ok
```

Now see what happens when you LOAD and try to LIST this IMMUNE program:

Chapter 7

```
LOAD "IMMUNE
Ok
RUN
I'm impregnable
Ok

LIST
Illegal function call
Ok
EDIT 10
Illegal function call
Ok
```

If you try to LIST or EDIT a protected program, you get an "Illegal function call" message. The only way you can change this program is to SAVE a copy of the original (in normal, unprotected mode) under a different name. Then you can modify the copy and re-SAVE it. (This is good to know, because many programs require continual modification.)

Building and Using Sequential Data Files

Data files are different from program files. A data file contains data, such as a list of names and addresses, the coordinates for a graphics illustration, the temperature in Tokyo for every day of the 20th century, etc. A data file is separate from a program file—in fact, one program might make use of several data files; or several programs can use the data from one file. Figure 7-4 illustrates the difference.

You can do a lot with BASIC without knowing about data files and their structure. But when you're programming for "real-world" applications, especially in business, you're certain to need data files.

One difference between data and program files is that you use a different set of statements to handle them. You store and retrieve program files with SAVE and LOAD, but you'll need a whole new set of statements for data files.

Although you don't use READ to get data from a file, you use a special form of INPUT that works on a data file somewhat the same way READ works on DATA. In fact, as shown in figure 7-5, you can think of a data file as a lot of data you're going to input to your program with a special "automatic" INPUT statement.

Input and Output to Files and Devices

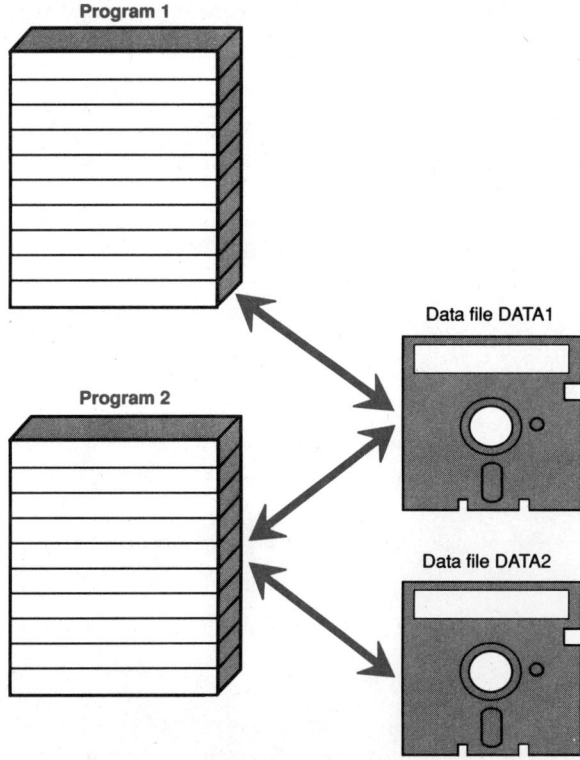

Fig. 7-4:   Data files are independent from programs.

```
DATA 17, 35, 4
READ A, B, C

DATA file #1  17, 35, 4........................97, 83,
21

FOR I = 1 TO 1000
    INPUT #1, A, B, C
NEXT
```

Fig. 7-5:   A data file and the special INPUT# statement work a lot like READ and DATA.

Sequential versus Random-Access Data Files

Data files contain data—even numbers—as a series of bytes, and the way BASIC interprets these bytes depends on the statements you use to save or read them. Depending on the statements, those bytes can be considered to be ASCII characters, integers, or single- or double-precision numbers.

Chapter 7

Data files can be arranged as *sequential* files or as *random-access* ones. Figure 7-6 shows the difference.

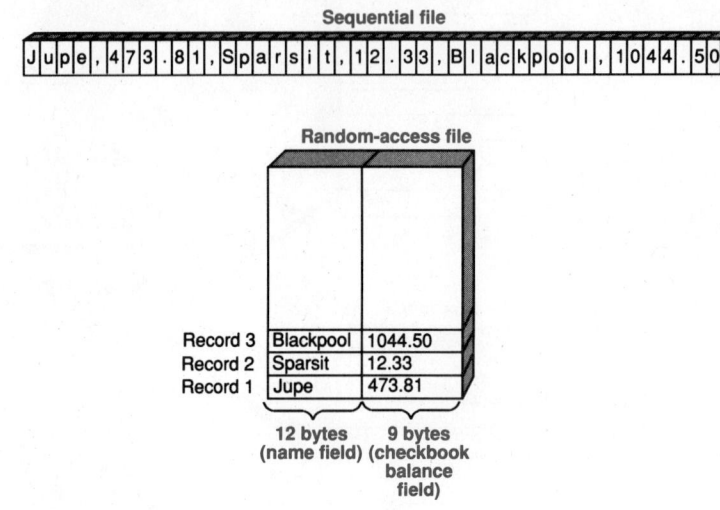

Fig. 7-6:   Data file structure.

In a sequential file, all data is arranged end-to-end, without extra spaces. The data elements run continuously from the beginning of the file to its end. Therefore, a list of names and checkbook balances would consist of the characters for a name, followed by the ASCII characters for a balance, followed by another name, followed by a balance, and so on.

Sequential files are very space-efficient, because they use virtually every byte. But it can be difficult—and slow—to find a specific piece of data (like a name or balance) because you have to search the data in sequence until you come to the right one. Also, it's not easy to change data in a sequential-access file. Suppose that you wanted to change Jupe's name to Jupe, S. There's no room for those extra characters, so you'd have to pull out all the data, add the additional characters to the name, and rewrite it all to the file—a time-consuming process, even for BASIC. For this reason, you should use sequential-access data files for applications in which you need to save disk space and in which the data won't change.

In a random-access file, data are contained in *records*, each with a specified number of bytes. (In figure 7-6, each record is 21 bytes.) Each record, in turn, is divided into *fields*. For example, each record might have a 12-byte field for the name, and a 9-byte field for the balance.

All the bytes allocated to each record are used; they're just filled with empty spaces if there's no data for them. That's why random-access files gulp much more disk space than the sequential-access type. But it's much faster and easier to search

Input and Output to Files and Devices

for data, and to change it, in a random-access file. Because each record and each field is guaranteed to be the same size, BASIC can bounce quickly from one record to the next to find a specific piece of data. Also, when you're revising data, the new data will take up the same amount of space as the old, so it's necessary only to read and replace the single record that's affected.

Putting Data into a Sequential File

In order to put data into a sequential file, use the following steps:

1. Open the file with OPEN
2. Write data to the file with PRINT# or WRITE#
3. Close the file with CLOSE

   Let's take a close look at these statements and how to use them.

OPEN a File

To open a file, you use the OPEN statement. Its general form is as follows:

```
100 OPEN "DATAFILE" FOR OUTPUT AS #N
```

or

```
100 OPEN O, #N, "DATAFILE"
```

    Both of these statements mean the same thing: "Open a file DATAFILE so that data can be output to it; position to the beginning of the file; and after this, refer to the file by the number N." When you specify OUTPUT (or O, as in the second statement above), the file is created if it doesn't exist, and your output will begin at the beginning of the file.
    If the file already exists, OPEN...FOR OUTPUT destroys any data already in the file and overwrites it with new data. To add data to an existing file, use OPEN...FOR APPEND, like this:

```
100 OPEN "DATAFILE" FOR APPEND AS #N
```

or

```
100 OPEN A, #N, "DATAFILE"
```

    These statements both mean, "open the file DATAFILE so that data can be appended to it; position to the end of the file; and after this refer to the file by the number N."

Chapter 7

Incidentally, you can omit the number sign (#) in front of the number if you want; however, using the number sign makes these statements easier to follow and understand, especially in a long program listing.

Now OPEN a file. You can give it a try now, right from the keyboard:

```
OPEN "SIXTIES" FOR OUTPUT AS #1
Ok
```

Well, that wasn't too difficult, was it? Let's look at how to get data into that file.

Use WRITE# to Put Data into a File

The simplest way to put data into a file is with the WRITE# statement. Its general form is as follows:

```
100 WRITE#N, A$, X, B$,...
```

This means, "write the variables A$, X, B$, and so on to file #N." You can write strings or numeric data—it doesn't matter as long as you read it back later into the same type of variables that were used to write it.

The WRITE# statement inserts commas between all items in the "A$, X, B$, ..." list, and separates each item by surrounding it with quotation marks. This will make it easier for you to separate the data when you read it later.

You can separate the items in the "A$, X, B$, ..." list with commas or semicolons. WRITE# doesn't put a blank in front of a positive number, but after the last item in the "A$, X, B$,..." list has been sent to the file, the statement sends a carriage return.

If you have OPENed the file SIXTIES as #1, as outlined above, the following statements put in the names of some of your favorite 60's rock groups. (Yes, you can execute the statements from the keyboard.)

```
WRITE #1, "Shirelles", "Chiffons", "Orlons"
Ok
```

One important point: Be sure you know how data is written to a sequential file, because you'll need that information later. For instance, if you WRITE data out to the file in the order of string variable, numeric variable, and string variable, then later you'll want to bring the data in from the file in the same order. The rule to remember is:

Read it the way you wrote it!

CLOSE a File

There's a third step to putting data into a file, and it's a very important one. Before doing anything else, as soon as you're done writing data, you should close the file using the CLOSE statement. Its general form is shown here:

```
CLOSE #N
```

This means, "close the file associated with number N." You can use the number sign (#) to specify the number, but you don't have to. Also, you can specify more than one file at the same time. If you use CLOSE without a number, all open files are closed.

Here are some examples of CLOSE statements.

```
100 CLOSE #1, #2
200 CLOSE 1, 2
300 CLOSE
```

The statement in line 100 means, "close the files associated with #1 and #2." The statement in line 200 means the same thing. Because the CLOSE statement in line 300 doesn't specify a number, it closes any files that are open at this time.

Once you CLOSE a file, it frees that number, so you can assign it to another file if you like.

To continue with our earlier keyboard example, you can CLOSE the file SIXTIES by typing

```
CLOSE 1
Ok
```

Your data is now in the file on a floppy or hard disk. If it's a floppy, you can take it out, trade it with your friends, carry it to school or work—the data remains on the disk, ready for use. Now let's see how we can get that data back out of the file.

How CLOSE Flushes the Buffer

When you assign a number to a file (such as #1 or 2), you're actually setting up a "buffer" between BASIC and the file. The buffer is a kind of holding tank (see fig. 7-7) that matches the speed of BASIC (fast) to that of the disk drive (relatively slow). The buffer operates in the background, so you're not usually aware of it—unless you commit the cardinal sin of forgetting to flush the buffer.

Chapter 7

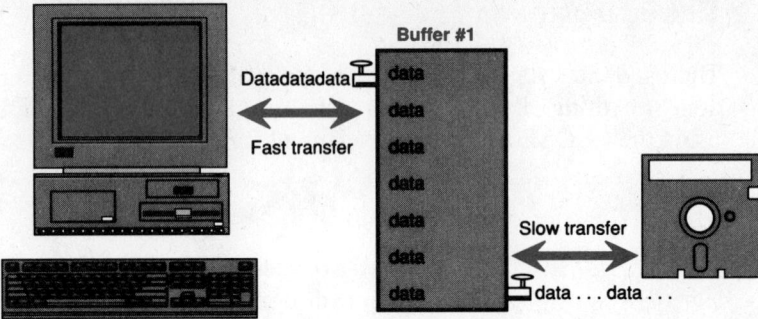

Fig. 7-7: A buffer is a holding tank for data.

The CLOSE statement (as well as a few other statements such as END and RUN) empties all data from the buffer to either the file or BASIC, depending on which way data is being transferred. It flushes the buffer and ensures that everything is in its proper place before continuing.

If you omit a CLOSE statement from your program, it's possible that some of your data might be left in the buffer and lost. This can happen if, for instance, you remove a disk from the drive without closing all files with CLOSE first. For best results, remember this rule:

Always use CLOSE statements to flush buffers!

Bringing Data In from a Sequential File

The steps you take to get data from a sequential file are similar to those used to put data in. Here are the steps to follow:

1. Open the file with OPEN
2. Input data from the file with INPUT# or LINE INPUT#
3. Close the file with CLOSE

This looks pretty familiar—after all, two of the three steps use our old friends OPEN and CLOSE. The only thing that looks different is that we use an INPUT# or LINE INPUT statement rather than WRITE# or PRINT#. There are some more subtle differences, too, as you'll soon see.

OPEN the File Again

Before you can retrieve data from a file, you have to (all together now) OPEN it again. Because you're inputting data from the file, instead of writing or printing to the file, you use the OPEN command in a slightly different manner. Here's the general form:

```
100 OPEN "DATAFILE" FOR INPUT AS #N
```

or

```
100 OPEN I, #N, "DATAFILE"
```

These two statements both mean, "open the file called DATAFILE for inputting data to BASIC, and assign it to number 1; start at the beginning of the file."

As you know, you can OPEN a file from within a program, or from the keyboard, like this:

```
OPEN "SIXTIES" FOR INPUT AS #3
```

Notice that you don't have to use the same number for the file. Once you've CLOSEd a file, you can OPEN it using any number. In fact, if you're opening and closing the same file at several different points in your program, you might want to use different file numbers to keep track of the number of times you OPEN and CLOSE it.

Now we're ready to get data back in from the file.

Use INPUT# to Get Data from the File

You can use the INPUT# statement to bring in data from a file. Here's the general form of the statement:

```
100 INPUT #N, var1, var2, var3, ...
```

This means, "read data items one by one from a sequential file; assign the first item to *var1*, the second to *var2*, the third to *var3*, and so on." It's similar to an ordinary INPUT statement, except that you don't see a question mark printed, and INPUT# can input several items of data in a row rather than just one.

INPUT# can handle numeric and string variables together:

```
100 INPUT #N, A$, X, B$
```

This statement reads the first data item into string variable A$, the second into numeric variable X, and the third into string variable B$. (You can see why it's

Chapter 7

important that you know how the data has been placed in the file.) INPUT# uses some special rules when it reads in data:

- When reading in strings, INPUT# looks for a double quotation mark (") and assumes that everything after it is part of that string until the next quotation mark.
- When reading in numeric quantities, INPUT# ignores leading spaces and line feeds. The first character is the start of the number, and the number is terminated when BASIC encounters a space, carriage return, line feed, or comma.

Why You Use the Number Sign for Files

INPUT# demonstrates why the number sign (#) is important. Suppose that you omit the number sign when referring to a file, and use an INPUT statement like this:

```
50 INPUT 3, A$
```

In line 50, BASIC thinks you mean keyboard INPUT, and responds by displaying a question mark and waiting for you to enter a value. If you want input from file #3, you have to specify it like this:

```
50 INPUT #3, A$
```

To avoid confusion, always use the number sign in every statement that refers to files—even though you don't have to.

Let's see what happens when we bring in data from the SIXTIES file:

```
INPUT #3, X$, Y$, Z$
Ok
PRINT X$, Y$, Z$
Shirelles      Chiffons       Orlons
Ok
```

There's your data, all right! The INPUT# statement started at the beginning of the file. The first piece of data in the file was the string Shirelles, and it was assigned to the first variable—that is, to X$. Chiffons, the second string in the file, was assigned to Y$; and Orlons was assigned to Z$.

The list of variables in an INPUT# statement must match up with the data in the file. Suppose that you have a file assigned to #3, and its data looks like that shown in figure 7-8.

Input and Output to Files and Devices

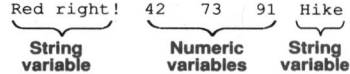

Fig. 7-8: Data in file assigned to #3.

You'd want an INPUT statement that looks like this:

```
100 INPUT #3, A$, X, Y, Z, B$
```

In order to input this data correctly, your INPUT statement must first bring in a string variable, then three numeric variables, then another string.

That, in a simple form, is how you handle sequential files. Before you continue, though, there's one final—and important—step to take.

Don't Forget to CLOSE the File!

You know what's next, don't you? That's right, you have to CLOSE the file. A few keystrokes do it:

```
CLOSE #3
Ok
```

Now the file is closed, and you're ready to move on.

Further Commands for Sequential Files

You have learned the rudiments of handling sequential files. But you'll need a little more information if you plan to work with files in the real world.

Detecting a File's End with EOF

When inputting data from large files—or even small ones—it can be difficult if not impossible to specify exactly how many pieces of data are in the file. And if you go past the end of the file during INPUT, you'll get an error. Luckily, BASIC data files have an end-of-file marker that you can detect with the EOF (end-of-file) function. When it hits the end of the file, your program can branch or change its execution accordingly.

297

Chapter 7

The general form of the EOF function is

```
100 X=EOF(N)
```

This means, "look for the end-of-file marker in file N; if it's not found, set X to zero (0) for false; when the end-of-file marker is found, set X to −1 for true."

The following short program illustrates the problem you can have if you try to INPUT more data than is in the file:

```
10 OPEN "SIXTIES" FOR OUTPUT AS #1
20 WRITE #1, "Shirelles", "Chiffons", "Orlons", "Pips"
30 CLOSE #1
40 OPEN "SIXTIES" FOR INPUT AS #1
50 FOR I=1 TO 10
60    INPUT #1, A$
70    PRINT A$
80 NEXT
90 CLOSE #1
100 END
```

Let's look closely at this: lines 10-30 open the file SIXTIES, put four data strings in it, and close the file. Then line 40 opens the file again, this time for input. The FOR...NEXT loop is set up to INPUT one string of data from the file and print it; the next time through the loop, the next string of data is INPUT, and so on.

Each INPUT# statement executed before the file is closed again takes the next piece (or pieces) of data. As shown in figure 7-9, INPUT# keeps a pointer to data in the file, much like the pointer kept by the READ instruction for DATA statements.

But look! There are only four strings in the file; however, because we're going through the loop 10 times, we're trying to INPUT 10 strings. What happens when we RUN the program? Here's the output:

```
Shirelles
Chiffons
Orlons
Pips
Input past end in 60
Ok
```

The program crashes, because after printing all four strings in the file, the pointer reaches the end and can go no further. This stops the loop with an error of "Input past end."

Input and Output to Files and Devices

To solve this problem, use the EOF function. One way to do it is replace the FOR...NEXT loop with a WHILE...WEND loop that executes only until the EOF becomes true. Or, to put it another way:

```
WHILE NOT EOF(1)
```

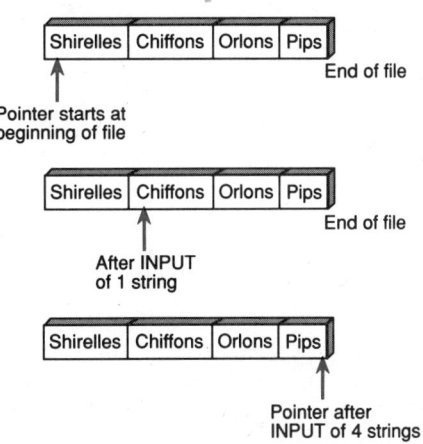

Fig. 7-9: Movement of the file pointer.

This means, "while the end-of-file function for file #1 is not true, keep going through the loop." It tells BASIC to crank through the WHILE...WEND loop just as it went through the FOR...NEXT loop—but to do it only as long as the EOF marker for file #1 is false. (Or, rather, as long as it's NOT true.) When BASIC bumps up against the end-of-file marker, EOF(1) becomes true, and execution falls silently and painlessly out of the loop. The new-and-improved program looks like this:

```
10 OPEN "SIXTIES" FOR OUTPUT AS #1
20 WRITE #1, "Shirelles", "Chiffons", "Orlons", "Pips"
30 CLOSE #1
40 OPEN "SIXTIES" FOR INPUT AS #1
50 WHILE NOT EOF(1)
60      INPUT #1, A$
70      PRINT A$
80 WEND
90 CLOSE #1
100 END
```

Chapter 7

When you run the program now, the results are decidedly better. The output is now error-free.

```
Shirelles
Chiffons
Orlons
Pips
Ok
```

Using LINE INPUT# to Get Data

The LINE INPUT# statement pulls data out of a file exactly as it's written. It looks for an entire "line"—that is, up to the next carriage return it finds in the file. The general form is

```
100 LINE INPUT #N, stringvar$
```

This means, "take all the characters in file N up to the next carriage return, and put them in string variable *stringvar$*." LINE INPUT# can accept up to 256 characters. It doesn't strip off quotation marks or commas, so it's especially useful in detecting just what is in an unknown file.

Try this little program to store cities and their temperatures in a sequential file.

```
10 OPEN "FIRE-ICE" FOR APPEND AS #1
20 PRINT "Input a city name"
30 INPUT CITY$
40 INPUT "Input a temperature"; TEMP
50 WRITE #1, CITY$, TEMP
60 CLOSE #1
70 OPEN "FIRE-ICE" FOR INPUT AS #1
80 WHILE EOF(1) <> -1
90     LINE INPUT #1, A$
100    PRINT A$
110 WEND
120 CLOSE #1
```

Now RUN the program and type today's temperature for Munich in degrees Celsius.

```
RUN
Input a city name
? Munich
```

```
Input a temperature? 3
"Munich",3
Ok
```

After you open the file FIRE-ICE for appending data in line 10, you are asked to input the name of a city, followed by a temperature. After you've completed the input, a WHILE...WEND loop uses the LINE INPUT# statement in line 90 to print each city and temperature. The city name is printed with quotation marks around it because that's actually how it is inside the file.

RUN the program a few more times and add some more cities and temperatures. After each run, the WHILE...WEND loop prints the complete contents of the file.

```
RUN
Input a city name
? Beijing
Input a temperature? -4
"Munich",3
"Beijing",-4
Ok

RUN
Input a city name
? Honolulu
Input a temperature? 17
"Munich",3
"Beijing",-4
"Honolulu",17
Ok
```

If, in line 10, we open the file FOR OUTPUT, any old cities and temperatures that are in that file are destroyed. Instead, we open it FOR APPEND, which means that new cities and temperatures are added onto the end of the file after any that already exist there.

Incidentally, the WHILE...WEND loop shows another way to write NOT EOF(1). The expression EOF(1)<>-1 means the same thing as NOT EOF(1). So the WHILE...WEND loop is executed until the EOF for file 1 becomes -1 (that is, true). Then the program falls out of the loop, closes the file, and ends.

Using PRINT# or PRINT# USING to Output Data

Besides WRITE#, there's another way to put data into a file. It's with the PRINT# or PRINT# USING statements. These statements write an image of the data to the file, just as their cousins PRINT and PRINT USING write an image to the monitor screen. The general form is as follows:

```
100 PRINT #N, A$; X; B$;...
200 PRINT USING string expression; A$, X; B$
```

Line 100 means, "write the variables `A$`, `X`, and `B$` to the file specified by number `N`." Line 200 means, "write the variables using the string expression as a format." (You'll find more about the formats in the description of PRINT USING in chapter 6 earlier in this book.)

The important thing to remember about PRINT# is that it prints to the file exactly the same way it prints to the screen. This means that it strips off the semicolons and quotation marks that separate the data. If you use commas to separate data, it even adds the extra spaces needed to print to the next field—just as an ordinary PRINT does!

As with PRINT, this means that to have a string that contains quotation marks, you must use the ASCII character for it, like this:

```
50 PRINT #1, "She said CHR$(34)Go away.CHR$(34) I went away."
```

This statement prints the following string to the file:

```
She said "Go away." I went away.
```

Closing a File with RESET—and Other Ways

RESET closes all disk files and writes the directory information to the diskette or hard disk. (It is exactly the same as CLOSE by itself, without a buffer number specified.)

The statements END, LOAD (without R), NEW, RUN, and SYSTEM all automatically close any open files, too. It's best, though, to always explicitly use CLOSE or RESET when you're done writing to or inputting from a file. Don't depend on END or another statement to do it for you.

A Sequential Telephone Number File

Now that we've examined sequential files and their commands, let's look at a practical example—a program that stores a list of names and telephone numbers for you.

Input and Output to Files and Devices

Remember that sequential files use much less memory than random-access files, but it's more difficult to change data in the file. The secret to altering a sequential file is to do it this way:

1. Bring the data out into an array.
2. Manipulate the data.
3. Read the new data back into the file.

That's what we're going to do in the Telephone List Program.

Opening the File for Input

The program opens a file called PHONLIST.DOC, and reads its contents into a pair of arrays. You can examine the complete list, add names or delete them, or get a display of any name you choose. You can print the list, too; and when you end the program, all your changes are automatically output back to the file.

Let's look at the code for the program. APPEND will create a file if the file doesn't already exist. So after naming the file in line 40, we begin in lines 80 and 90 by OPENing the file for APPEND, then closing it immediately. This prevents a later "File not found" error that results if you try to open a nonexistent file for INPUT. This technique lets you change to a new file for each list—you might want to change the name of FILENAME$ in line 40 to BUSINESS or FRIENDS, for instance.

```
40 FILENAME$ = "PHONELST.DOC"
50 '
60 DIM P$(256), T$(256)
70 REM-Account for a brand-new file
80 OPEN FILENAME$ FOR APPEND AS #1
90 CLOSE #1
```

Line 60 reserves space for two arrays, one for persons (P$) and one for their telephone numbers (T$). The program begins by reading in the names and telephone numbers that are now in the file:

```
100 OPEN FILENAME$ FOR INPUT AS #1
110 RECORDS=0
120 WHILE NOT EOF(1)
130     RECORDS=RECORDS+1
140     INPUT #1, P$(RECORDS)
150     INPUT #1, T$(RECORDS)
160 WEND
170 CLOSE #1
```

Chapter 7

In line 100, we OPEN the file as #1 again, this time for INPUT. The WHILE...WEND loop in lines 120-160 uses INPUT# statements to read in existing names and numbers from the file. This loop reads in data until it hits the end of the file; then the statement WHILE NOT EOF(1) is no longer true, and execution drops out of the loop and continues.

This WHILE...WEND loop also does something else for us. It sets up a counter, RECORDS, that keeps track of the number of records of data in the file. When you learn about random-access files, you'll see how you can specify record length. For now, just think of a record as a single entry—one person's name accompanied by one telephone number (see fig. 7-10).

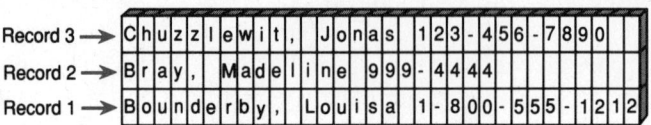

Fig. 7-10: Records in the telephone list file.

Although data in the file is actually all jammed up, with one piece of data following another one, we know that each person's name is followed by a telephone number; there are no names without numbers. (How do we know this? Because that's how we output data to the file in the first place. "Read it the way you wrote it," remember?) So we can assume that each "record" will consist of two variables: a name and a number. We just don't know how long each will be.

Once we're done reading in all data, we CLOSE the file. The things we're going to do—searches and comparisons and deletions—are lightning-fast if done with arrays in BASIC, but slower than last year's microprocessor if done in the file itself.

Next we call a sorting subroutine that guarantees the data will be sorted correctly when its input from the file.

```
180 '
190 GOSUB 7000 'Call sort subroutine for initial sort
200 '
```

Don't worry about the sort subroutine now. We'll come back to it in a little bit, after you've seen how data will be placed into the arrays.

The Menu Loop

Now let's look at the "heart" of the program. It's another WHILE...WEND loop, and it displays the menu for the telephone list. Once execution enters this loop, it can fall

Input and Output to Files and Devices

out only if you press the number 6 (or Ctrl-Break, but that's not very elegant) on your keyboard.

```
210 REM-Display menu
220 WHILE MENUNUM <> 6
230     CLS
240     REM-Display the menu
250     PRINT  "TELEPHONE LIST"
260     PRINT "Press the number for your choice"
270     PRINT "1 - Display all persons and telephone numbers"
280     PRINT "2 - Add a person and telephone number to the list"
290     PRINT "3 - Delete a person and number"
300     PRINT "4 - Find the telephone number for a person"
310     PRINT "5 - Print the entire list"
320     PRINT "6 - Exit and save the list"
330     INPUT MENUNUM
340     CLS
350     ON MENUNUM GOSUB 1000, 2000, 3000, 4000, 5000, 6000
360 WEND
370 END
```

Take a good look at this loop. If you didn't have the INPUT MENUNUM statement in line 330, it would run and run and run. But the INPUT statement halts execution to wait for you to type a menu number from 1-6. When you do type a number in this range, the ON...GOSUB statement branches execution to one of the subroutines listed. If you type a 1, execution branches to line 1000, a 2 sends you to line 2000, and so on.

We've seen the menu for the program; now let's examine its hard-working subroutines one by one.

Displaying the List

The subroutine beginning at line 1000 displays your list of person's names and telephone numbers. Notice that we don't reach into the file for this information—instead, we use the arrays P$ and T$, like this:

```
1000 REM-Display the complete list
1010 '
1020 PRINT: PRINT "TELEPHONE LIST": PRINT
1030 FOR NUMREC = 1 TO RECORDS
1040     PRINT P$(NUMREC) TAB(30) T$(NUMREC)
1050 NEXT NUMREC
```

Chapter 7

```
1060 GOSUB 8000 'Call subroutine to wait for a key press
1070 RETURN
1080 '
```

    This prints a heading, "TELEPHONE LIST," followed by the elements of both arrays—names and telephone numbers—side by side. The variable RECORDS, remember, is a counter that keeps track of the total number of records. NUMREC is the loop counter and number of the current record. So `P$(1)` might be "Bounderby, Louisa", while `T$(1)` might be "1-800-555-1212." The PRINT statement in line 1040 prints the name beginning at the left margin, and the telephone number beginning in column 30.

    Because we've gone to all this trouble to print the telephone list, we don't want to erase it right away. Line 1060 calls a subroutine that waits for you to press a key before execution RETURNS to the loop and the menu display again.

Adding a Person

If you select "2" from the menu, to add a person's name and telephone number, execution branches to the subroutine beginning with line 2000. The LINE INPUT PERSON$ statement lets you type a person's full name, with commas and spaces; the program instructs you to put the last name first so that the names can be sorted meaningfully. The LINE INPUT TELNUM$ statement gives you an equally free hand in how you type the telephone number. (In fact, you don't have to type a number here; you could put in a dollar balance, trenchant character assessment, or a sweetheart's name to be printed romantically next to the first name.)

```
2000 REM-Add a name
2010 '
2020 PRINT "Type the name of a person, last name first"
2030 LINE INPUT PERSON$
2040 PRINT "Now type that person's telephone number"
2050 LINE INPUT TELNUM$
2060 IF PERSON$ = "" OR TELNUM$="" THEN RETURN
2070 RECORDS=RECORDS+1
2080 P$(RECORDS)=PERSON$
2090 T$(RECORDS)=TELNUM$
2100 CLS
2110 PRINT P$(RECORDS);", "; T$(RECORDS); " added to list"
2120 GOSUB 8000 'Call subroutine to wait for key press
2130 GOSUB 7000 'Call sort subroutine
2140 RETURN
2150 '
```

The IF PERSON$... statement in line 2060 returns execution to the menu loop if you just press Return without entering at least one character for both PERSON$ and TELNUM$. This is pretty important, because it makes sure that both "fields" in each record have something in them. It also prevents your array (and your file) from filling up with blanks.

Once you've typed something for both the name and the number, then number of RECORDS is incremented by one. At this point, we don't care where in the array the new name and number are placed, because we're going to sort the array just before we return to the menu loop. So the new person's name is added to the end of array P$, and the new telephone number is added to T$.

Again, to give you time to verify what you've added to the list, the program waits for you to press a key before continuing. Then the program calls the sort subroutine beginning at line 7000.

The Sort Subroutine

Lines 7020-7070 perform a bubble sort on the array, "bubbling" the names into alphabetical order. By doing sorting in a subroutine, we don't have to sort except when needed, saving valuable milliseconds for other tasks. By calling the sort subroutine every time there's a change, we guarantee that the array is sorted before you choose the next menu item. This means that when you add a record (one person's name and telephone number), the list is sorted before you see it again.

```
7000 REM-Sort subroutine
7010 '
7020 FOR J=1 TO (RECORDS-1)
7030    FOR K=(J+1) TO RECORDS
7040       IF P$(K)<P$(J) THEN
                 SWAP P$(K), P$(J):
                 SWAP T$(K), T$(J)
7050    NEXT K
7060 NEXT J
7070 RETURN
```

Deleting a Person

The delete subroutine begins in line 3000. You are asked to type the name of a person, and LINE INPUT statement places that name into variable DELPERSON$. Then we set a flag (which we named FLAG) to 0; we'll use this to tell us whether the name we typed is actually in the array. A FOR...NEXT loop checks every element of the P$ array looking for an exact match of name you typed.

Chapter 7

```
3000 REM-Delete a person from the list
3010 '
3020 LINE INPUT "Whom do you want to delete?  "; DELPERSON$
3030 FLAG=0
3040 FOR NUMREC = 1 TO RECORDS
3050    IF DELPERSON$=P$(NUMREC) THEN GOSUB 3500:
        FLAG=1 'Call delete subroutine and set flag
3060 NEXT NUMREC
3070 IF FLAG=0 THEN PRINT DELPERSON$ " not found"
3080 GOSUB 8000 'Call subroutine to wait for a key press
3090 GOSUB 7000 'Call the sort subroutine
3100 RETURN
3500 REM-Subroutine to delete name and number
3510 CLS
3520 PRINT "Person found"
3530 PRINT P$(NUMREC); ", ";T$(NUMREC); " deleted from list"
3540 FOR R=NUMREC TO RECORDS
3550    P$(R)=P$(R+1): T$(R)=T$(R+1) 'Moves all
            other names up one record
3560 NEXT R
3570 RECORDS=RECORDS-1
3580 RETURN
3590 '
```

If a match is found, this subroutine saves the record number (that is, the value of the array subscript) in NUMREC, then branches to another subroutine that performs the actual deletion.

The delete subroutine begins at line 3500. It removes the person's name from array P$ and the person's telephone number from T$. The actual "deletion" is done by a FOR...NEXT loop that begins with the next element after the one to delete, and copies each successively lower name and telephone number into the array element above it.

For example, suppose that NUMREC is 5. To remove person P$(5), the program begins by copying P$(6) into P$(5), then P$(7) into P$(6), and so on. It does the same thing with the T$ array. Figure 7-11 illustrates the copying procedure.

When all elements have been copied into the ones above them, the subroutine executes the statement RECORDS=RECORDS −1 to reduce by one the number of elements in the array. So, only the last array element is actually deleted—the others are simply all moved up by one.

Input and Output to Files and Devices

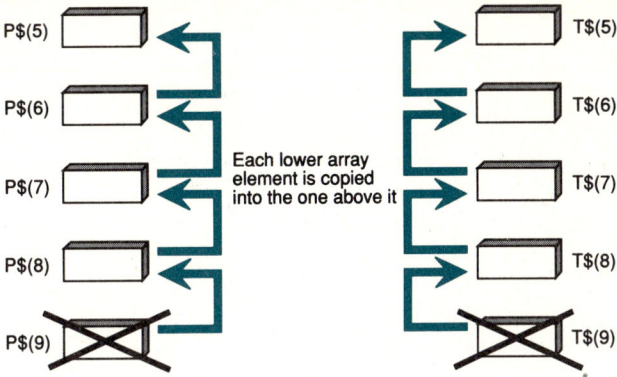

Fig. 7-11: Deleting an array element.

There's another part to the IF...THEN statement that calls the delete subroutine. If DELPERSON$ (the person to delete) is found in the array, this statement sets FLAG to 1, and we don't need to worry about it any longer.

However, if DELPERSON$ doesn't match any of the names in the array P$, FLAG remains set to 0, and the following statement shows that the program couldn't find the person:

```
3070 IF FLAG=0 THEN PRINT DELPERSON$ " not found"
```

Finding a Person

Especially when your telephone list grows in size, it may be easier to have BASIC find a number for you instead of looking it up yourself. This program's directory assistance begins in line 4000. After you are prompted to type a person's name, the LINE INPUT statement assigns the name to the variable FINDPERSON$. As with a deletion, the program uses a FOR...NEXT loop that begins with the first element of the P$ array and looks for a match with FINDPERSON$. When a match is found, the subroutine prints the name, P$(NUMREC), and the associated telephone number, T$ (NUMREC).

```
4000 REM-Find one person and the telephone number
4010 '
4020 PRINT "Whose number do you want to find?"
4030 LINE INPUT "Type the name, last name first: "; FINDPERSON$
4040 FLAG=0
4050 CLS
4060 FOR NUMREC = 1 TO RECORDS
```

Chapter 7

```
4070     IF FINDPERSON$=P$(NUMREC) THEN PRI.NT P$(NUMREC)
              TAB(30) T$(NUMREC): FLAG=1
4080 NEXT
4090 IF FLAG=0 THEN PRINT FINDPERSON$ " not found"
4100 GOSUB 8000 'Call subroutine to wait for a key press
4110 RETURN
4120 '
```

As with the delete subroutine, the FLAG is set to 0 when the subroutine begins running, and if the name is found it's set to 1. But if FINDPERSON$ isn't found, an IF...THEN statement prints the message "not found."

Printing the List

For a hard-copy printout of the telephone list, you call the print subroutine that begins in line 5000. This subroutine uses NUMREC as a counter for a FOR...NEXT loop. As NUMREC is increased by one each time through the loop, the LPRINT statement prints the name P$(NUMREC) on the printer, tabs over to column 30, then prints the telephone number T$(NUMREC).

```
5000 REM-Print the entire list
5010 '
5020 PRINT "Printing the list"
5030 LPRINT: LPRINT "TELEPHONE LIST": LPRINT
5040 FOR NUMREC=1 TO RECORDS
5050     LPRINT P$(NUMREC) TAB(30) T$(NUMREC)
5060 NEXT
5070 RETURN
5080 '
```

The subroutine also displays the message, "Printing the list," on the screen so that you know what's happening.

Hints for Printing

If you have a laser printer, you'll have to send a form feed to the printer after the last entry in the list has been printed. Merely insert this statement in the program just before the RETURN:

```
5065 LPRINT CHR$(12)
```

This sends the form feed (ASCII character 12) to the printer, causing it to advance to the top of the next page—and printing your final page for you before it advances.

Input and Output to Files and Devices

If your printer is attached to something other than your computer's LPT1 port, you might have to redirect output to the printer, as described earlier in this chapter.

Outputting to the File

When you're satisfied that the telephone list is just the way you want it, press 6 to exit the menu loop. The program branches to line 6000, and your file FILENAME$ is opened for OUTPUT.

```
6000 REM-Output revised list to the file, then end
6010 '
6020 OPEN FILENAME$ FOR OUTPUT AS #1
6030 PRINT "Saving file " FILENAME$
6040 FOR NUMREC=1 TO RECORDS
6050    WRITE #1, P$(NUMREC), T$(NUMREC)
6060 NEXT NUMREC
6070 CLOSE #1
6080 PRINT "Program ends"
6090 END
6100 '
```

With the updated telephone list stored in the arrays P$ and T$, we can save it in the file. We want our fresh, new list of names and numbers there, unsullied by any old data. So we OPEN the file for OUTPUT, which will destroy anything remaining in the file when our new list is put in.

Yet another FOR...NEXT loop cycles through the array. This time, though, each element of the array is copied into the file by the WRITE #1 statement. The structure of the file, with records consisting of two fields each, is set up by this loop.

The Waiting Subroutine

Line 8000 is the subroutine to wait for a key press. Whenever this subroutine is called (and it's called by many of the other subroutines in the program), it prompts you to "Press any key to continue" and then waits for any key.

```
8000 REM-Subroutine to wait for a key press
8010 '
8020 PRINT: PRINT "Press any key to continue"
8030 WHILE INKEY$ = "": WEND 'Loop waits for any key
8040 RETURN
```

Line 8030 is a complete WHILE...WEND loop that uses INKEY$ to detect a key press. As long as no key is pressed, INKEY$ is the null string; but as soon as you hit a key, execution falls out of the loop and returns to the calling location.

Chapter 7

Running the Program

Let's run the program. First, type the names and numbers of some of our oldest and dearest friends.

```
RUN
TELEPHONE LIST
Press the number for your choice
1 - Display all persons and telephone numbers
2 - Add a person and telephone number to the list
3 - Delete a person and number
4 - Find the telephone number for a person
5 - Print the entire list
6 - Exit and save the list
? 2

Type the name of a person, last name first
Bounderby, Louisa

Now type that person's telephone number
1-800-555-1212

Bounderby, Louisa, 1-800-555-1212 added to list

Press any key to continue

TELEPHONE LIST
Press the number for your choice
1 - Display all persons and telephone numbers
2 - Add a person and telephone number to the list
3 - Delete a person and number
4 - Find the telephone number for a person
5 - Print the entire list
6 - Exit and save the list
? 2

Type the name of a person, last name first
Chuzzlewit, Jonas

Now type that person's telephone number
123-456-7890

Chuzzlewit, Jonas, 123-456-7890 added to list

Press any key to continue
```

Got the idea? We'll go a little faster, omitting the menu for now (although it's still on your screen when you run the program):

```
TELEPHONE LIST
Press the number for your choice
? 2
Type the name of a person, last name first
Squeers, Wackford
Now type that person's telephone number
456-7596
Squeers, Wackford, 456-7596 added to list

Press any key to continue

TELEPHONE LIST
Press the number for your choice
? 2
Type the name of a person, last name first
Bray, Madeline
Now type that person's telephone number
999-4444
Bray, Madeline, 999-4444 added to list

Press any key to continue
```

Now let's see what the list looks like. Press 1 to choose the display of persons and telephone numbers.

```
TELEPHONE LIST
Press the number for your choice
? 1
Bounderby, Louisa          1-800-555-1212
Bray, Madeline             999-4444
Chuzzlewit, Jonas          123-456-7890
Squeers, Wackford          456-7596
```

Not bad! No matter how you enter the names, they're all sorted in ASCII order. Madeline Bray, it turns out, has left for a monastery in Tibet; to expunge her from the telephone list, choose 3:

```
Press the number for your choice
? 3
```

Chapter 7

```
Whom do you want to delete?  Bray, Madeline
Person found
Bray, Madeline, 999-4444 deleted from list

Press any key to continue

Press the number for your choice
? 1
Bounderby, Louisa               1-800-555-1212
Chuzzlewit, Jonas               123-456-7890
Squeers, Wackford               456-7596
```

You can see that Madeline is gone from our list. Try looking up the telephone number of your buddy Wackford Squeers.

```
Press the number for your choice
? 4
Whose number do you want to find?
Type the name, with the last name first:  Squeers, Wackford
Squeers, Wackford               456-7596
```

Now see whether Madeline Bray has mysteriously reappeared.

```
? 4
Whose number do you want to find?
Type the name, last name first:  Bray, Madeline

Bray, Madeline not found
```

Nope! She's gone for good. Now if you press menu number 5 to print the list, here's what you see on the screen while the program is outputting to the printer:

```
Printing the list
```

And when you finally decide the list is complete, you simply press 6 to exit the program. This automatically saves your telephone list on the disk.

```
TELEPHONE LIST
Press the number for your choice
1 - Display all persons and telephone numbers
2 - Add a person and telephone number to the list
3 - Delete a person and number
```

```
               4 - Find the telephone number for a person
               5 - Print the entire list
               6 - Exit and save the list
               ? 6

               Saving file PHONELST.DOC
               Program ends
               Ok
```

Elsewhere on these pages you'll find the complete program listing, all together.

```
10 REM-PHONLIST
20 REM-Sequential file telephone list
30 REM
40 FILENAME$ = "PHONELST.DOC"
50 '
60 DIM P$(256), T$(256)
70 REM-Account for a brand-new file
80 OPEN FILENAME$ FOR APPEND AS #1
90 CLOSE #1
100 OPEN FILENAME$ FOR INPUT AS #1
110 RECORDS=0
120 WHILE NOT EOF(1)
130     RECORDS=RECORDS+1
140     INPUT #1, P$(RECORDS)
150     INPUT #1, T$(RECORDS)
160 WEND
170 CLOSE #1
180 '
190 GOSUB 7000 'Call sort subroutine for initial sort
200 '
210 REM-Display menu
220 WHILE MENUNUM <> 6
230     CLS
240     REM-Display the menu
250     PRINT  "TELEPHONE LIST"
260     PRINT "Press the number for your choice"
270     PRINT "1 - Display all persons and telephone numbers"
280     PRINT "2 - Add a person and telephone number to the list"
290     PRINT "3 - Delete a person and number"
300     PRINT "4 - Find the telephone number for a person"
310     PRINT "5 - Print the entire list"
```

Chapter 7

```
320        PRINT "6 - Exit and save the list"
330        INPUT MENUNUM
340        CLS
350        ON MENUNUM GOSUB 1000, 2000, 3000, 4000, 5000, 6000
360 WEND
370 END
380 '
1000 REM-Display the complete list
1010 '
1020 PRINT: PRINT "TELEPHONE LIST": PRINT
1030 FOR NUMREC = 1 TO RECORDS
1040     PRINT P$(NUMREC) TAB(30) T$(NUMREC)
1050 NEXT NUMREC
1060 GOSUB 8000 'Call subroutine to wait for a key press
1070 RETURN
1080 '
2000 REM-Add a name
2010 '
2020 PRINT "Type the name of a person, last name first"
2030 LINE INPUT PERSON$
2040 PRINT "Now type that person's telephone number"
2050 LINE INPUT TELNUM$
2060 IF PERSON$ = "" OR TELNUM$="" THEN RETURN
2070 RECORDS=RECORDS+1
2080 P$(RECORDS)=PERSON$
2090 T$(RECORDS)=TELNUM$
2100 CLS
2110 PRINT P$(RECORDS);", "; T$(RECORDS); " added to list"
2120 GOSUB 8000 'Call subroutine to wait for key press
2130 GOSUB 7000 'Call sort subroutine
2140 RETURN
2150 '
3000 REM-Delete a person from the list
3010 '
3020 LINE INPUT "Whom do you want to delete?   "; DELPERSON$
3030 FLAG=0
3040 FOR NUMREC = 1 TO RECORDS
3050     IF DELPERSON$=P$(NUMREC) THEN GOSUB 3500:
         FLAG=1 'Call delete subroutine and set flag
3060 NEXT NUMREC
3070 IF FLAG=0 THEN PRINT DELPERSON$ " not found"
3080 GOSUB 8000 'Call subroutine to wait for a key press
3090 GOSUB 7000 'Call the sort subroutine
```

```
3100 RETURN
3500 REM-Subroutine to delete name and number
3510 CLS
3520 PRINT "Person found"
3530 PRINT P$(NUMREC); ", ";T$(NUMREC); " deleted from list"
3540 FOR R=NUMREC TO RECORDS
3550     P$(R)=P$(R+1): T$(R)=T$(R+1) 'Moves all
            other names up one record
3560 NEXT R
3570 RECORDS=RECORDS-1
3580 RETURN
3590 '
4000 REM-Find one person and the telephone number
4010 '
4020 PRINT "Whose number do you want to find?"
4030 LINE INPUT "Type the name, last name first: "; FINDPERSON$
4040 FLAG=0
4050 CLS
4060 FOR NUMREC = 1 TO RECORDS
4070     IF FINDPERSON$=P$(NUMREC) THEN PRINT P$(NUMREC)
            TAB(30) T$(NUMREC): FLAG=1
4080 NEXT
4090 IF FLAG=0 THEN PRINT FINDPERSON$ " not found"
4100 GOSUB 8000 'Call subroutine to wait for a key press
4110 RETURN
4120 '
5000 REM-Print the entire list
5010 '
5020 PRINT "Printing the list"
5030 LPRINT: LPRINT "TELEPHONE LIST": LPRINT
5040 FOR NUMREC=1 TO RECORDS
5050     LPRINT P$(NUMREC) TAB(30) T$(NUMREC)
5060 NEXT
5070 RETURN
5080 '
6000 REM-Output revised list to the file, then end
6010 '
6020 OPEN FILENAME$ FOR OUTPUT AS #1
6030 PRINT "Saving file " FILENAME$
6040 FOR NUMREC=1 TO RECORDS
6050     WRITE #1, P$(NUMREC), T$(NUMREC)
6060 NEXT NUMREC
6070 CLOSE #1
```

```
6080 PRINT "Program ends"
6090 END
6100 '
7000 REM-Sort subroutine
7010 '
7020 FOR J=1 TO (RECORDS-1)
7030     FOR K=(J+1) TO RECORDS
7040         IF P$(K)<P$(J) THEN
                    SWAP P$(K), P$(J):
                    SWAP T$(K), T$(J)
7050     NEXT K
7060 NEXT J
7070 RETURN
7080 '
8000 REM-Subroutine to wait for a key press
8010 '
8020 PRINT: PRINT "Press any key to continue"
8030 WHILE INKEY$ = "": WEND 'Loop waits for any key
8040 RETURN
```

This telephone list is just an example, of course. You could use the same technique to create lists with much larger numbers of elements: client addresses, baseball averages, expenses, frequent-flier miles, and more.

Random Access Files

The sequential file structure shoehorns the most data into your files, but it's not always the best solution. After all, in an era of giant hard disks and optical storage, you have to worry less and less about every byte of memory. Random access files make it a lot easier to find and change data, making them ideal for "real-world" applications like mailing lists, expense accounts, patient and customer records, accounting systems, and the like.

What Is a Random Access File?

A random access file consists of many records, and each record has several fields. For instance, a customer list file might have its records and fields set up as shown in figure 7-12.

Input and Output to Files and Devices

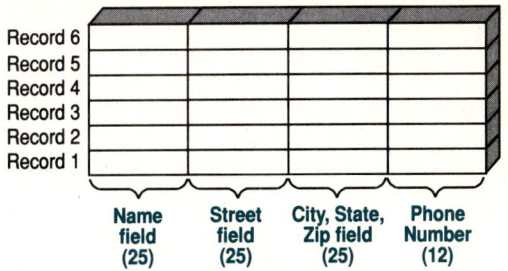

Fig. 7-12: Random access file—customer list>.

Fields have fixed sizes, whether they are filled or not. In our example, the sizes allocated to the customer list file are

`Name`	25 characters
`Street`	25 characters
`City, State, Zip`	25 characters
`Phone number`	12 characters
`Total record length`	87 characters

The total length of each record is 87 characters. If all the data is to be string data, then that means each record will require 87 bytes (because each character requires one byte).

Because each record and each field is a specific size, it's easy for BASIC to locate any specific field. For instance, you can quickly find the telephone number of the customer in record 4 by specifying, in effect, "record 4, the phone number field."

Now let's see how we can put data in and get it out of a random access file.

Putting Data into a Random Access File

Putting data into a random access file is a little different procedure than with sequential files. Here are the steps to follow:

1. Use OPEN to open the file in random access mode, and specify record length.

2. Use FIELD to specify the fields and the length of each field.

3. Use LSET or RSET to place data into the file buffer.

4. Use PUT# to write data from the buffer into the file itself.

Chapter 7

Set Record Length with OPEN

We start off by opening a file, using our old friend the OPEN statement. For a random access file, you use it like this:

```
100 OPEN "FILENAME" AS #N LEN=L
```

This means, "open the file FILENAME as a random access file, with a buffer number of N and a record length of L bytes." You don't have to specify FOR RANDOM (although you can), because RANDOM is the default mode. If you don't specify LEN=, the default is 128 bytes. So these three statements are the same.

```
100 OPEN "MYFILE" FOR RANDOM AS #2 LEN=128
100 OPEN "MYFILE" AS #2 LEN=128
100 OPEN "MYFILE" AS #2
```

All these statements will cause BASIC to open a file called MYFILE as a random access file, with the record length set at 128 bytes and using buffer #2.

You can try opening a random access file from the keyboard. Enter the following:

```
OPEN "KBDFILE" AS #2 LEN=50
Ok
```

You've just opened a random access file called KBDFILE. It has a record length of 50 bytes, and from now on you'll refer to it by its buffer number, that is, #1.

Set the Fields with FIELD

The FIELD statement allocates space in the buffer for each one of the fields. It's pretty easy to use; here's how it looks:

```
100 FIELD #N, W1 AS A$, W2 AS B$, ...
```

This means, "allocate the following space in buffer N: a width of W1 bytes for variable A$; W2 bytes for variable B$; and so on." The FIELD statement depends on the OPEN statement earlier—you can't have more total space allocated to the different field widths than you specified in the OPEN...LEN= statement earlier.

Look at this example:

```
100 OPEN "SCORES" AS #1 LEN=25
110 FIELD #1, HERO$ AS 20, POINTS$ AS 5
```

Line 100 opens a path to the file SCORES as buffer #1, with a total record length of 25 bytes. The FIELD statement in line 120 sets one field (HERO$) of 20 bytes, and another field (POINTS$) of 5 bytes.

Incidentally, any variables you use in the field name (here they're HERO$ and POINTS$) are special. They point to locations in the file buffer and should not be used in INPUT or LET statements, or in any other assignments. In fact, we'll say it again:

If you've used a variable in a FIELD statement, don't reuse it with INPUT or LET!

To set some fields from the keyboard, you can type

```
FIELD 2, 25 AS CUSTNAME$, 25 AS STREET$
Ok
```

This allocates a field of 25 bytes for CUSTNAME$ and 25 bytes for STREET$. FIELD allocates space only in the buffer; it doesn't actually move any data.

Move Data into the Buffer with LSET or RSET

Once you've set up the record length and the fields, you can begin moving data into the buffer. For this, you use the LSET or RSET command to specify whether the data begins at the right or left side of the field. Here is the general form of these statements:

```
100 LSET A$="String"
200 RSET A$="String"
```

Line 100 means, "put String into the buffer field in the space provided by FIELD variable A$; begin the characters at the left-hand side of the field." Line 100 is similar, except that the characters are right-justified within the field.

Why is it so important to specify whether a quantity begins on the right or left? Because if the "String" doesn't fill up the field, you want to know where the empty spaces will be. LSET begins writing on the left of the field, so spaces will be on the right. (RSET is just the opposite.) Also, if "String" is larger than the field, you'll lose some characters; LSET begins at the left, so any characters you lose will be the less important ones on the right-hand side of the data value.

Chapter 7

If you've been working through the simple keyboard example, you can use LSET to fill the buffer you created earlier:

```
LSET CUSTNAME$="Oliver Twist"
Ok
LSET STREET$="10 Downing Street"
Ok
```

What you have just done is filled the buffer with all the information for one record—a CUSTNAME$ and a STREET$. This information isn't in the file yet. But you'll change that soon enough!

PUT Data into the File

With one record's worth of data in the buffer, you use the PUT statement to empty those fields into the file and get ready for more input. The general form of the statement is

```
100 PUT #N, R
```

This means, "empty buffer number N to its file; put the data into record R in the file." You can omit the number sign (#) in front of the buffer number. You can also omit the record number R; in this case, the data is PUT into the record after the one accessed by the previous PUT statement.

Here's how to PUT data into the file in our keyboard example:

```
PUT #2, 1
```

This means you'll put whatever is in buffer #2 into record 1 of the file.

Notice that you can be very specific with PUT. You can choose to PUT data directly into record 163 or 1222. And as you'll see, you can get it out with equal ease.

To end this portion of our keyboard example, close the file:

```
CLOSE #2
Ok
```

A Short Input Example

To see how to put data into a random access file, you can enter this short program:

```
10 REM-CREATE CUSTOMER LIST
20 REM
30 OPEN "CUSTOMER" AS #1 LEN=87
```

```
40 FIELD 1, 25 AS CUSTNAME$, 25 AS STREET$, 25 AS CITY$,
      12 AS PHONE$
50 PRINT
60 INPUT "Input customer number"; CUST%
70 WHILE (CUST%>0) AND (CUST%<101)
80      LINE INPUT "Name ?          "; N$
90      LINE INPUT "Street ?        "; S$
100     LINE INPUT "City, ST Zip ?  "; C$
110     LINE INPUT "Phone ?         "; P$
120     LSET CUSTNAME$=N$
130     LSET STREET$=S$
140     LSET CITY$=C$
150     LSET PHONE$=P$
160     PUT #1, CUST%
170     PRINT "Customer added"
180     PRINT
190     INPUT "Input customer number"; CUST%
200 WEND
210 CLOSE
220 END
```

This brief program sets up a customer list. Line 30 opens CUSTOMER (via buffer #1) as a random access file with a record length of 87 bytes. The FIELD statement in line 40 establishes fields of 25 characters each for name, street, and city; and a field of 12 characters for the telephone number.

The integer variable CUST%, which the user inputs as "Customer number," is actually the record number within the file. After line 60 prompts you for the first "customer number," the WHILE...WEND loop keeps prodding you for more information until you finally enter a customer number of less than 1 or greater than 100.

Each time through the loop, you are asked to input a customer number and a name (N$), street (S$), city (C$), and telephone number (P$). You can skip an entry or two—it doesn't matter.(The space is still reserved for that field in the buffer, though.)

Now see how one of the quantities you input is written to the buffer. In line 80, when you respond to the LINE INPUT prompt for "Name?", your typed input goes into variable N$. Later, in line 120, the LSET statement reads the contents of N$ into field variable CUSTNAME$. LSET begins writing at the left side of the CUSTNAME$ field.

After the LSET statements in lines 120-150 place all your inputs into their proper fields in the buffer, you're ready to dump the buffer into the file and prepare for new input. If, say, the customer number CUST% is 5, the PUT statement in line 160 copies the buffer into record 5 in the file. Then the WHILE...WEND loop prompts you for another "Customer number" and starts again.

Here's what you see as you type some customer information:

```
RUN
Input customer number? 1
Name ?          Frank Cheerybyle
Street ?        123 Maypole
City, ST Zip ?  Epping Forest, CA, 94041
Phone ?         408-555-1212
Customer added

Input customer number?
```

Because you specified a record number (whoops, "customer number") of 1, Frank Cheerybyle's data is shoveled into record 1 of the file. Now add a little more data:

```
Input customer number? 2
Name ?          Tetsuro Muranaka
Street ?        2, 5, Nibancho, Chiyoda-ku
City, ST Zip ?  Tokyo 102, Japan
Phone ?         011-81-3-263-9800
Customer added

Input customer number? 3
Name ?          Tommy Traddles
Street ?        Salem House
City, ST Zip ?  London, England
Phone ?         01-634-4403
Customer added
```

When you're ready to quit, just enter a customer number outside the range of 1-100. A simple RETURN will do it, too, because this input is given a value of zero.

```
Input customer number? 102
Ok
```

Well, the information for Frank, Tetsuro, and Tommy is all safely stored in the random access file CUSTOMER. Now let's see how we can get that data.

Getting Data from Random Access File

Extracting specific pieces of data from a random access file is a lot easier than from sequential files. All you have to do is specify the record that you want to see.

Input and Output to Files and Devices

Naturally, the program that gets the data out must have its buffer set up with the same FIELDs as the original program that wrote the data. This isn't much of a problem in most real-world programs, because the same program that writes to a file also reads from it. But it's something to keep in mind if you are using one program for writing and another for reading.

Here's the sequence of events to get data from a random access file:

1. Open the file in random access mode, and specify record length.
2. Use FIELD to specify the fields and the length of each field.
3. Use GET# to bring data from the file into the buffer.
4. Use program statements to PRINT the data or use it.

Specify Record Length with OPEN

You use the OPEN statement to declare a buffer and the record length, just as you did when you put data into the file. Be sure that the record length is the same for reading as it was when the data was written. (Read it like you wrote it!)

For instance, if you worked through the earlier keyboard example, you should have KBDFILE on your disk. You can open it for random access this way:

```
OPEN "KBDFILE" AS #3 LEN=50
Ok
```

Here's what's wonderful about random access files: Once you open a file, you can read from it or write to it in any order that you please. So in a program that does both (as in most real-world applications), you only have to use a single OPEN statement.

Set the FIELDs

You set the buffer fields using FIELD, just as you do when putting data into a file. And a program that writes and reads to a file needs only a single FIELD statement—you don't have to repeat it.

If you've opened KBDFILE from the keyboard, you can set the fields this way:

```
FIELD #3, 25 AS CUST$, 25 AS ST$
Ok
```

Notice that, although you should keep the same fields and field sizes, you don't have to use the same actual names for field variables that you did when you put data into the file. In fact, you can execute any number of FIELD statements for the same

Chapter 7

file, each with different variable names, and all those statements can be in effect at the same time. (Of course, this isn't a good idea, because things could get pretty confusing!)

GET Data from the File

Now that you've established the record size with OPEN and the fields with FIELD, you can get data from the file. Not surprisingly, the statement you use is called GET#, and its basic form looks like this:

```
100 GET #N, R
```

This means, "get record R from the file referenced by buffer N, and put that data into the buffer." You can omit the number sign (#) in front of the buffer number. You can also omit the record number R. If you omit R, the GET statement gets data from the next file record after the last GET. The GW-BASIC language allows up to 16,777,215 records per file.

To GET data from the file in our keyboard example, you can type the following:

```
GET #3, 1
```

This statement gets record 1 from the file and puts it into buffer #3. Now the data is ready to use.

Use the Data

After a GET, the buffer contains one record's worth of data. To use the data, you can read it from the buffer with INPUT# or LINE INPUT#. (Remember, don't use INPUT or LET for this purpose!) Or you can PRINT the data using PRINT, as shown here:

```
PRINT CUST$, ST$
Oliver Twist                    10 Downing Street
```

Output from the Earlier Example

If you entered and ran the earlier example program to create a customer list in a random access file, you can use this code to view different records in the list:

326

Input and Output to Files and Devices

```
10 REM-VIEW CUSTOMER LIST
20 REM
30 OPEN "CUSTOMER" AS #1 LEN=87
40 FIELD 1, 25 AS CUSTNAME$, 25 AS STREET$, 25 AS CITY$, 12
      AS PHONE$
50 PRINT
60 INPUT "Input customer number"; CUST%
70 WHILE (CUST%>0) AND (CUST%<101)
80      GET #1, CUST%
90      PRINT "      "; CUSTNAME$
100     PRINT "      "; STREET$
110     PRINT "      "; CITY$
120     PRINT "      "; PHONE$
130     PRINT
140     INPUT "Input customer number"; CUST%
150 WEND
160 CLOSE
170 END
```

As with the earlier program, the file CUSTOMER is opened with a record length of 87 bytes. The FIELD statement is also the same as in the earlier example; it sets fields of CUSTNAME$, STREET$, and CITY$, which are all 25 characters each. It also sets a field of 12 characters for PHONE$.

Like the earlier example, you are prompted for an initial customer number CUST%, and then a WHILE...WEND loop prompts for additional numbers. Each customer number (you enter them with the INPUT statements in lines 60 and 140) is actually the number for a specific record in the file.

Suppose that the program is waiting for input at line 140, and you type a "3" in response to the prompt for "Customer number." This sets CUST% to 3, so the GET statement in line 80 gets record number 3 and copies it into buffer #1. The GET statement fills each field in the buffer with the information from record 3.

To see the information, you simply PRINT it using the statements in lines 90-120. Unlike INPUT and LET, PRINT doesn't affect the field variables, so you can use their actual names. Here's what happens if you specify customer number 3:

```
Run
Input customer number? 3
      Tommy Traddles
      Salem House
      London, England
      01-634-4403
```

There's Tommy, all right! What about the other information in the file?

```
Input customer number? 1
    Frank Cheerybyle
    123 Maypole
    Epping Forest, CA, 94041
    408-555-1212

Input customer number? 2
    Tetsuro Muranaka
    2, 5, Nibancho, Chiyoda-k
    Tokyo 102, Japan
    011-81-3-263
```

Notice that in record 2 we had typed an address that was too long for the field. The original LSET statement that put this address into the buffer began writing at the left, so the only character lost was at the end of the address, not at the beginning.

What About Empty Records?

If a record is empty, this program gets it anyway, and what you see as a result of the PRINT statements are several lines of blanks. As your programs get more sophisticated, you'll want to account for empty records so that you don't waste time trying to read them.

One way to handle this is to put some oddball character, like an asterisk, as the first character of every record of a file before you ever start writing data to it. When you write data to a record, the asterisk will be wiped out. But if you GET a record from the file and the first character is an asterisk, you know it's an empty record and you don't have to print it.

Besides LSET and RSET, you can use PRINT#, PRINT# USING, and WRITE# to fill the fields in a random buffer.

Additional Things You Should Know About Files

You've seen the basics of files and file management. Now let's look at some further tricks to help you manage your data and data files.

More About OPEN

OPEN is one of the most important and versatile statements in the BASIC language. You use OPEN not only for working with files, but also when you're working with devices such as modems.

Input and Output to Files and Devices

OPEN has a number of options you can use. We won't discuss all options in detail at this point, but they're all there in your bag of BASIC tricks, ready to help.

OPEN can be written in either of two forms. We'll start by expanding a little on the general form of the OPEN statement, as follows:

```
OPEN filename [FOR mode] [ACCESS access] [lock] AS
[#] file number [LEN=reclen]
```

(The brackets around an item mean it's optional—you don't have to include it when you write the statement.)

The Mode Option

The *mode* actually determines the initial positioning within the file, like this:

- **RANDOM**   Default. Random input or output.

- **INPUT**   Positions to beginning of the file. Produces "File not found" error if file doesn't exist.

- **OUTPUT**   Positions to the beginning of the file and creates file if it doesn't exist.

- **APPEND**   Positions to end of the file and creates file if it doesn't exist.

The other syntax you can use for OPEN is

```
OPEN mode, [#] file number, filename [,reclen]
```

In this type of statement, you indicate the *mode* with single letters, this way:

- O   Sequential output mode

- I   Sequential input mode

- R   Random input/output mode

- A   Position to end of file

The ACCESS Option

The ACCESS tells what kind of access is allowed for a file once it's open. You can specify the type of ACCESS as READ, WRITE, or READ WRITE; these are "paired" with *lock* items as outlined in the following section.

Chapter 7

Lock Items

If your data files are to be used on a network, you can use the *lock* item to safeguard important data. On a network, many programs—in many computers—might be reading and writing to the same file. The lock item lets you lock a file so that no one else on a network can write to it or read from it. You can specify just who can have access to the file and how much can be done with it. See table 7-1 for your options.

Table 7-1: Locking modes.

Access	Mode	Meaning
none	none	Default; no access is specified, and the file can be opened any number of times by anyone else on the network.
none	SHARED	No restrictions, except that the default mode isn't allowed.
READ	LOCK	Deny read mode; nobody else on the network can get read access to this file.
WRITE	LOCK	Deny write mode; prevents file from being opened for write access by anyone else on the network.
READ WRITE	LOCK	Exclusive mode; you have exclusive access to the file now, and nobody else can access it.

The lock item doesn't protect the file and allow only you access forever. It controls access only after you've OPENed the file using LOCK. When you CLOSE it again, the file lies there, naked and unprotected, ready for its data to be pillaged by other network users.

You can also use the LOCK statement to restrict access to specified records of data; more about the LOCK statement in a moment.

Multiple Numbers for a File

You can OPEN a file under only a single file number if you're outputting or appending to the file. But for INPUT from the file, you can assign different numbers to it, like this:

```
100 OPEN "SNGLFILE" FOR OUTPUT AS #1
110 OPEN "SNGLFILE" FOR OUTPUT AS #3
```

Input and Output to Files and Devices

Finding Where You Are with LOC

Sometimes you need to know the present location where you are in a file. And for this purpose, BASIC presents you with the LOC (location) function. The general form of LOC is

```
X=LOC (N)
```

This means, "find the present location in buffer N and return that value to variable X." With random access files, LOC gives you the record number of the latest GET or PUT statement. With sequential files, it names the number of 128-byte blocks that were output or input since the file was opened.

You can use LOC to keep track of the actual record number of the file with a simple statement like the following:

```
645 PRINT "The current record number is"; LOC (1)
646 IF LOC(1) > 100 THEN END
```

You also use LOC in communications to return the number of characters waiting to be read in the input buffer.

The Length of File (LOF) Function

Sometimes you want to make decisions based on the size of a file. That's where the LOF (length of file) function comes in. Its general form is shown here:

```
100 X=LOF(N)
```

This means, "return the number of bytes allocated to file N and put the result in X." LOF can tell you whether a file has anything in it, and you can branch execution accordingly, as follows:

```
10 OPEN "CUSTOMER" AS #1 LEN = 87
20 IF LOF(1) > 0 GOSUB 1000
 .
 .
1000 PRINT "File not empty" :RETURN
```

This example branches execution to tell you whether a file is not empty when you OPEN it.

Chapter 7

Protecting Data Files with LOCK

You already know how to protect program files; now we'll explore how you can prevent unauthorized entry to your data as well—an important concern, especially in a network environment. You'll use the LOCK and UNLOCK statements to seal your data tight and make it available again.

LOCKing a Data File

You use the LOCK statement to lock an entire data file, or certain records within the file. The file must be open and a file number assigned. Then you use LOCK, as shown here:

```
100 LOCK #N
120 LOCK #N, X TO Y
```

Line 100 means, "restrict access to file N." The command in line 120 means, "restrict access to records X through Y in file N." You can restrict access while the file is open, but you should always UNLOCK the file or records before you end the program or close the file.

Here are some other ways to use LOCK:

```
130 LOCK #1, 5
140 LOCK #2, TO 100
```

Line 130 locks only record 5 in file #1. Line 140 locks all records from 1 to 100 in file #2. Incidentally, if you try to specify records in a sequential access file that's been opened for input or output, you can't do it: the entire file is locked.

Unlocking the Data

Not surprisingly, UNLOCK frees a file or specified records for input and output again. You should pair up LOCK and UNLOCK statements, like this:

```
100 LOCK #1, 10 TO 50
120 LOCK #1, 51 TO 100
.
.
780 UNLOCK #1, 10 TO 50
790 UNLOCK #1, 51 TO 100
```

Input and Output to Files and Devices

One thing to remember about LOCK is that it's for short-term data protection. But if you fail to UNLOCK files before you CLOSE them, you can mess up future access to them on a network. Remember:

Always UNLOCK all files before you CLOSE them!

Other Devices

Besides printers and files, BASIC can control and access other devices, such as a light pen, joystick, modem, and more. GW-BASIC offers a number of statements specifically designed for handling these devices.

Still More About OPEN

You can use OPEN to open buffers for devices such as a printer or a communications port just as you do for files. The devices you can open and their modes are presented in table 7-2.

Table 7-2: Devices and OPEN modes.

Specifier in OPEN	Device	Modes You Can Use
A:, B:, etc.	Disk drive	All modes
KYBD:	Keyboard	INPUT only
SCRN:	Screen	OUTPUT only
LPT1:	Line printer 1	OUTPUT only
LPT2:	Line printer 2	OUTPUT only
LPT3:	Line printer 3	OUTPUT only
COM1:	Serial communications port 1	INPUT, OUTPUT or RANDOM
COM2:	Serial communications port 2	INPUT, OUTPUT or RANDOM

You OPEN a buffer for any of these devices the same way that you do for a file. For instance:

```
100 OPEN "SCRN:" FOR OUTPUT AS #2
```

Line 100 opens the screen for output as buffer #2.

Trap Those Devices!

Many times you'll want to "trap" the activity of a device. When you set up a trap, BASIC checks for activity after every instruction it executes. The trap itself contains a branch to a subroutine that may process the activity or send a message.

The ON KEY statement, which was explained in an earlier chapter, is an example of a trap. When a key is pressed, this statement registers the press and branches execution. You can also trap activity from communication ports, a light pen, the trigger from a joystick, the internal timer, and playing music.

Regardless of the device whose activity you want to trap, the procedure is much the same:

1. Set up the trap with an ON statement like ON COM or ON STRIG. This trap contains a GOSUB statement that will be executed if the event happens.

2. Enable the trap with a statement like COM(1) ON or STRIG(0) ON.

The ON Statements

All ON statements have the same general form:

```
100 ON event GOSUB N
```

This means, "watch for the *event*, and if it happens, execute the subroutine beginning with line N." After this statement (and if the event is turned on with the *event* ON statement), BASIC begins looking for the event. As it executes a program, BASIC checks after each line to see that the event has happened. When the event does occur, execution immediately branches to the subroutine and executes it before continuing. See table 7-3 for a list of the ON statements and their events.

Table 7-3: ON Statements and Events.

ON Statements	Events
ON COM(N)	Traps COM port 1 or 2
ON KEY(N)	Traps the press of a key
ON PEN	Traps the light pen
ON PLAY(N)	Traps music played by BASIC
ON STRIG(N)	Traps trigger from joystick
ON TIMER(N)	Traps internal timer

The Event ON Statement

Once you've set up the trap with the subroutine, you still must enable the trap. You do this with an event-ON statement. The general form is as follows:

```
100 event (N) ON
500 event (N) OFF
700 event (N) STOP
```

The event-ON statement means, "turn on the trapping of this event." The event-OFF statement means, "turn off trapping of this event."

The event-STOP statement means, "remember the activity of this event but don't execute the subroutine in the ON event statement now; execute the subroutine as soon as the event-ON statement is executed again." The event-STOP statement is a way of trapping an event but deferring any action on it until later. This can be useful for parts of your program that shouldn't be interrupted during processing.

Using a Light Pen

If you have a light pen, you can point it at the screen (or touch it to the screen, depending on the type of pen), then trap its activity by using the ON PEN and PEN statements. (There's only one pen, so ON PEN has no N after it.) The light pen also has a function associated with it:

```
X=PEN(N)
```

This means, "find the light pen coordinates or pen status and place the result in variable X." The value for N determines what value X receives, as shown in table 7-4.

Table 7-4: Arguments for PEN.

Value of N	What X receives
0	−1 if PEN was down since last poll; otherwise 0
1	X-pixel coordinate when PEN was last activated. Range is 0-319 (medium resolution) or 0-639 (high resolution).
2	Y-pixel coordinate when PEN was last activated. Range is 0-199.
3	Current PEN switch value: −1 if down, 0 if up.
4	Last known valid X-pixel coordinate. Range is 0-319 (medium resolution) or 0-639 (high resolution).
5	Last known Y-pixel coordinate. Range is 0-199.
6	Last character row position when PEN was last activated. Range is 1-24.
7	Last character column position when PEN was last activated. Range is 1-40 or 1-80, depending on screen width.
8	Last known valid character row. Range is 1-24.
9	Last known valid character column position. Range is 1-40 or 1-80, depending on screen width.

A single trap of the light pen doesn't usually do you much good. Here's an example of how to trap the activity of the light pen:

```
10 ON PEN GOSUB 500
20 PEN ON
 .
 .
500 FOR I=1 TO 10000
510 L1=PEN(8)
520 L2=PEN(9)
530 PRINT "ROW ="; L1; "COLUMN ="; L2
540 NEXT
550 RETURN
```

This example prints the row and column of the pen as it is moved around the screen.

Getting Happiness from a Joystick

To trap the controls of a joystick, begin by setting up the trap with the ON STRIG(N), then enable the trap with STRIG(N) ON. You trap each button separately, using the value for N as shown in table 7-5.

Table 7-5: Arguments for STRIG.

Value of N	Joystick button trapped
0	Button A1
2	Button B1
4	Button A2
6	Button B2

Using STICK with a Joystick

The STICK function returns the X- and Y-coordinates of a pair of joysticks. The function is used as follows:

```
100 C=STICK(N)
```

This means, "find the coordinate specified by N and put the value in variable C." The value of N can be in the range of 0 to 3, and the resulting coordinates are shown in Table 7-6.

Table 7-6: Arguments for STICK.

Value of N	Coordinate
0	X-coordinate of joystick A (also see below)
1	Y-coordinate of joystick A
2	X-coordinate of joystick B
3	Y-coordinate of joystick B

Using an N with a value of zero can store the X- and Y-coordinates for both joystick A and joystick B in successive function calls.

Increasing BASIC Communications Skills

The GW-BASIC library offers several statements to help you write communications software in this language.

Opening a COM Port

To open a communications port, you use a special form of the OPEN statement:

```
100 OPEN "COM [n]: [speed] [,parity][,data][,stop],
    [RS][,CS[n]][,DS[n]][,CD[n]][,LF][,PE]"
    AS [#] filenum [LEN=number]
```

This means, "open COM port *n*, using the specified parameters, as buffer number *filenum*."

There are a lot of parameters here, although they'll simply default if you don't specify them. You need them because, in communications between two computers or between a computer and a modem, both ends have to be set the same. They must use the same speed, they have to expect the same size for one byte of data, they have to use the same kind of error-checking, and so on.

Being able to specify all those different parameters with OPEN COM[n] ensures that you can match whatever is happening on the other end of the RS-232-C interface used in communications. You don't usually need to know exactly what each of these parameters does, as long as you match what's happening at the other end of the RS-232-C line. But for your information, we will discuss what all those parameters mean.

COM[n] can be COM1 or COM2. The *speed*, which is a measure of bits per second—how much information is being transferred from one system to another—can be 75, 110, 150, 300, 600, 1200, 1800, 2400, 4800, or 9600. The default is 300 bps, so this is probably one parameter you'll always want to include, because 300 bps is slooooooow.

The *parity* is a form of error-checking. An extra bit is added to each byte so that the sum of the bits is always even, odd, and so forth. Parity is shown in table 7-7.

Table 7-7: Specifying Parity.

What You Specify	What It Means
S	SPACE
M	MARK
O	ODD
E	EVEN (default)
N	NONE

Input and Output to Files and Devices

The *data* field indicates how many data bits form a character for send and receive; the default is 7 bits, but you can specify 4, 5, 6, 7, or 8 data bits. You can't specify 4 data bits parity of none (N) or 8 data bits with any parity *other* than none.

The *stop* parameter is the number of stop bits. You can specify 1 or 2 stop bits here; if you don't specify the number of stop bits, all speeds except 75 and 110 bps transmit 2 stop bits.

Besides choosing the way data is sent, you can also select the actual RS-232-C line signal options as shown in Table 7-8. These are the signals that control how control is passed between devices—who's sending, who's receiving, and so on. The value for *n* is the number of milliseconds for the signal before a device timeout occurs.

Table 7-8: RS-232-C Line Signal Options.

Option	What It Does
RS	Suppresses RTS (request to send) signal
CS[n]	Controls CTS (clear to send), default is 1000 ms
DS[n]	Controls DSR (data set ready), default is 1000 ms
CD[n]	Controls CD (carrier detect), default is 0 ms
LF	Sends a line feed at each Carriage Return
PE	Enables parity checking

Here is an example of how you use the OPEN COM statement:

```
100 OPEN "COM1:1200,N,8" AS #1
```

Line 100 opens communications port 1 at a speed of 1200 bits per second, with no parity and 8 data bits, and assigns this port to buffer #1.

Trapping COM Port Activity

You can trap COM ports 1 or 2. First use ON COM to define the communications port you're going to trap and what action will be taken, then turn on the trapping with the COM(N) statement. Here's an example of how to use ON COM and COM(N):

```
100 OPEN "COM1:1200,N,8" AS #1
110 ON COM(1) GOSUB 500
120 COM(1) ON
    .
    .
500 PRINT "Incoming modem traffic!" : RETURN
```

Chapter 7

Lines 110 and 120 enable trapping of activity on COM port 1, which could have a modem connected to it. After enabling the trap, BASIC checks for activity after it executes every statement. If the modem sends a signal, you get a display on the screen to tell you.

You should use this trap only for long transmissions; trying to trap single-character messages at the high speeds of today's modems can cause the COM interrupt buffer to overflow.

Using LOC for Communications

The LOC(N) function, you'll recall, returns the value of the present location in a file. It can also be a big help in communications, because it can show how many characters are waiting to be read in the input buffer.

The input buffer (or receive buffer) in BASIC is where information is placed when it arrives from the RS-232-C interface. It usually holds up to 256 characters. You can use LOC to detect when the input buffer has been read, so that a program can signal the sending system to send another bufferful of information. Here's an example:

```
10 OPEN "COM1: 1200, N, 8" AS #1
20 WHILE NOT EOF(1)
30     IF LOC(1) > 128 THEN PRINT #1, CHR$(19): SUSPEND=1
40     BUFFER$=INPUT$ (LOC(1), #1)
50     PRINT BUFFER$
60     IF SUSPEND=1 THEN PRINT #1, CHR$(17): SUSPEND=0
70 WEND
```

In this short section of code, we open a communications port, COM1, which is physically connected to a modem. In this case, we've specified 1200 bits per second speed, no parity, 8 data bits. Then we enter the WHILE...WEND loop to read data coming in from the modem. We let 128 characters come into buffer #1. Then the IF LOC(1)>128 statement is true (we're located past character 128 of the buffer) and sends a CHR$(19) to the modem. (CHR$(19) is the ASCII code for XOFF in this case, and it tells the modem to "stop sending data.")

Now we use LOC again, this time to place the characters that are in the buffer into the variable called BUFFER$. Remember, LOC(1) is set at 128, so the statement BUFFER$=INPUT$ (LOC(1), #1) tells BASIC to read 128 characters from buffer #1 into BUFFER$. Then we print the contents of that variable on the screen, and when we're done printing, we send a CHR$(17) to the modem. (CHR$(17) is the ASCII character that signals XON to the modem to tell it to send information again.)

When no more information is being sent from the modem, reading buffer #1 produces an end-of-file signal, and execution falls out of the WHILE...WEND loop.

Other I/O Aids

This section shows some additional "bells and whistles" contained in BASIC to help you handle input and output to devices, including printers.

Returning a Device Error

Earlier in this book, you wrote a simple error-trapping routine. BASIC has some sophisticated "built-in" ways of handling certain errors, too, such as ERDEV and ERDEV$.

The ERDEV and ERDEV$ variables show you the value of a device error and the name of the device causing the error. The general form of these variables is as follows:

```
X=ERDEV
A$=ERDEV$
```

The top statement means, "look at the error code and place the value into X." The bottom statement means, "put the name of the error-causing device in variable A$." This name is an eight-byte character device name, such as "LPT1," or a two-byte block device name, such as "A:".

For instance, if the printer is out of paper, here's what you might see for ERDEV and ERDEV$:

```
PRINT ERDEV$
LPT1
Ok
PRINT ERDEV
-32759
Ok
```

Chapter 9, *Advanced GW-BASIC*, provides more information on different errors and how to handle them.

File Management

If you're already familiar with MS-DOS, you'll have little trouble handling the file management statements of GW-BASIC. You specify directories and paths much the same way, although BASIC is a little pickier about the need for quotation marks around file paths.

Counting Files

Use the FILES statement to see a list of all files on the current directory, as follows:

```
FILES
```

You'll see a list of all files on the current directory. To see what's in a different directory, just add the necessary information to the FILES command, like this:

```
FILES "A:\MYSUB\"
```

You'll get a display of all the files in that subdirectory. You can use wildcards and question marks, just as in MS-DOS, to narrow down the display further:

```
10 FILES "*.BAS"
20 FILES "DATA?.*"
```

Line 10 displays all files with the .BAS extension. Line 20 shows you all files named with the word DATA followed by any character, and with any extension after the period. Your display might look like this:

```
DATA1.BAS       DATA2.DOC       DATA2.          DATA9.ASC
```

Changing Names

Use the NAME command to change the name of a file, like this:

```
NAME "OLDFILE" AS "NEWFILE"
```

This means, "change the name of the file OLDFILE to NEWFILE." The new file is placed in the same location on the diskette, with a new name. For example:

```
NAME "MYFILE.BAS" AS "YOURFILE.BAS"
```

This renames the file MYFILE.BAS and changes its name to YOURFILE.BAS.

Killing Files Softly

To delete a file from the current directory, use the KILL statement. The form is:

```
KILL "FILENAME.EXT"
```

Input and Output to Files and Devices

This means, "erase the file FILENAME.EXT from the current directory." As with MS-DOS file commands, you can specify wildcards for KILLing. For instance, to delete all files with the extension ".MYF", you could type:

```
KILL "*.MYF"
```

And you can, of course, specify a pathname for the deletion, too:

```
100 KILL "A:\FILES\*.*"
```

Line 100 deletes all files in the subdirectory FILES on the disk in drive A:. Unlike MS-DOS, BASIC doesn't give you an "Are you sure?" message before it makes the deletion. So be careful using wildcards this way!

Making and Removing Directories

Like MS-DOS, GW-BASIC allows you to add and remove directories. The commands are similar:

```
MKDIR "pathname"
RMDIR "pathname"
```

These statements mean, "make the directory specified by pathname," and "remove the directory specified by pathname." For instance, here's how you would create a directory called FILES on drive A, then remove a directory named TEMP on drive B:

```
MKDIR "A:\FILES"
RMDIR "B\TEMP"
```

As with MS-DOS, before you can delete a directory, it must be completely empty of all files except "." and "..". (Unlike DOS, however, you can't abbreviate MKDIR and MD, nor can you abbreviate the other BASIC commands CHDIR and RMDIR.)

Changing Directories with CHDIR

The CHDIR command changes from one working directory to another. (It's just like typing "CD" if you're in MS-DOS.") The general form is:

```
CHDIR "PATHNAME"
```

343

This means, "change the working directory to be the one specified by the pathname." Here is an example:

```
10 SAVE "FILE-A"
20 CHDIR "ASCFILES"
30 SAVE "FILE-A", A
```

This example saves the current program as a normal binary file. Then it changes the working directory to ASCFILES and saves the program as an ASCII file in *that* directory.

Setting the Environment

The environment string table is a global table that can be used by any program that runs—not only BASIC programs. It contains statements that look like this:

```
Environment variable = string
```

The environment table can contain such elements as the PATH statement, which is used by many programs to search for their files, and it can contain special variables that tell programs where to look for their data files. You can examine and modify this table using the ENVIRON statement and the ENVIRON$ function.

Using ENVIRON to Change the Environment

While MS-DOS has the PATH command, GW-BASIC has ENVIRON to let you look at and modify the environment. The general form is as follows:

```
ENVIRON A$
```

This means, "change the environment according to the string `A$`." The string A$ must be of a specific form, like this:

```
parameter=text
```

The "parameter" is the name of the parameter. It may be "path" or another parameter from MS-DOS. It must be separated from the "text" by a space or an equals sign. If the parameter already exists in the environment file, it's deleted and the new one is added at the end.

Here's how you would add a PATH parameter to create a default path to the directory FILES on drive A:

```
ENVIRON "PATH=A:\FILES"
```

Input and Output to Files and Devices

Reading the Environment with ENVIRON$

You can use ENVIRON$ to determine the current environment. The general form is as follows:

```
A$=ENVIRON$("P$")
A$=ENVIRON(N)
```

The top expression means, "return the parameter specified by `P$` and put the result in `A$`." The second expression means, "return the Nth parameter in the environment string and put the result in `A$`." Unlike most BASIC statements, ENVIRON$ is sensitive to uppercase and lowercase characters.

Here's how you can read just the PATH parameter:

```
PRINT ENVIRON$("PATH")
A:\FILES
Ok
```

Here's a little program that reads the first 10 parameters from the environment table:

```
10 FOR I = 1 TO 10
20    PRINT ENVIRON$(I)
30 NEXT
```

This is an example of the output from the short program above. (Your output may be different.)

```
RUN
COMSPEC=C:\COMMAND.COM
PATH=A:\FILES


Ok
```

Review Questions

1. What would you type to save the current program as an ASCII file named PROGRAM5.BAS?

2. You're creating a data file containing a list of names, addresses, and telephone and fax numbers of worldwide sales managers (some 200 in all). There's a lot of turnover in your organization, so you expect the list to change rather frequently. What type of file structure should you use, and why?

Chapter 7

3. You are given a sequential data file, but you don't know what its contents look like nor how they are formatted. What statement would you use to "read" the file initially, so that you could determine how to set up your input routines later?

4. What's the cardinal rule on variables you've used in a FIELD statement?

5. The following section of code locks up records 1 to 100 in the file specified by #3. What's wrong with it?

```
1250 LOCK #3, 1 TO 100
1260 END
```

6. Explain the output from this program:

```
10 OPEN "LIT-101" FOR OUTPUT AS #1
20 PRINT #1, "Holden Caulfield",5,"Hester Prynne",2
30 CLOSE #1
40 OPEN "LIT-101" FOR INPUT AS #2
50 WHILE EOF(2) <> -1
60      LINE INPUT #2, A$
70      PRINT A$
80 WEND
90 CLOSE #2
100 END
Ok
RUN
Holden Caulfield             5                  Hester Prynne    2
```

7. Write a short section of code to print the contents of 10 records from the random access file BATTERUP. Each record is 36 bytes long, and is set up with fields like this:

   Name - up to 30 characters

   Number of times at bat - 3 characters

   Number of hits - 3 characters

8. This loop always produces an "Input past end" error. What's wrong?

```
90 WHILE EOF(2) <> 1
100 LINE INPUT #2, A$
110 PRINT A$
120 WEND
```

9. Write a statement that will change the PATH environment variable to C:\BATCHFLS.

10. Exercise: Combine the two example programs for random access files into a single program that allows you to choose whether you want to add information to the CUSTOMER file or read information from it. You should be able to use a single OPEN and FIELD statement at the beginning of the program.

Chapter 8

The BASIC Screen, Graphics, and Sound

Chapter **8**

The BASIC Screen, Graphics, and Sound

Most people are happier when they're allowed to give full rein to their creativity. That's why you should particularly enjoy this introduction to BASIC's graphics and sound functions. Not that programming isn't creative all by itself, of course; you've probably already broken new programming ground, or at least tried improvements and modifications to the programs elsewhere in this book. But when your output includes dazzling color graphics and brilliant music, well, it can be pretty rewarding.

You don't add graphics to your programs just for fun, either. Using the graphics statements in this chapter, you can transmogrify reams of dull data into eye-catching output. And just by looking at a bar or pie chart, you can size up a situation or opportunity. In programming, as elsewhere, a picture is often worth a thousand words.

What You'll Learn in this Chapter

In this chapter you'll learn

- How to draw graphs using ordinary text characters
- The difference between the graphics screen and the alphanumeric screen
- Switching to the appropriate graphics resolution for your system
- Drawing simple shapes, changing colors, and manipulating lines on the screen—with a little animation thrown in!
- Making beautiful music with BASIC's built-in sound features

Chapter 8

Using the Text Screen

We're going to discuss the special graphics functions in a minute. But before turning to graphics, let's see what we can do with the "ordinary" display screen, the one you see when you first load BASIC.

About the Standard Text Screen

When you first load BASIC, the display is a text screen—it's set to show alphabetic characters and numbers only. Although BASIC has many different kinds of graphics statements, they don't affect this ordinary display, and you can't use them to "draw" on the screen yet.

The text screen itself (see fig. 8-1) is 80 columns wide by 25 lines high, so there's room for 80 characters or spaces on each line, and space for a total of 25 lines of text. (The 25th line is used by the function key display, but you can use KEY OFF to make it available for text display.)

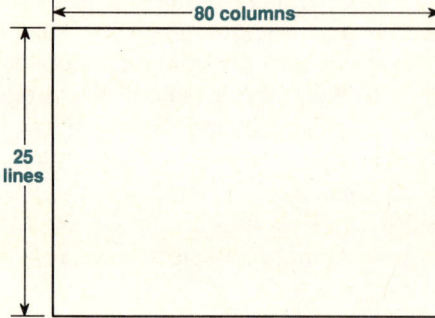

Fig. 8-1:   The text display screen.

Video Plotting with TAB

You don't need fancy graphics statements to produce art and charts in BASIC. No indeed! We can do some pretty neat graphing just by using TAB and equations.

For example, suppose that we wanted to plot the values of a simple equation such as X = Y. Consider that the Y axis is down the screen (0 is at top) and the X axis is across the screen (0 is at the left). As shown in figure 8-2, imagine that an (X,Y) of (0,0) is at the top left, while an (X,Y) of (24,79) is at the lower right. Later you'll see that the text screen actually goes from (1,1) to (25,80).

352

The BASIC Screen, Graphics, and Sound

Fig. 8-2: Plotting on the screen.

Now look what happens with this program.

```
10 FOR Y = 1 To 15 : X = Y
20 PRINT TAB(X) "*"
30 NEXT
RUN
 *
  *
   *
    *
     *
      *
       *
        *
         *
          *
           *
            *
             *
              *
               *
```

Here we have a FOR...NEXT loop which increments through 15 values of Y. The variable Y is set to equal the value of X, then we TAB X spaces to the right and print an asterisk character. Because the equation is X = Y, we get a slanted line. The slant isn't 45 degrees, as would be expected, because the vertical spacing on the terminal doesn't equal the horizontal spacing. There are more than three times as many horizontal column positions as there are vertical positions. Because the spacing is not equal, there will be some distortion in your graphs.

Chapter 8

In the example X = Y, we have a *linear equation*. Linear equations produce straight lines of different angles and different offsets on the screen. However, we can also print curved-line graphs. Consider the equation X = Y * Y/10. Can you tell how the RUN of this program would look?

```
10 FOR Y = 1 TO 10
20 X = Y * Y/10
30 PRINT TAB(X) "*"
40 NEXT
```

Table 8-1 illustrates what happens in this case. The equation X = Y * Y/10 generates decimal fractions between 0 and 10. When Y is 1, X * X/10 is 0.1; and because we can TAB only an integer number of spaces, TAB(X) is zero. A RUN of the program produces the graph shown in figure 8-3.

Table 8-1: Using TAB with decimal numbers.

Y	X = (Y * Y/10)	TAB(X)
1	0.1	0
2	0.4	0
3	0.9	0
4	1.6	1
5	2.5	2
6	3.6	3
7	4.9	4
8	6.4	6
9	8.1	8
10	10.0	10

The BASIC Screen, Graphics, and Sound

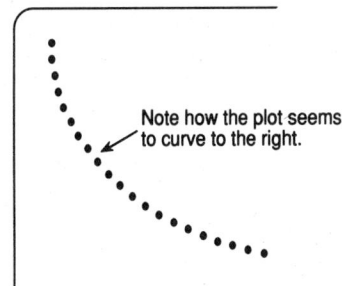

Fig. 8-3: Graph using Tab with decimal numbers.

Plotting the SIN on the Screen

We can take advantage of some of the more powerful BASIC numeric functions in our graphing. The trigonometric functions SIN, COS, and ATN can be easily used to create harmonic curves for biorhythms, music analysis, modulation studies, and so on. As an example, we can use the formula X = SIN(Y) to calculate the value of the X coordinate we want to TAB out to. Because Y is in radians (rather than degrees) for the trig functions, we will make it vary from 0 to 6.28, which is one full circle in radians. We will use a FOR...NEXT loop with a variable STEP size to control the number of points of the curve that are displayed.

To make things even more interesting, we can make the string that gets PRINTed a message. Remember that this message can be any characters on the keyboard. Here is the program:

```
10 INC = .3
20 FOR Y = 0 TO 6.28 STEP INC
30     X = SIN(Y)
40     X = X * 15 + 15
50     PRINT TAB(X) "SINE"
60 NEXT
```

Note that we changed X in statement 40 to X * 15 + 15. This is because X = SIN(Y) produces decimal fractions between −1 and +1, and we cannot TAB a negative number of spaces. Therefore we multiply X by 15 so that the numbers produced are in the range −15 to +15, and then add 15 so that the numbers are offset to 0 to 30. (To print to the full screen width, we could increase the width to 80 by writing X = 40 * X + 40.)

Here is a RUN of the program:

```
RUN
              SINE
                SINE
                  SINE
                    SINE
                     SINE
                      SINE
                      SINE
                     SINE
                    SINE
                  SINE
                SINE
              SINE
            SINE
          SINE
        SINE
      SINE
     SINE
    SINE
    SINE
    SINE
      SINE
        SINE
          SINE
Ok
```

Switching Line Length with WIDTH

One simple way to control the screen output is with the WIDTH statement. WIDTH switches the display between lines that are 80 characters wide (what you've probably used all along) and 40 characters. The general form is as follows:

```
100 WIDTH 40
200 WIDTH 80
```

Line 100 means, "set the line width in the display to 40 characters per line." Line 200 means, "set the line width to 80 characters per line." These are your only two choices for the display, although you can specify different line widths for the printer or other devices.

Let's see what happens to our sine program if we change the line width to 40 characters per line. Add line 5 to the program, as shown here:

```
5 WIDTH 40
```

The BASIC Screen, Graphics, and Sound

This changes the line width to 40 characters per line before the PRINT statements in the FOR...NEXT loop, so everything is printed at the new line width:

```
5 WIDTH 40
10 INC =.3
20 FOR Y=0 TO 6.28 STEP INC
30      X=SIN(Y)
40      X=X*15+15
50      PRINT TAB(X) "SINE"
60 NEXT

RUN
```

The output now looks like that shown in figure 8-4.
To switch your screen back to an 80-character line, use this statement:

```
WIDTH 80
Ok
```

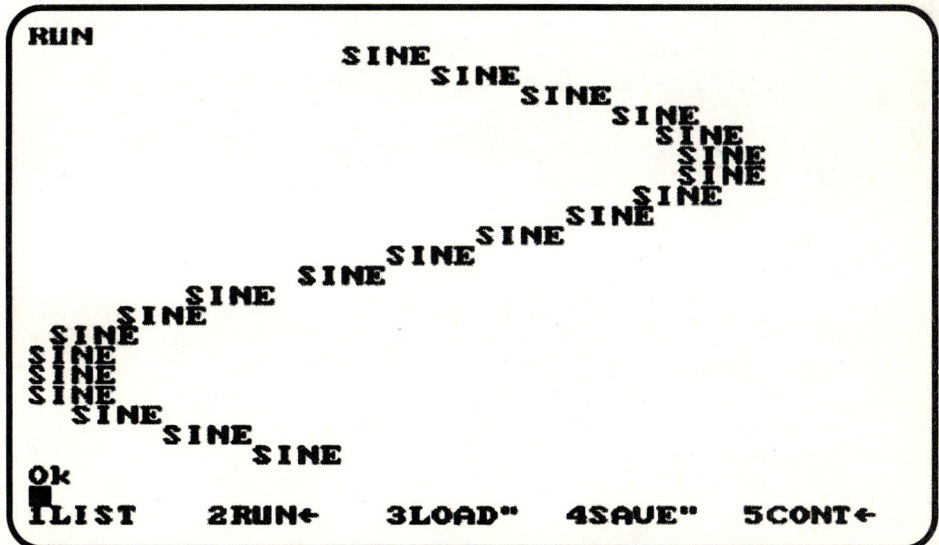

Fig. 8-4: The sine program printed with 40 characters per line.

If Your Display Isn't IBM...

If you have a display adapter that doesn't follow one of the IBM standards (the IBM standards are CGA, EGA, or VGA), you won't be able to do some of the things

Chapter 8

explained in this chapter. For instance, if you have a Hercules graphics adapter, you won't be able to change the screen width or use GW-BASIC's graphics screen modes. If this happens to you, you may be able to obtain the special version of BASIC for that adapter, or you may be able to use public domain software such as HGC.IBM and SIM.CGA to provide graphics capabilities in BASIC.

Going Where You Want—And Finding Where You've Been

In order to make the fullest use of that vast expanse of screen in front of you, the BASIC language contains statements and functions for placing and locating the cursor. As explained elsewhere in this book, the POS (position) function tells you the current position of the cursor within a line. You can use CSRLIN (cursor line) to tell you the actual line number of the cursor, while LOCATE places the cursor anywhere on the screen. Let's see how you can put these functions to use.

How to LOCATE Anywhere

The screen cursor, you remember, is the place where PRINTing begins and where you type INPUT. And you're not stuck with beginning on the first line in the left-hand margin, either. You can use the LOCATE statement to place the cursor anywhere on the screen so that printing or input begins there. Having trouble finding the cursor? LOCATE can cure that for you, too. The general form is as follows:

```
100 LOCATE R, C, CS, A, B
```

This means, "place the cursor at row R column C; specify whether it's on or off with CS; and specify cursor scanning from START to STOP." You can leave any of these parameters unchanged by simply typing the comma without a number.

The row and column can be anywhere on the current screen. R can be 1 through 25, and C can be 1 through 80. The value for CS can be either 0 or 1; a 0 means "cursor is invisible," whereas a 1 means "cursor is visible."

The variables A and B indicate scan lines for the cursor. Their range is 0 to 31. For the largest possible cursor on the screen, specify a scan line A of 0 and B of 31, like this:

```
LOCATE , , ,0, 31
Ok
```

Here's a small program that bounces the cursor randomly around the screen, printing at a different location each time:

```
10 CLS
20 RANDOMIZE TIMER
30 FOR I = 1 TO 10
```

The BASIC Screen, Graphics, and Sound

```
40          R=INT(1 + RND*23)       'Randomizes the row
50          C=INT(1 + RND*79)       'Randomizes the column
60          LOCATE R,C,0
70          PRINT "I'm here!"
80 NEXT
Ok
RUN
```

The RANDOMIZE TIMER statement in line 20 makes sure that the random number generator function, RND, starts with a different "seed" for each iteration. Each time through the short FOR...NEXT loop, the value for R (row) is set to a random integer in the range from 1 to 24, then C (column) is set to a random number from 1 to 80. The LOCATE statement places the cursor at the row and column called for by those random numbers. The results are all over the screen.

```
                    I'm here!
                                                                    I'm here!
                                                    I'm here!
                                I'm here!
I'm here!
                                                                I'm here!
                                                                I'm here!
I'm here!
                    I'm here!
                                        I'm here!
```

If one of the "I'm here!" phrases would be broken because the random LOCATE statement would place it too close to the right-hand edge of the screen, BASIC simply prints the entire phrase all together at the beginning of the following line.

How CSRLIN Helps Get You Back

The CSRLIN (it means "cursor line") variable tells where the cursor is currently positioned. Its general form is as follows:

```
100 Y=CSRLIN
```

This means, "detect the current line of the cursor and put the result in variable Y." It should be pretty clear that this value will be in the range of 1 to 25, because that's the number of lines on the BASIC screen.

How do we use CSRLIN? If you ran the small program above, you noticed that the cursor wound up in a left-hand row that was one row after the final LOCATE statement executed by the loop. It was probably nowhere near where it was when you originally typed RUN.

Chapter 8

One common use of LOCATE during a running program is to print a message or provide for input in another part of the screen from where the main action is happening. Here's a program that shows how it's done:

```
10 REM-RELOCATOR
20 KEY OFF: CLS
30 WHILE INKEY$<>CHR$(27)
40      PRINT "This simulates a high-powered business program"
50      PRINT "printing data on the screen, while down below"
60      PRINT "a prompt tells you how to stop the thing"
70      Y=CSRLIN
80      X=POS(0)
90      GOSUB 130
100 WEND
110 END
120 '
130 REM-Subroutine to show prompt on line 25 of the screen
140 LOCATE 25,1
150 PRINT "PRESS THE [ESC] KEY TO EXIT"
160 LOCATE X,Y
170 RETURN
```

This program has a WHILE...WEND loop that simulates the action of a much larger program printing data on the screen. Each time through the loop, the cursor line is recorded in variable Y, and the cursor position on that line is recorded in variable X. Then the program branches to the prompting subroutine in line 130.

The subroutine LOCATEs the cursor at line 25, column 1 of the screen. This is in the lower left-hand corner, in the space in which the function key labels are usually displayed. (Remember, we turned them off with the KEY OFF statement earlier in the program.) The subroutine then prints a message to tell you how to exit the program, and uses the LOCATE statement to return the cursor to the top portion of your screen. The effect is that the program appears to be doing two things at once—printing data and displaying a prompt.

```
This simulates a high-powered business program
printing data on the screen, while down below
a prompt tells you how to stop the thing
This simulates a high-powered business program
printing data on the screen, while down below
a prompt tells you how to stop the thing




PRESS THE [ESC] KEY TO EXIT
```

BASIC Graphics

Nobody but another programmer cares about your actual code. But everyone responds to a colorful, eye-popping, fast-changing display. And while you can get some pretty remarkable effects using only the plain-vanilla text screen, BASIC has an entire suite of specialized commands just to help you create dazzling displays of graphics. Whether for business, education, or just plain fun and games, the graphics statements help you get the most out of BASIC.

BASIC's Other Screens

Up to now, you haven't had to give much thought to the screen BASIC uses. It's simple: Type or execute a statement such as PRINT "HELLO" and the characters are written across the screen, beginning at the left.

Actually, though, the IBM PC and its clones have several internal screen modes. When BASIC "wakes up," it's automatically set for screen mode 0, which can handle only text. Although you can do a lot with this screen alone (including simple graphs), you'll have to switch to a different screen mode if you want to use BASIC's graphics statements to draw those intricate, detailed displays we were talking about.

Changing the SCREEN Mode

You use the SCREEN statement to change screen modes. This statement lets you switch back and forth between a text-only display and a text-and-graphics display. You use the SCREEN statement like this:

```
SCREEN 0
SCREEN 1
SCREEN 2
```

This means, "set the screen for mode 0, or mode 1, or mode 2." SCREEN 0 is the mode in effect at "wake-up," so it's what you use when you do the examples in any other chapter of this book. When SCREEN 0 is in effect, you can put only text on the screen.

There are also other modes you can put in effect. Your choice of mode depends largely on what kind of a graphics display and hardware you have. Virtually all IBM-compatible computers can be switched between SCREEN 0, SCREEN 1, and SCREEN 2, however.

SCREEN 1, shown in figure 8-5(a), is the medium-resolution graphics mode. It shows 40 characters of text on a line instead of 80, but you can have four colors active. Characters look "fat" and appear twice as wide as those on screen 2.

Chapter 8

SCREEN 2, shown in figure 8-5(b), is the high-resolution graphics mode. In this screen mode you can display 80 characters of text per line, in two colors. When SCREEN 2 is active, the text looks just the way you're used to seeing it, except that you can also use graphics statements.

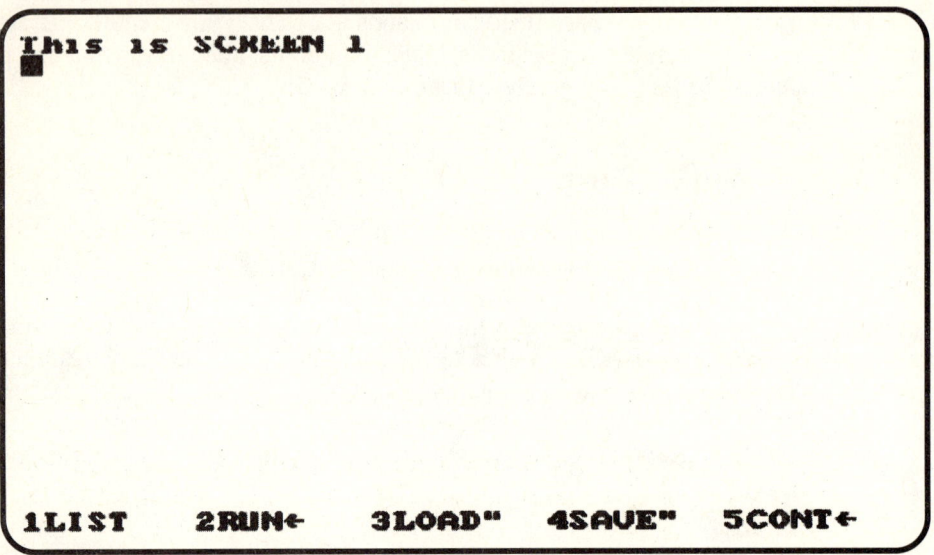

a) SCREEN 1.

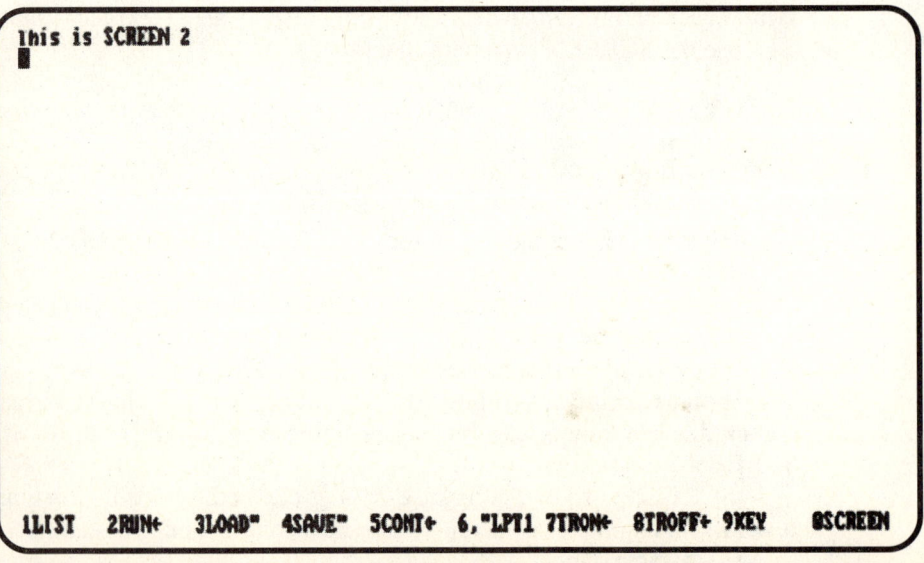

b) SCREEN 2.

Figure 8-5: BASIC's graphics screens 1 and 2.

The BASIC Screen, Graphics, and Sound

You can switch modes from the keyboard or in a program, and the switch remains active until you execute another SCREEN statement or type the SYSTEM command.

Plotting Points

Once you've turned on a graphics screen, what can you do with it? One thing you can do is plot points. Graphics points are kind of like pennies or yen or sous—one isn't worth very much by itself, but if you have a couple thousand, you can do a lot.

Using PSET to Plot Points

Each PSET (point set) statement plots a single point on the graphics screen. The general form is as follows:

```
100 PSET (X,Y)
200 PSET (X,Y), C
```

Line 100 means, "plot a single point in the foreground color on the graphics screen at the coordinates specified by X and Y." (By "foreground color" we mean the current drawing color—and with BASIC's default foreground color, that means in turn that the point will be visible.) Line 200 means, "plot the point in color C."

To try it on your own screen, you can type these statements from the keyboard:

```
SCREEN 1
Ok
PSET (160, 100)
Ok
```

This plots a point almost in the center of your screen. (You might have to look hard to find it.) Now, how did we do that?

BASIC's Good Coordination

Remember that the ordinary text screen (SCREEN 0) was 80 columns wide by 25 rows long. Using LOCATE, you could put the cursor down—and type a character, if you wanted—at any one of those 2000 locations, with pinpoint accuracy.

The graphics screens (selected by SCREEN 1 and SCREEN 2) have many more locations available. Screen 1 is a grid that is 320 points wide by 200 points high, and screen 2 is 640 points by 200 points. (These points are actually called *pixels*, or picture elements.) The upper left-hand point is at location 0, 0. On the screen, we say that this address, or location of a point, is the *physical coordinates* of that point.

Chapter 8

As shown in figure 8-6, when you specified PSET (160, 100) on screen 1, it meant that point was put on the screen 160 points along the X-axis from 0, and 100 points along the Y-axis. The point farthest away from (0,0), in the lower right corner of screen 1, is at coordinates of (319, 199). So, plotting a point with PSET (160, 100) puts the point almost in the center of the screen.

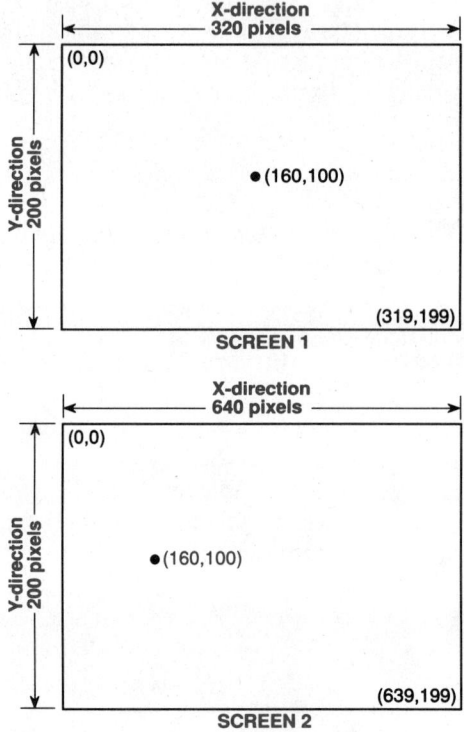

Fig. 8-6: Coordinates on graphics screens.

For screen 2, the point in the lower right corner of the screen is (639, 199). So, plotting a point at coordinates (160, 100) puts it in the middle of the Y-axis, all right, but in the left quarter of the Y-axis.

The BASIC Screen, Graphics, and Sound

Armed with PSET and our knowledge of screens 1 and 2, we can explore their boundaries. For instance, here's a program that plots a few hundred points on screen 1:

```
10 SCREEN 1: CLS: KEY OFF
20 FOR X=0 TO 319
30    Y=X*(200/320)
40    PSET (X,Y)
50 NEXT
```

Line 10 is an initialization routine; it sets up BASIC for graphics screen 1, clears the screen, and turns off the function key labels at the bottom. Then we set up a FOR...NEXT loop for a value of X from 0 to 319. Inside the loop, for each value of X, we set Y equal to (200/320) times X. Finally, we plot each of the points using PSET (X,Y). And voila! A diagonal line that marches across the screen from the top left to lower right (see fig. 8-7).

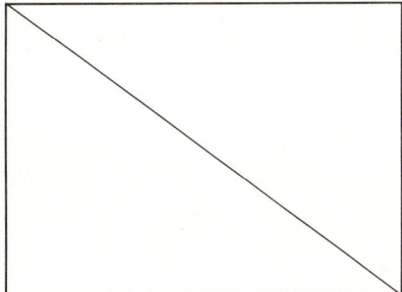

Fig. 8-7: Using PSET to "draw" a diagonal.

If the Y-axis and the X-axis were of equal length, our job would be simpler, because line 30 would look like this:

```
30    Y=X
```

Because they aren't the same, though, we multiply X by 200/320, which is the ratio of the number of Y points to the number of X points, to make sure that we have a diagonal from one corner of the screen to the opposite corner.

Chapter 8

Let's use the same technique with FOR...NEXT and PSET to draw a diagonal on screen 2.

```
10 SCREEN 2: CLS: KEY OFF
20 FOR X=0 TO 639
30     Y=X*(200/640)
40     PSET (X,Y)
50 NEXT
```

This time you change line 10 to turn on screen 2, and you change lines 20 and 30 to account for X values from 0 to 639. In addition, you need to multiply by 200/640, which is the ratio of the number of points in Y to those in X.

Outside the Realm

You can specify points anywhere on the screen—or even off of it. PSET lets you plot to locations that you'll never see. For instance, this is a legal PSET statement:

```
120 PSET (5000, 990)
```

It's legal, all right, but of course, you can't see the point. This means that if your graphics program doesn't appear to be producing anything, you just might be drawing out in never-never land. The only restrictions on PSET are that you can't go outside the range of BASIC integers; that is, −32768 to 32767.

Unplotting Points with PRESET

Pictures are nice, but once you've drawn on the screen, you'll often want to change part of that drawing. You may want to update a graph or animate a character in a game. To do this, you need to selectively erase points or lines.

How can you erase a line? The harsh, brutal way is with CLS, of course—but this clears everything on the screen. A much more elegant (and useful) solution is to simply change selected points back to the screen's background color. You can do this with the PRESET statement.

PRESET is just like PSET, except that it "wakes up" set to the background color of the screen. If you have a monochrome monitor with white letters on a black background, PRESET plots each point in black. And what you'll see will be nothing—the point is there, but it's the same color as the screen, so you don't see it.

Here's a short program that draws a diagonal with PSET, then "erases" it with PRESET:

```
10 SCREEN 2: CLS: KEY OFF
20 FOR X=0 TO 639
30    Y=X*(200/640)
40    PSET (X,Y)
50 NEXT
60 FOR X=0 TO 639
70    Y=X*(200/640)
80    PRESET (X,Y)
90 NEXT
```

We've added a second FOR...NEXT loop to the diagonal program. The only difference is that instead of plotting points with PSET, we plot exactly the same points using PRESET. When you RUN this program, you see what happens: The first loop "draws" a diagonal line made up of points, and the second loop "erases" the line by plotting the same points in the background color.

Another Way to Erase

You can change the color for PSET or PRESET, using this form:

```
100 PSET (X, Y), C
100 PRESET (X, Y), C
```

The value for C is the color attribute—it indicates what color the plotted point will be. A value of 0 means, "plot this point in the background color," whereas numbers of 1 and greater mean, "plot this point in another color." That is, a 0 is invisible, and 1, 2, 3, and so on are visible. PSET "wakes up" with a default value for C set so that it's visible; and PRESET wakes up set to 0.

This leads us to another way to plot, then erase, a point—just plot it once using PSET with the color attribute set for a visible color, then change the color attribute to 0 and plot it again. Here's an example:

```
10 SCREEN 2: CLS: KEY OFF
20 C=1
30 GOSUB 70
40 C=0
50 GOSUB 70
60 END
70 FOR X=0 TO 639
80    Y=X*(200/640)
```

Chapter 8

```
 90     PSET (X,Y), C
100 NEXT
110 RETURN
```

Here, the program begins by setting C equal to 1 (C=1). So, the first time the subroutine call to line 70 runs the FOR...NEXT loop, each point is plotted in the color specified by attribute 1. (We'll discuss what that color can be later in this chapter.) After the Return, the color is set to the background color with the C=0 statement; then the subroutine is called again and the points are "erased." So another way to plot and then erase a line is to plot the same points first in a foreground color, then in the background color.

Stepping Out with PSET and PRESET

There's still another way you can use PSET and PRESET: You can combine each one with STEP. The general form is

```
100 PSET STEP (X,Y)
110 PRESET STEP (X,Y)
```

Both of these mean, "from the current point, move X points along the X-axis and Y points along the Y-axis, and plot the next point." Here's an example:

```
10 SCREEN 2: CLS
20 PSET (0,0)
30 FOR I=0 TO 100
40    PSET STEP (4,1)
50 NEXT
```

When you RUN this little program, you get a series of dots plotted down to the right from 0,0. The first dot is placed at coordinate (0,0).

Figure 8-8 illustrates how PSET STEP works. The first time through the loop, PSET moves four places along the X-axis and one place along the Y-axis, then plots another point. Therefore, the second point plotted (the first one within the loop) is at (5,1). When the loop is executed again, PSET moves another 4 steps to the right and 1 down, and this time plots a point at (9,2). Each time through the loop, PSET moves another 4 steps to the left and 1 down. This is called *relative* positioning, because each STEP is relative to the last one.

The BASIC Screen, Graphics, and Sound

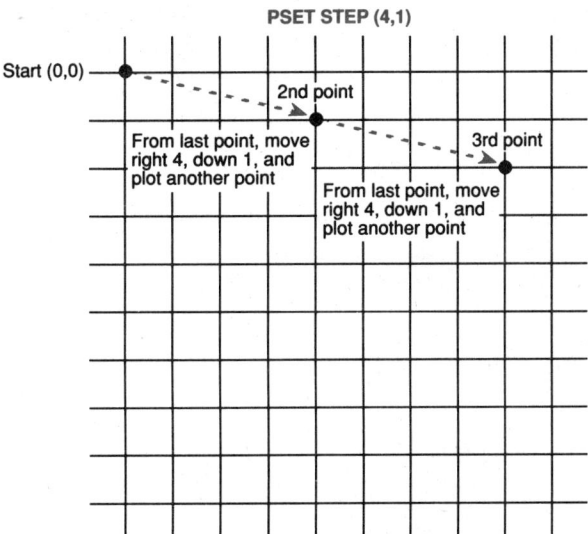

Fig. 8-8:   Relative plotting with PSET.

Coordinates—Your Way

Suppose we're trying to plot that old sine curve again, this time on the graphics screen. We want to display the sines of angles from 0 to 720 degrees, and we know that all values will be between 1 and −1. It appears that first we'll have to go through some convoluted calculations to make values in this range appear on a screen that goes from (0,0) to (319, 199), or (0,0) to (639, 199). Let's see, 720 divided by 320 is 2, carry 80...

Stop right there! There's good news: You don't need to convert your problem to fit the physical coordinates of one of BASIC's graphics screens. Instead, you can use screen coordinates to suit the range of values in your problem. The WINDOW statement does it for you.

The general form of the statement is as follows:

```
100 WINDOW (X1, Y1) - (X2, Y2)
200 WINDOW SCREEN (X1, Y1) - (X2, Y2)
```

Line 100 means, "define the graphics space as a window with a coordinate system that begins at point (X1, Y1) in the lower left corner and extends to coordinates (X2, Y2) in the upper right corner." Because the lowest coordinates are

369

Chapter 8

in the lower left corner (rather than the upper left), this system is like the Cartesian coordinates you probably remember from illustrations in trigonometry or mathematics books. Figure 8-9 shows how WINDOW and WINDOW SCREEN work.

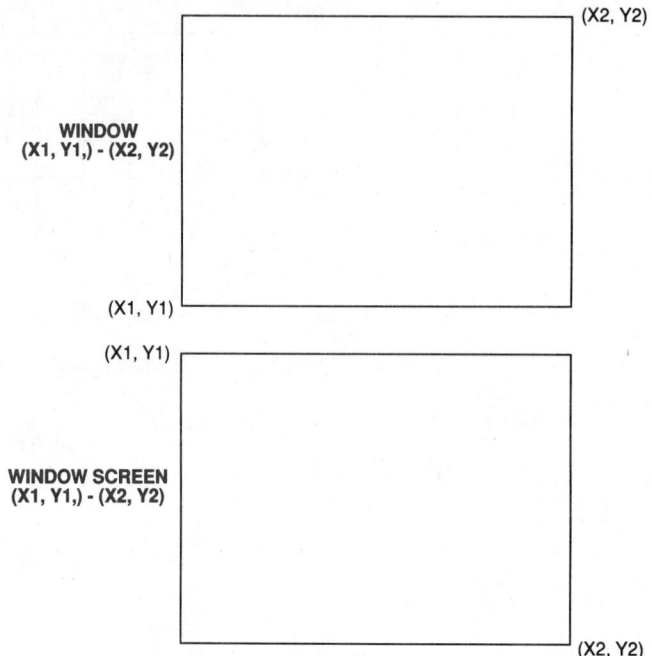

Fig. 8-9: WINDOW sets coordinates the way you want them.

Line 200, with the SCREEN attribute added, means, "define the graphics space as a window with a coordinate system that begins at point (X1, Y1) in the upper left corner and extends to coordinates (X2, Y2) in the lower right corner." (This is the way you see the actual coordinates of the graphics screens.)

For instance, to turn your graphics screen into a 10 x 10 grid, you would use this statement:

```
WINDOW (0, 0) - (10, 10)
```

After the above statement, all BASIC graphics statements assume that your screen looks like a grid of 10 cells by 10 cells, with cell (0,0) in the lower right corner of the screen, and cell (10, 10) in the upper right (see fig. 8-10).

The BASIC Screen, Graphics, and Sound

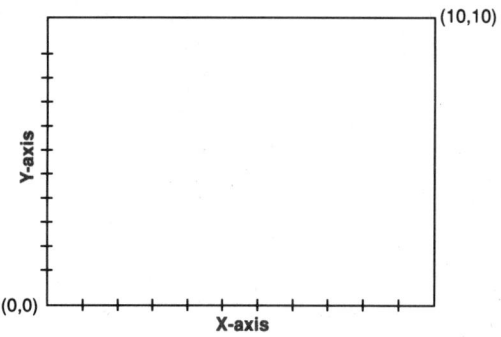

Fig. 8-10: 10 x 10 grid.

To use the default screen size for SCREEN 1, but do it in traditional Cartesian coordinates, you could specify a statement of WINDOW (160,100) – (319,0).

Now let's return to that sine problem for a moment. We said that we wanted to see a plot of the sine of every angle from 0 to 720 degrees, and that the sine is in the range from –1 to 1. That means we might want a window with these dimensions on it, as shown in figure 8-11.

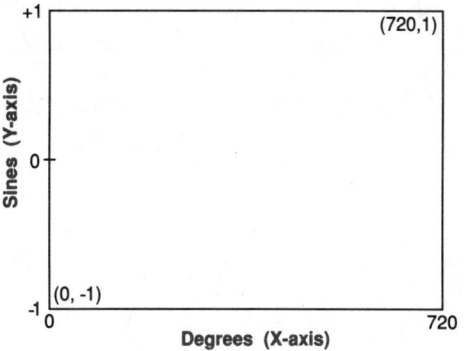

Fig. 8-11: Window to plot the sines of angles from 0-720 degrees.

The following statement gives you the dimensions you want:

```
WINDOW (0, -1) - (720, 1)
```

371

Chapter 8

This statement turns your screen into a window whose X-axis is from 0 to 720, and whose Y-axis extends from −1 to +1. Now we use this statement in a program to plot those sines:

```
10 REM-SINES
20 '
30 SCREEN 2: CLS: KEY OFF
40 PI=3.14159
50 RAD2DEG=PI/180
60 WINDOW (0,-1) - (720, 1)
70 FOR X=0 TO 720
80    Y=SIN(X*RAD2DEG)
90    PSET (X,Y)
100 NEXT X
110 END
```

That should do it! First we initialize the program for screen 2, clear the screen, then turn off the function key display. Next we specify a value for pi and use it to calculate RAD2DEG, a variable that will convert radians (which BASIC requires for trigonometric functions such as SIN) to degrees (what we need here for our display).

We set the FOR...NEXT loop to plot the sine for every angle from 0 to 720 degrees. Because we've set the screen up with a WINDOW statement, the curve fits the screen exactly (see fig. 8-12).

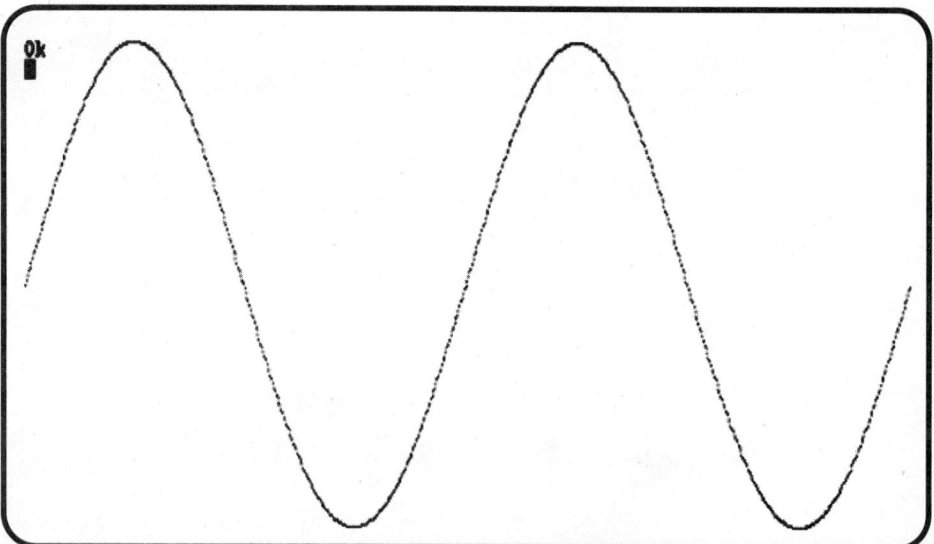

Fig. 8-12:   Plot of sines from 0 to 720 degrees.

What If You Use a Different Screen?

Notice that, with WINDOW, it doesn't matter which SCREEN you use. The WINDOW statement sets the screen coordinates up the way you want. You can change the sine plotting program to SCREEN 1 and the result looks pretty much the same. The only difference is the resolution.

Your last WINDOW statement stays active until you execute RUN or another WINDOW statement. If you change SCREENs after WINDOW, the coordinates default to the ones for that SCREEN. But the easiest way to return to the standard physical coordinates is to just use a plain WINDOW statement without any coordinates, as follows:

```
100 WINDOW
```

Drawing Lines and Boxes

Although there are situations when it's advantageous to use loops with PSET statements, there's an easier way to draw a straight line between two points. It's the LINE statement, and you can use it for drawing not only lines, but also boxes, and filled boxes. Here's the simplest form:

```
100 LINE (X1, Y1) - (X2, Y2)
200 LINE - (X2, Y2)
```

Line 100 means, "draw a line from the point specified by coordinates X1 and Y1 to the point specified by coordinates X2 and Y2." Line 200 means, "draw a line from the last point referenced to the point specified by coordinates X2 and Y2." Line 200 lets you easily draw from point to point to point.

Let's see how to use LINE. To draw a diagonal line on screen 2, you'd type

```
SCREEN 2
Ok
LINE (0,0) - (639, 199)
```

Chapter 8

This statement draws a line from the upper left corner of the screen (coordinates 0,0) to the lower right corner of screen 2 (coordinates 639, 199). To draw shapes, you can draw several lines, as follows:

```
10 CLS
20 LINE (20,20)-(300, 20)
30 LINE (300, 20) - (300, 100)
40 LINE (300, 100) - (20, 100)
50 LINE (20, 100) - (20, 20)
60 END
```

The program above draws a rectangle by drawing a line from one point to another, then from that point to another, and so on. A better way to do this is to use LINE – (X2, Y2) to draw all lines after the first one:

```
10 CLS
20 LINE (20,20)-(300, 20)
30 LINE - (300, 100)
40 LINE - (20, 100)
50 LINE - (20, 20)
60 END
```

Here's a short program that links random lines on your screen. You can press the Esc key to stop it. Output from the program can cover your screen with lines, as shown in figure 8-13.

```
10 SCREEN 2: CLS: KEY OFF
20 WINDOW (0,0) - (1,1)
30 RANDOMIZE TIMER
40 PSET (.5, .5)
50 PRINT "Press ESC to stop"
60 WHILE INKEY$ <> CHR$(27)
70      LINE -(RND(1), RND(1))
80 WEND
90 WINDOW
100 END
```

Because the numbers returned by RND fall into the range of 0 to 1, we set a WINDOW with coordinates (0,0) to (1, 1). The program first plots a point at the very center of the screen (coordinates 0.5, 0.5). Then it enters the WHILE...WEND loop. Each time through the loop, the LINE – ((RND(1), RND(1)) statement draws a line from the last point to a new, random point. If you let this program run long enough, it can completely fill up your screen.

374

The BASIC Screen, Graphics, and Sound

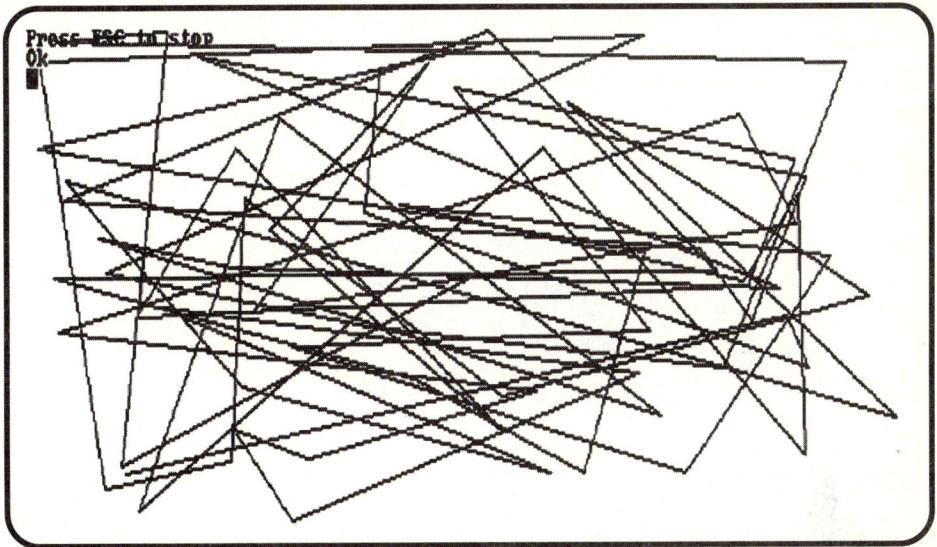

Fig. 8-13: Linked random lines on your screen.

When you exit the WHILE...WHEN loop by pressing the Esc key, the WINDOW statement in line 90 resets your screen to its normal coordinates.

Little Boxes

You know how to draw rectangles by connecting lines. But there's an even easier way to draw rectangles; you simply add "B" (for *box*) to the LINE statement, like this:

```
100 LINE (X1, Y1) - (X2, Y2) , , B
200 LINE (X1, Y1) - (X2, Y2) , , B F
```

Line 100 means, "draw a box with the beginning corner at coordinates X1 and Y1, and the ending corner at coordinates X2 and Y2." Line 200 means, "fill the box with the foreground color." Be sure to put the two commas in there—they're "placeholders" for additional attributes to specify color or intensity. (We'll discuss color in a minute.)

The upper left corner of the rectangle in the program shown earlier was at coordinates 20, 20; and the lower right corner was at coordinates 300, 100. To draw the rectangle with a single statement, enter the following:

```
LINE (20,20) - (300,100) ,, B
```

Chapter 8

To draw the filled rectangle shown in figure 8-14, enter the following:

```
LINE (20,20) - (300,100) ,, B F
```

Fig. 8-14: Filled box drawn with LINE.

More About LINE

You can choose several options for LINE. Here's the full form of the LINE statement:

```
100 LINE [(X1,Y1)] - (X2, Y2) [,[attribute] [,B][F][,style]
```

As you know, X1 and Y1 specify the starting point of the line, and X2 and Y2 mark the end point. The *attribute* specifies the color and intensity of the pixels that are displayed. Your choices for color depend on the type of hardware you have and on which SCREEN you have specified; you'll find a list for the most common configurations in Appendix G.

The B means, "draw a box" and F means "filled box." As for *style*, you can use it for normal lines and boxes but not for filled boxes. The *style* attribute is a 16-bit integer mask you can use to specify the style of the line. Because you can specify the

376

mask as a hexadecimal quantity, you can produce dashed lines, with dashes that are fat or thin. For example, this program produces two different dashed lines:

```
10 SCREEN 2: CLS
20 LINE (0,80) - (300, 80), , ,&HFF00
30 LINE (0,160) - (300,160), , ,&HCCCC
```

The bit pattern of a hexadecimal FF00 produces fat dashes, as shown in figure 8-15, whereas the CCCC mask makes dashes that are thinner. You can experiment with hexadecimal quantities for the *style* attribute to get dashed lines the way you want them.

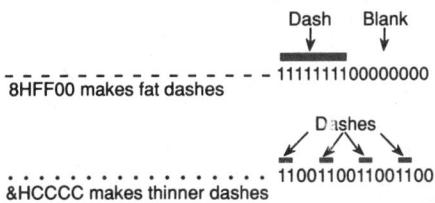

Fig. 8-15: Controlling line style.

For each tiny increment of the line, you see only the locations where there are 1's in the bit pattern used in the LINE statement.

Because you can specify the mask as a hexadecimal quantity, start by sketching how the 16 bits in the mask should be arranged to produce the pattern you want. Then refer to Appendix B to see how to convert that bit pattern into a hexadecimal quantity that you can plug into the LINE statement. Here's a valuable hint: for a dotted line, use &HAAAA, which gives a bit pattern of 1010101010101010.

The Background for Dashed Lines

If you are drawing lines using the *style* attribute, remember that the 0 bits don't turn off the background color, they let it be displayed. So, if you have a background that's yellow and you want a blue-and-green dashed line, you first can draw a solid green line, then draw a dotted blue line over it.

Drawing Circles and Arcs

In BASIC, a circle is much more than a circle. Circles are important drawing elements because they let you create things such as pie charts, arcs, parabolas, and the like. It's easy to draw circles in BASIC using the CIRCLE statement.

Chapter 8

A Simple CIRCLE

With one of the graphics screens active, you can draw a CIRCLE using this general form:

```
100 CIRCLE (X, Y), R
```

This means, "draw a circle whose center is at coordinates X, Y and whose radius is R units."

Here's how you can draw a circle in the middle of screen 2:

```
10 SCREEN 2: CLS: KEY OFF
20 CIRCLE (320, 100), 125
```

RUN this little program, and you come up with a circle on the screen (see fig. 8-16). Line 10 clears the screen and sets it for screen 2. Then the CIRCLE statement in line 20 draws the circle; it puts the center at coordinates 320, 100, and creates a circle with a radius of 125 units.

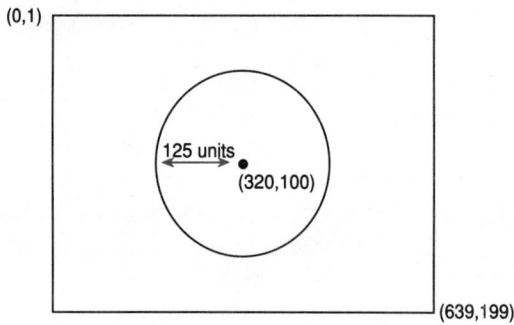

Fig. 8-16: Drawing a circle.

To draw an expanding universe of circles, stick the CIRCLE statement inside a FOR...NEXT loop that changes the radius, and add a few more statements to the program:

```
10 SCREEN 2: CLS: KEY OFF
20 WHILE INKEY$<> CHR$(13)  'Carriage return to exit
30     CLS
40     FOR R=20 TO 200 STEP 20
50         CIRCLE (320,100), R
60     NEXT R
70 WEND
```

The BASIC Screen, Graphics, and Sound

Here you've created a WHILE...WEND loop that you can exit by pressing the Enter key. Inside this loop is another loop that draws a circle; each time through the loop, the center of the circle remains the same, but 20 is added to the radius and a new circle is drawn. The circles seem to expand outward like the universe, as shown in figure 8-17. When the FOR...NEXT loop has drawn 10 circles, the screen is cleared and drawing begins again.

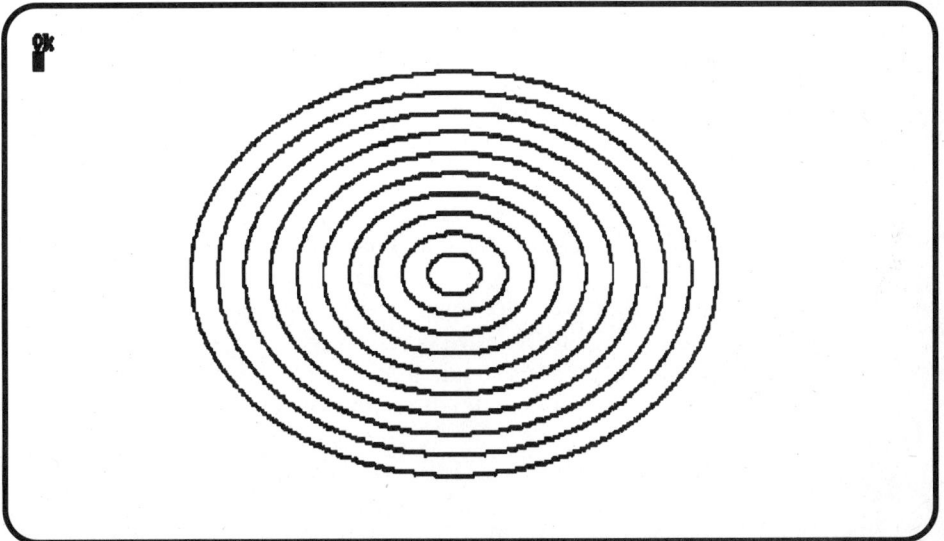

Fig. 8-17: The expanding universe.

The Complete CIRCLE Statement

The CIRCLE statement lets you select not only the center and the radius, but several optional items as well. Here's the full statement in its general forms:

```
100 CIRCLE (X,Y) ,R, C, , , A
200 CIRCLE (X,Y) ,R, C, S, E, A
```

The statement in line 100 means, "draw a circle with a radius of R, a color of C, and centered at coordinates X,Y; draw it with an aspect ratio of A." The aspect ratio A is the ratio of the X-axis to the Y-axis necessary to show a perfect circle on your screen.

Chapter 8

The statement in line 200 draws a partial circle. It means, "draw a part of a circle with a radius of R, a color of C, and centered at coordinates X,Y; draw from a starting angle of S radians counterclockwise to an ending angle of E radians; and draw it with an aspect ratio of A."

Incidentally, the parameters for color, start, end, and aspect ratio are all optional—you don't have to include them. However, if you omit, say, the parameter for color (C), but want to include the one for start (S), you'll have to add a comma as a placeholder.

A Quick Cartesian Review

For graphics, it will help if you remember the conventions of Cartesian coordinates, which you can see in figure 8-18. In this system, there is an imaginary horizontal line called the X-axis, and a vertical line called the Y-axis. The intersection of these two lines is called the *origin*. If each line is measured in equal-length units, then you can specify any point by referring to it by a pair of numbers—its address along the X-axis and that along the Y-axis. So, a point that's out 4 units along the X-axis and 2 units along the Y-axis is at (4,2). The origin, clearly, is at (0,0).

Angles for curved lines and circles are measured counterclockwise. (In GW-BASIC, angles are assumed in radians, but you can convert them to degrees, if you want.)

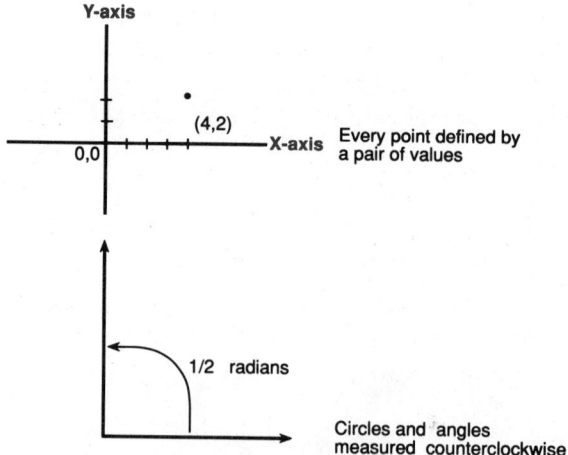

Fig. 8-18:   Principles of Cartesian coordinates.

Don't forget that BASIC puts the origin (0,0) in the upper left corner of your screen, not the center. To see the origin in the center of the screen, you can use the WINDOW statement.

The BASIC Screen, Graphics, and Sound

With the Cartesian system, to find any point on a circle, you can use the formulas shown in figure 8-19.

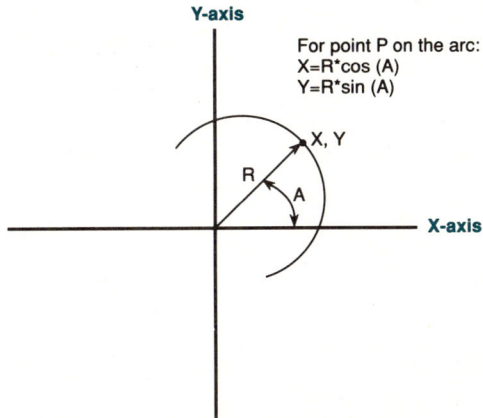

Fig. 8-19:   Finding a point on an arc.

Semicircles and Pie Wedges

In CIRCLE, the values for start and end (S and E) are in radians, and they can be from −2 pi to 2 pi. For instance, here's how to draw a semi-expanding universe of semicircles that begin at 0 radians and go to pi radians:

```
10 SCREEN 2: CLS: KEY OFF
20 WHILE INKEY$<> CHR#(13)   'Carriage return
30     CLS
40     FOR R=20 TO 200 STEP 20
50         CIRCLE (320,100), R, , 0, 3.1416
60     NEXT R
70 WEND
```

Now the CIRCLE statement in line 50 starts at an angle of 0 radians (that is, 0 degrees), and draws halfway around the screen (to pi radians, or 180 degrees). You get semicircles instead of circles for the output. (See figure 8-20.)

Chapter 8

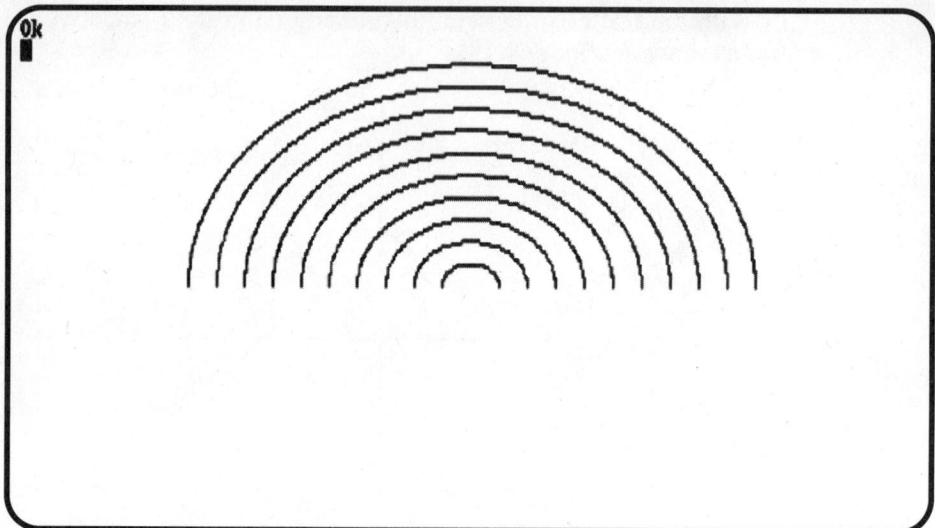

Fig. 8-20: Drawing semicircles.

If you use a negative number for either S or E, the starting or ending point of the circle is connected to the center (that is, to X,Y) with a line. (That's all a minus sign does in this statement, too—it doesn't change the direction or the angle.)

Let's make a pie wedge by closing off the ends of the circle segments. Change line 50 so that it looks like this:

```
50          CIRCLE (320,100), R, , -.0001, -2
```

Notice how you did this. You wanted to start at 0 degrees, using a start angle with a negative number, to close off the ends of the arcs and create a pie wedge. But BASIC doesn't recognize a negative 0, so you use the tiniest little negative number, .0001, instead. For the end angle, you use another negative number, this time 2 radians. The result is the series of semicircles shown in figure 8-21. They begin at 0 radians (well, almost 0, anyway) and go to 2 radians. The negative numbers for S and E draw the extra lines to the center that turn the result into a pie wedge.

General Pies

In the words of an old Chinese proverb, "a picture is worth more than ten thousand words." BASIC's graphics language can speak volumes, turning business or personal data into charts and graphs. Graphic representations are not only pleasing to the eye, they also make it easy to spot trends and get an overall view of a situation

The BASIC Screen, Graphics, and Sound

at a glance. Line graphs are well suited to showing trends, whereas pie charts are handy for comparing quantities—such as the market share controlled by each of several companies.

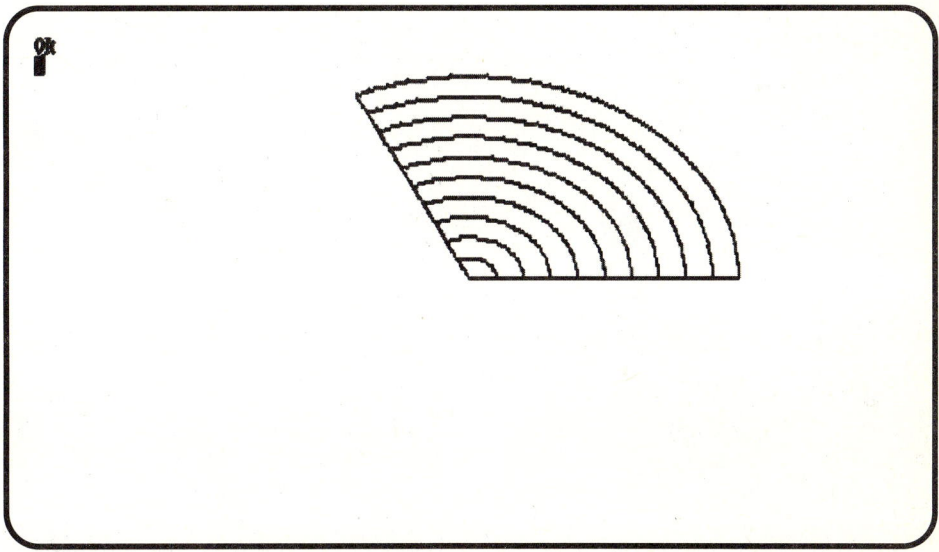

Fig. 8-21: Use negative numbers for start and end to produce a pie wedge.

For instance, suppose that our company is selling wobulators, and we want to be able to eyeball a chart and tell how we're doing in our major markets. Now that we know how to draw a single pie wedge, we can make a pie chart. We'll make a general pie chart, one that can be used for any number of segments.

```
10 REM-GENERAL PIES
20 SCREEN 1: CLS: KEY OFF
30 PI=3.14159
40 DEF FN ANGLE(A)=2*PI*A/100
```

After the initialization, in which we set screen 1, clear the screen, and turn off the keys, we define a value for PI. We use this value right away to define a function, DEF FN ANGLE(A). What does this function do? It converts percent into angle. After we input a quantity of wobulators for each region, we'll first calculate what percentage that is of the total sales. Then we'll use the function DEF FN ANGLE(A)=2*PI*A/100 to convert that percentage into an angle (in radians) on the circle. For instance, if we knew that one particular wedge was 25% of the total, and a circle is 2*PI radians, the angle for that wedge should be 1/2 PI.

383

Chapter 8

Next we define all the variables for the CIRCLE statement. We set S (the start for the CIRCLE statement) to 0, then specify the center of the screen with CNTX and CNTY; we'll use these in the CIRCLE statement later on. Using a RADIUS of 75 will give us a nice-sized circle; you can set the ASPECT for a circle that looks good on your monitor.

```
50 S=0
60 CNTX=160
70 CNTY=100
80 RADIUS=75
90 ASPECT =5/6
```

This is a general program, so it asks, "How many wedges for the pie?" and waits for INPUT from the keyboard. You enter N, the number of items. Then the DIM statement dimensions an array called WEDGE to hold the number of wedges you want. A FOR...NEXT loop reads in the amount of each item.

```
100 INPUT "How many wedges for the pie ";N
110 DIM WEDGE(N)
120 FOR I=1 TO N
130     PRINT "Wedge # ";I;
140     INPUT WEDGE(I)
150     T=T+WEDGE(I)
160 NEXT
```

Each time through the loop, you are asked to input the WEDGE for that number. For instance, if region 1 had sold 50 wobulators, you'd input a WEDGE of 50. The total number of wobulators (or anything else, because this is a general-use program) is kept in the variable T. Each time through the loop, the latest WEDGE(I) is added to T.

Next, the program clears the screen to prepare it for the pie. Another FOR...NEXT loop begins in line 180; it counts from 1 to the number (N) of wedges. Each time through the loop, the current wedge is scaled into a percentage of the total by the statement WEDGE(I)=WEDGE(I)*100/T. Here's how it works: Suppose that the total number of wobulators is 200, and this WEDGE(I) is 50. Then 50 times 100 is 5000, and that divided by 200 is 25. That means this WEDGE(I) will be 25% of the circle.

In line 200, the program takes the value for percent of the circle and uses it in the function that returns the angle in radians for this portion of the circle. Thus if we know this wedge segment should be 25% of the circle, the function W=FN ANGLE(WEDGE(I)) returns a value for W of 2*PI*25/100 = 1/2 PI.

The BASIC Screen, Graphics, and Sound

```
170 CLS
180 FOR I=1 TO N
190     WEDGE(I)=WEDGE(I)*100/T
200     W=FN ANGLE(WEDGE(I))
210     E=S+W
220     IF E>2*PI THEN E=0
230     CIRCLE (CNTX, CNTY), RADIUS , 1, -S, -E, ASPECT
240     S=E
250 NEXT
260 END
```

Before beginning the first loop, the start angle is set to 0 radians. The wedge angle, W, is added to the start angle, S, to calculate the end angle, E, for the first wedge, WEDGE(1). At the end of the loop (line 240), S is set to E; this sets S so that WEDGE(2) will begin where WEDGE(1) ends. The next time through the loop, the angle W is calculated for WEDGE(2), and so on, until all the wedges have been calculated and drawn (see fig. 8-22).

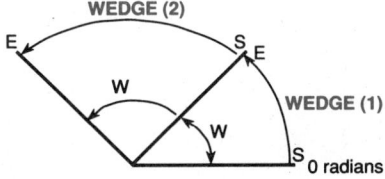

Fig. 8-22: Each time through the loop, a new wedge is drawn.

The CIRCLE statement in line 230 draws each wedge. The center points CNTX, CNTY, and the RADIUS were defined earlier in the program. The wedge is drawn from an angle of S radians to an angle of E radians.

Let's run this program to see what worldwide wobulator sales are doing. Here are the sales figures for each region, hot off the fax machine:

Worldwide Wobulator Sales for the Year

Region Number	Location	Sales in Units
1	Africa	48
2	Europe and Middle East	73
3	North and South America	17
4	Australasia	34

Let's see how these figures look on the pie chart.

```
RUN
How many wedges for the pie ? 4
Wedge # 1 ? 48
Wedge # 2 ? 73
Wedge # 3 ? 17
Wedge # 4 ? 34
```

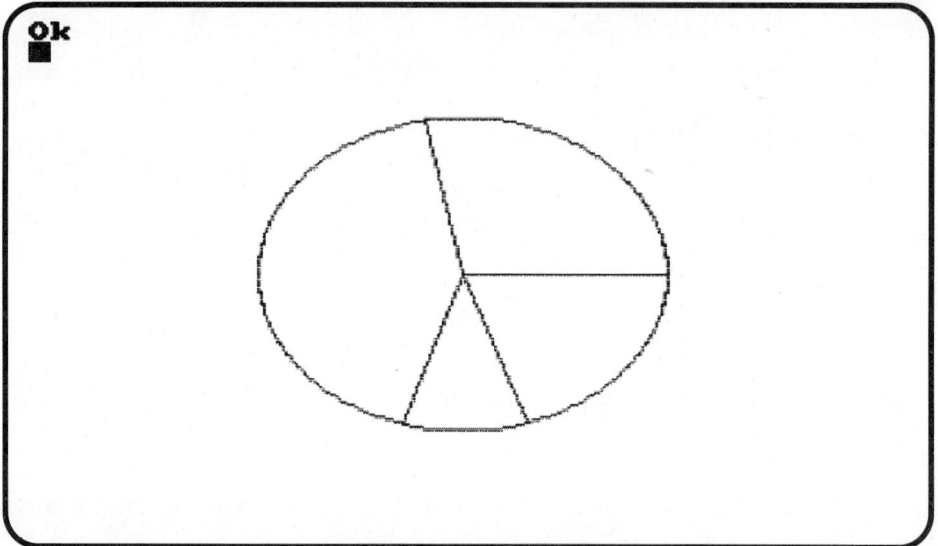

Fig. 8-23: A pie with one wedge for each region.

Figure 8-23 shows the resulting pie. The program draws one wedge for each region, so we can see the relative size. Here's the complete program:

```
10 REM-GENERAL PIES
20 SCREEN 1: CLS: KEY OFF
30 PI=3.14159
40 DEF FN ANGLE(A)=2*PI*A/100
50 S=0
60 CNTX=160
70 CNTY=100
80 RADIUS=75
90 ASPECT =5/6
```

```
100 INPUT "How many wedges for the pie ";N
110 DIM WEDGE(N)
120 FOR I=1 TO N
130     PRINT "Wedge # ";I;
140     INPUT WEDGE(I)
150     T=T+WEDGE(I)
160 NEXT
170 CLS
180 FOR I=1 TO N
190     WEDGE(I)=WEDGE(I)*100/T
200     W=FN ANGLE(WEDGE(I))
210     E=S+W
220     IF E>2*PI THEN E=0
230     CIRCLE (CNTX, CNTY), RADIUS , 1, -S, -E, ASPECT
240     S=E
250 NEXT
260 END
```

How the Aspect Ratio Affects Circles

When you draw a circle or part of a circle on the screen, is it weirdly shaped—flattened out like a watermelon? It's because of the *aspect ratio* of the screen. Your screen isn't really square—instead, it's a rectangle, and each individual *cell* of that screen is wider than it is long.

The aspect ratio of many monitors is 4 to 3. This means that a screen 9 inches wide is only 27/4, or 6 3/4 inches tall. When you specify SCREEN 1 or SCREEN 2, you automatically set the value for the aspect used by CIRCLE so that a round circle is drawn on this monitor. But if your monitor has a different aspect ratio, or if you specify a WINDOW, you might have to change the *aspect* of the CIRCLE you draw.

By changing the aspect ratio at which you draw circles or arcs, you can create ellipses that are long and thin like a dirigible.

The Labeled Pie

Your pie chart is looking good, but right now there's no way to tell which region is which. Let's draw a label on the screen for each wedge. We don't have to change the

Chapter 8

main part of the program much—we'll simply add a subroutine call after the wedge is drawn in the FOR...NEXT loop, as follows:

```
180 FOR I=1 TO N
190     WEDGE(I)=WEDGE(I)*100/T
200     W=FN ANGLE(WEDGE(I))
210     E=S+W
220     IF E>2*PI THEN E=0
230     CIRCLE (CNTX, CNTY), RADIUS , 1, -S, -E, ASPECT
240     GOSUB 280 'Call to labeling subroutine
250     S=E
260 NEXT
270 END
```

We've added a line and renumbered the program, so that now line 240 is a call to a subroutine. The subroutine will print the wedge number in each wedge so that we can identify it. Here's the subroutine:

```
280 X=CNTX + RADIUS*.5 * COS((S+E)/2)
290 Y=CNTY + RADIUS*.5 * SIN((S+E)/2)
300 ROW=1+(200-Y)/8
310 COL=1+X/8
320 LOCATE ROW, COL
330 PRINT I
340 RETURN
```

We're going to start the label somewhere near the center of the wedge. Now, for a circle around point (0,0), we can find any point on the circle by computing the values for the X and Y coordinates this way:

```
X= RADIUS * COS(ANGLE)
Y= RADIUS * SIN(ANGLE)
```

Figure 8-24 shows how to find a point on the circle. Knowing how to find any point on the curve, we can find the X and the Y of the midpoint along the curve between E and S this way:

```
X=RADIUS*COS((S+E)/2)
Y=RADIUS*SIN((S+E)/2)
```

However, as shown in figure 8-25, we want to point the label within the wedge. So we actually want a point not on the edge of the circle, but near the middle of the wedge, about halfway along the radius.

The BASIC Screen, Graphics, and Sound

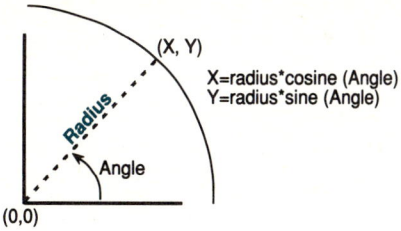

Fig. 8-24: Finding a point on a curve.

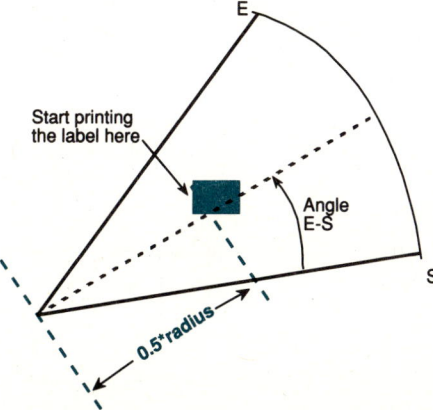

Fig. 8-25: Finding the center of the wedge.

Also, we have to account for an origin (0,0) that's not at (0,0) on the screen. Therefore, to calculate the (x,y) coordinates where we want to put the label, we can use this code:

```
280 X=CNTX + RADIUS*.5 * COS((S+E)/2)
290 Y=CNTY + RADIUS*.5 * SIN((S+E)/2)
```

Now we're ready to LOCATE the cursor at this point and begin printing labels...aren't we?

Not quite yet. Remember, LOCATE knows nothing about Cartesian coordinates. LOCATE assumes that you're going to give it the row and then the column where it is to locate the cursor. So, you have to convert the (x,y) coordinates to the screen's (row, column) system.

Chapter 8

```
300 ROW=1+(200-Y)/8
310 COL=1+X/8
```

That should do it. We're using SCREEN 1, which has 40 columns and 25 rows. To convert the Y-value to rows, we subtract it from 200 (the width of graphics screen 1), divide it by 8 (the ratio of 320 x-values to 40 rows) and add 1 (to make sure that we don't wind up with an illegal row of zero). We perform a similar conversion for columns.

Finally, we LOCATE the cursor in the row and column and print the number of this region. Don't forget that although graphics statements like CIRCLE are set up for coordinates in the order (x, y), the LOCATE statement is just backwards—it assumes that the first number of the pair is the row, and the second is the column. Be careful that you don't get mixed up!

Why Variables Are Better

To keep things simple in this program, we've used "hard-coded" numbers to represent quantities like screen width and height. But in a real-world program, you'd want to use variables instead. By using variables, declaring them all in one section of the program, and even letting the user change them, you can make a program easier to use by more people. In this program, using variables for screen width and height would allow you to quickly change them for different screen modes.

Here's a run of the modified program, followed by its complete listing. You can see the labels in figure 8-26.

```
RUN
How many wedges for the pie ? 4
Wedge # 1 ? 48
Wedge # 2 ? 73
Wedge # 3 ? 17
Wedge # 4 ? 34
```

```
10 REM-LABELED PIE
20 SCREEN 1: CLS: KEY OFF
30 PI=3.14159
40 DEF FN ANGLE(A)=2*PI*A/100
50 S=0
60 CNTX=160
70 CNTY=100
```

The BASIC Screen, Graphics, and Sound

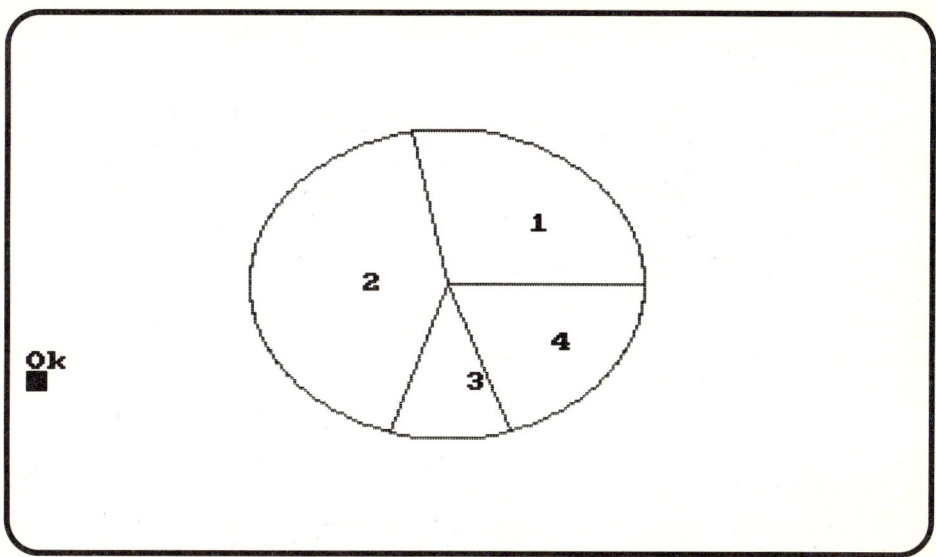

Fig. 8-26: Output from the labeled pie program.

```
80 RADIUS=75
90 ASPECT =5/6
100 INPUT "How many wedges for the pie ";N
110 DIM WEDGE(N)
120 FOR I=1 TO N
130     PRINT "Wedge # ";I;
140     INPUT WEDGE(I)
150     T=T+WEDGE(I)
160 NEXT
170 CLS
180 FOR I=1 TO N
190     WEDGE(I)=WEDGE(I)*100/T
200     W=FN ANGLE(WEDGE(I))
210     E=S+W
220     IF E>2*PI THEN E=0
230     CIRCLE (CNTX, CNTY), RADIUS , 1, -S, -E, ASPECT
240     GOSUB 280
250     S=E
260 NEXT
270 END
280 X=CNTX + RADIUS*.5 * COS((S+E)/2)
```

```
290 Y=CNTY + RADIUS*.5 * SIN((S+E)/2)
300 ROW=1+(200-Y)/8
310 COL=1+X/8
320 LOCATE ROW, COL
330 PRINT I
340 RETURN
```

In the output from the program, notice that the number 3 doesn't appear to be in the center of the wedge. That's because the LOCATE statement can deal only with whole character positions, which means it can't center well in narrow segments.

Colorful Graphics

Adding cascades of color can make your programs more enjoyable and interactive. In order to take fullest advantage of your monitor and the graphics card in your computer, however, remember that BASIC's handling of color varies with the type of hardware you have. (For details of just what color options are available, refer to Appendix G.)

Monochrome users, take note: Even if you don't have a color monitor, don't skip this section—BASIC's color options are helpful even with some monochrome monitors.

To apply color effectively in your BASIC statements, you have to understand the relationship between the SCREEN statement and the COLOR statement, with its PALETTE argument. (You'll also need to consider the PALETTE statement if you have EGA.)

Changing Colors

When you first load BASIC on your computer, it "wakes up" set for certain default conditions. You'll see SCREEN 0 (the text screen). As illustrated in figure 8-27, you'll see the screen itself in a background color (perhaps white), and letters you type in a contrasting foreground color (perhaps black) that makes them easy to read.

You can change the background and foreground colors to suit your own taste. The default color, and what you can change them to, depend on the hardware and color monitor you're using.

Everything You Wanted to Know About SCREEN

Your choice of SCREEN statements depends on what kind of a monitor and what sort of hardware you have. The graphics illustrations in this book use only SCREEN 1 and SCREEN 2, because these will work with any IBM-compatible color system.

However, GW-BASIC can be used to specify other screens as well, giving you more display and color options than you have with just screens 1 and 2.

Remember, the general form of the SCREEN statement looks like this:

```
100 SCREEN [MODE][,[COLORSWITCH]][,APAGE][,VPAGE]]
```

The brackets show parts of the statement that are optional, and you don't have to include them. But if you want to use any of these parameters, you'll find the explanations for them below.

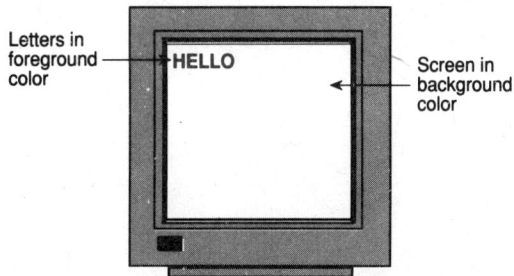

Fig. 8-27: Background and foreground colors.

What Kind of System Do You Have?

If you're not sure whether your particular computer allows you to specify a particular BASIC screen, just type SCREEN, followed by the number. The computer won't blow up if you're wrong—it will merely give you an "Illegal function call" error.

If you have MDA (which means IBM Monochrome Display Adapter) and a monochrome display, you can use text mode only; you can't use any of the graphics statements like SCREEN or PSET.

CGA is the IBM Color Graphics Adapter, the simplest form of IBM-compatible color. If you have CGA and a color monitor, you'll be able to display up to four colors at a time, chosen from among 16 colors. EGA is the IBM Enhanced Graphics Adapter. With EGA and a standard color display, you can show 16 colors on the screen at the same time.

There are other combinations of hardware and monitors, but the three mentioned here are the most common. If you're lucky enough to have VGA, the GW-BASIC language treats it as if it was EGA, but you don't get any "extra" resolution. To take full advantage of VGA, you'll need an enhanced form of BASIC such as QuickBASIC.

Chapter 8

Viewing Color on a Monochrome Monitor

Even if you don't have a color monitor, you may be able to see "color." It all depends on what type of graphics adapter you're using. For instance, if you have a CGA and a monochrome monitor, black and white are displayed as black and white. Colors, however, are displayed as combinations of black and white dots. So even on a monochrome monitor, you'll be able to see the difference between "red" and "green." You should know, however, that some combinations of foreground and background colors that would be visible and attractive on a color monitor are almost impossible to read if you're looking at a monochrome display.

Table 8-2 shows a list of common hardware configurations and what SCREENs you can use with them:

Table 8-2: Computer hardWARE AND screen MODE.

Graphics Adapter and Display	Type SCREEN Modes Allowed
MDA with monochrome display	SCREEN 0: monochrome display, text mode only.
CGA with color display	SCREEN 0, 1, 2: text mode, and medium- and high-resolution color graphics
EGA with color display	SCREEN 0, 1, 2, 7, and 8
EGA with enhanced color display	SCREEN 0, 1, 2, 7, 8, and 9. SCREEN 9 is the highest resolution graphics for EGA.
EGA with monochrome display	SCREEN 10: monochrome graphics at very high resolution
VGA	Treated like EGA by GW-BASIC

The graphics examples in this book use SCREEN 1 or SCREEN 2, so they'll all run if you have the minimum configuration—CGA and a color monitor. If you have a more powerful and exotic system, you can do a lot more; get in there and experiment!

SCREEN Modes

The following discussion is a breakdown of the different MODE options for the SCREEN statement:

SCREEN 0: This is the screen GW-BASIC "wakes up" in. It's for text mode only, and allows a screen that's 40 columns x 25 rows or 80 columns x 25 rows. You can assign any of 16 colors to either of 2 attributes, so you can display a "monochrome" screen that's, say, red on green. If you have EGA, you can assign colors to 16 attributes, which means you can display 16 colors at once.

SCREEN 1: This screen has medium-resolution graphics (320 x 200 pixels). It also has text mode (40 columns x 25 rows). You can assign 16 colors to any of 4 attributes.

SCREEN 2: This screen has high-resolution graphics (640 x 200 pixels) and text mode (80 columns x 25 rows). You can assign 16 colors to either of 2 attributes.

SCREEN 7: This is a more colorful version of SCREEN 1, for EGA only; you can't specify SCREEN 7 if you only have CGA. SCREEN 7 gives medium-resolution graphics at 320 x 200 pixels, a 40 x 25 text format, and up to 16 screen colors at one time. It also gives you 2 memory pages with 64 Kbytes of total memory, 4 pages with 128 Kbytes, or 8 pages with 256 Kbytes total. You can use this mode with the IBM color display or the enhanced color display.

SCREEN 8: This is similar to SCREEN 2 except that it's for EGA only, and it can use either the normal color display or the enhanced color display. It has high-resolution graphics at 640 x 350 pixels, an 80 x 25 text format with characters that are 8 pixels x 14 pixels, and up to 16 screen colors at one time. As with SCREEN 7, this screen has 1, 2, or 4 memory pages, with 64K, 128K, or 256K of total memory assigned to them.

SCREEN 9: You need EGA and enhanced color display for SCREEN 9, which gives you the 640 x 350 pixel enhanced-resolution graphics and an 80 x 25 text format with 8-pixel x 14-pixel characters. With ordinary EGA memory you can choose from among 16 colors and have any 4 on the screen at once; if you have additional EGA memory (over 64K), you can use as many as 64 colors, with 16 on the screen at once. You also get two display pages (with 256K of EGA memory installed).

SCREEN 10: This mode is for displaying monochrome graphics on the IBM monochrome display. It gives you 640 x 350 enhanced-resolution graphics, 80 x 25 text format with 8- x 14-pixel characters, and assignment of up to 9 pseudo-colors, with as many as 4 on the screen at once. There are 2 display pages if you have 256K of EGA memory installed.

The Colorswitch

The COLORSWITCH variable is used with SCREEN statements for composite monitors and televisions used as monitors. The COLORSWITCH variable can be either 0 or nonzero; a 0 means "display black and white only," whereas a nonzero value means "display color." (The meanings are just the opposite for SCREEN 0.)

Switching Pages

In SCREENs 7, 8, 9, and 10, you can use screen *pages*. These are really areas of memory in which an entire screen is stored during drawing and other operations, while you look at a different screen. The APAGE and VPAGE arguments of the SCREEN statement indicate which page is *active* (that is, which one is being written on) and which page is *visible*. Because redrawing is not being done on the screen, but elsewhere in memory, it's much faster to use paging for applications like animation. Here's how it's done:

```
1200 SCREEN 8, , 2, 1
 .
 .
1300 SCREEN 8, , 1, 2
```

After line 1200 above, you see page 2 on the screen, but any graphics statements like LINE or CIRCLE are "written" to page 1. In line 1300, the program switches so that page 1 is now visible on the screen, and any drawing is done to page 2.

The COLOR Statement

The easiest way to change color for all screens except SCREEN 2 is with the COLOR statement. This changes the background color, and it can change the colors displayed in the foreground, too. The general form is as follows:

```
100 COLOR F, B, BDR
```

This means, "set the foreground color to F, the background color to B, and the border color to BDR."

The actual colors available depend on the display, the graphics adapter, and what SCREEN you're using.

Using COLOR for the Text Screen

BASIC wakes up set for the text screen (SCREEN 0), and you can use the COLOR statement with this SCREEN. Just look at all the colors available!

Attribute Number	Color
0	Black
1	Blue
2	Green
3	Cyan
4	Red
5	Magenta
6	Brown
7	White

The BASIC Screen, Graphics, and Sound

Attribute Number	Color
8	Gray
9	Light blue
10	Light green
11	Light cyan
12	Light red
13	Light magenta
14	Yellow
15	High-intensity white

You can use 0-7 for the background, and all 15 numbers for the foreground. For blinking foreground characters, add 16 to these numbers. For instance, the default foreground color attribute for the text screen is 7 (white). To change to blinking foreground characters, type

```
SCREEN 0
Ok
COLOR 23
Ok (blinks on and off)
```

Now let's write a little program that changes the display to show black characters on a white background, then back to the normal display:

```
10 SCREEN 0
20 PRINT "This is displayed in the normal colors"
30 COLOR 0, 7
40 PRINT: PRINT "This is displayed in reverse video"
50 COLOR 7, 0
60 PRINT: PRINT "This is displayed in the normal colors again"

RUN
This is displayed in the normal colors
This is displayed in reverse video
This is displayed in the normal colors again
```

Using COLOR for Graphics SCREEN 1

You can't use COLOR with graphics SCREEN 2, but COLOR is very important for SCREEN 1. You use a slightly different syntax:

```
100 COLOR B, PAL
```

Chapter 8

This means, "set the background color to B, and the foreground color to a palette of colors." You can choose the background color B from numbers 0-7 (of the numbers BASIC uses to select color):

```
Number      Background Color

0           Black
1           Blue
2           Green
3           Cyan
4           Red
5           Magenta
6           Brown
7           White
```

For the foreground—what you'll use for actual characters, lines, circles, and other shapes—you choose one of two palettes. For systems without EGA, the default palette colors are

Palette 0:

Attribute
Number   Color

0   Background
1   Green
2   Red
3   Yellow

Palette 1:

Attribute
Number   Color

0   Background
1   Cyan
2   Magenta
3   White

All colors are combinations of three primary colors—and each of these palettes gives you all the primary colors you need to form other colors (see fig. 8-28).

The BASIC Screen, Graphics, and Sound

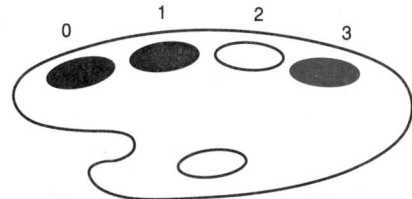

Fig. 8-28: The COLOR palette has 3 foreground colors and a background color.

Here's a small program that draws rectangles and fills them with the primary colors available to you:

```
10 REM-COLORS
20 REM-This program shows the primary colors for SCREEN 1
30 REM-with the COLOR,0 and COLOR,1 statements
40 CLS
50 SCREEN 1
60 COLOR 0,0
70 LINE (10,10)-(300,20),0,BF
80 LINE (10,30)-(300,40),1,BF
90 LINE (10,50)-(300,60),2,BF
100 LINE (10,70)-(300,80),3,BF
110 LOCATE 25,1
120 PRINT "Press ESC to change palettes"
130 WHILE INKEY$<>CHR$(27):WEND
140 COLOR 0,1
150 LINE (10,110)-(300,120),0,BF
160 LINE (10,130)-(300,140),1,BF
170 LINE (10,150)-(300,160),2,BF
180 LINE (10,170)-(300,180),3,BF
190 LOCATE 1,1
200 PRINT "COLOR 0,0"
210 LOCATE 12, 1
220 PRINT "COLOR 0,1"
230 KEY OFF
```

When you RUN the program on a CGA system, it specifies SCREEN 1 and COLOR 0,0, so you see rectangles drawn with palette 0; that is, green, red, and brown. The WHILE...WEND loop in line 130 waits for you to press the Esc key.

Chapter 8

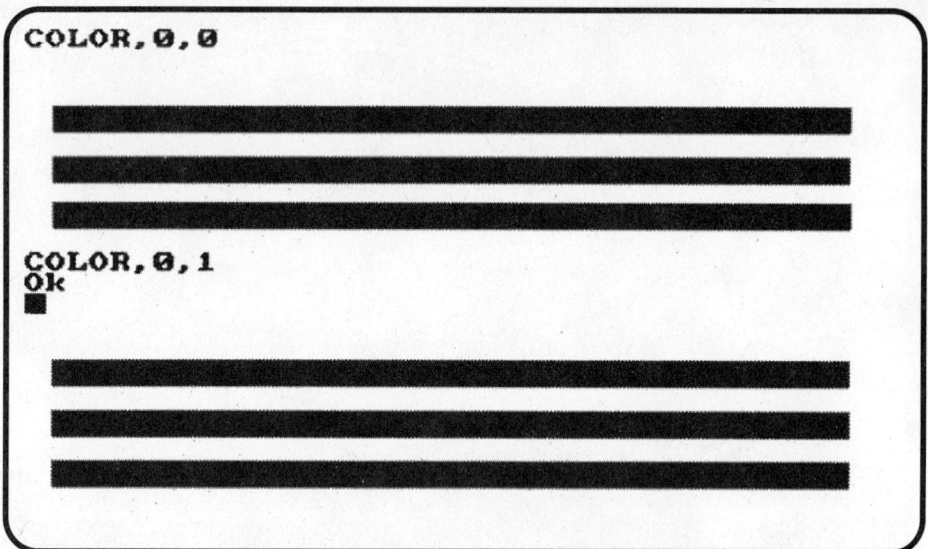

Fig. 8-29: Output from the program showing the COLOR palette for SCREEN 1.

When you press Esc, the program executes a COLOR 0,1 statement that specifies palette 1, so the colors in new boxes (shown in fig. 8-29) are cyan, magenta, and white. The boxes you drew previously also are changed, because although the *attributes* are the same (1, 2, and 3), the *colors* to which the attributes refer are not. Remember:

When you change COLOR palettes, all graphics on the screen are changed—not just those drawn since the change.

Colors and Attributes

So far, we've been throwing the word *color* around pretty loosely when we've talked about statements such as LINE and CIRCLE. But actually, these statements don't refer to a color—they refer to an *attribute*. The actual colors themselves depend on your hardware, and on what you've specified with the SCREEN, COLOR, and PALETTE statements. The attribute is just a *pointer* to a color.

Here's an example. The LINE statement in line 30 below draws a line with an attribute of 2. Because you've specified palette 0 with the COLOR statement, that means the line is drawn in red. The STOP statement in line 40 lets you see the line (Use CONT to continue after you've viewed the lines.)

The BASIC Screen, Graphics, and Sound

```
10 SCREEN 1: CLS
20 COLOR 0,0
30 LINE (10,10)-(50,50), 2
40 STOP
50 COLOR 0,1
60 LINE (10,10)-(50,50), 2
```

Now look at line 60. It's the same statement as line 30, with the same attribute, 2. But now, because the COLOR statement in line 50 changed the palette, the line is drawn in magenta. Attributes are powerful tools to help you, because they can change an entire screen of colors with a single command.

The palette you specify in the COLOR statement is the one that's used in SCREEN 1 by statements such as LINE and CIRCLE. For instance, here's how you could see—if you were so inclined—a green rectangle on a magenta background using the CGA:

```
10 SCREEN 1: CLS
20 COLOR 5, 0
30 LINE (10,10)-(300,20), 1, BF
```

The COLOR 5,0 statement in line 20 gives you a background color of magenta (5) and palette 0; then the LINE statement in line 30 draws a line and fills it with the color assigned to attribute 1 of that palette, which is green. If you don't specify a color in drawing statements like LINE and CIRCLE, they default to attribute 3, which is the color white in palette 1, or yellow (CGA) or brown (EGA) in palette 0. (If you're having trouble reading the screen now, type COLOR 0,1 to get back to black and white.)

Applying Other Palettes of Color (EGA Only)

If your computer is equipped with a color monitor and the IBM enhanced graphics adapter (EGA) or an equivalent, your output can really get colorful. That's because with EGA you can take advantage of the PALETTE and PALETTE USING statements to change the palettes beyond the two sets of colors you get with the COLOR statement.

The PALETTE Statement

The PALETTE statement lets you change colors in the palette to whatever you want. The general form is as follows:

```
100 PALETTE A, C
```

Chapter 8

This means, "set attribute A in the current palette for color C." You see, when you specify color, you actually specify an *attribute* associated with that color.

Remember the COLOR statement? If you specify an attribute of 3 with VGA, it means "brown" for palette 0, but it means "white" if you're using palette 1. The PALETTE statement takes this concept much further. You can actually change the color associated with any attribute. For instance,

```
PALETTE 3, 7
```

The statement above changes attribute 3 to color 7 (white). It makes the change for any line, circle, letter, or anything else that's on the screen and has been drawn or written using attribute 3.

Here's a short program that illustrates how PALETTE can change the way your screen looks. (Remember, you'll need EGA to see its effects).

```
10 SCREEN 1: CLS: KEY OFF
20 PRINT "Press RETURN to continue"
30 COLOR 0,0
40 GOSUB 90
50 WHILE INKEY$<> CHR$(13):WEND
60 PALETTE 2,2
70 GOSUB 90
80 END
90 LINE (10,50)-(100,80),1,BF
100 LINE (10,100)-(100,120),2, BF
110 RETURN
```

Line 30 of the program gets the color palette 0,0, then the subroutine call draws two filled rectangles: One (line 90) is filled with the color assigned to attribute 1, which is green; and the other is filled with the color assigned to attribute 2, which is now red. The program uses a WHILE...WEND loop to wait while we examine the two rectangles, then we can press Return to continue.

The PALETTE 2,2 statement in line 60 changes the palette so that now attribute 2 also "points" to color 2. A quick look at the color chart shows us that color 2 is green. So now, instead of a green rectangle followed by a red one, the subroutine draws two green rectangles.

PALETTE USING

PALETTE lets you modify one attribute at a time. The PALETTE USING statement can change all attributes to different colors at once. Here's the general form:

```
PALETTE USING A(I)
```

This means, "set attributes to refer to the entire palette of colors, using the value of element A(I) as the color of the first attribute, A(I+1) as the color referred to by the second attribute, and so on." The array has to be dimensioned first, and it has to be large enough to hold all the palette entries after A(I).

For instance, suppose that you just inherited several long and complex graphics programs, all very colorful and detailed. However, you're partial to the colors red and black, and you don't want to see anything else. This short section of code shows how to use PALETTE USING to set all attributes so that they refer to one of these two colors. (You'll need EGA and an EGA-supported SCREEN mode, such as 7, to run this little program.)

```
10 REM-ROUGE ET NOIRE
20 DIM P%(16)
30 FOR I=0 TO 4
40     P%(I)=4
50 NEXT I
60 FOR I=5 TO 15
70     P%(I)=0
80 NEXT
90 PALETTE USING P%(0)
```

Figure 8-30 show's what's happening here. The array P% is dimensioned to hold 16 colors. Then elements P(0) through P(4) are set by the first FOR...NEXT loop to hold the number 4—which is the color red. Then a second FOR...NEXT loop fills the rest of the array with 0, which is the color for black.

The PALETTE USING P%(0) statement begins with element P%(0) of the array and assigns its value (4) to attribute 0. Then it assigns the value of element P%(1) to attribute 1, etc. The result is that attributes from 0 through 4 are all set to the color red (4), while attributes from 5 through 15 are assigned to black (0).

What About Color on SCREEN 2?

Your graphics SCREEN 2 is great for high-resolution graphics, but it comes up a little short in the color department. Where SCREEN 1 lets you choose from a background color and a palette of three colors, SCREEN 2 gives you only the background color and one foreground color at one time.

On a monitor using the CGA, you can't change colors in SCREEN 2—you're stuck with the default foreground and background colors. If you have EGA, then you can use the PALETTE statement to change colors, but you still can specify only two (foreground and background) at any one time. But then, you'll probably want to use one of the SCREEN modes that supports EGA, such as the flashy and colorful SCREEN 8.

Chapter 8

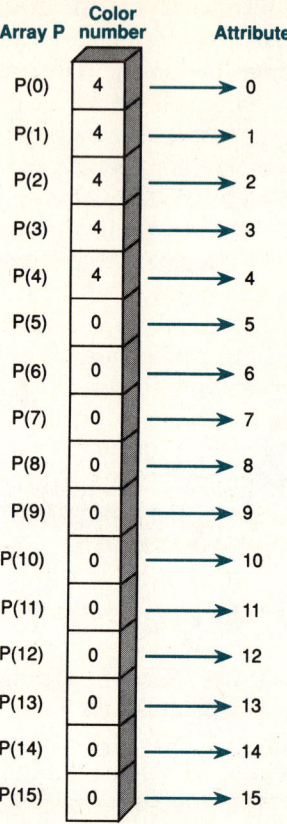

Fig. 8-30: Setting all attributes to red or black.

Filling Large Areas with Color

As you know, the LINE statement lets you draw rectangles and fill them with color, but what about other shapes? Circles, stars, irregular shapes—no matter what the figure is, if it has a border, it can be filled with color using the PAINT statement.

The BASIC Screen, Graphics, and Sound

Filling In with PAINT

The general forms of the PAINT statement are shown here:

```
100 PAINT (X,Y),P
200 PAINT (X,Y), P, BDR
300 PAINT (X,Y), P, BDR, BACK
```

Line 100 means, "start painting at point X, Y, using the color of attribute P; paint every pixel continuously until a border with the attribute P is reached."

Line 200 means the same thing, except that it paints until a color specified by the attribute BDR is reached. Line 300 adds a BACK variable, which specifies a background tile pattern or a color to skip. (More about using BACK in a minute.)

Try this small program that draws a circle and fills it with color:

```
10 SCREEN 1: CLS: KEY OFF
20 CIRCLE (160,100), 50
30 PAINT (160,100)
```

When you RUN the program, line 20 draws a circle with the center at coordinates (160,100), and with a radius of 50. Because you didn't specify a color, the circle is drawn in the foreground color.

Then the PAINT statement in line 30 takes over. It begins painting from the center of the circle, using the foreground color. It fills in all directions, spreading out and flooding the circle with color. PAINTing stops only when it comes to a line (actually, when it comes to a point) in the foreground color—or in the color you specify with the border attribute, B.

To fill the circle, you don't have to begin in its center, just as long as you set the PAINT statement to start somewhere within its borders. For instance, you can change the X,Y coordinates in the PAINT statement to (140,80), and the effect is the same. However, if you try to begin on a border of a shape—like the circumference of the circle—PAINT has no effect.

What if you "miss" and don't begin to PAINT inside the circle? Change the program as follows:

```
10 SCREEN 1: CLS: KEY OFF
20 CIRCLE (160,100), 50
30 PAINT (10,10)
RUN
```

See what happens? Because you specified the beginning of the PAINT outside the circle, it paints everything on the screen except the circle.

405

Chapter 8

If you have several shapes with different colors, use the border attribute, B, to tell PAINT how far to go. PAINT rides roughshod over other borders until it comes to a border with the attribute you specify. Here's an example:

```
10 SCREEN 1: CLS: KEY OFF
20 LINE (10,10)-(150,150),2,B
30 CIRCLE (50, 50), 25, 3
40 PAINT (50,50),2
```

This little program draws a circle inside a rectangle. The lines of the rectangle are in color attribute 2, whereas those of the circle are in color attribute 3. The PAINT statement starts filling from the center of the circle. It continues filling outward until it comes to a border with the specified color attribute—that is, 2. Because the border of the circle is in attribute 3, it's painted right over as PAINT chugs out to the edges of the rectangle (drawn in attribute 2) before it stops.

If a shape is extremely jagged or has many surfaces, PAINT can cause an "Out of memory" error.

PAINT Tiling

You can use the PAINT command to give *tiled* patterns. To create a tiled pattern, you specify a tile mask by using a string instead of the paint attribute P. Try the following:

```
10 CLS: SCREEN 2
20 CIRCLE (160,100), 50
30 PAINT (160,100), "<"
RUN
```

The program draws a circle with its center at (160,100) and a radius of 50 on screen 2. Then the PAINT statement fills the circle. The < character is called the tile mask. Because you've used the string character < in the PAINT statement, it produces the circle painted with bold stripes shown in figure 8-31.

The tile mask is one byte (8 bits) wide, and can be from 1 to 64 bytes long. In our example, the tile mask was the "less than" character (<), whose bit pattern is 00111100. This masks half of each byte of painting, allowing half to be seen. Figure 8-32 shows how the bit pattern of the mask covers half the painted area.

Notice that the shape of the character itself doesn't matter—it's the binary value of the character's ASCII code that you're after. (For a further discussion of conversions between decimal and binary numbers, refer to Appendix B.)

The BASIC Screen, Graphics, and Sound

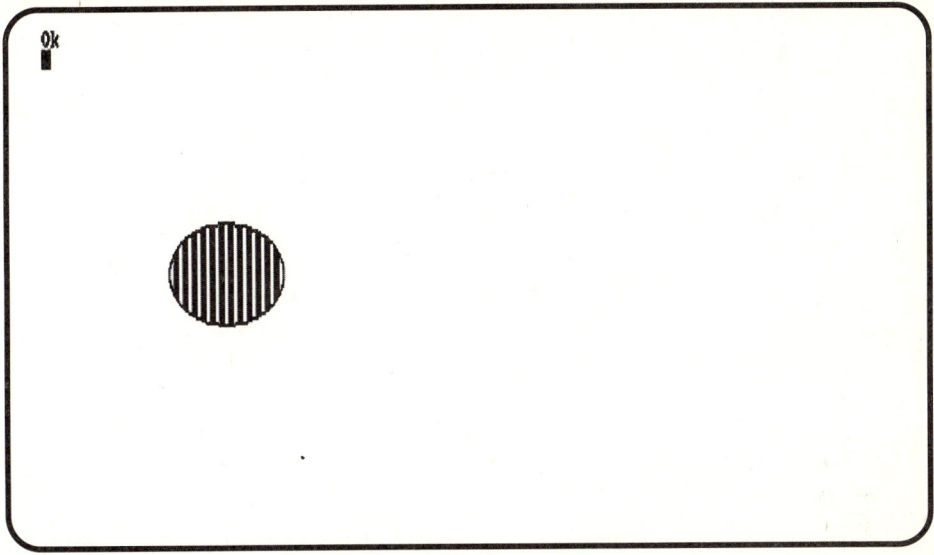

Fig. 8-31: PAINT with tiling.

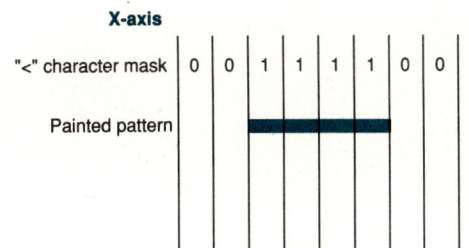

Fig. 8-32: The bit pattern for < masks half the PAINTed area.

Each successive byte (that is, each successive character) appears at a new Y-coordinate. Therefore you can string bytes together to create patterns. Here's a small program that fills the same circle with a wavy sawtooth pattern:

```
10 CLS: SCREEN 2
20 CIRCLE (160,100), 50
30 PAINT (160,100), CHR$(15)+"<"+"p"+"<"+CHR$(15)
RUN
```

407

Chapter 8

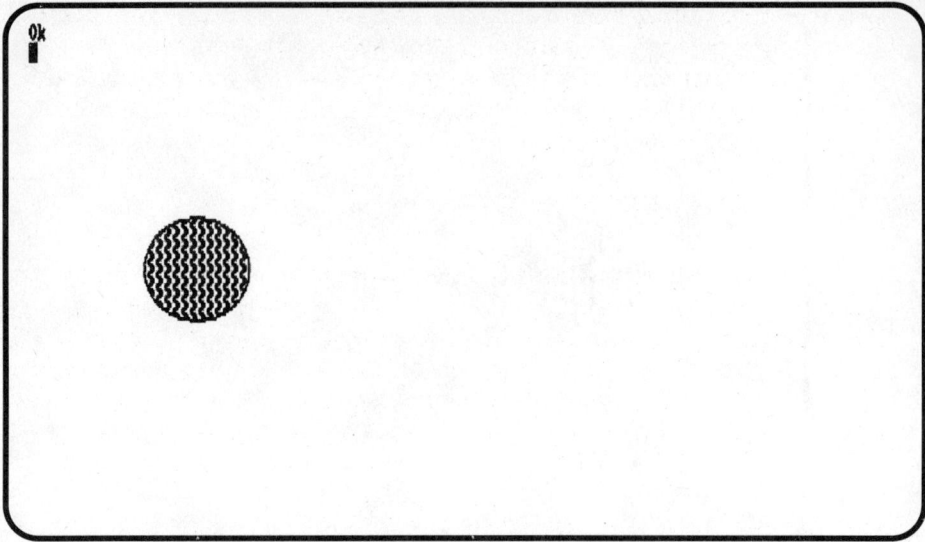

a) The sawtooth pattern produced.

PAINT (160, 100), CHR$(15)+"<"+"p"+"<"+CHR$(15)

CHR$(15)	00001111	1st byte
<	00111100	2nd byte
p	11110000	3rd byte
<	00111100	4th byte
CHR$(15)	00001111	5th byte

b) The mask that produces the sawtooth pattern.

Figure 8-33: Painting a sawtooth pattern.

The first byte, CHR$(15), produces a mask of 00001111. The next byte, the < character, produces 00111100, and the third byte, p, produces 11110000. Seen in succession, these produce one of the wavy lines you see within the circle.

In SCREEN 1, each pixel is two bits wide. Each two bits of the tile mask give the attribute for one of the four possible colors.

The Background Attribute

With PAINT, you can specify background this way:

```
300 PAINT (X,Y), P, BDR, BACK
```

The BASIC Screen, Graphics, and Sound

The background attribute is a single-byte (one-character) value that specifies a color byte or tile pattern for PAINT to ignore when it's checking for a boundary. The background attribute lets you PAINT, say, alternating green and blue lines on a blue background. Without specifying a value for BACK, this is impossible.

Fancy Things with Windows

Up to now, you've been mixing text and graphics on your screen pretty much with impunity. And you've already noticed that when you want a screen address, you have to specify statements such as LOCATE, using the row, column format; whereas, for CIRCLE, LINE, and other graphics statements, you use the x,y format.

That's because BASIC actually gives you access to at least two screens. One is for text, the other for graphics. You haven't separated them yet—but you're about to.

What a VIEW!

If you want to see only graphics in an area, without the intrusion of text, you can use the VIEW statement. Its general form is

```
100 VIEW (X1,Y1) - (X2,Y2)
200 VIEW (X1,Y1) - (X2, Y2) F, B
```

Line 100 means, "set a graphics viewport from coordinates X1,Y1 to X2,Y2." Line 200 adds optional parameters to let you fill the viewport with the color assigned to attribute F, or to add a border in the color assigned to attribute B.

After you've defined a graphics viewport, any points plotted in it are relative; that is, X1 and Y1 are added to them before plotting. Try this example:

```
10 SCREEN 2: CLS: KEY OFF
20 VIEW (200,100)-(350,150), ,1
30 CIRCLE (75,25), 25
```

When you RUN this program, the VIEW statement creates a tiny little graphics viewport in the lower center of the screen, gives it a border, and then it draws a circle in the center of the viewport (see fig. 8-34).

The CIRCLE statement uses the relative coordinates of the viewport—that is, it assumes the upper left corner of the viewport is (0,0), and calculates from there. Because this particular viewport runs from (0,0) to (150,50), no matter where it's located on the screen, the center of the viewport is at (75,25). From now on, that's your graphics area—the rectangle that's 150 x 50 in size. If you draw circles or lines, or plot points, that little square is where they'll wind up.

Chapter 8

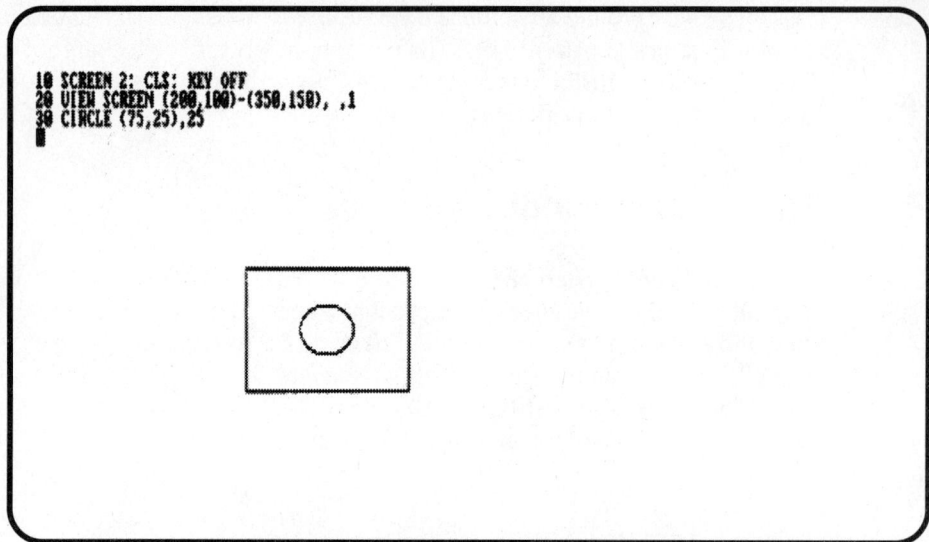

Fig. 8-34:   Making a graphics viewport.

To use actual coordinates in the VIEW statement, add the word SCREEN, like this:

```
100 VIEW SCREEN (X1,Y1)-(X2,Y2)
```

Now you're using the actual screen coordinates. So, to put the viewport in the same place on the screen—and the circle in the same place within the viewport—you'll need to change the CIRCLE statement so that it's drawn using real coordinates, not relative ones:

```
10 SCREEN 2: CLS: KEY OFF
20 VIEW (200,100)-(350,150), ,1
30 CIRCLE (275,125), 25
```

CLS clears only the screen specified by the latest VIEW statement. If you want to clear the entire screen, use VIEW with no coordinates specified, then use CLS.

Setting Text Boundaries with VIEW PRINT

There's another statement you can use to set up your screen the way you want. VIEW PRINT sets the boundaries of the screen's text window. The general form is the following:

```
100 VIEW PRINT T TO B
```

This means, "use the area from top line T on the screen to bottom line B as the text window." All scrolling and cursor movement now takes place in this area, as do statements like LOCATE and PRINT.

Here's a short program that combines VIEW and VIEW PRINT to partition your display into a text window and a graphics window.

```
10 SCREEN 2: CLS: KEY OFF
20 VIEW PRINT 15 TO 24
30 VIEW (0,0) - (639,100),1,1
40 CIRCLE (320, 50), 50, 0
50 LIST
```

In line 20, the VIEW PRINT 15 TO 24 statement means that the text window will be rows 15 through 24 on the screen—that is, the lower portion of your display. The VIEW statement in line 30 sets the top portion of the screen to a graphics viewport, and paints the screen in the foreground color. After dividing the screen, the program LISTs itself in the text window and draws a circle in the graphics window (see fig. 8-35). If you like, try typing some more LIST statements; you'll see that scrolling and listing all take place in only the text part of the screen.

After a RUN of the program, CLS clears only the graphics viewport, because this is the last one that was specified. If you specify VIEW PRINT without top and bottom rows, it specifies the entire screen for text input—this is how BASIC is set up when you first load it.

Other Graphics Statements

Computer games and animated displays are fun to use, but the program code necessary for these applications can be very complex. This section explains some more advanced graphics statements which are excellent for performing real-world jobs, including animation and games.

Chapter 8

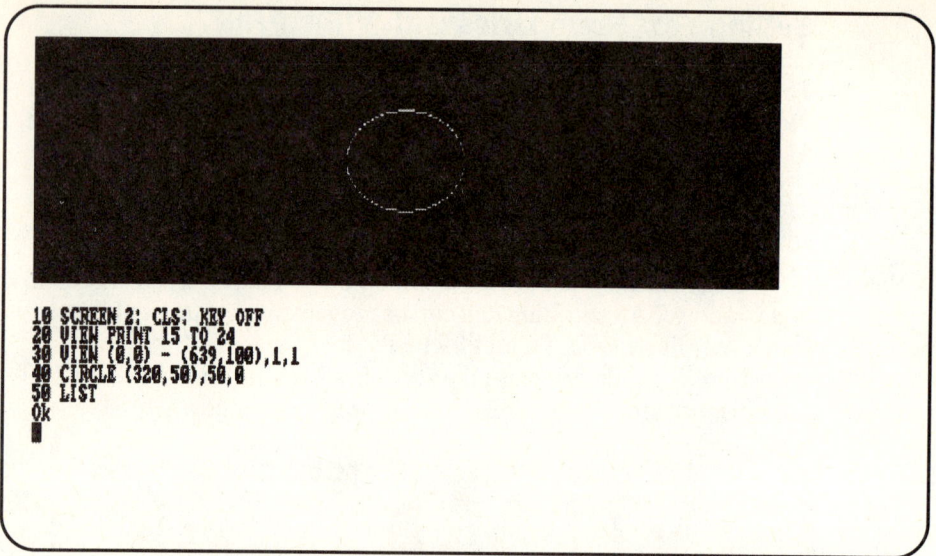

Fig. 8-35: VIEW and VIEW PRINT give separate text and graphics screens.

Looking for People Who Like to DRAW

One very useful statement is DRAW. In fact, DRAW is more than just a single statement—it's actually a sub-language of its own, complete with several different commands. A single DRAW statement can draw a complex shape and fill it in, skip to another part of the screen and draw another shape there, and so on. It can accomplish what otherwise might take you several ordinary BASIC statements.

The general form of DRAW is simple:

```
100 DRAW A$
```

This means, "begin at the last specified point and draw using the commands in string `A$`." If you don't have a last point specified on the screen, DRAW begins at the center. The actual DRAW commands handle movement, rotation, color, and scaling, and they're shown in Table 8-3.

Table 8-3: DRAW commands.

Command	Action
U*n*	Move up the amount specified by *n*
D*n*	Move down the specified amount
R*n*	Move right the amount specified by *n*
L*n*	Move left the amount specified by *n*
E*n*	Move diagonally up and right the amount specified by *n*
F*n*	Move diagonally down and right the amount specified by *n*
G*n*	Move diagonally down and left the amount specified by *n*
H*n*	Move diagonally up and left the amount specified by *n*
M*x,y*	Move to point *x, y* and draw a line from the current position; or, if *x* and *y* are preceded by a + or – sign, move relative to the current position
B	After one of the drawing commands above, move but don't draw
N	After one of the drawing commands above, move, but return to the original position when done
A*n*	Set angle *n* using the numbers 0 through 3 for *n*. 0 means 0 degrees, 1 means 90 degrees, 2 means 180 degrees, and 3 means 270 degrees.
TA*n*	Turn an angle of *n* degrees. Turn counterclockwise if positive, clockwise if negative
C*n*	Set color, as in the COLOR and PALETTE statements
S*n*	Scale the following drawing. S1, S2, S3 are reductions, S4 is the default (no scaling), and S5 through S255 are enlargements
P*c,b*	Paints the figure in the color *p*, with outline color *b*. You have to specify both quantities, and you cannot perform tiling
X*string, variable*	Executes a substring from within a string, like GOSUB; *variable* is optional

Chapter 8

This short program features a DRAW statement that draws a box:

```
10 SCREEN 1: CLS: KEY OFF
20 DRAW "U50 L50 D50 R50"
```

In line 20, DRAW begins at the center of the screen, point (160,100), because you didn't name a starting point. It draws up 50 units, then left 50 units, then down 50 units, and finally right 50 units. The result is a box on the screen.

You can use variables within the DRAW statement; just add equals signs and separate them with semicolons. Here's another way to draw the same box, but this time you'll fill it with the foreground color:

```
10 SCREEN 1: CLS: KEY OFF
20 N=50
30 BOX$="C3; U=N; L=N; D=N; R=N; BM-10,-10; P2,3"
40 DRAW BOX$
```

As you can see, if you use variables within the DRAW string, you must assign most of them with the equals sign and separate them with semicolons. In this example, the commands you assign to the string variable BOX$ draw the box on the screen in the color assigned to attribute 3 (C3). The box is drawn using the value of 50 for N. When the box is completely drawn (after executing R=N), the last point is in the lower right corner of the box. The next command, BM-10,-10, means, "move back 10 and up 10 without drawing; this prepares for the paint command. Finally, the command P2,3 fills the box with the color assigned to attribute 2; like PAINT, it draws until it reaches a border in the color assigned to attribute 3. The DRAW BOX$ statement in line 40 actually does the drawing, using the string BOX$ that was created earlier in the program.

Here's another program that shows some of the things you can do with DRAW. It draws a rocket, then jerks the rocket around in a circle by its nose.

```
10 SCREEN 1: CLS: KEY OFF
20 ROCKET$="TA=DEG; S4 F5 D30 F10 D10 H10 L10 G10 U10
    E10 U30 E5"
30 FOR DEG=0 TO 360 STEP 10
40      DRAW "C1" + ROCKET$
50      DRAW "C0" + ROCKET$
60 NEXT DEG
```

The DRAW string ROCKET$ contains the drawing commands necessary to get the rocket on the screen. The S4 in the string scales the rocket; to increase the size of the rocket, you could change this to "S5" or even higher. The TA=DEG in the ROCKET$ string specifies that the turning angle will be an angle of DEG degrees.

414

The BASIC Screen, Graphics, and Sound

The actual DRAW statements are within the FOR...NEXT loop. The first time through the loop, DEG=0, and the rocket is drawn at an angle of 0 degrees. It's drawn in the foreground color by the statement DRAW "C1" + ROCKET$. Then, as quickly as it's drawn, the rocket is "erased" by the DRAW "C0" + ROCKET$ statement. (It's actually redrawn in the background color, 0, which erases it.) Each time through the loop, the rocket is redrawn and erased at a new turning angle. The overall effect is of a rocket rotating around its nose for 360 degrees (see fig. 8-36).

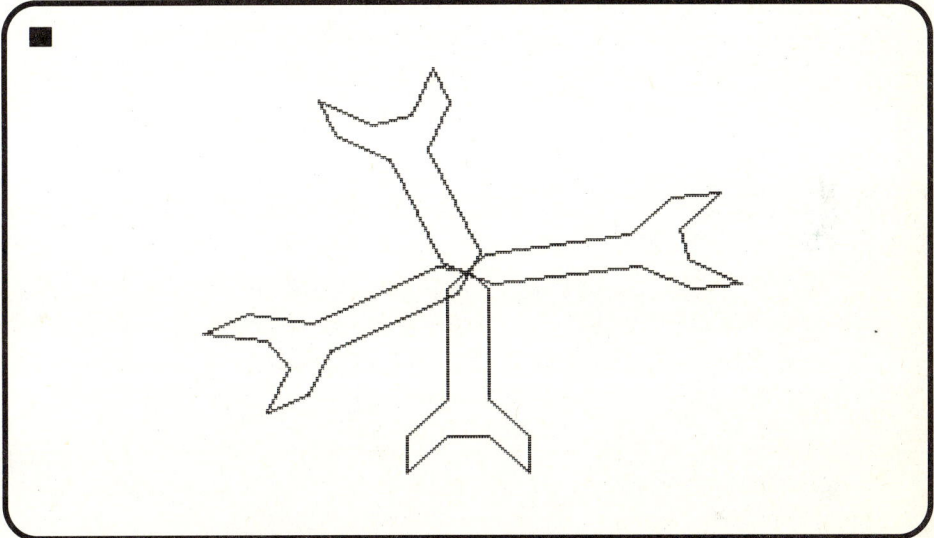

Fig. 8-36: Rotating a rocket with DRAW.

Besides showing the DRAW statement, this little program also illustrates one of the principles of animation—drawing a shape, erasing it quickly, then redrawing it in a new location.

Using PUT and GET

The PUT and GET statements are also very helpful in animation, or when you need to quickly draw the same pattern in many locations. To use them, you dimension an array, GET a section of the screen into the array, then PUT that section anywhere on the screen.

Chapter 8

The GET Statement

The GET statement gets a specified area of the graphics screen, and anything in it. It takes all the points within that area, including lines, circles, color attributes, and anything else. The general form of the statement is as follows:

```
GET (X1,Y1)-(X2,Y2), ARRAY
```

This means, "get every point in the rectangle from coordinates X1,Y1 to coordinates X2,Y2, and copy them into ARRAY." You have to dimension the array before executing the GET statement, just as you do with any array.

PUT

Once you've copied an area using GET, you can use PUT to place it anywhere on the screen. The general form of PUT is as follows:

```
PUT (X,Y), ARRAY
```

This means, "put the image in ARRAY on the screen, with the top left corner of the image at coordinates X,Y."

Smiling Jack

Here's an example program. It draws the face of Smiling Jack on the screen. Then it GETs that face and PUTs it at random locations. Smiling Jack can pop up anywhere!

```
10 REM-SMILING JACK
20 DIM F(1000)
30 SCREEN 1: COLOR 0,0: CLS
40 CX=50
50 CY=50
60 GOSUB 140
70 GET (0,0)-(100,100),F
80 WHILE INKEY$=""
90     CLS
100    PUT (219*RND, 99*RND),F
110    FOR I=1 TO 1000: NEXT
120 WEND
130 END
140 REM-Draw Smiling Jack
```

416

```
150 CIRCLE (CX, CY), 50
160 CIRCLE (CX+12,CY-6),8
170 CIRCLE (CX-8, CY-6), 8
180 CIRCLE (CX, CY), 30, ,3, 0
190 LINE (0,0)-(100,100),,B
200 RETURN
```

The program begins by dimensioning an array, F, to 1000 elements. After initialization to SCREEN 1, the program defines CX and CY as 50 each, then goes off to the subroutine beginning with line 140. The subroutine draws a face centered on coordinates (50,50), and surrounds the face with a rectangle. The entire drawing is from coordinates (0,0) to (100,100).

When the program returns from the subroutine, the GET statement in line 70 gets everything on your screen that's included in a rectangle drawn from (0,0) to (100,100). That includes the box you drew and the face inside it. All the points within that space are copied into array F.

Now comes the fun part. Within the WHILE...WEND loop, the PUT statement places the contents of the array—containing our buddy Smiling Jack—onto the screen. Where he's PUT depends on the coordinates of the PUT statement—and those are a pair of random numbers. Smiling Jack's face pops up all over the screen. The FOR...NEXT loop in line 110 is a delay that makes sure you'll get a good look at Jack before he decamps for the next location (see fig. 8-37).

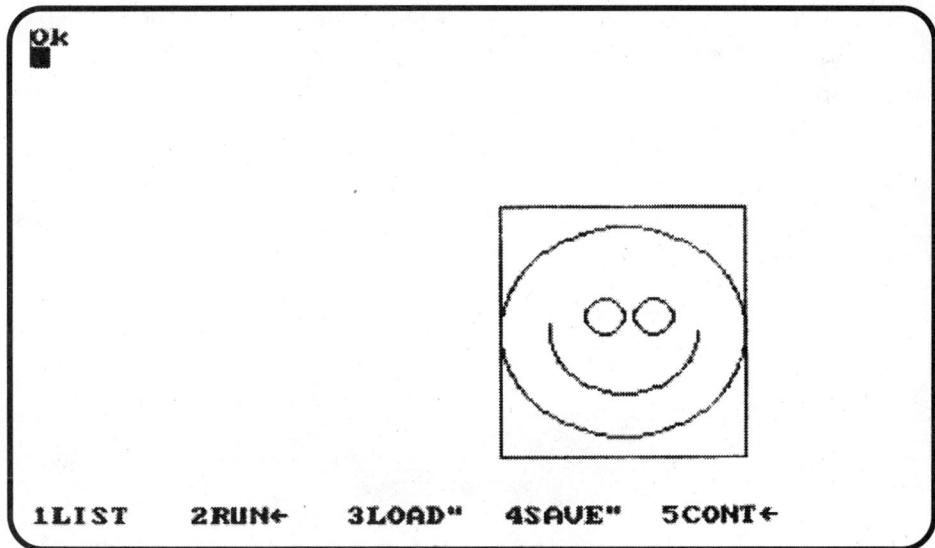

Fig. 8-37: Smiling Jack.

How Big Should an Array Be?

One question you need to answer when using GET is, "what minimum size of array will I need?" We used a rough figure of 1000 in the example above, but if you want to get specific, you'll need to know the SCREEN you're using, and how many bits per pixel the screen has. First you figure out how many total bytes you'll need, using these formulas:

Number of bytes to GET = 4 + INT(X*bits per pixel + 7)/8) * Y

where

X = ABS(X2-X1) + 1
Y = ABS(Y2-Y1) + 1

For Smiling Jack, we used SCREEN 1, which has 2 bits per pixel. The value for X is 101 (that is, 100 – 0 + 1), and the value for Y is also 101. So, the number of bytes we need to store in the array is 4 + ((101*2) + 7)/8) * 101 = 2643 bytes.

OK, that's the number of bytes we need. But this is a numeric array, remember, not a string array. The number of bytes we can store in each element of a numeric array depends on the type of storage: integer, single precision, or double precision.

Array Type	Storage
Integer	2 bytes per element
Single precision	4 bytes per element
Double precision	8 bytes per element

In our example, then, we're using the default single-precision array, so we need 2643/4=661 elements. DIM F(661) should do the trick.

More about PUT

The PUT statement lets you specify modes for placing the image on the screen. You do this with specific words, like this:

```
100 PUT (x,y), array, XOR
200 PUT (x,y), array, PSET
300 PUT (x,y), array, PRESET
400 PUT (x,y), array, AND
500 PUT (x,y), array, OR
```

If you don't specify a mode, PUT wakes up set to XOR the image. When you XOR an image onto a complex background on the screen, it covers anything on the screen without destroying the background. If you then use another PUT statement to XOR that same image to the same spot again, the image is erased and the background restored. This is especially useful in animation—it's how you can draw a rascally rabbit racing across a lawn, and leave the lawn intact after he passes.

PUT with PSET mode transfers the image onto the screen without regard for what is already there. PRESET is similar to PSET, except that it reverses the color of the image. AND puts the image down on the screen only if an image already exists there, while OR superimposes the image onto the existing one.

Copying Pages with PCOPY

The screen you see in front of you is actually a screen "page" in memory. The size of the page depends on your graphics adapter and which SCREEN you're using. Appendix G shows graphics information, including page sizes, for most hardware and SCREEN combinations.

If you have the IBM enhanced graphics adapter (or its equivalent) and EGA memory, you can use multiple screen pages. This can speed up graphics redrawing and animation, because one page is displayed while you write or draw on the other. The PCOPY statement is a way of copying one screen to another; it's much faster than completely redrawing the screen.

The general form of the statement is as follows:

```
100 PCOPY S, D
```

This means, "copy the source page S to destination page D." Both S and D are determined by the amount of video memory you have, and by the size per page of the SCREEN.

For instance, if you're using SCREEN 7 with 64K of EGA memory, you can use this statement to copy PAGE 1 to PAGE 2:

```
10 PCOPY 1, 2
```

Using the POINT Function

With the different SCREEN sizes and all the different drawing statements in BASIC, it's easy to get lost. When you want to know the coordinates of the latest graphics point, or what color that point is, you can use the POINT function.

Chapter 8

Finding the Coordinates

To find the graphics coordinates of the current point, use the POINT function with arguments of 0 through 3, like this:

```
100 X = POINT (0)
200 Y = POINT (1)
300 XW = POINT (2)
400 YW = POINT (3)
```

Line 100 means, "find the current physical X-coordinate, and put that value in X." Line 200 finds the current physical Y-coordinate.

When you use POINT(2) and POINT(3), these functions find the current logical X-coordinate if you're using a WINDOW. If you're not using a WINDOW, they're the same as POINT(0) and POINT(1).

Reading the Color with POINT

The POINT function can also read the color at a location, so that your programs can make decisions based on that color. Used in this way, the general form of POINT is shown here:

```
100 P=POINT (X,Y)
```

This means, "find the color attribute of the point at coordinates (X,Y), and put that value in variable P." If the point is out of range, you'll see a –1 in P.

Translating Coordinates with PMAP

The PMAP function is useful in graphics for mapping expressions to coordinates on your screen. Like the POINT function, it uses numbers 0 through 3, like this:

```
100 X = PMAP (0, N)
200 Y = PMAP (1, N)
300 XW = PMAP (2, N)
400 YW = PMAP (3, N)
```

Line 100 has a 0 in the parentheses after PMAP. It means, "map the logical expression or coordinate N to physical coordinate X." Line 200 maps N to physical coordinate Y.

Lines 300 and 400, containing the numbers 2 and 3 in the parentheses, map physical expressions to logical coordinates.

You can use this function to translate coordinates between the physical screen and the ones you define with WINDOW and VIEW.

Making Music and Sound

You might already be using the BEEP statement to signal the end of a program process, an error, or just to wake yourself up from time to time. GW-BASIC, though, is outfitted with sound and musical abilities that go far beyond the mere BEEP. As you'll soon see, you can create everything from sound effects to sonatas.

The SOUND Machine

The SOUND statement generates sounds through your computer's speaker. You can be very specific about each SOUND, because you can name both the exact frequency and the duration of the sound. Here's the general form:

```
100 SOUND F, D
```

This means, "output a sound through the computer's speaker that is F Hertz (cycles per second) in frequency and D clock ticks long."

The Music Writer

Here's a program that turns your computer into a piano. When you press a function key at the top of the keyboard, it sounds a note—just like a piano. It also records your notes on the screen, to help you write music.

The program uses several ON KEY statements to specify the action to take if that key is pressed. For instance, if you press key 4, execution will branch immediately to the subroutine beginning in line 490. Here, the frequency 523.25 Hertz—that's middle C on a real piano—is sounded for a duration of 2 clock ticks. Pressing other keys branches execution to other subroutines, which give different notes.

```
120 ON KEY(4) GOSUB 490
130 KEY 4, "C"
 .
 .
 .
490 REM-Middle C
500 PRINT "C";
510 SOUND 523.25, 2: RETURN
```

Chapter 8

For each key, we also display a label showing what the key is. So, key 4 will be the key for C, and we'll see that label in the display.

Before we can use the function keys, we need to turn them on with the KEY ON statement. This is handled by a FOR...NEXT loop:

```
260 FOR K=1 TO 10
270     KEY(K) ON
280 NEXT
```

Finally, we display the title and program instructions, and use a WHILE...WEND loop to allow us to exit when the spacebar is pressed.

```
300 KEY ON
310 PRINT TAB(30) "MUSIC WRITER"
320 PRINT: PRINT TAB(20) "The function keys are your
       piano keys"
330 PRINT: PRINT TAB(25) "Press the spacebar to exit"
340 PRINT
350 WHILE INKEY$ <> CHR$(32): WEND
360 END
```

If you want, type the code for the complete program and try your hand at composing a song, or playing one of your favorites!

```
10 REM-MUSIC WRITER
20 REM
30 REM-Set variables
40 DEFINT K
50 REM-Set up function keys as piano keys
60 ON KEY(1) GOSUB 370
70 KEY 1, "G"
80 ON KEY(2) GOSUB 410
90 KEY 2, "A"
100 ON KEY(3) GOSUB 450
110 KEY 3, "B"
120 ON KEY(4) GOSUB 490
130 KEY 4, "C"
140 ON KEY(5) GOSUB 530
150 KEY 5, "D"
160 ON KEY(6) GOSUB 570
170 KEY 6, "E"
180 ON KEY(7) GOSUB 610
190 KEY 7, "F"
```

```
200 ON KEY(8) GOSUB 650
210 KEY 8, "G"
220 ON KEY(9) GOSUB 690
230 KEY 9, "A"
240 ON KEY(10) GOSUB 730
250 KEY 10, "B"
260 FOR K=1 TO 10
270     KEY(K) ON
280 NEXT
290 CLS
300 KEY ON
310 PRINT TAB(30) "MUSIC WRITER"
320 PRINT: PRINT TAB(20) "The function keys are your piano keys"
330 PRINT: PRINT TAB(25) "Press the spacebar to exit"
340 PRINT
350 WHILE INKEY$ <> " ":WEND
360 END
370 REM-G
380 PRINT "G";
390 SOUND 392, 2: RETURN
400 '
410 REM-A
420 PRINT "A";
430 SOUND 440, 2: RETURN
440 '
450 REM-B
460 PRINT "B";
470 SOUND 493.88, 2: RETURN
480 '
490 REM-Middle C
500 PRINT "C";
510 SOUND 523.25, 2: RETURN
520 '
530 REM-D
540 PRINT "D";
550 SOUND 587.33, 2: RETURN
560 '
570 REM-E
580 PRINT "E";
590 SOUND 659.26, 2: RETURN
600 '
610 REM-F
620 PRINT "F";
```

Chapter 8

```
630 SOUND 698.46, 2: RETURN
640 '
650 REM-G
660 PRINT "G";
670 SOUND 783.99, 2: RETURN
680 '
690 REM-A
700 PRINT "A";
710 SOUND 880, 2: RETURN
720 '
730 REM-B
740 PRINT "B";
750 SOUND 987.77, 2: RETURN
```

How to PLAY Music

BASIC has a high-level music command language that lets you compose and play music using simple strings of notes. You can even put music in the background, playing while BASIC is performing its other wonders on the screen.

The PLAY statement gives you access to BASIC's music-making talents. Here's its general form:

```
PLAY S$
```

This means, "play all the notes in that string." What's in the string is shown in Table 8-4.

Table 8-4: Music commands in the PLAY string.

String	Action
A-G[#,+,–]	Notes A through G; # or + follow a note for sharp, – follows for a flat.
L*n*	Length of each note, 1-64; L4 is quarter note, L1 a full note. Use *n* after a note to change only that note's length.
MF	Music in foreground; runs PLAY and SOUND statements in foreground, so each note finishes before computer performs another task.
MB	Music in background; allows PLAY and SOUND to be executed in background, while other actions continue. Background music buffer holds up to 32 notes at one time.

The BASIC Screen, Graphics, and Sound

String	Action
MN	Music normal; each note plays 7/8 of time determined by length L.
ML	Music legato; each note plays full time determined by L.
MS	Music staccato; each note plays 3/4 of time determined by length L.
Nn	Play note n, in the range 0-84, covering 7 octaves. N0 is a rest.
On	Octave n, in the range 0-6, covering 7 octaves. Default is 4, the octave containing middle C.
Pn	Pause n, in the range 0-64.
Tn	Tempo, n L4's in a minute, in the range 32-255; default is 120.
.(period)	Increases playing time of note by 3/2 x L x T. You can place multiple periods after a note to changed its playing time.
X*string*	Executes a substring.
>n	Before a note, means play it and subsequent notes in the next higher octave. Use more to change more than one octave.
<n	Before the note, means play it and subsequent notes in the next lower octave. Use more to change more than one octave.

Here's an example you can try:

```
10 HYMN$= "MN O3 GB O4 DDDDDGD <B8 >C8 DDC O3 AG"
20 PLAY HYMN$
```

The string HYMN$ contains the commands for a simple tune, well-known to many people. MN specifies normal music, and O3 starts off in the third octave. (It's capital O3 remember, not 03.) The O4 changes to the fourth octave, and the notes DDDDDGD are played, followed by a 1/8 note B and C. The "less than" symbol (<) shifts down one octave from the present one (because we're currently in the fourth octave, it's the same as O3 would be in this case), and the "greater than" symbol (>) shifts back up after this single note. The next notes, DDC, are played in the fourth octave, and the final AG are played in the third octave again.

This music sublanguage is very similar to the DRAW sublanguage. You can use values for n or you can use constants. If you use constants, you need an equals sign before the constant and a semicolon after it, like this:

```
10 N=3
20 PLAY "MF O=N; BCB"
```

This short example plays the notes BCB in the third octave.

425

Using ON PLAY for Background Music

Background music is specified with an `MB` in the string of notes. The difference between foreground and background is, for an `MB` string (that is, music in the background) BASIC continues executing other statements while the music plays. For an `MF` string (music foreground), BASIC waits politely until the music has played before continuing.

You use the ON PLAY(N) and PLAY ON statements to set up a background music trap. The basic form is as follows:

```
100 PLAY ON
200 ON PLAY (N) GOSUB NNN
```

Line 100 enables the trap; line 200 shows where to branch if the trap occurs. Line 200 means, "on the Nth note from the end of the background music buffer, go to subroutine NNN and execute it." The background music is unaffected by the subroutine call.

Once you've specified background music, you can place up to 32 notes in a buffer to be played. BASIC continues execution while the music is playing. Trapping background music is similar to trapping other events with ON statements (such as ON KEY and ON COM).

Here's an example that illustrates the technique:

```
10 HYMN$= "MB O3 GB O4 DDDDDGD <B8 >C8 DDC O3 AG"
20 PLAY ON
30 PLAY HYMN$
40 WHILE INKEY$=""
50   PRINT "Press any key to exit..."
60   ON PLAY (4) GOSUB 100
70 WEND
80 END
90 '
100 PRINT "Warning: Only 4 notes left!"
110 RETURN
```

To begin with, we change the first two characters in the HYMN$ string to `MB` for music in the background. Then we use the PLAY ON statement to enable the trap. In line 30, the "hymn" starts playing, but execution continues into the WHILE...WEND loop as the music plays delightfully in the background. When only four notes of the ditty remain in the buffer, the subroutine is executed and you see a warning message flash by.

The BASIC Screen, Graphics, and Sound

Review Questions

1. Explain the main differences between the graphics SCREEN 1 and SCREEN 2 using CGA.

2. Write a program that uses PSET (rather than CIRCLE) to draw a circle centered in the middle of SCREEN 2. Use a radius of 50 and the following formulas:

   ```
   X = radius * cosine(a)
   Y = radius * sine(a)
   ```

3. You want to plot the daily movement of one of your holdings on the stock market for a year. At its height, the stock price was 50; at its lowest, it fell to 30 points. Write a WINDOW statement that plots days along the X-axis and price along the Y-axis for these ranges.

4. What statements should you modify in the Labeled Pie program to change it for screen 2? You should produce output similar to figure 8-26, but still use the wedges shown.

5. What does this program do?

   ```
   10 SCREEN 1: CLS: KEY OFF
   20 LINE (10,10)-(150,150),2,B
   30 CIRCLE (50, 50), 25, 3
   40 PAINT (50,50),3
   ```

6. You're planning to GET a picture of a house that covers the coordinates (0,0) to (100,100) in screen 1. Write a DIM statement to store HOUSE in an integer array.

7. Where will the following statement place the cursor on the screen?

   ```
   15 LOCATE 15,0
   ```

8. Can you predict the result of this program?

   ```
   10 CLS: SCREEN 1: KEY OFF
   20 LINE (10,10)-(100,100), 3, B
   30 PAINT (50,50), 1, 2
   ```

9. What is the duration in minutes of the longest sound you can specify with SOUND?

10. Exercise: Write an animation program to move a box from one side of the screen to the other, then back again.

Chapter 9

Advanced
GW-BASIC

Chapter **9**

Advanced GW-BASIC

What you've learned about GW-BASIC to this point is sufficient for you to write powerful, complex programs that accomplish dozens of real-world tasks. Nevertheless, good programmers are always looking for whatever can provide that extra edge. In this chapter, you'll learn about advanced BASIC and other features that can increase the usability or speed of your programs, and add professional polish.

What You'll Learn in this Chapter

Up to now in this book, BASIC has existed in its own private world, insulated for the most part from the system and other programs around it. In this chapter, you'll see how a single BASIC program is linked to your computer hardware, to other programs, and to other languages. You'll learn how to:

- Economize on disk space by using number-string conversions
- Write to and read from any byte in computer memory
- Save and restore entire chunks of computer memory
- Save your art in files with permanence that Michelangelo never dreamed of
- Call DOS commands and assembly language programs from BASIC
- Set BASIC parameters such as stack size, number of files that can be open, and highest memory location
- Handle errors creatively

Chapter 9

Using Conversions for Economy

LSET and RSET are the preferred ways of moving data in and out of a random file buffer, but to use these statements, all your data must be strings. This means that if you have numeric data, it must first be converted. You could use STR$ to convert numbers to their string representations before putting them into the file buffer, and then use VAL to convert them back to numbers when you extract them from the file. There's a better way, though, using BASIC functions that save you disk space and let you be very specific about what types of conversions you perform.

Number-String Conversions with MKI$, MKS$, and MKD$

What do you do if you're sitting there with a handful of numbers you want to save in a random file? Simple—you convert them to strings with MKI$ (convert integer to string), MKS$ (convert single-precision number to string), or MKD$ (convert double-precision number to string). Here are the general forms of these functions:

```
100 A$ = MKI$(N%)
200 B$ = MKS$(N!)
300 C$ = MKD$(N#)
```

The MKI$ function in line 100 means, "convert the integer N% to a string and place it in the variable A$." The MKS$ function in line 200 converts a single-precision number to a string, while MKD$ converts a double-precision number into a string, as shown in line 300.

Before you learn how to use these functions in detail, take a look at the other side of the coin—functions that convert strings back to numeric variables.

String-Number Conversions with CVI, CVS, and CVD

Three functions, CVI (convert to integer), CVS (convert to single precision), and CVD (convert to double precision) convert strings to numbers. The general form is as follows:

```
100 A% = CVI(A$)
200 B! = CVS(B$)
300 C# = CVD(C$)
```

Line 100 means, "convert the 2-byte string A$ to an integer, and put the result in variable A%." The CVD function in line 200 converts a 4-byte string B$ to single-precision numeric variable B!; while the CVD function in line 300 converts an 8-byte string to a double-precision number and stores it in C#.

Advanced GW-BASIC

Let's say that you want to save the integer 1234567 in a random file. You can convert the number to its string representation using STR$, like this:

```
100 A$=STR$(1234567)
```

Then, when you bring the string back out, you can convert it back to a numeric quantity using VAL. This works fine, but the number requires one byte of disk storage for each of the seven characters, rather than the two bytes needed to store an integer. If you have a lot of numbers, this can gobble up disk space in a hurry.

Now let's see how that same number might be stored using MKS$ and retrieved with CVI. Here's a short program that illustrates the process:

```
10 M!=1234567!
20 A$=MKS$(M!)
30 PRINT "A$ is "A$
40 N!=CVS(A$)
50 PRINT "N! is"N!

RUN
A$ is 8┤■Ó
N! is 1234567
Ok
```

In line 20, the MKS$ function converts the single-precision number 1234567 to string A$. When you PRINT A$ in line 30, you can see that this string contains nothing that looks very useful—the important thing is that it's only 4 bytes long. In line 40 we use CVS to convert string A$ back to a single-precision variable, N!. And when we print the result, there's our original number again.

Why is this such a big deal? Because before storing numeric values, you can convert them to strings to save space on a disk or other storage medium. Then when you read the data from disk into a program, you can use CVI, CVS, and CVD to convert those strings back into numbers that you can add, subtract, multiply, and divide.

In simple programs, saving memory and disk space is not very important, and the 360,000 or 1,200,000 bytes of storage available on a floppy disk seems like an infinite amount. However, as you begin to write programs that handle more and more data, it's pretty easy to gobble up an entire floppy disk—or even a hard disk. One way to cut down on the amount of storage space needed is with the conversions using MKI$-CVI, MKS$-CVS, and MKD$-CVD.

Chapter 9

Multiple BASIC Programs

Although the examples in this book have purposely been kept simple, BASIC programs can become quite large and complex. Add to this the memory requirements of large graphics images and those of programs other than BASIC, and it's possible that your programs will grow until a single program won't fit into memory.

Or consider the Worldwide Travel Companion: it's a large (and, unfortunately, still largely mythical) program chock full of information about travel. When you go to any country, you just fire up the program, and it gives you a dictionary and phrasebook in the local language, converts from amounts in the local currency to other currencies, lists hotels and restaurants, and draws maps.

The question is, how does the program provide such detailed information for every country on the face of the globe? You could do it with one big subroutine for each country—for a total of 150-plus—but think of the wasted memory, especially if you're traveling only in Europe. All those extra subroutines would just sit idle most of the time, while one was working!

There's a better way to handle programs that are very large, or that need access to multiple modules. You can break them up into several programs, then use CHAIN or CHAIN MERGE to link them together. These statements let one program call another from disk to replace all or part of it in memory.

Using CHAIN to Link Programs

The CHAIN statement brings in a new program and starts running it. The general form is as follows:

```
100 CHAIN "FILENAME"
200 CHAIN "FILENAME", NNN
300 CHAIN "FILENAME", NNN, DELETE NN-NN
400 CHAIN "FILENAME", NNN, ALL
```

When encountered in a running program, line 100 means, "erase all lines of the current program, bring in the program FILENAME, and begin running it from its first line." Line 200 means, "bring in FILENAME and begin running it at line NNN." Line 300 means, "bring in FILENAME, run it, then delete lines NN-NN from memory."

The ALL in the CHAIN statement in line 400 specifies that all variables are to be passed to the called program. What does "passing variables" mean? Think about this: suppose that the calling program assigns to a variable, NAME$, the name "Barnaby." Now if a second program is chained into memory, and one line contains the instruction PRINT NAME$, what happens? Nothing—unless you specify ALL to "pass" all variables to the new program. Passing is a way of defining those variables so that they mean the same thing in the new program as they did before the **CHAIN** statement.

You can use CHAIN to load one program after another and run it (see fig. 9-1). For instance, PROG1 is executed and uses CHAIN to replace itself in memory with PROG2. Then PROG2 runs until it encounters a CHAIN statement, whereupon it brings in PROG3 to replace itself, and so on. Each program completely replaces the former one, no matter what the line numbers are.

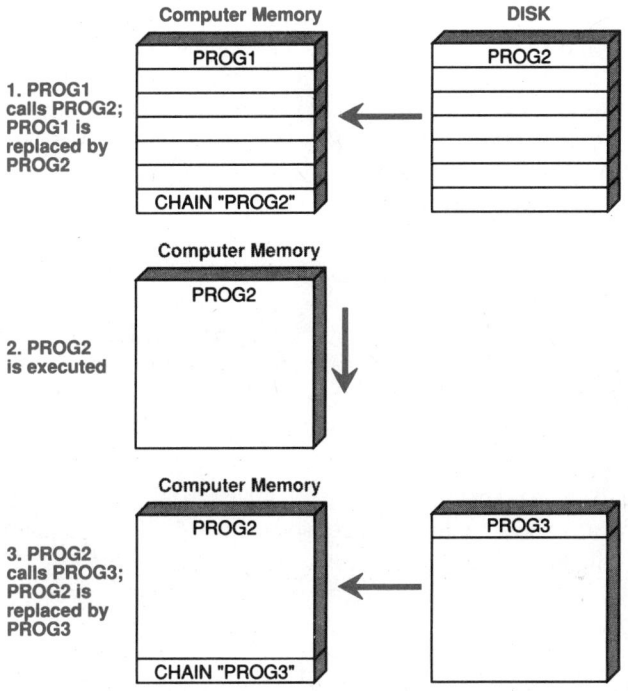

Fig. 9-1: With CHAIN, each successive program replaces the previous one.

Here's a simple example of chaining two programs together. First, save a program for PROG1:

```
10 REM-PROG1
20 DIM A(100)
30 PRINT "PROG1 now running"
40 FOR I=1 TO 100
50     A(I)=SQR(I)
60 NEXT
70 CHAIN "PROG2",,ALL
80 END
```

```
SAVE"PROG1
Ok
```

This little program, which we save as PROG1, creates an array, A. It dimensions the array for 100 elements, then fills the array with the square roots of numbers from 1 to 100. Then in line 70, PROG1 is going to CHAIN "PROG2". The ALL at the end of the CHAIN statement means that all variables will be passed to PROG2.

Now enter the code for PROG2 and save it:

```
100 REM-PROG2
110 PRINT "PROG2 now running"
120 FOR I=1 TO 100
130     PRINT A(I);
140 NEXT

SAVE"PROG2
Ok
```

In this simple illustration, the second program exists just to print the results of the first. Notice that even though you want to print an array of 100 elements, you don't have to use a DIM statement in PROG2; you've already dimensioned array A in PROG1. And because you specify ALL in the CHAIN statement in PROG1, the entire array and the memory reserved for it by DIM is passed to PROG2.

Ah, but will this work? Let's see—you SAVEd PROG1, you SAVEd PROG2. The time has come to give it a try. LOAD the first program and start it running, then stand back and watch the results:

```
LOAD"PROG1
Ok

RUN
PROG1 now running

PROG2 now running
 1   1.414214   1.732051   2   2.236068   (etc.)
 9.949874   10
Ok
```

How about that! PROG1 calculated the squares, and PROG2 printed them. Let's see what program is loaded now:

Advanced GW-BASIC

```
LIST
100 REM-PROG2
110 PRINT "PROG2 now running"
120 FOR I=1 TO 100
130     PRINT A(I);
140 NEXT
```

PROG1 has disappeared (it's still safely tucked away on disk, of course), and was replaced by PROG2. The line numbers of the calling program and the new program don't matter for simple CHAIN statements—the new program shoves the old program rudely aside and takes over.

Using COMMON

When using CHAIN, if you don't want to pass any variables to the new program, just omit ALL. This means that a variable like A or NAME$, even though it appears in both programs, is independent—there's no connection between the value of a variable A in one program and its value in another. If you want to pass some variables, while leaving others independent, you can use the COMMON statement just before CHAIN. The general form of COMMON is as follows:

```
100 COMMON A, B$, C(), D$, ...
```

This means, "in the next CHAIN statement, pass only variables A, B$, array C, and D$ to the new program." Notice that you use parentheses for arrays.

Here's an example:

```
10 COMMON A, NAME$, TEMP()
20 CHAIN "PRNTPRGM", 1000
```

This section of code replaces the current program in memory with PRNTPRGM, passes variables A and NAME$ and the array TEMP to PRNTPRGM, and starts PRNTPRGM running beginning at line 1000. Except for the variables in the COMMON statement, any other variables in PRNTPRGM are "unique" to that program. Even if the calling program contains a variable called I, and PRNTPRGM also contains a variable called I, they are not related in any way.

The most obvious advantage of passing only a specified set of variables is to save memory. But you can also think about this: suppose that you have a program 1 that contains a variable, SWEETHEART$. Program 2 also contains a very important variable with the same name, SWEETHEART$, but with a different string assigned to it. Now if you're in program 1 and you CHAIN ALL, the string you've defined there for SWEETHEART$ will replace the SWEETHEART$ for program 2. Program 2's SWEETHEART$ is lost forever. Here is the moral:

437

Chapter 9

If you have a valuable variable in the called program, use COMMON to specify exactly what variables will be passed.

Nondestructive Merging with CHAIN MERGE

When you want to bring in part or all of a second program while leaving the current program intact, you can use the CHAIN MERGE statement. The general form is the following:

```
100 CHAIN MERGE "FILENAME"
200 CHAIN MERGE "FILENAME", NNN
300 CHAIN MERGE "FILENAME", NNN , ALL
400 CHAIN MERGE "FILENAME", NNN, DELETE NN-NN
```

When executed in the current program, line 100 means, "merge the program contained in the ASCII file FILENAME with the current program; if the same line numbers exist in both programs, replace those in the current program with lines from FILENAME; and begin execution with the lowest-numbered of the new lines." The other options for CHAIN MERGE, such as NNN, ALL, and DELETE, operate as they do for CHAIN.

Unlike CHAIN, the CHAIN MERGE statement doesn't destroy the current program—it brings in only selected lines, leaving the rest of the current program intact. Another difference is that CHAIN MERGE requires that the program to be merged must be an ASCII file, such as one that is saved using the A option:

```
100 SAVE "FILENAME", A
```

Let's consider the Worldwide Travel Companion program again. Here we want to keep some program lines while replacing others. For instance, the program might perform some initialization in lines 10-100, define phrases and currency conversion rates in lines 100-1000, and display the menu and print the output in lines 1000-5000. For any country, the initialization, the menu, and printing are all the same. The only portion that differs from country to country happens to be the phrasebook and currency conversions in lines 100-1000. Looks like a good candidate for CHAIN MERGE!

If we use CHAIN MERGE, BASIC lets you bring in only those lines 100-1000 from another program. The rest of the program can stay intact. When you're in France, you can CHAIN MERGE lines 100-1000 for that country, and when you go to Japan or Mexico, you simply CHAIN MERGE the lines for that country (see fig. 9-2). Each of these "modules" is a separate program that consists only of lines in the range 100-1000.

Advanced GW-BASIC

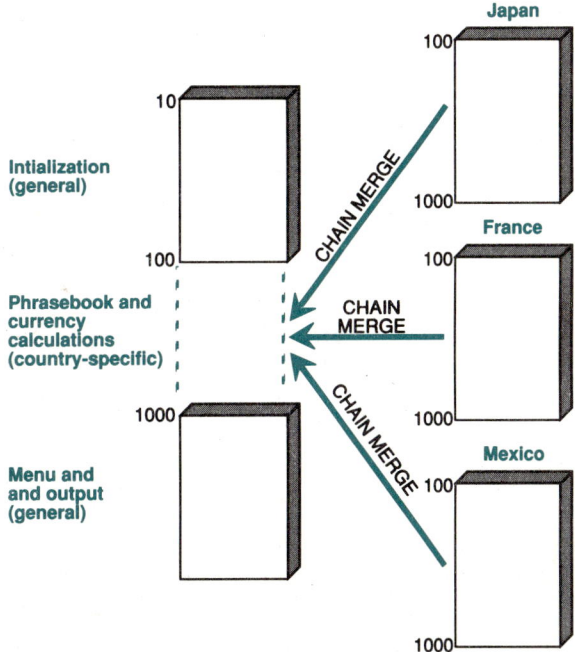

Fig. 9-2: CHAIN MERGE brings in selected program lines.

Let's see how we might handle this. We begin with initialization in lines 10-100, and some beginning variables in lines 100-1000:

```
10 REM-WORLDWIDE TRAVEL COMPANION
20 '
30 CLS
40 '
50 'Country information from file begins at line 100
60 '
100 REM-Program for USA
101 COUNTRY$="the USA"
102 GREETING$="Hello"
103 DOLCONVERT=1/1
104 CURRENCY$="dollar"
105 HOTELSRCH$="Is there a hotel near here?"
999 '
```

Chapter 9

Eventually we're going to be using CHAIN MERGE to replace those lines 100-999. But for now, we'll define *starting values* for all the variables we're going to use:

COUNTRY$ is the name of the country
GREETING$ is how you say "Hello" in that country
DOLCONVERT is the conversion rate from that country's currency into dollars
CURRENCY$ is the unit of currency (francs, pesos, yen, etc.)
HOTELSRCH$ is a phrase for locating a hotel

To begin with, we've defined these all for the USA, but they'll change whenever we change countries.

Next we print the menu. This remains the same no matter what country we're in:

```
1000 PRINT: PRINT "WORLDWIDE TRAVEL COMPANION"
1010 '
1020 WHILE N <> 5
1030     PRINT
1040     'Main menu
1050     PRINT: PRINT "Press 1 to check or change the country"
1060     PRINT "Press 2 for greetings"
1070     PRINT "Press 3 to find a hotel"
1080     PRINT "Press 4 for currency conversion"
1090     PRINT "Press 5 to exit and save your changes"
1100     INPUT "What is your choice"; N
1110     ON N GOSUB 2000, 3000, 4000, 5000
1120 WEND
1130 SAVE "WORLD"
1140 CLS
1150 END
1160 '
```

The heart of the menu section is a WHILE...WEND loop that waits for you to input a number N. If N is 1, execution branches to the subroutine beginning at line 2000; if it's 2, execution branches to line 3000, and so on. If you type a 5, execution falls out of the WHILE...WEND loop, and this file is saved as WORLD.

The most interesting subroutine is the one that changes the country-specific information. With the menu displayed, if you type 1, execution branches to line 2000.

Advanced GW-BASIC

```
2000 'Subroutine to check or change the country"
2010 CLS
2020 PRINT "Currently set for "COUNTRY$
2030 PRINT "Do you want to change to another country (Y/N)?"
2040 INPUT ANS$
2050 WHILE LEFT$(ANS$,1)= "Y" OR LEFT$(ANS$,1)= "y"
2060     PRINT "Type country to change to"
2070     LINE INPUT COUNTRY$
2080     'Country file is merged beginning at line 100
2090     CHAIN MERGE LEFT$(COUNTRY$,8), 100
2100     ANS$=""
2110 WEND
2120 RETURN
2130 '
```

The subroutine shows the current value of COUNTRY$. (So, the first time you run the program, line 2020 prints "Currently set for the USA.") Then you are asked whether you want to change to another country. Your answer is recorded as the variable ANS$, then the WHILE statement checks to see whether the leftmost character of your answer is a "Y" (or a "y"). When you answer "Y" or "yes" or anything beginning with an upper- or lowercase Y, execution goes into the WHILE...WEND loop and you're asked to type the name of a country to change to. The LINE INPUT statement takes the name you type here and assigns it to the variable COUNTRY$; for now, this is actually the filename of the country file.

Now comes the CHAIN MERGE statement. Line 2090 brings in a country file and starts executing it at line 100. Note that using LEFT$ (COUNTRY$, 8) in the CHAIN MERGE statement prevents you from trying to call a file whose name is longer than 8 characters.

The country files all contain lists of variables in lines 100-1000. For instance, here's the country file for JAPAN:

```
100 REM-Program for Japan
101 COUNTRY$="Japan"
102 GREETING$="Ohayo gozaimasu"
103 DOLCONVERT=1/150
104 CURRENCY$="Yen"
105 HOTELSRCH$="Kono chikaku ni hoteru ga arimasu ka?"
```

Chapter 9

The program file "JAPAN.BAS" sets the variables for this particular country. (Naturally, a large, full-fledged program might contain arrays with entire lists of phrases, verb conjugations, a dictionary, spelling checker, and more.) You don't need to pass any variables to this section of code because it will be run when it's brought in by CHAIN MERGE, setting all the variables (including COUNTRY$) for the desired country.

Once the country program has been merged, we want to exit from the WHILE...WEND loop, so in line 2100 we set ANS$ to a null string. Because ANS$ is no longer "Y" or "y," execution falls out of the loop and returns to the main menu.

The remainder of the program uses the variables from the merged program for printing phrases and performing currency conversions. Here's the subroutine for printing a greeting:

```
3000 'Subroutine for greeting
3010 CLS
3020 PRINT: PRINT "To say 'Hello' in "COUNTRY$
3030 PRINT "you say '"GREETING$"'"
3040 RETURN
3050 '
```

Line 3030 prints the current value of GREETING$; if you've just merged the program file JAPAN, the greeting is "Ohayo gozaimasu."

Here's the subroutine to find a hotel:

```
4000 'Subroutine to find a hotel
4010 CLS
4020 PRINT: PRINT "For a hotel in "COUNTRY$", ask this question:"
4030 PRINT "'"HOTELSRCH$"'"
4040 RETURN
4050 '
```

This subroutine uses the current value of COUNTRY$ (which for Japan is "Japan") and that of HOTELSRCH$ (which for Japan is "Kono chikaku ni hoteru ga arimasu ka?").

The currency conversion subroutine looks like this:

```
5000 'Subroutine for currency conversion
5010 CLS
5020 PRINT: PRINT "What's the price in "CURRENCY$ "(s)?"
5030 INPUT AMT
5040 DOLLARS=AMT*DOLCONVERT
```

Advanced GW-BASIC

```
5050 PRINT: PRINT AMT; CURRENCY$ "(s) equals";
5060 PRINT USING "$$######,.##"; DOLLARS
5070 RETURN
```

This subroutine asks for the price in the current value of the variable CURRENCY$ (that's "Yen" in Japan). You enter an AMT at the INPUT statement in line 5030, and the program uses the DOLCONVERT variable to convert the amount to dollars. Then the subroutine prints the amount, the type of currency, and the dollar equivalent.

If you want to run the program, begin by creating some country-specific program files, such as these for Japan, France, and Mexico. Be sure to save them as ASCII files, using a comma and an "A" after the filename:

```
NEW
Ok
100 REM-Program for Japan
101 COUNTRY$="Japan"
102 GREETING$="Ohayo gozaimasu"
103 DOLCONVERT=1/150
104 CURRENCY$="Yen"
105 HOTELSRCH$="Kono chikaku ni hoteru ga arimasu ka?"

SAVE "JAPAN", A
Ok

NEW
Ok
100 REM-Program for France
101 COUNTRY$="France"
102 GREETING$="Bonjour"
103 DOLCONVERT=.1778
104 CURRENCY$="Franc"
105 HOTELSRCH$="Y-a-t-il un hotel pres d'ici?"

SAVE "FRANCE",A
Ok

NEW
Ok
100 REM-Program for Mexico
101 COUNTRY$="Mexico"
102 GREETING$="Buenos dias"
```

Chapter 9

```
103 DOLCONVERT=.000351
104 CURRENCY$="Peso"
105 HOTELSRCH$="Hay alguno hotel cerca de aqui?"

SAVE "MEXICO",A
Ok
```

Then load the code for the main Worldwide Travel Companion:

```
10 REM-WORLDWIDE TRAVEL COMPANION
20 '
30 CLS
40 '
50 'Country information from file begins at line 100
60 '
100 REM-Program for USA
101 COUNTRY$="the USA"
102 GREETING$="Hello"
103 DOLCONVERT=1/1
104 CURRENCY$="dollar"
105 HOTELSRCH$="Is there a hotel near here?"
999 '
1000 PRINT: PRINT "WORLDWIDE TRAVEL COMPANION"
1010 '
1020 WHILE N <> 5
1030     PRINT
1040     'Main menu
1050     PRINT: PRINT "Press 1 to check or change the country"
1060     PRINT "Press 2 for greetings"
1070     PRINT "Press 3 to find a hotel"
1080     PRINT "Press 4 for currency conversion"
1090     PRINT "Press 5 to exit and save your changes"
1100     INPUT "What is your choice"; N
1110     ON N GOSUB 2000, 3000, 4000, 5000
1120 WEND
1130 SAVE "WORLD"
1140 CLS
1150 END
1160 '
2000 'Subroutine to check or change the country"
```

```
2010 CLS
2020 PRINT "Currently set for "COUNTRY$
2030 PRINT "Do you want to change to another country (Y/N)?"
2040 INPUT ANS$
2050 WHILE LEFT$(ANS$,1)= "Y" OR LEFT$(ANS$,1)= "y"
2060     PRINT "Type country to change to"
2070     LINE INPUT COUNTRY$
2080     'Country file is merged beginning at line 100
2090     CHAIN MERGE LEFT$(COUNTRY$,8), 100
2100     ANS$=""
2110 WEND
2120 RETURN
2130 '
3000 'Subroutine for greeting
3010 CLS
3020 PRINT: PRINT "To say 'Hello' in "COUNTRY$
3030 PRINT "you say '"GREETING$"'"
3040 RETURN
3050 '
4000 'Subroutine to find a hotel
4010 CLS
4020 PRINT: PRINT "For a hotel in "COUNTRY$", ask this question:"
4030 PRINT "'"HOTELSRCH$"'"
4040 RETURN
4050 '
5000 'Subroutine for currency conversion
5010 CLS
5020 PRINT: PRINT "What's the price in "CURRENCY$ "(s)?"
5030 INPUT AMT
5040 DOLLARS=AMT*DOLCONVERT
5050 PRINT: PRINT AMT; CURRENCY$ "(s) equals";
5060 PRINT USING "$$######,.##"; DOLLARS
5070 RETURN

SAVE "WORLD"
Ok
```

Now it's time to travel. Tuck the Worldwide Travel Companion under your arm and jet off to ... let's start in Mexico. First, notice that the Companion "wakes up" in the USA:

Chapter 9

```
RUN

WORLDWIDE TRAVEL COMPANION


Press 1 to check or change the country
Press 2 for greetings
Press 3 to find a hotel
Press 4 for currency conversion
Press 5 to exit and save your changes
What is your choice? 1

Currently set for the USA
Do you want to change to another country (Y/N)?
```

To change to Mexico, answer "Y" and enter the name of that country:

```
? Y
Type country to change to
MEXICO

WORLDWIDE TRAVEL COMPANION


Press 1 to change countries
Press 2 for greetings
Press 3 to find a hotel
Press 4 for currency conversion
Press 5 to exit and save your changes
What is your choice?
```

Let's see how to say "hello" in Mexico:

```
What is your choice? 2

To say 'Hello' in Mexico
you say 'Buenos dias'
```

It would be nice to stay around a little longer, but our jet-setting tour is off to France. Here's how you'd find a hotel there:

```
What is your choice? 1
Currently set for Mexico
```

446

```
Do you want to change to another country (Y/N)?
? Y
Type country to change to
FRANCE

WORLDWIDE TRAVEL COMPANION


Press 1 to change countries
Press 2 for greetings
Press 3 to find a hotel
Press 4 for currency conversion
Press 5 to exit and save your changes
What is your choice? 3

For a hotel in France, ask this question:
'Y-a-t-il un hotel pres d'ici?'
```

France was wonderful, but there's no time to waste with this tour. We now find ourselves in a Tokyo coffee shop, inquiring about the price of a cup of Mocha Java. It's only 600 yen; but how much is that? The Companion can tell us:

```
What is your choice? 1
Currently set for France
Do you want to change to another country (Y/N)?
? Y
Type country to change to
JAPAN

WORLDWIDE TRAVEL COMPANION


Press 1 to change countries
Press 2 for greetings
Press 3 to find a hotel
Press 4 for currency conversion
Press 5 to exit and save your changes
What is your choice? 4

What's the price in Yen(s)?
? 600

   600 Yen(s) equals          $4.00
```

Chapter 9

At those prices, perhaps we'd better shut down the Travel Companion and head for home:

```
Press 5 to exit and save your changes
What is your choice? 5
Ok
```

The next time you fire up the Travel Companion, it will be initialized with the variables in lines 100-1000—and these are now set for Japan, as you can see if you LIST the program. So as long as you're in Japan, you don't have to change the country information. Only when you go to another country do you need to call upon CHAIN MERGE to bring in a new set of variables.

Hexadecimal and Octal Conversions

As it happens, numeric conversions are an all-too-frequent fact of life in programming circles. Certain quantities, such as memory addresses, are usually given in hexadecimal notation because base 16 is a multiple of the base 2 (binary) system that is the natural numbering system for computers. If you have trouble with any of the numbering systems, refer to Appendix B for a detailed and helpful discussion, and to Appendix C for a chart that shows ASCII characters and their equivalent values as binary, octal, decimal, and hexadecimal quantities.

Four functions are used for conversions between decimal quantities (the kind you're used to seeing) and hexadecimal or octal quantities. The general forms are as follows:

```
10 HEX$(N)
20 OCT$(N)
30 &HNNNN
40 &ONNNN
```

HEX$(N) means, "Convert the decimal number N to HEXadecimal notation."

OCT$(N) means, "Convert the decimal N to OCTal notation."

&HNNNN means, "Convert the hexadecimal number NNNN to decimal notation."

&ONNNN means, "Convert the octal number NNNN to decimal notation."

In the preceding definitions, N represents either a decimal number or a variable which has the value of that number. NNNN represents a hexadecimal or octal number.

These four functions are used to convert numbers back and forth between hexadecimal (or octal) notation and decimal notation. They are very useful functions, especially if you will be using any assembly-language routines with your

Advanced GW-BASIC

BASIC program. (For a discussion of hex ("hex" is a shortened form of "hexadecimal") and octal numbers, read Appendix B, *Numbering Systems*.)

HEX$ (or OCT$) takes the value of a numeric variable or constant and turns it into a string variable which is the hex (or octal) equivalent of that value. For example, if you execute the statement PRINT HEX$(255), your computer will print FF, which is the hex equivalent of the decimal number 255.

Here's a program that will print the first 16 decimal numbers and their hex equivalents:

```
10 FOR D = 0 TO 15
20 H$ = HEX$(D)
30 PRINT D; H$
40 NEXT D


RUN
 0  0
 1  1
 2  2
 3  3
 4  4
 5  5
 6  6
 7  7
 8  8
 9  9
 10 A
 11 B
 12 C
 13 D
 14 E
 15 F
```

HEX$ and OCT$ are useful if you want to see what the hex or octal representation of a number is. However, you can't use the converted form of the number in numerical calculations, because it is a string variable. In other words, an expression like `PRINT HEX$(127) + 2` is not legal.

&H and &O convert the hex or octal representations of numbers into decimal form. (This is the opposite of HEX$ and OCT$.) A limitation of &H and &O is that they work only with constants, not variables. In other words, you can write &H7FF0, in which 7FF0 is a hexadecimal number, but you can't write &HX, in which X is a variable whose value is a hexadecimal number. This restricts the use of &H and &O to situations in which you know what values you will want to convert. You can't, for example, use &H and &O to convert values you type into a program with an INPUT statement.

449

Chapter 9

This is no problem, though, because you can write a short program that will take hexadecimal values and display them in decimal. Try this:

```
10 INPUT "HEX ";H$
20 D$ = "&H" + H$
30 PRINT "HEX "D$ " IS";VAL(D$);"IN DECIMAL"
```

When you RUN this program, you can type values in hex and see their decimal equivalents:

```
RUN
HEX ? BC
HEX &HBC IS 188 IN DECIMAL
RUN
HEX ? AD
HEX &HAD IS 173 IN DECIMAL
```

&H is often used for converting addresses, because computer addresses are frequently expressed in hex form.

Manipulating Memory Directly

Using most of BASIC's statements, you don't have to worry much about memory. After all, BASIC takes care of storing and fetching the values of your variables, and you usually don't care precisely where in memory those variables reside.

Both BASIC and the DOS operating system, however, do have specific memory locations where important information is placed, and on occasion you may want to make a decision based on what's there. Or you might actually want to manipulate a memory location or two. GW-BASIC contains statements that let you examine and directly manipulate computer memory.

A complete discussion of computer memory could (and does) occupy entire volumes. We'll give you a few highlights here.

A Little About Memory

GW-BASIC runs under MS-DOS, so its memory addressing depends on this operating system. In MS-DOS, computer memory is made up of a large number of individual addresses, with each address storing 1 byte of data. Memory addresses begin with address 0 and continue up from there; they're usually specified as hexadecimal numbers, as shown in figure 9-3.

Advanced GW-BASIC

Some portions of computer memory in MS-DOS are allocated when you first *boot up*; for instance, the area beginning with hexadecimal address B8000 and continuing to BC000 is dedicated to the text screen for the CGA and EGA displays. Other areas are reserved for other functions. There's also an area for user programs and DOS. When you load GW-BASIC, it's loaded into this user-program area.

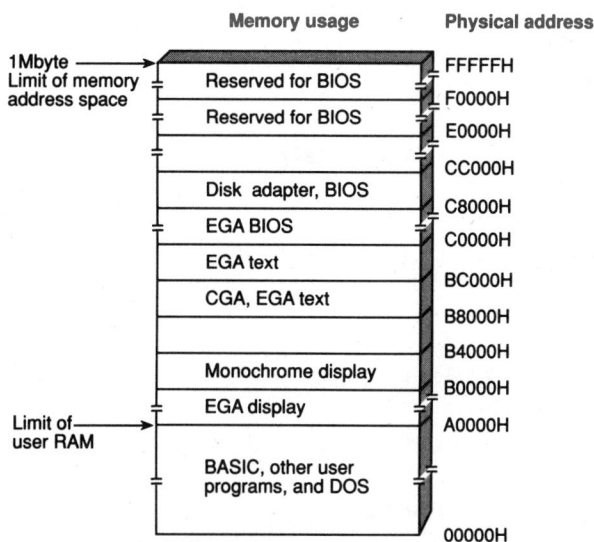

Fig. 9-3: Memory usage in MS-DOS.

Accessing Memory Through Segments

Due to the design of the computer's internal microprocessor, you can't simply say, "access memory location 16000." Instead, you have to specify an address as consisting of a 64-Kbyte "segment" plus the address offset from the segment. In fact, you'll sometimes see addresses written in the notation *segment: offset*, with four digits for each.

Within the area of memory used by BASIC are its code segment (CS), data segment (DS), stack segment (SS), and extra segment (ES). There's an instruction pointer (IP) within the central processing unit that keeps track of the next instruction to be processed in the code segment. There's also a stack pointer (SP) to keep track of what's happening in the stack segment. If you don't specify a segment, any addresses you specify for BASIC's memory-manipulating functions will be within BASIC's data segment.

Chapter 9

Outside the area of memory used by BASIC, in other areas of memory, are other segments. For instance, the color graphics screen begins at the segment address B800. You access these segments directly in BASIC by using the DEF SEG statement.

DEF SEG

DEF SEG lets you assign a current segment address, which can then be used by other statements. The general form is as follows:

```
100 DEF SEG = &HNNN
```

This means, "specify the segment address hexadecimal NNN for the next BLOAD, BSAVE, CALL, PEEK, POKE, or USR statement." If you don't specify &HNNN, the default is the beginning of the data segment (DS).

Segment addresses are shifted 4 bits (that is, 1 hexadecimal digit) to the left from the actual address. So, to specify the beginning of memory for the EGA-CGA text screen (which begins at address &HB8000), you'd use this DEF SEG statement:

```
100 DEF SEG = &HB800
```

DEF SEG is used to set up the "starting point" for the statements BLOAD, BSAVE, CALL, PEEK, POKE, and USR. If you don't specify a DEF SEG, the GW-BASIC language assumes that you mean the data segment used by GW-BASIC itself.

Saving and Loading Chunks of Memory

There are times when you'll want to save entire sections of memory to a disk. Other times, it's convenient to be able to bring back what was in that memory, or to load a program to a specific location. When you want to work with large sections of memory at a time, you can call on BSAVE and BLOAD.

Storing Memory with BSAVE

The BSAVE statement is for saving portions of memory on disk. The general form is as follows:

```
100 BSAVE "FILENAME", OFFSET, LENGTH
```

This means, "save the contents of memory beginning OFFSET addresses after the latest DEF SEG, and continuing through LENGTH bytes; save memory in the file FILENAME." Both OFFSET and LENGTH can be anywhere from 0 to 65535.

Advanced GW-BASIC

With BSAVE, you can save machine language programs, and you can also save the graphics screen, allowing you to store your pictures on disk for future use. Before a BSAVE, make sure that you specify a DEF SEG; the OFFSET begins counting from the current DEF SEG.

Bringing Memory Back with BLOAD

BLOAD is what you use to bring back from disk the sections of memory you've saved with BSAVE. The general form is as follows:

```
100 BLOAD "FILENAME"
200 BLOAD "FILENAME", NNN
```

Line 100 means, "load the image file FILENAME back into the same locations in memory from which it was BSAVEd."

Line 200 lets you specify an offset; it means, "load the image file FILENAME into memory beginning NNN bytes offset from the segment address specified in the last DEF SEG statement." You should be careful using this form, though, because with it you can load that image file anywhere in memory—even right on top of a part of memory that's supposed to be used for other tasks. In short, you can really mess things up!

Here's an example of how you might use BLOAD:

```
100 DEF SEG = &HB800
110 BLOAD "MY-ART", 0
```

The DEF SEG statement specifies the segment beginning with address hexadecimal B8000. (The segment address is shifted 4 bits to the left from the actual address; that's why you specify it as B800 instead of B8000.) Then, because the offset NNN is 0, the BLOAD statement loads the image file MY-ART into this segment beginning with the first address of the segment.

You can use BLOAD and BSAVE for loading and saving machine language programs, and for saving and reproducing the graphics screen.

Graphics Memory

The IBM PC uses what is called a "memory-mapped" display format: What is on the screen at any time is contained in a specific area of memory. The memory contains 1's and 0's, and each memory location controls one pixel on the screen. This particular area of memory is being scanned constantly by the computer, so that any change made to one of these memory locations is instantly seen on the screen.

Chapter 9

When we manipulate graphics, such as drawing a line, PSETting a point, or changing the color of the background, we are actually changing what's in certain memory locations. You can address these memory locations directly, specifying them with decimal values or with hexadecimal values (using the &H convention).

Saving the Graphics Screen

Here's the problem: You've turned into a real PC Picasso, a veritable Gauguin of GW-BASIC, wielding the colors and graphics statements to produce masterworks that have the art world at your feet. But your fame, unfortunately, is fleeting, because each time you turn off the computer or do something so simple as LISTing a program, your latest illustration is overwritten. However the dynamic duo of BSAVE and BLOAD are ready to ride to your aid, letting you save each picture in its own file, and bringing your masterpieces back on the screen one by one.

One way to draw a perspective view of a cylinder is to draw a circle, change the point of origin and radius and draw another circle, and so on. To see how, try this short program on your computer:

```
10 SCREEN 1: CLS
20 FOR I=1 TO 100 STEP 10
30     CIRCLE (160, I), I
40 NEXT I
```

This little program begins with the center of the circle at the top center of SCREEN 1 (that is, at 160,0). The first time through the FOR...NEXT loop, a tiny circle with a radius of 1 pixel is drawn. Then the center of the circle is moved down 10 pixels, and a circle with a radius of 11 pixels is drawn. The next time through the loop, the center of the circle is another 10 pixels closer to the bottom of the screen, and another circle is drawn; this time the radius is 21 pixels. By the time the FOR...NEXT loop hits the end of its I's, the circles have created a drawing that looks like a perspective view of a cylinder (see fig. 9-4).

By varying the amount of change of the point of origin, you can change the perspective of the cylinder; and by changing the colors each time through the loop, you can get some truly brilliant effects. The following program not only lets you exercise your creativity, but, thanks to BLOAD and BSAVE, it also archives your creation on disk and brings it back if you want.

The main part of the program is simple enough: a series of subroutine calls to draw the cylinder, save it to disk, then bring the cylinder back to the screen.

```
10 REM-SAVING CYLINDERS
20 SCREEN 1: CLS: KEY OFF
30 GOSUB 90  'Draw the cylinders
40 GOSUB 210 'Save the cylinder
50 GOSUB 260 'Get the cylinder back
60 END
```

454

Advanced GW-BASIC

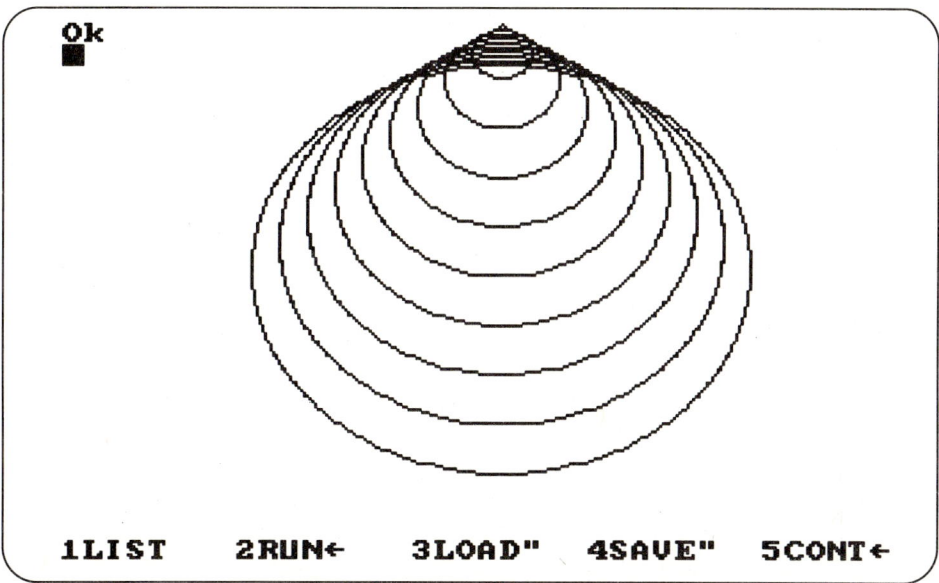

Fig. 9-4: A cylinder is drawn by changing the radius and origin of circles.

Line 20 sets BASIC for graphics screen 1 and clears the screen. Then the subroutine calls occur to draw the cylinder, save it to disk, and return it to the screen.

In the subroutine to draw the cylinder, you are asked in line 100 to input the CHANGE—that is, the distance between the centers of circles. It could be .5 unit, it could be 1.1, it could be 10; this is where your creativity comes in. You also get a choice of locations along the Y-axis to BEGIN. To begin somewhere on the screen, the location will need to be in the range of 0-199.

```
80 'Subroutine to draw the cylinder
90 COLOR 0, PAL
100 INPUT "Input the change"; CHANGE
110 INPUT "Where do I begin, 0-199"; BEGIN
120 CLS
130 FOR R=1 TO 100
140     CIRCLE (160, BEGIN+R*CHANGE),R, COL
150     COL=COL+1
160     IF COL>5 THEN PAL=PAL+1: COL=0
170     IF PAL=1 THEN PAL=0
180 NEXT
190 RETURN
```

Chapter 9

Once you've input the amount of CHANGE and where to BEGIN, the program executes a FOR...NEXT loop over and over again. Each time through the loop, a circle is drawn with a different radius and in a different color. When the color attribute, COL, becomes greater than 5, the program switches palettes (PAL specifies the palette), and begins coloring with attribute 0 in the new palette. The result is a series of colorful circles or a cylinder, depending on the value for CHANGE.

Once you've completed the drawing, the program returns and calls the second subroutine:

```
210 'Subroutine to save the cylinder
220 DEF SEG=&HB800
230 BSAVE "CYLINDER",0,16384
240 RETURN
```

It's pretty simple, really. The DEF SEG statement in line 220 specifies the beginning of the segment as hexadecimal address B800, which is the very beginning of where the graphics screen is mapped in memory. Then the BSAVE statement in the next line saves the contents of every memory location between 0 (that is location B800 itself) and 16384 (the end of the memory containing the graphics screen). The screen is saved in a file called CYLINDER, and you can call this file up with BLOAD or copy it to another file if you like.

Before exiting, the program lets you verify what's in the file. You are asked whether you want to see the cylinder again, and your answer is placed in the variable A$ by the INPUT statement. If you answer "Yes" (or, for that matter, if you answer "yes" or "Y" or "y" or even "yahoo") the leftmost 1 character of A$ is "Y" or "y" and the program clears the screen, then uses BLOAD to bring back the cylinder to the screen.

```
260 'Subroutine to bring back the cylinder
270 INPUT "Do you want to see it again (Y/N)"; A$
280 IF LEFT$(A$,1)="Y" OR LEFT$(A$,1)="y", THEN CLS:
    BLOAD "CYLINDER"
290 RETURN
```

Because no address is specified for BLOAD, the cylinder goes back to the same memory locations from whence it came—that is, to that area of memory containing the graphics screen.

Here's one run of the program, with its output shown in figure 9-5:

```
RUN
Input the change? 1.5
Where do I begin, 0-199? 0
```

Advanced GW-BASIC

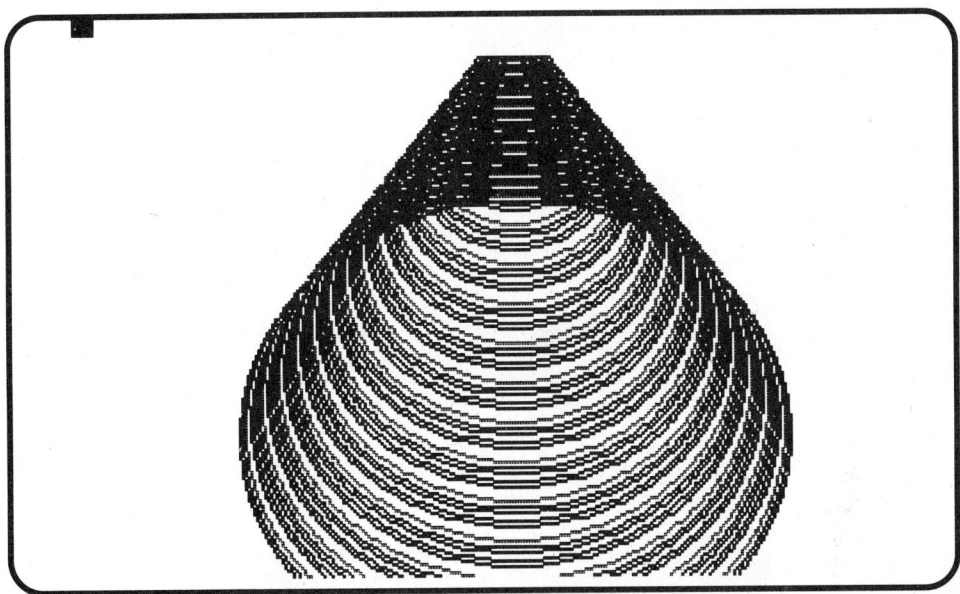

Fig. 9-5: One run of the cylinder-creating program.

Once you've drawn the cylinder, you get a chance to verify what's in the CYLINDER file:

```
Do you want to see it again (Y/N)? Y
```

The complete program is shown below.

```
10 REM-SAVING CYLINDERS
20 SCREEN 1: CLS: KEY OFF
30 GOSUB 90 'Draw the cylinders
40 GOSUB 210 'Save the cylinder
50 GOSUB 260 'Get the cylinder back
60 END
70 '
80 'Subroutine to draw the cylinder
90 COLOR 0, PAL
100 INPUT "Input the change"; CHANGE
110 INPUT "Where do I begin, 0-199"; BEGIN
120 CLS
130 FOR R=1 TO 100
140     CIRCLE (160, BEGIN+R*CHANGE),R, COL
150     COL=COL+1
160     IF COL>5 THEN PAL=PAL+1: COL=0
```

457

Chapter 9

```
170      IF PAL=1 THEN PAL=0
180 NEXT
190 RETURN
200 '
210 'Subroutine to save the cylinder
220 DEF SEG=&HB800
230 BSAVE "CYLINDER",0,16384
240 RETURN
250 '
260 'Subroutine to bring back the cylinder
270 INPUT "Do you want to see it again (Y/N)"; A$
280 IF LEFT$(A$,1)="Y" OR LEFT$(A$,1)="y", THEN CLS:
    BLOAD "CYLINDER"
290 RETURN
```

Using PEEK and POKE

PEEK and POKE allow direct control over individual memory locations from BASIC. Recall that a memory location is made up of 8 bits, which we commonly referred to as a *byte*. An 8-bit byte can represent a number between 0 and 255. Thus, a single memory byte can hold a number between 0 and 255. Also recall that BASIC's memory can have up to approximately 64,000 of these memory locations. In an MS-DOS computer, there can be 1,000,000 bytes or more.

The memory is visualized as a huge ladder of memory cells or locations. We can see that each location has a fixed address and can be made to contain any number between 0 and 255. POKE puts data into a memory location, while PEEK "reads" it. We can visualize the operation of PEEK and POKE as shown in figure 9-6:

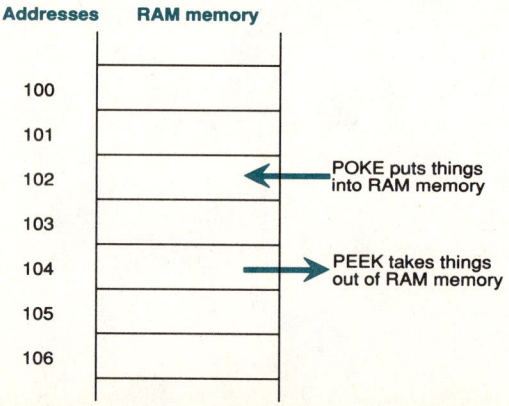

Fig. 9-6: Comparing PEEK and POKE.

458

Advanced GW-BASIC

The POKE Statement

In BASIC, we can place a number (0-255) in any of these memory locations with POKE. POKE works like this:

```
100 POKE A, D
```

This means, "put the data, D, into the memory location specified by the last DEF SEG statement + A." We say that A is the *offset*.

Here, A is a positive integer expression, variable, or constant. It varies from 0 up to 65535. D is a number or expression between 0 and 255 that you want to go into location A.

For example,

```
POKE 800,127
```

causes the memory location offset 800 bytes from the last DEF SEG specification to be filled with the value 127. The previous contents of this location are lost. And consider this:

```
100 FOR I = 800 TO 1000: POKE I,15: NEXT I
```

This example causes memory offsets 800 to 1000 to be filled with the number 15. We can say that POKE writes data into memory.

The PEEK Function

The keyword PEEK does the complementary function of POKE. PEEK is used to read data from memory. PEEK is a function and therefore is used like this:

```
100 X = PEEK(A)
```

This means, "look at the memory location specified by the last DEF SEG statement + A; put the value of that memory location in variable X."

Here the variable X is set to the value found in memory offset A by PEEKing at A. Being a function, PEEK returns a value to a variable. The argument of PEEK is the memory address A, which can be an expression, variable, or an integer constant. It must not exceed the memory range of your computer.

For example,

Chapter 9

```
X = PEEK(4096)
```

causes X to be set to the number found in the memory location specified by the last DEF SEG statement + 4096. And:

```
 90 DEF SEG=1000
100 FOR I = 0 TO 1023
110    PRINT PEEK (I)
120 NEXT I
```

causes the contents of memory locations 1000 to 2023 to be printed on the screen. (We sometimes refer to this as a memory dump.) Note that PEEK(I) may appear alone in the PRINT statement, because it is an expression that returns a value.

Using Conversions with PEEK and POKE

If you want to PEEK into the hex memory address 7AB0, you don't need to convert offset 7AB0 to its decimal equivalent (which is 31488). You can simply write:

```
PRINT PEEK (&H7AB0)
```

&H is also useful if you want to POKE a machine-language routine into memory. If you use &H, you don't need to convert the hex values (the ones that the routine was originally written in) into decimal values. For example, suppose that you want to POKE a five-byte routine into memory starting at location AA. The five bytes you want to POKE are 7A, 2B, 3C, 00, and FF. This program will do it:

```
 5  DEF SEG = &HB800
10  FOR J = 0 TO 4
20     READ B
30     POKE B, &H7AB0 + J
40  NEXT J
50  DATA &H7A,&H2B,&H3C,&H00,&HFF
```

In this program, we READ the first value, 7A (hex), from the list of DATA items, then POKE it into address AA (hex). The next time through the loop, we read the next item, 2B, and POKE it into address AA plus 1, which is AB. The process continues until all five values have been POKEed in.

Machine language is what actually operates the microprocessor (the "heart" of your computer). Machine language has its own instructions, rules of usage, and formatting conventions. It uses special codes and instructions that look like this:

```
LDA F000
```

Advanced GW-BASIC

To the computer this means, "load the accumulator register inside the microprocessor with data that is located at memory address F000 (F000 is a hexadecimal address which equals 61440 in decimal)." There are other machine language instructions for the microprocessor, and these allow data to be moved back and forth between registers inside the microprocessor, data to be placed in memory or read from memory into the microprocessor, simple binary arithmetic to be performed, and so on. In essence, the machine language program controls the elementary logic of the microprocessor operations.

Machine language programs allow us to do things that would be very difficult, if not impossible, to do with BASIC alone. A machine language program can be placed in an area of memory that is not occupied by BASIC. It has a starting address somewhere in the free memory space not used by BASIC, and it is treated like a special form of subroutine.

Why use machine language when we have BASIC at hand? For one thing, machine language routines run much faster than BASIC, making them the choice for faster graphics and calculations. Animation is another area in which machine language can be superior.

Using CALL

The machine language subroutine has its own return statement, usually designated by the instruction RET. What CALL does is provide a way for us to branch out of BASIC and execute a specific machine language subroutine. The machine language program performs instructions until it finds the RET instruction, which is usually at the end of the program. RET tells the computer to transfer control back to BASIC and exit from the machine language program. BASIC begins executing again as if nothing happened. The format of the CALL statement is something like the GOSUB statement:

```
100 CALL M, (A, B$, C---)
```

This means, "call the machine language subroutine that begins at address M, and pass to it variables A, B$, C, etc."on

The M represents the memory address that is offset from the most recent DEF SEG statement; it specifies the beginning of the user's machine language program. It might also be the address of a machine language program provided in the system's firmware or monitor. This means you can take advantage of the many machine language utility subroutines that are available in the operating system of the computer. As an example of how to visualize the CALL statement, imagine that you want to use a machine language subroutine that begins at an offset memory location of 10; and then later in your BASIC program you want to use one that begins at a location offset by 20. The sequence might look like that shown in figure 9-7.

461

Chapter 9

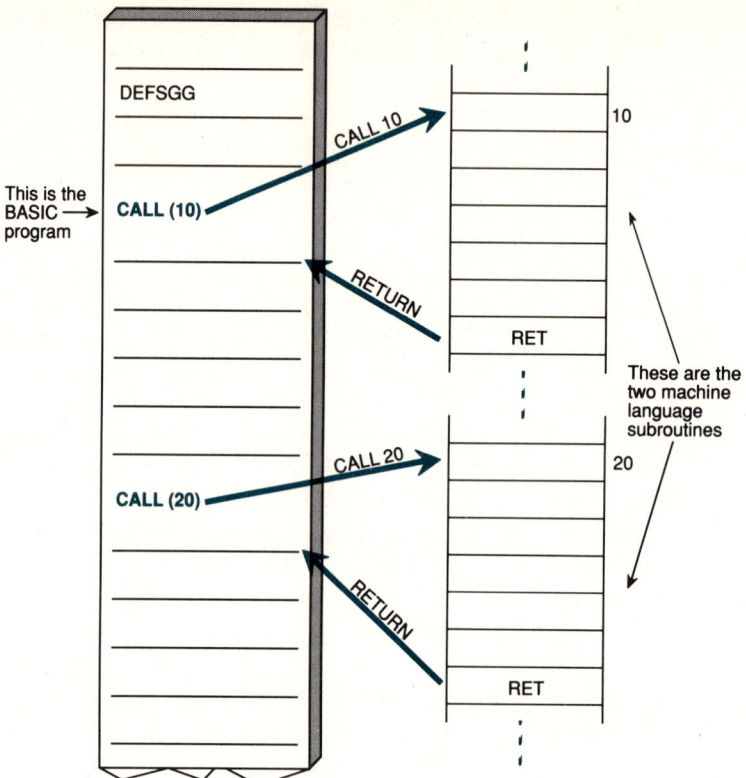

Fig. 9-7: CALLing machine language subroutines.

What we have here are two machine language subroutines located in memory, one starting at a location offset by 10 from the latest DEF SEG statement, and the other starting at a location offset by 20. The BASIC program executes one statement at a time until the first CALL is found. Then the CALL 10 statement sends the computer off to execute the machine language program that starts at location 10 in RAM (or ROM in some cases). None of the variables or arrays are changed in the BASIC program, and their values are automatically saved by BASIC when it leaves the main program. The machine language program then performs its specific function. When the RET is encountered, control is sent back to the next statement after the CALL in BASIC. The second CALL 20 works in the same manner.

What can we do with the CALL statement and the subroutines it can access? There are literally hundreds of uses for machine language programs; we will outline just a few of the more popular uses here.

Advanced GW-BASIC

Because of its microprocessor-controlling capabilities, machine language programs can do things extremely fast, and they can even test for the presence of a particular processor.

You can also use CALL and never write a bit of machine language, if you use CALL to access a machine language program that is provided already in ROM or in the operating system. Utility routines that might be available include programs that home the cursor and clear the screen, clear the cursor from end of page or end of line, produce a line feed, scroll up or down one line of text, and so on. What actually happens when the call is made is that the address in the CALL specifies a utility machine language subroutine that performs the desired function, without you doing anything. Exit is the same as in the normal CALL statement. For example, if a machine language routine to home the cursor and clear the screen is at address 936 of the &H2000 segment, you could do the following:

```
100 DEG SEG = &H2000
110 CALL 936
```

(Note that this is a purely hypothetical example.)

PEEKing and POKEing into Screen Memory

By now you are probably wondering what is so special about direct memory access with PEEK and POKE. There are many uses, including the following:

- Controlling external devices
- Controlling screen information (graphics)
- Setting option switches in the BASIC operating system

One particularly useful application of PEEK and POKE involves manipulating characters and graphics on the screen without using PRINT or graphics statements. This technique is made possible by the special chunk of RAM memory called the screen memory. The computer automatically scans these memory locations, converts the contents to a specific ASCII character, and then displays the characters on the screen in a unique position.

Remember that graphics SCREEN 1 contained 16,384 bytes of information—that's how much memory we needed for it in its file when we saved it with BSAVE. We say that SCREEN 1 has a page size of 16 Kbytes.

The text screen (SCREEN 0) is a little different. In its 80-column text mode, it has a page size of about 4,000 bytes. In this mode, the screen is 80 columns wide by 25 rows high, as shown in figure 9-8. Two bytes are allocated in memory for each position on the screen; the first byte contains the character, and the second byte contains the color attribute for that character.

Chapter 9

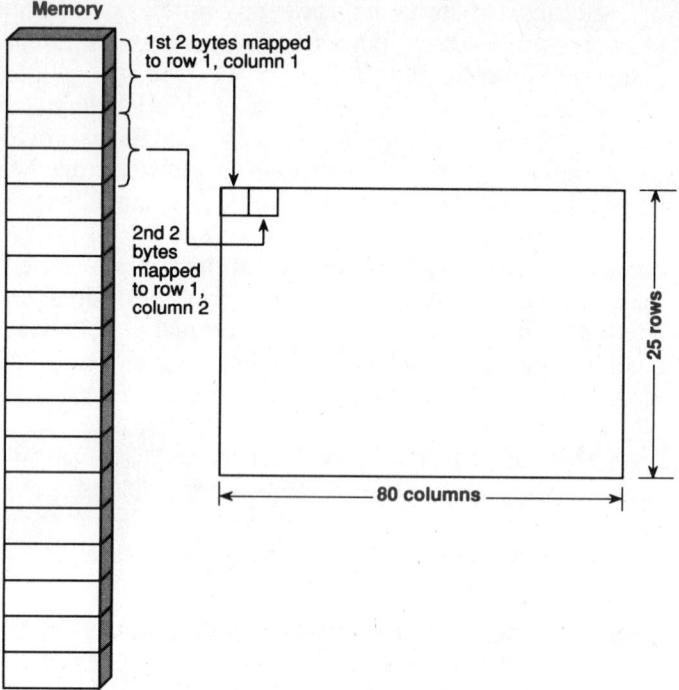

Fig. 9-8: Text screen memory mapping for 80 x 25 SCREEN 0.

Here's how to use POKE to put an "A" in the center of the text screen:

```
10 CLS: SCREEN 0: WIDTH 80
20 DEF SEG = &HB800
30 POKE 2000, 65
40 POKE 2001, 20
50 END
```

Line 10 clears the screen and sets it for the text screen with a width of 80 characters. The DEF SEG statement in line 20 sets the segment for the beginning of the graphics memory. Then the POKE statement in line 30 places an "A" (ASCII 65) in location 2000—which happens to be the center of the 80-column text screen. The POKE statement in line 40 changes the attribute of the "A" so that it appears as reverse video.

You can PEEK at these values, too. Just use the following little program (and don't clear the screen!).

Advanced GW-BASIC

```
10 X=PEEK (2000)
20 Y=PEEK (2001)
30 PRINT X, Y

RUN
 65    20
Ok
```

Using Mixed-Language Routines

One of the advantages of BASIC is that you can mix it with computer languages other than BASIC. For instance, you can load and call DOS commands or routines that are written in assembly language (also called machine language).

Another Way to Call Assembly Language Programs

Besides CALL, you can also use the USR statement to call assembly language subroutines. Before you can use USR, you must first use DEF USR (similar to the way you use DEF SEG) to tell BASIC where to find them.

Preparations with DEF USR

The DEF USR statement sets up assembly language subroutine calls; it actually tells BASIC where to find those subroutines. The general form is as follows:

```
100 DEF USR = S
200 DEF USR N = S
```

Line 100 means, "define the starting address of the assembly language subroutine; define it as an offset of S bytes from the absolute address specified by DEF SEG." The starting address S has to be an integer.

If you have more than one assembly language subroutine, you can specify the address for each one using DEF USR with a number N, as shown in line 200. Line 200 means, "define the starting address of assembly language subroutine N." This number N can be an integer from 0-9. It corresponds to the number "N" in the USR function (more about USR in a moment), and means that you can have up to 10 individual USR statements in a single BASIC program.

Chapter 9

Using USR

The USR function is one way of calling assembly language subroutines. It calls these subroutines just as ordinary BASIC functions are called. The general form is as follows:

```
Y = USR N (X)
```

This means, "call assembly language subroutine N, using the X specified in parentheses, and put the result in Y." If you don't specify N, BASIC assumes that you mean 0. If the subroutine doesn't need an X, you still need the parentheses, with a dummy argument (such as 0) inside.

If you remember how you used DEF FN and FN, you'll see that using DEF USR and USR is very similar.

The "X" in USR is called the *argument*. It can be an expression, or a numeric or string variable. Its value gets "sent," or passed, to the machine language program that you call. The value "returned" by the USR function ends up in the variable to the left of the equal sign, in this case the Y. Usually it is the same "type" (string or numeric) as the argument passed by USR.

USR uses function call syntax, so it can return a value directly to an expression in your BASIC program. For example,

```
TIME 2 = USR1 (TIME)
```

USR can receive only one variable from the calling program, however, whereas CALL can receive multiple variables.

Combining DEF USR and USR

An example of a call to an assembly language subroutine is shown here:

```
100 DEF USR3 = 24000
        .
        .
        .
500 M = USR3(Z + 2)
```

Here statement 100 says that machine language routine number 3 starts at address 24000 decimal. Then line 500 "calls" this routine, sending the value of Z + 2 to the routine. (The routine would, of course, have been set up previously by the program, by either being POKEd in with DATA statements or BLOADed off the disk into memory.) The routine then executes and does something with the value of Z + 2. The resultant value is sent back to the BASIC program and put in variable M in line 500.

Advanced GW-BASIC

The proper use of USR requires a firm understanding of machine language programming, so you should use it with caution. You can, of course, use the USR function without passing variables. In this case the variable to the left of the equal sign would be a *dummy*, as would the variable in the argument. Dummy means it's not used by the program but still must appear in the statement for it to work correctly.

Locating Variables with VARPTR

If you intend to pass a variable, array, or file information to an assembly language subroutine, you can't do it by simply specifying the name, because assembly language routines recognize only addresses. You can use the VARPTR function to produce the address of the variable you need. The general form is as follows:

```
100 X = VARPTR (N)
```

Line 100 means, "find the physical address in the computer of the first byte of variable N, and put that address in X." Here's a simple example:

```
10 A = 125
20 X = VARPTR(A)
30 PRINT X

RUN
 4765
```

This tiny little program shows you where the address of the variable A is located in your computer's memory. It's located at address 4765 (in decimal). Naturally, this address might be different on your own computer.

Incidentally, make sure that you assign all simple variables like A, B$, C, etc., before you use VARPTR to find an array. Array addresses change whenever you assign a new simple variable.

How BASIC Variables Are Stored

At this point, we need to explain a little about how BASIC stores variables in your computer's memory.

As you know, the computer's memory is divided into units called *bytes*. Each byte is 8 bits long, so a byte can have any of 256 possible values, from 0 to 255. (This is explained in more detail in Appendix B, *Numbering Systems*.) Each byte has a separate *address* so that BASIC can tell one byte of memory from another. The value of each BASIC variable is stored in memory, and depending on which type the variable is (integer, single- or double-precision, or string), it takes up a different

Chapter 9

number of bytes. You can see some of these types of variables, and how they're stored, in figure 9-9.

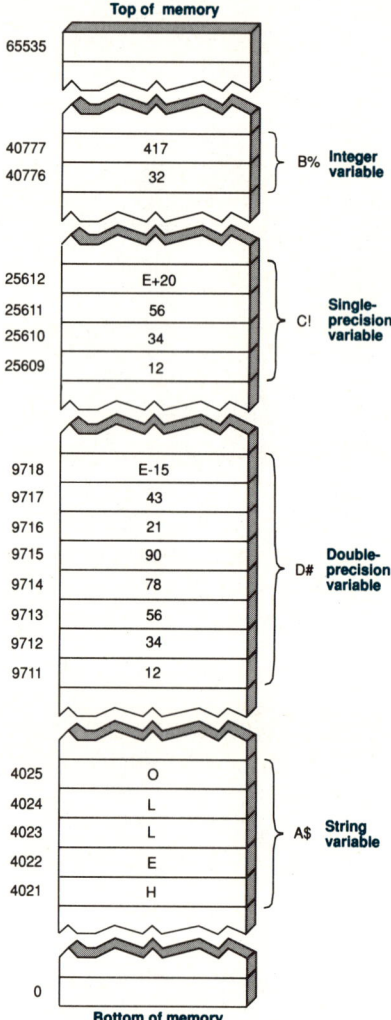

Fig. 9-9: Variables in memory.

When writing ordinary BASIC programs, you don't usually need to know where your variables are stored in memory or how many bytes each one requires. BASIC takes care of these "housekeeping" chores without any help from the programmer. However, if you are writing an assembly-language or machine-

Advanced GW-BASIC

language program to work with your BASIC program, then you usually need to know more about variable storage.

Suppose, for example, that you want an assembly-language program to take a particular string variable, already generated in your BASIC program, check it for lowercase letters, and convert any that it finds to uppercase. (Or you might want to count the number of words in a string, or remove carriage returns. Assembly language can do all sorts of things.) For your assembly-language program to do this, it must know where the string is; that is, it must know its address in memory. You can tell it where the string is by using VARPTR to find the string in your BASIC program, and then by "passing" (that is, communicating) the information to the assembly-language program with DEF USR. The instructions to do this might look like this:

```
10 S$ = "THIS IS THE STRING."
20 A = VARPTR(S$)
30 D = USR1(A)
```

Of course, you have to know what to do with the address A inside your assembly-language program, and that is beyond the scope of this book.

However, even if you aren't going to use assembly language, VARPTR can be an interesting tool for exploring the inner workings of how BASIC stores numbers and text.

Integer Variables

Using VARPTR, let's figure out how variables are stored. We'll start with integers, which are the simplest of the four types of variables. Type this program:

```
10 INPUT "Input an integer J%"; J%
20 V = VARPTR(J%) : PRINT V
30 PRINT PEEK(V)
40 PRINT PEEK(V + 1)
```

We'll start by setting an integer variable, J%, equal to a value of 3. Then we set V equal to the VARPTR of J%. That is, VARPTR(J%) will return the address of the first byte where the value of J% is stored, and assign it to V, which we then print. But integers required two bytes of storage. Why? Because one byte contains 8 bits, which is enough to represent only values up to 255. Two bytes, however, have 16 bits, enough for values up to 256 times 256, which is 65536.

Actually, one bit is used as a *sign bit* to indicate whether the number is positive or negative, so that the range of values is cut in half: from 32767 to −32768. (See the description of two's complement arithmetic in Appendix B, for a further explanation of this.) In any case, J% is stored in two bytes. We have found the address of the first byte, and the second byte is located in memory immediately after the first one; that is, in address V plus 1.

Now that we know where our variable J% is stored, we can look at its value using the PEEK function, which returns the contents of a particular memory location. In line 30 of our example program, we use the PEEK function to look at the first byte of J%, and in line 40 we look at the second byte.

Let's RUN the program, input a 3, and see what happens. In line 20 we will find the address where J% is stored. This address will vary a great deal, depending not only on what kind of computer you are using and how much memory you have, but also on whether you already have other programs in memory. Let's say this address turns out to be 4777. (All numbers in this discussion are decimal numbers.) We assign this number to V. Next we PEEK into V, which is an address with a value of 4777, and then we PEEK into the next address, V + 1, which is 4778. We print the values stored in these two addresses:

```
RUN
 4777
 3
 0
Ok
```

The 4777 is the address of the first byte where J% is stored, the 3 is the contents of the first byte, and the 0 is the contents of the second byte. Because the value we set J% to was 3, we can deduce that the address contains the lower part of J% (the 3), and 4778 contains the upper part, which is 0. We call the lower part of the number the *least significant byte*, or LSB, and the upper part we call the *most significant byte*, or MSB. The LSB holds the lower 8 bits of the number, and the MSB holds the upper 8 bits.

To get a feel for this, try changing the value of J% and running the program again. For values of J% up to 255 you will find that this value appears, unaltered, in the LSB, and the MSB remains zero. But when you set J% to 256 and RUN the program, something different happens. Now the LSB is 0, and the MSB is 1. Why? Because the LSB was "full" when it contained a value of 255, so that adding one more caused it to become zero, with 1 to "carry" into the MSB. This is just like what happens when you add a 1 to a 9: the 9 (the one's column) is already full, so adding a 1 causes it to become 0, and a 1 to appear in the next column over. Figure 9-10 shows how a bit is "carried" from the least significant byte to the most significant byte.

What happens if J% is 257? The LSB will be 1, and the MSB will remain 1. If J% is 258, then LSB = 2 and MSB = 1. As we count upward, the MSB will remain at 1 until J% is 512 (which is 2 times 256), at which point it will become 2. When J% is 32767, both the LSB and the MSB will be full; trying to add one more will cause an OVERFLOW error.

Advanced GW-BASIC

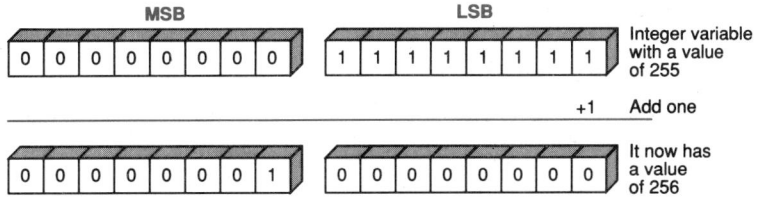

Fig. 9-10: Carrying a bit from the LSB to the MSB.

We summarize this here:

```
Value of J%        MSB              LSB
      0              0                0
      1              0                1
      2              0                2
    254              0              254
    255              0              255
    256              1                0
    257              1                1
    258              1                2
    510              1              254
    511              1              255
    512              2                0
    513              2                1
    514              2                2
  32765            127              253
  32766            127              254
  32777            127              255
  32768        (cannot be represented)
```

Every time we add 256 more units to the LSB, we increase the value of the MSB by one. This gives us a rule (sometimes called an "algorithm") for figuring out the value J% if we know the values of the LSB and the MSB.

```
J% = LSB + (MSB * 256)
```

So, if you PEEK into memory and find the LSB and the MSB of a particular integer, you can find the decimal value of the integer by multiplying the MSB by 256 and then adding the LSB. Similarly, if you know the decimal value of an integer, you can find the values of the LSB and the MSB:

```
MSB = INT (J%/256)
LSB = J% MOD 256
```

The other variable types are more complex and require more bytes of memory storage than integers do.

Single-Precision Variables

Single-precision variables require four bytes, arranged this way:

    Y = LSB of mantissa
V + 1 = Next most significant byte (NMSB) of mantissa
V + 2 = MSB of mantissa, with one sign bit
V + 3 = exponent, with one sign bit

(For a discussion of *mantissa* and *exponent*, refer to Appendix F, Exponential Notation.)

Here's a small program that prints the addresses of the first 10 elements in an array of cubes:

```
10 DIM S(50)
20 FOR I=0 TO 50
30     S(I)=I^3
40 NEXT
50 FOR J=0 TO 9
60     PRINT VARPTR(S(J))
70 NEXT
Ok

RUN
 4835
 4839
 4843
 4847
 4851
 4855
 4859
 4863
 4867
 4871
Ok
```

Because S is an array of single-precision variables, the addresses are 4 bytes apart.

Double-Precision Variables

Double-precision variables require 8 bytes of memory, arranged like this:

    V = LSB of mantissa
V + 1 = NMSB of mantissa
V + 2 = NMSB of mantissa
V + 3 = NMSB of mantissa
V + 4 = NMSB of mantissa
V + 5 = NMSB of mantissa
V + 6 = MSB of mantissa
V + 7 = exponent

String Variables

String variables are stored somewhat differently than numeric variables. Instead of pointing to the string itself, VARPTR returns the first of three addresses, the first of which is the length of the string, and the last two of which are pointers to the actual location of the string in memory.

    V = length of string
V + 1 = LSB of address where string starts
V + 2 = MSB of address where string starts

To show how VARPTR is used to find a string in memory, let's look at the following program, which will find a string and print it out by PEEKing at the values of the characters it finds in memory.

```
10 S$ = "THIS IS THE STRING"
20 V = VARPTR(S$)
30 L = PEEK(V)
40 A = PEEK(V +1) + (256 * PEEK(V +2))
50 '
60 FOR J = 1 TO L
70 PRINT CHR$ (PEEK(A + J - 1));
80 NEXT J
```

This program first finds the variable pointer V for the string S$. Then it finds L, the length of the string, which is stored in the first address pointed to by V. The second and third addresses pointed to by V contain the address where the string starts. We reconstruct this address by multiplying its MSB by 256 and adding the LSB. The result is A.

Chapter 9

To print the string, we set up a loop to count through the number of characters, L, in the string. The first character is at address A, the second at A + 1, and the last at A + L - 1. We PEEK at each location, then change the numeric value we find there to a string value with the CHR$ function, and print it out.

Figure 9-11 shows how the pointers are arranged for a string variable.

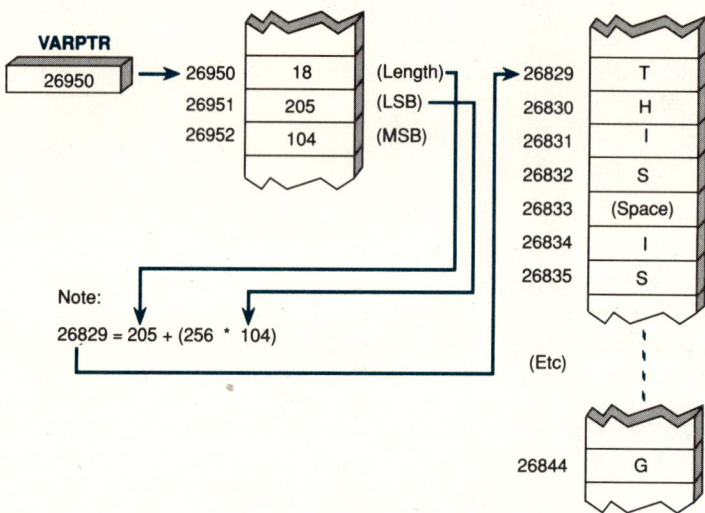

Fig. 9-11: String variable storage.

VARPTR returns a value, 26950, which is a pointer to the three locations that hold the following: first, the length of the string, which is 18 (in 26950); second, the LSB of the address, which is 205 (in location 26951); and last, the MSB of the address, which is 104 (in location 26952). We can calculate the actual address where the string starts by multiplying the MSB of the address by 256 and adding the LSB, which gives us 26829. Remember that all these addresses will be different on your computer.

Also, keep the following in mind: When using VARPTR, you should place the VARPTR statement as close as possible in your program to the place where the value it returns will be used. For instance, it should go immediately before the USR statement, if you are going to use the value it returns in an assembly-language routine. The reason for this is that BASIC is constantly changing the storage locations of the string variables in memory. It does this when you change the length of a string variable in your program, and it also occasionally does it all by itself to compact existing strings into the smallest possible space. So, if you use VARPTR to get an address in one part of your program, and then do some string variable operations before you make use of the address, it might well have changed before you use it!

Arrays and Assembly Language

When passing arrays to assembly language subroutines, the address you're usually most concerned with is that of the beginning element of the array. You can determine the base element with a statement like this:

```
X = VARPTR (A(0))
```

This finds the beginning element (element 0) of array A, and puts its address in X.

Using VARPTR with Files and Devices

When a file or device is open, GW-BASIC maintains a *file control block* that contains information about it. This FCB, as it is called, is an area of computer memory containing information such as the mode in which the file was opened, the number of bytes left in the input buffer, the record number, and more. You can use VARPTR to access any of this information or to pass it to a subroutine.

The general form of VARPTR used with files and devices is the following:

```
200 X = VARPTR (#N)
```

This means, "find the physical address in the computer of the first byte of the file control block for file (or device) N, and put that address in X."

Because of the amount of information in the FCB, the actual FIELD data buffer that holds data being written to or read from the file begins 188 bytes after the address returned by VARPTR.

Finding a Variable with VARPTR$

The VARPTR$ function gives you another way to find—or use—a variable's address, and find out more about the variable besides. The general form is as follows:

```
100 A$ = VARPTR$(X)
```

This means, "find the address of variable X and place the value along with information about the variable into A$." The information in A$ appears like this:

Byte 0   Variable type:
                    2   integer
                    3   string
                    4   single precision
                    5   double precision

Byte 1	Least significant byte of address
Byte 2	Most significant byte of address

As with VARPTR, if you want to use VARPTR$ to determine or use the beginning address of an array, make sure you have assigned all simple variables (such as A, B$, C, and so on) earlier in the program. Array addresses change whenever you assign a new simple variable.

How SHELL Summons DOS Commands and Other BASIC Programs

The SHELL statement lets you call MS-DOS commands and other BASIC programs, while retaining control within the calling program. In a sense, SHELL is like a giant GOSUB statement, except that instead of specifying a line number, you're calling an entire program or statement.

The general form of SHELL is as follows:

```
100 SHELL A$
```

This means, "run the program as specified in `A$`, then return." The string `A$` contains the name of the program, along with arguments if needed.

The simplest example of SHELL is when you use it with no string specified; in this case, it goes to MS-DOS. Unlike SYSTEM, which is a permanent exit, SHELL lets you go temporarily to MS-DOS, execute a command or two, then return to BASIC by typing EXIT. If you have BASIC on your screen now, try this example. (Insert the MS-DOS work disk into the disk drive first.)

```
SHELL

A> DIR/W
GWBASIC    EXE      GRAFX1      BAS       ROCKET      BAS

A> EXIT
Ok
```

Here you used SHELL to slip over to MS-DOS for a moment, and looked at a directory of files on drive A with the DIR command. Satisfied that all was in order, you then typed EXIT and you were instantly back in GW-BASIC.

If you've been using the FILES statement in BASIC to show you a list of the files on a disk, you know that it doesn't give you as much file information (such as date and time the file was last modified) as you find from the DIR command in MS-DOS. Also, wouldn't it be nice to have an alphabetical listing of those files?

Advanced GW-BASIC

Here's a short program that uses SHELL and the piping capabilities of MS-DOS to give you a file containing an alphabetical list of all your BASIC programs. (For best results with this program, make sure that your BASIC programs and MS-DOS are on the same disk—or at least that they're easily accessible.)

```
10 SHELL "DIR *.BAS | SORT > PROGS"
20 OPEN "PROGS" FOR INPUT AS #1
30 WHILE EOF (1) <>-1
40      INPUT #1, L$
50      PRINT L$
60 WEND
70 END
```

The SHELL statement in line 10 employs the DIR command in DOS. But instead of putting the directory on the screen, the pipe symbol (|) means to sort the directory to a file called PROGS. The command inside the quotation marks is exactly the same as if you'd typed it from the DOS prompt. It takes the DIR command, sorts its output in alphabetical and numerical order, and puts the result in the file PROGS. So after line 10, PROGS contains an alphabetical listing of your BASIC files.

After executing line 10, execution returns to BASIC. Line 20 opens PROGS for input, and the WHILE...WEND loop in lines 30-60 inputs one string (that is, one filename) at a time and prints it on the screen, until the end of the file is reached. Output from the program is an alphabetic listing of your BASIC programs:

```
14 File(s)     189440 bytes free
  BAR2    BAS     1844   6-15-90    1:25p
  BARCHT  BAS     2322   6-14-90    1:04a
  BBOX    BAS      249   6-13-90   11:43p
  COLREC  BAS     3547   6-17-90    2:35p
  .
  .
  TEMP    BAS      139   6-19-90    1:38p
  VPDEMO  BAS     2788   6-18-90   10:32p
  ZOOM    BAS      242   6-17-90    4:56p
Ok
```

If the DOS external commands such as SORT are in a directory and aren't available to BASIC, it's no problem to add their directory path within the SHELL statement, like this:

```
10 SHELL "DIR C:\DOS \*.BAS > FILE1"
```

Chapter 9

SHELL isn't limited to calling DOS commands, of course. You can use SHELL to call compiled programs (that is, .EXE or .COM files) from other languages.

Accessing I/O Ports

The IBM PC and compatible computers have special input and output locations called I/O ports. The purpose of the I/O ports is to provide a method for communicating 8-bit data from the computer to and from the outside world. The IBM computer uses memory-mapped I/O, which means any memory location can serve as an I/O port. The hardware engineer can decode these special addresses and easily hook up various devices to them such as keyboards, external displays and lights, d/a and a/d converters, speakers, and so on.

Ports are different from the memory locations; in fact, the port at location &HF0 and memory location &HF0 are not related at all. You use different statements to access and control ports than you do with memory locations.

In order to access ports from a BASIC program, two special keywords called INP and OUT are provided.

The INP Function

INP is a function statement which accepts an integer byte argument (0-65535) specifying the port and which returns an 8-bit value from the port. The value of the 8 bits is determined by what kind of device is connected to the port, and how many bits are being used.

The general form of INP is as follows:

```
X = INP (N)
```

This means, "get the current value contained in port address N and place the value in X."

As an example of using INP, let's find out what the current value of the speaker port is. The speaker port happens to be at port address &H61, so you can try this from the keyboard:

```
PRINT INP(&H61)
  48
Ok
```

Assuming that the speaker is off, you have just shown the value that keeps it silent. With 48 applied to the speaker port, it sits there in blissful silence. (The actual value for silence varies, depending on your computer.)

Advanced GW-BASIC

The Out Statement

In BASIC, the OUT statement performs the complementary function to the INP statement. OUT sends an 8-bit value in the range of 0-255 to a specified output port in the range of 0 to 65535. Here's the general form:

```
OUT H,J
```

This means, "send byte J to port address H." An important point about ports is that once you change a value there, it stays changed. For instance, here's a little program that outputs a bit pattern to port &H61 that happens to turn on the speaker:

```
10 PORT=INP (&H61)
20 OUT &H61, &H3
30 FOR I = 1 TO 100
40      PRINT "Sounding"
50 NEXT
60 OUT &H61, PORT
70 PRINT "Port value for silence:" PORT
```

If you run this program, you get several seconds of the speaker's beep, followed by blessed silence again. The output looks like this:

```
RUN
Sounding
Sounding
.
.
Sounding
Sounding
Port value for silence: 48
Ok
```

In line 10, we save the old value of the port. Then we use the OUT statement to send a hexadecimal 3 to the speaker port. This turns the speaker port on—and it stays on until we use another OUT statement to restore the port to its former status, before we started monkeying with it.

It's ALWAYS a good idea, when working with machine language ports, to save the previous or known value of the port before you try to use OUT to send anything to the port. Machine ports maintain the last value that was sent to them, so if you OUT something that locks up the keyboard, makes the speaker whistle, or flashes the screen in 4/4 time, you're going to be stuck with that little feature until you reboot or figure out how to correct the problem.

Chapter 9

How to WAIT for a Port's Input

Unlike other ways of suspending execution while waiting for input, such as WHILE...WEND, the WAIT statement doesn't need a partner—it can wait for an input all by itself. However, WAIT is used only to wait for input from a machine language port. The general form is as follows:

```
100 WAIT P, N
```

Line 100 means, "if the value at machine port P ANDed with N produces any bit set, continue; otherwise wait." This means that:

If a bit at P is:	And the corresponding bit of N is:	Then the result is:
0	0	0 (wait)
0	1	0 (wait)
1	0	0 (wait)
1	1	1 (continue)

As long as the result is zero, execution is suspended at the WAIT statement. When the result becomes a "1," execution continues. You can see that without input from the specified machine port, it's pretty easy for WAIT to become an endless loop, suspending execution forever. You can exit by pressing Ctrl-Break.

Here's an example of a typical WAIT statement:

```
500 WAIT 28, 3
```

Line 500 causes the program to wait until either bit 0 or bit 1 of port 28 is set. There's another way to specify WAIT. It's like this:

```
200 WAIT P, N, J
```

This means, "take the data at port P, XOR it with integer J, and then AND the result with integer N; continue if any resulting bit is a 1."

The purpose of WAIT, as the name implies, is to cause the program to wait until an external device has reached a certain state. This is useful, for example, if a device cannot input information as fast as the computer can read it. Usually in this case the device will set a "flag" when it is ready to have its information read using an INP statement. A flag can consist of a single bit set in a particular input port.

Let's assume that this flag is the third bit from the right in port 255 (as shown in figure 9-12). The WAIT instruction will then have the following form:

Advanced GW-BASIC

```
WAIT 255, 4
```

Here 255 is the number of the port, (just as in an OUT statement), and the 4 is a number which will be logically ANDed with the value read in at port 255. In this case, because 4 has a binary value of 00000100, only the third bit from the right will be examined by the WAIT statement. If the result is 0, then the WAIT statement is repeated. It will be repeated until the bit changes to a 1, at which time the program will go on to the statement following the WAIT.

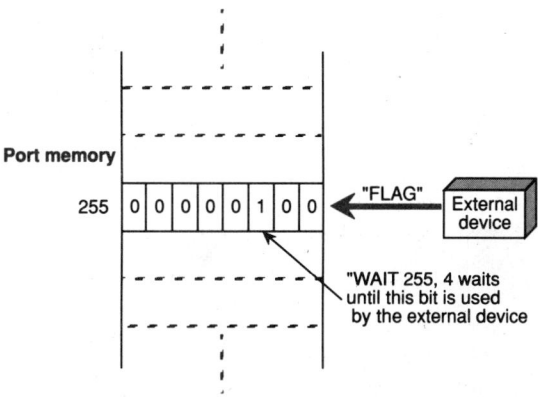

Fig. 9-12:   WAITing for input to a port.

Dealing with Errors—Creatively

Until now you might have assumed that, if an error occurred in your program, BASIC would, as inevitably as death and taxes, exit from the program, print an error message (like "Syntax error"), and revert to the BASIC monitor mode with an "OK" message. This is what BASIC normally does. The process works all right while you are developing and debugging a program, because you get immediate feedback on any mistakes you've made and you can then make the needed corrections. But once the program is finished and in the hands of a user, such cryptic error messages are not so useful. The last thing you want the user to have to deal with is the sudden appearance of a phrase like "Overflow error in line 290" on the screen, followed by the program "bombing" (ceasing to operate).

Some errors are not caused by the programmer, but might be the result of bad input on the part of the user, so that even a correctly written program is no assurance

Chapter 9

that errors will not occur when the program is run. Is there some way that we can keep errors from "bombing" the program? The answer to that question is the subject of this section.

ON ERROR GOTO and RESUME—Confronting Your Errors

ON ERROR GOTO N means, "ON the occurrence of any kind of ERROR, GOTO line number N and execute the routine there, without causing an error message."

RESUME M means "The error has been handled, so RESUME the regular program, at line number M."

ON ERROR GOTO and RESUME, taken together, provide a way for the programs you write to take over the job of processing errors from BASIC. ON ERROR GOTO provides a way to transfer control from your program to the routine you write to handle errors, and RESUME provides a way to get back to the program.

As an example, look at this program for finding factorials:

```
10 INPUT"NUMBER"; N
20 F = 1
30 F = F * N
40 N = N - 1
50 IF N>0 THEN GOTO 30
60 PRINT "FACTORIAL IS"; F
70 GOTO 10
```

For the purpose of this illustration, we'll use a bad programming practice—an IF statement and a GOTO, rather than the WHILE...WEND loop.

If you type this program and experiment with it, you will find that it works fine for comparatively small values of N: say, up to about 33. When you tried to input a larger number, 34 for example, the program "bombed" and BASIC printed "Overflow."

Here's how the results of running the factorial program might have looked if you had typed some large numbers:

```
NUMBER? 32
FACTORIAL IS 2.631308E + 35
NUMBER? 33
FACTORIAL IS 8.683317E + 36
NUMBER? 34
Overflow
FACTORIAL IS 1.701412E + 38
```

What's going on here? Why do we get an error message? Well, the problem is that your computer can handle numbers only up to a certain size, and the factorial of

Advanced GW-BASIC

a number like 34 is a really huge number—in fact, it is 37 digits long! When numbers get this large, BASIC says, "I give up, it's too big for me, help!" That's what the "Overflow" error message means: that a number was too large for BASIC to handle.

So, if you used this factorial routine in a program that other people would use, then every time they attempted to type too large a number, BASIC would print the error message and bomb the program—and users might wish they had used someone else's program instead of yours.

Is there a way to avoid having the program bomb when the numbers get too big? There certainly is: by using ON ERROR GOTO and RESUME. Let's modify the program like this:

```
5 ON ERROR GOTO 100
10 INPUT"NUMBER"; N
20 F = 1
30 F = F * N
40 N = N - 1
50 IF N>0 THEN GOTO 30
60 PRINT"FACTORIAL IS"; F
70 GOTO 10
100 REM-ERROR-CATCHING ROUTINE
110 PRINT"TOO LARGE A NUMBER."
120 RESUME 10
```

As you see, we've inserted a new line 5, "ON ERROR GOTO 100." This line tells BASIC, "Don't do anything now, but if an error occurs in the program, don't print the usual error message and bomb the program; just go to line 100 and start executing the instructions there." It's important to realize that this line has no immediate effect on the program—in fact, it has no effect at all unless an error occurs.

We've also added the new lines 100 and 120. These lines deal with any error that occurs. (If no errors occur, this routine will never be executed.) This kind of routine is often called an *error-trapping* routine, because its purpose is to "trap" errors before they can do any harm. In this particular case, the only thing that the routine does—if an error occurs and control passes to the routine—is to print a message, "TOO LARGE A NUMBER." The message tells users of the program that they can't expect the computer to correctly handle the factorial of this number N; it's too large.

Then, to return to the main program, the error-trapping routine executes the RESUME 10 instruction in line 120 to return control to line 10. RESUME not only takes you back to the main program, it also has the effect of "resetting" the ON ERROR GOTO statement, so that when the next error is detected control will pass again to the error-trapping routine. If you returned to the main program without using RESUME (with a GOTO, for example), then when the next error occurred, BASIC would handle it in the "normal" way, by taking over, bombing the program, and printing an error message.

Chapter 9

RESUME can be followed—as it is here—by the line number in the main program to which you want control to return from the error-trapping routine. You can also say RESUME 0, or simply RESUME. These statements will cause BASIC to go back and resume execution of the program at the same line in which the error occurred. If you do this, you have to be sure the error has been corrected before you execute the RESUME. Otherwise, control will go back to the line with the error in it, and because the error is still there, BASIC will head right back to the error-trapping routine, creating an endless loop. (You could avoid this by having the error-trapping routine reset N to the largest value BASIC can handle.) You can also say RESUME NEXT, which will cause control to resume at the line following the line in which the error occurred.

Try out the program. It works fine, doesn't it? No matter how large a number you type, the program answers it with "TOO LARGE A NUMBER" and goes right back to ask "NUMBER?" again.

There are, however, some possible pitfalls in the use of ON ERROR GOTO, things that could cause trouble if you're not aware of them.

One such pitfall is this: Once an error occurs, and you're in the error-trapping routine, you shouldn't let another error happen before you go back to the main program with the RESUME statement. If you do, the error-trapping routine will not trap it—control will return to BASIC, which will bomb the program and print its own error message in the usual way.

Another possible pitfall is that once you've executed the ON ERROR GOTO statement, then any error, no matter what it is or where it is in the program, will cause control to go to the error-trapping routine. This is true even of errors you make in direct statements in the monitor mode. For instance, if you typed LISP instead of LIST to list your program, control would go immediately to your error-trapping routine, even though your program wasn't even running at the time. The best way to avoid these problems is to execute the statement, ON ERROR GOTO 0, when you no longer expect the particular error that your error routine is intended to trap. This statement has the effect of cancelling your original ON ERROR GOTO N statement, so that errors will cause the normal BASIC error messages instead of going to your routine. We'll give an example of how to do this in the next section in which we discuss ERR and ERL.

ERR and ERL—What Was the Error, and Where Did It Happen?

ERR and ERL have similar functions, so we will describe them together here. They are both typically used in an error-trapping routine to give the routine information about the error. (For a discussion of error-trapping, see the previous section about ON ERROR GOTO and RESUME.) Often, they are used simply to ensure that the error which occurred is the one you expected (the one the error-trapping routine is designed to deal with) and not a more serious, unexpected error.

Advanced GW-BASIC

ERR means, "What was the number of the error?"

ERL means, "On what line number did the error occur?"

To create an "unexpected" error, try making a typing mistake in one of the lines of the factorial program described in the last section. For example, change the word INPUT in line 10 to INPIT. Now RUN the program. What happens? You would expect BASIC to recognize the error, halt execution of the program, print "SYNTAX ERROR," and then wait in the command mode for you to tell it what to do. But no—it prints out "TOO LARGE A NUMBER." Why? Because in line 5 you told it, "ON ERROR GOTO 100," and that's what it does faithfully—no matter what the error is—until you tell it to do otherwise. Although this is what you want if the error is really caused by inputting too large a number, it isn't very useful if the error is something else, like writing INPIT instead of INPUT.

Let's change the error-trapping routine so that it is a little more discriminating—that is, so that it can respond differently to different errors. We'll have it check not only that the error is the same kind of error we expected (that is, the same error number), we'll also have it check that the error took place on the same program line that we expected it to. To do this, we add line 105, making the program look like this:

```
5 ON ERROR GOTO 100
10 INPUT"NUMBER"; N
20 F = 1
30 F = F * N
40 N = N - 1
50 IF N>0 THEN GOTO 30
60 PRINT"FACTORIAL IS"; F
70 GOTO 10
100 REM-ERROR-TRAPPING ROUTINE
105 IF ERR <> 6 OR ERL <> 30 THEN ON ERROR GOTO 0
110 PRINT"TOO LARGE A NUMBER."
120 RESUME 10
```

Now when an error occurs, the error-trapping routine first checks to see whether ERR (the error number) is equal to 6, which is the number of the Overflow error. Then it checks to see whether ERL (the line number where the error occurred) is equal to 30, which is the line number where we expect the overflow error to occur (because this is where the factorials—which might cause overflow—are generated by multiplication). If either of these conditions is not true, then the routine knows that an unanticipated error has taken place, one which the routine cannot deal with itself. At this point, in order to turn control back over to BASIC so the proper error message can be printed, the routine executes an ON ERROR GOTO 0 statement. This has the effect of cancelling the ON ERROR GOTO 100 statement in line 5, and control then goes back to the BASIC monitor, which prints the appropriate error message. Notice that control does not go to line number 0.

485

ERROR—Stirring Up Trouble

ERROR N means, "Make BASIC think that ERROR number N has occurred."

This statement has the effect of imitating (simulating) an error, so that BASIC thinks one has taken place when in fact no error has occurred. Now why would we want BASIC to think that an error had taken place? The usual reason is that we want to test an error-trapping routine. (See the preceding discussions of ON ERROR GOTO, RESUME, and ERR and ERL.) Let's try out this idea, using the factorial program with the error-trapping routine. We'll make only one change in this program: we'll leave off the part of line 105 that says OR ERL <> 30. The reason for this will be explained later.

```
  5 ON ERROR GOTO 100
 10 INPUT"NUMBER"; N
 20 F = 1
 30 F = F * N
 40 N = N - 1
 50 IF N>0 THEN GOTO 30
 60 PRINT"FACTORIAL IS"; F
 70 GOTO 10
100 REM-ERROR-TRAPPING ROUTINE
105 IF ERROR <> 6 THEN ON ERROR GOTO 0
110 PRINT"TOO LARGE A NUMBER"
120 RESUME 10
```

RUN the program. When you type in a number which is too large, the program will "trap" to the error-handling routine in line 100 and print "TOO LARGE A NUMBER." Now, instead of actually causing an error by inputting too large a number, let's just "imitate" an error. Break into the program by typing "break" (or Control-C or Control-Break) so that BASIC halts execution of the program and returns to the monitor mode, printing "Ok."

Now type "ERROR 6" (the overflow error). Lo and behold, the error-trapping routine is executed in exactly the same way as it was when we typed in too large a number. So we have checked out the operation of the error-trapping routine without having a real error take place. Of course, in this example it's easy to generate a real error by typing too large a number, so that the ERROR statement isn't essential to checking out the error-trapping routine. But some errors are difficult to cause when you want them—those relating to malfunction of a disk unit, for example—and in these cases ERROR is a very useful function.

Notice that the reason we had to delete the OR ERL <> 30 part of line 105 is that, if we imitate the error in command mode by typing ERROR 6 as explained above, then the error is no longer taking place in line 30. So, if the routine checks to see that it did happen in line 30 and finds that it didn't, it will come to the mistaken conclusion that an unanticipated error has occurred. The routine will then execute the ON ERROR GOTO 0 part of the statement, which will cause BASIC to print "Overflow" instead of the "TOO LARGE A NUMBER" message that we want.

ERROR Used as an Extended Form of GOSUB

ERROR can also be used in another way, one the designers of BASIC probably didn't think of. In the following program we will use ERROR not to imitate an error, but almost as if it were a normal GOSUB statement. The advantage of using ERROR rather than GOSUB is that when an ERROR statement is executed, ERR is automatically set to the error number N (specified by the number N in ERROR N), and ERL is set to the line number where the error occurred. It can be very useful for a subroutine to be able to figure out the line number from which it was called, and it can also be useful to be able to pass an *argument* (a number with different values) to the subroutine from the program which calls it.

Here's a program which shows how this might be done. The program asks for the user's name and age. If the name is longer than 15 characters, the program prints, "Please use a shorter name." If the age is less than 3 years or greater than 80, the program assumes that the user has made a nonserious reply and prints, "Please be honest." (If you really are more than 80 or less than 3 years old, you can change line 50 accordingly!)

```
10 ON ERROR GOTO 80
20 INPUT"Please enter your last name"; LN$
30 IF LEN(LN$) > 15 THEN ERROR 38
40 INPUT"and your age"; AG
50 IF AG<3 OR AG>80 THEN ERROR 38
60 PRINT"THANK YOU."
70 END
80 REM-ERROR-TRAPPING ROUTINE
90 IF ERR <> 38 THEN ON ERROR GOTO 0    'Unexpected Error
100 IF ERL = 30 THEN PRINT"Use a shorter name." : RESUME 20
110 IF ERL = 50 THEN PRINT"Please be honest." : RESUME 40
120 ON ERROR GOTO 0    'Unexpected line number
```

In this program we use the ERROR statement to branch to the error-trapping routine at line 80 if either the name is too long or the age is less than 3 or more than 80. Neither of these conditions is really an "error," of course. We are simply using the error-handling statements to permit the routine to figure out which part of the main program called the routine.

Chapter 9

Let's go through this step by step for the case of the user typing an inappropriate age; 120, for example.

The first line of the program makes BASIC aware that, in the event of an error, control should go to line 80. Then the program asks for the user's last name and age. If, when asked for age, the user types (for example) 120, then in line 50 the program will see that AG is greater than 80 and will go on to the next part of the statement, which is ERROR 38. (Actually, any valid error number could be used here.) Executing this statement takes us immediately to the error-trapping routine on line 90. There, on line 90, we first verify that the error is the one we expect (that is, number 38). If it isn't, we assume that a "real" error (that is, one we hadn't anticipated, such as a syntax error) has taken place, and execute the ON ERROR GOTO 0 statement so that control will return to BASIC to deal with the error in the normal way. However, if the error is number 38, we then go on to check what line number it occurred on, using the ERL function. In this case, it occurred on line number 50, so we will execute the second part of line 110, which is

```
PRINT"Please be honest." : RESUME 40
```

Control will then go back to line 40, where the user will again be asked to input the value for age. If the error routine has not been called from either of the expected line numbers, 30 or 50, then it goes on to execute the "ON ERROR GOTO 0" statement in line 120, which will return control to BASIC to deal with a normal error.

When to Use an Error-Trapping Routine

You probably won't need to use any of the error-trapping terms we have been discussing when you are writing and debugging your program. In fact, in these stages of program development, error-trapping routines might even be a disadvantage, because you want BASIC to tell you about any errors in your program.

However, to make a finished program as "user-proof" as possible, it can often be an advantage to include an error-trapping routine to deal with all the errors which you can imagine being made by users of the program. No matter what the user of your program does, it is almost always better to have the program keep running and deal with the error itself, rather than bombing and turning control back over to BASIC. This way you can print the kind of error message you want to, rather than letting a BASIC error message reveal to the user that you have failed to foresee something the program or the user might do.

And if your error-trapping routine can't figure out what sort of error the user made, it can always print some sort of outrageous general-purpose error message, such as, "WE REGRET TO INFORM YOU THAT YOU HAVE VIOLATED SECTION 6SJ7 OF THE COMPUTER USER'S GUIDE. CONSIDERING THE DEGREE OF YOUR INCOMPETENCE WE HAVE NO CHOICE BUT TO TERMINATE THIS PROGRAM. GOODBYE!"

Advanced GW-BASIC

Of course there is no "Section 6SJ7" (and no "Computer User's Guide" either, for that matter). But perhaps this will be so demoralizing that the user of your program will fail to notice that you have not anticipated whatever error it was that caused the message! (Actually we're just kidding about this. In fact, it might not be such a good idea for your program to completely take over the error-handling process.) Just try to ensure that the user gets error messages that are clear and useful from whatever source.

Controlling and Reading Device Drivers

Peripheral devices, such as printers and disk drives that you attach to your computer, are controlled by small programs called *device drivers*. These drivers translate program instructions into commands the device can understand. DOS includes some standard device drivers, such as LPT2 and COM1, and you can usually use them without worry.

If for some reason you've written your own drivers to replace standard ones like LPT2 and COM1, you can use the IOCTL statement and IOCTL$ function. The problem with device drivers is that sometimes they do their job too well. For instance, if you write your own printer driver to replace LPT2, you might want the driver to respond to the command string PW40 to change the page width to 40 characters. But the driver will simply pass this to the printer.

The IOCTL statement and IOCTL$ function help you to control and get responses from character device drivers. Here are their general forms:

```
100 IOCTL #N, A$
200 B$ =IOCTL$ (#N)
```

Line 100 means, "send the command string in `A$` to the open device `N`." The string A$ is a command string that in practice usually is two or three characters long (although it can be up to 255 bytes long, with commands separated by semicolons.)

Line 200 means, "get a control data string from the open device `N` and put it in variable `A$`." This function is usually used after an IOCTL statement to get the response from the device driver.

Here's a brief example.

```
100 OPEN "LPT2:" FOR INPUT AS #2
110 IOCTL #2, "PW40"
120 RESPONSE$=IOCTL$(#1)
130 PRINT RESPONSE$
```

This brief bit of code opens a device driver called "LPT2:" as buffer #2, and the IOCTL statement in line 110 sends the command PW40 (which, depending on how the device driver is written, might be a command to change page width to 40 characters). Line 120 reads back the response from the device driver to the variable RESPONSE$.

Having GW-BASIC Your Way

We've come right back to where you began learning about BASIC—in MS-DOS, at the so-called GW-BASIC *command line*. When you first load GW-BASIC, you can change several parameters so that it dovetails better with what you're doing at the moment. Remember, to load GW-BASIC without changing any of the default parameters, you simply type GWBASIC.

The BASIC Command Line

Here's the full line you can type to load GW-BASIC, showing all the options available:

```
GWBASIC filename <stdin> >stdout /F:n /I /S:n /C:n /M:n, n /D
```

All of these parameters are optional. You can specify any *n* as a decimal value, as octal (with &O), or as hexadecimal (&H).

Automatic RUN

If you specify a *filename* that's the name of a BASIC program file, that program begins running automatically. For instance,

```
A> GWBASIC MYFILE.BAS
```

This loads GW-BASIC, then loads the file MYFILE.BAS and begins running it. Notice that you don't have to put quotation marks around the file name.

Standard Input File

The <*stdin* parameter specifies a standard input file for BASIC. You can use it if you want to run a BASIC program from the DOS command line and have it read data from a file rather than from the keyboard.

Advanced GW-BASIC

Directing Output

If you specify >*filename* when you start GW-BASIC, it means that everything appearing on the BASIC text screen is also logged in the file *filename*. This is an excellent way to keep track of your progress as you write and debug a program. You can also use this form to output to a printer or other device. To append to a file, use >> rather than >. For instance,

```
A> GWBASIC >> LOGFILE.TXT
```

Typing the above statement to load GW-BASIC causes everything that's printed on the text screen to be appended onto the file LOGFILE.TXT. BASIC creates the file if it isn't already there.

You can use both the "less than" symbol (<) and the "greater than" symbol (>) together to start from the command line, get input from a file, and save output into another file—all without operator intervention. Here's an example:

```
A> GWBASIC SORTER.BAS < NAMES > LIST
```

This command line runs the BASIC program SORTER, has it read from the file NAMES, and puts the output into the file LIST.

Maximum Number of Files

Using /F:*n* specifies the maximum number of files that can be opened at the same time while a GW-BASIC program is being executed. The default is 3 files. To use /F, you also must specify /I on the same line.

Using /I causes GW-BASIC to allocate the space needed for file operations.

Maximum File Record Length

Using /S:*n* sets the maximum record length, in bytes, for files. You can't exceed this maximum record length, even using OPEN. The default is 128 bytes, and the maximum record length you can specify is 32767 bytes.

Serial Communications

Using /C:*n* lets you determine how many bytes are allocated for the receive buffer for each RS-232-C communications card present in the computer. The default for the receive buffer is 256 bytes. If you specify /C:*n*, it means *n* bytes are allocated for each receive buffer, and 128 bytes for each transmit buffer. Using /C:0 allocates no space for these buffers, and disables BASIC support for RS-232-C.

Chapter 9

Maximum Block Size and Memory Location

Using /M:*n* sets the highest memory location used by GW-BASIC, and /M*n*, *n* also determines the maximum block size.

If you're going to use machine language subroutines with BASIC, use /M to specify the highest memory location that BASIC can use, then load the machine language subroutines into memory above that location. The maximum block size, which is in multiples of 16, is used to reserve that space (the space above the highest memory location) for those machine language subroutines. Here's an example:

```
C> GWBASIC /M: 16000
```

This loads GW-BASIC so that it uses only the first 16 Kbytes of its available memory, leaving 48 Kbytes for user programs. Instead of something like "60300 Bytes free" on the screen, here's what you see when GW-BASIC is loaded:

```
10766 Bytes free
```

Double-Precision Results in Some Functions

To allow certain functions to produce double-precision results, use /D when you load GW-BASIC. This makes BASIC use about 3000 more bytes of space, but it allows ATN, COS, EXP, LOG, SIN, SQR, and TAN to return answers that are double-precision numbers rather than single precision.

Here's an example of a longer GW-BASIC command line:

```
A> GWBASIC /F:5 /C:0 /D
```

This command line allows five user files to be open at one time (F:5), disables serial communications support (C:0), and allows the trigonometric and mathematics functions to return double-precision results.

The CLEAR Statement

CLEAR is another way you have control over just how BASIC uses computer memory. With CLEAR, you can specify the end of memory and reserve stack space for GW-BASIC. Moreover, CLEAR gives you a way to reset all variables to zero. The general form is as follows:

```
100 CLEAR
110 CLEAR, M
120 CLEAR, M, S
```

Advanced GW-BASIC

CLEAR by itself, as in line 100, takes care of all these tasks for you:

- Closes all files
- Resets stack and string space
- Clears user variables and COMMON variables
- Releases disk buffers
- Turns off any SOUND
- Sets any PLAY statements for foreground
- Sets the light PEN to OFF
- Sets the joystick STRIG to OFF
- Disables ON ERROR trapping

If, as in line 110, you add the memory expression, M, in number of bytes, you set the maximum number of bytes available for use by BASIC. If you add S (also in number of bytes), as in line 120, you can specify the size of the stack used by GW-BASIC. (The default is 512 bytes or 1/8 of available memory, whichever is smaller.)

Look at this CLEAR statement, for instance:

```
CLEAR , 32768, 1024
```

This statement zeroes all variables and strings, protects memory above decimal address 32768, and reserves 1,024 bytes for use by the GW-BASIC stack.

Review Questions

1. You're pulling data out of a file. The data have been converted from double-precision variables to strings with the MKD$ function. What function should you apply to each piece of data to convert it back to a double-precision numeric variable?

2. Write program lines that allow a program to replace itself with the program METER.BAS, passing the variable VOLTAGE and the array CURRENT to the program.

3. Write a short program that subtracts hexadecimal D0 from hexadecimal F00. What is the answer?

Chapter 9

4. What is the effect of the following program?

```
10 CLS:SCREEN 0: WIDTH 80
20 DEF SEG = &HB800
30 FOR C=320 TO 639 STEP 2
40      POKE C, 88
50 NEXT C
60 END
```

5. What statements would you use to print the beginning address in memory of the string array COLLEGES$?

6. How can you use MS-DOS commands in your BASIC programs?

7. What is the purpose of the RESUME statement?

8. What statement would you use to simulate a "Disk not ready" error in a program? (The error code for "Disk not ready" is 71.)

9. How would you get maximum accuracy from this program line?

```
1230 X=SIN(M)
```

10. Exercise: Write a program called PROG-A that saves the graphics screen to disk, then write a second program, PROG-B, to recall and display the graphics screen. Have PROG-A chain PROG-B to perform the actual display.

Chapter 10

The Fabulous Fractal

Chapter **10**

The Fabulous Fractal

This chapter describes some of the more important steps in creating fractal pictures. Fractal pictures are stunningly beautiful works of computer-generated art that don't lose detail as you zoom in on them. You can create them in BASIC on your own computer.

You may know of fractals as the Mandelbrot set. Math buffs know the Mandelbrot definition, given in Roger T. Stevens' book, *Fractal Programming in Turbo Pascal*. "A fractal is a curve whose Hausdorff-Besicovitch dimension is larger than its Euclidean dimension." Whew! Happily, the programming steps necessary to create fractals are easier to understand than their definition.

What You'll Learn in this Chapter

This chapter won't be devoted to the higher math necessary to understand all about fractals; you should refer to the Suggested Reading List if you want to know more. Instead, we will give the elementary definitions you'll need to write a fractal program. Then we will use traditional program design steps such as flowcharting and pseudocoding to design a program that will show us what a fractal looks like. We will use the flowcharts, pseudocode, *top-down*, *bottom-up*, and *dynamic* design methods to actually "walk through" by hand what the program is telling the computer to do. These steps are important when attacking a large project and when trying to *debug* (fix problems in) a program of any size. We will also discuss design considerations such as hardware compatibility and optimization. The program design methods that you will learn in this chapter will serve you well as you design and code larger programs of your own.

You may be wondering whether fractals serve a purpose besides just looking neat. In fact, fractals are a big aid in understanding our universe, and they're useful in "cutting-edge" sciences like chaos theory. For fractals at least, beauty IS more than skin deep.

Chapter 10

You can find an example of a fractal in figure 10-1. Although the small black-and-white picture can't do it justice, you can see how amazing a full-screen, color fractal will look.

Fig. 10-1: A fabulous fractal picture.

Our goal in designing this program is to show a full-screen color fractal while making it easy to change the fractal formula. (Different formulas, of course, produce different shapes on the screen.) Also, we'll want to make the program easy to change when we want to run it on a different type of screen. In other words, we want to structure our program so that it is flexible and easy to tailor to our needs, even as our needs change. For this reason, we'll emphasize "dynamic" design.

To show fractals really well, you need a high-resolution screen and plenty of colors—the more colors the better. Unfortunately, CGA screens have neither enough resolution nor a wide enough range of colors to show fractals to their best advantage. We're recommending a color EGA screen as the minimum screen type for this fractal program, and the EGA card should have 256K of video memory. Because we've practiced dynamic design, though, even if you have only CGA you'll be able to make a few minor changes to the program and view fractals on your monitor.

Initial Planning

To start our "plan of attack," we must decide what we want our fractal program to do and how to do it. As we said above, our goal in designing this program is to show a full-screen color fractal, so we must plan how to present that on a monitor.

Minimum Requirements

Fractals require high resolution or a good number of colors, preferably both. GW-BASIC supports the CGA (Color Graphics Adapter) and EGA (Enhanced Graphics Adapter) screen types. The CGA in its highest resolution mode (640 by 200 pixels) supports only two colors—black and white. In its most colorful mode the CGA has only four colors and its resolution is only 320 by 200 pixels. Although black-and-white fractals do look good, they need a much higher resolution than 640 by 200 pixels. And some fractals do look good at a low resolution of 320 by 200 pixels, but they need more than the four colors CGA offers.

Because it's our only other choice, let's look at the EGA. The EGA's highest resolution mode is 640 by 350 pixels, and that mode has 16 colors—wonderful for detailed fractals. There is also a 320-by-200-pixel mode with 16 colors that should work well for less detailed fractals.

Although we recommend the EGA, we want this program to support other screen modes as well. We'll try the CGA, just to see how it works, and perhaps we'll experiment with other EGA modes, too. If you have BASIC language that supports VGA, the dynamic design used in our fractal program should be able to accommodate the higher resolution that the VGA offers.

Two Considerations: Speed and Size

Because fractals are mostly math, you'd think the computer should be able to blast right through them. Unfortunately, when you think about the amount of math that a fractal requires, you realize that even a fast computer is going to need some time to "think" about it. For example, at the highest resolution of an EGA (which is 640 by 350 pixels), there are 224,000 pixels affected by mathematical operations. You'd take a long time, too, if you had to deal with almost a quarter million math problems!

The fractals we present in this chapter took about four-and-a-half hours to run on a 16-megahertz 386SX system. This figure is for the high-resolution EGA (640 by 350 pixels); it falls to about an hour and twenty minutes in the medium-resolution 320-by-200-pixel EGA mode. If you run the fractal program on an 80286 AT-type system or an 8088 XT-type system, you can expect slower performance.

You can increase the speed of the fractal program if you use the QuickBASIC or PowerBASIC compilers rather than GW-BASIC. Also, if you use the QuickBASIC or PowerBASIC compilers, the fractal program can take advantage of an 80x87 math coprocessor if your machine has one. A math coprocessor can increase the speed of a fractal program several times over, but remember that GW-BASIC doesn't know how to take advantage of one.

Now you're probably scratching your head at the prospect of tying up your computer for four hours (or more) at a time. You're right, of course; even diehard fractal fans wouldn't do that. Luckily, GW-BASIC gives us another option. After

Chapter 10

each picture is drawn, we will save it to disk. Then whenever we want to view the fractal, we can run another program that simply loads in the picture we've already saved. That way if you come up with a particularly interesting fractal formula, you can show it to others—without their having to wait four and a half hours! You could even put the picture files on a disk or upload them to a bulletin board system.

These picture files require over 112 Kbytes of storage, so some type of disk drive is also required. It can be a 5 1/4" floppy disk, a 3 1/2" floppy disk, or a hard drive. Remember that there must be at least 112 Kbytes available before you start the fractal program. If there isn't enough storage available or there is no disk, the fractal program will "crash" and you'll lose the four-and-a-half hours you spent making the fractal picture.

Choosing the Fractal

What type of fractal should we create? If you look at any of the books in the Suggested Reading List at the end of this chapter, you'll see that every mathematician in the world has a fractal method named after him or her. What we looked for in designing this program was a fractal method that was quickly and easily translated from mathematical language into GW-BASIC. We chose the Escape Time Algorithm, as presented by Michael Barnsley in his book, *Fractals Everywhere*.

The Escape Time Algorithm (or ETA for short) meets both our qualifications for a fractal program—speed and simplicity. It is quick, processing almost 900 pixels per minute. And the algorithm is easily converted into GW-BASIC program statements, as we will discover.

Pseudocode or Flowchart?

Without getting into the technical mathematics behind the ETA, we can say that it is a procedure to determine the color of a specific pixel on the screen. We apply the fractal formulas enough times until the values pass a cutoff point. When a value passes the cutoff point, we draw the point in the appropriate color. We continue this process for all columns and rows on the screen.

How can we go from this mathematical explanation of a procedure to working GW-BASIC code? That's where pseudocode and "top-down" design come in.

Pseudocode Is the Real Thing

Pseudocode is a kind of shorthand—you just write down directions for what you're going to do, without paying much attention to actual programming statements. Top-down design means that we start with the BIG picture, and add details as we proceed.

The Fabulous Fractal

Let's start by adding a little more detail, and summarize what we're going to do in the fractal program as follows:

```
Initialize
    For each column...
        For each row...
            Calculate initial X and Y
            Until we pass the cutoff point...
            Calculate the formulas
            Keep track of how many times we do the formulas
Draw the point at the current column and row
```

See how logically the pseudocode is laid out? That's to help us write the program later. For example, notice how parts of the pseudocode are indented; these indents show that the program is supposed to do all the things after the indent, using one of GW-BASIC's control flow loops. In fact, it's common to write pseudocode with additional lines that show where you'll use control flow loops, like this:

```
Initialize
For each column...
|   For each row...
|   |   Calculate initial X and Y
|   |   Until we pass the cutoff point...
|   |   |   Calculate the formulas
|   |   |   Keep track of how many times we do the formulas
|   |   Draw the point at the current column and row
```

We call this *top-down* pseudocode because it deals with the most general concepts (the *top*) first, and works "down" through progressively greater detail until we come to specific tasks. As we go farther down the pseudocode, or indent farther right, the pseudocode gets more detailed.

In our above example, the line "For each column..." is the least detailed (or most general, whichever way you prefer to look at it) and the lines "Calculate the formulas" and "Keep track of how many times we do the formulas" are most detailed (or least general).

Usually, the least detailed items are those that cover the most areas but that are executed least often; and the most detailed items are those that cover the least area but executed most often. In our example, the line "Initialize" is the least detailed and is executed least often (only once); the line "Calculate the formulas," however, is the most detailed and will be executed the most (640 × 350 = 224,000 times on an EGA screen 9).

The pseudocode we saw earlier is generic; it has almost no detail whatsoever. Let's use a "watered-down" version of Dr. Barnsley's definition of the Escape Time

Algorithm to develop a new set of pseudocode. The ETA says to keep track of how many times it takes for the squares of the fractal variables to pass some fixed limit. Fortunately, GW-BASIC gives us the ^ exponentiation operator to do the squaring (remember that squaring is the same as raising to the power of two). The first fractal formulas we will use look pretty simple:

```
X = 2 * X
Y = 2 * Y
```

Let's call these the *target* formulas because they draw the lower right hand corner of a set of concentric ellipses, a lot like an archery target. When we add these formulas, our new pseudocode might look like this:

```
Initialize
For each column... (0 TO 639)
|    For each row... (0 TO 349)
|    |    Calculate initial X and Y
|    |    While X^2 + Y^2 <= the cutoff point
|    |    |    X = 2 * X
|    |    |    Y = 2 * Y
|    |    |    Increment count
|    |    Draw the point at the current column and row
```

As you can see, this is getting more and more like "real" GW-BASIC code. In fact, the two formula lines:

```
X = 2 * X
Y = 2 * Y
```

are simply GW-BASIC program lines.

Pseudocode combines ease and efficiency; it is easy to use because it's in plain English, and it is efficient because it can easily be turned into GW-BASIC statements. (That's also a tribute to GW-BASIC's English-like syntax.)

Flowcharting

There is one other common way to document your GW-BASIC program before you actually write it, and that is flowcharting. Flowcharts use symbols to distinguish between different types of program lines; for example, the triangle indicates a decision-making statement, usually an IF. Flowcharting is popular because it can be more precise than pseudocode. However, with precision comes more work. Flowcharts can indeed be tedious things to produce, because you have to draw the symbols, put text descriptions in them, and then draw lines in between them. Depending on the project, flowcharting is sometimes worth the extra effort. Figure 10-2 has a flowchart representing the pseudocode above.

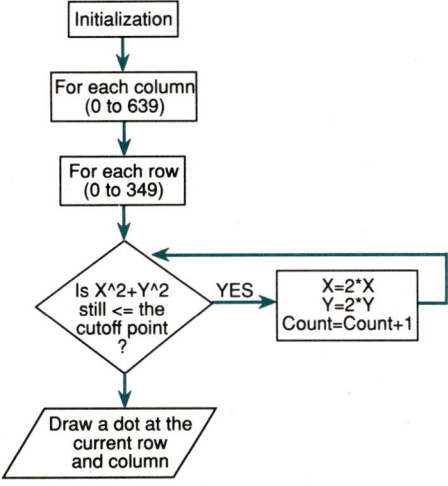

Fig. 10-2: Flowchart.

Adding to the General Program

As we look at our "draft" pseudocode and flowchart, we ask ourselves: "Is there anything else that I should add?" At the beginning of this chapter, we identified the need to save the fractal image to disk for later viewing. No problem! We won't save the image until it's finished being displayed, so we can simply tack on the following pseudocode:

```
Save screen image to disk files
```

or the flowchart fragment in figure 10-3.

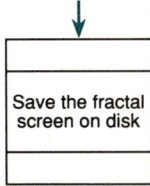

Fig. 10-3: Flowchart fragment for saving fractal image.

503

Chapter 10

Note that in both the pseudocode and flowchart fragment, we've "hidden" the details about the actual process of saving the image to disk; we treat that process as a "black box" that does its work without interfering with other parts of the program. We shouldn't have to worry about it as long as it does its job.

Because our pseudocode and flowchart seem simple and manageable, maybe we could add some other features just for the fun of it. The PALETTE statement from Chapter 8 is a good candidate. By manipulating the EGA's color palette, we can simulate motion of the fractals on the screen. Again, we treat this color palette manipulation as a black box—at this point in the programming process we don't care how it's done. Let's add the following pseudocode:

```
Manipulate EGA color palette to simulate motion
```

or the flowchart fragment in figure 10-4.

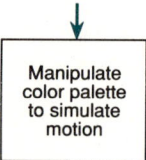

Fig. 10-4:   Flowchart fragment for color palette manipulation.

Because our current design saves the fractal image to disk, let's add still another feature, a program to load the disk images to the screen. This program doesn't have to do the calculations of our fractal program, so it is even smaller. Take a look at the pseudocode that follows, and the flowchart in figure 10-5.

```
Initialize
Load screen image from disk files
Manipulate EGA color palette to simulate motion
```

Dynamic Design

One of our design goals was *dynamic* design; but just exactly what is it? Dynamic design is thoughtful anticipation in a program. If you can anticipate that the user will want some other feature, make it easy to add that feature in the future.

Dynamic design makes just as much sense for the programmer as it does the user. For instance, what happens two years down the road when the user wants more features? If you've practiced dynamic design and let the program easily accept

The Fabulous Fractal

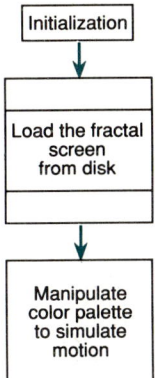

Fig. 10-5: Flowchart for the program to load a fractal.

changes, you'll be safe; otherwise you might be facing a costly program "hack"—a lot of extra work just to "squeeze" the feature in place.

Here are some of the obvious places where dynamic design is important:

- *Screen color.* For a long time, most people had monochrome monitors, so it wasn't a big deal if the user couldn't change how the program looked. However, as color monitors became more common, people resented having dumb, old programs that still used only black and white in their screens. Worse, some programs today still insist on setting whatever colors the original programmer thought looked best, resulting in some bright and garish screens. Dynamic design, however, allows the use of multiple colors.

- *Disk drives.* Before hard drives were in common use, many programs let you use only floppy drives A: and B:, and would give error messages if you tried using hard drives C: or D:. Dynamic design lets the user pick from any drive.

In our fractal program, we'll use dynamic design in one important area: graphics resolution. GW-BASIC now supports only the CGA and EGA graphics adapters, but perhaps someday it will support the VGA or Hercules graphics adapters. (If you have VGA, you can use the EGA-supported screens, of course, but you don't get any "extra" resolution because you've got VGA.) We want to be able to easily add VGA graphics to our fractal program.

In our pseudocode and flowchart, we have an entry called "Initialization." We left it vague on purpose, but it will take care of setting the proper screen graphics mode. If we make it easy for the user to specify the graphics mode, we will have taken a big step toward dynamic design.

505

Chapter 10

The Final Flowchart

We've gone about as far as we can go in the design phase. It's time to start coding. But first, take a look at our current pseudocode, as well as the final flowchart (fig. 10-6) with all the bells and whistles.

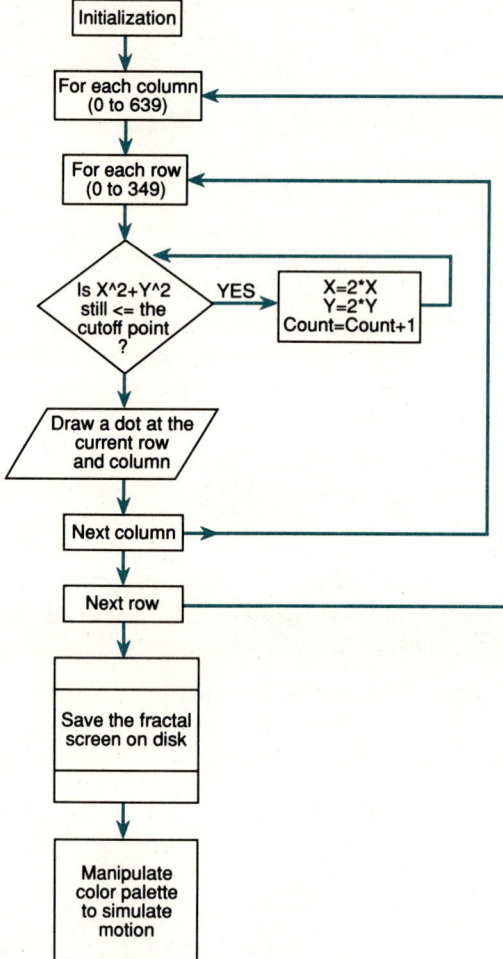

Fig. 10-6: Final flowchart.

```
Initialize
For each column... (0 TO 639)
│    For each row... (0 TO 349)
```

```
|         |     Calculate initial X and Y
|         |     While X^2 + Y^2 <= the cutoff point
|         |     |     X = 2 * X
|         |     |     Y = 2 * Y
|         |     |     Increment count
|         |     Draw the point at the current column and row
|         Save screen image to disk files
|         Manipulate EGA color palette to simulate motion
```

Biting the Bullet—Writing the Program

With our pseudocode and flowchart in place, we are now ready for the next step in the programming process—actually writing sections of code corresponding to the lines in our pseudocode or boxes in our flowcharts. Because one of our design ideals was *top-down* programming, we will try to follow the structure of our pseudocode and flowcharts from the top down as we actually write the code.

The Main Program Loops

The first things we'll write are the main *loops* of the program. In this fractal program, these main loops do the real work. Remember that in a larger program, you'd probably separate the work into several small subroutines and do the real work in the subroutines.

```
70  FOR X1% = 1 TO MAXCOLUMNS%            ' for each column
80      FOR Y1% = 1 TO MAXROWS%            ' for each row
90          X = X1% / MAXCOLUMNS%          ' calculate initial X & Y
100         Y = Y1% / MAXROWS%             ' for column and row
110         COUNT% = 0                     ' start at count of 0
120         WHILE X * X + Y * Y <= LIMIT%  ' until X & Y pass
125                                        ' the LIMIT% cutoff point
130             '----------------------------------------
140                                        ' insert other formulas here,
150                                        ' instead of the following two lines
160                                        ' put ' REM marks in front of other lines
170             '----------------------------------------
180             X = 2 * X                  ' -----------------
190             Y = 2 * Y                  ' "target" formulas
200                                        ' -----------------
210             COUNT% = COUNT% + 1        ' keep track of number passes
220         WEND                           ' when reached cutoff point,
230         PSET (X1%, Y1%), COUNT%        ' draw the point in the
```

Chapter 10

```
232                                             ' appropriate color
235             ' SOUND 100 * COUNT%, 1         ' sound tone (optional)
240    NEXT                                     ' do the next row
250 NEXT                                        ' do the next column
```

Note that we use "%" percent signs on the variables X1%, Y1%, and COUNT%. These signs denote integer variables. As a general rule, you should use integer variables wherever you can; and because X1% is going to range between 1 and 640 for an EGA, we don't need a floating point variable. The same applies to Y1% and COUNT%. Because integer variables are faster than floating point variables, the more you can use integers, the more time you'll save. And in a slow program like this fractal, we'll need to squeeze out every little bit of time we can.

The heart of the main program is a WHILE...WEND loop (starting at line 120 and ending at line 220) that runs through the formulas until the sum of the squares passes the cutoff point. Because the fractal formulas are calculated in that WHILE...WEND loop, it is the most important loop in creating the fractal.

How does this program compare to the pseudocode and flowcharts we've done? Well, in this fractal program the main loops correspond to the pseudocode and flowchart except for the initialization and last two lines in pseudocode, or those symbols in the flowchart. Program line 70 matches up with the pseudocode "For each column" line, and program line 210 matches up with the pseudocode "Increment count" line, for example. The same holds true for our flowchart; the third box in the flowchart matches with program line 80, the first parallelogram matches with program line 230, and so on.

Saving the Fractal to Disk

The next part of the program we'll look at is the routine to save the fractal image to disk. This routine is *hardware-specific*, which means that it relies on certain features of the IBM Enhanced Graphics Adapter. Luckily, almost 100% of the EGA-compatible adapters are at least compatible enough to work. Most VGA adapters are EGA-compatible, so they too should operate OK with the fractal program.

The EGA/VGA Save Routine

Here is the save routine for EGA adapters:

```
300 DEF SEG = &HA000                    ' switch to EGA video memory
310 SIZE% = 28000                       ' each plane is 28,000 bytes long
320 OUT &H3CE, 4: OUT &H3CF, 0: BSAVE "FRACTAL.BLU", 0, SIZE%
330 OUT &H3CE, 4: OUT &H3CF, 1: BSAVE "FRACTAL.GRN", 0, SIZE%
340 OUT &H3CE, 4: OUT &H3CF, 2: BSAVE "FRACTAL.RED", 0, SIZE%
```

The Fabulous Fractal

```
350 OUT &H3CE, 4: OUT &H3CF, 3: BSAVE "FRACTAL.INT", 0, SIZE%
360 OUT &H3CE, 4: OUT &H3CF, 0
370 DEF SEG                                            ' switch back
```

This save routine uses the BSAVE statement (which is explained in Chapter 8) and the OUT and DEF SEG statements (which you'll find in Chapter 9). Don't worry if you don't know exactly how this routine works; it assumes a lot of hardware knowledge that is beyond the scope of this book.

The EGA organizes its memory in four color *planes*. It's easiest to think of these planes as color transparencies, one each for blue, green, red and a "bright" transparency. If you mix a blue and a green transparency, for example, you'll get turquoise. The EGA works in a similar manner. You change the colors in the planes one at a time. Combining the colors of the three color planes gives you up to eight colors, and the "brightness" plane gives you an additional eight bright colors. The VGA has planes like the EGA, but the CGA has none.

Line 300 turns GW-BASIC's attention to the area of memory that the EGA uses; and lines 320-360 each saves a portion of the picture—one of the four color planes— using BSAVE. The OUT statements are the hardware-specific portions of this program. Each statement outputs a byte to a specific hardware port; the byte tells the EGA adapter to switch to a different color plane.

These OUT statements will not work on the CGA adapter, but they do work on most VGA adapters.

The CGA Save Routine

If you are adapting this fractal program to run on a computer using CGA, you'll have to remove lines 300-370 and replace them. Because the CGA doesn't have color planes like the EGA and VGA, the CGA save routine is simpler. All we need to do is save the single section of memory where the CGA stores the graphics image. Here is a replacement for lines 300-370:

```
300 DEF SEG = &HB800                ' switch to CGA video memory
310 BSAVE "FRACTAL.CGA", 0, 16383          ' save CGA image
320 DEF SEG                                    ' switch back
```

Flash and Dazzle

The last section of the fractal program is the *flash* routine, which manipulates the EGA palette colors to make it appear as if the fractal is moving. VGA adapters have an enhanced, but compatible, color palette capability, so the EGA flash routine will run unchanged on a VGA. If you have CGA, however, you'll have to modify the routine somewhat.

EGA/VGA Flash Routine

Here is the EGA flash routine:

```
430 DIM COLORS%(15)                         ' set up the initial colors
440 FOR TEMP% = 0 TO 15                     ' of the EGA palette
450     COLORS%(TEMP%) = TEMP%              ' This will flash the screen
460 NEXT                                    ' colors of the fractal
470 WHILE INKEY$ = ""                       ' unless the user hits a key
480     FOR TEMP% = 0 TO 15                 ' switch the EGA palette to
490         COLORS%(TEMP%) = (COLORS%(TEMP%) + 1) MOD 64
500     NEXT
510     PALETTE USING COLORS%(0)            ' rotate the colors
520 WEND                                    ' on the screen
```

To modify the color palette, we use GW-BASIC's PALETTE statement (see Chapter 8 for details). The PALETTE statement is similar to the OUT statement we used to save the fractal image to disk—it is hardware-dependent, requiring an EGA adapter. PALETTE is a lot nicer, though, because you don't need the confusing code numbers used by the OUT statement.

The first thing we do in this flash routine is set up an array, COLOR%, for the initial palette colors. We then use a WHILE...WEND loop to save the numbers 0 through 15 in this array, because these are the color numbers of the standard 16 colors. (The EGA supports up to 64 colors, though only 16 simultaneously.)

We then enter another WHILE...WEND loop, this time going again and again through the loop WHILE INKEY$ = "". What does this do? Because INKEY$ returns a null string ("") when no key has been pressed, GW-BASIC will run through this WHILE...WEND loop until the user presses a key to stop the program. After the WEND statement, the program ends.

Within the WHILE...WEND loop, we enter another loop, the FOR...NEXT loop. In the FOR...NEXT loop we increment the contents of the palette color array and then use the MOD operator to see whether the color has passed 63. Because 64 is the maximum number of EGA colors, and because those colors are numbered 0 through 63, we want to "trap" illegal color numbers and reduce them back down to numbers in the proper range.

We then execute the PALETTE USING statement, which instantly switches the palette colors. Successive color numbers usually appear next to each other; therefore as each color is incremented, it "moves" across the screen, usually from left to right.

Not even Rembrandt's works were loved by everyone, and this flash routine is an example of an area that some people might find annoying. Because we've practiced dynamic design, you can safely delete lines 430-520 with no ill effects.

CGA Flashing

CGA adapters can't use the PALETTE or PALETTE USING statements, so if you're adapting this fractal program to run on a CGA-adapted computer, you must remove lines 430-520 and replace them with another routine. Although the CGA doesn't have the full color palette capabilities of the EGA, it can use GW-BASIC's COLOR statement to do something similar to the EGA flash routine. We simply switch all the screen colors on a CGA to a different set. (See Chapter 8 for more details about COLOR.) Because we aren't "rotating" through all the colors, this routine is much shorter than the EGA routine:

```
470 WHILE INKEY$ = ""
480 COLOR , 0                       ' switch CGA palette colors
490 FOR X = 1 TO 1000: NEXT         ' pause a bit
500 COLOR , 1                       ' switch CGA palette colors
510 FOR X = 1 TO 1000: NEXT         ' pause a bit
520 WEND
```

Initialization and Dynamic Design

The last part of the program we'll look at is the initialization routine, whose biggest responsibility will be to set up the right graphics mode using the SCREEN statement. This routine will also be where most of our dynamic design comes from.

Remember that we decided we would use the high-resolution EGA mode with colors? That's screen mode 9, so we can initialize with the following statement:

```
SCREEN 9
```

Simple enough. You now have a 640 by 350 graphics screen with 16 simultaneous colors. But, as we talked about, what if we wanted to use the 320 by 200 graphics screen with 16 colors? If you take a look back at lines 70, 80, 90, 100 and 120 of the main program, you'll see we use variables like MAXCOLUMNS%, MAXROWS%, and LIMIT%. By using these variables instead of the actual "hard-coded" numbers 640 or 350, the only changes we need to make are in our initialization routine. If we make these changes, the rest of the program will fall in line and use the new layout.

For example, our initialization routine for using screen mode 9 is:

```
10 KEY OFF                          ' turn off key labels
20 LIMIT% = 200                     ' cutoff point
30 SCREEN 9                         ' high res EGA
40 MAXROWS% = 350                   ' 350 rows
50 MAXCOLUMNS% = 640                ' 640 columns
```

Chapter 10

Just a couple of changes to the initialization routine and we can use screen mode 7, with 320 by 200 resolution.

```
10 KEY OFF                              ' turn off key labels
20 LIMIT% = 200                         ' cutoff point
30 SCREEN 7                             ' medium res EGA
40 MAXROWS% = 200                       ' 200 rows
50 MAXCOLUMNS% = 320                    ' 320 columns
```

This is the place where you could make the changes to use CGA adapters, too. You could pick screen mode 1, which has 320 by 200 resolution with only four colors, or maybe screen mode 2, which has 640 by 200 resolution with only two colors. The initialization for screen mode 1 would look like this:

```
10 KEY OFF                              ' turn off key labels
20 LIMIT% = 200                         ' cutoff point
30 SCREEN 1                             ' medium res CGA
40 MAXROWS% = 200                       ' 200 rows
50 MAXCOLUMNS% = 320                    ' 320 columns
```

If you want to use CGA, try your hand at writing the initialization routine for screen mode 2, which has 640 columns and 200 rows with only two colors.

It looks like we're in business, with a complete fractal program, doesn't it? The truth is that not everything is perfect yet. Read on for details.

A View from the Bottom Up

Now that we have written code, we can look more closely at the fractal program. And what we see in this "bottom up" view shows some areas for improvement.

Gaining Speed

When a program takes up to four-and-a-half hours to run, you should always be on the lookout for ways to speed it up. Optimizing, as this is called, is important because sometimes even a small change can have a dramatic speed improvement.

As we can see by our pseudocode, the fractal program spends most of its time in the WHILE...WEND loop, calculating the fractal formulas. Is there some way we can simplify these calculations? Well, the lines within the WHILE...WEND loop look pretty straightforward, but what about the WHILE...WEND loop itself? Our WHILE statement uses exponentiation (raising to a power). But because it's only raising to the second power, we could rewrite the WHILE statement using simpler multiplication, as follows:

The Fabulous Fractal

```
120            WHILE X * X + Y * Y <= LIMIT%
```

As a matter of fact, exponentiation is much slower than multiplication when you're only squaring or cubing a number. On one system, this simple change sped up these fractal formulas to run in under fifteen minutes, down from almost an hour and a half before the change!

CGA Changes

We've shown how to convert the fractal program to run on a CGA, but are there other kinds of problems with this display adapter? Here's one: the Escape Time Algorithm routinely gives color numbers of 12 and 13. Displaying these colors is no problem for EGA and VGA, with their 16 colors, but it's not possible on a CGA because even in screen mode 1 (320 by 200 pixels) CGA has only four colors. To modify the program to run on a CGA, we must somehow reduce these high color numbers down to the range of a CGA.

The easiest way to do this reduction is by division; if we divide the actual color number by 4, most of the color numbers will fall into the CGA range. So, to use the fractal program with CGA, change the following lines:

```
55 COLORDIVISOR% = 4              ' Divides actual color into CGA range

230        PSET (X1%, Y1%), COUNT% \ COLORDIVISOR%
232                    ' draw the point in the appropriate color
```

Note that in line 230 we use the \ operator for integer division. Integer math, as we've already discussed, is much faster than floating point math. Every little bit helps!

Other Fractal Formulas

Working from the bottom up, we can take advantage of our dynamic design to plug in another, more interesting fractal formula. Michael Barnsley, in his book *Fractals Everywhere*, gives a formula for the Sierpinski triangle, a triangle built upon smaller and smaller triangles. Converted to GW-BASIC code, that Sierpinski triangle looks like this:

```
180 IF Y <= .5 THEN 185 ELSE X = 2 * X: Y = 2 * Y - 1: GOTO 200
185 IF X <= .5 THEN 190 ELSE X = 2 * X - 1: Y = 2 * Y: GOTO 200
190 X = 2 * X: Y = 2 * Y
200 ' -------------------- triangle formulas --------------------
```

Note that these lines replace the lines in the original "target" formula. You should also notice that this formula is more complex than the original formula, so it will be slower.

Presenting—The Fabulous Fractal Programs

Here it is: in the color corner, weighing in at only 55 lines, including comments, it's the Fabulous Fractal Program!

Writing the Fabulous Fractal program wasn't hard at all, was it? It may have sounded difficult at the outset, but when we broke down the problem, it became a series of simple tasks. And that's really what all programming is—breaking things down into more digestible pieces and then putting them together in a working program. The hard (but most enjoyable and creative) part is PLANNING your program, not writing it. Happy fractaling!

Fractals for EGA/VGA

Here's the complete program for use with EGA systems:

```
5 REM-FABULOUS FRACTALS FOR EGA/VGA
10 KEY OFF                                    ' turn off key labels
20 LIMIT% = 200                               ' cutoff point
30 SCREEN 9                     ' hi-res EGA (640x350x16 colors)
40 MAXROWS% = 350                             ' 350 rows
50 MAXCOLUMNS% = 640                          ' 640 columns
60          ' Change the above variables if you change screen modes
70 FOR X1% = 1 TO MAXCOLUMNS%                 ' for each column
80     FOR Y1% = 1 TO MAXROWS%                ' for each row
90         X = X1% / MAXCOLUMNS%    ' calculate initial X & Y
100        Y = Y1% / MAXROWS%       ' for column and row
110        COUNT% = 0               ' start at count of 0
120        WHILE X * X + Y * Y <= LIMIT%      ' until X & Y pass
125                                 ' the LIMIT% cutoff point
130              ' ----------------------------------------
140                      ' insert other formulas here,
150                  ' instead of the following two lines
160              ' put ' REM marks in front of other lines
170              ' ----------------------------------------
180            X = 2 * X             ' ------------------
190            Y = 2 * Y             ' "target" formulas
200                                  ' ------------------
```

```
210              COUNT% = COUNT% + 1  ' keep track of number passes
220          WEND                     ' when reached cutoff point,
230          PSET (X1%, Y1%), COUNT%  ' draw the point in the
232                                   ' appropriate color
235          ' SOUND 100 * COUNT%, 1  ' sound tone (optional)
240      NEXT                         ' do the next row
250 NEXT                              ' do the next column
260 '===============================================================
270 'when finished, save the screen to disk
280 'thanks to Ethan Winer of Crescent Software for this routine
290 '===============================================================
300 DEF SEG = &HA000                  ' switch to EGA video memory
310 SIZE% = 28000                     ' each plane is 28,000 bytes long
320 OUT &H3CE, 4: OUT &H3CF, 0: BSAVE "FRACTAL.BLU", 0, SIZE%
330 OUT &H3CE, 4: OUT &H3CF, 1: BSAVE "FRACTAL.GRN", 0, SIZE%
340 OUT &H3CE, 4: OUT &H3CF, 2: BSAVE "FRACTAL.RED", 0, SIZE%
350 OUT &H3CE, 4: OUT &H3CF, 3: BSAVE "FRACTAL.INT", 0, SIZE%
360 OUT &H3CE, 4: OUT &H3CF, 0
370 DEF SEG                                            ' switch back
380 '===============================================================
390 ' Note:   Use the SHOWE.BAS program to load these pictures
400 '===============================================================
410 ' NOTE:   THE FOLLOWING CODE ONLY WORKS FOR EGAs!
420 '===============================================================
430 DIM COLORS%(15)                   ' set up the initial colors
440 FOR TEMP% = 0 TO 15               ' of the EGA palette
450     COLORS%(TEMP%) = TEMP%        ' This will flash the screen
460 NEXT                              ' colors of the fractal
470 WHILE INKEY$ = ""                 ' unless the user hits a key
480    FOR TEMP% = 0 TO 15            ' switch the EGA palette to
490        COLORS%(TEMP%) = (COLORS%(TEMP%) + 1) MOD 64
500    NEXT
510    PALETTE USING COLORS%(0)                ' rotate the colors
520 WEND                                       ' on the screen
FRACTAL.BAS
```

Fractals for CGA

This is the program as modified for system with CGA:

```
5 REM-FABULOUS FRACTALS FOR CGA
10 KEY OFF                                    ' turn off key labels
```

Chapter 10

```
20 LIMIT% = 1500                                  ' cutoff point
30 SCREEN 1                         ' med-res CGA (320x200x4 colors)
40 MAXROWS% = 200                                      ' 200 rows
50 MAXCOLUMNS% = 320                                ' 320 columns
55 COLORDIVISOR% = 4           ' Divides actual color into CGA range
60          ' Change the above variables if you change screen modes
70 FOR X1% = 1 TO MAXCOLUMNS%                     ' for each column
80     FOR Y1% = 1 TO MAXROWS%                       ' for each row
90         X = X1% / MAXCOLUMNS%        ' calculate initial X & Y
100        Y = Y1% / MAXROWS%            ' for column and row
110        COUNT% = 0                       ' start at count of 0
120        WHILE X * X + Y * Y <= LIMIT%     ' until X & Y pass
125                                        ' the LIMIT% cutoff point
130                        ' ---------------------------------------
140                              ' insert other formulae here,
150                        ' instead of the following two lines
160                  ' put ' REM marks in front of other lines
170                        ' ---------------------------------------
180            X = 2 * X                 ' ------------------
190            Y = 2 * Y                        ' "target" formulae
200                                       ' ------------------
210            COUNT% = COUNT% + 1 ' keep track of number passes
220        WEND                        ' when reached cutoff point,
230        PSET (X1%, Y1%), COUNT% \ COLORDIVISOR%
232                       ' draw the point in the appropriate color
235          ' SOUND 100 * COUNT%, 1        ' sound tone (optional)
240     NEXT                                     ' do the next row
250 NEXT                                       ' do the next column
260 '==============================================================
270 'when finished, save the screen to disk
290 '==============================================================
300 DEF SEG = &HB800                  ' switch to CGA video memory
310 BSAVE "FRACTAL.CGA", 0, 16383              ' save CGA image
320 DEF SEG                                         ' switch back
380 '==============================================================
390 ' Note:  Use the SHOWC.BAS program to load these pictures
400 '==============================================================
410 ' This code works for a CGA
420 '==============================================================
470 WHILE INKEY$ = ""
480 COLOR , 0                         ' switch CGA palette colors
490 FOR X = 1 TO 1000: NEXT                        ' pause a bit
500 COLOR , 1                         ' switch CGA palette colors
```

```
510 FOR X = 1 TO 1000: NEXT                            ' pause a bit
520 WEND
```

Triangular Fractals

This program produces fractals based on the Sierpinski triangle, a triangle built upon smaller and smaller triangles.

```
5   REM-TRIANGLE FRACTALS FOR CGA
10  KEY OFF                                     ' turn off key labels
20  LIMIT% = 1500                                      ' cutoff point
30  SCREEN 1                         ' med-res CGA (320x200x4 colors)
40  MAXROWS% = 200                                          ' 200 rows
50  MAXCOLUMNS% = 320                                    ' 320 columns
55  COLORDIVISOR% = 4          ' Divides actual color into CGA range
60       ' Change the above variables if you change screen modes
70  FOR X1% = 1 TO MAXCOLUMNS%                        ' for each column
80      FOR Y1% = 1 TO MAXROWS%                          ' for each row
90          X = X1% / MAXCOLUMNS%          ' calculate initial X & Y
100         Y = Y1% / MAXROWS%               ' for column and row
110         COUNT% = 0                       ' start at count of 0
120         WHILE X * X + Y * Y <= LIMIT%    ' until X & Y pass
125                                          ' the LIMIT% cutoff point
130              ' ---------------------------------------------
140                             ' insert other formulae here,
150                         ' instead of the following two lines
160                     ' put ' REM marks in front of other lines
170              ' ---------------------------------------------
180 IF Y <= .5 THEN 181 ELSE X = 2 * X: Y = 2 * Y - 1: GOTO 200
181 IF X <= .5 THEN 182 ELSE X = 2 * X - 1: Y = 2 * Y: GOTO 200
182 X = 2 * X: Y = 2 * Y
200 ' ------------------- triangle formulae --------------------
210             COUNT% = COUNT% + 1 ' keep track of number passes
220         WEND                     ' when reached cutoff point,
230         PSET (X1%, Y1%), COUNT% \ COLORDIVISOR%
232                     ' draw the point in the appropriate color
235         ' SOUND 100 * COUNT%, 1       ' sound tone (optional)
240     NEXT                                    ' do the next row
250 NEXT                                        ' do the next column
260 '=============================================================
270 'when finished, save the screen to disk
290 '=============================================================
```

Chapter 10

```
300 DEF SEG = &HB800                        ' switch to CGA video memory
310 BSAVE "FRACTAL.CGA", 0, 16383                       ' save CGA image
320 DEF SEG                                             ' switch back
380 '================================================================
390 ' Note:  Use the SHOWC.BAS program to load these pictures
400 '================================================================
410 ' This code works for a CGA
420 '================================================================
470 WHILE INKEY$ = ""
480 COLOR , 0                               ' switch CGA palette colors
490 FOR X = 1 TO 1000: NEXT                              ' pause a bit
500 COLOR , 1                               ' switch CGA palette colors
510 FOR X = 1 TO 1000: NEXT                              ' pause a bit
520 WEND
```

Viewing the Fractal Again

Your fractal programs save the images to disk. The two short programs below bring those images back for repeated viewing. Use the following program if you've saved your image using the fractal program for EGA:

```
1 REM-LOADING AN EGA FRACTAL ("SHOWE.BAS")
10 SCREEN 9
20 DEF SEG = &HA000
30 OUT &H3C4, 2: OUT &H3C5, 1: BLOAD "FRACTAL.BLU", 0
40 OUT &H3C4, 2: OUT &H3C5, 2: BLOAD "FRACTAL.GRN", 0
50 OUT &H3C4, 2: OUT &H3C5, 4: BLOAD "FRACTAL.RED", 0
60 OUT &H3C4, 2: OUT &H3C5, 8: BLOAD "FRACTAL.INT", 0
70 OUT &H3C4, 2: OUT &H3C5, 15
80 DIM PALETTEARRAY%(16)
90 FOR TEMP% = 1 TO 16
100 PALETTEARRAY%(TEMP%) = TEMP%
110 NEXT
120 WHILE INKEY$ = ""
130 FOR TEMP% = 1 TO 16
140     PALETTEARRAY%(TEMP%) = (PALETTEARRAY%(TEMP%) + 1) MOD 64
150 NEXT
160 PALETTEARRAY USING PALETTEARRAY%(0)
170 WEND
```

The Fabulous Fractal

If you've saved your image as a CGA fractal, you can use the following program to display it again:

```
1 REM-SHOWING A CGA FRACTAL ("SHOWC.BAS")
10 SCREEN 1                        ' CGA med-res (320x200x4 colors)
20 DEF SEG = &HB800                 ' switch to CGA video memory
30 BLOAD "FRACTAL.CGA"              ' load CGA memory
40 DEF SEG                          ' switch back
120 WHILE INKEY$ = ""
130 COLOR , 0                       ' switch CGA palette colors
140 FOR X = 1 TO 1000: NEXT         ' pause a bit
150 COLOR , 1                       ' switch CGA palette colors
160 FOR X = 1 TO 1000: NEXT         ' pause a bit
170 WEND
```

Suggested Reading List

Michael Barnsley. *Fractals Everywhere*. Boston: Academic Press, Harcourt Brace Jovanovich, 1989.

Michael Barnsley. *The Desktop Fractal Design System*. Boston: Academic Press, Harcourt Brace Jovanovich, 1990.

Roger T. Stevens. *Fractal Programming in Turbo Pascal*. Redwood City: M&T, 1990.

Appendixes

A	BASIC Quick Reference Guide	523
B	Numbering Systems	561
C	ASCII—Numeric Conversions and Keyboard Scan Codes	585
D	Tips to Save Memory	597
E	Speed Hints	601
F	Exponential (Scientific) Notation	603
G	Information for Graphics	609
H	Answers to Review Questions	615

Appendix A

BASIC Quick Reference Guide

In this quick reference guide, quantities in brackets ([ ]) are optional.

ABS
Syntax:
ABS(*n*)

```
100 PRINT ABS (-5*8)
```

Displays the absolute value (40) of the expression.

ASC
Syntax:
ASC(*s$*)

```
100 A$="TEST"
110 PRINT ASC(A$)
```

The ASCII code of the first character of A$ is printed. For the capital letter T, the value is 84.

ATN
Syntax:
ATN(*x*)

```
100 PRINT ATN(3)
```

Displays the arctangent of 3 radians.

Appendix A

AUTO
Syntax:
AUTO [*line number*][,[*increment*]]
AUTO .[,[*increment*]]

```
100 AUTO 1000,50
```

Automatically numbers each new program line using steps of 50 and beginning with line 1000.

BEEP
Syntax:
BEEP

```
100 IF X < 100 THEN BEEP
```

If X is less than 100 the speaker emits a single beep.

BLOAD
Syntax:
BLOAD *filename*[,*offset*]

```
100 DEF SEG=&HB800
110 BLOAD "MYART",0
```

Loads a file called MYART that has been previously BSAVEd into memory at *offset*=0 of the segment beginning at HB8000.

BSAVE
Syntax:
BSAVE *filename*, *offset*, *length*

```
100 DEF SEG=&HB800
110 BSAVE "MYART", 0, &H320
```

Saves an image of the memory area in segment HB8000 starting at *offset*=0 and ending at *offset*=320. The image is written to a disk file called MYART.

CALL
Syntax:
CALL *numvar*[(*variables*)]

```
100 DEF SEG=&H800
110 STARTHERE=0
120 CALL STARTHERE(A,B$,C)
```

Calls a machine language subroutines that begins at *offset*=0 of segment H8000 and passes variables A,B$, and C to the called routine.

CDBL
Syntax:
CDBL(*x*)

```
100 PRINT CBDL(X)
```

Converts the value X to a double-precision number.

CHAIN
Syntax:
CHAIN [MERGE] *filename*[,[*line number*][,[ALL][DELETE *range*]]]

```
100 CHAIN "C:PROG2", 50, ALL
```

Transfers control to PROG2, which begins execution at line 50, and passes ALL variables to PROG2.

CHDIR
Syntax:
CHDIR *pathname*

```
100 CHDIR "B:PIX"
```

Changes directory to the directory PIX on drive B.

CHR$
Syntax:
CHR$(*n*)

```
100 PRINT CHR$(65)
```

Converts the value 65 to the equivalent ASCII code character, which is the capital letter A.

Appendix A

CINT
Syntax:
CINT(*x*)

```
100 PRINT CINT(35.87)
```

Converts the value 35.87 to the integer value 36.

CIRCLE
Syntax:
CIRCLE(*xcenter,ycenter*),*radius*[,[*color*][,[*start*],[*end*][,*aspect*]]]

```
100 CIRCLE (160,100), 20
```

Draws a circle with center at X=160, Y=100, and a radius of 20.

CLEAR
Syntax:
CLEAR[,[*expression1*][,*expression2*]]

```
100 CLEAR 20000, 10000
```

Sets string variables to null, numeric variables to zero, and closes all open files. CLEARs all memory used for data without erasing current program; sets maximum workspace=20,000 bytes; sets stack size=10,000 bytes.

CLOSE
Syntax:
CLOSE [[#]*filenumber*[,[#]*filenumber*]...]

```
100 CLOSE
```

Closes all open files and devices.

CLS
Syntax:
CLS[*n*]

```
100 CLS
```

Clears the screen and homes the cursor.

BASIC Quick Reference Guide

COLOR
Syntax:
COLOR [*foreground*][,[*background*]][,*border*]]
COLOR [*background*][,[*palette*]]
COLOR [*foreground*][,[*background*]]

```
100 SCREEN 1
110 COLOR 1,0
```

Sets background color to blue and selects palette 0 in SCREEN 1.

COM(*n*)
Syntax:
COM(*n*) ON
COM(*n*) OFF
COM(*n*) STOP

```
100 COM(2) ON
110 ON COM(2) GOSUB 1000
```

Enables trapping of communications adapter #2; when trapped, execution branches to subroutine beginning at line 1000.

COMMON
Syntax:
COMMON *variables*

```
100 COMMON A,B(),C$
110 CHAIN "A:PROG2"
```

Passes variables A, array B( ), and C$ to PROG2.

CONT
Syntax:
CONT

```
100 CONT
```

Continues program execution after a break.

COS
Syntax:
COS(*x*)

527

Appendix A

```
100 PRINT COS(5)
```

Displays the cosine of an angle of 5 radians.

CSNG
Syntax:
CSNG(*x*)

```
100 PRINT CSNG(12.34567891)
```

Converts the double-precision value 12.34567891 to the single precision value 12.34568.

CSRLIN
Syntax:
y=CSRLIN

```
100 Y=CSRLIN
```

Stores the value of the current cursor line number in the variable Y.

CVD
Syntax:
CVD *(8-byte string)*

```
100 X=CVD(N$)
```

Converts the 8-byte string variable N$ to a double-precision numeric value X.

CVI
Syntax:
CVI(*2-byte string*)

```
100 X=CVI(N$)
```

Converts the 2-byte string variable N$ to an integer variable X.

CVS
Syntax:
CVS(*4-byte string*)

```
100 X=CVS(N$)
```

Converts the 4-byte string variable N$ to a single-precision numeric variable X.

DATA
Syntax:
DATA *constants*

```
100 DATA 12, 78.9788, "DEGREES"
110 READ M, T, A$
```

Stores the constants 12, 78.9788, and "DEGREES" for reading by the READ statement.

DATE$
Syntax:
As a variable: *a$=DATE$*
As a statement: DATE$=*a$*

```
100 DATE$="10/31/83"
110 PRINT DATE$
```

Sets and retrieves the current date.

DEF FN
Syntax:
DEF FN *name[arguments] expression*

```
100 PI=3.14159
110 DEF FNAREA(R)=PI*R^2
120 INPUT "RADIUS?",RAD
130 PRINT"AREA=";FNAREA(RAD)
```

Defines a user-written function that calculates area of a circle from its radius.

DEF INT/SNG/DBL/STR
Syntax:
DEF*type letters*

```
100 DEFINT A-B
110 DEFSNG C-D,X-Z
120 DEFSTR E-W
```

Variables whose names begin with A or B are integers, those beginning with C, D, X, Y, or Z are single-precision numbers, and those beginning with E through W are string variables.

Appendix A

DEF SEG
Syntax:
DEF SEG [*address*]

```
100 DEF SEG=&HB800
```

Defines the segment in memory that will be accessed by BLOAD, BSAVE, CALL, PEEK, POKE, or USR. Segment addresses are shifted 4 bits left, so HB8000 (the area of the color screen buffer) is specified as &HB800.

DEF USR
Syntax:
DEF USER[*n*]=*integer*

```
100 DEF SEG=0
110 DEF USR2=16000
120 X=USR2
```

Defines a machine language subroutine called USR(2) that begins at *offset*=16000 of the current segment.

DELETE
Syntax:
DELETE [*line number1*][*–line number 2*]
DELETE *line number1–*

```
100 DELETE 2000-3500
```

Erases lines 2000-3500.

DIM
Syntax:
DIM *variable*(*subscripts*)[,*variables*(*subscripts*)]...

```
100 DIM A$(20), X(40)
```

Allocates space in memory for up to 21 elements of array A$, and 41 elements of array X.

DRAW
Syntax:
DRAW *string expression*

BASIC Quick Reference Guide

```
100 SCREEN 1
110 DRAW "U40 R20 D40 L20
```

Draws a box 40 units high and 20 units wide.

EDIT
Syntax:
EDIT *line number*
EDIT .

```
100 EDIT 85
```

Displays line 85 for editing.

END
Syntax:
END

```
100 END
```

Terminates program execution, closes all files, and returns to command level.

ENVIRON
Syntax:
ENVIRON *string*

```
100 ENVIRON "PATH=A:\"
```

Sets the path parameter in the BASIC environment table to the root directory on the A: drive.

ENVIRON$
Syntax:
*v$*=ENVIRON$(*parmid*)
*v$*=ENVIRON$(*nthparm*)

```
100 PRINT ENVIRON$(1)
```

Displays the current contents of the first string in the environment table.

EOF
Syntax:
x=EOF(*file number*)

531

```
100 IF EOF(2) THEN END
```

Checks for an end-of-file condition when reading from sequential file #2. Returns −1 (true) when found, 0 (false) if not found.

ERASE
Syntax:
ERASE *list of array variables*

```
100 ERASE ARRAY1, TEST5
```

Erases arrays ARRAY1 and TEST5 from memory.

ERDEV
Syntax:
ERDEV

```
100 PRINT ERDEV
```

Displays a number containing a device error code.

ERDEV$
Syntax:
ERDEV$

```
100 PRINT ERDEV$
```

Displays the name of the device causing an error.

ERL
Syntax:
x=ERL

```
100 IF ERL=500 THEN GOSUB 1000
```

If the error occured in line 500, execute the subroutine beginning at line 1000.

ERR
Syntax:
x=ERR

```
100 IF ERR=6 THEN GOTO 500
```

If error code=6 (Overflow) then GOTO the error-handling routine beginning at line 500.

ERROR
Syntax:
ERROR *integer expression*

```
100 ON ERROR GOSUB 1000
120 IF X>500 THEN ERROR 333
130 IF ERR=333 THEN END
ERROR 6
```

Defines a new error code to be handled by your program. In command mode, prints message for any given error.

EXP
Syntax:
EXP(*x*)

```
100 PRINT EXP(3)
```

Displays the value of the number *e* raised to the third power.

EXTERR
Syntax:
EXTERR(*n*)
n = 0,1,2,3

```
100 PRINT EXTERR(0)
```

Returns MS-DOS "Extended" error information when DOS functions are performed.

FIELD
Syntax:
FIELD [#] *filenumber, width* AS *stringvar* [*,width* AS *stringvar*]...

```
100 FIELD #1, 30 AS A$, 50 AS B$
```

Allocates space for variables A$ and B$ in random file buffer #1.

FILES
Syntax:
FILES [*pathname*]

```
100 FILES "C:\TEMP\"
```

Displays all files in the TEMP directory on drive C.

Appendix A

FIX
Syntax:
FIX(*x*)

```
100 PRINT FIX(34.56)
```

Displays the integer digits (34) of the number 34.56.

FOR...NEXT
Syntax:
FOR *variable*=*x* TO *y* [STEP *z*]
NEXT [*variable*][,*variable*...]

```
100 FOR I=1 TO 200 STEP 5
110 NEXT I
```

Advances the counter I five steps at a time each time NEXT is executed until the count reaches 200.

FRE
Syntax:
FRE(*s$*)
FRE(*x*)

```
100 PRINT FRE(0)
```

Displays the number of unused bytes of memory. Arguments are dummy arguments.

GET (for Files)
Syntax:
GET[#]*file number*[,*record number*]

```
100 OPEN "DATAFILE" AS #1
110 FIELD 1, 30 AS CUSTNAME$, 40 AS ADDRESS$
120 GET 1
```

Reads a record from the random file DATAFILE.

GET (for Graphics)
Syntax:
GET (*x1*, *y1*)–(*x2*, *y2*), *array name*

```
100 GET (10,10)-(200,120), "MYART"
```

BASIC Quick Reference Guide

Saves the contents of the screen within the rectangle whose opposite corners are (10,10) and (200, 120) into an array named MYART.

GOSUB...RETURN
Syntax:
GOSUB *line number*
RETURN [*line number*]

```
110 GOSUB 400
120 PRINT "Back from subrroutine":END
400 PRINT "Off at subroutine":RETURN
```

Goes to a subroutine at line 400; then returns to the statement following the GOSUB.

GOTO
Syntax:
GOTO *line number*

```
100 GOTO 120
110 PRINT "NEVER HAPPEN"
120 PRINT "CONTINUING"
```

Skips line 110, goes to line 120 and continues execution from there.

HEX$
Syntax:
*v$*=HEX$(*x*)

```
100 H$=HEX$(29)
110 PRINT H$
```

Converts the decimal value 29 to the hexadecimal value 1D.

IF
Syntax:
IF *expression*[,] THEN *statement(s)*[,]ELSE *statement(s)*]
IF *expression*[,]GOTO *line number*[[,]ELSE *statement(s)*]

```
100 IF A=12.37 THEN GOTO 30 ELSE STOP
```

If A=12.37 is true, then branch to line 30; otherwise, stop execution.

Appendix A

INKEY$
Syntax:
v$=INKEY

```
100 PRINT "PRESS ANY KEY"
110 A$=INKEY$
120 IF A$="" THEN 100
```

Reads a character from the keyboard and assigns it to a variable called A$. If no key is pressed, execution returns to line 100 and loops until a key is pressed.

INP
Syntax:
INP(*n*)

```
100 A=INP(&8H3B0)
```

Reads input from one byte of the machine port that begins with number 3B0 hex, and assigns it to variable A.

INPUT
Syntax:
INPUT[;][*prompt string,*] *list of variables*
INPUT[;][*prompt string,*] *list of variables*

```
100 INPUT "Type your name";N$
```

Waits for keyboard input while displaying the quoted prompt string; then assigns the keyboard input to variable N$.

INPUT#
Syntax:
INPUT# *file number, list of variables*

```
100 OPEN "DATAFILE" FOR INPUT AS #1
110 INPUT #1, A$
```

Reads the variable A$ from the open file.

INPUT$
Syntax:
INPUT$ (*x*[,[#]*file number*)]

```
100 A$=INPUT$(20)
```

Reads a string of 20 characters from the keyboard and assigns them to A$.

INSTR
Syntax:
INSTR([n,]x$,y$)

```
100 A$="ABCDEFG"
110 B$="B"
130 PRINT INSTR(A$,B$)
```

Searches for the first occurence of B$ within A$ and displays the position (2) where the match begins.

INT
Syntax:
INT(x)

```
100 PRINT INT(-3.87)
```

Truncates –3.87 to a whole number, displaying the largest integer (–4) that is less than or equal to –3.87.

IOCTL
Syntax:
IOCTL[#]*file number,string*

```
100 OPEN "O", #2,"LPT1:"
110 IOCTL #2, "WD44"
```

Passes control data (WD44) to open device #2; the control data could be a command for a user-written driver.

IOCTL$
Syntax:
IOCTL$([#]*file number*)

```
100 IF IOCTL$(2)="99" THEN PRINT "OK"
```

Reads the control data string from a user-written character device driver on open device #2.

Appendix A

KEY
Syntax:
KEY *key number, string expression*
KEY *n*,CHR$(*hexcode*]) + CHR$(*scan code*)
KEY ON
KEY OFF
KEY LIST

```
100 KEY 5, "PRINT"
```

Sets function key F5 as a typing aid that puts the word PRINT on the screen.

KEY(*n*)
Syntax:
KEY(*n*) ON
KEY(*n*) OFF
KEY(*n*) STOP

```
100 ON KEY(10) GOSUB 5000
110 KEY (10) ON
```

Allows trapping of function key F10; if function key F10 is pressed, execution branches to subroutine in line 5000.

KILL
Syntax:
KILL *filename*

```
100 KILL "A:MYPROG.BAS"
```

Erases the file on drive A called MYPROG.BAS.

LEFT$
Syntax:
LEFT$(*x$,n*)

```
100 A$="Waite Group"
110 PRINT LEFT$(A$,5)
```

Displays the leftmost 5 characters (Waite) of the string A$.

LEN
Syntax:
LEN(*s$*)

```
100 A$="Help me, Rhonda"
110 PRINT LEN(A$)
```

Displays the length (15) of the string A$.

LET
Syntax:
[LET] *variable=expression*

```
100 LET X=50
```

Assigns the value 50 to the variable X.

LINE
Syntax:
LINE [*(x1,y1)*]–*(x2,y2)* [,[*attribute*][,B[F]][,*style*]]

```
100 LINE (10,10)-(50,50),2,B
```

Draws a box using color attribute 2 whose opposite corners are (10,10) and (50,50).

LINE INPUT
Syntax:
LINE INPUT[;][*prompt string,*]*string variable*

```
100 LINE INPUT "Address?";C$
```

Reads an entire line of input, including delimiters, into variable C$.

LINE INPUT#
Syntax:
LINE INPUT # *file number, string variable*

```
100 OPEN "PLACES" FOR INPUT AS #1
110 LINE INPUT #1, CITY$
```

Reads an entire line from the open file PLACES and assigns it to the variable CITY$.

LIST
Syntax:
LIST [*line number*][–*line number*][,*filename*]

Appendix A

LIST [*line number–*][*,filename*]

```
100 LIST 10-200
```

Displays a listing of lines 10–200 of the program in memory.

LLIST
Syntax:
LLIST [*line number*][*–line number*]
LLIST [*line number–*]

```
100 LLIST
```

Prints a complete program listing on the printer.

LOAD
Syntax:
LOAD *filename*[,R]

```
100 LOAD "MYPROG"
```

Loads the program MYPROG from a disk into memory.

LOC
Syntax:
LOC(*file number*)

```
100 PRINT LOC(1)
```

Displays the current position in the file opened as #1.

LOCATE
Syntax:
LOCATE [*row*][,[*column*][,[*cursor*][,[*start*][,*stop*]]]]

```
100 LOCATE 21, 40
```

Positions the cursor at row 21, column 40.

LOCK
Syntax:
LOCK [#]*n*[,[*record number*][TO *record number*]

```
100 LOCK #1, 1 TO 20
```

Restricts access to records 1 to 20 of file opened as #1.

LOF
Syntax:
LOF(*file number*)

```
100 PRINT LOF(1)
```

Displays length in bytes of file opened as #1.

LOG
Syntax:
LOG(*x*)

```
100 PRINT LOG(10)
```

Displays the natural logarithm (2.302585) of 10.

LPOS
Syntax:
LPOS(*x*)

```
100 PRINT LPOS(0)
```

Displays the position of the print head in the print buffer. The 0 is a dummy argument.

LPRINT
Syntax:
LPRINT [*list of expressions*][;]

```
100 LPRINT "HELLO"
```

Prints the word HELLO on the printer.

LPRINT USING
Syntax
LPRINT USING *string expression*; *list of expressions*[;]

```
100 LPRINT USING "###.##";123.4567
```

Prints the expression 123.4567 on the printer using the quoted format. Printed copy reads 123.46.

Appendix A

LSET
Syntax:
LSET *string variable = string expression*

```
100 LSET N$=YOURNAME$
```

Moves the contents of YOURNAME$ into the random file buffer named N$ and left-justifies that field.

MERGE
Syntax:
MERGE *filename*

```
100 MERGE "PROG2
```

Merges the lines of ASCII file PROG2 with the lines of the current program in memory. Duplicate line numbers are replaced by the lines in PROG2.

MID$
Syntax:
MID$(*x$,n*[,*m*])
MID$(*string1, n,* [,*m*])=*string 2*

```
100 A$="LOOKING GOOD"
110 PRINT MID$(A$, 5, 3)
```

Starting with the 5th character, display the next 3 characters (ING).

MKD$
Syntax:
MKD$ (*double-precision expression*)

```
100 T$=MKD$(TONS)
```

Converts the value of the double-precision variable TONS to a string variable T$.

MKDIR
Syntax:
MKDIR *pathname*

```
100 MKDIR "TEMPS"
```

Creates a directory called TEMPS.

MKI$
Syntax:
MKI$(*integer expression*)

```
100 C$=MKI$(COUNTER)
```

Converts the value of the integer variable COUNTER to a string variable.

MKS$
Syntax:
MKS$(*single-precision expression*)

```
100 B$=MKS$(BALANCE)
```

Converts the single-precision variable BALANCE to a string variable B$.

NAME
Syntax:
NAME *old filename* AS *new filename*

```
100 NAME "MYPROG.BAS" AS "YOURPROG.BAS"
```

Renames the file MYPROG to the new name YOURPROG.

NEW
Syntax:
NEW

```
100 NEW
```

Clears current program and all variables from memory.

OCT$
Syntax:
OCT$(*x*)

```
100 PRINT OCT$(19)
```

Converts the decimal value (19) to the equivalent octal value (23).

ON COM(n)
Syntax:
ON COM ([*n*]) GOSUB *line number*

Appendix A

```
100 ON COM(1) GOSUB 1000
```

When activity is detected in communications adapter #1, branch to line 1000.

ON ERROR GOTO
Syntax:
ON ERROR GOTO *line number*

```
100 ON ERROR GOTO 500
```

When any error occurs, branch to line 500.

ON KEY(n)
Syntax:
ON KEY(*n*) GOSUB *line number*

```
100 ON KEY(4) GOSUB 1000
```

When function key F4 is pressed, branch to line 1000.

ON PEN
Syntax:
ON PEN GOSUB *line number*

```
100 ON PEN GOSUB 2000
```

When light pen is detected, branch to line 2000.

ON PLAY(n)
Syntax:
ON PLAY (*n*) GOSUB *line number*

```
100 ON PLAY(10) GOSUB 500
```

When music is playing in the background and 10 notes remain in the buffer, branch to line 500.

ON STRIG(n)
Syntax:
ON STRIG (*n*) GOSUB *line number*

```
100 ON STRIG(4) GOSUB 5000
```

When joystick trigger button A2 is pressed, branch to line 5000.

ON TIMER (n)
Syntax:
ON TIMER *(n)* GOSUB *line number*

```
100 ON TIMER (60) GOSUB 5000
110 TIMER ON
```

When 60 seconds have elapsed since the TIMER ON statement, branch to line 5000.

ON...GOSUB
Syntax:
ON *expression* GOSUB *line numbers*

```
100 ON N GOSUB 500, 700, 330
```

If N=1, GOSUB 500; if N=2, GOSUB 700; if N=3, GOSUB 330.

ON...GOTO
Syntax:
ON *expression* GOTO *line numbers*

```
100 ON N GOTO 500, 700, 330
```

If N=1, GOTO 500; if N=2, GOTO 700; if N=3, GOTO 330.

OPEN
Syntax:
OPEN *mode*,[#]*file number*,*filename*[,*reclen*]
OPEN *filename* [FOR *mode*[ACCESS *access*][*lock*] AS [#] *file number*
[LEN = *reclen*]

```
100 OPEN "O",#1,"DATAFILE"
```

Opens a device or file called DATAFILE to receive output as file #1.

OPEN "COM (n)
Syntax:
OPEN "COM[*n*]:[,*speed*][*parity*][,*data*][,*stop*][,RS][,CS[*n*]][,DS[*n*]][,CD[*n*]][,LF]
[,PE]" AS[#]*filename* [LEN=*number*]

```
100 OPEN "COM2:" AS 2
```

Opens communications adapter #2 for communications.

Appendix A

OPTION BASE
Syntax:
OPTION BASE 0
OPTION BASE 1

```
100 OPTION BASE 1
```

Sets the subscript of the lowest-numbered array element as 1.

OUT
Syntax:
OUT *h*, *j*

```
100 OUT 853, 3
```

Sends a value of 3 to machine port 853.

PAINT
Syntax:
PAINT (*x-start*, *y-start*)[,*paint attribute*[,*border attribute*][,*background attribute*]]

```
100 LINE (10, 10)-(50, 50), 3, 8
110 PAINT (20, 40), 1, 2
```

Fills the interior of the box drawn by LINE with a color attribute 1 starting at point (20, 40).

PALETTE, PALETTE USING
Syntax:
PALETTE [*attribute*,*color*]
PALETTE USING *integer array name (arrayindex)*

```
100 SCREEN 1
110 PALETTE 1, 6
```

Changes the color for attribute 1 to brown (6). This statement works only on systems with EGA adapters.

PCOPY
Syntax:
PCOPY *sourcepage*, *destinationpage*

BASIC Quick Reference Guide

```
100 PCOPY 1,2
```

Copies page 1 of the current screen buffer to page 2.

PEEK
Syntax:
PEEK(*a*)

```
100 PRINT PEEK (4782)
```

Displays the value stored in memory location 4782.

PEN
Syntax:
As a statement:
PEN ON
PEN OFF
PEN STOP
As a function:
$x = P(n)$

```
100 X=PEN(1)
110 PRINT X
```

Displays the x-pixel coordinate when the light pen was last activated.

PLAY
Syntax:
PLAY *string expression*

```
100 PLAY HYMN$
```

Plays music as defined by contents of HYMN$.

PLAY(n)
Syntax:
PLAY(*n*)

```
100 PRINT PLAY(0)
```

Displays the number of notes remaining in the music background buffer. The variable *n* is a dummy argument.

547

Appendix A

PMAP
Syntax:
x = PMAP (*expression, function*)

```
100 WINDOW (-1,-1)-(1,1)
110 PSET (PMAP (150,2), PMAP(50,3))
```

Maintains the WINDOW logical coordinates for all statements, but plots a point at physical coordinates (150, 50).

POINT
Syntax:
POINT(*x,y*)
POINT(*function*)

```
100 C=POINT(100,205)
```

Reads the color attribute of the point at screen location (100,20) and assigns it to variable C.

POKE
Syntax:
POKE *offset, data*

```
100 SCREEN 0
110 DEF SEG = &HB800
120 POKE 320, 65
```

Writes an "A" (ASCII value 65) into the memory location that is offset 320 bytes above segment address hexadecimal B8000.

POS
Syntax:
POS (*c*)

```
100 IF POS(0)>50 THEN PRINT CHR$(13)
```

If the cursor column position is beyond 50, then perform a carriage return. The *c* is a dummy argument.

PRINT
Syntax:
PRINT [*list of expressions*][;]
?[*list of expressions*][;]

BASIC Quick Reference Guide

```
100 PRINT "Hello"
```

Displays the word Hello on the screen.

PRINT #
Syntax:
PRINT #*n, list of expressions*

```
100 PRINT #1, "FILE", F1
```

Writes the word FILE and the variable F1 to the sequential file opened as #1.

PRINT USING
Syntax:
PRINT USING *string expression;list of expressions*[;]

```
100 PRINT USING "###.##";123.4567
```

Uses the quoted format to display the expression, causing 123.4567 to be displayed as 123.46.

PRINT # USING
Syntax:
PRINT USING #*file number* ,[USING *string*]; *list of expressions*

```
100 PRINT #1 USING "###.##";COST
```

Writes the value of the variable COST to the sequential file open as #1; uses the format specified in the quotes.

PSET and PRESET
Syntax:
PSET(*x,y*)[,*color*]
PRESET(*x,y*[,*color*]

```
100 PSET (160,100)
110 PRESET (160,100)
```

PSET draws a point at coordinates (160, 100) in the foreground color. PRESET removes the same point.

Appendix A

PUT (for Files)
Syntax:
PUT [#] *file number* [,*record number*]

```
100 PUT #1, 5
```

Writes data into record 5 of the random access file that has been opened as #1; file must be OPEN, and data must have been LSET or RSET into random buffer #1.

PUT (for Graphics)
Syntax:
PUT(*x,y*), *array*[, *action verb*]

```
100 SCREEN 1
110 PUT (100,40),MYART
```

Takes the bit image that was saved with GET in the array called MYART and puts it on the graphics screen with the upper left corner of the image at location (100,40).

RANDOMIZE
Syntax:
RANDOMIZE [*expression*]
RANDOMIZE TIMER

```
100 RANDOMIZE (1000)
```

Reseeds the random number generator with the number 1000 to produce a new sequence of numbers.

READ
Syntax:
READ *list of variables*

```
100 DATA 36, 47, 29
110 READ A, B, C
```

Reads the three values from the DATA statement and assigns them as follows: A=36, B=47, C=29.

REM
Syntax:
REM[*comment*]
'[*comment*]

```
100 REM Ignore this statement
```

Inserts a nonexecutable remark.

RENUM
Syntax:
RENUM[*new number*],[*old number*][,*increment*R]]

```
100 RENUM 1000, 50, 10
```

Renumbers the program beginning with current line number 50, so that line 50 becomes line 1000, and subsequent lines are in increments of 10 (1010, 1020, etc.).

RESET
Syntax:
RESET

```
100 RESET
```

Closes all open disk files.

RESTORE
Syntax:
RESTORE[*line number*]

```
100 RESTORE
```

Causes the next READ statement to begin reading at the first DATA statement in the program.

RESUME
Syntax:
RESUME
RESUME 0
RESUME NEXT
RESUME *line number*

Appendix A

```
100 RESUME 500
```

Following an error recovery procedure, causes execution to resume at line 500.

RETURN
Syntax:
RETURN [*line number*]

```
100 RETURN
```

Causes execution to return to the line following the GOSUB that initiated the branch to this subroutine.

RIGHT$
Syntax:
RIGHT$(*x$*,i)

```
100 W$="LONESOME"
110 PRINT RIGHT$(W$,2)
```

Displays the rightmost 2 characters (ME) of the string LONESOME.

RMDIR
Syntax:
RMDIR *pathname*

```
100 RMDIR "A:TEMP"
```

Removes the directory called TEMP from the A drive.

RND
Syntax:
RND[(*x*)]

```
100 X=INT(RND*11)
```

Yields random integers in the range 0 to 10.

RSET
Syntax:
RSET *string variable = string expression*

```
100 RSET N$=YOURNAME$
```

Moves the contents of YOURNAME$ into the random file buffer named N$ and right-justifies that field.

RUN
Syntax:
RUN [*line number*[,R]]
RUN *filename*[,R]

```
100 RUN
```

Executes the current program in memory.

SAVE
Syntax:
SAVE *filename*,[,A]
SAVE *filename*,[,P]

```
100 SAVE "PROG4",A
```

Saves the program in memory using the name PROG4 as an ASCII file.

SCREEN (Function)
Syntax:
x=SCREEN(*row,column*)[,z]

```
100 PRINT SCREEN(20,40)
```

Displays the ASCII code for the character on the screen at row 20, column 40.

SCREEN (Statement)
Syntax:
SCREEN [*mode*] [,[*colorswitch*]] [,[*apage*][,[*vpage*]]

```
100 SCREEN 1
```

Switches screen to medium resolution graphics mode.

SGN
Syntax:
SGN(*x*)

```
100 PRINT SGN(X)
```

Displays the sign (as −1, 0, or 1) of the variable X.

Appendix A

SHELL
Syntax:
SHELL [*string*]

```
100 SHELL
```

Loads DOS; current BASIC program remains in memory, and you can type EXIT to return to BASIC and continue running the program.

SIN
Syntax:
SIN(*x*)

```
100 PRINT SIN(2)
```

Displays the sine of an angle of 2 radians.

SOUND
Syntax:
SOUND *frequency, duration*

```
100 SOUND 440, 18
```

Produces a sound of 440 Hertz for a duration of 18 clock ticks (1 second).

SPACE$
Syntax:
SPACE$(*x*)

```
100 S$=SPACE$(20)
110 PRINT S$; "HEADER"
```

Prints a string of 20 spaces; then prints the word HEADER.

SPC
Syntax:
SPC(*n*)

```
100 PRINT SPC(30)
```

Prints 30 spaces.

BASIC Quick Reference Guide

SQR
Syntax:
SQR(*x*)

```
100 PRINT SQR(144)
```

Displays the square root (12) of the value 144.

STICK
Syntax:
x=STICK(*n*)

```
100 Y=STICK(1)
```

Returns y-coordinate of joystick A and assigns it to variable Y.

STOP
Syntax:
STOP

```
100 STOP
```

Halts program execution and issues message "Break in 100".

STR$
Syntax:
STR$(*x*)

```
100 PRINT LEN (STR$(121))
```

Treats the numeric expression 121 as a string expression and displays the length.

STRIG
Syntax:
STRIG ON
STRIG OFF
x=STRIG(*n*)

```
100 STRIG ON
110 X=STRIG(1)
120 PRINT X
```

Displays –1 if joystick trigger A1 is currently pressed, 0 if not pressed.

Appendix A

STRIG(n)
Syntax:
STRIG(*n*) ON
STRIG(*n*) OFF
STRIG(*n*) STOP

```
100 STRIG(0) ON
```

Enables trapping of joystick button A1 by the ON STRIG(*n*) statement.

STRING$
Syntax:
STRING$(*n,j*)
STRING$(*n,x$*)

```
100 A$=STRING$(10,42)
110 PRINT A$;"FILE 1";A$
```

Displays a string consisting of ASCII character 42 (*) repeated 10 times; then prints the words FILE 1; then displays 10 more asterisks.

SWAP
Syntax:
SWAP *variable 1, variable2*

```
100 SWAP A$,Z$
```

Exchanges the values of variables A$ and Z$.

SYSTEM
Syntax:
SYSTEM

```
100 SYSTEM
```

Returns to MS-DOS.

TAB
Syntax:
TAB(*n*)

```
100 PRINT TAB(25) "HELLO"
```

Moves cursor to column 25 on the screen, then displays the word HELLO.

BASIC Quick Reference Guide

TAN
Syntax:
TAN(x)

```
100 PRINT TAN(2)
```

Prints the tangent of an angle of 2 radians.

TIME$
Syntax:
TIME$ = *string expression*
string expression = TIME$

```
100 TIME$ = "10:23:00"
110 PRINT TIME$
```

Sets the current time to 10:23:00 and prints the current time.

TIMER
Syntax:
v = TIMER

```
100 PRINT TIMER
```

Displays the number of seconds elapsed since midnight or since system reset.

TRON and TROFF
Syntax:
TRON
TROFF

```
100 TRON
110 REM Code to be traced
500 TROFF
```

Traces execution of program statements between line 100 and line 500.

UNLOCK
Syntax:
UNLOCK [#]n[,[record number] [TO record number]

```
100 UNLOCK #1, 1 TO 10
```

Unlocks records 1 to 10 in file opened as #1.

Appendix A

USR
Syntax:
v = USR[*n*](*argument*)

```
100 DEF USR3=&HF000
110 C=USR3 (M^3)
```

Calls the machine language subroutine USR3, located beginning at memory address hexadecimal F000, and supplies argument (M^3).

VAL
Syntax:
VAL(*s$*)

```
100 TELNUM$="9998880"
110 PRINT VAL(TELNUM$)
```

Prints the numeric value of the string "9998880".

VARPTR
Syntax:
VARPTR (*variable name*)
VARPTR (*#file number*)

```
100 PRINT VARPTR$ (X)
```

Displays the memory location of the variable X.

VARPTR$
Syntax:
VARPTR$ (*variable*)

```
100 PRINT VARPTR(A$)
```

Returns a 3-byte string containing the type and memory location of the variable A$.

VIEW
Syntax:
VIEW [[SCREEN][*x1*, *y1*)–(*x2*, *y2*) [,[*fill*[,[*border*]]]]

```
100 VIEW (0,0)-(319,100)
```

Defines a rectangular section of the screen whose opposite corners are (0,0) and (319,100) as the graphics viewport into which the contents of WINDOW are mapped.

VIEW PRINT
Syntax:
VIEW PRINT [*topline* TO *bottomline*]

```
100 VIEW PRINT 1 TO 10
```

Sets boundaries of screen text window to the area between the 1st and 10th row on the screen.

WAIT
Syntax:
WAIT *port number n*[*,j*]

```
100 WAIT 24, 2
```

Causes the program to wait until port 24 receives a 2 as input.

WHILE...WEND
Syntax:
WHILE *expression*
[*loop statements*]
WEND

```
100 X=0
110 WHILE X=0
120     INPUT X
130     Y=Y + X
140 WEND
150 PRINT "TOTAL=";Y
```

Causes the statements between WHILE and WEND to loop until a nonzero value for X is input.

WIDTH
Syntax:
WIDTH *size*
WIDTH *file number, size*
WIDTH *"device", size*

Appendix A

```
100 WIDTH "LPT1:", 40
```

Sets the printer width to 40 characters per line.

WINDOW
Syntax:
WINDOW[[SCREEN]($x1,y1$)-($x2,y2$)]

```
100 WINDOW (0, 0)-(10, 10)
```

Defines screen as a window so that the lower left-hand corner is coordinates (0,0) and the upper right-hand corner is coordinates (10, 10).

WRITE
Syntax:
WRITE[*list of expressions*]

```
100 A=10: B=20: C$="Goodbye."
110 WRITE A,B,C$
```

Similar to PRINT, but inserts commas and quotes. Example displays 10,20,"Goodbye."

WRITE #
Syntax:
WRITE #*file number*, *list of expressions*

```
100 WRITE #1, A$, B$
```

Writes the variables A$ and B$ to the sequential file opened as #1. Automatically inserts commas between items and quotes around strings.

Appendix B

Numbering Systems

"What's one and one and one and one and one and one and one and one and one and one?"
"I don't know," said Alice. "I lost count."
"She can't do addition," said the Red Queen.
(Lewis Carroll, *Through the Looking Glass*)

No one knows when the first number was recorded, but most likely it dates back to Biblical times. Among the oldest system of numbers was that of the Chinese, which was first based on a system of laying sticks in patterns and later was based on symbols drawn with pen and ink (fig. B-1).

Chinese "stick" number system.

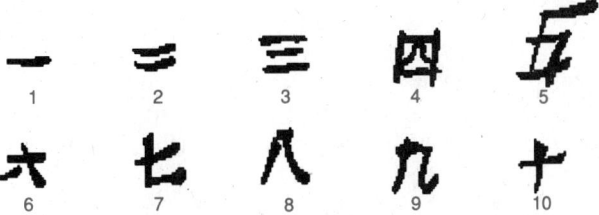

Chinese "pen-and-ink" number systems.

Fig. B-1: First number systems.

Appendix B

Calculating in these number systems was exceedingly difficult. This was because each time the basic numerals were exceeded, a new numeral had to be invented. In Roman numerals, when you needed to count above 100, you used a C, and above 1000, an M. The real problem came when these numbers had to be multiplied. The actual process of counting took place on counting boards, such as the Chinese abacus, where answers were converted back to the notation system.

Our current decimal system is much more streamlined than those of the ancient civilizations. We have only to learn the 10 basic symbols and the positional notation system in order to count to any number. For example, what is the meaning of the number 256? In positional notation, the value of each digit is determined by its position. The four in 4000 has a different value than the four in 400. Thus, in 256, we have three digits and each must be "interpreted" in light of where it is in order and relation to the other digits. We learn that the rightmost digit is interpreted as the number of "ones," the next to the left as the number of "tens," and the next digit as "hundreds." The general formula for representing numbers in the decimal system using positional notation is as follows:

$$a_1 10^{n-1} + a_2 10^{n-2} + \ldots + a_n$$

which is expressed as $a_1 a_2 a_3 \ldots a_n$, in which n is the number of digits to the left of the decimal point. Therefore,

$$256 = (2 \times 10^2) + (5 \times 10^1) + (6 \times 10^0)$$
$$= 2 \text{ hundreds} + 5 \text{ tens} + 6 \text{ ones}$$

In the decimal system we use 10 as the basic multiplier. We call 10 the *base* or *radix*. Most of recorded history shows mankind counting in the decimal system (base 10). However, it is not difficult to imagine a race of one-armed people who used the quinary system (base 5). Moreover, we see examples of the duodecimal system in clocks, rulers, the dozen, and so on.

The Binary System

Although the seventeenth-century German mathematician Leibnitz was given most of the credit for invention of the binary number system with a base of 2, it was probably the ancient Chinese who realized the simple and natural way of representing numbers as powers of 2.

Numbering Systems

Early computers used relays and switches as their basic elements. The operation of a switch or a relay is itself binary in nature. A switch can either be on (1) or off (0). Modern computers use tiny integrated circuits, each containing tens of thousands of gates, or transistors. These gates can be set in one or two *states*: on, or off. As a matter of fact, the more distinctly different the two states, the more reliable the computer's operation.

The idea is to make the devices work in such a manner that even slight changes in their characteristics will not affect the operation. The best way of doing this is to use a *bistable* device, which has two states.

If a bistable device is in stable state X, an energy pulse will drive it to state Y; and if the bistable component is in stable state Y, an energy pulse will drive it to state X. It is easy for a bistable component to represent the number 0 or 1:

stable state X = 1
stable state Y = 0

Counting

The same type of positional notation used in the decimal system is used in the binary, because there are only two possible states for a numeral: either we count the position value or we don't count it. The general rule is as follows: The binary number $a_1 a_2 a_3 \ldots a_n$ is expressed in decimal as:

$$a_1 2^{n-1} + a_2 2^{n-2} + \ldots + a_n$$

Therefore, the binary number 11010 is converted to decimal as follows:

$$N = a_1 2^{5-1} + a_2 2^{4-1} + a_3 2^{3-1} + a_4 2^{2-1} + a_5 2^{1-1}$$
$$= a_1 16 + a_2 8 + a_3 4 + a_4 2 + a_5 1$$

Substituting the values for a_1, a_2, a_3, a_4, and a_5:

$$11010 = (1 \times 16) + (1 \times 8) + (0 \times 4) + (1 \times 2) + (0 \times 1)$$
$$= (16 + 8 + 0 + 2 + 0)$$
$$= 26 \text{ (decimal system)}$$

Appendix B

Table B-1 lists the first 20 binary numbers.

Table B-1: The first 20 binary numbers.

Decimal	Binary	Decimal	Binary
1	1	11	1011
2	10	12	1100
3	11	13	1101
4	100	14	1110
5	101	15	1111
6	110	16	10000
7	111	17	10001
8	1000	18	10010
9	1001	19	10011
10	1010	20	10100

A simpler way to convert binary numbers to decimal is to use a weighting table (fig. B-2). This is simply a reduction of the expansion formula just presented. Write down the value of the positions in the binary number over the binary digits, arrange them as an addition, and add them.

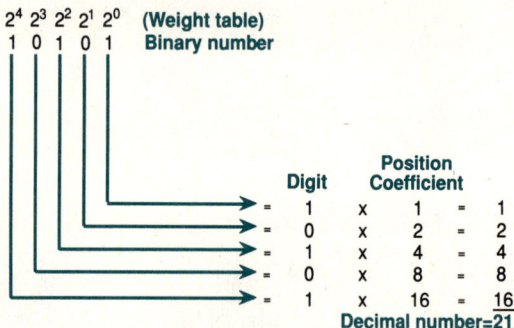

Fig. B-2: Binary-to-decimal conversion using the weighting method.

Frequently we will want to convert in the opposite direction, from decimal to binary. For this method, we repeatedly divide the decimal number by 2, and the remainder after each division is used to indicate the coefficients of the binary number

Numbering Systems

to be formed. Fig. B-3 shows the conversion of 47_{10} to binary. Note that decimal 47 is written 47_{10} and that binary numbers are given the subscript 2 if there is danger of confusing the number systems.

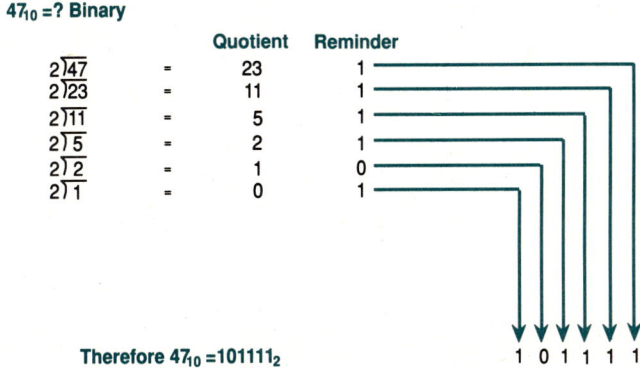

Fig. B-3: Decimal-to-binary conversion using the division method.

Fractional numbers are treated in the same manner as in the decimal system. In the decimal system:

$$0.128 = (1 \times 10^{-1}) + (2 \times 10^{-2}) + (8 \times 10^{-3})$$

In the binary system:

$$0.101 = (1 \times 2^{-1}) + (0 \times 2^{-2}) + (1 \times 2^{-3})$$

Binary Addition and Subtraction

Addition in binary is as easy as addition in decimal, and follows the same rules. In adding decimal 1 + 8, we get a sum of 9. This is the highest-value digit. Adding 1 to 9 requires that we change the digit back to 0 and carry 1. Similarly, adding binary 0 + 1, we reach the highest-value binary digit, 1. Adding 1 to 1 requires that we change the 1 back to a 0 and carry 1, that is, 1 + 1 = 10. Thus, for example, add binary 101 to 111:

$$\begin{array}{rcl} 101_2 & = & 5_{10} \\ + \ 111_2 & = & 7_{10} \\ \hline 1100_2 & = & 12_{10} \end{array}$$

565

Appendix B

The four rules of binary addition are as follows:

$0 + 0 = 0$
$0 + 1 = 1$
$1 + 0 = 1$
$1 + 1 = 0$, carry 1

Here are some examples:

Binary	Decimal	Binary	Decimal
101	5	11.01	3 1/4
+ 110	6	101.11	5 3/4
1011	11	1001.00	9

Subtraction is just inverted addition. It is necessary to establish a convention for subtracting a large digit from a small digit. This condition occurs in binary math when we subtract a 1 from 0. The remainder is 1, and we borrow 1 from the column to the left. Just as in decimal subtraction, if the digit on the left is a 1, we make it a zero, and if it's a zero, we make it a 1. The rules for binary subtraction are:

$0 - 0 = 0$
$1 - 0 = 1$
$1 - 1 = 0$
$0 - 1 = 1$, borrow 1

Here are two examples:

Binary	Decimal	Binary	Decimal
10000	16	110.01	6 1/4
− 11	− 3	− 100.1	− 4 1/2
1101	13	1.11	1 3/4

Binary Multiplication and Division

There are only four basic multiplications to remember in the binary system, rather than the usual 100 we memorize in the decimal system. The binary multiplication table is as follows:

$0 \times 0 = 0$
$1 \times 0 = 0$
$0 \times 1 = 0$
$1 \times 1 = 1$

The following examples illustrate how easy binary multiplication is compared with decimal. The rule to remember is, "copy the multiplicand if the multiplier is a 1, and copy all 0's if the multiplier is a 0. Then add down, as in decimal multiplication."

```
   Binary        Decimal        Binary        Decimal
    1100           12             1.01          1.25
  x 1010         x  10          x 10.1        x  2.5
    0000           120             101           625
    1100                          1010           250
   0000                          11.001         3.125
  1100
 1111000
```

Binary division is also very simple. Division by zero is forbidden (meaningless), just as in decimal division. The binary division table is as follows:

$$\frac{0}{1} = 0 \qquad \frac{1}{1} = 1$$

Examples of binary division are:

```
       Binary              Decimal
         101                  5
    101)11001              5)25
         101
          101
          101
```

Because of the difficult binary additions and subtractions that result when the numbers are large, octal or hexadecimal notation is often used.

Representing Binary Numbers

Information in digital computers of today is processed by the switching and storing of electrical signals. Computers operating in the binary number system need represent only one of two values (1 and 0) at a time. A single wire can be utilized for this purpose. A method for representing a binary digit on a signal line is shown in fig. B-4(a). In this method a small positive voltage is used to represent a 0, and a large positive dc voltage is used to represent a 1.

Much importance is placed on the actual voltage values used to represent the binary digit. Usually, the circuitry used to transmit and receive these signals determines the range of voltages. The ideal circuit is one in which the two logic levels are far apart, as shown in fig. B-4(b).

Appendix B

Note that the "1" signal is positive with respect to the "0" signal. This convention could also have been reversed, that is, the more negative signal called a "1" and the more positive signal a "0," as shown in fig. B-4(c). Usually, one convention is chosen by the designer and then used throughout a computer.

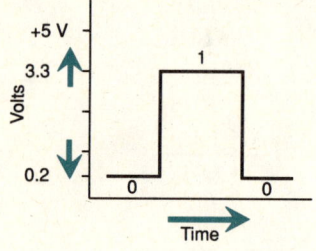

(a) Binary digit representation (TTL).

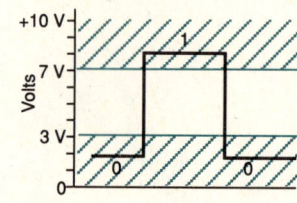

(b) Binary digit representation (CMOS).

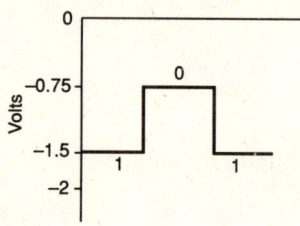

(c) Binary digit representation—negative logic (ECL).

Fig. B-4: Representing binary numbers.

Pulse Representation of Binary Numbers

Binary digits are often transmitted and received as a burst of pulses. Fig. B-5(a) shows a system in which a positive pulse represents a 1 and a negative pulse a 0. The signal line remains at some in-between value when no pulse is being sent. This technique is used frequently in magnetic recording, and is called *return-to-zero* (RZ) encoding.

Numbering Systems

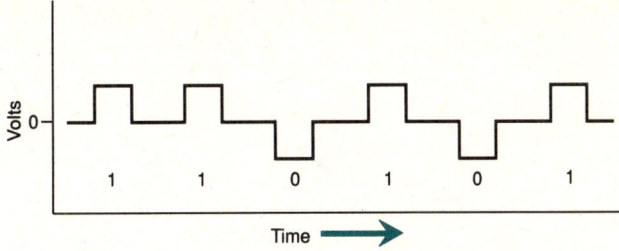

(a) RZ method of representing binary digits.

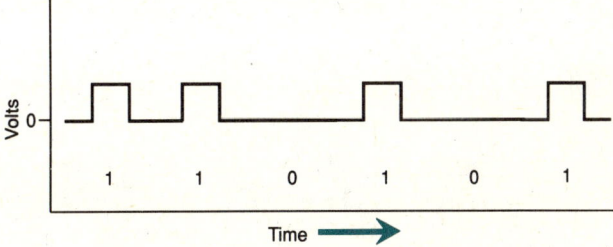

(b) NRZ method of representing binary digits.

Fig. B-5: Pulse representation of binary numbers.

A more popular technique is shown in fig. B-5(b). A 1 is represented by a pulse, and a 0 is no pulse. The receive circuitry must keep in synchronization with the incoming signal in order to know when a binary digit is occurring. This technique is called *non-return-to-zero* (NRZ) encoding.

Serial and Parallel Transmission

So far, methods of representing and transmitting a single binary digit have been illustrated. We will find that it is often necessary to transmit complete binary numbers, which is accomplished by transmitting each binary digit over its own wire. Thus, an *n*-digit binary number would require *n* wires or signal lines. This is called *parallel transmission*. Fig. B-6(a) illustrates an 8-bit binary number (10010101) being transmitted over eight parallel lines. In such a system, each line is assigned a different weight, based on the positional notation of the binary number system. The leftmost binary digit is assigned the weight of 2^{n-1}, in which *n* is the number of binary digits (8 in this case).

569

Appendix B

The other method of transmitting binary data is called *serial transmission*. In this method, the signals representing the binary digits are transmitted one at a time in sequence, usually starting with the rightmost digit, as shown in Fig. B-6(b). This method requires some synchronization in order to distinguish several 0's or 1's that follow each other in a sequence. It is also much slower than parallel transmission.

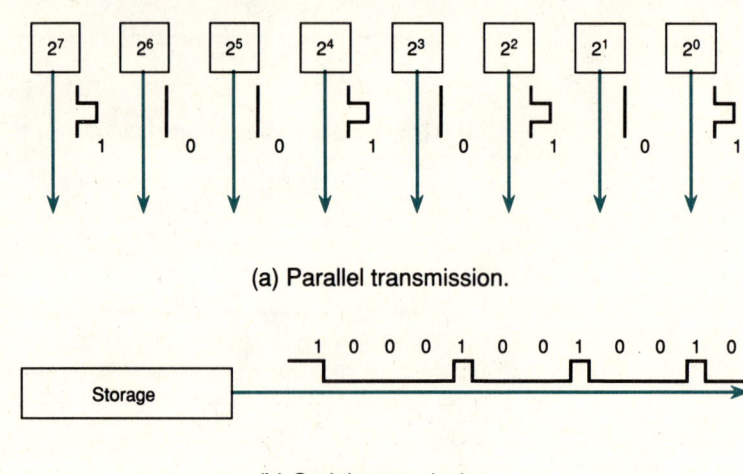

(a) Parallel transmission.

(b) Serial transmission.

Fig. B-6: Parallel and serial transmission.

Negative Numbers

The normal way to express a negative number is to place a minus sign in front of the number. When a negative number is subtracted from a positive number, we *change the sign and add*. For example, 256 − (−128) = 256 + 128 = 384.

Digital computers use binary storage devices to store and represent binary digits. Seven such devices can represent the binary numbers from 0000000 to 1111111 (0 to 127_{10}). If we wish to increase the range to include the negative numbers from 0000000 to −1111111, however, we need another binary digit, or bit. This bit is called the *sign bit* and is placed in front of the most significant digit of the binary number.

The convention for the sign bit is as follows: If the sign bit is 0, the number is positive; if the sign bit is a 1, the number is negative. The remaining digits form the absolute value of the number. This numerical storage mode is called *signed binary*. Fig. B-7(a) shows signed binary numbers from +127 to −127, and the signed binary number line is shown in Fig. B-7(b).

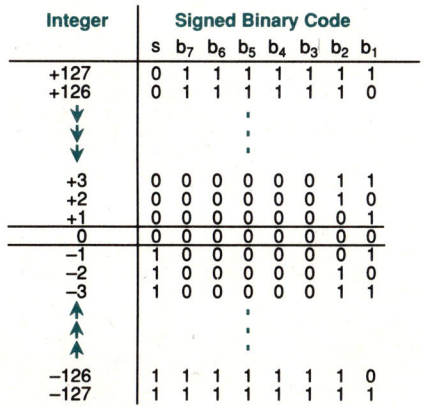

(a) Seven-bit magnitude table.

(b) Signed binary number line (seventh-bit magnitude).

Fig. B-7: Signed binary code.

Signed binary, although frequently used, has a few minor flaws that make it less flexible than other codes for negative numbers. Any arithmetic operation requires checking the sign bit and then either adding or subtracting the numerical values, based on the signs.

Appendix B

The Use of Complements

The use of complemented binary numbers makes it possible to add or subtract numbers using only circuitry for addition. To see how negative numbers are used in the computer, consider a mechanical register, such as a car mileage indicator, being rotated backwards. A five-digit register approaching and passing through zero would read as follows:

```
00005
00004
00003
00002
00001
00000
99999
99998
99997
```
etc.

It should be clear that the number 99998 corresponds to −2. Furthermore, if we add

```
  00005
+ 99998
1 00003
```

and ignore the carry to the left, we have effectively formed the operation of subtraction: 5 − 2 = 3.

The number 99998 is called the *ten's complement* of 2. The ten's complement of any decimal number may be formed by subtracting each digit of the number from 9, then adding 1 to the least significant digit of the number formed. For example,

Normal subtraction		*Ten's complement subtraction*
89 − 23 ── 66	89 − 23 ──	89 + 77 ── →1 66 DROP CARRY

Two's Complement

The two's complement is the binary equivalent of the ten's complement in the decimal system. It is defined as that number which, when added to the original number, will result in a sum of zero, ignoring the carry. The following example points this out:

```
         1101     Number
         0011     Two's complement
      →10000      Sum
   ⌊IGNORE CARRY
```

The easiest method of finding the two's complement of a binary number is to first find the one's complement, which is formed by setting each bit to the opposite value:

```
11011101     Number
00100010     One's complement
```

The two's complement of the number is then obtained by adding 1 to the least significant digit of the one's complement:

```
11011101     Number
00100010     One's complement
      +1     Add one
00100011     Two's complement
```

The complete signed two's complement code is obtained for negative numbers by using a 1 for the sign bit, and two's complement for the magnitude of the number. Fig. B-8(a) shows the signed two's complement code, and its number line is shown in fig. B-8(b).

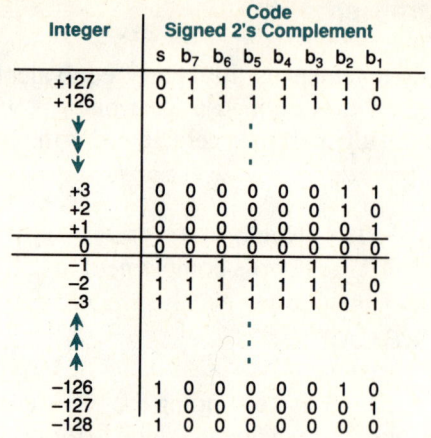

(a) Seven-bit magnitude table.

(b) Two's complement number line.

Fig. B-8: Signed two's complement code.

In contrast to the signed binary code, in the signed two's complement code, numbers can be added without regard to their signs and the result will always be correct. The following examples should make this clear:

$$
\begin{array}{rr}
0000101 & 5 \\
+\ 1111110 & +(-2) \\
\hline
\rightarrow 1\ 0000011 & 3 \\
\text{IGNORE} &
\end{array}
\qquad
\begin{array}{rr}
1111011 & -5 \\
+\ 0000010 & +(+2) \\
\hline
1111101 & (-3)
\end{array}
\qquad
\begin{array}{rr}
1111011 & -5 \\
+\ 1111110 & +(-2) \\
\hline
\rightarrow 1\ 1111001 & (-7) \\
\text{IGNORE} &
\end{array}
$$

Notice that it is impossible to add +64 to +64 in a 7-bit code and −128 to −128 in an 8-bit code. Also note that in comparing the two systems, signed binary and two's complement, the largest negative two's complement number that can be represented in 8 bits is −128, whereas in signed binary it's −127. Changing a negative integer from signed binary to two's complement requires simply complementing all bits except the sign bit, and adding 1.

Binary-Coded Number Representation

Because computers operate in the binary number system, while people use the decimal system it was only natural that some intermediate system was developed. Computers, and some calculators and "intelligent" instruments, use a *binary-coded decimal* system. In such systems, a group of binary bits is used to represent each of the 10 decimal digits.

The binary-coded decimal (BCD) system is called a *weighted binary code* with the weights 8, 4, 2, and 1, as shown in Table B-2 later in this section. Notice that 4 binary bits are required for each decimal digit, and that each digit is assigned a weight: the leftmost bit has a weight of 8; the rightmost bit a weight of 1.

There's a slight problem with using 4 bits to represent 10 decimal values. Because $2^4 = 16$, the 4 bits could actually represent 16 values. However, the next choice down, 3 bits, allows only 2^3, or 8, possible digits, which is insufficient. To represent the decimal number 127 in BCD, 12 binary bits are required rather than seven if we use pure binary:

```
   1       2       7
 0001    0010    0111
```

The BCD system has another property that makes it less flexible for binary computation in the computer. The difficulty lies in forming complements of its numbers. As was pointed out, it is common practice to perform subtraction by complementing the subtrahend and adding 1. When the BCD 8–4–2–1 system is used, the complement formed by inverting all the bits may produce an illegal BCD digit. For example, complementing the BCD number 0010 (2_{10}) gives 1101 (13_{10}), which is not a BCD code.

To solve this problem, several other codes have been developed. One code is the "excess-three" code, which is formed by adding 3 to the decimal number and then forming the BCD code. For example,

```
    4         Number
   +3         Add for excess-three
   ──
    7
    7  =  0111   Convert 7 to BCD
```

Table B-2 also shows the excess-three codes for the 10 decimal digits. Now the complement of the excess-three code doesn't form any illegal BCD digits, that is, 10_{10} or above.

The excess-three code is not a weighted code, because the sum of the bits does not equal the number being represented. On the other hand, the BCD 8–4–2–1 code is weighted but forms illegal complements.

A weighted code that does form legal complements is the 2–4–2–1 code in table B-2.

Appendix B

Table B-2: Binary-coded number representation.

Decimal Digit	Binary Coded Decimal	Excess-3 Coded Binary	2-4-2-1 Coded Binary Weight of Bit			
			2	4	2	1
0	0000	0011	0	0	0	0
1	0001	0100	0	0	0	1
2	0010	0101	0	0	1	0
3	0011	0110	0	0	1	1
4	0100	0111	0	1	0	0
5	0101	1000	1	0	1	1
6	0110	1001	1	1	0	0
7	0111	1010	1	1	0	1
8	1000	1011	1	1	1	0
9	1001	1100	1	1	1	1

Octal Number System

It is probably quite evident by now that the binary number system, although nice for computers, is a little cumbersome for human usage. For example, communicating binary 11011010 over a telephone would be "one-one-zero-one-one-zero-one-zero," which is quite a mouthful. Also, it is easy to make errors when adding and subtracting large binary numbers. The octal (base 8) number system alleviates most of these problems and was formerly used frequently when talking about computers. It has largely been replaced by hexadecimal (base 16) notation in microcomputer literature.

The octal system uses the digits 0 through 7 in forming numbers. Table B-3 shows octal numbers and their decimal equivalents.

Numbering Systems

Table B-3: First 13 Octal digits.

Decimal	Octal	Binary	Decimal	Octal	Binary
0	0	0	7	7	111
1	1	1	8	10	1000
2	2	10	9	11	1001
3	3	11	10	12	1010
4	4	100	11	13	1011
5	5	101	12	14	1100
6	6	110	13	15	1101

Octal numbers are converted to decimal numbers by using the same expansion formula as that used in binary-to-decimal conversion, except that 8 is used for the base instead of 2.

$$
\begin{aligned}
\text{(Octal) } 167 &= (1 \times 8^2) + (6 \times 8^1) + (7 \times 8^0) \\
&= (1 \times 64) + (6 \times 8) + (7 \times 1) \\
&= 64 + 48 + 7 \\
&= 119 \text{ (Decimal)}
\end{aligned}
$$

A weighting table (fig. B-9) is a quick way to convert octal values to decimal.

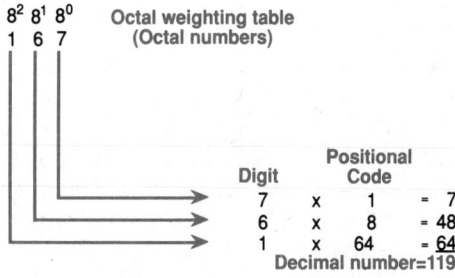

Fig. B-9: Octal-to-decimal conversion.

Appendix B

Octal is a convenient way of recording values stored in binary registers. This is accomplished by using a grouping method to convert the binary value to its octal equivalent. The binary number is grouped by threes, starting with the bit corresponding to $2^0 = 1$ and grouping to the left of it. Then each binary group is converted to its octal equivalent. For example, convert 11110101 to octal:

```
   011        110        101      Binary number
    3          6          5       Octal equivalent
 ↗
Implied 0
```

The largest 8-bit octal number is 377_8, and the largest 7-bit octal number is 177_8. Negative octal numbers in 8-bit signed two's complement cover 377_8 (-1_{10}) to 200_8 (-128_{10}).

Conversion from decimal to octal is performed by repeated division by 8 and using the remainder as a digit in the octal number being formed. Fig. B-10 illustrates this method.

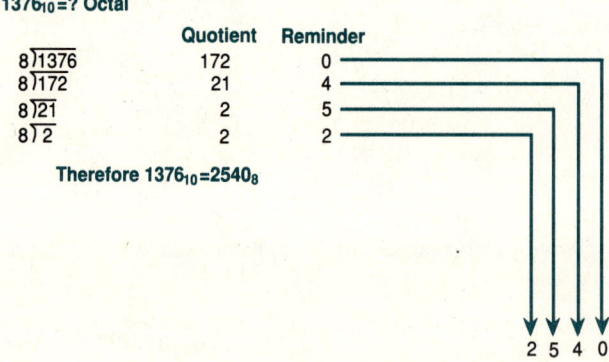

Fig. B-10:   Decimal-to-octal conversion.

Addition in Octal

Octal addition is easy if we remember the following rules (which we will find also apply to hexadecimal):

1. If the sum of any column is equal to or greater than the base of the system being used, the base must be subtracted from the sum to obtain the final result of the column.

2. If the sum of any column is equal to or greater than the base, there will be a carry, equal to the number of times the base was subtracted.

3. If the result of any column is less than the base, the base is not subtracted and no carry will be generated.

Examples:

```
Octal    Decimal              Octal      Decimal
  5       = 5                   35    =    29
 +3       = 3                  +63   =    +51
  8                          1 10  8
 -8                           -8 -8
 10       = 8                1 2  0   =    80
```

Octal Subtraction

Octal subtraction can be performed directly or in the complemented mode by using addition. In direct subtraction, whenever a borrow is needed, an 8 is borrowed and added to the number. For example,

$2022_8 - 1234_8 = ?$

$$\begin{array}{r} 2022_8 \\ 1234_8 \\ \hline 566_8 \end{array}$$

Octal subtraction can also be performed by finding the eight's complement and adding. The eight's complement is found by adding 1 to the seven's complement. The seven's complement of the number may be found by subtracting each digit from 7. For example,

$377_8 - 261_8 = ?$

a)
```
     777
    -261        (Second number)
     516        7's complement
    + 1
     517        8's complement
```
b)
```
     377        (First number)
    +517        8's complement of 261
    9 9 14
   -8 -8 -8
    1 1 6  = 116₈
```

Appendix B

Octal Multiplication

Octal multiplication is performed by using an octal multiplication table (see Table B-4) in the same manner as a decimal table would be used. All additions are done by using the rules for octal addition. For example,

$$17_8 \times 6_8 = ? \qquad 177_8 \times 27_8 = ?$$

```
       Octal         Decimal              Octal         Decimal
          17    =       15                  177    =      127
         x 6    =      x 6                  x27    =      x23
       1 11  2          90                 1371           381
      – 0 –8 –0                              376           254
       1  3  2  = 132₈               5 11 13  1          2921
                                    – 0 – 8 – 8 – 0
                                     5  3  5  1 = 5351₈
```

Numbers are multiplied by looking up the result in the table. The result of any product larger than 7 (the radix or base) is carried and then octally added to the next product. The results are then summed up by using octal addition.

Table B-4: Octal multiplication table.

x	0	1	2	3	4	5	6	7
0	0	0	0	0	0	0	0	0
1	0	1	2	3	4	5	6	7
2	0	2	4	6	10	12	14	16
3	0	3	6	11	14	17	22	25
4	0	4	10	14	20	24	30	34
5	0	5	12	17	24	31	36	43
6	0	6	14	22	30	36	44	52
7	0	7	16	25	34	43	52	61

Octal Division

Octal division uses the same principles as decimal division. All multiplication and subtraction involved, however, must be done in octal. Refer to table B-4, the octal multiplication table. Some examples include:

$$144 \div 2_8 = ?$$

$$\frac{144_8}{2_8} = \frac{100_{100}}{2_{10}} = 50_{10} = 62_8$$

$62_8 \div 2_8 = ?$

$$2 \overline{)62} \quad 31 = 31_8 = 25_{10}$$
$$\underline{6}$$
$$02$$
$$\underline{2}$$
$$0$$

$1714_8 \div 22_8 = ?$

$$22 \overline{)1714} \quad 66 = 66_8 = 54_{10}$$
$$\underline{154}$$
$$154$$
$$\underline{154}$$

The Hexadecimal System

Hexadecimal is now more important than octal as a computer number system. "Hex" uses the radix 16 and, therefore, has 16 digits. The first 10 digits are represented by the decimal digits 0 through 9, and the remaining six are indicated by the letters A, B, C, D, E, and F. There is nothing special about these letters, and any other letters could have been used. Table B-5 shows the first 16 hexadecimal digits.

Table B-5: First 16 hexadecimal digits.

Binary	Hexadecimal	Decimal
0000	0	0
0001	1	1
0010	2	2
0011	3	3
0100	4	4
0101	5	5
0110	6	6
0111	7	7

(continued)

Appendix B

Table B-5: *(continued)*

Binary	Hexadecimal	Decimal
1000	8	8
1001	9	9
1010	A	10
1011	B	11
1100	C	12
1101	D	13
1110	E	14
1111	F	15

Binary numbers are easily converted to hex by grouping the bits in groups of four, starting on the right, converting the results to decimal, and then converting to hex. For example,

1000	1010	1101	Binary
8	10	13	Decimal
8	A	D	Hex = $8AD_{16}$

As you can probably tell, hex is preferred over octal whenever the binary number to be represented is 16 bits or more, which is the case in today's PCs. This is because the hex code is more compact than the octal equivalent.

Conversion from hexadecimal to decimal is straightforward but time-consuming. The expansion formula, or a weighting table with an intermediary hex-to-decimal conversion, is used as shown in fig. B-11.

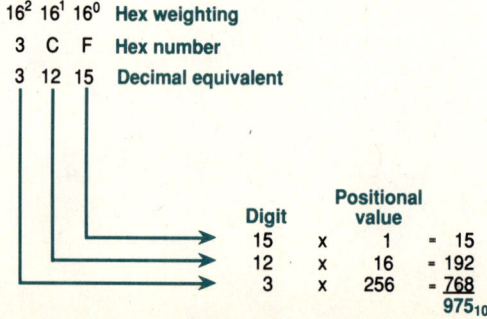

Fig. B-11: Hexadecimal-to-decimal conversion.

Conversion from decimal to hex is performed by repeatedly dividing by 16 and converting the remainder to a hex digit. The quotient becomes the next number to divide. This is shown in fig. B-12.

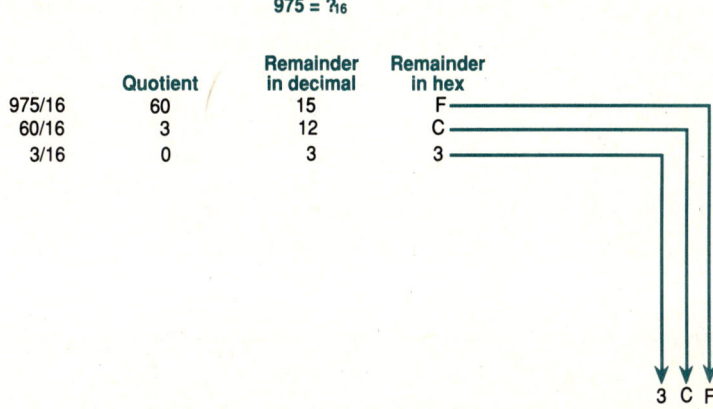

Fig. B-12:   Decimal-to-hexadecimal conversion.

Hexadecimal Addition

Addition in hex is similar to the addition procedure for octal, except that the hex digits are first converted to decimal. For example,

$$
\begin{array}{r}
3CF + 2AD = ? \\
+2AD = +2\ \ 10\ \ 13 \\
\underline{3CF}\underline{3\ \ 12\ \ 15} \\
6\ \ 23\ \ 28 \\
\underline{-0-16-16} \\
6\ \ \ \ 7\ \ 12 = 67C
\end{array}
$$

Appendix B

Subtraction in Hexadecimal

Subtraction in hex may be accomplished by either the direct or the complement method. In the direct method, the hex digits are converted to decimal. If a borrow is required, 16 is added to the desired number and the digit borrowed from is decreased by 1. In the complement method, the sixteen's complement of the subtrahend is determined and the two numbers are added. The sixteen's complement is found by adding 1 to the fifteen's complement. The fifteen's complement is found by subtracting each of the hex digits from F. For example,

$$2BD - 1CE = ?$$

```
   FFF   =    15    15    15
 − 1CE       − 1    12    14    Second number
              14     3     1    15's complement
                          + 1
              14     3     2    16's complement
   2BD   =   + 2    11    13    First number
        →1    16    14    15
             −16    −0    −0
                                = EF (answer)
 IGNORE CARRY
```

Hexadecimal Multiplication

Direct hex multiplication is rather tedious and time-consuming. This is because there are 256 entries in a hex multiplication table. The best method is to convert to decimal by using the expansion polynomial, and then convert back from decimal to hex after computation.

Appendix **C**

ASCII—Numeric Conversions and Keyboard Scan Codes

Decimal-Hexadecimal-Octal-Binary-ASCII Numerical Conversion

DEC X_{10}	HEX X_{16}	OCT X_8	P	Binary X_2	ASCII
0	00	00	0	000 0000	NUL
1	01	01	1	000 0001	SOH
2	02	02	1	000 0010	STX
3	03	03	0	000 0011	ETX
4	04	04	1	000 0100	EOT
5	05	05	0	000 0101	ENQ
6	06	06	0	000 0110	ACK
7	07	07	1	000 0111	BEL
8	08	10	1	000 1000	BS
9	09	11	0	000 1001	HT
10	0A	12	0	000 1010	LF

Appendix C

DEC X_{10}	HEX X_{16}	OCT X_8	Binary P X_2			ASCII
11	0B	13	1	000	1011	VT
12	0C	14	0	000	1100	FF
13	0D	15	1	000	1101	CR
14	0E	16	1	000	1110	SO
15	0F	17	0	000	1111	SI
16	10	20	1	001	0000	DLE
17	11	21	0	001	0001	DC1
18	12	22	0	001	0010	DC2
19	13	23	1	001	0011	DC3
20	14	24	0	001	0100	DC4
21	15	25	1	001	0101	NAK
22	16	26	1	001	0110	SYN
23	17	27	0	001	0111	ETB
24	18	30	0	001	1000	CAN
25	19	31	1	001	1001	EM
26	1A	32	1	001	1010	SUB
27	1B	33	0	001	1011	ESC
28	1C	34	1	001	1100	FS
29	1D	35	0	001	1101	GS
30	1E	36	0	001	1110	RS
31	1F	37	1	001	1111	US
32	20	40	1	010	0000	SP
33	21	41	0	010	0001	!
34	22	42	0	010	0010	"
35	23	43	1	010	0011	#
36	24	44	0	010	0100	$
37	25	45	1	010	0101	%

ASCII—Numeric Conversions and Keyboard Scan Codes

DEC X_{10}	HEX X_{16}	OCT X_8	Binary P	X_2		ASCII
38	26	46	1	010	0110	&
39	27	47	0	010	0111	'
40	28	50	0	010	1000	(
41	29	51	1	010	1001	)
42	2A	52	1	010	1010	*
43	2B	53	0	010	1011	+
44	2C	54	1	010	1100	,
45	2D	55	0	010	1101	-
46	2E	56	0	010	1110	.
47	2F	57	1	010	1111	/
48	30	60	0	011	0000	0
49	31	61	1	011	0001	1
50	32	62	1	011	0010	2
51	33	63	0	011	0011	3
52	34	64	1	011	0100	4
53	35	65	0	011	0101	5
54	36	66	0	011	0110	6
55	37	67	1	011	0111	7
56	38	70	1	011	1000	8
57	39	71	0	011	1001	9
58	3A	72	0	011	1010	:
59	3B	73	1	011	1011	;
60	3C	74	0	011	1100	<
61	3D	75	1	011	1101	=
62	3E	76	1	011	1110	>
63	3F	77	0	011	1111	?
64	40	100	1	100	0000	@

Appendix C

DEC X_{10}	HEX X_{16}	OCT X_8	Binary P X_2	ASCII
65	41	101	0 100 0001	A
66	42	102	0 100 0010	B
67	43	103	1 100 0011	C
68	44	104	0 100 0100	D
69	45	105	1 100 0101	E
70	46	106	1 100 0110	F
71	47	107	0 100 0111	G
72	48	110	0 100 1000	H
73	49	111	1 100 1001	I
74	4A	112	1 100 1010	J
75	4B	113	0 100 1011	K
76	4C	114	1 100 1100	L
77	4D	115	0 100 1101	M
78	4E	116	0 100 1110	N
79	4F	117	1 100 1111	O
80	50	120	0 101 0000	P
81	51	121	1 101 0001	Q
82	52	122	1 101 0010	R
83	53	123	0 101 0011	S
84	54	124	1 101 0100	T
85	55	125	0 101 0101	U
86	56	126	0 101 0110	V
87	57	127	1 101 0111	W
88	58	130	1 101 1000	X
89	59	131	0 101 1001	Y
90	5A	132	0 101 1010	Z
91	5B	133	1 101 1011	[

ASCII—Numeric Conversions and Keyboard Scan Codes

DEC X_{10}	HEX X_{16}	OCT X_8	P	Binary X_2	ASCII
92	5C	134	0	101 1100	\
93	5D	135	1	101 1101	]
94	5E	136	1	101 1110	^
95	5F	137	0	101 1111	_
96	60	140	0	110 0000	`
97	61	141	1	110 0001	a
98	62	142	1	110 0010	b
99	63	143	0	110 0011	c
100	64	144	1	110 0100	d
101	65	145	0	110 0101	e
102	66	146	0	110 0110	f
103	67	147	1	110 0111	g
104	68	150	1	110 1000	h
105	69	151	0	110 1001	i
106	6A	152	0	110 1010	j
107	6B	153	1	110 1011	k
108	6C	154	0	110 1100	l
109	6D	155	1	110 1101	m
110	6E	156	1	110 1110	n
111	6F	157	0	110 1111	o
112	70	160	1	111 0000	p
113	71	161	0	111 0001	q
114	72	162	0	111 0010	r
115	73	163	1	111 0011	s
116	74	164	0	111 0100	t
117	75	165	1	111 0101	u
118	76	166	1	111 0110	v

Appendix C

DEC X_{10}	HEX X_{16}	OCT X_8	Binary P X_2	ASCII
119	77	167	0 111 0111	w
120	78	170	0 111 1000	x
121	79	171	1 111 1001	y
122	7A	172	1 111 1010	z
123	7B	173	0 111 1011	R
124	7C	174	1 111 1100	/
125	7D	175	0 111 1101	T
126	7E	176	0 111 1110	~
127	7F	177	1 111 1111	DEL

P = Parity bit; "1" for odd number of 1's, "0" for even number of 1's

ASCII Definitions

Although ASCII codes from 1-32 (decimal) have specific names, their functions are often defined differently depending on the application. These ASCII code definitions stem from when ASCII was used ONLY for communications.

ACK (Acknowledgment)—Used as a general "yes" answer to various queries, but it also sometimes indicates, "I received your last transmission and I'm ready for your next."

ASCII—American Standard Code for Information Interchange.

BEL (Bell)—Activates a bell, beeper, or other audible alarm.

BS (Backspace)—Moves the carriage, print head, or cursor back one space or position.

CAN (Cancel)—Indicates that the material in the previous transmission is to be disregarded. The amount of material is decided by the user.

CR (Carriage Return, or Return)—Moves carriage, print head, or cursor back to beginning of line. On most computers, the Return key causes both a CR and a FF (Form feed).

DC1-DC4 (Device Controls)—These are used to control the user's terminal or similar devices. There are no standard functions assigned, except that DC4 frequently means stop. The CCITT suggests a number of possible assignments; in general, they prefer using the first two controls for *on*, and the last two for *off*, and DC2 and DC4 to refer to the more important device. In some systems, these codes are labeled XON, TAPE, XOFF, and TAPE, respectively. X means transmitter, and TAPE AND TAPE means tape on and tape off. These labels are found on the keytops of some older terminals.

DEL (Delete)—Used to delete a character. It is called RUBOUT on some terminals. It is not strictly a control character since it is not grouped with the other ASCII control characters. The DEL function has binary all-ones bit pattern ($1111\ 1111_2$), and the reason for this is historic: the only way to erase a bit pattern punched into paper tape was to punch out all the holes so that the resulting pattern was equivalent to a null. ASCII still considers DEL equivalent to a null, although many operating systems use it to erase the preceding character.

DLE (Data Link Escape)—This control function uses a special type of escape sequence specifically used for controlling the data line and transmission facilities.

EM (End of Medium)—This is used to indicate the end of paper tape (or other storage medium) or that this is the end of the material on the medium.

ENQ (Enquiry)—This is usually used for requesting identification or status information. In some systems, this code is called WRU—"Who are you?"

EOT (End of Transmission)—Code used to mark end of transmission after one or more messages.

ESC (Escape)—This code marks the beginning of an escape sequence. An escape sequence consists of a series of codes which, as a group, have a special meaning, usually a control function. On some terminals, ESC is called ALT MODE.

ETB (End of Transmission Block)—This code is used when it is desired to break up a long message into blocks. ETB is used to mark block boundaries. The blocks usually have nothing to do with the format of the message being transmitted.

ETX (End of Text)—This code is used to mark the end of a text. See SOH. This code was originally called EOM, "End Of Message," and may be labeled as such on some terminals.

FF (Form Feed)—Advance to the top of next page.

FS, GS, RS, US (File, Group, Record and Unit Separator)—These are a set of codes that are used as "information separators" for delimiting portions of information. There is no standard usage, except that FS is expected to refer to the largest division, and US to the smallest.

HT (Horizontal Tab)—Used to tab carriage, print wheel, or cursor to the next predetermined stop on the same line. It is usually up to the user to decide where the horizontal tab stops are to be positioned.

LF (Line Feed)—This code moves the carriage, print head, or cursor down one line. Most systems combine CR (carriage return) with LF, and new line is then called new line (NL).

NAK (Negative Acknowledgment)—Used to indicate No in answer to various queries. It is sometimes defined as "I received your last transmission, but it had errors and I'm awaiting a retransmission."

NUL (Null)—This code is used mainly as a space filler. See also SYN.

SI (Shift In)—Used after an SO code to indicate that codes revert to normal ASCII meaning.

Appendix C

SO (Shift Out)—Indicates that bit patterns to follow will have meanings outside the standard ASCII set and will continue to do so until SI is entered.

SOH (Start Of Heading)—This code is used to mark the beginning of a heading, when headings are used in messages along with text. Headings usually state the name and location of an addressee. This code was originally called SOM, "Start Of Message."

STX (Start of Text)—Used as a marker for beginning of text and end of heading (if used). Was originally called EOA, "End Of Address."

SUB (Substitute)—Indicates a character that is to be used to take the place of a character known to be wrong.

SYN (Synchronous Idle)—Some high-speed data communications systems use synchronized clocks at the transmitter and receiver ends. During idle periods, when there are no bit patterns to enable the receiver's clock to track the transmitter's, the receive may drift out of sync. Every transmission following an idle period is therefore replaced by three or four SYN characters. The SYN code has a bit pattern that enables the receiver not only to lock onto the transmitter's clock, but also to determine the beginning and end points of each character. SYN characters may also be used to fill short idle periods to maintain synchronization, hence the name.

VT (Vertical Tab)—Used to tab the carriage, print head, or cursor to the next predetermined stop (usually a line).

Key Scan Codes

This table shows scan codes for the keys on the 101-key IBM keyboard. Scan codes are used in key trapping by the KEY statement.

Key	Decimal Scan Code
Esc	01
1/!	02
2/@	03
3/#	04
4$	05
5/%	06
6/^	07
7/&	08
8/*	09
9/(	10

ASCII—Numeric Conversions and Keyboard Scan Codes

Key	Decimal Scan Code
0/)	11
-/_	12
=/+	13
Backspace	14
Tab	15
Q	16
W	17
E	18
R	19
T	20
Y	21
U	22
I	23
O	24
P	25
[/{	26
]/}	27
Enter	28
Ctrl	29
A	30
S	31
D	32
F	33
G	34
H	35
J	36
K	37
L	38

Appendix C

Key	Decimal Scan Code
;/:	39
'/"	40
'/~	41
Left Shift	42
|	43
Z	44
X	45
C	46
V	47
B	48
N	49
M	50
,/<	51
./>	52
//?	53
Right Shift	54
*/Prtsc	55
Alt	56
Spacebar	57
Caps Lock	58
F1	59
F2	60
F3	61
F4	62
F5	63
F6	64
F7	65
F8	66

ASCII—Numeric Conversions and Keyboard Scan Codes

Key	Decimal Scan Code
F9	67
F10	68
Num Lock	69
Scroll Lock	70
7/Home	71
8/Cursor Up	72
9/Pgup	73
-	74
4/Cursor Left	75
5	76
6/Cursor Right	77
+	78
1/End	79
2/Cursor Down	80
3/Pgdn	81
0/Ins	82
./Del	83

Appendix **D**

Tips to Save Memory

When writing a big program, you might often encounter an error statement in BASIC such as "Out of memory." This indicates that your program is too large for the amount of memory space (64 Kbytes) allowed for BASIC. To determine the number of bytes consumed by your application program, you can use the FRE (free) function as follows:

```
PRINT FRE(0)
 1024
Ok
```

The FRE function returns the number of bytes "unused" by the current program. Thus we have 1024 bytes unused and still available.

This is all nice, but there is a Murphy's law that states:

FOR EVERY "K" BYTES OF AVAILABLE MEMORY, A PROGRAM WILL EXCEED THIS AMOUNT BY 256 BYTES.

Thus, you will eventually be faced with the prospect of figuring out how to shorten your program. Here are some "space-slashing" techniques you can apply to help keep the program smaller and save valuable memory space.

1. *Use multiple statements per line*. There is a small amount of overhead associated with each line in the program. Putting as many statements as possible on a line will cut down the number of bytes used by your program. A single line can usually contain up to 255 characters.

597

Appendix D

2. *Delete all REM statements*. This is only a good idea if you don't want anyone to understand how your program works. Each REM statement uses at least one byte of memory plus the number of bytes in the text of the REM statement. For example, the statement

```
100 REM PROGRAM WRITTEN BY RAMON PEABODY
```

uses up 5 + 1 + 33 or 39 bytes.

In the statement,

```
200 I = I + 1: REM INCREMENT INDEX
```

the REM uses 18 bytes of memory including the colon before REM. The ' symbol used here would consume one less byte because no colon is required.

3. *Use integers rather than single-precision variables*. Integer variables are stored in 2 bytes; single precisions are stored in 4 bytes. Thus, use integer variables in FOR...NEXT loops and whenever large accurate numbers are not needed. Use integer arrays instead of real single-precision arrays to save space consumed by arrays.

You can force a variable to be an integer variable using a DEFINT statement at the beginning of your program, or the % sign after the variable name, as in A% or A%(I,J). DEFINT I-N would make all variables beginning with the letters I, J, K, L, M, N integer variables.

4. *Use variables rather than constants*. Suppose that you use the constant 3.14159 ten times in your program. If you insert a statement,

```
10 PI = 3.14159
```

in the program, and use PI rather than 3.14159 each time it is needed, you will save 40 bytes. This will also result in a speed improvement, as explained in Appendix E.

5. *A program does not have to end with an END statement*. This will save bytes.

6. *Re-use the same variables*. (Do not do this if you wish absolute clarity in your programs.) If you have a variable S that is used to hold a temporary result in one part of the program, and you need a temporary variable later in your program, use S again. Or if you have many separate FOR...NEXT loops, the same index may be used over in each loop. Or, if you are asking the user to give a YES or NO answer to two different questions at two different times during the execution of the program, use the same temporary variable A$ to store the reply.

Tips to Save Memory

7. *Use GOSUBs.* These can be used to execute sections of program statements that perform identical actions.

8. *Remember to use the zero elements of matrices; for example, X(0), BETA(0), etc.* If you have a ten-element array required by a program use DIM ARRAY(9), and call the first element ARRAY(0) and the last element ARRAY(9).

Appendix **E**

Speed Hints

Whenever you create programs that contain long, complex mathematical equations and functions, or programs with long FOR...NEXT loops (such as those found in sorting arrays), you are likely to run into a speed problem. Although the computer runs at microsecond rates, BASIC takes many steps to "understand" the statement it is to execute, and many more steps to set things up so that the statement can be executed.

The following list of hints can be used to improve the execution time of your programs. Notice that some of these hints are the same as those used to decrease the space used by your program (see Appendix D). This means that in many cases you can increase the efficiency of both the speed and the size of your programs at the same time.

1. *Use variables rather than constants.* (This is the most important speed hint of all.) It takes more time to convert a constant to its floating point representation than it does to fetch the value of a simple or matrix integer variable. This is especially important within FOR...NEXT loops or other code that is executed repeatedly.

2. *For variables used often, define them at the beginning of a program.* Variables that are encountered first during the execution of a BASIC program are allocated at the start of the *variable table* (a special table BASIC sets up to determine the line number of a variable's first definition). This means that a statement such as `10 X = 0: Y = 4; Z = 8` will place X first, Y second, and Z third in the variable symbol table (assuming that line 10 is the first statement executed in the program). Later in the program, when BASIC finds a reference to the variable X, it will search only one entry in the symbol table to find X, two entries to find Y, and three entries to find Z.

601

Appendix E

3. *Use NEXT statements without the index variable when possible.* NEXT is somewhat faster than NEXT I because no check is made to see whether the variable specified in the NEXT statement is the same as the variable in the most recent FOR statement.

4. *Frequently referenced lines should be placed at the beginning of the program.* During program execution, when BASIC encounters a new line reference such as GOTO 100, it scans the entire user program starting at the lowest-numbered line until it finds the referenced line number. Therefore, frequently referenced lines should be placed as early in the program as possible.

5. *In FOR...NEXT loops use integer variables rather than single-precision variables.* It takes much longer to increment a single-precision variable in a loop than an integer variable.

6. *Write around remarks.* Prevent BASIC from having to "read" remarks on GOTOs and GOSUBs by putting remarks before the line number referenced. For instance,

```
500 GOSUB 1000
    .
    .
998 REM - Print subroutine
999 REM - This prints the number of widgets
1000 PRINT"There are"; WIDGETS; "widgets"
1010 RETURN
```

Appendix **F**

Exponential (Scientific) Notation

Exponential notation, which is also sometimes called scientific notation, is a way of representing numbers that are too large or too small to write conveniently in the ordinary way. When BASIC prints numbers with an E in the middle of them, like 4.78245E + 10, it is using exponential notation. In this appendix we will describe what exponential notation is, why it is useful, and how to convert between exponential and "normal" notation.

    Computers are capable of storing and performing arithmetic on very large (and very small) numbers. Just how large a number can a computer store? Would you believe one billion billion billion billion? That certainly sounds large, but it's no problem. What would a number this big actually look like written down? Let's figure it out. Think for a minute about the number *one thousand*. It is written as a 1 followed by 3 zeros: 1000. A million, which is a thousand times a thousand, or one thousand thousand, is a one with 6 zeros: 1,000,000. And a billion, which is a thousand times a million, or one thousand million, is a one with nine zeros after it: 1,000,000,000.

    Perhaps you've noticed something here: When we multiply large numbers like one thousand and one million together, we can easily find the answer just by adding up how many zeros there are in the numbers. So, one thousand, with 3 zeros, times one thousand, with 3 more zeros, equals one million, with 6 zeros (because 3 plus 3 is 6); and one thousand, with 3 zeros, times one million, with 6 zeros, is one billion, which has 9 zeros (because 3 plus 6 is 9).

    Using this idea, let's figure out how many zeros there are in one billion billion billion billion. Since we've already decided that there are 9 zeros in one billion, we can add 9 zeros to 9 more zeros and conclude that there are 18 zeros in one billion times one billion, which is a billion billion. There must be 18 plus 18 or 36 zeros in

Appendix F

a billion billion times a billion billion, which is a billion billion billion billion. So there's our answer: BASIC can handle numbers up to one billion billion billion billion, which is a one followed by 36 zeros, Printed, it looks like this:

1,000,000,000,000,000,000,000,000,000,000,000,000

To give yourself an idea just how big numbers like this really are, consider this: The universe is thought to be about 14 billion years old. That's 4.2 hundred million billion seconds. The speed of light is about 300,000 kilometers per second, which is 300 billion millimeters per second. (A millimeter is about the thickness of the lead in a pencil.) Multiplying the age of the universe in seconds by the speed of light in millimeters per second, we arrive at the conclusion that if a ray of light had started out at the beginning of the universe, it would have covered a distance, up to the present, of 126 billion billion billion millimeters. This written out is as follows:

126,000,000,000,000,000,000,000,000,000.0 mm

That's still a good bit smaller than the size of the number BASIC can handle.
"That's all very well," you might be saying, "but how could I type a number with all those zeros, or read it out again? I would probably make a mistake and type the wrong number of zeros, or not count correctly how many there are on the screen."

That's a good point. To simplify the reading and writing of large numbers, mathematicians invented a whole new way of writing numbers, called exponential notation. The idea behind exponential notation is this: instead of writing down all the zeros in a big number, we just write down how many zeros there are. How many zeros in a thousand? Three. In exponential notation, you write the number of zeros after the letter E, (which, of course, stands for "Exponential"). So, for one thousand we write 1E + 3. (The 1 before the E means one (1) thousand, and we'll explain the plus sign later.) How do we write one million? It has 6 zeros, so we write 1E + 6. How do we write one billion billion billion billion? Easy: we know it has 36 zeros, so we write 1E + 36. That's a lot more practical than writing out all those zeros, isn't it? This way of writing numbers—exponential notation—is how your computer stores single- and double-precision numbers, and how it prints numbers that are too large to print normally.

The number that follows the E in exponential notation, and represents the number of zeros in the number, is called the *exponent* of the number.

If you want to see BASIC print a number in exponential notation, type the following (in command mode):

```
PRINT 10000 * 10000
```

Exponential (Scientific) Notation

This is ten thousand (which has 4 zeros) times ten thousand (another 4 zeros), so BASIC should respond with:

```
1E + 08
```

which represents one hundred million, a number with 8 zeros. You can experiment with this, typing different values and seeing how BASIC responds.

But, you say, suppose I want to talk about a more complicated number? Do I always have to talk about one (1) of something, like one thousand or one million? Could we represent 2.75 million in exponential notation, for instance? No problem. To represent 2.75 million, we write 2.75E + 6. If we wanted to represent one hundred and twenty-five thousand (125,000), we would write 1.25E + 5. Six hundred (600) would be 6E + 2, and so on. This number, which goes to the left of the E in exponential notation, is called the *mantissa*. It is written with its first digit to the left of the decimal place, and any other digits to the right.

As you can see, a number written in exponential notation has three parts: first, the mantissa, which is the original number, but written with the decimal point to the right of the leftmost digit; second, the exponent, which is the number of zeros in the number; and third, a letter E to separate the mantissa and the exponent.

Seems pretty easy, but actually there's something we have to be careful of. Until now we have referred to the exponent (the number on the right of the E) as representing how many zeros there are in the number. Actually, this was a slight simplification. What the exponent really represents is how many digits (which may or may not be zeros) there are to the right of the first (leftmost) digit in the number. For instance, as we said previously, 2.75 million (or 2,750,000) is 2.75E + 6 in exponential notation. We write 6 after the E, not because there are 6 zeros in the number (there are 4), but because there are 6 digits following the 2, which is the leftmost or "most significant" digit.

Another way to think of the exponent is this: It tells you how many times you must multiply the mantissa (the number on the left of the E) by ten. Why is this true? Because multiplying a number by ten is the same as adding a zero on the right of the number. Or, if the number is a decimal fraction—with zeros to the right of its decimal point—we can say that multiplying by ten is the same as moving the decimal point to the right one place.

Using this idea, let's figure out what 4.234E + 4 is in normal numbers. 4.234 times 10 is 42.34. Multiply by ten again and you get 423.4, and a third time is 4234. Multiply by ten a fourth time and you get 42340, which is the number as we would normally write it, in nonexponential notation. We've multiplied 4.234 by ten 4 times, which moved the decimal point 4 places to the right. Ten times ten times ten times ten is ten thousand (10 * 10 * 10 * 10 = 10000), or 1E + 4. So, 42340 is 4.234 times ten thousand, or 4.234E + 4.

Appendix F

Let's convert 9,321,000 to exponential notation. That's 9 million and a bit left over. How do we write one million in exponential notation? One million is a thousand times one thousand, and because one thousand is 10 multiplied by itself 3 times, a million is 10 multiplied by itself 6 times. For any number of millions, whether 1 million, 2 million, or 9 million, we take the number of millions and multiply it by ten, 6 times. So 9,321,000 = 9.321 * 10 * 10 * 10 * 10 * 10 * 10. And, of course, the easy way to write this is 9.321E + 6.

Let's compress these examples into some simple rules for converting to and from exponential notation.

RULE 1: To convert the "normal" representation of a number larger than 1 to exponential notation, move the decimal point to the left until there is only one digit to the left of the decimal point; chop off any trailing zeros on the right of the number; write an E after the number and follow it with a plus sign; and after the E and the plus sign, write down how many times you had to move the decimal point.

For example,

```
3 6 0 0 0.        Start with this
3.6 0 0 0
    4 3 2 1       Move the decimal point until only 1 digit is still on the left
3.6E + 4          Erase any trailing zeros and write E and the exponent
```

RULE 2: To convert from exponential notation to normal representation, move the decimal point to the right the number of times indicated by the exponent, filling in any zeros that are necessary; and erase the E, the plus sign, and the exponent.

For example,

```
8.7645E + 3       Start with this
8.7 6 5.4 E + 3
  1 2 3           Move the decimal point the number of times indicated
                  by the exponent
8765.4            Erase the E and the exponent
```

Small numbers, as well as large ones, can be represented by using exponential notation. How small? Would you believe one billion billion billionth? That's a decimal point followed by 35 zeros and a 1, like this

```
0.00000000000000000000000000000000001
```

Exponential (Scientific) Notation

In exponential notation we would write 1E −36. (This is where you find out about the plus sign that we promised earlier we would explain.) As you can see, with large numbers the sign of the exponent is positive, and with small numbers it is negative. But 1E − 36 is a very, very small number. For convenience, let's think about something larger, like one one-hundredth, or 0.01. In exponential notation this is 1E − 2. How do we know that? Well, for one thing, we'd have to move the decimal place 2 places to the right in order for the 1 to be to the left of the decimal point. Also, where a positive exponent means to multiply the number by ten the number of times indicated by the exponent, a negative exponent means to divide it by ten that many times. If we divide 1 by 10 once we get 0.1, and if we divide it again we get 0.01. That's two divisions by ten, so the exponent must be a negative 2. Other examples of negative exponents are as follows:

```
0.00275      is  2.75E - 3
0.99999      is  9.9999E - 1
0.000512     is  5.12E - 4
0.00000002   is  2E - 8
```

We can now write down two more rules, this time for handling exponential notation with small numbers:

RULE 3: To convert a number that is smaller than one to exponential notation, move the decimal point to the right until there is one digit to the left of the decimal point; write an E and a minus sign after the number; and after the minus sign, write how many times you had to move the decimal point.

For example,

```
.000275              Start with this

0 0 0 2. 7 5         Move the decimal point until there is only one digit to
1 2 3 4              left

2.75E - 4            Add the E and the negative exponent.
```

RULE 4: To convert a number which is smaller than one, from exponential notation to normal representation, move the decimal point to the right the number of places indicated by the exponent, adding zeros if necessary, and erase the exponent.

```
9.99E -3             Start with this

0 0 9. 9 9 E - 3
3 2 1                Move the decimal point

.00999               Erase the E and the exponent
```

Appendix F

Now we need to talk about something that can be quite confusing, that is, negative numbers in exponential notation. The thing to keep in mind here is, don't confuse negative exponents with negative numbers! The sign of the exponent and the sign of the number (which is the same thing as the sign of the mantissa of the number) are two entirely different things. So far we have talked about only positive numbers—that is, numbers greater than 0. These positive numbers can be either large numbers with an exponent greater than 0, or small numbers with an exponent smaller than zero. (Actually, to have a positive exponent a number doesn't have to be all that large; if it is greater than one it has a positive exponent, and if it is smaller than one it has a negative exponent.)

Similarly, a negative number—that is, one less than zero—can either be "large" and have an exponent greater than zero, or it can be small and have an exponent less than zero.

Table F-1 summarizes these combinations.

Table F-1: Ranges of numbers in exponential notation.

Example of Number	Sign of Number	Sign of Exponent Notation	Number in Exponential	Range of Numbers
478	+	+	4.78E + 2	Very large positive to +1
.0478	+	−	4.78E − 2	+1 to 0
−.0478	−	−	−4.78E − 2	0 to −1
−478	−	+	−4.78E +	−1 to very large negative

All we're really saying here is that a very large number (which, because it is large, has a positive exponent) can be either positive or negative; and that a very small number (which, because it's small, has a negative exponent) can also be either positive or negative.

BASIC is one of the best teachers of exponential notation. Type some large numbers, do some arithmetic with them in the command mode, experiment a little, and pretty soon you'll find exponential notation almost as easy as the regular, "old fashioned" way of writing numbers.

Appendix G

Information for Graphics

Colors

The following table shows the colors and the numbers associated with them:

Table G-1: Colors in BASIC.

Color Display Number	Color	Monochrome Display Number	Color
0	Black	0	Off
1	Blue		(Underlined)
2	Green	1	On
3	Cyan	1	On
4	Red	1	On
5	Magenta	1	On
6	Brown	1	On
7	White	1	On
8	Gray	0	Off
9	Light blue		High intensity (Underlined)
10	Light green	2	High intensity
11	Light cyan	2	High intensity

(continued)

Appendix G

Table G-1: (*continued*)

Color Display		Monochrome Display	
Number	Color	Number	Color
12	Light red	2	High intensity
13	Light magenta	2	High intensity
14	Yellow	2	High intensity
15	High intensity white	0	Off

Screen Modes

Table G-2: Screen 0.

Monitor	Adapter	Attribute Range	Color Range	Default Foreground Attribute	Default Foreground Color
Monochrome	MDPA	NA	0-2	7	1
Monochrome	EGA	0-15	0-2	7	1
Color	EGA	NA	0-15 (normal) 16-31 (blinking)	7	7
IBM Enhanced Color Display	EGA	0-15 (normal) 16-31 (blinking)	0-15	7	7

Resolution	EGA Memory	Pages	Page Size
40-column text	NA	1	2K
80-column text	NA	1	4K

Information for Graphics

Table G-3: Screen 1.

Monitor	Adapter	Attribute Range	Color Range	Default Foreground Attribute	Default Foreground Color
Color	CGA	NA	0-3	3	15
IBM Enhanced Color Display	EGA	0-3	0-15	3	15

Resolution	EGA Memory	Pages	Page Size
320 x 200 pixels	NA	1	2K

Table G-4: Screen 2.

Monitor	Adapter	Attribute Range	Color Range	Default Foreground Attribute	Default Foreground Color
Color	CGA	NA	0-1	1	15
IBM Enhanced Color Display	EGA	0-1	0-15	1	15

Resolution	EGA Memory	Pages	Page Size
640 x 200 pixels	NA	1	16K

Appendix G

Table G-5: Screen 7.

Monitor	Adapter	Attribute Range	Color Range	Default Foreground Attribute	Default Foreground Color
IBM Enhanced Color Display	EGA	0-15	0-15	15	15

Resolution	EGA Memory	Pages	Page Size
320 x 200 pixels	64K	2	32K
	128K	4	32K
	256K	8	32K

Table G-6: Screen 8.

Monitor	Adapter	Attribute Range	Color Range	Default Foreground Attribute	Default Foreground Color
IBM Enhanced Color Display	EGA	0-15	0-15	15	15

Resolution	EGA Memory	Pages	Page Size
640 x 200 pixels	64K	1	64K
	128K	2	64K
	256K	4	64K

Information for Graphics

Table G-7: Screen 9.

Monitor	Adapter	Attribute Range	Color Range	Default Foreground Attribute	Default Foreground Color
IBM Enhanced Color Display	EGA	0-3	0-15	3	15
IBM Enhanced Color Display	EGA (more than 64K EGA memory)	0-15	0-63	15	63

Resolution	EGA Memory	Pages	Page Size
640 x 350 pixels	64K	1	64K
	128K	1	128K
	256K	2	128K

Table G-8: Screen 10.

Monitor	Adapter	Attribute Range	Color Range	Default Foreground Attribute	Default Foreground Color
Monochrome	EGA	0-3	0-8	3	8

Resolution	EGA Memory	Pages	Page Size
640 x 350 pixels	128K	1	128K
	256K	2	128K

Appendix G

Table G-9: Default attributes for SCREEN 10, monochrome display.

Attribute Value	Displayed Pseudo-Color
0	Off
1	On, normal intensity
2	Blink
3	On, high intensity

Table G-10: Color values for SCREEN 10, monochrome display.

Color Value	Displayed Pseudo-Color
0	Off
1	Blink, off to on
2	Blink, off to high intensity
3	Blink, on to off
4	On
5	Blink, on to high intensity
6	Blink, high intensity to off
7	Blink, high intensity to on
8	High intensity

Appendix H

Answers to Review Questions

Chapter 1

1. Only a and d are correct.
2. This line will do it:

   ```
   50 PRINT WORD4$; WORD2$; WORD3$, WORD1$
   ```

3. PRINT 5*(28-7*(8+2))/2. The answer is −105.
4. Only a and d are legal variable names.
5. The value of C remains at 0. (It's really undefined in the program.)
6. You use END, because STOP always produces the "Break" message.
7. At the end, A has the "pea," the value 1; B and C are zero.
8. RENUM 500, 100, 100
9. You can use EDIT 80, or LIST 80.

Appendix H

Chapter 2

1. It counts down from 100 to 50 and prints the numbers on the screen.

2. The program is as follows:

   ```
   10 FOR I=0 TO 100 STEP 2
   20 T=T+I
   30 NEXT
   40 PRINT T
   ```

3. Although this will work, to be useful the variable XX should be on the left of the equals sign, like this:

   ```
   50 IF XX=10 THEN PRINT "TRUE"
   ```

4. The program displays UNEQUAL because in ABS(INT(–7.9)), the INT is done first. Then ABS is performed on that quantity, yielding 8. In the expression INT (ABS(–7.9)), the ABS is done first, yielding 7.9; INT then takes the integer portion (7) of that quantity.

5.
   ```
   110 IF ANSWER$="Y" OR ANSWER$="y" THEN END
   ```

6.
   ```
   10 INPUT NUM
   20 ON NUM GOSUB 50, 770, 100
   ```

7. The revised program might look like this:

   ```
   10 INPUT AMOUNT
   15 GOSUB 100
   20 PRINT AMOUNT
   30 END
   100 AMOUNT = AMOUNT * 1.07
   110 RETURN
   ```

8. Use TRON to trace execution, TROFF to turn off tracing.

9. The program never stops; you'll have to press Ctrl-Break.

Answers to Review Questions

Chapter 3

1. Use DIM N(100).

2. This statement will do it all:

   ```
   DIM MONTHS$(12), ROOTS(99), WORKERS (10, 52)
   ```

3. While a program is running, ERASE is used to release memory dimensioned for arrays, and it can also be used to redimension during a running program.

4. The program lacks a DIM statement.

5.
   ```
   10 DIM MONTH$(12), T(12)
   20 FOR I= 1 TO 12
   30    INPUT "Month"; MONTH$(I)
   40    INPUT "Average temperature"; T(I)
   50 NEXT
   60 FOR I = 1 TO 12
   70    PRINT MONTH$(I); T(I)
   80    X = X + T(I)
   90 NEXT
   100 PRINT "Average yearly temperature is"; X/12
   ```

6. If you use OPTION BASE 0, all arrays begin with element 0; OPTION BASE 1 means that the first subscript for all arrays will be 1.

7. No.

8. The first time through the general input subroutine beginning at line 6000, I is set to 1. So you could change line 6040 to an instruction like the following one, to make sure that the user has to input the date if it's the first time this subroutine is called.

   ```
   6040 IF I=1 THEN INPUT "Input date";DAY$(I):
           D$=DAY$(I):
           GOTO 6110
   ```

9. No. The array consists of 300 x 50 elements. The number of dimensions is different from the number of elements; an array can contain any number of elements, depending only on the memory available.

617

Appendix H

Chapter 4

1. The output looks like this:

   ```
   10    40
   20    30
   ```

   All data is READ in line 10, so the program runs as if the RESTORE statement is not there.

2. Here's the answer:

   ```
   10 OPTION BASE 1
   20 DIM M$(12)
   30 DATA "Jan", "Feb", "Mar", "Apr", "May", "Jun"
   40 DATA "Jul", "Aug", "Sep", "Oct", "Nov", "Dec"
   50 FOR I=1 TO 12
   60    READ M$(I)
   70 NEXT
   ```

3. First use the cosine of angle A to find side C, the distance from the tee to point B:

   $$\text{Side C} = \frac{150}{\text{COS(A)}} = \frac{150}{\text{COS(40*(3.14159/180))}} = 195.811 \text{ yards}$$

   Then use the tangent to find side D:

   $$\text{Side D} = 150\,(\text{TAN(A)}) = 150*\text{TAN}(40*(3.14159/180)) = 125.8648 \text{ yards}$$

   Finally, add the two distances together:

   $$195.811 + 125.8648 = 321.6759$$

   Did you remember to convert the angles to radians before calculating the sine and tangent?

4. The result of 5 MOD 3 is 2. The result of integer division (note the backslash!) of 15 by 2 is 7. So, the answer is 7.

5. The instruction IF X AND 2 THEN PRINT "OK" masks all but the second bit.

6. The rightmost digit (the "3") has no meaning.

7. 4 bytes for the value, plus 3 bytes for the variable name.

8. They take up less memory, and they're faster in any kind of arithmetic operation and in loops.
9. Try DEFINT A-M, W-Z.

Chapter 5

1. Press Enter to print "OUT OF LOOP."
2. You could use INPUT$(2).
3. This program finds *and* three times, because it begins reading from the 10th character in the string. (N=10.)
4. You press the X key (capital X).
5. One solution is shown here:

```
10 A$ = "LOOKOUT"
20 B$ = LEFT$(A$,4)
30 C$ = RIGHT$(A$,3)
40 PRINT C$; B$
```

6. PRINT CHR$(61)
7. X = ASC("Queequeg")
8. CHR$(12)
9. INPUT$ does not "echo" what's being typed. It merely accepts characters.

Chapter 6

1. One statement is the following:

```
30 PRINT USING "**$####,.##"; A, B, C, D, E
```

Appendix H

2. You'll see a "graph" of the square roots of every 10th number from 10 to 200, like this:

```
       *
        *
         *
          *
           *
            *
             *
              *
               *
                *
                *
                 *
                 *
                  *
                  *
                   *
                   *
                    *
                     *
                     *
```

3. The cursor left (left-arrow) key will cause a beep.

4. A combination of Alt and the lowercase h key.

5. You could use the following:

```
KEY 10, "RENUM" + CHR$(13)
```

6. TIMER shows the number of seconds past midnight, so the time is 25200 divided by 3600, or about 7:00 am.

7. You would use DELETE 20-40 to eliminate the FOR...NEXT loop.

8. Here's a simple program that will do the job:

```
10 DEF FN FTOC(F)=5*(F-32)/9
20 PRINT FN FTOC(40)
```

The answer is 4.44 degrees Celsius.

9. The STRING$ statement will do it.

Chapter 7

1. You could type:

   ```
   SAVE "PROGRAM5", A
   ```

2. A random-access file is the choice, because the amount of data (200 names) is small, and random-access files make it easier to find and modify data within the file.

3. The LINE INPUT# statement shows string data with quotation marks and numeric data as numbers, with commas separating them so that you can see exactly what's in the file.

4. Don't use FIELDed variables in INPUT or LET statements. Use LSET/RSET instead.

5. LOCK is for short-term locking of data files. You should always UNLOCK data records before ending the program.

6. The PRINT #1 statement in line 20 uses commas to separate data items, causing the spaces needed to put these items in the next field to appear in the file. It's just like when you PRINT to the screen.

7. Here's a little program that will do the job:

   ```
   10 OPEN "BATTERUP" AS #1 LEN=36
   20 FIELD #1, 30 AS GUYSNAME$, 3 AS BATS$, 3 AS HITS$
   30 FOR BATTER% = 1 TO 10
   40    GET #1, BATTER%
   50    PRINT GUYSNAME$, BATS$, HITS$
   60 NEXT BATTER%
   70 CLOSE #1
   80 END
   ```

8. "True" for the EOF function is –1, not 1. So line 90 should read:

   ```
   90 WHILE EOF(2) <> -1
   ```

9. You can type:

   ```
   ENVIRON "PATH=C:\BATCHFLS"
   ```

Appendix H

Chapter 8

1. SCREEN 1 is medium-resolution graphics (320 x 200 pixels), with four colors on the screen at once. SCREEN 2 is high-resolution graphics (640 x 200 pixels), with two colors on the screen.

2. Here's one possible solution:

   ```
   10 SCREEN 2:CLS
   20 PSET (320,100)
   30 R=50
   40 PI=3.14159
   50 DEF FNDEG(ANGLE)=ANGLE*PI/180
   60 FOR A=1 TO 360
   70     PSET (320+R*COS(FNDEG(A)), 100+R*SIN(FNDEG(A)))
   80 NEXT
   90 END
   ```

   To get a circle instead of an ellipse on your screen, you may need to multiply the sine by a fraction.

3. You could use:

   ```
   WINDOW (0, 30) - (365, 50)
   ```

4. You should change the SCREEN statement and the value for CNTX (but not CNTY). Here's what you need to change:

   ```
   20 SCREEN 2: CLS: KEY OFF
   .
   .
   60 CNTX=320
   ```

5. The program draws a rectangle with the color specified by attribute 2, draws a circle inside it, then fills the circle with the color specified by attribute 3.

6. DIM HOUSE%(1322) will be just enough space.

7. Nowhere. You get an error, because LOCATE is for the text screen, and both columns and rows are numbered beginning with 1. LOCATE 15,1 is a legal statement.

8. The LINE statement draws a box, using the color assigned to attribute 3. Then the PAINT statement fills the *entire screen* with color; although it begins PAINTing from within the box, PAINT looks for a border with an attribute of 2. Not finding this attribute, it continues past the border of the box and fills the screen with color.

Answers to Review Questions

9. About 60 minutes; you can have sounds up to 65535 clock ticks in duration, and there are 18.2 clock ticks per second.

Chapter 9

1. You use CVD to convert back to double-precision numbers.
2. These two lines will do it:

```
100 COMMON VOLTAGE, CURRENT ()
110 CHAIN "METER"
```

3. The answer is E30. Here's a program that will produce the answer:

```
10 A=&HF00
20 B=&HD0
30 C=A-B 'Decimal arithmetic
40 D$=HEX$C 'Convert answer back to hex
50 PRINT D$
```

4. The program fills rows 3 and 4 of the text screen with capital X's.
5. You could use the following:

```
100 A=VARPTR(COLLEGES$())
110 PRINT A
```

6. You use SHELL to call DOS commands and other executable (.COM and .EXE) programs.
7. RESUME takes execution back to a specific line number after an error is handled.
8. You'd insert the statement ERROR 71 at the point where you wanted to simulate the error.
9. When you load GW-BASIC, specify /D, like this:

```
GWBASIC /D
```

This permits some functions, including SIN, to produce double-precision results.

Index

Symbols

" (quotation marks), 282
! (exclamation point) type declaration character, 177
(number sign) type declaration character, 177, 296
(pound sign) type declaration character, 176 238
$ (dollar sign) type declaration character, 52, 177
% (percent sign) type declaration character, 177
\ (backslash) integer division symbol, 196-197

A

ABS function statement, 85
absolute value, 85
ACCESS statement, 329
actual parameters, 266
ADD command statement, 37
addition, 39
algorithms, 471
Alt key, 255
altitude, calculating, 192
American Standard Code for Information Interchange, 212
amortization
    loan formula, 60
    schedules, 95
AND logical operator, 199-201, 205
angles, converting to degrees, 185-186
animation, 412-415
answers to review questions, 615-623
APAGE argument, 395
applications
    business, 4-5
    educational, 6-8
    entertainment, 5-6, 88-89
    scientific, 7
arcs, drawing, 377

arctangents
    calculating, 190-191
    trigonometric functions, 184
arguments
    APAGE, 395
    VPAGE, 395
arithmetic operators, 38
arrays, 116-125, 137
    dimensions, 119
    double-precision, 418
    dual-subscripted, 120
    initializing
        with DATA and READ, 161-162
        with FOR...NEXT, 161
    integer, 418
    look-up tables, 123-124
    maximum number of dimensions, 131
    multiple, 119
    numeric, 418
    passing to subroutines, 475
    retrieving data, 139
    setting for metric conversion, 163-164
    single-precision, 418
    size, 418
    three-dimensional, 120
    TYPE, 134
ASCII
    as program files, 285
    characters, 214
    extended characters, 223
    function, 212-213
    loading program files, 284
    saving program files, 284
    tables, 212
aspect ratios, 387
assembly language programs, see machine language programs, 465
* (asterisk) operator, 40

625

ATN trigonometric function, 184, 355
attributes, 376, 400-401, 409
AUTO command statement, 33-34
AUTOEXEC.BAT DOS file, 279
automatic
    line numbers, 32-34
    type conversions, 182
averages, 48

B

background
    attribute, 409
    music, 426
\ (backslash) integer division symbol, 196-197
BASIC
    commands, *see* statements, 23
    starting, 20
BEEP command statement, 32
binary formats, 284
binary numbering systems, 562-565
    addition, 565-566
    binary coded decimal system, 575
    binary coded number representation, 575-576
    complements, 572
    division, 566-567
    multiplication, 566-567
    negative numbers, 570-571
    numbers, 567
    parallel transmission, 569-570
    pulse representation, 568-569
    serial transmission, 569-570
    subtraction, 565-566
    two's complement, 573-574
    weighted binary code, 575
bit-coding, 205
bits, 199
    sign, 469
blank spaces, inserting, 57
blinking foreground, 397
BLOAD statement, 452-453
booting up, 451
borders, printing, 240
boundaries, setting in text, 411
boxes, drawing, 373
BSAVE statement, 452-453
bubble sorting, 268-269
buffers, 293
    filling, 322
    moving data into, 321
    opening, 333

business applications, 4, 5
    Customer Billing, 5
    General Ledger (GL), 5
    Inventory Control, 5
    Mailing Label Preparation, 5
    Order Processing, 5
bytes, 199
    least significant, 470-471
    most significant, 470-471
    stringing together, 407

C

calculating
    altitude, 192
    arctangents, 190-191
    cosines, 187-188
    height, 188-189
    interest, 96
    monthly interest, 95
    monthly payments, 96
    sine, 185
    tangents, 188
CALL statement, 461-463
Caps Lock key, 255
Cartesian coordinates, 380
CDBL(X) type conversion, 181-182
center, finding on wedges, 388
centering titles, 245
CGA
    (IBM Color Graphics Adapter), 393
    flash routine, 511
    save routine, 509
CHAIN MERGE statement, 438-447
CHAIN statement, 434-437
characters
    converting to numeric values, 218-219
    extended ASCII, 223
    single, 221
CHDIR command statement, 343
CHR$ string function, 214-215
CINT numeric function, 196
CINT(X)
    numeric function, 195
    type conversion, 181-182
CIRCLE statement, 378-379, 381, 409
circles
    drawing, 377-378
    filling with color, 405-406
    finding points, 388
circumflex character, 40

Index

CLEAR statement, 492-493
CLOSE statement, 293
closing, data files, 293, 297
CLS (clear screen) command, 22
COLOR statement, 396-397
colors, 400-403, 609-610
   attributes, 400-401
   available, 396
   changing on monitors, 393
   default, 398
   erasing, 367-368
   filling
      areas, 404, 406
      circles, 406
   on monitors, 392
   pointers, 400-401
   primary, 398-399
   reading in graphics, 420
   viewing on monochrome monitors, 394
COLORSWITCH variable, 395
columns, 42-44
COM ports, 339
   opening, 340
command lines, 490
command references, 523–560
commands
   DOS, DIR, 477
   DRAW, 413-414
   music, 424-425
   STEP, 76
commas, 41-44
commissions, figuring, 175-176
COMMON statement, 437
communication ports, *see* COM ports,
communications software, 338
concatenation, 53
conditional branches, 76, 92
Control-Break sequence, 91
conversions, 460
   defining types automatically, 182
   factors, 163
   metric, 162-166, 168
   numeric, 448, 585
   decimal, 448-450
      hexadecimal, 448-450
      octal, 448-450
   octal, 448-450
   setting arrays, 163-164
   string-number, 432
converting
   angles to degrees, 185-186
   characters to numeric values, 218-219

   numeric values to characters, 219
   Y-values to rows, 390
coordinates, translating, 420-421
copying
   characters into strings, 217
   pages, 419
   to floppy disk, 14-16
   to hard disk, 13
   to work disk, 16-19
   with GET statement, 416
COS trigonometric function, 184, 355
cosines
   trigonometric function, 184
   calculating, 187-188
CS (code segment) code, 451
CSNG(X) type conversion, 181-182
CSRLIN function statement, 358-359
Ctrl key, 255
CUBE function statement, 266
currency conversion subroutine, 442
current segment addresses, 452
cursor
   lines, 359
   positions, 264
curves, finding points, 388
CVD function statement, 432
CVI function statement, 432-433
CVS function statement, 432
cylinders
   changing perspectives, 454
   drawing, 454-457

D

dashed lines, drawing, 377
DATA command statement, 156-164
data files, 280, 288, 457
   adding data, 291
   closing, 293, 297
   inputting into random access files, 323-324
   moving into buffers, 321
   opening, 291
   outputting, 301
   protecting, 332
   random-access, 289
   reading, 164
      from memory, 459
   retrieving
      data, 294-296, 301
      from arrays, 139
      from files, 300-301, 324-328

627

data files
    running out, 162
    segments, 452
    sequential, 289, 291, 294
    storing in files, 280
    unlocking, 332
data pointers, 157, 159-160
DATE$ string variable, 59
dates
    inputting, 135
    printing, 58, 253-254
debugging, 29
decimals
    aligning points, 236
    numeric conversion, 448-450
DEF FN statement, 265
DEF SEG statement, 452
DEF USR statement, 465
defaults
    colors, 398
    paths, 344
    variables, 179
DEFDBL type declaration definition, 179
DEFINT type declaration definition, 179
DEFSNG type declaration definition, 179
DEFSTR type declaration definition, 179
DELETE statement, 262-263
delete subroutine, 307-308
deleting
    files from directories, 342
    lines, 35
device drivers, 489
devices, trapping, 334
dialects, 4
DIM statement, 121-122
dimensions, 119
DIR DOS command, 477
direct
    modes, 23, 39
    output, 491
    statements, 27
directories
    changing, 343
    creating, 343
    deleting files, 342
    removing, 343
    specifying paths, 282
disk files, closing, 302
DIVIDE command statement, 38
documentation, 63-64
$ (dollar sign) type declaration character, 52, 177

DOS, 12, 450
    AUTOEXEC.BAT files, 279
    commands
        DIR, 477
        MODE, 279
    exiting to temporarily, 476-477
    redirection statements, 278
    returning to, 23
double commas, 44
double-precision arrays, 418
double-precision numbers, 492
double-precision variables, 175-176, 193, 473
DRAW command statements, 412-415
drawing
    arcs, 377
    boxes, 373
    circles, 377-378
    cylinders, 456-457
    dashed lines, 377
    lines, 373
    pie wedges, 382
    pies, 383
    rectangles, 374
    semicircles, 382
DS (data segment) code, 451
dual dimensional arrays, 120
dynamic designs, 504
    disk drives, 505
    screen color, 505

E

EDIT command statement, 35
educational applications, 6-8
EGA, 401
EGA (IBM Enhanced Graphics Adapter), 393
EGA flash routine, 510
EGA save routine, 509
EGA/VGA save routine, 508-509
elements, 116
ELSE command, 78
END command statement, 30-31
endless loop, 90-91
engineering specifications, 126
entertainment applications, 5-6, 88-89
ENVIRON statement, 344
ENVIRON$ string function, 345
environment string table, 344
EOF function, 297, 299
EQV logical operator, 199, 203

Index

ERASE command statement, 123
erasing
    colors, 367-368
    points, 367-368
ERDEV variable, 341
ERDEV$ variable, 341
ERL statement, 485
ERR statement, 485
ERROR statement, 486-487
error-checking subroutine, 106, 108-110
error-trapping routines, 483-489
errors, 481-488
    line numbers, 485
    messages, 486
    numbers, 485
ES (extra segment) code, 451
! (exclamation point) type declaration character, 177
exiting, temporarily to DOS, 476-477
EXP logarithmic function, 191
expense account program, 99-103, 107-110, 126
    ending, 143
    input screen, 127
    inputting dates, 137
    inputting expenses, 134
    menus, 99, 128
    output screen, 126-127
    printing, 145-146
    running, 143-145
    variables, 130
expense account reports
    inputting dates, 135
    totaling, 101
exponential notations, 170, 172, 603-608
exponentiation, 40-41
extended keys, 255

F

F1 (LIST) function key, 250
F2 (RUN<-) function key, 250
F3 (LOAD") function key, 250
F4 (SAVE") function key, 66, 250
F5 (CONT<-) function key, 250
F6 (,"LPT1:"<-) function key, 250
F7 (TRON<-) function key, 250
F8 (TROFF<-) function key, 250
F9 (KEY) function key, 250
F10 (SCREEN O,O,O<-) function key, 250
FCB (file control block), 475

FIELD statement, 321
filenames, 491
files
    ASCII, 284
    buffers, moving data, 432
    counting, 342
    data, 280, 288-289, 291, 294-297, 301
        protecting, 332
        unlocking, 332
    deleting from current directory, 342
    disk, 302
    length, 331
    listing, 342
    maximum length, 491
    program, 280
        as ASCII, 285
        loading ASCII, 284
        saving as ASCII, 284
    protecting, 287
    random saving numbers, 432
    random access, 318, 321
        inputting data, 320
        setting fields, 321
    saving on disk, 281
    standard input, 490
    storing data, 280
    telephone data, running, 312-314
    telephone number, 302-304
        adding a person, 306-307
        deleting a person, 307-308
        displaying lists, 305
        finding a person, 309
        outputting to file, 311
        printing, 310
        running, 314, 316, 318
FILES statement, 342
FIX numeric function, 196
FIX(X) numeric function, 195
flash routine, 509
floppy disk, 10
    copying to, 14-16
    inserting, 11
    single drives, 16
flowcharts, 129, 502-506
    inputting expenses, 135
    overall, 128
FN CUBE function statement, 265
FOR loop statement, 74-76
FOR...NEXT loop statement, 76, 80, 117, 161, 174
foreground, blinking, 397

629

FORM FEED key, 278
formal parameters, 266
formulas
    amortization loan, 60
    simple loan, 60
fractals, 500, 512, 513
    CGA flash routine, 511
    CGA save routine, 509
    color, 498
    dynamic designs, 504
        disk drives, 505
        screen color, 505
    EGA flash routine, 510
    EGA save routine, 509
    flash routine, 509
    flowcharts, 502-504, 506
    hardware requirements, 499
    hardware specific, 508
    initialization routine, 511-512
    modifying
        for a CGA, 513, 515-516
        for an EGA, 514-515
    pseudocodes, 500-504
    reviewing, 518-519
    saving to disk, 508
    target formulas, 502
    top-down pseudocode, 501
    triangular, 517-518
    writing loops, 507-508
fractions, measuring, 174
FRE command statement, 262
FRE function statement, 597-598
FRE(0) command statement, 124
function call syntax, 466
function keys, 21, 422
    F1 (LIST), 250
    F2 (RUN<-), 250
    F3 (LOAD"), 250
    F4 (SAVE"), 66, 250
    F5 (CONT<-), 250
    F6 (,"LPT1:<-), 250
    F7 (TRON<-), 250
    F8 (TROFF<-), 250
    F9 (KEY), 250
    F10 (SCREEN O,O,O<-), 250
    redefining, 251
function statements, *see* statements, 81
functions
    ASC, 212-213
    combining, 87
    CSRLIN, 358
    CUBE, 266

CVD, 432
CVI, 432-433
CVS, 432
defining, 266
EOF, 297, 299
FN CUBE, 265
INSTR, 227-228
LOF, 331
math, 37-41
numeric, *see* numeric functions, 248
PMAP, 420
POINT, 419-420
POS, 358
SPC, 249
string
    ENVIRON$, 345
    HEX$, 449
    IOCTL$, 489
    OCT$, 449
    VARPTR$, 475
TIMER, 257
using, 266
VAL, 218
writing your own, 265

G

games, 5-6, 88-89, 245-249
general input subroutines, 136
GET statement, 327, 416, 418
GET# statement, 326
global tables, 344
GOSUB command statement, 104-105
GOTO statement, 89-90, 92-93
GRANDTOTAL command statement, 142
graphics
    adding colors, 392
    clearing, 411
    colors, 609-610
    finding
        coordinates, 420
        points, 419
    manipulating characters on screen, 463
    memory, 453
    placing, 417-418
        with PUT statement, 416
    reading colors, 420
    saving screens, 454-455
    screens, 363, 365, 371-372,
        378, 383, 416, 454, 456-457
        modes, 610-614

Index

transferring, 419
viewing, 409
viewports, 409

H

hard disk, 10
    copying to, 13
hardware configurations, 394
hardware requirements, 9, 11, 357, 361, 394-395, 419, 499
hardware specific, 508
headers, printing, 240
headings, printing, 141
height, calculating, 188-189
HEX$ string function, 449
hexadecimal numbering system
    addition, 583
    digits, 581-582
    multiplication, 584
    numeric conversion, 448-450
    subtraction, 584
hypotenuse, finding, 184

I

I/O aids, 341
I/O ports, 478-479
    memory-mapped, 478
IBM Color Graphics Adapter, *see* CGA, 393
IBM Monochrome Display Adapter, see MDA, 393
IF loop statement, 93
IF...THEN loop statement, 76-77, 92
IF...THEN...ELSE loop statement, 79
IMP logical operator, 199, 204
index values, 99
indirect statements, 27
initialization, 131, 511-512
INKEY$ variable, 221-223
INP function statement, 478
INPUT command statement, 53-55, 226
INPUT# statement, 295-296
INPUT$ string function, 223-224
INSTR function statement, 227-228
INT function statement, 82-84
INT numeric function, 196
INT(X) function statement, 82
INT(X) numeric function, 195
integers
    arrays, 418

converting numbers, 82
storing variables, 56, 169, 173-174, 194, 469-471
interest
    amount paid, 97
    calculating, 96
    monthly, 95
IOCTL statement, 489
IOCTL$ string function, 489
IP (instructional pointer), 451
iteration, 74

J-K

joysticks, 337
key combinations, trapping, 254
KEY LIST statement, 250
KEY OFF command statement, 21
KEY ON command statement, 21
KEY statement, 251
KEY(N) OFF statement, 253
KEY(N) ON statement, 253
KEY(N) statement, 252
KEY(N) STOP statement, 253
keys
    Alt, 255
    Caps Lock, 255
    Ctrl, 255
    extended, 255
    FORM FEED, 278
    latched, 255-256
    Left Shift, 255
    ON LINE, 278
    Right Shift, 255
    trapping, 252-254
keystrokes
    logging, 286
    recording, 285
keywords, 24
KILL statement, 342

L

labels, 52-53
language programs
    machine, 460-466, 475
    saving, 453
laser printers, 278
latched keys, 255-256
least significant byte (LSB), 470-471

631

Left Shift key, 255
LEFT$ string function, 215
left-justified, 43
LEN(A$) string function, 220
LET command statement, 48-49
light pens, 335, 336
LINE INPUT statement, 225-226
LINE INPUT# statement, 300-301
line numbers, 26-27
    automatic, 32-34
    editing, 35
    running, 30
LINE statement, 376
linear equations, 354
lines, 42
    breaking, 79
    deleting, 35
    drawing, 373
    removing, 262
LIST command statement, 29
listing statements, 28-29
LLIST command statement, 277
LOAD command statement, 66
LOAD statement, 282-284
loans
    payments, 61
    calculating, 62
LOC statement, 331, 340
LOCATE statement, 358-360, 389
LOCK statement, 332
LOF function statement, 331
LOG logarithmic function statement, 191
logarithmic functions, 191-192
    EXP, 191
    LOG, 191
logical operators, 78
    AND, 199, 201, 205
    EQV, 199, 203
    IMP, 199, 204
    NOT, 199, 204
    OR, 199, 202
    stringing together, 200
    XOR, 199, 202
look-up tables, 123-124
looping, 74-75
loops
    endless, 90-91
    menu, 132, 304
    WHILE...WEND, 508
    writing, 507-508
LPRINT command statement, 279
LPRINT USING statement, 279

LSB (least significant byte), 470-471
LSET statement, 432

M

machine language programs, 460-461, 465
    accessing, 463
    inputting to ports, 480
    locating variables, 467
    passing arrays to subroutines, 475
    receiving variables, 466
    specifying addresses, 465
    storing variables, 469
    subroutines, 461-462
        calling, 466
        finding, 465
masking, 205
math functions, 37-41
MAX variable, 107
maximum block size, 492
maximum elements, 121
MDA (IBM Monochrome Display Adapter), 393
memory, 21, 451, 456, 597-598
    direct access, 463
    graphics, 453-455, 457
    individual locations, 458-459
    loading, 452
    locating strings, 473
    manipulating, 450
    offsets, 459
    reading data, 459
    retrieving, 453
    saving chunks, 452
    screens, 463
    segment addresses, 452
    storing, 452
    unused, 262
memory-mapped display format, 453
memory-mapped I/O port, 478
menu loops, 304
menu-selection routines, 222
menus, 128, 132
    loops, 132
    writing routines, 131
messages, moving, 57
metric conversion program, 165-168
metrics, converting, 162
MID$ string function, 215, 217
minimum configuration, 9
– (minus sign) operator, 39
MKD$ string function, 432

MKI$ string function, 432
MKS$ string function, 432
MOD operator, 197-198
MODE DOS command, 279
modes, 329
   locking, 330
   PSET, 419
   SCREEN 0, 394
   SCREEN 1, 395
   SCREEN 10, 395
   SCREEN 2, 395
   SCREEN 7, 395
   SCREEN 8, 395
   SCREEN 9, 395
modulus, 197
monitors, 392, 395
   changing screen colors, 393
   viewing color on monochrome, 394
monthly interest, 95
   payments, 61, 97
      calculating, 96
      printing, 96
   rates, 61
most significant byte (MSB), 470-471
moving data in random file buffers, 432
MS-DOS, see DOS, 450
MSB (most significant byte), 470-471
multiple programs, 434
multiple-letter variables, 51
multiplication, 39
MULTIPLY command statement, 38
music, 424
   background, 426
      trapping, 426
music commands, 424-425
music sounds, 421

N

NAME command statement, 342
names, changing, 342
NEXT loop statement, 74-75
NOT logical operator, 199, 204
null string, 215
(number sign) type declaration character, 177, 296
numbering systems
   binary, 562-567
      addition, 565-566
      coded decimal system, 575
      coded number representation, 575-576
      division, 566-567
      multiplication, 566-567
      negative numbers, 570-571
      parallel transmission, 569-570
      pulse representation, 568-569
      serial transmission, 569-570
      subtraction, 565-566
      two's complement, 573-574
      weighted binary code, 575
   complements, 572
   hexadecimal
      addition, 583
      digits, 581-582
      multiplication, 584
      subtraction, 584
   numeric conversions, 585
   octal, 576
      addition, 578
      digits, 577-579
      division, 581
      multiplication, 580
numbers
   converting to integers, 82
   inserting, 236
   mixing with strings, 45
   negative, 38
   positive, 38
   prime, 198
   printing, 238
   random, 85-86, 88, 248
   rounding off, 195-196
   saving in random files, 432
numeric conversions, 585
   decimal, 448-450
   hexadecimal, 448-450
numeric functions, 194
   CINT, 196
   CINT(X), 195
   FIX, 196
   FIX(X), 195
   INT, 196
   INT(X), 195
   RND, 248, 259
   SGN, 193-194
   SQR, 183-184
   TAN, 188
numeric values
   converting characters, 218-219
   storing, 433
numeric variables, 56, 82

O

OCT$ string function, 449
octal numbering system, 576
    addition, 578
    conversion, 448-450
    digits, 577-579
    division, 581
    multiplication, 580
ON ERROR GOTO statement, 482, 484
ON KEY statement, 252-253
ON LINE key, 278
ON PEN statement, 335
ON PLAY(N) statement, 426
ON statement, 334
ON TIMER statement, 259
ON...GOSUB loop statement, 105
ON...GOTO loop statement, 99
OPEN statement, 291, 328, 333
opening data files, 291
operators, 38
    * (asterisk), 40
    + (plus sign), 39
    – (minus sign), 39
    / (slash), 40
    logical, 78
    logical, *see also* logical operators, 199
    MOD, 197-199
OPTION BASE 1 statement, 131
OR logical operator, 199, 202
origin, 380
OUT function statement, 478-479
overall flowchart, 128

P

pages
    active, 395
    copying, 419
    screening, 395
    visible, 396
PAINT command statement, 405-406
PALETTE 2 statement, 402
PALETTE statement, 402
PALETTE USING statement, 402-403
parameters
    actual, 266
    formal, 266
    stop, 339
parentheses, 39
parity, 338

payroll, 241-244
PCOPY statement, 419
PEEK statement, 458, 460, 463-464
PEN statement, 335
% (percent sign) type declaration character, 177
peripherals, 275
physical coordinates, 363
piano sounds, 421-422, 424
pie charts, 383-385, 387-388
pixels, 363
PLAY ON statement, 426
PLAY statement, 424-425
+ (plus sign) operator, 39
PMAP function, 420
POINT function, 419-420
points
    erasing, 366, 368
    finding
    in graphics, 419
        on circles, 388
        on curves, 388
    plotting, 363
POKE statement, 458-460, 463
ports
    accessing from BASIC, 478
    COM, 338-340
    I/O, 478-479
    waiting for input, 480
POS function statement, 358, 264
(pound sign), 238
precision of value, 169
PRESET statement, 366, 368
primary
    colors, 398
    commands, 399
prime numbers, 83, 198
primes, 84
PRINT command statement, 41-42, 45
PRINT USING command statement, 146
PRINT USING statement, 236-239
PRINT# statement, 301
PRINT# USING statement, 301
printers
    laser, 278
    listing programs, 277
    problems, 278
    sending output to, 279
    setting up, 278
printing
    borders, 240
    dates, 58, 253-254
    expense account program, 145-146

Index

general headings, 141
headers, 240
hints, 310
monthly payments, 96
multiple arrays, 119
numbers, 238
spaces, 249
strings, 237, 474
SUBTOTAL, 142
subtotals, 132
telephone number file, 310
time, 58, 253-254
to serial ports, 278
program files, 280
    ASCII, 285
        loading, 284
        saving as, 284
programs
    debugging, 29
    editing, 35
    expense account, 99-100, 102-103, 108-110, 126, 128
        menus, 99
    expense accounts, 107
    interrupting, 91
    language, 453, 460-466
    linking, 434-437
    merging, 438-446
    modes, 23-26
    multiple, 434
    removing lines, 262
    renumbering, 36-37
    retrieving, 66, 282-283
    running, 26, 30
    saving as ASCII files, 283-284
    stopping, 30
    tracing, 93-94
prompt, 9
protecting files, 287
PSET statement, 364, 368, 419
pseudocodes, 500-504
PUT statement, 322, 415-416, 418

Q-R

quotation marks, 54
random access files, 318, 321
    buffers, moving data, 432
    inputting data, 319, 322-324
    numbers, 88
    retrieving data, 324-328
    saving numbers, 432
    setting fields, 321
RANDOMIZE TIMER statement, 248, 359
RATE command statement, 61
ratios, 387
READ command statement, 156-164
rebooting, 12
recording keystrokes, 285-286
rectangles, drawing, 374
redirection statements, 278
reflex tester, 258
relative positioning, 368
REM command statement, 63
removing
    directories, 343
    statements, 29
RENUM command statement, 36
renumbering lines, 36-37
reseed, 86
reserved words, 58
RESET statement, 302
RESTORE command statement, 160
RESUME statement, 482, 484
RET statement, 461
retrieving
    data from files, 295-296, 301
    memory, 453
    programs, 66, 283
returning
    strings, 212
    to DOS, 23
review questions, 67-69, 111-112, 122, 150-151, 206-207, 230, 270-271, 345-346, 427, 493-494
    answers, 615–623
Right Shift key, 255
RIGHT$ string function, 215-216
RND function statement, 85-86
RND numeric function, 248, 259
rounding off numbers, 195-196
RS-232-C interface, 340
RS-232-C line signal options, 339
RSET statement, 432
RUN command statement, 29
running programs, 30

S

SAVE command statement, 65
SAVE statement, 281, 283-284

saving
    chunks of memory, 452
    EGA/VGA routine, 508-509
    fractals
        CGA save routine, 509
        EGA save routine, 509
        to disk, 508
    graphics screens, 454-455
    language programs, 453
    numbers in a random file, 432
    on disk, 281
    programs, 65, 283
scientific applications, 7
scientific notation, *see* exponential notation, 603-608
SCREEN 0 mode, 394
SCREEN 1 mode, 395, 463
SCREEN 2 mode, 395, 403
SCREEN 7 mode, 395
SCREEN 8 mode, 395
SCREEN 9 mode, 395
SCREEN 10 mode, 395
SCREEN statement, 361, 392
screens
    BASIC, 20-21
    changing modes, 361
    clearing, 22
    colors, 505
    coordinates, 410
    cursor movements, 359-360
    graphics, 363, 365, 371-372, 378, 383, 454-457
        saving, 454
        transferring, 419
        viewing, 409
    input, 127
    linking lines, 374
    manipulating characters, 463
    memory, 463
    modes, 610-614
    output, 126-127
    plotting, 355
    text, 352, 396
segment addresses, 452
    current, 452
    default, 452
segment: offset, 451
semicircles, 382
semicolons, 45
serial
    communications, 491
    printing to ports, 278
SGN numeric function, 193-194

SHELL statement, 476-478
sign bits, 469
simple loan formula, 60
SIN trigonometric function, 184, 355
sines
    calculating, 185
    creating tables, 186
    trigonometric function, 184
single
    characters, 221
    letter variables, 51
    precision arrays, 418
    precision variables, 169-173, 177, 472
/ (slash) operator, 40
soft keys, 21-22
software communications, 338
sort subroutine, 307
sorting bubble, 268-269
SOUND statement, 421
sounds
    music, 421, 424, 426
    piano, 421-422, 424
SPACE$ string function, 245-247
SPACE$(N) string function, 245
spaces, printing, 249
SPC function statement, 249
speed hints, 601-602
SQR numeric function, 183-184
square roots, 183-184
SS (stack segment) code, 451
standard input files, 490
starting
    BASIC, 20
    using working disk, 19
    values, 440
statements, 26, 28
    ACCESS, 329
    BLOAD, 452-453
    BSAVE, 452-453
    CALL, 461-463
    CHAIN, 434-437
    CHAIN MERGE, 438-447
    CIRCLE, 378-379, 381, 409
    CLEAR, 492-493
    CLOSE, 293
    COLOR, 396-397
    KEY(N), 252
    COMMON, 437
    CSRLIN, 359
    DEF FN, 265
    DEF SEG, 452
    DEF USR, 465

636

Index

DELETE, 262-263
DIM, 121-122
direct, 27
DOS, LPRINT, 279
DRAW, 412, 414-415
ENVIRON, 344
ERL, 485
ERR, 485
ERROR, 486-487
FIELD, 321
FILES, 342
GET, 327, 416, 418
GET#, 326
GOTO, 89-93
indirect, 27
INPUT, 226
INPUT#, 295-296
IOCTL, 489
KEY, 251
KEY(N) OFF, 253
KEY(N) ON, 253
KEY(N) STOP, 253
KILL, 342
LINE, 376
LINE INPUT, 225-226
LINE INPUT#, 300-301
listing, 28-29
LOAD, 282-284
LOC, 331-340
LOCATE, 358-360, 389
LOCK, 332
LPRINT USING, 279
LSET, 432
ON, 334
ON ERROR GOTO, 482, 484
ON KEY, 252-253
ON PEN, 335
ON PLAY(N), 426
ON TIMER, 259
OPEN, 291, 328, 333
OPTION BASE 1, 131
PAINT, 405
PALETTE, 402
PALETTE 2, 402
PALETTE USING, 402-403
PCOPY, 419
PEEK, 458, 460, 463-464
PEN, 335
PLAY, 424-425
PLAY ON, 426
POKE, 458-460, 463
POS, 264

PRESET, 366, 368
PRINT USING, 236-239
PRINT#, 301
PRINT# USING, 301
PSET, 364, 368
PUT, 322, 415-416, 418
RANDOMIZE TIMER, 248, 359
redirection, 278
removing, 29
RESET, 302
RESUME, 482, 484
RET, 461
RSET, 432
SAVE, 281, 283-284
SCREEN, 361, 392
SCREEN 1, 463
SCREEN 2, 403
SHELL, 476-478
SOUND, 421
STICK, 337
STRIG, 337
STRIG(N), 337
STRIG(N) ON, 337
SWAP, 267
TIMER, 261
TIMER ON, 259
UNLOCK, 332
USR, 465-466
VARPTR, 469, 473-475
VIEW, 409, 411
VIEW PRINT, 411
WAIT, 480
WIDTH, 356-357
WINDOW, 370, 373
WINDOW SCREEN, 370
WRITE#, 292
command
    ADD, 37
    AUTO, 33-34
    BEEP, 32
    CHDIR, 343
    CLS (clear screen), 22
    DATA, 156-164
    DIVIDE, 38
    EDIT, 35
    ELSE, 78
    END, 30-31
    ERASE, 123
    FOR, 74
    FRE, 262
    FRE(0), 124
    GOSUB, 104-105

637

statements
   command
      GRANDTOTAL, 142
      INPUT, 53-55
      KEY OFF, 21
      KEY ON, 21
      LET, 48-49
      LIST, 28-29
      LLIST, 277
      LOAD, 66
      MULTIPLY, 38
      NAME, 342
      PAINT, 406
      PRINT, 41-42, 45
      PRINT USING, 146
      RATE, 61
      READ, 156-164
      REM, 63
      RENUM, 36
      RESTORE, 160
      RUN, 29
      SAVE, 65
      STOP, 31
      SUBTOTAL, 142
      SUBTRACT, 37
      SYSTEM, 23
      TAB, 56, 58
      TROFF, 93-94
      TRON, 93-94
   function
      ABS, 85
      FRE, 597-598
      INP, 478
      INT, 82, 84
      INT(X), 82
      OUT, 478, 479
      RANDOMIZE, 86
      RND, 85-86
      TIMER, 87
   loop
      FOR, 75-76
      FOR...NEXT, 117, 161, 174
      IF, 93
      IF...THEN, 76-77, 92
      IF...THEN...ELSE, 79
      NEXT, 74-75
      ON...GOSUB, 105
      ON...GOTO, 99
      WHILE-WEND, 83
      WHILE...WEND, 80, 508
      writing, 507-508
STEP loop statement, 76
STICK statement, 337
STOP command statement, 31
stop parameters, 339
storing
   integer variables, 470-471
   numeric values, 433
   variables, 467, 469
STR$ string function, 219
STRIG statement, 337
STRIG(N) ON statement, 337
STRIG(N) statement, 337
string functions
   CHR$, 214-215
   ENVIRON$, 345
   HEX$, 449
   INPUT$, 223-224
   IOCTL$, 489
   LEFT$, 215
   LEN(A$), 220
   MID$, 215, 217
   MKD$, 432
   MKI$, 432
   MKS$, 432
   OCT$, 449
   RIGHT$, 215-216
   SPACE$, 245-247
   SPACE$(N), 245
   STR$, 219
   STRING$, 240
   VARPTR$, 475
string variables, 51, 56, 212, 473-474
   DATE$, 59
   TIME$, 59
STRING$ string function, 240
string-number conversions, 432
strings, 26, 54
   adding, 229
   bytes, 407
   conversions, 432
   converting to numeric quantity, 433
   copying characters into, 217
   defining lengths, 220
   formatting expressions, 237
   locating, 469, 473
   mixing with numbers, 45
   null, 215
   printing, 237, 474
   retrieving, 433
   returning, 212
   searching for, 227
   tables, 344
   variables, 473-474
style attribute, 377
subroutines, 103, 105-110

Index

branching off, 135
delete, 307-308
error-checking, 106, 108-110
general input, 136
in machine language programs, 465
inputting dates, 138
passing arrays, 475
sorting, 307
waiting, 311
subscripted variables, 116, 118
substrings, 215
SUBTOTAL command statement, 142
subtotals, printing, 132
SUBTRACT command statement, 37
SWAP statement, 267
Syntax error message, 25
SYSTEM command statement, 23
system disk, 10-11

T

T.D.C.s (type declaration characters), 177
TAB, 352, 354
TAB command statement, 56, 58
tables
    environmental strings, 344
    global, 344
TAN numeric function, 188
TAN trigonometric function, 184
tangents
    calculating, 188
    trigonometric function, 184
target formulas, 502
telephone data files, 312-314
telephone number files, 302-304
    adding a person, 306-307
    deleting a person, 307-308
    displaying lists, 305
    finding a person, 309
    outputting to file, 311
    printing, 310
    running, 314, 316, 318
term, 60
text, setting boundaries, 411
text screens, 352, 396
three-dimensional arrays, 120
tile masks, 406
tiled patterns, 406
time, printing, 58, 253-254
TIME$ string variable, 59
TIMER function statement, 87, 257, 261

TIMER ON statement, 259
timers, trapping, 260-261
titles, centering, 245
tracing programs, 93-94
trapping
    background music, 426
    COM ports, 339
    devices, 334
    errors, 483-486
triangular fractals, 517-518
trigonometric functions
    arctangent, 184
    ATN, 184, 355
    COS, 184, 355
    cosine, 184
    SIN, 184, 355
    sine, 184
    TAN, 184
    tangent, 184
TROFF command statement, 93-94
TRON command statement, 93-94
truncate, 82
truth tables, 200
TYPE array, 134
type conversions
    CDBL(X), 181-182
    CINT(X), 181-182
    CSNG(X), 181-182
type declaration characters (T.D.C.s), 177
    ! (exclamation point), 177
    #, 176
    # (number sign), 177
    $ (number sign), 177
    % (percent sign), 177
type declaration definitions
    DEFDBL, 179
    DEFINT, 179
    DEFSNG, 179
    DEFSTR, 179

U-V

UNLOCK statement, 332
USR statement, 465-466
VAL function statement, 218
values
    absolute, 85
    assigning
        to labels, 53
        to variables, 47, 131
    exchanging in variables, 267

values
    index, 99
    of variables, 46-49
    precision, 169
variables, 46-50, 390-392, 437
    assigning values, 47, 131
    COLORSWITCH, 395
    converting, 181
    declaring, 130
    default, 179
    defining types automatically, 178-180
    double-precision, 175-176, 193, 473
    ERDEV, 341
    ERDEV$, 341
    exchanging values, 267
    expense account program, 130
    INKEY$, 221-223
    integer, 56, 169, 173-174, 194, 469-471
    lists, 130
    locating, 475
        in machine language programs, 467
    MAX, 107
    multiple-letter, 51
    names, 50
    numeric, 56
        rounding off, 82
    receiving in machine language programs, 466
    resetting to zero, 492-493
    separating with commas, 52
    single-letter, 51
    single-precision, 169-173, 177, 472
    starting values, 440
    storing, 467, 469
        in machine language programs, 469
    string, 51, 56, 212, 473, 474
    subscript, 116, 118
    types, 178
    value of, 46-49
VARPTR statement, 469, 473-475
VARPTR$ string function, 475
VIEW PRINT statement, 411
VIEW statement, 409, 411
viewports, 409
VPAGE argument, 395

W

WAIT statement, 480
waiting subroutine, 311
wedges, 384
    finding the center, 388
WHILE...WEND loop statement, 79-80, 83, 508
WIDTH statement, 356-357
WINDOW SCREEN statement, 370
WINDOW statement, 370, 373
work disk, 12
    copying to, 16-19
    starting from, 19
wraparound, 265
WRITE# statement, 292

X

X-axis, 380
XOR logical operator, 199, 202

Y

Y-axis, 380
yearly interest rate, 61

```
K$ = INKEY$
IF K$ = CHR$(27) THEN 1000
1000 SYSTEM.

S=1 : START=TIMER:
WHILE TIMER < START + S
WEND.
```

The Waite Group Library

If you enjoyed this book, you may be interested in these additional subjects and titles from The Waite Group and SAMS. Reader level is as follows: ★ = introductory, ★★ = intermediate, ★★★ = advanced, Δ = all levels. You can order these books by calling 1-800-628-7360.

Level	Title	Catalog #	Price	
	— C and C++ Programming Language —			
Tutorial, Unix & ANSI				
★	The New C Primer Plus, Waite and Prata	22687	$29.95	NEW
★	C: Step-by-Step, Waite and Prata	22651	$29.95	
★★	C++ Programming, Berry	22619	$29.95	
Tutorial, Product Specific				
★	Microsoft C Programming for the PC, Second Edition, Lafore	22738	$29.95	NEW
★	Turbo C Programming for the PC, Revised Edition, Lafore	22660	$29.95	
★	C Programming Using Turbo C++, Lafore	22737	$29.95	
Reference, Product Specific				
★★	Microsoft C Bible, 2nd Edition, Barkakati	22736	$29.95	
★★	Quick C Bible, Barkakati	22632	$29.95	
★★	Turbo C Bible, Barkakati	22631	$29.95	
★★	Turbo C++ Bible, Barkakati	22742	$29.95	NEW
★★	Essential Guide to Turbo C, Barkakati	22675	$9.95	
★★	Essential Guide to Microsoft C, Barkakati	22674	$9.95	
	— DOS and OS/2 Operating System —			
Tutorial, General Users				
★	Discovering MS-DOS, O'Day	22407	$19.95	
★	Understanding MS-DOS, Second Edition, The Waite Group	27087	$17.95	NEW
Tutorial/Reference, General Users				
★★	MS-DOS Bible, Third Edition, Simrin	22693	$24.95	
Δ	Using PC DOS, The Waite Group	22679	$29.95	
Tutorial/Reference, Power Users				
★★	Tricks of the MS-DOS Masters, Second Edition, The Waite Group	22717	$29.95	NEW
Tutorial, Programmers				
★★★	MS-DOS Developer's Guide, Second Edition, The Waite Group	22630	$29.95	
	— UNIX Operating System —			
Tutorial, General Users				
★	UNIX System V Primer, Revised Edition, Waite, Prata, and Martin	22570	$29.95	
★★	UNIX System V Bible, Prata and Martin	22562	$29.95	
★	UNIX Primer Plus, Second Edition, Waite, Prata, Martin	22729	$29.95	
Tutorial/Reference, Power Users and Programmers				
★★	Tricks of the UNIX Masters, Sage	22449	$29.95	
	— Assembly Language —			
Tutorial/Reference, General Users				
★★	Microsoft Macro Assembler Bible, Barkakati	22659	$29.95	
★★	The Waite Group's Turbo Assembler Bible, Syck	22716	$29.95	NEW
	— Macintosh —			
Tutorial, General Users				
★	HyperTalk Bible, The Waite Group	48430	$24.95	
★	Tricks of the HyperTalk Masters, Edited by The Waite Group	48431	$24.95	

The Waite Group

100 Shoreline Highway, Suite 285   Mill Valley, CA 94941   (415) 331-0575
Compuserve: 75146,3515   usenet:mitch@well.sf.ca.usa   MCI Mail: The Waite Group

Dear Reader:

Thank you for considering the purchase of our book. Readers have come to know products from **The Waite Group** for the care and quality we put into them. Let me tell you a little about our group and how we make our books.

It started in 1976 when I could not find a computer book that really taught me anything. The books that were available talked down to people, lacked illustrations and examples, were poorly laid out, and were written as if you already understood all the terminology. So I set out to write a good book about microcomputers. This was to be a special book—very graphic, with a friendly and casual style, and filled with examples. The result was an instant best-seller.

Over the years, I developed this approach into a "formula" (nothing really secret here, just a lot of hard work—I am a crazy man about technical accuracy and high-quality illustrations). I began to find writers who wanted to write books in this way. This led to co-authoring and then to multiple-author books and many more titles (over seventy titles currently on the market). As The Waite Group author base grew, I trained a group of editors to manage our products. We now have a team devoted to putting together the best possible book package and maintaining the high standard of our existing books.

We greatly appreciate and use any advice our readers send us (and you send us a lot). We have discovered that our readers are detail nuts: you want indexes that really work, tables of contents that dig deeply into the subject, illustrations, tons of examples, reference cards, and more.

This new introductory book on GW-BASIC combines the elements that have made our other tutorial books for beginners, like *The Waite Group's BASIC Programming Primer* and *The Waite Group's New C Primer Plus*, so successful. It features a gentle, friendly, handholding, and step-by-step approach that features many illustrations and example programs that are fun and practical.

Even if you're a new computer user and have never programmed before, this book will take you from how to insert a BASIC disk into your PC all the way to writing BASIC programs that can talk in the computer's native tongue—assembly language. In between you'll learn how to write games, applications, and nifty graphics programs that will amaze your friends, as well as learning the fundamentals of computer programming.

If you want to get more information on using your PC and working with DOS, check out *The Waite Group's Discovering MS-DOS* or *Understanding MS-DOS*, Second Edition. If you like this book and want to learn how to program using C language, take a look at our best-selling *New C Primer-Plus*, Second Edition. A list of all our titles follows this letter. In fact, let us know what topics you've been unable to find and we'll try to write about them.

Thanks again for considering the purchase of this title. If you care to tell me anything you like (or don't like) about the book, please write or send email to the addresses on this letterhead.

Sincerely,

Mitchell Waite
The Waite Group

Code Typing Eliminator

Companion Disk Saves Time

There is absolutely no reason why anyone today would type in the program listings for a computer book unless they wanted to learn how to type. Suppose your time is worth $40 per hour (a not unusual rate for today's programmer). If it takes you 10 minutes to type in and debug a half page of code, then typing all the listings in this book will take you at least 1000 minutes, or 16.6 hours. At $40 per hour, that's $664. Contrast this with the $19.95 (+ postage) it takes to buy a disk with the code already on it. The companion disk for this book comes with all the major listings in each chapter, including the fractal program and a fractal demo.

Ordering Details

Use order blank below. Order product CD-7 (GW-BASIC Primer Plus Companion Disk). Please specify 5.25-inch or 3.5-inch diskettes.
Price: $19.95. CA Residents add 7% sales tax. Shipping and handling: United States–UPS Ground: $3 for 1st unit, $1 each additional. UPS 2nd day: $6 for 1st unit, $2 each additional. COD add $3. Canada–UPS Ground: add $7 for first unit, $1 each additional. Overseas–U.S. Airmail: $14 for each unit. No shipments to PO Boxes.

Make check or Money Order payable to The Waite Group, Inc. VISA and MasterCard orders also accepted. Call for bulk or institutional orders.

 **Companion Disk for The Waite Group's GW-BASIC Primer Plus**

100 Shoreline Hwy, Suite A-285, Mill Valley, CA, 94941, (415) 331-0575. FAX: (415) 331-1075. CIS: 75146,3515

GWB-CD7-900713

ORDER FORM Please specify 5.25-inch or 3.5-inch diskettes.

California residents add 7% sales tax. Shipping and handling: United States–UPS Ground: $3 for first unit, $1 each additional. UPS 2nd day: $6 for first unit, $2 each additional. COD add $3. Canada–UPS Ground: add $7 for first unit, $1 each additional. Overseas–U.S. Airmail: $14 for each unit. UPS will not ship to PO Boxes.

Please circle shipping instructions
☐ Send free Waite Group catalog

Qty	Product Description	Format	Unit Price	Total
	Master C training system (#CBT-1)	☐ 3.5-inch ☐ 5.25-inch	$49.95	
	GW-BASIC Primer Companion Disk (#CD-7)	☐ 3.5-inch ☐ 5.25-inch	$19.95	

Name: _____

Address: _____

Country _____

Phone _____

Subtotal	
Tax (CA only)	
Shipping & Handling	
COD charge ($3)	
Total Due	

Please bill my credit card
☐ Visa   ☐ MasterCard
Card Number _____

Expiration Date _____

Signature required for credit card _____

The Waite Group, 100 Shoreline Hwy, Suite A-285, Mill Valley, CA, 94941, (415) 331-0575. FAX: 331-1075. CIS: 75146,3515

The Waite Group's
GW-BASIC
Primer Plus

Waite Group Reader Feedback Card

SAMS

Help Us Make A Better Book

To better serve our readers, we would like your opinion on the contents and quality of this book. Please fill out this card and return it to *The Waite Group*, 100 Shoreline Hwy., Suite A-285, Mill Valley, CA, 94941 (415) 331-0575.

Name _____
Company _____
Address _____
City _____
State _____ ZIP _____ Phone _____

1. How would you rate the content of this book?

   ☐ Excellent   ☐ Fair
   ☐ Very Good   ☐ Below Average
   ☐ Good   ☐ Poor

2. What were the things you liked *most* about this book?

   ☐ Pace   ☐ Listings   ☐ Ref. Card
   ☐ Content   ☐ Price   ☐ 2nd Color
   ☐ Writing Style ☐ Format   ☐ Appendixes
   ☐ Accuracy   ☐ Cover   ☐ Illustrations
   ☐ Examples   ☐ Index   ☐ Construction

3. Please explain the one thing you liked *most* about this book.
   _____
   _____

4. What were the things you liked *least* about this book?

   ☐ Pace   ☐ Listings   ☐ Ref. Card
   ☐ Content   ☐ Price   ☐ 2nd Color
   ☐ Writing Style ☐ Format   ☐ Appendixes
   ☐ Accuracy   ☐ Cover   ☐ Illustrations
   ☐ Examples   ☐ Index   ☐ Construction

5. Please explain the one thing you liked *least* about this book.
   _____
   _____

6. How do you use this book? For work, recreation, look-up, self-training, classroom, etc?
   _____
   _____
   _____
   _____

7. Would you be interested in a disk-based course that teaches how to use BASIC? What would you pay for this course?
   _____

8. Where did you purchase this particular book?

   ☐ Book Chain   ☐ Direct Mail
   ☐ Small Book Store ☐ Book Club
   ☐ Computer Store   ☐ School Book Store
   ☐ Other: _____

9. Can you name another similar book you like better than this one, or one that is as good, and tell us why?
   _____
   _____

10. How many Waite Group books do you own? _____

11. What are your favorite Waite Group books?
    _____
    _____

12. What topics or specific titles would you like to see The Waite Group develop?
    _____
    _____

13. Have you programmed before?
    _____

14. How did you learn about this book?
    _____

15. Any other comments you have about this book or other Waite Group titles?
    _____
    _____
    _____

16. ☐ Check here to receive a free Waite Group catalog.

Fold Here

From:

Place Stamp Here

The Waite Group, Inc.
100 Shoreline Highway, Suite A–285
Mill Valley, CA 94941

Staple or tape here